# ADJUSTMENT AND GROWTH IN A CHANGING WORLD

## SECOND EDITION

# ■ ADJUSTMENT AND GROWTH IN A CHANGING WORLD

## SECOND EDITION

VINCE NAPOLI

JAMES M. KILBRIDE

DONALD E. TEBBS

Miami-Dade Community College
Miami, Florida

WEST PUBLISHING COMPANY

St. Paul   New York   Los Angeles   San Francisco

Library of Congress Cataloging in Publication Data

Napoli, Vince.
    Adjustment & growth in a changing world.

    Bibliography: p.
    Includes index.
    1. Self-actualization (Psychology) 2. Adjustment (Psychology) 3. Identity (Psychology) 4. Interpersonal relations. I. Kilbride, James M. II. Tebbs, Donald E. III. Title. IV. Title: Adjustment and growth in a changing world.
BF637.S4N365 1985        158        84-17404
ISBN 0-314-85280-8


**Copyediting:** Beverly Peavler,
               Naples Editing Service
**Composition and Artwork:** Carlisle Graphics

**Cover Photograph**
David Brownell, Image Bank.

**Chapter One**
3 Micheal Hayman, Stock Boston; 6 Ira Berger, Woodfin Camp & Associates; 9 Photo Researchers, Inc; 14 Sepp Seitz, Woodfin Camp & Associates; 15 Nicholas Sapieha, Stock Boston; 16 Jim Anderson, Woodfin Camp & Associates.

**Chapter Two**
23 Robert V. Eckert, Jr., EKM-Nepenthe; 36 Paolo Koch, Photo Researchers, Inc.; 45 Christa Armstrong, Photo Researchers, Inc.; 49 Frank Siteman, EKM-Nepenthe.

**Chapter Three**
57 Mary Ellen Mark, Archive Pictures, Inc.; 59 Joseph Szabo, Photo Researchers, Inc.; 62 Suzanne Szasz, Photo Researchers, Inc.; 70 Mary Ellen Mark, Archive Pictures, Inc.; 73 Jim Howard, Freelance Photographers Guild; 75 Randy Matusow, Monkmeyer; 78 William Patrick Rotegon, Freelance Photographer Guild; 79 Robert J. Bennett, Freelance Photographers Guild.

**Chapter Four**
87 Tim Davis, Photo Researchers, Inc; 91 Cartoon by Kim Pickering; 96 Richard Laird, Freelance Photographers Guild; 101 Myron Wood, Photo Researchers, Inc.; 103 (left) E. Alan McGee, Freelance Photographers Guild; 103 (right) A & A Graphics, Freelance Photographers Guild; 110 Rhonda Galyn, Photo Researchers, Inc.; 113 Stan Pantonc, Photo Researchers, Inc.; 115 Bettina Cirone, Photo Researchers, Inc.; 123 Freelance Photographers Guild.

**Chapter Five**
133 Peter Menzel, Stock Boston; 134 George Malave, Stock Boston; 138 Cartoon by Kim Pickering; 141 Win McIntyre, Photo Researchers, Inc.; 149 (top left) Mark Antman, Stock Boston; 149 (top right) Richard Balzer, Stock Boston; 149 (bottom left) Micheal Hayman, Stock Boston; 149 (bottom right) Owen Franken, Stock Boston; 151 Russel Abraham, Stock Boston; 153 Bill Anderson, Monkmeyer; 157 U.S. Department of Defense, Marine Coprs Photo; 159 Cartoon by Kim Pickering; 161 Cartoon by Kim Pickering; 162 Joe Kelly, Archive; 165 Cartoon by Kim Pickering.

**Chapter Six**
175 David Aronson, Stock Boston; 180 James R. Holland, Stock Boston; 183 EKM-Nepenthe; 191 Jerry Berndt, Stock Boston; 197 Peter Southwick, Stock Boston; 200 Stock, Boston; 205 Frank Siteman, EKM-Nepenthe.

*credits continued after index*

# ■ CONTENTS

**5**

# COGNITIVE SELF 132

# 6

## EMOTIONAL SELF 174

## STRESS 217

## STRESS 218

## SELF AND OTHERS 263

## SOCIALIZATION 264

## 9

# GROUP DYNAMICS AND LEADERSHIP 294

# V

## INTERPERSONAL ADJUSTMENT 327

# 10

## COMMUNICATION 328

# 11

## INTIMACY 356

# 14

# PSYCHOTHERAPY  438

# ■ PREFACE

## FOCUS

To lead an effective and fulfilling life, a person must do two things—adjust and grow. This book deals with adjustment and growth on two levels, the level of people in general and the level of *you* in particular. The material that deals with people in general tends to be theoretical, although specific devices have been used to ground this theoretical material in a base of reality. The material that deals with you in particular is practical; it should help you in your own adjustment and growth.

*Adjustment and Growth in a Changing World,* second edition, is a text on the psychology of adjustment. It is concerned with the practical application of psychological principles to everyday life.

The book is organized on one level in a topical progression from a consideration of the individual to a consideration of interpersonal relationships. On another level is a second organizational pattern interwoven with the first: a progression from personal awareness to evaluation to change. This developmental pattern—from awareness to evaluation to change—is consistent with the general pattern of problem solving. That is, first we become aware of a problem; then we decide what to do about it; and finally, we design and carry out specific action plans geared to solve the problem. Hence, the book helps you first to become aware of and to evaluate your own patterns of adjustment and growth and then to make changes as you deem necessary or desirable.

## ORGANIZATION

The book contains an introduction, six major parts, a conclusion, and a special section that consists of four personal action plans. The introduction is particularly useful because it deals with a topic that can be applied to any textbook you might use: study techniques. In addition, the introduction shows how a distinctive approach to learning, the SQ3R study method, has been employed in this book. We suggest that you read the introduction carefully before moving to Part I.

Part I presents an overview of the psychology of adjustment. It includes considerations of the processes of adjustment and growth, personality theories, and the concept of self-esteem. Part II surveys the physical, cognitive, and emotional aspects of individual identity. Stress is the subject of Part III. Here you will have the opportunity to ponder the effects of stress on your own well-being. Part IV considers the relationship of self to others, including significant people and social structures that have contributed to our personal identity. It also discusses group dynamics and leadership. Interpersonal adjustment and growth are analyzed in Part V. This part should help you to understand your communication style and to improve your communication with others, as well as to understand the impact of intimacy on your personal growth and the means by which intimacy is either facilitated or thwarted. Part VI focuses on a variety of factors involved when things go wrong for the individual. It includes a survey of maladjustive responses and of approaches that may be used to facilitate a return to healthy functioning.

The conclusion examines goal setting and decision making. Having learned about major concepts involved in the psychology of adjustment and having been encouraged to apply those concepts to yourself, you are now provided with a step-by-step process that you may use to direct and guide desired changes in your life.

Finally, there is the special section containing four Personal Action Plans designed to help you manage your own growth. The first plan deals with time management; the second, with self-help in general and quitting smoking in particular; the third, with stress reduction; and the fourth, with career choice.

## MAJOR CHANGES IN THIS EDITION

We have benefited from an enormous amount of feedback on the first edition from scores of instructors and hundreds of students. This feedback has led to several major changes in this edition.

First, we have completely reorganized the material in the text to a form that lends itself to a better development of ideas. The chapter on adjustment now appears at the beginning of Part I, "Overview of Adjustment." We have eliminated the chapter on sexuality, although much of the information it contained now appears in appropriate sections of the chapters on physical self, intimacy, and maladjustment. The chapter on socialization now introduces Part IV, "Self and Others," and the chapter on individuals and groups now immediately follows it. The chapter on communication has been moved to the beginning of Part V, "Interpersonal Adjustment." We have divided the chapter on intimacy into two chapters, "Intimacy" and "Barriers to Intimacy," and moved them to Part V. The psychotherapy chapter now appears at the end of Part VI, "Maladjustment and Psychotherapy." The material on life decisions and life goals has been moved to the conclusion. Finally, four of the Self-Managements now comprise the special section Personal Action Plans.

Second, we have substantially rewritten and reorganized material within chapters. For example, the chapter on personality contains additional material on Erikson, Bandura and Walters, and Maslow as alternatives to the positions of Freud, Skinner, and Rogers. The chapter on physical self includes a new section on life extension as well as new material on sociobiology and an enlarged section on attribution theory. We have condensed the discussion of emotional theory in the chapter on emotional self. The chapter on socialization contains a new section on the life cycle. We have completely rewritten the chapter on group dynamics and leadership to provide a more appropriate balance between these two topics. Along with these and other changes and additions to the material has come an attempt to tie factual and theoretical information to a consideration of the reader's adjustment patterns. Of course, we have updated research and statistics. In addition, we have added one new chapter, "Maladjustment." The material on sexual disorders and substance abuse has been of particular interest to many reviewers.

Third, several new or changed special features function as study aids for the reader. All the study aids have received consistently positive feedback from both student and teacher reviewers. Short anecdotes, many of them based on actual people and situations, are interspersed through the chapters. Also interspersed through the chapters are Cases in Point. These may take the form of short, insight-provoking exercises, research data, or factual explanations dealing with significant concepts. Each chapter begins with an organizational outline of the chapter. We have replaced the question-and-answer format used in the first edition with a three-level organization represented by headings and two levels of subheadings. The focus, review questions, summary, and glossary sections of the chapters have been retained. The selected readings section for each chapter also remains, although its form has been changed from a bibliographical essay to an annotated bibliography that is shorter and that contains a blend of longer, classical writings (such as Erikson's *Childhood and Society*) and shorter, more popular writings (such as articles from *Psychology Today*). In short, *Adjustment and Growth in a Changing World* has been thoroughly revised.

## ANCILLARY MATERIALS

There are two companion pieces to *Adjustment and Growth in a Changing World*—one for the student and one for the instructor. Both have been written by us, the authors of the text. The *Study Guide to Accompany Adjustment and Growth in a Changing World* includes a listing of the major terms and concepts from each chapter and several exercises, including short quizzes, designed to help students master the concepts. We have found that students who complete these exercises tend to make relatively good class grades (C or better); therefore, we recommend use of the study guide.

In addition, the study guide contains a new section of nine personal action plans that may be used by students for their own personal growth or by instructors as a basis for class-related activity.

The *Instructor's Manual to Accompany Adjustment and Growth in a Changing World* is provided to all instructors who adopt the book.

## ACKNOWLEDGMENTS

This book is the product of the efforts of literally hundreds of people. Many students and teachers have helped us by offering constructive criticisms. We also have been helped by many in the editorial and production departments of West Publishing. We thank all of you for your help.

We offer special thanks to the following individuals, who acted as principal critical reviewers:

| | |
|---|---|
| L. Jim Anthis | Stephan Link |
| Georgette Daughterty | Robert Petty |
| Gary Dean | Linda Schwartz |
| Thomas Dodamead | Doris Skelton |
| Lane Gerber | Don Stanley |
| Chuck Hobgood | Mary Vlahos |
| Arnold LeUnes | Webster White |

Finally, we owe a particular debt of gratitude to Flora Napoli, whose encouragement, help, and guidance were invaluable not only in the preparation of first drafts for this manuscript but for those of the first edition as well.

Vince Napoli
James M. Kilbride
Donald E. Tebbs

# ■INTRODUCTION

## STUDYING TO UNDERSTAND AND REMEMBER

How much will you have to adjust your schedule to meet the demands of this course on adjustment? Your answer will depend on the level of your **study skills.** Below are four definitions of studying. Check the one that best describes your present approach.

Studying is:
1. Reading the pages over and over until the information sinks in. _____
2. Reading the text until I understand what I am reading. _____
3. Reading the chapter and underlining the important parts. _____
4. Using my mind to acquire knowledge. _____

The goal of using special study techniques is to learn as much as possible in the shortest time and to retain what is learned. Let's look at how psychologists evaluate the definitions listed above in light of that goal.

**1. Reading and rereading.** Passive reading—simply looking at the words while "waiting for good things to happen" (Locke, 1975)—is of little help in learning. Repeating the process simply adds frustration and wastes time.

**2. Reading for understanding**. The task of learning is to understand and remember what you read so that you are able to explain it to others or to apply it when necessary. Many college students confuse understanding what they are reading with being able to recall what they have read—a fatal error. We must go beyond what we read as we are reading it. We must literally make the new information a part of ourselves.

**3. Reading and underlining**. Underlining is perhaps the most used, and abused, study method. It is a useful tool for noting what is important to make learning and review easier. However, it is not learning. It is an I.O.U., a promise of future learning. "Underlining says, 'Look, I'm picking out the real meat so I can concentrate on it—some other time'" (Elliott, 1966, p. 48).

**4. Using the mind to acquire knowledge**. This definition offers little specific help in teaching us how to study, but it does give us a starting point. We can use our minds to improve our ability to learn. We can learn good study methods, incorporate them into our system of study, and monitor our study behavior in terms of these methods until they become a part of us.

## ELEMENTS OF A STUDY PLAN

The following suggestions can form the basis of a personal action plan for studying that can improve performance while allowing more time for activities other than studying. Samuel Smith (1970) reports that "students can save from one-quarter to one-third of their time if they systematize their efforts in accordance with the chief principles of learning." Each element in this plan has merit, and each should be given consideration, *but the plan should not be used in a mechanical fashion*. Select from these elements and build a personal plan to meet your unique needs. Any plan is better than no plan at all.

Before Studying

I. **A time for study**. Robinson (1970) reports that "students may actually be strangers to their own relative abilities" (p. 5). Most students underestimate the time they need to learn, work, play, and in general enjoy whatever it is they are doing while they are attending college. Planning pays. (See our personal action plans on managing time.)

II. **A place for study**. Study in a well-equipped workplace. Create a situation that will prompt you to go to work quickly, concentrate fully, and perform effectively. A suitable study place should provide:

   A. Freedom from external distractions.

      1. Low levels of noise and no unexpected noises. Even background music increases inattention and decreases performance. For this reason students who study in the library generally outperform those who study in the dorm.

      2. Good lighting, free from glare or flicker. Invest in a study lamp—it will last for decades.

      3. Infrequent interruptions. Choose a place away from the flow of traffic and out of eye contact with others.

   B. Freedom from internal distractions.

      1. Internal distractions such as boredom, fear, or confusion may invade even the best workplace. (See IV: A climate for study.)

      2. Do not complain about the lack of a "perfect place to study." Just change what you can, and then try to study only at that place. Also, *only* study at that place: eat, daydream, and so on elsewhere.

III. **Equipment for study**. In addition to the text, keep the following on hand: calendar, clock, college dictionary, loose-leaf notebook and scratch paper, pen and pencil, reading stand (to hold your place and free your hands for note-taking), bookshelf, and, if possible, typewriter and/or printer and personal computer. Do not allow the lack of needed supplies to become a source of distraction. Restock regularly.

IV. **A climate for study**. There is no substitute for high interest and motivation when it comes to learning something. A positive, confident, and determined attitude toward the task at hand produces a climate in which knowledge and personal satisfaction abound.

   The personal action plans in this text as well as class discussions and activities will give you opportunities to gain self-awareness, clarify values, set goals, and in general reduce the number and intensity of internal distractions that can be so destructive to study. Your skill in studying should grow as the course unfolds.

V. **A unit of study**. How many pages of text should you attempt to cover during one study effort? Some factors to consider when selecting the size of your study unit include the following:

   A. The amount attempted should be the most you can permanently learn in one continuous sitting. "The measure of study is the amount permanently learned" (Elliott, 1966).

   B. Studying is not like reading; it is *work*. Therefore fatigue, boredom, and memory span limit the amount of learning to be attempted.

C. Small units are more easily learned than large units.
1. You can make each small unit a piece of a larger, meaningful unit, not an arbitrary chunk.
2. You can overlearn small, manageable units. *Overlearning* means continuing to rehearse and review material that you understand and remember. *Overlearning* is good, because practicing material already learned reduces forgetting.

Time yourself as you study to learn exactly how long it takes you to permanently learn a given number of pages of text. Ehrlich (1976) reports that ten pages an hour is not an uncommon rate.

## During Study

Active study, involving your body as well as your mind, will help you to understand and remember what you read. The suggestions that follow are drawn from the work of many study theorists. In turn, all writers on effective study have been influenced by the pioneering work of F. P. Robinson. In 1941 Robinson introduced the famous *SQ3R* (survey, question, read, recite, review) study method. Each of Robinson's elements follow, along with suggestions that confirm and extend his system. **We encourage you to select from these elements and increase your range of study skills.** When you find yourself in your place of study at the appointed time, in a positive mood, surrounded by the proper equipment and supplies, and committed for a limited time to learn and remember a definite unit of work, you have already begun well. Here are some suggestions to help you complete your study task.

## SQ3R TECHNIQUES

### Steps in Studying

**STEP 1:**
**SURVEY**

I. Read the chapter overview (at the beginning of each part—see page 1, for example), the chapter outline, and the focus to learn the five or six major ideas of the chapter and to become involved with its contents. These few minutes provide you with knowledge of the major theme of the chapter, its important ideas, and how they flow together. This knowledge will give you a permanent framework of "tags" or "pegs" around which you can cluster the myriad of detail that is to come.

**STEP 2:**
**QUESTION**

II. This text has been carefully constructed to present meaningful "chunks" of information under three levels of headings. When the symbol ■ appears before a heading, *convert the heading into a question!* For example, *the heading* " ■ Diseases of Adaptation" can be quickly turned into the question "What are diseases of adaptation, and how do they come about?" Such questions will direct your reading.

**STEP 3:**
**READ**

III. Now, carefully read the information under the heading *with the intention of answering the question that you have just posed.* This step gives purpose and direction to your reading and makes it possible for you to be selective in what you commit to memory.

*As you read:*

A. **Actively challenge the material**. Each paragraph, at times each sentence, contains an idea you can support or question from your own background. According to Locke (1975), it is essential that you "make a habit of understanding each concept the first time you encounter it" (p. 23). Then, make an effort to learn the idea immediately. Classify the information, for example, in some way that is meaningful to you and related to the topic under study. Integrate it into what you already know. This creates a rich network of associations that makes the information easier to recall.

B. **Allow time to emotionally and intellectually respond to what you are reading**. How do you feel about it? What is its significance? What are its implications? Try to take a stand for or against the ideas under discussion. This will get your ego involved and make recall easier.

C. **Involve your whole body in active participation by marking your textbook**. Why mark up a textbook? Because if done correctly, marking identifies important ideas and makes reviewing easier. It is essential that you understand what is important before you mark up your text. *Do not underline as you read*.

   1. Finish reading the entire passage before making any marks.
   2. Wait a brief period to allow for your analysis and reaction.
   3. Mark only the essential idea and its supporting detail.
   4. When taking notes, use your own words plus key phrases from the text. Symbols and abbreviations are useful, as are color codes. Use marginal notes to emphasize material that your professor has elaborated on in class.

IV. Stop reading at intervals and play back to yourself what you have just read. "Say aloud the full idea in your own words," advises Walter Pauk (1974). Then restate the same idea using the technical terminology of the text. **STEP 4: RECITE**

A. **Why recitation?** Because active responding is a form of self-test.
   1. It keeps you focused on your task.
   2. It gives you knowledge of your progress.
   3. It reduces anxiety.
   4. It allows you to reconstruct the new material, to make it a part of you.
   5. It gives you helpful practice.

B. **How much recitation?** Spend at least half your total study time in active recitation (Pauk, 1974).

C. **What should be recited?** Everything you think important enough to be understood and remembered should be recited. Try to reproduce your recorded notes without looking at them.

D. **What type of recitation?** Every possible type of recitation, using as many of your faculties as possible, should be employed. Speak, write, and act. In your imagination, challenge yourself to recite accurately and completely by playing the role of a debater, teacher, or consultant. After reciting, *revise* your notes and underlinings to make later review more effective.

### After Studying

**STEP 5:**
**REVIEW**

V. Do you quickly forget? Most of us forget as much as 50 percent of what we read immediately after reading. After completing your study unit, review the information you wish to remember. Review is most effective at three times: just after study, just before rest, and just before examinations. *Why is review so necessary?* It is essential because:

- It takes a while after learning for information to be stored in our memories. Immediate recall prevents its being lost prior to storage.
- Mental review can effectively replace worrying and so reduce anxiety.
- Review is a form of practice, which promotes retention.
- Review helps you concentrate on your central task of understanding and remembering.
- Review gives you knowledge of what you still need to know, suggestions for revision of notes, and directions for rereading.

*At the end of each unit of study:*

A. **Set high standards for your immediate recall**. Do not try for perfect recall, but demand the main idea and its supporting details. After all, you will never be able to remember what you did not commit to memory in the first place. *Do not confuse understanding what you read as you read it with knowing the material.*

B. **Distribute your practice sessions**. Space your reviews at intervals prior to exams. Eliminate cramming as your only review activity.

**Consider these ideas when reviewing:**

1. Use mnemonic devices. These are memory tricks. Making the first letters of the names of the Great Lakes into the word HOME, for example, is a mnemonic device for remembering the names of the lakes. You just think of the letter H in the word *home*, and Lake Huron comes to mind, and so on.
2. Use active recall. Do not engage in another session of passive reading or looking at your notes.
3. Practice first without notes, then with notes. Revise your notes and underlinings as needed.
4. Avoid mental mumbling. Recall specifics using complete sentences.
5. State the relationship among the details you have learned under each major topic, along with the main ideas you learned from the chapter overview.

*At the end of a study session:*

This is the time for you to reflect, to consolidate your progress and your approach by asking yourself two final questions:

A. **What is the meaning of what I have just learned?**
B. **Have I followed the process for studying that is best for me?**

*After an examination:*

After each examination, review your study methods in light of their results so that your knowledge, understanding, and study skills will continue to grow. Learning is a lifelong joy that goes far beyond this textbook or this course.

## ELEMENTS OF YOUR SQ3R TEXT

This text has been written with your study needs in mind. If you are aware of its unique style and structure, you can build its features into your study plan. Your SQ3R text includes:

*1.* **A table of contents** to provide you with an outline of the entire work and access to its parts.

*2.* **A preface and an introduction** to make you aware of the approach, general assumptions, and central values of the authors of the text.

*3.* **Sectional introductions** to help you focus on the major themes to be explored in the chapters that immediately follow.

*4.* **Fourteen individual chapters** to present major ideas, principles, and practices in the psychology of human adjustment.

*5.* **Chapter outlines** to present an overview of each chapter.

*6.* **Selected readings** at the end of each chapter to provide you with resources for greater understanding of the concepts presented.

*7.* **A conclusion at the end of the text** to relate the information presented in the chapters to the text's central theme—adjustment and growth in a changing world.

*8.* **An index and a glossary** to provide you with ready access to authors, subjects, and terms presented in the text. New terms appear in boldface type when introduced in the text, and a glossary of all these terms is included at the end of each chapter.

*9.* **An appendix** to offer you the opportunity to establish **personal action plans**. Personal action plans allow you to put theory into practice in areas of your own personal growth. These self-regulation exercises are *the single most important feature of your text*. They make it possible for you to actively direct your behavior toward a more satisfying and effective lifestyle. See "Managing Growth" in Chapter One for an overview of the theory supporting the construction of these exercises.

*10.* **Type faces** of different colors and sizes to draw attention to important ideas or facts.

*11.* **Pictures, charts, and graphs** to visually depict information presented in the chapter.

**A study guide** is also available. This workbook provides *nine supplementary personal action plans* in addition to behavioral objectives, student response exercises, vocabulary lists, and practice tests. Students who elect to use the *study guide* have been found to outperform those who do not by significant margins. We strongly recommend its use.

## CHAPTER FORMAT

Each chapter contains these elements of the SQ3R plan:

SURVEY          *1.* A **focus** plus **chapter outlines** and a **summary** to interest and involve you in the topics to be presented.

QUESTION    2. ■ **Headings** designed to be converted into questions to give purpose and direction to your study. The **summary** is also drawn from the chapter headings, so that you can use it to turn each of the major portions of the chapter into questions for a final self-quiz.

READ    3. **Anecdotes** and **cases in point** to provide further insight into the psychology of adjustment. Each *anecdote* describes a fictional incident suggested by the text material, while each *case in point* is either: (a) a research-based example, (b) a real-life case study, or (c) a student response questionnaire or an insight-provoking exercise. **Selected readings** are included to encourage you to read further in areas of interest developed in the body of the text.

RECITE    4. **Review questions** and **What do you think?** questions are built into each major section to encourage you to think reflectively and to test your memory and understanding as you study your text.

REVIEW    5. A **summary** to draw together the ideas and supporting facts presented in the chapter. **Chapter outlines** are also useful for review. **Illustrations** highlight important information or provide human interest.

## REFERENCES

Elliott, H. C. *The Effective Student: A Constructive Method of Study*. New York: Harper & Row, 1966.

Ehrlich, E. *How to Study Better and Get Higher Marks*. New York: Thomas Y. Crowell, 1976.

Locke, E. A. *A Guide to Effective Study*. New York: Springer Publishing Company, 1975.

Mahoney, M. J. *Cognition and Behavior Modification*. Cambridge, Mass.: Bollinger, 1974.

Morgan, C. T., and Deese, J. *How to Study*. New York: McGraw-Hill, 1957.

Pauk, W. *How to Study in College*. Boston: Houghton Mifflin, 1974.

Robinson, F. P. *Effective Study*, Fourth Edition. New York: Harper & Row, 1970.

Smith, S. *Best Methods of Study*. New York: Barnes & Noble, 1958.

Watson, D. L., and Tharp, R. G. *Self-Directed Behavior: Self-Modification for Personal Adjustment*. Monterey, Calif.: Brooks/Cole, 1972.

# ■ ADJUSTMENT AND GROWTH IN A CHANGING WORLD
## SECOND EDITION

Part I provides an overview of the psychology of adjustment by looking at the processes of adjustment and growth, at personality theories, and at the concept of self-esteem.

Chapter 1 analyzes the processes of adjustment and growth. It examines criteria for the adequacy of any individual response and any adjustment strategy and points out significant differences between the adjustment of humans and that of other living organisms. It also introduces an approach to behavior management that, when mastered, will be extremely useful in your own adjustment and growth.

Chapter 2 provides an overview of personality—one of the fundamental concepts upon which the psychology of adjustment is built. Early in the chapter, we suggest that body, mind, emotions, and behavior are interdependent. This interdependency is explored and reexplored throughout the book.

In Chapter 2, the concept of a personality model is introduced, and three broad approaches to personality models are briefly defined. Most of the chapter is devoted to an exploration of three specific personality models, one for each of the three approaches. In addition, an alternative for each model is provided. In reading this material, you will become familiar not only with several specific personality models but with three general approaches to adjustment that are dealt with in one way or another throughout the book.

Chapter 3 examines a critically important part of our self-concept—self-esteem, the degree to which we value ourselves or feel worthy. This examination is particularly important because our level of self-esteem may influence our adjustment and growth patterns more than any other personality factor.

# OVERVIEW OF ADJUSTMENT

# 1

# ADJUSTMENT AND GROWTH

## QUIZ: THE BEST-ADJUSTED PERSON

Below are brief descriptions of three people. Read each description carefully and determine who of the three people is the best adjusted. Then write an explanation of your view.

*1.* Ellen is a married, thirty-two-year-old stockbroker. Although she shares a mutually exlcusive sexual relationship with her husband, she has a strong sexual attraction to several men in her brokerage firm. Believing it morally wrong for her to be attracted to men other than her husband, Ellen has remained unaware of her sexual desires by using her 'excess' sexual energy to jog several times a week. Through her sublimation, Ellen is able to maintain an acceptable self-image as well as to keep herself in good physical health. Generally, she is happy with herself.

*2.* George is a fifty-four-year-old business executive. For many years, he has thought of himself as having all the necessary characteristics to become president of a large corporation, which he has strived to do. Within the past few years, however, George has been passed over twice for promotions that would have moved him from a middle- to an upper-management position. Recently, he has come to the realistic conclusion that he does not have what it takes to hold an upper-management job. Rather than fooling himself, George has accepted his career limitations and is exploring some of his other, untapped potentialities. Generally, he is happy with himself.

*3.* Herbie is a twenty-year-old college student who has been experiencing frustration because of his poor grades. Although he was able to get through high school with reasonably good grades, Herbie has recently become aware that his longstanding habit of cramming before exams is not working well in college. Consequently, he has made a conscious attempt to alter his study habits. His grades are improving and, generally, he is happy with himself.

Explanation: I believe _____ is the best-

adjusted person because _____

_____

_____

_____

**ADJUSTMENT
AND
GROWTH**

## DISCUSSION: ADJUSTMENT AND GROWTH

It is possible that in completing the quiz you raised more questions than you answered. For example, can good adjustment really include self-deception? Is good adjustment always measured only in relation to the self (as opposed to other people and/or the environment)? Is personal happiness always a criterion by which good adjustment can be measured? Is good adjustment a state of being or an ongoing process? Can we speak of good adjustment without the intrusion of value judgments? Is there a universal standard by which good adjustment can be measured?

In this chapter, we will consider these and other questions. We will focus on adjustment and growth in general, on the adjustment and growth of living organisms, and, most particularly, on the adjustment and growth of human beings.

### ■ Defining Adjustment and Growth

**Adjustment** refers to the individual's response to the physical, psychological, and social demands of the self, other people, and the environment. Thus, adjustment is concerned with how we respond to stimuli. Learning to meet the demands of a college environment is a matter of adjustment.

**Growth** refers to the individual's changing his or her thoughts, feelings, or behaviors regarding the self, others, or the environment. Growth involves internal change. Learning to control my temper so that I may improve the quality of my interpersonal relationships is a matter of growth.

The concepts *adjustment* and *growth* are complementary, but each has different emphasis. Adjustment emphasizes the impact of the environment on our attempt to meet our needs. Growth emphasizes internal motivation. We adjust because we sense that environmental demands will overwhelm us if we do not adjust; we grow because we are not satisfied with our responses to our selves, others, or the environment.

Both Sam and Helen were shocked to find that their fifteen-year-old son, Michael, had become addicted to cocaine. What had happened? They knew this kind of thing occurred in other families, but they never believed it could happen in theirs. How could Michael have done such a thing?

After the initial shock, they placed Michael in a drug counseling program to help him give up drugs and cope effectively with his problems. At the same time, Sam and Helen joined another therapy group designed to help them deal with Michael and their feelings towards him.

Today, five years later, Michael has completely given up his drug habit and is well on his way to becoming an honors student at the state university. He has learned from his mistakes and is committed to avoid making the same errors again.

Sam and Helen are trying to provide Michael with as much support as they can. They are proud of his current achievements and have accepted completely the financial burden of seeing him through school. Deep down, however, both of them fear that he will again turn to drugs. Sam and Helen have adjusted; Michael has grown.

**WHAT DO YOU THINK?**
■ Have Michael's parents also grown?
■ If so, in what ways?

## ■ Measuring Adjustment

Scholars have not been able to agree on a universal standard by which to measure adjustment. Rather, they have adopted a variety of standards, each reflecting the theoretical orientations and **values** of its proponents. Consider the following examples.

Sigmund Freud viewed good adjustment as the individual's effective use of self-deception to satisfy simultaneously the demands of his or her desires and conscience. Accordingly, the description of Ellen in the Focus reveals that she is a very well-adjusted person.

Carl Rogers, on the other hand, sees self-deception as maladjustment, because it interferes with the fulfillment of one's potential. Thus, Rogers would not characterize Ellen as well adjusted. He would, however, say that George exhibits excellent adjustment, because he has accepted his true limitations in one area and is actively exploring his potentialities in others.

Behaviorists such as B. F. Skinner tend to view good adjustment from a third perspective. They emphasize learned behavior that allows the individual to cope successfully with situational demands. According to this view, Herbie displays good adjustment, because he has learned to alter his study habits and, as a result, is making better grades.

There are many other conceptions of good adjustment. Those of several scholars—including Freud, Rogers, and Skinner—are dealt with in other chapters of this book. The important point here is that each scholar's conception of good adjustment rests upon his or her theoretical orientation and values.

*See Chapter 2 for further discussion of the ideas of Freud, Rogers and Skinner.*

## ■ Adjustment and Value Judgments

It is impossible to evaluate good adjustment without making value judgments. In fact, the very use of the word *good* tells us that value judgments are being made. That, however, is not a condemnation of any definition of good adjustment, for value judgments may be based on logic. For example, if, as Freud

---

## CASE IN POINT

Reread the explanation you wrote in the Focus. What are the values inherent in your judgment of which person was best adjusted?

_____

_____

_____

_____

What is the logic behind these values?

_____

_____

_____

_____

One cannot decide what comprises good adjustment without making value judgements; however, there may be excellent reasons for making such value judgments.

suggests, there are inevitable conflicts between the demands of desires and conscience, and if these conflicts produce great (and potentially psychologically disabling) tensions for the individual, then self-deception (which can reduce the tensions) can only be defined as good adjustment. This is not to say that Freud necessarily liked the idea of lying to oneself. Rather, he saw self-deception as the *only* means available to avoid maladjustment. Hence, in Freud's view, self-deception *must* be valued for a logical reason. In like manner, other scholars have come to hold their values for similar, logical reasons.

## DISCUSSION: SOCIAL VALUES AND ADJUSTMENT

While it appears true that some conceptions of good adjustment are based on logically derived value judgments, it also seems true that others are based on socially and culturally determined values. We in the United States, for example, tend to place great emphasis on winning through competition. Thus, it would not be unusual to find Americans defining good adjustment in the following terms: the more one is able to compete successfully, the better adjusted one is. Other cultures, however, may place little or no emphasis on competitive prowess. The Zuni Indians, for instance, have held the value of moderation in such high esteem that "in contests of skill like their footraces, if a man wins habitually he is debarred from running" (Benedict, 1934, p. 99). Therefore, when considering the adequacy of an adaptive response, we must consider social and cultural factors as well as individual needs.

■ Being "number 1" might be important to many, but some cultures do not place such great emphasis on winning.

## ■ American Values and Adjustments

A few of the values Americans have traditionally used as barometers of good adjustment are self-reliance, initiative, an ability to get along well with others, self-control, and personal happiness. The following, more extensive listing is taken from Scott (1968, pp. 976–977).

### GENERAL ADAPTIVE CAPACITY

Adaptability
Flexibility
Mastery of the environment
Capacity to meet and deal with a changing world

Successful behavior
Modifiability of behavior, according to its favorable or unfavorable consequences
Capacity to formulate ends and implement them

### CAPACITY FOR SELF-GRATIFICATION

Genital sexuality (ability to achieve orgasm)
Gratification of one's needs
Enjoyment of life activities

Spontaneity of action
Feeling of relaxed participation in the present moment
Ability to direct one's behavior to one's own benefit

### COMPETENCE IN INTERPERSONAL ROLES

Fulfilling one's social role
Role-appropriate behavior
Adjustment in social relations
Behavior eliciting social approval
Interpersonal competence

Using relevant help
Commitment to others
Social responsibility
Steady employment
Ability to work and love
Participation in social activities

### INTELLECTUAL CAPACITY

Accuracy of perception
Efficient mental functioning
Cognitive adequacy
Good sense
Rationality
Contact with reality

Knowledge of self
Problem-solving capacity
Intelligence
Broad awareness and deep comprehension of human experience

### EMOTIONAL AND MOTIVATIONAL CONTROL

Frustration tolerance
Ability to handle anxiety
Morality
Courage
Self-control
Virtue

Resistance to stress
Morale
Conscience
Ego strength
Honesty

### WHOLESOME ATTITUDES TOWARD PEOPLE

Altruism
Concern for others
Trust
Liking for people

Warmth toward people
Capacity for intimacy
Empathy

### PRODUCTIVITY

Contribution to society

Initiative

### AUTONOMY

Emotional independence
Identity

Self-reliance
Detachment

## MATURE INTEGRATION

Self-actualization
Personal growth
Unifying philosophy of life
Balance between opposing forces
Mutually compatible motives
Self-utilization

Ability to handle impulses, energies, and
   conflicts in an integrative way
Maintaining consistency
Complex level of integration
Maturity

## FAVORABLE ATTITUDES TOWARD SELF

Sense of mastery
Satisfaction with one's
   accomplishments
Acceptance of self
Self-respect
Optimism
Happiness

Favorable self-image
Feeling of freedom and self-determination
Freedom from inferiority feelings
Confidence in ability to meet and solve
   problems

**WHAT DO YOU THINK?**

- In your own life, has the display of a particular value ever been functional in one situation but dysfunctional in another?
- What were some of the consequences for you?
- What did you learn from these experiences?

### ■ Individual Needs

Living up to the values in Scott's listing would not necessarily make a person well adjusted. A consideration of cultural and social factors may be useful in making judgments concerning adjustment, but individual needs must be considered, too. For example, while it may be generally true that Americans value trusting others, in some situations a display of trust could be maladjustive for the individual. (Would you, for instance, trust a stranger with your life's savings?) Thus, a person who *never* displays trust in others might be considered somewhat maladjusted from the American point of view, but a person who *always* displays trust might be considered equally maladjusted.

REVIEW
QUESTIONS

*1.* Scholars have not been able to agree on a universal standard by which to measure good adjustment. T F
*2.* When considering adjustment, behaviorists emphasize the role of learning. T F
*3.* It is easy to decide what comprises good adjustment without making value judgments. T F
*4.* One must take into consideration social and cultural factors as well as individual needs when considering the adequacy of an adaptive response. T F
*5.* A person who never displays trust in others is remarkably well adjusted from the American point of view. T F
*The answers to these review questions are on page 20.*

## DISCUSSION: ADJUSTMENT AND INDIVIDUAL NEEDS

### ■ Survival Value

*See the discussion of inclusive fitness in Chapter 4.*

Perhaps the most basic criterion we can use to judge the adequacy of any response is its ultimate survival value. Does the behavior contribute to the ultimate survival of either the individual or his or her gene pool? If so, it may be considered adjustive; if not, it may be considered maladjustive.

■ Many people remember the Great Depression of the 1930's as a time of economic compromise.

In this view, one must take into account not only what an individual is doing at the moment but the long-term implications of this behavior. Delaying, avoiding, distorting, or retreating from reality may seem dysfunctional at first glance but may ultimately ensure survival. For example, running away from danger might prove to be a much better response than facing up to it.

By analyzing the transactions that actually take place between the individual and the environment in the light of ultimate survival value, we begin to realize that many situations can be dealt with successfully only through compromise or even resignation. "Events may occur that require us to give in, relinquish things we would have liked, perhaps change direction or restrict the range of our activities. We may have no recourse but to accept a permanent impoverishment of our lives and try to make the best of it" (White, 1976, p. 20). In this view, compromise becomes essential for survival.

## ■ Growth

Survival value is not the only criterion by which to judge an individual response. Another fundamental criterion is personal growth. Does the behavior contribute to the personal growth of the organism? If so, then it may be considered adjustive; if not, it may be considered maladjustive.

One aspect of growth is the expansion of the organism at the expense of its environment. That is, a growing organism is constantly taking materials from outside itself and transforming them into parts of its own. This expansion may be physical, like the bodily growth that takes place when a person eats food. It may be psychological, like the mental growth that takes place when a person learns from experience. Or it may be social, like the interpersonal growth that takes place when a person acquires communication skills.

*See Chapter 10 for a consideration of communication skills.*

■ Autonomy

Another aspect of growth is autonomy (self-governance). Living organisms are to a degree governed from within. Environmental forces may impinge on them, but they have an internal tendency to resist these forces. In this sense, growth becomes the movement toward an increase in autonomy.

> *Aggressiveness, combativeness, the urge for mastery, domination, or some equivalent urge or drive or trait is assumed probably by all students of personality. All these various concepts imply that the human being has a characteristic tendency toward self-deter- mination, that is, a tendency to resist external influences and to subordinate the forces of the physical and social environment to its own sphere of influences (Angyal, 1941, p. 49).*

Thus, all adjustment involves a kind of compromise—an attempt to balance the effects of internal and external demands so that personal growth as well as survival is achieved. Note that adjustive compromise does not mean abandoning everything we believe is important simply in order to survive. A strategic retreat today may ensure the drive forward tomorrow. Note also that adjustive com- promise not only permits survival and personal growth but ensures that both the individual and the environment will be changed as a result of their interaction.

> Susan is pleased with herself. At twenty-eight she has a challenging job, her own apartment, money in the bank, and a variety of creative pursuits. In short, she is managing her life well. However, things have not always gone so smoothly.
>
> Just a few years ago Susan was caught in the seeming dilemma so many young people face these days. At twenty-two she had been accepted into the law school at the university in her home town. Her parents, who were willing to pay the expenses for her schooling, insisted that she live at home in order to save money.
>
> Susan, an adult by virtually any standard, wanted the personal freedom that typically accompanies adulthood. Her parents, on the other hand, wanted her to follow the somewhat rigid guidelines they had set for her. If she pressed for personal freedom, she would lose the financial backing she so desperately needed to get through school. If she submitted to the guidelines, she would retain the financial backing but lose her personal freedom.
>
> In the long run it appears she chose correctly, for today she has the benefits of both her education and her personal freedom.

## DISCUSSION: ADJUSTMENT STRATEGIES

### ■ A Choice of Strategies

We can imagine few situations in which no choice among responses is available. In essence, each potential choice may be viewed as a strategy of adjustment, and the adequacy of each may be judged according to certain criteria. Consider for example, the following situation. You are alone at night, camping out in a tent. You are fairly deep in the woods, and, to your knowledge, there are no other people within shouting distance. You hear a strange noise coming from some nearby bushes. What are your potential adjustment strategies?

One strategy is to approach the bushes directly. In that case, an immediate confrontation with whatever is making the noise is likely. Another strategy is to look closely and listen carefully to find out what is making the noise, while at the same time maintaining some distance so that an immediate confrontation is less likely. A third strategy is to turn and run away to avoid confrontation altogether. And a fourth strategy is to hide quietly in your tent, another way to avoid confrontation.

## ■ Evaluating Strategies

Three criteria are particularly useful in judging the adequacy of an adjustment strategy. The criteria involve the strategy's value in helping the organism: (1) to secure adequate information about the environment, (2) to maintain the internal conditions necessary for action and for processing information, and (3) to maintain autonomy, or freedom of movement (White, 1976, p. 20). Generally, all three criteria must be met for an organism to interact successfully with the environment, and all must be met simultaneously. Let's consider each of the criteria and then apply them to the four adjustment strategies suggested in the example above.

It seems obvious that the organism must have adequate information about the environment to respond adequately. Certainly all of us recognize that action based on too little information can be disastrous. But too much information may be just as harmful. The flooding of our senses with information often leads to confusion that, at least temporarily, immobilizes us. Thus, behavior geared to obtain more information when we do not have enough and behavior geared to cut down on information when we are receiving too much are both adjustive.

Maintaining the internal conditions necessary for action and for processing information is also critical. If, for example, you become so anxious about your performance on your final biology exam that you cannot concentrate when taking the test, you may flunk the test even though you know the material well. Hence, behavior such as remaining calm in the midst of an intense situation is adjustive.

It is also of critical importance to maintain autonomy and freedom of movement. How can any organism adjust if it cannot move? Generally, behaviors

**WHAT DO YOU THINK?**

■ Can you think of any other adjustment strategies that might be used in this situation?
■ Would these other strategies be superior or inferior to those mentioned in the text?
■ Why?

## CASE IN POINT

Think about some situation in which you acted without first obtaining adequate information. (Perhaps you bought something without fully understanding either the product or the sales transaction.) What was the outcome?

_____

_____

_____

_____

Now, think about some situation in which you failed to act because you were confused by too much information. What was the outcome?

_____

_____

_____

Is the concept of securing adequate information too theoretical for application in the "real world?"

that allow the greatest freedom of movement are the most functional, provided they do not interfere with either the securing of adequate information about the environment or the maintaining of the internal conditions necessary for action and for processing information.

Now let us apply these three criteria to the example given earlier. The first adjustment strategy mentioned in the example is to approach the bushes directly on hearing the strange noise. From the standpoint of securing adequate information, this appears to be a good strategy. It also seems to imply that you, the actor, are relatively calm. Remember, however, that all three criteria must be applied simultaneously. From the standpoint of maintaining autonomy, this appears a poor strategy, because it restricts rather than enhances freedom of movement. Can you imagine approaching the bushes only to find a grizzly bear waiting for you?

The second adjustment strategy is looking and listening while maintaining some distance. This appears to be a good strategy, because it seems to meet all three criteria. You are obtaining needed information, remaining calm, and keeping options open.

The third strategy is to turn and run away. Clearly, this is a poor choice. You do not have adequate information, and you have already panicked. The fourth strategy (to sit quietly and hide) is also poor. You have not obtained adequate information, and you have become totally immobile.

6. Two criteria by which to judge the adequacy of any response are its ultimate _____ value and its contribution to the personal _____ of the organism.

7. A particularly important process that leads not only to the survival but to the growth of organisms is _____ .

8. One aspect of growth is the _____ of the organism; another is movement toward an increase in _____ .

9. It is useful to think of each potential choice by the organism as a _____ of adjustment.

10. The three criteria for judging the adequacy of an adjustment strategy involve: (1) securing _____ _____ , (2) maintaining _____ _____ necessary for action and for processing information, and (3) maintaining_____ , or freedom of _____ .

*The answers to these review questions are on page 20.*

## DISCUSSION: HUMAN PSYCHOLOGICAL AND SOCIAL ADJUSTMENT AND GROWTH

Adjustment and growth occur on biological, psychological, and social levels. In the preceding section, we focused primarily on biological adjustment as we applied adjustment criteria to specific behaviors and strategies. The discussion was universal in that the principles given may be applied not only to humans but to all other animals as well. In this section, we will consider human psychological and social adjustment and growth.

## ■ Human Adjustment and Growth

Human adjustment and growth are different from those of other animals with regard to three significant dimensions: time, language, and morality. Humans have the unique ability to relate to events in terms of the past and the future as well as the present. We can make judgments about today's behavior in the light of goals we hope someday to attain. Similarly, we can use yesterday's successes or failures as standards by which to judge today's or even tomorrow's behavior. Hence, we have the ability not only to sort out current information and respond to the current situation but also to set goals, to plan actions, to act in accordance with that plan, and to evaluate actions in terms of their effectiveness in achieving our goals. It appears that other animals do not match us in these abilities.

*The conclusion contains a complete description of the process of goal setting.*

The language capabilities of humans allow us to accumulate, store, and transmit an enormous amount of information of many types and qualities. We can express opinions ("I believe it is going to rain"), feelings ("I love you"), and hard facts ("George Washington was the first president of the United States"). We can talk about something without its being present ("Last summer, I visited the Grand Canyon. It was an awesome experience") and we can refer to entities whose very existence cannot be objectively verified—that is, known to our senses ("God is omnipresent"). Other animals may communicate with one another on a rudimentary level, but none can begin to compare with humans with regard to length, depth, and breadth of language use.

As human beings, we also are capable of making moral judgments; we differentiate between good and evil. The culture of every human society contains a code of ethics that guides and directs behavior. Through the socialization process, we learn and come to accept an ethical code and, eventually, to experience guilt when we violate it. No one has been able to demonstrate that other animals have such moral capabilities.

*See Chapter 8 for an overview of socialization.*

Thus, time, language, and morality provide human beings with a world of experience eminently larger than that of other animals. And to the degree that our experiential world is larger, our adjustment and growth strategies are more intricate and complex.

## ■ Human Adjustment and Growth Strategies

■ *Securing Information*   Other animals are restricted to their immediate cognitive field when they search for information, but humans can secure information about things even when those things are not present. Thus, a person may obtain information that will help her solve an interpersonal problem she is having at work by talking with other people, by reading a book, or even by taking a course in the psychology of adjustment. When evaluating human adjustment and growth, we must consider the variety of informational strategies available as well as how well those strategies are being carried out.

■ Humans can secure information about things even when those things are not present.

Chapter 3 examines the concept of self-esteem.

See Chapters 2 and 7 for discussions of defensive behavior.

See the discussion of impression management in Chapter 4.

**WHAT DO YOU THINK?**

■ Can you think of a situation in which your level of self-esteem affected your ability to adjust?
■ Do you think self-esteem is really an important factor in adjustment?
■ Why or why not?

■ *Internal Conditions*   Human beings must maintain and, if possible, enhance their level of self-esteem. However, no one has been able to demonstrate clearly that other animals have a conscious idea of who and what they are, much less a need to maintain a positive evaluation of themselves. Hence, self-esteem is a factor that separates humans from other animals.

When a person begins to believe that he or she is incapable, unfit, or unworthy, that person invariably adopts one of two mental postures: emotional depression or **defensive behavior** (an attempt to cope through some form of self-deception). Either is likely to upset the person's internal equilibrium to the point that efficiency in both action and information processing is impaired.

David had been working at the firm for only a few months when the United Way campaign was launched. Because the firm was so small it did not take long before each person knew the amount of every other person's pledge.

Unfortunately, David could not afford to pledge as much as most of the others because he had recently lost money on several bad investments in the stock market. All of this left him in a mild state of depression and, in an attempt to convince himself that he really was just as good as the next person, David made the largest pledge of all.

Moreover, the ramifications of maintaining self-esteem are so wide that any adaptive strategy that fails to take it into account is unlikely to succeed.

*Almost any situation that is not completely familiar, even casual and superficial contacts with new people, even discussing the day's news, can touch off internal questions like, "What sort of impression am I making?" "How well am I dealing with this?" "What kind of a person am I showing myself to be?" When self-esteem is tender or when the situation is strongly challenging, such questions, even if only vaguely felt, can lead to anxiety, shame, or guilt with their threat of further disorganization [White, 1976, p. 31].*

■ *Autonomy or Freedom of Movement*   Our strategy for maintaining autonomy, or freedom of movement, is unique in two ways: (1) it involves an *expanded time factor,* and (2) it involves powerful *psychological* and *social factors.* One aspect of the expanded time factor is its *future dimension.* We can plan for the future in such a way that we are likely to have more options when we get there. It is quite possible, for example, that you are now selecting and preparing for some future occupation. Your planning can take into account projected income and job opportunities, as well as the anticipated capacity of a particular job to meet your growth needs and/or to be a stepping stone to other jobs that will meet those needs.

*See the Personal Action Plan on Career Choice.*

Another aspect of the expanded time factor may be called the *duration dimension*—the "things take time" concept. In many instances, adjustment strategies are not devised instantly but develop and change over time. For example, grieving for a time immediately following the death of a loved one may enhance adjustment more than attempting too quickly to resume usual activities. A person can move more effectively toward greater freedom of movement in the long run by consciously choosing less freedom of movement at the moment.

The psychological and social factors related to autonomy, or freedom of movement, are connected with self-esteem and morality. If our self-esteem is to be high, we must believe our actions are correct and/or moral. Conversely, if we believe our actions are incorrect and/or immoral, our self-esteem will be low. Generally, high self-esteem is a liberating factor that leads to greater autonomy, and low self-esteem is a debilitating factor that leads to less autonomy.

Since societies define correct and moral behavior in terms of their rules, it would appear that all we need do is conform to the rules of our society to attain high self-esteem and, thereby, autonomy. The problem here, though, is that each person has the ability to define morality on his or her own terms, regardless

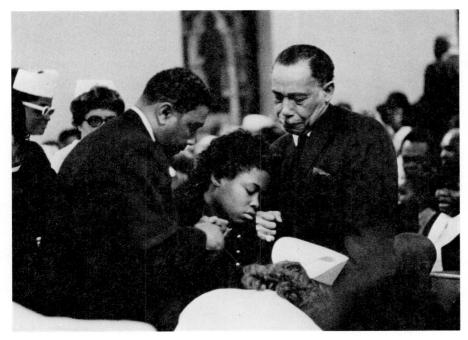

■ A period of grief immediately following the death of a loved one may facilitate adjustment and growth.

■ Do you think drug
dealers are
autonomous? Would
they have high or
low self-esteem?
How would you
answer the same
question with regard
to their customers?

what society preaches. Suppose, for instance, that your society had evolved as
its major criterion of personal success the acquisition of material goods (that is,
a successful person is one who has accumulated a lot of things, particularly
expensive things). But suppose that material goods hold little value for you and
that you define personal success in terms of qualities such as honesty, integrity,
fidelity, and so on. (In other words, you define a successful person as one who
is honest, regardless of whether he or she is wealthy.) In this case, it appears
that you may attain high self-esteem and autonomy by *not* conforming to your
society's rules.

Autonomy, however, is not attained merely by either blindly conforming to
or steadfastly deviating from society's rules. Rather, autonomy is attained by
making independent judgments in the light of personal needs. In some instances,
these judgments may coincide with the rules; in others, they may not. In any
case, the conscious nonconformist is no more autonomous than the person who
always conforms.

*See the discussion of
Maslow's hierarchy of
needs in Chapter 8.*

REVIEW
QUESTIONS

*11.* Human adjustment is different from that of other animals with regard to three
significant dimensions: time, language, and morality. T F
*12.* Only humans transmit information from one member of the species to another.
T F
*13.* Many animals seem to plan their futures. T F
*14.* Humans are different from other animals in that they maintain and, if possible,
enhance their level of self-esteem. T F
*15.* Adjustment strategies often develop and change over time. T F
*16.* It is necessary to become a social deviant to attain autonomy. T F
*The answers to these questions are on page 20.*

## DISCUSSION: MANAGING GROWTH

Thus far, this chapter has provided an overview of the processes of adjustment and growth. It has discussed the general nature of adjustment and growth and the relationship of adjustment to both social values and individual needs. It also has dealt with adjustment strategies and human psychological and social adjustment and growth. Now, the chapter's final section will consider a specific approach you may use to manage your own growth.

### ■ ABCs of Behavior

The approach comes from Watson and Tharp (1972). It is their version of *cognitive-behavioral theory* and they call it the **ABCs of behavior.** Let's begin with B, your *behavior* itself. This category includes all you think, or feel, or do. Eye blinks, hunger pangs, fear responses, and problem solving are all behaviors. Such behaviors can be observed or inferred, and some can be evaluated *by you* as: (1) excessive—too much eating, worrying, daydreaming, and so on; (2) deficient—too little studying, smiling, exercising, and so on; and/or (3) inappropriate—eating the wrong foods, mistaking intentions, talking negatively about yourself, and so on.

*See Chapter 5 for a description of cognitive-behavioral theory.*

The approach holds that all behavior comes under the immediate control of *C*, its *consequences*. Consider the effect your behavior has on you and your environment. Pleasurable consequences strengthen or maintain behavior. For example, the smile that evokes a warm hug will likely be repeated, as will the smile that softens another person's anger.

In the long run, however, our behavior comes under the control of *A*, its *antecedents*. Antecedents, stimuli present just prior to the behavior's being emitted, may evoke or maintain that behavior. For instance, hearing a strange noise while camping in the woods might cause us to "freeze." In time, control may shift from immediate consequences to *anticipated consequences,* which depend on our perception of the situation in which the behavior unfolds. Our memories allow us to interpret present situations in terms of the past. Thus, we come to respond, or behave, in terms of what we expect to happen, based on our beliefs about past events. For example, we may hear a noise, believe it signals danger (it could be the grizzly bear), and resort to screaming because we have come to view ourselves as too slow and weak to run or fight. In this way our behavior may come under the control of its antecedents.

Knowing about the *ABC* approach can help you direct your own behavior in three ways. First, it explains why you behave as you do (the *A* and *C* parts). Second, it gives you three specific areas (*A, B,* and *C*) to consider when creating a plan for changing your behavior. Third, it allows you to regulate your motivations, beliefs, and actions by monitoring your *ABCs* in specific situations and altering them in terms of your progress toward whatever goals you have selected.

### ■ Applying the ABCs

Suppose you are dissatisfied with your excessive display of anger. You keep a record of your outbursts (*behavior*) and discover that they occur under certain conditions (*antecedents*) at home: in the evening; in the presence of your parents;

*Emotions are the subject matter of Chapter 6.*

*The relationship between the individual and the group is considered in Chapter 9, intimacy in Chapter 11, and barriers to intimacy in Chapter 12.*

after much negative thinking about what you see as the unfair pressure your parents are placing upon you; and during discussions of household duties or social activities. Moreover, you find that your anger supports your negative thoughts, relieves your tension, intimidates your parents, and frequently helps you to get your way—even though it destroys the warmth and closeness between you and your parents and leads to remorse (*consequences*).

You decide to attack this unwanted anger on three fronts: (1) *To change antecedents,* you reduce the stimuli that trigger your anger by avoiding certain topics in the evening and by **cognitively restructuring** your thoughts to exclude the notion that your parents are placing excessive pressure on you. (2) *To change behaviors,* you select a response that is **incompatible** with anger—such as a sincere compliment—and use the evening appearance of your parents as a signal for you to search for such a compliment and deliver it sincerely. (3) *To change consequences,* you arrange (contract) with yourself to make some reward **contingent** on your carrying out *A* and *B* above. For example, you may grant yourself one half-hour of free time *if,* and only if, you avoid excessive negative thoughts during the evening. Further, you may grant yourself one half-hour of listening to your favorite music *if,* and only if, that evening you notice something positive about your parents and communicate that observation to them.

As you gain skill and success in directing your behavior, you will raise the standards by which you judge success (you will strive for even less frequent, less intense, and less prolonged anger, for example); and you will change your earned pleasures (**reinforcers**) to include more self-praise. You will also increase the number of times you must meet your standards before you may earn and consume your reinforcers. In this way you can establish a new, less angry pattern of interacting with your parents; and more satisfying evenings will emerge as easy as *ABC.*

### ■ Personal Action Plans

Near the end of this text (see page 481) are four Personal Action Plans designed to help you manage your own growth. The first deals with time management, an area of critical concern for all who desire personal success and fulfillment. The second explores self-help and provides both a general model of self-help and a specific application of the model to a personal problem: how to quit smoking cigarettes. Stress is the subject of the third plan, which concentrates on stress reduction and provides a plan for managing stress. The fourth plan focuses on careers. In addition, Personal Action Plans in the *Study Guide* cover a variety of areas, from personality traits to communication to intimacy.

*Chapter 13 focuses on maladjustment, and Chapter 14 deals with psychotherapy.*

REVIEW
QUESTIONS

*17.* Watson and Tharp call their approach to cognitive-behavioral theory the _____ \_\_\_\_ _____ .

*18.* This approach holds that all behavior comes under the *immediate* control of its _____ .

*19.* In the long run, however, Watson and Tharp maintain that our behavior comes under the control of its _____ .

*20.* Problem behaviors may be evaluated as _____ , _____ , or

_____ .

*The answers to these questions are on page 20.*

## SUMMARY

■ *Adjustment* refers to the individual's response to the physical, psychological, and social demands of the self, other people, and the environment. *Growth* refers to the individual's changing his or her thoughts, feelings, or behaviors regarding the self, others, or the environment. Thus, adjustment emphasizes the impact of the environment, while growth emphasizes internal motivation.

■ There is no universal standard by which to measure adjustment. Scholars have adopted a variety of standards, each reflecting the theoretical orientations and values of its proponents.

■ When judging the adequacy of an adaptive response, we must consider social and cultural factors as well as individual needs.

■ Perhaps the most basic criterion we can use to judge the adequacy of response is its ultimate survival value.

■ Another fundamental criterion by which to judge a response is its contribution to the personal growth of the organism.

■ Growth includes both the expansion of the organism at the expense of its environment and its movement toward an increase in autonomy (self-governance).

■ We may view each potential adjustive choice as a strategy of adjustment, and the adequacy of each may be judged according to whether it helps the organism (1) to secure adequate information about the environment, (2) to maintain the internal conditions necessary for action and for processing information, and (3) to maintain autonomy, or freedom of movement. Generally, all three criteria must be met for an organism to interact successfully with the environment, and all must be met simultaneously.

■ Human adjustment is different from that of other animals with regard to three significant dimensions: time, language, and morality. As a result, our world of experience is eminently larger than that of other animals, and our adjustment strategies more complex.

■ Unlike other animals, humans (1) are not restricted to their immediate cognitive field when securing information, (2) must maintain and, if possible, enhance their level of self-esteem, and (3) can consciously set goals and modify long-range adjustment strategies.

■ The autonomous person is one who makes independent judgments in the light of his or her own needs, regardless of what society preaches.

■ We can manage our own personal growth. A useful approach to self-management is Watson and Tharp's *ABCs* of behavior.

## SELECTED READINGS

Browne, *How I Found Freedom in an Unfree World*. New York: Avon, 1973. A consideration of how we can achieve freedom through personal change.

Moos, R. H., ed. *Human Adaptation: Coping with Life Crisis*. Lexington, Mass.: D. C. Heath, 1976. An anthology that deals first with adjustment in a general sense and then with adjustment to a wide variety of life crises, ranging from those encountered in developmental life transitions, such as marriage and parenthood, to those encountered in unusual situations, such as skyjacking.

Oldenburg, R., and Brissett, D. "The Essential Hangout," *Psychology Today* (April 1980): 82–84. The quality of life of many of us depends almost exclusively on our families and jobs, two institutional structures that tend to disappoint us because we expect too much from them. This article argues that what we need is a "third place," an informal spot away from both home and office where we feel free enough to be ourselves.

Rogers, C. R. *Carl Rogers on Personal Power.* New York: Delacorte, 1977. An examination of how the individual may use personal resources to improve the quality of his or her life.

Zimbardo, P. G. "The Age of Indifference." *Psychology Today* (August 1980): 71–76. A noted psychologist's warning of the destructive influence, both to the individual and to society, of the trend toward isolation and indifference.

## GLOSSARY

**ABCs of behavior:** the *antecedents* of behavior, the *behavior* itself, and the *consequences* of behavior. These are determined by a critical analysis of the situation.

**adjustment:** the individual's response to the physical, psychological, and social demands of the self, other people, and the environment.

**autonomy:** self-governance.

**cognitive restructuring:** altering thoughts that needlessly produce negative emotions and inappropriate behaviors.

**contingency:** a specified relationship between a given response and the occurrence of a reinforcer. *If, then* statements are contingency statements.

**defensive behavior (defense):** an attempt to cope through some form of self-deception. For Freud (see Chapter 2), the unconscious ego process by which we reduce tension from moral anxiety by deceiving ourselves.

**growth:** The process by which the individual changes his or her thoughts, feelings, or behaviors regarding the self, others, or the environment.

**incompatible response:** a response that prevents unwanted behavior from being emitted. For example, you cannot drink water and inhale smoke at the same time.

**reinforcement:** the process by which a perceived reward is associated with an emitted behavior. The perceived reward is called a **reinforcer.** B. F. Skinner (see Chapter 2) holds that reinforcement always increases the probability that an emitted behavior will be repeated.

**value:** an idea of something's being intrinsically desirable. Examples: honesty, freedom, beauty.

## REFERENCES

Angyal, A. *Foundations for a Science of Personality.* New York: Commonwealth Fund, 1941.

Benedict, R. *Patterns of Culture.* Boston: Houghton Mifflin, 1934.

Scott, W. A. "Conceptions of Normality." In *Handbook of Personality Theory and Research.* Edited by E. F. Borgatta and W. W. Lambert. Chicago: Rand McNally, 1968.

Watson, D. L., and Tharp, R. G. *Self-Directed Behavior: Self-modification for Personal Adjustment.* Monterey, Calif.: Brooks/Cole, 1972.

White, R. W. "Strategies of Adaptation: An Attempt at Systematic Description." In *Human Adaptation: Coping with Life Crises.* Edited by R. H. Moos. Lexington, Mass.: D. C. Heath, 1976.

## ANSWERS TO REVIEW QUESTIONS

**Page 8.** *1.* T  *2.* T  *3.* F  *4.* T  *5.* F

**Page 12.** *6.* survival, growth
*7.* compromise  *8.* expansion, autonomy
*9.* strategy  *10.* adequate information; internal conditions; autonomy, movement

**Page 16.** *11.* T  *12.* F  *13.* F  *14.* T  *15.* T  *16.* F

**Page 19.** *17. ABCs* of behavior  *18.* consequences
*19.* antecedents  *20.* excessive, deficient, inappropriate

# 2

# PERSONALITY

FOCUS
## Who am I?

I am a living being who shares certain similarities with others, but who is separate and distinct from any other being that has ever lived. I have my own genetic inheritance, my own way of approaching reality, and my own patterns of thoughts, feelings, and actions.

I have a vast store of memories. I am capable of making instantaneous adjustments to new situations and of planning for my future. I can communicate with others on highly abstract levels and understand my place in the universe.

I can love and hate. I experience anger, pity, jealousy, awe, and just indifference. I sympathize and empathize with other beings. I make rules and then decide either to live by or to break them. I change continually.

Who am I? I am a human being.

## PERSONALITY

## DISCUSSION: PERSONALITY

The question "Who am I?" is as old as human questioning. It has been asked by philosophers, theologians, writers, artists, and scientists, as well as by you and me and most other people who have ever lived. Within the last hundred years many psychologists have attempted to investigate this question scientifically. The concept of **personality** has emerged from their work.

### ■ Defining Personality

*Personality* may be defined as the individual's unique and dynamic pattern of thoughts, feelings, and actions. It is important to realize that scholars disagree on specific definitions of the term *personality* and that a great number of definitions have been given. Most psychologists, however, agree that at least three characteristics should be taken into account: *uniqueness* (no two personalities are exactly alike), *adaptability* (personality can change), and *organization* (a personality is not just a collection of behaviors; it is a patterned response to the environment that shows some degree of consistency).

### ■ Describing Personality

Psychologists describe personality in much the same way most of us do: by **traits** and by **types**. Suppose, for instance, you are asked to describe the personality of a girl you know. One approach is to list some of the consistent characteristics of her personality — her traits. You might say she is honest, loyal, fun-loving, persistent, and so on. Generally, the description that emerges from the trait approach emphasizes the uniqueness rather than the organization of the personality. If you compare the personality of the girl with that of a boy who also is honest and loyal but who is relatively indifferent to having fun and who is not especially persistent, you are struck with the uniqueness of each.

Another approach is to describe personality as a type: a set of interrelated traits that seem to form a consistent pattern. For example, you might refer to people who are sociable, good-natured, humorous, and impulsive as *extroverted* personalities. Notice that the traits mentioned seem relatively consistent with one another. Thus, the type approach emphasizes organization rather than uniqueness.

While each of these approaches emphasizes a different attribute of personality, neither does so to the exclusion of the other. That is, although the trait approach emphasizes uniqueness, it is still possible to find some degree of consistency among the traits expressed in a given personality. And although the type approach emphasizes organization, it is possible to find inconsistency among the traits expressed in a given type of personality. The same principle holds true for the third personality characteristic we have mentioned—adaptability. Personality can change, but the amount and kind of change may vary from one individual to the next. We might also note that while some traits (such as self-esteem) seem to be subject to great change, others (such as introversion/extroversion) appear to be relatively stable. Thus, personality is both stable and adaptable.

**WHAT DO YOU THINK?**

■ What personality traits of your own do you consider to be very positive?
■ What are some positive personality traits you see in others?
■ In what ways are you unique?
■ If you had to create a name for the type of personality you think yours is, what would it be? Why?

CASE IN POINT
## Genetics and Personality

The thyroid glands secrete a hormone, called thyroxin, that governs the rate of metabolism. If your body had secreted too little thyroxin when you were a child, you would be short, have a pot belly and a protruding tongue, and be mentally retarded. If your body secreted too little thyroxin in adulthood, you would be physically sluggish, less alert, and have a lower degree of motivation. If your thyroid produced too much thyroxin, on the other hand, you would be nervous and irritable and probably would eat large amounts of food.

### ■ Factors That Influence Personality

One factor that may influence personality is **genetic inheritance.** For example, the genetically controlled production of certain hormones may cause a person to display certain behavioral or emotional reactions.

Diet, exercise, rest, and general physical health are other factors that may influence personality. Indeed, modern scientific information suggests that an intricate relationship exists among body, mind, emotions, and behavior, with each affecting the others in their functioning. For example, a man who fails to get enough sleep may eventually begin to experience a kind of depression that causes him to become irritable and to behave erratically. His fellow workers, in turn, may begin to respond to him as though he were nothing but a grouch, which may further depress him, and so on. As you can easily see, many factors, both learned and unlearned, influence personality.

### ■ Personality Development

We are not born with personalities completely formed. The newborn must mature and must have many interactions with the environment before personality development is complete. Indeed, while some scholars believe our personality development is completed while we are relatively young (about six years old is the low figure), others take the position that personalities never stop developing. In this chapter and the next, we will examine several positions taken on this issue.

### ■ Personality Models

A **personality model** is a logically organized general description of what a personality is and how it works. It contains basic assumptions about the nature of people and provides clues to predict how people will respond under given circumstances. In a sense, all of us rely on personality models from time to time. For example, we may believe that people are basically good or bad, selfish or giving, honest or dishonest, smart or stupid; and our actions are often based on these assumptions.

Scholars construct personality models that are much more detailed and more logically consistent than the models most of us have devised. Nevertheless, scholars who have constructed personality models disagree widely on at least four major issues: (1) *determinants* (what are the factors that determine, or cause, personality); (2) *structure* (what are its component parts); (3) *dynamics* (how do these parts interact with each other and how does the personality interact with the environment); and, as we have briefly mentioned, (4) *development* (how does the personality grow and change).

Although there is a great variety of personality models, each differing in some aspects from all the others, they may be divided into three basic approaches: *conflict, learning-centered,* and *fulfillment*. Each approach rests on a particular assumption about the nature of human beings.

REVIEW
QUESTIONS

*1.* Personality includes thoughts, feelings, and actions. T F

*2.* Genetic inheritance, diet, exercise, and learning may all affect personality. T F

*3.* The two main approaches to personality description are trait theories and behavior theories. T F

*4.* Scholars often disagree on how personality is structured. T F

*5.* One characteristic of personality is that once it is formed, it cannot be changed. T F

*6.* A personality model is a logically organized general description of what a personality is and how it works. T F

*The answers to these review questions are on page 54.*

## DISCUSSION: A CONFLICT MODEL—PSYCHOANALYSIS

### ■ Freud and Psychoanalysis

The basic assumption of the conflict approach is that a clash between two opposing forces shapes personality. Older versions of the conflict approach identified a clash between good and evil; modern versions identify conflicts between social and psychological forces, such as conflict between social rules and the individual's personal desires. Many scholars have constructed personality models based on the conflict approach, but the most influential is Sigmund Freud (1856–1939), the originator of **psychoanalysis.**[1]

---

1. The volume of Freud's work is large, and his later thought varies, sometimes considerably, from his earlier thought. Our discussion attempts to present the mainstream of his ideas concerning personality in a reasonably consistent and coherent fashion. It is drawn primarily from the following works (title and year originally published are given): *The Interpretation of Dreams* (1900), *The Psychopathology of Everyday Life* (1904), *Beyond the Pleasure Principle* (1920), *The Ego and the Id* (1923), *Civilization and Its Discontents* (1930), *New Introductory Lectures on Psychoanalysis* (1933), and *An Outline of Psychoanalysis* (1940). It is perhaps appropriate to emphasize that the ideas presented in this section are Freud's. These ideas may or may not be consistent with other theorists' views of personality or with what today's scholarship generally concedes to be correct with regard to personality functioning. Our purpose here is to provide an example of a conflict model of personality. Models representing other approaches appear later in this chapter and in other chapters of this book.

Freud's impact on the field of psychology has been enormous. While many have come to challenge the basic concepts of psychoanalysis, both as personality theory and as psychotherapy, some of these concepts—unconscious functioning, including defensive behavior; the critical influence of the relationship between parent and child on the child's development; and the role of transference in the therapeutic relationship—are essential to a general understanding of psychological adjustment and maladjustment.

*See Chapter 14 for a discussion of transference.*

## ■ Drives

The opposing forces Freud saw as shaping personality are the self-serving demands of the individual and the **communal** demands of society. Freud believed that when we are born, we are, in a psychological sense, a mass of drives that demand immediate gratification.[2] In the beginning, our most pressing drive is to obtain the air, food, and water we need for physical self-preservation. Most of us are able to meet our self-preservation demands relatively easily; ultimately, they usually do not cause great conflict for us, because society does not oppose our gratifying them. Our other major drives, however, do cause great conflict, because society places many restrictions on their gratification. These are our drives for sex and aggression. Like the self-preservation drive, the drives for sex and aggression are with us when we are born; but unlike the self-preservation drive, they are incompletely developed and take time to mature.

Freud believed all drives have four characteristics: a *source*, an *energy*, an *aim*, and an *object*. The source is always biological. The energy is the tension caused by the source. The aim is to reduce the tension, and the object is the means by which the tension is reduced. Consider an example: the hunger drive emanates from biological functioning in the gastrointestinal tract. When you have not eaten recently, the fluid level in the mucous membranes of your gastrointestinal tract goes down (source). This drying up creates a bodily tension experienced mentally as hunger pains (energy). You want to reduce the tension (aim), and you will do so by seeking out and eating food (object).

We should note that Freud saw a very close connection between the body and the mind. He believed the source and the object of a drive manifest themselves in a person's mind as a *wish* and that the energy and the aim of a drive are experienced as *uncomfortable emotions*. Our wishes and uncomfortable emotions are therefore expressions of biological requirements.

We should also note that in Freud's view the basic thrust of our biological requirements is to avoid pain and enhance pleasure. Our drives create painful tension, and we seek pleasure through tension reduction. To eat food when we are hungry, for example, is pleasurable. In this sense, Freud saw the basic nature of the individual as self-serving.

## ■ Personality Structure—Id, Ego, Superego

Freud referred to all our basic drives collectively as the **id.** Since it is only a collection of drives, the id is not rational. It cannot think, perceive, remember,

---

2. There are many translations of Freud's writings into English. Sometimes the German word *Trieb* is translated as *drive*; other times, as *instinct*. We have chosen to use *drive* rather than *instinct* because we believe it is closer to what Freud meant.

or act to gratify its own demands. If the personality were only an id, we would not have the power to recognize our drives or to direct ourselves to act in ways that would gratify them. But Freud recognized that there is more to a personality than just self-serving drives. People do possess rational faculties. These faculties develop as we mature physiologically and learn to fend for ourselves. Freud referred to our rational faculties collectively as the **ego.** With both an id and an ego we have the means to experience our wishes and emotions and to act on them. (When the ego functions to help gratify the id, it is operating according to what Freud called the *pleasure principle.*)

The id and the ego do not comprise a complete personality. A third component depends on what we learn from others. We are reared in a society—a web of relationships with rules and regulations that will not permit us to do whatever we want whenever and however we want. As we grow up we learn these rules. When we break them, we are punished by other people. Punishment, or even the threat of punishment, increases tension within us; we experience this tension mentally as anxiety (a general fear or apprehension). Freud called this fear of punishment **reality anxiety.** Like all tension, it is painful. In this case we reduce the tension by obeying the rules. (When the ego functions to help reduce tension and anxiety by using realistic, problem-solving methods, it is operating according to what Freud called the *reality principle.*)

As time goes by, we learn the rules, remember them, and finally accept them. When this happens, the third and last part of the personality is complete. Freud calls this part the **superego.** It is a set of moral ideas that reflect society's rules, or what Freud referred to as the "internalized values of society." The superego allows us to make moral judgments about our thoughts and actions. When we think or do something opposed to the superego, we experience a guilty conscience, the kind of tension Freud called **moral anxiety.** As with reality anxiety, we reduce moral anxiety by obeying the rules.

### ■ Conflict and Defense

Freud believed that we invariably find ourselves in situations in which our desires conflict with our moral beliefs. For example, suppose you are a young man who has been taught and has accepted the belief that it is immoral to have sexual intercourse outside marriage. However, both you and your girlfriend want to have sexual intercourse. In essence, your id would say, "I want her so badly it hurts." But your superego would say, "You will be hurt by terrible guilt feelings if you go to bed with her." In this case, if you do have sexual intercourse, you will reduce the tension of your sex drive but will also experience pain in the form of moral anxiety. If you do not have sexual relations, you will not experience moral anxiety, but you will feel pain in the form of increasing sexual tension.

Freud believed that tension from the id and the superego could be reduced simultaneously in only one way—through **defense.** Defense involves deceiving ourselves so that we remain unaware of our true wishes. Reconsider the example given earlier. Suppose you actually go to bed with your girlfriend. Having committed what you believe is an immoral act, you can escape the pain of moral anxiety by convincing yourself that it was she and not you who really wanted sex. Furthermore, you can convince yourself that if you had not satisfied her sexual desire, you would have lost the relationship you have with her. If you really believe either of these things, you will have less reason to feel the pain of guilt.

## ■ The Nature of Defense

The foregoing explanation of defense presents a problem: How could you tell yourself a lie and believe that lie if you were aware you were lying? The answer is that you would not know you were deceiving yourself. Let us explain. According to Freud, the mind operates on three levels: the **unconscious**, the **preconscious**, and the **conscious**. The unconscious is composed of the aspects of our functioning of which we are totally unaware. Unconscious behavior is so far removed from our awareness that, even if the behavior were pointed out to us, we would deny that it existed. The preconscious is composed of the aspects of our functioning of which we are not immediately aware, but which are accessible if we concentrate on them. For example, people with nervous habits such as tapping their pencils on their desks when taking a test are often unaware of this behavior. However, if you point out the behavior to such a person, he or she will become aware of it. Finally, the conscious is composed of everything of which we are immediately aware.

Defense takes place in the unconscious. In the situation involving you and your girlfriend, then, you would be able to believe your own lie because you would be totally unaware that you were deceiving yourself. The form of defense used in this example is called *rationalization* (offering reasonable and acceptable explanations for unreasonable and unacceptable behavior). Freud's work has been considerably extended in this area; consequently, many forms of defense have been identified. They will be discussed in some detail in Chapter 7. The important point here is that defense is an unconscious process and, according to Freud, a function of the ego. Defense is essential in that it allows us to resolve the apparent dilemma we face when what we wish is in direct conflict with what we believe to be morally right. Without defense, we would be unable to reduce tensions sufficiently to maintain adequate adjustment.

## ■ Psychosexual Stages of Development

Freud believed personality emerges in a series of **psychosexual stages of development.** The first three stages are dominated by conflicts related to gratification of the sexual drive. If these conflicts are adequately resolved, a mature and relatively well-adjusted personality will develop; if not, the resultant personality will be immature and maladjusted. Each stage is identified by distinctive characteristics and forms of defense.

### ■ *Oral Stage*
The first stage begins at birth and lasts approximately one year. It is called the *oral* stage because infants obtain sexual gratification primarily through oral activities (sucking, chewing, eating, and so on). Infants who receive the optimal amount of sexual gratification will develop adjustive personality traits and will proceed to the next stage of development with their personalities unharmed. If either too indulged or too frustrated with regard to oral activities,

**WHAT DO YOU THINK?**

■ Do you believe it is true, as Freud suggests, that conflicts between what we desire and what we believe to be morally right are inevitable?

■ What are some defensive behaviors you have seen displayed by other people?

■ Have others tried to point out some of your own defensive behaviors to you? What are they?

■ Can defensive behavior lead to adequate adjustment? Under what conditions? When might it be maladaptive?

however, infants will become **fixated** in the oral stage. This means that, while they will proceed to subsequent stages of development, they will also retain the unresolved psychological conflicts of the oral stage. Fixations can occur in any of the first three stages, according to Freud, and they always produce adjustment problems in adult life. For example, oral characters (persons fixated in the oral stage) with a background of overindulgence might display gullibility as adults; that is, their pleasure from oral overindulgence might be translated into their "swallowing" almost anything they are told. Conversely, an oral fixation caused by frustration might lead to suspiciousness. *Projection* (attributing to others one's own objectionable characteristics and motives) is a major defense of the oral character.

■ *Anal Stage*   The *anal* stage begins at the end of the oral stage and lasts until the child is approximately two to three years old. During the anal stage the child obtains sexual gratification primarily through voiding or withholding the voiding of the bowels. Toilet training becomes the primary area of potential conscious conflict between parent and child. Anal fixation is associated with stinginess/overgenerosity, stubbornness/acquiescence, and orderliness/messiness. For example, the anal character with a background of frustration might be particularly stubborn as an adult. A major defense of the anal character is *reaction-formation* (replacing true wishes and impulses with directly opposite wishes and impulses). For example, the meticulously clean person might really be renouncing a tendency to be messy.

■ *Phallic Stage*   The third stage is the *phallic* stage, which lasts from about age three to age five or six. The emphasis here is on genital activity. The child obtains gratification primarily through heterosexual interaction (usually with other children in the form of sexual "show and tell") and through masturbation. During the phallic stage the child experiences the **Oedipus complex**, in which the child competes with the parent of the same sex for the affection of the parent of the opposite sex.[3] Children's feelings about their parents may become very intense during this period. The boy, although he is unaware of it, and probably does not know quite how to do it, wants to possess his mother sexually. He views his father, who is infinitely more powerful than he, as the major competitor for his mother's affection and fears that his father will punish him for his desires.

The boy's growing resentment and fear of his father eventually lead to **castration anxiety**, a fear that his father will castrate him or mutilate his genitals (the source of his lustful feelings). In turn, castration anxiety leads to **identification** with the father, a process through which the boy incorporates the father's characteristics into his own personality. Through this identification, the boy is able to reduce the tension that stems from castration anxiety and, ultimately, to resolve his Oedipus conflict. By identifying with his father, he comes

---

3. Freud used the term *Oedipus complex* to identify the major conflict in the phallic stage for *both* boys and girls. Some scholars use the term *Electra complex* to identify the conflict for the girl, but Freud did not care for the use of this term.

to accept his father and the relationship between his parents. His father is no longer a competitor, but a kind of hero, a model after which to pattern his behavior. Now the boy can treat his mother with harmless, tender affection.

A girl may also have intense feelings, particularly when she experiences **penis envy**, a feeling of inadequacy at her lack of a visible sexual appendage. Holding her mother responsible for her castrated condition, the girl rejects her positive feelings for her mother. At the same time, she transfers her love to her father, because he has the organ she lacks, and she wants him to share it with her. Freud believed, however, that the daughter's love for her father (and, ultimately, for all men) is tainted by envy precisely because of the reason she is attracted to him in the first place—because he has something she lacks. Freud believed women are able to compensate somewhat for the lack of a penis when they give birth, particularly if the baby is a boy. Like boys, girls resolve the Oedipus conflict through the process of identification. However, unlike boys, girls do not experience the intense fear associated with castration anxiety. Rather, it is an awareness of the realistic barriers that prevent sexual gratification with her father that leads the girl to identify with her mother.

As in the oral and anal stages, the individual may become fixated in the phallic stage. Phallic fixation is associated with vanity/self-hatred, pride/humility, and stylishness/plainness. Thus, the phallic character who was overindulged might be vain as an adult. The major defense of the phallic character is *repression* (forcefully remaining unaware of unpleasant memories or impulses).

For Freud, these first three stages are so important that the major part of what we might call our character is developed by the time we are about six years old. However, he also believed that part of our development takes place after six.

■ *Latency*  The *latency* stage lasts from approximately age six until puberty. During this time, the sexual drive becomes temporarily inactive. Consequently, no major new conflict related to the sexual drive takes place, and there can be no fixation.

■ *Genital Stage*  The fifth and last stage, lasts from puberty until death. The sexual drive is active once again, but in a more mature fashion. The self-centered gratifications expressed in the oral, anal, and phallic stages give way to mutual gratifications expressed through caring and responsibility in heterosexual relationships. The individual matures into a responsible and productive member of society. Conflicts occur from time to time, but they are not as severe as in the first three stages, and no new fixation can take place. Of course, fixations from earlier stages may cause adjustment problems, sometimes severe. The major defense in the genital stage is *sublimation* (substituting a socially acceptable activity for an unacceptable one). A person with a very strong aggressive drive, for example, might divert the aggressive energy into volunteer work rather than picking fights with other people.

Table 2.1 summarizes Freud's psychosexual stages of development.

TABLE 2.1
Freud's Psychosexual Stages

|  | ORAL STAGE | ANAL STAGE | PHALLIC STAGE | LATENCY | GENITAL STAGE |
|---|---|---|---|---|---|
| Approx- mate age | Birth to 1 year | 1 year to 2 or 3 years | 3 years to 5 or 6 years | 6 years to puberty | Puberty death |
| Sexual gratifi- cation | Sucking chewing eating | Voiding or with- holding voiding of bowels | Masturba- tion, hetereo-sex- ual interaction | Inactive | Mature hetereo- sexual re- relationships |
| Possible fixation | Yes | Yes | Yes | No | No |
| Major de- fense mechanism | Projection | Reaction- formation | Repression | None | Sublima- tion |

## ■ Erickson's Alternative View

*See Chapter 8 for a further consideration of the life cycle.*

Freud did not identify substages within the genital stage, but other scholars had postulated a **life cycle** that inclused additional stages during adulthood. Erik Erickson (b. 1902), a student of Freud, has modified Freud's view by adding three stages of development and by emphasizing the social rather than the sexual nature of the conflicts we must contend with in each stage. Thus, Erikson speaks of eight *psychosocial* stages of development. Table 2.2 lists the major conflicts (Erickson calls them *crises*) associated with each stage and the age range within which the stage occurs.

■ *Trust versus Mistrust*   During the first year, the infant is totally dependent on others. If the infant's caretakers are relatively consistent and generous in the love, care, and attention they provide, the infant develops a basic trust with which to approach life. If the love, care, and attention are inconsistent or in-adequate, then the infant develops mistrust. Erikson maintains that the amount of trust or mistrust developed in this stage affects the way the individual ap-proaches all later relationships.

■ *Autonomy versus Doubt and Shame*   During the second and third years, the child, although still dependent, learns to do some things for himself or herself. To walk, talk, and decide to comply or refuse to comply with directions are all actions within the child's prerogative. During this same period, the child is expected to master the social demands of bowel and toilet training. When these skills are mastered, the child develops a sense of autonomy (self-governance). Failure to achieve such mastery produces a sense of shame and self-doubt. The self-assurance that accompanies success or the shame and doubt that accompany failure affect the person's self-concept throughout life.

■ *Initiative versus Guilt*   Preschool children are well on their way toward social independence. Fully capable of initiating their own behavior, they can make independent decisions—a process that involves risk. The problem here for the child is to make decisions that are correct, or, at least, acceptable. Correct or

TABLE 2.2
Erickson's Psychosocial Stages

| CRISES (CONFLICTS) | AGE RANGES |
|---|---|
| Trust versus mistrust | First year |
| Autonomy versus doubt and shame | Second and third years |
| Initiative versus guilt | Preschool age (4-5) |
| Industry versus inferiority | School age (6-11) |
| Identity versus identity confusion | Adolescence (12-18) |
| Intimacy versus isolation | Young adulthood |
| Intimacy versus isolation | Middle age |
| Generativity versus stagnation | Old age |
| Integrity versus despair | |

acceptable decisions are approved by others, encouraging the child to risk future initiatives. But incorrect or unacceptable decisions are not approved and often bring punishment, leading to a sense of guilt that can inhibit future initiatives.

■ *Industry versus Inferiority*  With school comes work, and school-age children may be rewarded in a variety of ways, from praise to A's, for doing their school work well. These rewards lead to the development of personal industry and a sense of accomplishment. Children who do not do well in school, however, invariably suffer from the negative feedback they receive. The result is a sense of inadequacy and inferiority.

■ *Identity versus Identity Confusion*  Adolescents attempt to forge a complete self-concept through integrating various aspects of self with the images others have of them. In other words, they seek a complete physical, psychological, and social identity. Erikson believes three areas are of crucial importance here: (1) the sexual area ("How well do I meet the requirements of my adult sex role?"); (2) the vocational area ("What will I be when I grow up?"); and (3) the social values area ("What are the appropriate moral principles by which to conduct my life?"). Firm answers to these questions provide the basis for a firm identity. Fragmented or confused answers lead to identity confusion.

■ *Intimacy versus Isolation*  Young adults seek intimate relationships with both opposite-sex and same-sex partners. By intimacy, Erikson (1963) means commitment to "concrete affiliations and partnerships and the ethical strength to abide by such commitments, even though they may call for significant sacrifices and compromises" (p. 263). Failure to form intimate relationships results in a sense of isolation.

*See Chapter 11 for a discussion of intimacy.*

> Carol, well into her fifties, has never been married and believes she never will be. She has had few intimate relationships in her life and seems to shy away from any man who attempts to become emotionally close to her. Now, few men even try. It was not always that way. When Carol was younger, more than one man tried to form an intimate relationship with her; but her inability to make a commitment kept the relationships at a superficial level. Even then, she sensed that she would always be lonely.

■ *Generativity versus Stagnation*  During middle age, persons become concerned with conditions beyond their own immediate development: "How can I make this a better world for future generations?" This seems an obvious concern for parents, but Erikson maintains it is a problem for nonparents as well. The failure to give of oneself to create better conditions for all human beings results in stagnant self-absorption, a kind of self-centeredness dysfunctional both for the individual and for society.

■ *Integrity versus Despair*   Old age is primarily a time to reflect on one's life and to integrate all past life experiences. Erikson (1968) refers to integrity as "the ego's accrued assurance of its proclivity for order and meaning. . . . It is the acceptance of one's one and only life cycle and of the people who have become significant to it as something that had to be and that, by necessity, permitted of no substitutions. It thus means a new and different love of one's parents, free from the wish that they should have been different, and an acceptance of the fact that one's life is one's own responsibility" (p.139). People who achieve integrity are therefore able to accept life and, when it comes, death. Failure to achieve integrity results in despair—a feeling of disgust with one's life and a belief that it is too late to start over. The person in despair is afraid of death.

REVIEW
QUESTIONS

---

*7.* The basic assumption of the_____approach is that a conflict between two opposing forces shapes personality.

*8.* According to Freud, the three structural components of personality are_____ _____, _____, and_____.

*9.* Freud argued that the basic nature of the individual is _____ while the basic nature of society is_____.

*10.* The kind of unconscious functioning by which we deceive ourselves about our true wishes is called_____.

*11.* A person who becomes psychologically arrested in a stage of development is said to be _____.

*12.* The great conflict associated with Freud's phallic stage is the_____ _____, which we eventually resolve through the process of_____ _____.

*13.* Erikson defines the major conflict of old age as_____versus _____.

*The answers to these review questions are on page 54.*

---

## DISCUSSION: A LEARNING-CENTERED MODEL— BEHAVIORISM

### ■ Skinner and Behaviorism

The basic assumption of the learning-centered approach is that *learning shapes personality.* Many scholars who have constructed personality models based on this approach pay scant attention to biologically based drives inferred from people's behavior or to emotional conflicts in people's minds. Instead, they focus on observable behavior and the observable conditions that may cause or determine it. Although some of these **behaviorists** consider internal determinants of behavior (perceptions, motives, attitudes, and so on) as well as external determinants (events in the physical and social environments), others are more extreme in their exclusive emphasis on environmental conditions. The most influential of these *radical behaviorists* is B. F. Skinner (b. 1904).[4]

### ■ Heredity versus Environment

Skinner recognizes that genetic factors can affect behavior. He argues, however, that no matter how much we learn about genetics, no adequate explanation of behavior can be achieved without a thorough understanding of how the environment affects it. In other words, both heredity and environment affect behavior, but Skinner prefers to concentrate on environment. In fact, he argues that environment ultimately determines a species's genetic characteristics. According to the principal of natural selection, he points out, it is the environment that determines what behaviors will allow members of a species to survive. When the successful members breed with one another, they transmit their adaptive characteristics to the next generation. So a species's genetic characteristics are ultimately determined by the environment. It appears that Skinner has good reason to emphasize environmental factors.

### ■ Conditioning

Environmental factors affect learning in two important ways, according to Skinner: one produces *respondent* behavior; another produces *operant* behavior. Respondent behavior is a reflexive type of behavior preceded by and elicited by a stimulus. For example, if someone placed a lit match directly under your hand, you would quickly pull your hand away. The sensation of extreme heat (the stimulus) would cause the respondent behavior of your pulling your hand away (the reflexive response). Early in the twentieth century, behaviorists discovered that respondent behavior could be *conditioned*. Suppose, for instance, each time the lit match were placed under your hand, someone rang a bell. Eventually, you would so strongly associate the heat (the original stimulus) with the sound of the bell (a neutral stimulus) that if the bell were rung, you would jerk back your hand, even if the lit match were not present. Skinner calls this process **respondent conditioning.** It is also called **classical conditioning.**

The early behaviorists made two other important discoveries. First, they found that a conditioned response would gradually diminish and eventually disappear if the neutral stimulus was never again paired with the original stimulus. For example, if you never again burned your hand when a bell was rung, eventually you would not jerk back your hand at the sound of a bell. This process is called **extinction.** Second, the early behaviorists found that the conditioned response

---

4. Skinner has produced many important books, from the 1930s through the 1970s. Our discussion is based on his work in general and, in particular, on *Science and Human Behavior* (1953), *Verbal Behavior* (1957), *Contingencies of Reinforcement* (1969), *Beyond Freedom and Dignity* (1971), and *About Behaviorism* (1974).

tended to generalize to similar but neutral stimuli (that is, you might jerk back your hand upon hearing a buzzer or a whistle as well as a bell). This is called **stimulus generalization**.

Respondent conditioning is obviously important in understanding how and why we display certain learned behavior, and Skinner recognizes its validity. However, he believes another concept, **operant conditioning**, explains our most significant responses to the environment.

Operant conditioning is the process in which an emitted behavior produces consequences that either increase or decrease the probability that the behavior will be repeated under similar circumstances in the future. Suppose, for example, you are visiting Las Vegas and you decide to try your luck with a slot machine. You have never been much of a gambler, so you decide to limit your gambling to a dollar. You put a quarter in the machine and pull the handle on four successive occasions. Each time, you win a dollar. The odds are that you will play again, regardless of your previous decision to gamble only one dollar. Why? Because each time you behaved in a particular way (played the machine), you were rewarded (the machine paid off), and you anticipate that if you display the same behavior again, you will be rewarded again. You have been operantly conditioned to play the machine because your behavior produced positive consequences. The process by which a behavior is made more likely to occur is called **reinforcement**.

Oscar's heart was pounding as he walked toward Sylvia. This was his first dance, and Sylvia was the prettiest girl in the room. Would she dance with him? He thought he would die if she refused. At the least, he would never go

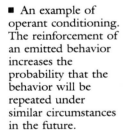

■ An example of operant conditioning. The reinforcement of an emitted behavior increases the probability that the behavior will be repeated under similar circumstances in the future.

to another dance. It had taken him a full half-hour to muster the courage to approach her. Several other boys had done so, and she had turned each of them down. Now, the moment of truth had arrived. He asked. She said yes. Now, Oscar can't wait until the next dance.

## ■ The Nature of Reinforcement

While it may appear simple at first glance, operant conditioning has many ramifications. To begin with, let us note an important difference between respondent conditioning and operant conditioning. In respondent conditioning, the stimulus always precedes the response; in operant conditioning, the stimulus follows the response. Thus, we may conclude that an organism that displays respondent behavior is essentially passive. It simply reacts to environmental stimuli. But an organism that displays operant behavior is essentially active. It emits behavior to produce consequences that, in turn, may serve as stimuli for future responses.

Skinner recognizes that human beings, even from early infancy, are active behavior emitters who produce a great variety of responses. Those that are reinforced are woven into conditioned-response patterns that represent our more significant everyday responses. For example, reading, writing, carrying out a particular work routine, and interacting in certain ways with friends are more significant than respondent behaviors such as jerking one's hand away from a flame or displaying fear on hearing an unexpected loud noise. Thus, Skinner considers personality to be primarily the operantly conditioned responses of the individual.

## ■ Types of Reinforcement

Reinforcement works in two ways: one has to do with the type of reinforcement, and the other concerns its regularity. Two types of reinforcement occur in operant conditioning—positive and negative. Both increase the probability that a response will be repeated. **Positive reinforcement** occurs when something perceived as pleasant follows a response. For example, playing the slot machine in the previous example led to the accumulation of money. It is important to realize that the learner must perceive the payoff as a reward; if not, the probability of the response's being repeated is not increased.

**Negative reinforcement** occurs when something perceived as unpleasant is removed after a response is emitted. For example, suppose you are in the library trying to study for an exam and are distracted by loud talk from a couple of people nearby. If you leave the room to get away from the noise, and thus are able to concentrate, you increase the probability that the next time you are in a similar situation, you will respond by leaving the room.

The second consideration with regard to reinforcement is its regularity. Some behaviors are **continuously reinforced**; that is, there is a payoff each time the behavior is emitted. For example, flicking the light switch in your bedroom results consistently in the light's going on. Your flicking the switch has been continuously reinforced; therefore, you continue to do it. Skinner has found that when the usual reinforcement is not forthcoming in such situations, the result is often disturbing and sometimes humorous. Thus, if you flick the switch and the light does not come on, your initial reaction might well be anger or laughter. Skinner has also found that continuously reinforced behaviors are extinguished rapidly if reinforcement ceases. If, for instance, the light does not turn on when you first flick the switch, you will not keep flicking the switch for long.

Many behaviors are not continuously reinforced; their reinforcement is said to be **intermittent**. When we engage in conditioned behavior that has been maintained by intermittent reinforcement, we are not disturbed when reinforcement is not forthcoming; so intermittently reinforced behaviors take longer to extinguish. Suppose, for example, you know your light switch isn't dependable. In this case, you will not become disturbed if you flick the switch and the light does not turn on. After all, you do not expect it to turn on every time. You may flick the switch for a long time before you give up on it. Thus, intermittent reinforcement is particularly important in repeated response patterns.

**WHAT DO YOU THINK?**

■ Can you identify any of your own behaviors that seem to be the product of respondent conditioning? What stimuli produce these behaviors?

■ What are some of your behavior habits?

■ Can you identify any reinforcers for them?

■ How can reinforcement be used to change behavior?

### ■ Reinforcement Schedules

Not all intermittent reinforcement is the same. The timing may vary considerably, as may the results. Different ways of delivering reinforcers are called *reinforcement schedules*. One kind of intermittent reinforcement is based on the passage of time. It is received on what Skinner calls an **interval schedule**. If the time interval between reinforcers is constant, the schedule is called a *fixed-interval* schedule. The couple that has sex once a week on Saturday night operates on a fixed-interval schedule. They tend to become amorous as Saturday night approaches but not to feel very sexual early in the week, particularly on Sunday morning. This pattern—a low rate of response that immediately follows each reinforcement and a gradual increase of response rate as the next reinforcement approaches—is typical of behavior reinforced at fixed intervals. On the other hand, if the time interval between reinforcers varies, the schedule is called a *variable-interval* schedule, and the behavior is emitted more constantly. Thus, the couple that has sex on an average of four times a month (the same average as in the previous example), but that does not know when the next sexual encounter will occur, will display amorous behavior more often.

Another kind of intermittent reinforcement is based on the amount of behavior emitted. It is received on a **ratio schedule**. If the number of responses required for each reinforcement is constant, the schedule is called a *fixed-ratio* schedule. The salesperson who works on commission operates on a fixed-ratio schedule. He or she must make a predetermined number of sales to earn a given commission. A large number of sales results in a very good living, so the commissioned salesperson often works very hard. Such high response rates are typical of behavior reinforced at fixed ratios (assuming that the required number of responses for reinforcement is not too large and that the individual does not become fatigued). If the number of responses required for reinforcement varies, the schedule is called a *variable-ratio* schedule. Here, because any response might result in reinforcement, a high, sustained rate of response is maintained. Our old friend, the slot machine, operates on a variable-ratio schedule, since it does not pay off predictably. Each failure increases the probability of subsequent success; thus, the more we lose, the more we play.

## CASE IN POINT
## Comparing Reinforcement Schedules

1. Identify one of your behaviors that has been reinforced on:
   a. A fixed-interval schedule.

   _____

   b. A variable-interval schedule.

   _____

2. Identify one of your behaviors that has been reinforced on:
   a. A fixed-ratio schedule.

   _____

   b. A variable-ratio schedule.

   _____

3. Which schedules produced the higher rate of response, fixed or variable schedules?

   _____

Skinner has identified a great variety of schedules that combine variable and fixed elements in many configurations. In a *concurrent* schedule, for example, two or more schedules operate at the same time and reinforcement can be received from any of them. According to operant psychologists, many of our behaviors are related to concurrent schedules.

Another common schedule is the *chained* schedule. Here, behavior reinforced by one stimulus produces a second stimulus, behavior reinforced by the second stimulus produces a third, and so on until a final payoff is received. For example, suppose you have decided to go to the movies tonight. A friend has told you about seeing a movie she described as great. You have always enjoyed the movies your friend has recommended, so you look in the newspaper to see if this particular movie is playing; and it is. The paper has always been correct on such matters, so you go to the theater. The theater is open, so you buy your ticket, and so on until you have seen (and enjoyed, we presume) the movie.

The first stimulus in the chain is a **discriminative stimulus**. A response is very likely to follow this stimulus, because it has been associated with reinforcement in the past (that is, you have been rewarded for following your friend's recommendations in the past; if you had not, you might not bother to look at the newspaper). Each succeeding stimulus in the chain is both a discriminative stimulus and a **conditioned reinforcer** (that is, looking at the newspaper is reinforced by finding an ad, which has in the past been associated with going to the theater to see the movie, and so on). Chaining accounts for many of our complex behaviors.

■ Punishment

According to the **law of effect**, a principle formulated by Edward Lee Thorndike, responses that lead to satisfying consequences are strengthened and therefore tend to be repeated, and responses that lead to unsatisfying consequences are weakened and therefore tend not to be repeated. Certainly punishment qualifies as an unsatisfying consequence; hence, punishment as well as reinforcement can condition behavior.

Skinner recognizes two types of punishment. One occurs when unpleasant consequences follow a response (for example, your request for a date is turned down); the other occurs when a reinforcer is removed after a response (that is, a child's allowance is taken away because she has misbehaved). However, Skinner has grave reservations regarding the use and effectiveness of punishment. He believes both types of punishment tend to suppress behaviors temporarily rather than weaken the overall tendency to respond. Thus, when punishment ceases, the behavior is likely to return. In addition, punishment may produce secondary consequences that are ultimately undesirable (as, for example, when a child punished for talking back to his parents later avoids standing up for his rights even when it is appropriate to do so).

A related Skinnerian concept is *aversive control,* in which threats are used to encourage expected behaviors. Thus, the boss threatens to fire the worker, the parent threatens to spank the child, the teacher threatens to fail the student, and so on. Skinner contends that aversive control, like punishment, is ultimately ineffective and may lead to undesirable secondary consequences. Thus, Skinner prefers the use of reinforcement to shape behavior.

### ■ Shaping

Many behaviors are so complicated that they must be learned in a series of steps. **Shaping** is the process of reinforcing at each step only those responses that come closest to approximating the desired behavior. For example, the student learning to write a high-school-level term paper might initially be rewarded just for putting some thoughts on paper. Eventually, however, more precise writing behavior (use of correct grammar, spelling, punctuation, sentence structure, paragraph structure, and so on) will be necessary for reinforcement to be received. Ultimately, only the production of a high-school-level term paper will be rewarded. A great many of our behaviors are shaped in this manner.

### ■ Thoughts and Feelings

Skinner recognizes thoughts and feelings as well as external behavior, but he believes that they, like external behavior, result from environmental conditions. According to Skinner, there are internal stimuli that arise from biological functioning and physical movement. These stimuli, unlike our overt behavior, are private experiences; they are directly experienced only by us as individuals. It is other people, however, who interpret these internal stimuli for us and who teach us the labels for them. Our parents, for example, observe our external behaviors, then tell us we are angry, embarrassed, loving, or indisposed. Ultimately, other people reinforce our acceptance of their interpretations.

As you may see, this process often leads to confusion. If, for instance, we have learned to label several slightly different internal sensations *anger*, it will be difficult for us to express, and for others to understand, exactly what we are feeling when we say, "I'm angry." Similarly, when we make such statements as "I love my car," "I love my dog," "I love my parents," "I love my spouse," and

---

## CASE IN POINT
## Conditioning Our Thoughts and Feelings

A child may experience sensations of arousal and exhilaration when standing at the edge of a balcony. The parents, however, observing the child's external behavior, may label her feelings as fear or excitement. Children later use these labels and superimpose them on their internal sensations, because they receive parental attention, sympathy, praise, and so on for doing so. In this way, we are conditioned to think and feel as we do.

---

"I love my God," do we really express the same feeling each time? It is no wonder that many of us know more about our external environments than we do about our own thoughts and feelings.

Another problem with internal sensations relates to whether they cause us to respond in certain ways. Have you ever heard statements such as "I lashed out at him (or her) because I was angry," or "I did poorly on the test because I felt depressed"? These statements indicate that the emotions caused the behavior. Skinner disagrees. He believes that if we look for what causes the emotion, we will also find what causes the behavior—and the answer is in the consequences. For example, the angry person experiences sensations that he or she has been conditioned to label *anger*, then lashes out because this behavior has produced a payoff in similar situations in the past. In like manner, the depressed person may feel low because of a general lack of reinforcement for his or her behavior. A lack of reinforcement for previous test-taking behavior may explain poor test results.

Skinner also denies that *drives* (in the sense Freud uses the word) can explain behavior. We do not behave a certain way because we have a strong (or weak) sex drive; we behave that way because we have been conditioned to behave that way. Thus, for Skinner, thoughts, feelings, and actions all are controlled by environment.

**WHAT DO YOU THINK?**

■ Do emotions cause behavior, or are both emotions and behavior caused by their consequences?

### ■ Bandura's and Walters's Alternative View

■ *Modeling* Two behaviorists, Albert Bandura and Richard H. Walters, have proposed a *social learning theory* that emphasizes internal as well as environmental factors in behavior. The theory focuses on **modeling** as the principal technique through which we learn; that is, we learn by observing the behaviors of other people who serve as models for us. In this view, what the observer primarily acquires from the model is a symbolic representation of a behavior and not stimulus-response connections. A child learning to swim, for example, does not just watch someone swim and then begin to swim himself. He observes, asks questions, receives information, and eventually, under supervision and with criticism, begins to take his first awkward but successful strokes. Thus, our uniquely human capacity to interpret reality, to formulate ideas and make judgments about what we observe, is more important than mere stimulus-response connections.

■ We learn many significant behaviors through the process of modeling.

Of course, trial and error accounts for some learning, but our most complex behaviors are learned through verbal instructions and the observation of models. In learning to speak a language, for example, the learner must have a model: "A child who is unfamiliar with the Polish language would never emit the Polish phrase for 'expectancy' even though the probability of reinforcement was 100 percent and the contingent reinforcer was exceedingly attractive. Obviously, in this particular example, the introduction of an important social variable—a verbalizing model—is an indispensible aspect of the learning process" (Bandura and Walters, 1963, p. 2).

■ *The Nature of Learning*   Learning requires more than exposure to a model, however. Attention, retention, reproduction, and motivation are needed as well.

- To begin with, the learner must direct *attention* to relevant cues and perceive those cues accurately (Bandura, 1969, 1971b). In other words, we must pay attention to what is important in the modeling situation.
- The learner must also *retain* symbols of the modeled behavior. We could not imitate a behavior if we had forgotten it. We recall the behavior by coding it into symbolic form (words or images).
- Next, memory is used to guide *reproduction* of the behavior. Merely acquiring and retaining an idea of what to do does not ensure skillful or even adequate performance. The learner must practice the behavior and make necessary adjustments as dictated by self-observation and feedback.
- Finally, the learner must be *motivated* to display the behavior. Rewards and punishments play a paramount role. If, for instance, you could dance the tango but were ridiculed each time you began to do that dance, then you would likely give up the tango.

■ *Vicarious Rewards and Punishments and Their Effects on Behavior*   Bandura and Walters agree with Skinner that rewards and punishments may operate directly on the learner's behavior; however, they believe rewards and punishments may also operate vicariously. That is, the learner may be affected by what he or she sees happening to a model. For example, if you observe a model being rewarded immediately after he or she displays a particular behavior, then you are more likely to imitate that behavior. Conversely, if the model is punished, you will not be likely to imitate the behavior.

According to Bandura (1971a, 1971b), the effects of vicarious rewards and punishments are regulated by six mechanisms:

1. *Information*—the observer may discover how to behave in ways that will be rewarded and how to avoid behaving in ways that will be punished.

2. *Incentive motivational effects*—the observer may begin to expect rewards similar to what the model has received when he or she displays behavior similar to the model's.

3. *Emotional arousal*—the observer may experience a general heightening of responsiveness that extends beyond the specific responses of the model. For instance, fear generated from observing a model being punished may not only keep the observer from imitating the model's behavior; it may also keep the observer from displaying *any* response. In this case, the observer may direct attention elsewhere or otherwise attempt to get away from the situation.

4. *Increased susceptibility to direct reinforcements*—the observer may become more accurate in his or her imitation in order to obtain direct reinforcement in the future.

5. *Modification of social status*—the observer may become aware that the model's (and, if the behavior is imitated, his or her own) social status may be increased or decreased through rewards and punishments.

6. *Alteration of valuation of reinforcing agents*—the observer may change his or her psychological posture toward a reinforcing agent if the agent is perceived to be abusing power. For example, if you observe a model receiving what you believe is unjust punishment, you may become aggressive toward the person dispensing the punishment.

Through these six mechanisms, the observational learner feels the effects of the model's rewards and punishments and modifies his or her own behavior accordingly.

---

*14.* Skinner argues that environment ultimately determines a species's genetic characteristics. T F

*15.* Our most significant responses to the environment are caused by respondent, or classical, conditioning. T F

*16.* In operant conditioning, the stimulus follows the response. T F

*17.* Reinforcement is the process by which a behavior is made more likely to occur. T F

*18.* Intermittent reinforcement occurs every time a particular stimulus occurs. T F

*19.* Extinction is the gradual dying out of a conditioned response. T F

*20.* Punishment occurs when unpleasant consequences follow a response or when a positive reinforcer is removed after a response. T F

*21.* Shaping is another name for the law of effect. T F

*22.* Skinner argues that a person's internal processes, such as thoughts and feelings, are conditioned, as a person's actions are. T F

*23.* Bandura and Walters claim that motivation has nothing to do with learning. T F

*24.* Information is one of the mechanisms that regulate the effects of vicarious rewards and punishments. T F

*The answers to these review questions are on page 54.*

## DISCUSSION: A FULFILLMENT MODEL—HUMANISM

### ■ Rogers and Humanism

The basic assumption of the fulfillment approach is that personality is shaped by a single force from within the person. Like the conflict and learning-centered approaches, the fulfillment approach has many adherents and many variations. Generally, fulfillment theorists reject the basic **determinism** of the other two approaches—the notion that behavior is caused by and can be explained by factors over which the individual has no control. Rather, they emphasize both freedom of choice for the individual and responsibility for one's own behavior. Scholars who support this position are often referred to as **humanists.** The most influential of the contemporary fulfillment theorists is Carl Rogers (b. 1902).[5]

### ■ Freedom and Control

You may recall that the conflict approach assumes that behavior is determined by and can be explained in terms of the conflict of two opposing forces. For Freud, the conflict is between the id and the superego. Through defense, the ego maintains equilibrium for the personality. In this view, about the best we can do is lie to ourselves to maintain adequate adjustment.

Behaviorism assumes that behavior is determined by and can be explained in terms of learning. For Skinner, learning is synonymous with conditioning, and our most significant learned responses are controlled by the environment through operant conditioning. In this view, concepts such as freedom of choice and responsibility for behavior are ultimately meaningless.

---

5. Like Freud and Skinner, Rogers has produced a large volume of work over an extended period. The following books and articles were particularly useful to our discussion of his ideas: " A Theory of Therapy, Personality, and Interpersonal Relationships, as Developed in the Client-Centered Framework" (1959, pp. 184–256); *On Becoming a Person* (1961); "Actualizing Tendency in Relation to 'Motives' and to Consciousness" (1963, pp.1–24); *Person to Person: The Problem of Being Human* (1967).

Rogers and other humanists are much more optimistic about the possibilities for human beings. They believe there is much more to human functioning than self-deception, or responses to environmental stimuli.

Rogers does not deny that the ultimate causes for human behavior lie outside the individual's control. However, he believes that we have freedom to choose among responses, within the limits of the factors that determine our behavior. We can, for instance, choose either to become aware of and to understand the factors that determine our behavior, or to ignore them. Through this kind of choice we can exercise responsibility for our behavior. Thus, Rogers accepts both determinism and freedom of choice, and he believes both concepts are useful in understanding human functioning.

## ■ The Actualizing Tendency

The force Rogers sees as shaping personality is the drive to actualize potentialities, to become what we are capable of becoming. Rogers believes that all living organisms possess this **actualizing tendency.** Like Freud's self-preservation drive, the actualizing tendency aims at maintaining life by pushing the organism to meet its needs for oxygen, food, and water. In addition, however, the actualizing tendency aims at enhancing life as it pushes the organism to *grow*. Growth can have involuntary aspects (biological changes that automatically take place over time, such as the development of a fetus from an embryo) and voluntary aspects (such as your conscious decision to become better educated by going to college).

■ These people are showing voluntary growth by actively pursuing a college education which will enhance their lives.

There are fundamental differences among Freud, Skinner, and Rogers on this issue. All three would agree that involuntary growth takes place, but there is no notion of voluntary growth in the Freudian and Skinnerian views. For Freud, unconscious functioning dominates our behavior, while Skinner holds that our choices are determined by environment.

## ■ Potentialities

**Potentialities** are the inherent capacities of the individual. Because Rogers views human beings as dynamic, growing, and free organisms, he does not believe it possible to specify what these potentialities are. However, he does indicate that all inherent potentialities of humans function to maintain and to enhance life.

Again, we see a significant difference among Freud, Skinner, and Rogers. The Freudian view holds that the aggressive drive may be turned inward and may ultimately result in suicide; therefore, suicide may be a function of human nature. The Skinnerian view holds that the only significant human potentiality is the ability to respond differentially to environmental stimuli. In contrast, the Rogerian view holds that we have many significant inherent potentialities, and that these work toward positive growth. Thus, a person may choose to commit suicide, but suicide (and other destructive behavior) is an expression of psychological maladjustment rather than an expression of human nature.

## ■ The Nature of Conflict

Unlike Freud, Rogers rejects the idea that conflict between the individual and society is inevitable. He believes that the maintenance and enhancement of the individual is consistent with society's communal requirements. Conflict, when it does occur, is an expression of maladjustment. For example, we lash out at people and act destructively in other ways only when we feel insecure, unworthy, depressed, and so on. Conversely, when we feel good about ourselves (secure, worthy, happy) we cooperate, reach out, and lend a helping hand. Therefore, we maintain and enhance our own lives when we maintain and enhance the lives of others. In this view, aggressiveness is an expression of maladjustment because it is not an expression of the basic life force, the actualizing tendency.

## ■ The Self-Actualizing Tendency

The actualizing tendency is our biological drive to become what we can become. As previously mentioned, all living organisms have this drive. Rogers assumes, however, that living organisms do not have identical potentialities; hence, the actualizing tendency does not express itself in the same way for all species. Human beings, for instance, experience psychological aspects of the actualizing tendency that do not occur in other life forms. One such aspect is the **self-actualizing tendency,** the drive to become what we think we are. Let us explain.

Rogers asserts that each of us has a **self**—a concious idea of who and what we are. Unlike the actualizing tendency, the self is not part of us when we are born. It develops over time as we gain the approval and disapproval of significant others in our environment (such as our parents). In other words, people make judgments about us and our behavior and tell us that we are good (or bad), smart (or stupid), kind (or mean), and so on. Eventually, we integrate this feedback into a conscious idea of who and what we are. Once we have developed this self-concept, we begin to make judgments about our own behavior, which, in turn, further defines our self-concept. We may, for example, evaluate our own thoughts, feelings, and actions as being more or less consistent with our self-concept. In this manner, we push to become what we think (and what others have originally taught us) we are. Thus, the self-actualizing tendency is manifested in our attempts to live up to our self-concept.

**WHAT DO YOU THINK?**

■ In what ways do you attempt to live up to your self-concept?
■ In what ways has your self-concept changed over the past five years?
■ Do these changes reflect an awareness of your potentialities, or are they attempts to meet standards set for you by other people?
■ Do we really have freedom of choice in our behaviors? If so, to what extent?

## ■ Potentialities and Self

Sometimes we strive to live up to standards that are outside the range of our potentialities. In these instances we may feel guilty and anxious and begin to behave defensively. Consider, for example, a boy who has been taught from early childhood that he has a superior intellect. He has incorporated the idea of being a little genius into his self-concept, but he really does not have extraordinary intellectual capacity. When he learns that his grade on a school test is less than A, he experiences guilt and anxiety for not living up to his expectations. In an attempt to maintain his self-concept, he will tell himself a lie. For instance, he may convince himself that he did not feel well when he took the test, or that the test was poorly constructed, or that it was unfair because it dealt with material not covered in the book. The boy in our example is maladjusted because, in his attempt to maintain a distorted self-concept, he works against the drive to actualize his potentialities. If he continues to display such maladjusted behavior, he will prevent himself from becoming all he could become.

Rogers provides a general description of the process by which inconsistencies between potentialities and self-concept arise. Significant others begin the process by giving us **conditional positive regard.** This means they accept, support, and respect us only some of the time (for example, when we behave the way they want us to behave). Our self-concept develops in accordance with their idea of who and what we should be. Soon we translate their "shoulds" into standards by which we judge the value of our thoughts, feelings, and actions—**conditions of worth.** Once we have established conditions of worth, we must meet them or display the guilt, anxiety, and defensive behavior previously mentioned. At this point, we find ourselves in a state of **incongruence,** in which we restrict the full expression of our potentialities. Thus, we are maladjusted.

If, however, we receive complete acceptance, support, and respect from significant others **(unconditional positive regard),** we will not develop conditions of worth. Without conditions of worth, we will not experience the guilt and anxiety or display the defensive behavior associated with them. We will be in a state of **congruence,** which will not restrict the full expression of our potentialities. Under these circumstances, there will be no inconsistency or conflict between our potentialities and our self-concept; on the contrary, our self-concept will reflect our potentialities. We will be adjusted. Rogers refers to this type of person as the *fully functioning person*.

Rogers recognizes that it is highly unlikely that fully functioning people exist; however, ideally it is possible that they could. This position is, of course, an extreme departure from the determinism and inherent pessimism of the Freudian view, in which conflict is inevitable. Moreover, Rogers argues that even if we display maladjusted behavior from time to time, we can do something about it. We can examine our thoughts, feelings, and actions. We can explore our own potentialities and be creative. We can learn to trust our own judgment and to reject inappropriate standards set for us by other people. Indeed, we can rearrange our self-concept so that it reflects our potentialities, thus eliminating the cause of our defensive behavior. And we can do all these things by conscious *choice,* a course of action unavailable to us in both the Freudian and Skinnerian views.

### ■ Maslow's Alternative View

Abraham Maslow (1908–1970), another humanist, concentrated on human needs and their relationship to the development of a person's full potential. According to Maslow, human needs unfold in a pyramidlike structure (see Figure 2.1). Each level of need in the pyramid emerges as the requirements of the preceding level are met.

■ *The Lower Levels of the Pyramid of Needs*   At the base of the pyramid are our physiological needs—our needs for food, air, rest, and so on. These are *unlearned* needs related to physical survival. Failure to meet them results in death. As previously mentioned, the aid of other people is initially indispensable in meeting physiological needs. When we have met these needs sufficiently, the next level of need emerges—the need for *safety.* We seek physical safety and psychological security so that we may feel free to act within our environment without fear or threat. Note that needs for safety are *learned,* as are all the needs above the physiological level in the pyramid.

When needs for safety have been satisfied, needs for *belongingness* and *love* arise. We want affection and appreciation from others, and we want to feel wanted as a social group member. Satisfaction of the needs for belongingness and love directly

FIGURE 2.1.
Maslow's perception
of human needs.

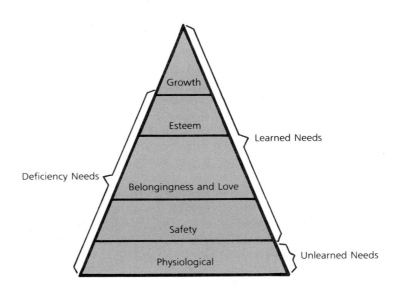

## CASE IN POINT
## The Learned Need for Safety

If you had been placed in a room with a poisonous snake when you were only a year old and you had not yet learned that poisonous snakes are dangerous, you probably would have approached the snake out of curiosity. You might have tried to hold it and perhaps to put it into your mouth. Contrast that image with the behavior you would display now if you were placed in a room with a poisonous snake.

You have learned to fear poisonous snakes for your safety's sake. Indeed, if you are like many people, this particular fear may have become generalized to include nonpoisonous snakes as well. Although it is possible to learn safety needs through observation of and reflection on direct life experiences, it is likely that you have learned many ideas related to safety through communication with other people.

depend on interaction with others; failure to satisfy these needs results in inadequate development.

The fourth level of the pyramid contains needs for *esteem*. We want respect, both from other people and from ourselves. These two types of needs for esteem share something in common, but they also differ. Both are concerned with meeting standards for achievement. However, we gain the respect of others by meeting *their* standards, while we gain self-respect by meeting *our own* standards. Generally, when we satisfy our needs for esteem, we feel good about ourselves and are confident that we can do whatever we choose to do. When we do not satisfy these needs, we feel frustrated, discouraged, inferior, and helpless.

■ We need the affection of others in order to become complete persons.

■ *Need Conflict*    In Maslow's view, we can attend to only one level of need at a time, so the needs cannot conflict. The person with unsatisfied needs for love and belongingness must attend to them before needs for esteem can be satisfied. Perhaps that is why the unloved superstar is such an unfulfilled person. He or she may be striving for self-respect or the respect of others without having first fulfilled the more basic need to get love and acceptance from others. Thus, although we do not have need conflicts, we may very well have need confusion.

It is important to understand that, in Maslow's view, we always function on the lowest level of unmet need at any given time. If, for example, you usually eat three meals a day and you miss breakfast, then by lunch time you will not be concerned with whether you are respected or loved. You will be concerned with satisfying your hunger. In such a situation, your needs for love and esteem are suspended until your need for food has been satisfied.

■ *Needs for Growth*    Maslow identified several needs related to growth, including needs for *self-actualization, understanding,* and *esthetics.* Maslow used the term *self-actualization* in virtually the same sense Rogers uses the term *actualizing tendency.* Hence, our need for self-actualization is our desire to fulfill our potential. Our need for understanding is our desire to reach the greatest levels of meaning and awareness of ourselves, others, and all aspects of the external environment. Our desire for beauty is reflected in our esthetic need.

There is a significant difference between the needs on the lower levels of the pyramid and the needs for growth. Maslow referred to the lower needs as *deficiency needs;* we act to meet these needs because we lack something. Once we have fulfilled the deficiency needs, we are free to become, to understand, and to appreciate all that we are capable of becoming, understanding, and appreciating. When we are actively engaged in fulfilling growth needs, we have reached the highest level of human development. Finally, we should note that at this level, as at all levels of the pyramid, human contact plays a vital role. We must have human contact if we are to become all we are capable of becoming.

*The role of human contact will be explored in Chapters 8 and 11.*

REVIEW
QUESTIONS

25. The doctrine that behavior is caused by and can be explained in terms of factors over which the individual has no control is called _____ .

26. The _____ _____ is the biologically based drive to become what we are capable of becoming.

27. Rogers refers to the inherent capacities of the individual as _____ _____ .

28. When we receive the complete acceptance, support, and respect of significant others, we are receiving _____ _____ _____ .

29. Conditions of worth typically lead to _____ , _____ , and _____ _____ .

30. Rogers calls our conscious idea of who and what we are our _____ .

31. Maslow's growth needs include the needs for _____ , _____ , and _____ .

*The answers to these review questions are on page 54.*

# SUMMARY

■ Many psychologists have attempted to investigate scientifically the question "Who am I?" The concept of personality has emerged from their work.

■ Although scholars often disagree on specific definitions of personality, they do agree that at least three characteristics should be taken into account: uniqueness, adaptability, and organization.

■ We may define *personality* as the individual's unique and dynamic pattern of thoughts, feelings, and actions.

■ Modern scientific information suggests that an intricate relationship exists among body, mind, emotions, and behavior, with each affecting the others in their functioning. Many factors, both learned and unlearned, influence personality.

■ Psychologists use two primary approaches to describe personality: by traits and by types. Generally, the trait approach emphasizes uniqueness, while the type approach emphasizes organization.

■ Psychologists also often provide broader, more general descriptions in the form of personality models. The major issues they address are the determinants, structure, dynamics, and development of personality.

■ The various personality models may be divided into three basic approaches: conflict, learning-centered, and fulfillment. The conflict approach (psychoanalysis) assumes that a conflict between two opposing forces shapes personality. The learning-centered approach (behaviorism) assumes that learning shapes personality. The fulfillment approach (humanism) assumes that a force that comes from within the individual shapes personality.

■ Sigmund Freud viewed the conflict between the self-serving demands of the individual and the communal demands of society as the determinants of personality.

■ Freud postulated a personality structure consisting of id (selfish demands), ego (rational functioning), and superego (society's rules). The conflict between the id and the superego is managed by the ego though its defensive functioning.

■ According to Freud, personality development proceeds through a series of five psychosexual stages, the first three of which are critical in the individual's character formation.

■ Erik Erikson has modified Freud's view by adding three stages of development and placing emphasis on the social rather than the sexual nature of the conflicts encountered in each stage. Erikson's stages are called psychosocial stages.

■ B. F. Skinner asserts that personality is determined primarily through learning.

■ Although he does not write about personality structure, Skinner believes the important structural component in human behavior is the ability to respond differentially to environmental stimuli.

■ Skinner treats personality dynamics in terms of respondent and operant conditioning; the more important of these is operant conditioning, because it explains our most significant responses.

■ Skinner explains development in terms of the individual's history of reinforcements.

■ Albert Bandura and Richard H. Walters have proposed a social learning theory that focuses on modeling as the principal technique through which we learn.

■ Carl Rogers holds that personality is determined by the degree of consistency between the individual's potentialities and self-concept.

■ Rogers believes personality structure consists of the actualizing tendency, the potentialities, and the self-concept. The individual pushes to behave consistently with his or her self-concept.

■ Conditional positive regard and conditions of worth lead to guilt, anxiety, defensive behavior, a state of incongruence, and, ultimately, maladjustment.

■ Unconditional positive regard and an absence of conditions of worth lead to a state of congruence, which, in itself, represents adjustment.

■ Rogers asserts that although initial development is heavily influenced by significant others, later development is a matter of conscious choice.

■ Abraham Maslow concentrated on human needs and their relationship to the development of a person's full potential. Our needs unfold in a pyramidlike structure, with each higher level of need emerging as the requirements of the preceding level are met.

## SELECTED READINGS

Bandura, A., and Walters, R. H. *Social Learning and Personality Development*. New York: Holt, Rinehart and Winston, 1963. A concise explanation of social learning theory and the role of modeling/imitation in personality development.

Erikson, E. H. *Childhood and Society*, 2d ed. New York: Norton, 1963. A detailed explanation of Erikson's psychosocial stages.

Freud, S. *An Outline of Psychoanalysis*. Revised, translated, and edited by J. Strachey. New York: Norton, 1969. Freud's very brief final work, which describes many of the ideas discussed in this chapter.

Hall, C. S., and Lindzey, G. *Theories of Personality*, 3d ed. New York: Wiley, 1978. One of the better general introductions to personality theory.

Janis, I. L.; Mahl, G. F.; Kagan, J.; and Holt, R. R. *Personality: Dynamics, Development, and Assessment*. New York: Harcourt, Brace & World, 1969. An excellent overview of personality.

Maslow, A. H. *Motivation and Personality*, 2d ed. New York: Harper & Row, 1970. A detailed explanation of Maslow's hierarchy of needs.

Milkman, H., and Sunderwirth, S. "The Chemistry of Craving." *Psychology Today* (October 1983): 36–44. An exploration of the hypothesis that personality determines how a person satisfies his or her compulsive needs.

Nye, R. D. *Three Psychologies: Perspectives from Freud, Skinner, and Rogers*, 2d ed. Monterey, Calif. Brooks/Cole, 1981. A brief introduction to the views of three theorists, including comparisons, contrasts, and criticisms.

Rogers, C. R. *On Becoming a Person*. Boston: Houghton Mifflin, 1961. Rogers's eloquent expression of his own brand of humanism.

Skinner, B. F. *About Behaviorism*. New York: Knopf, 1974. The authoritative guide to Skinner's ideas about behaviorism.

## GLOSSARY

**actualizing tendency:** the biologically based drive to become what we are capable of becoming.

**behaviorist:** a psychologist who focuses on observable behavior and on the observable conditions that may cause behavior. Behaviorists often experiment with animals such as rats and pigeons to identify behavioral principles that can be applied to human behavior. Sometimes they experiment with humans as well.

**castration anxiety:** a young boy's fear that his father will damage his genitals.

**communal:** pertaining to the people of the community.

**conditional positive regard:** partial acceptance, support, and respect from significant others.

**conditioned reinforcer:** a stimulus that has become a reinforcer because of its past association with other positive consequences.

**conditions of worth:** standards by which we judge our own value, taught to us by other people.

**congruence:** the condition in which there is no conflict between potentialities and self-concept.

**conscious:** the part of the mind containing everything of which we are immediately aware.

**continuous reinforcement:** reinforcement that occurs each time a particular behavior is emitted.

**defense:** the process by which we reduce the tension from moral anxiety by deceiving ourselves. It is an unconscious function of the ego.

**determinism:** the doctrine that behavior is caused by and can be explained in terms of factors over which the individual has no control.

**discriminative stimulus:** a stimulus that elicits a response associated with a high probability of reinforcement in the past.

**ego:** the rational part of our personality, which develops as we mature physiologically and learn to fend for ourselves. Thinking, perceiving, and remembering are aspects of ego functioning.

**extinction:** the gradual dying out of a conditioned response.

**fixation:** arrestment in a particular psychosexual stage of development.

**genetic inheritance:** the unique physical characteristics of the individual (such as eye color, body frame, blood type) that are biologically transmitted from parents to child.

**humanist:** scholar who views humans as having free choice of and responsibility for their own behavior.

**id:** our personality at birth, which consists of the biologically based drives for preservation, sex, and aggression. The id is inherently self-serving and irrational.

**identification:** the process of incorporating the characteristics of another person into one's own personality.

**incongruence:** the state in which the full expression of one's potentialities is restricted.

**intermittent reinforcement:** reinforcement that does not occur each time a particular behavior is emitted.

**interval schedule:** a pattern of reinforcement based on the passage of time. If the interval is constant, it is called a fixed-interval schedule; if the interval varies, it is called a variable-interval schedule.

**law of effect:** a behavioral principle that states that responses leading to satisfying consequences are strengthened and therefore tend to be repeated, and responses leading to unsatisfying consequences are weakened and therefore tend not to be repeated.

**life cycle:** the general sequence of events in our physical, psychological, and social development as we progress from infancy through old age.

**modeling:** the process in which a learner observes a behavior, formulates ideas and makes judgments about the behavior, and attempts to imitate the behavior.

**moral anxiety:** a fear caused by guilt.

**negative reinforcement:** the removal of something perceived as unpleasant from a situation after a response is emitted.

**Oedipus complex:** conflict during the phallic stage in which the child competes with the parent of the same sex for the affection of the parent of the opposite sex. Freud considered this the major conflict in each person's life.

**operant conditioning:** a kind of learning in which an emitted behavior produces consequences that either increase or decrease the probability that the behavior will be repeated under similar circumstances in the future.

**penis envy:** a young girl's feeling of inadequacy at her lack of a penis.

**personality:** the individual's unique and dynamic pattern of thoughts, feelings, and actions.

**personality model:** a logically organized general description of what a personality is and how it works.

**personality trait:** a personality characteristic consistently expressed by an individual.

**personality type:** a set of interrelated personality traits that form a consistent pattern.

**positive reinforcement:** the introduction of something perceived as pleasant following a response.

**potentialities:** the inherent capacities with which the individual is born.

**preconscious:** the part of the mind containing the aspects of our functioning of which we are not immediately aware, but which are accessible if we concentrate on them.

**psychoanalysis:** Sigmund Freud's system of psychological thought. It includes both a theory of personality and a therapeutic method. (See Chapter 14.)

**psychosexual stages of development:** five successive levels of personality development identified by particular personality traits. The first three stages are dominated by conflicts related to sexual gratification.

**ratio schedule:** a pattern of reinforcement based on the amount of behavior emitted. Ratio schedules may be fixed or variable.

**reality anxiety:** a fear that we will be punished for breaking the rules.

**reinforcement:** the process by which a perceived reward is associated with an emitted behavior. The perceived reward is called a **reinforcer.** Skinner holds that reinforcement always increases the probability that an emitted behavior will be repeated.

**respondent conditioning:** a kind of learning in which a neutral stimulus is substituted for a stimulus that causes a reflexive response; the neutral stimulus comes to cause same reflexive response. Also called **classical conditioning.**

**self:** a conscious idea of who and what we are; may also be referred to as self-image or self-concept.

**self-actualizing tendency:** the drive to become what we think we are.

**shaping:** the process of reinforcing at successive steps the responses that come closest to approximating the desired behavior.

**stimulus generalization:** the repetition of a response conditioned by one stimulus in the presence of similar but neutral stimuli.

**superego:** the part of our personality that represents society's rules and regulations.

**unconditional positive regard:**    complete acceptance, support, and respect from significant others.

**unconscious:**    the part of the mind containing the
aspects of our functioning of which we are totally
unaware.

## REFERENCES

Bandura, A. *Principles of Behavior Modification.* New
York: Holt, Rinehart and Winston, 1969.

———. "Analysis of Modeling Processes." In *Psychological Modeling: Conflicting Theories,* edited by
A. Bandura. Chicago: Aldine-Atherton, 1971(a).

———. *Social Learning Theory.* Morristown, N.J.:
General Learning Press, 1971(b).

Bandura, A., and Walters, R. H. *Social Learning and
Personality Development.* New York: Holt,
Rinehart and Winston, 1963.

Erikson, E. H. *Childhood and Society,* 2d ed. New York:
Norton, 1963.

———. *Identity: Youth and Crisis.* New York: Norton, 1968.

Freud, S. *Beyond the Pleasure Principle.* Revised, translated, and edited by J. Strachey. New York:
Liveright, 1961. First German edition, 1920.

———. *Civilization and Its Discontents.* Translated and
edited by J. Strachey. New York: Norton, 1961.
First German edition, 1930.

———. *The Ego and the Id.* Translated and edited by
J. Strachey. New York: Norton, 1961. First
German edition, 1923.

———. *The Interpretation of Dreams.* Translated and
edited by J. Strachey. New York: Avon, 1965.
First German edition, 1900.

———. *New Introductory Lectures on Psycho-Analysis.*
Translated and edited by J. Strachey. New York:
Norton, 1965. First German edition, 1933.

———. *An Outline of Psycho-Analysis.* Revised, translated, and edited by J. Strachey. New York:
Norton, 1969. First German edition, 1940.

———. *The Psychopathology of Everyday Life.* Translated
by A. Tyson; edited with an introduction and
additional notes by J. Strachey. New York: Norton, 1966. First German edition, 1904.

Maslow, A. H. *Motivation and Personality,* 2d ed. New
York: Harper & Row, 1970.

Rogers, C. R. "Actualizing Tendency in Reaction to
'Motives' and to Consciousness." In *Nebraska
Symposium on Motivation,* edited by M. R. Jones.
Lincoln: University of Nebraska Press, 1963.

———. *On Becoming a Person.* Boston: Houghton
Mifflin, 1961.

———. "A Theory of Therapy, Personality, and In-
terpersonal Relationships, as Developed in the
Client-Centered Framework." In *Psychology: A
Study of a Science,* vol. 3, edited by S. Koch.
New York: McGraw-Hill, 1959.

Rogers, C., and Stevens, B. *Person to Person: The Problem of Being Human.* Lafayette, Calif.: Real People Press, 1967.

Skinner, B. F. *About Behaviorism.* New York: Knopf,
1974.

———. *Beyond Freedom and Dignity.* New York:
Knopf, 1971.

———. *Contingencies of Reinforcement: A Theoretical
Analysis.* New York: Appleton-Century-Crofts,
1969.

———. *Science and Human Behavior.* New York: Macmillan, 1953.

———. *Verbal Behavior.* New York: Appleton-Century-Crofts, 1957.

## ANSWERS TO REVIEW QUESTIONS

**Page 26.**  *1.* T  *2.* T  *3.* F  *4.* T  *5.* F  *6.* T
**Page 34.**  *7.* conflict  *8.* id, ego, superego  *9.* self-
serving, communal  *10.* defense
*11.* fixated  *12.* Oedipus
complex, identification  *13.* integrity, despair
**Page 44.**  *14.* T  *15.* F  *16.* T  *17.* T  *18.* F

*19.* T *20.* T  *21.* F  *22.* T  *23.* F  *24.* T
**Page 50.**  *25.* determinism  *26.* actualizing
tendency  *27.* potentialities  *28.* unconditional
positive regard  *29.* guilt, anxiety, defensive
behavior  *30.* self  *31.* self-actualization,
understanding, esthetics

# 3

# SELF-ESTEEM

Think of a time when you felt happy,
alive, and fulfilled as a human being. What
was happening in your life that supported
these feelings? Who were the people who
shared in your happiness? Spend a few
moments relishing every thought and
feeling as you allow yourself to
reexperience this satisfying moment. Stay
with your feelings, if you wish, before
reading on.

Now, think of a time when you felt low
and perhaps unloved and when your
worth as a person was in question. What
events surrounded this period? How did
you behave toward yourself and toward
others? What did you do to change the
way you felt about yourself?

Think of another time when you were
neither extremely happy nor extremely
unhappy but felt generally okay. This type
of feeling may apply to you more often
than either of the others. However, on
occasion you may notice that something
triggers a mood swing in either a positive
or a negative direction. Identify some
triggers that usually result in a positive
mood swing. Identify some triggers that
tend to bring you down. When you are
temporarily down, what do you do to
help yourself get back up again? Spend a
few moments thinking about how you feel
right now.

**SELF-ESTEEM**

*See Chapter 2 for discussions of personality and self-concept.*

## DISCUSSION: DEFINING SELF-ESTEEM

The range of feelings described in the focus results from what psychologists call the level of **self-esteem**. We know that some people exhibit characteristics of low self-esteem for long periods. We also know that other people enjoy long periods of high self-esteem. Still others (probably most of us) are somewhere between, with occasional fluctuations from high to low, low to high, and back again. We can experience these ups and downs in a single day or even in a moment. In this chapter, we will discuss the characteristics of various levels of self-esteem, the effects of earlier development on our level of self-esteem, and most important, the maintenance of positive self-esteem as a lifelong process.

Self-esteem is perhaps the most important part of our self-concept. More specifically, it is the degree to which we value ourselves, or the degree to which we feel worthwhile. Psychological development throughout life is greatly affected by this self-judgment. It is probably the single most important factor determining our feelings, attitudes, values, behaviors, and goals (Branden, 1969). Canfield and Wells (1975) believe that the enhancement and preservation of our self-esteem is our highest value.

Abraham Maslow (1970) wrote that all people in our society (with a few pathological exceptions) have a need or desire for a stable, firmly based, usually high evaluation of themselves—in other words, for self-respect and self-esteem—as well as for the esteem of others.

- The need for *self-respect and self-esteem* is the desire for strength, achievement, adequacy, mastery and competence, confidence in the face of others, independence, and freedom.

- The need for the *esteem of others* is the desire for reputation or prestige (defined as respect or esteem from other people), status, fame and glory, dominance, recognition, attention, importance, dignity, or appreciation.

These needs require *feedback* from others assuring us that we are highly regarded and appreciated. As our need for self-esteem is satisfied, we begin to realize that our lives have meaning, and we begin to feel more useful and better able to make choices for ourselves and to direct our own lives.

### ■ Levels of Self-Esteem

The best indicator of the level of your self-esteem is the way you behave. *Behavior* is an acting out of the basic attitudes (beliefs) we hold and of the feelings we are experiencing. In turn, our behavior reinforces our attitudes and affects the way we view ourselves and, hence, the way we feel. It also greatly affects our relationships with others. Others are often more aware of our behavior than we are; so we can learn much about ourselves by objectively viewing our behavior from their perspectives.

**WHAT DO YOU THINK?**

■ How do you generally describe the condition of your self-esteem?

The intent of this chapter is to help you sharpen your awareness of yourself so you can identify personal characteristics that affect your level of self-esteem. We hope you will also discover how your level of self-esteem affects the way you live your life and what you can do to maintain a more positive self-esteem.

# DISCUSSION: DEVELOPMENT OF SELF-ESTEEM

The present condition of our self-esteem results most from the psychological environment in which we grew up and matured. Within this environment, other people (adults) had a greater effect on the development of our self-esteem than any other factor. The people who influence us serve as *models* for the development of our *attitudes, values, and behaviors*. The development of our self-esteem depends not only on what we learn from others, however; it also results from what we learn from experiencing life independently.

*See Chapter 11 for more about intimacy and maternal and paternal love.*

## ■ Influential People

Our teachers are parents, siblings, close relatives, school teachers, playmates, and many others. Some of these people may still influence us. Others may no longer be directly involved in our lives, but what we learned from them may have a dramatic effect on the way we live.

### ■ *Parents*
For most of us, parents have been the most significant influence in shaping us as people. They are, with few exceptions, our major sources of security, love, and other need fulfillment. When parents love us as we need to be loved and treat us as human beings of worth and value, we grow up in a psychologically healthy environment and probably will enjoy positive self-esteem in later life. However, when parents are too involved in their own problems to be able to love us, or even to conceive of us as unique individuals, it is difficult for us to develop positive self-esteem. Family cohesion and harmony has been determined to be a significant variable in the development of a positive self-esteem in children (Cooper, Holman, and Braithwaite, 1983). Conflict and

**WHAT DO YOU THINK?**

■ Do you plan to have children someday?

■ If so, why? If not, why not?

■ What are your earliest recollections of esteem-building experiences?

■ What experiences do you remember from your elementary school days? high school days?

■ The experience of growing up often has its lonely moments.

tension within the family often result in an environment that negatively affects the developing child. Karen Horney (1956) states that parents often unknowingly impede their children's psychological development by being erratic, dominating, overprotective, intimidating, irritable, overexacting, overindulgent, partial to other siblings, hypocritical, or indifferent.

Low self-esteem usually develops as a result of parents', and others', failing to understand the needs of children. This lack of understanding often makes children confused about how and when to let their needs be known. The confusion results in a serious dilemma. Children—impressionable, vulnerable, and dependent on adults for their survival—are seldom able to understand that sometimes adults make mistakes, too.

Sullivan (1953) believes that for some this childhood dilemma develops into a survival attitude toward life that profoundly affects the individual's interpersonal relationships and self-esteem. He refers to this survival attitude as the **malevolent attitude**.

The *malevolent attitude* is the belief that one really lives among enemies. Sullivan believes it is perhaps the greatest disaster that can happen in the childhood phase of personality development. The child comes to personify himself or herself as something detestable that will always be treated badly, and these beliefs often result in failure to achieve life goals. "I don't deserve this" or "I am unlovable" are examples of unconscious decisions that affect moods, relationships, physical health, and ability to succeed.

> Keith grew up in a home where he was treated as an unwanted nuisance. His father and mother worked six days a week and often came home tired and unhappy. Consequently, they spent very little time and energy helping Keith meet his needs. The rare expressions of affection or love shown toward him usually resulted from their feelings of guilt. Out of desperation, Keith occasionally reached out to his mother, who frequently screamed, "Get away! Can't you see I'm busy?" His father usually responded to his requests by saying, "I can't now! Wait 'til later." Unfortunately, later became never.
>
> These repeated responses taught Keith that he could not depend on his mother or father for love and affection. He soon learned that it was disadvantageous to show any need for affection. In response to his unfulfilled needs, Keith lashed out at his parents, teachers, and peers. Their negative responses to his behavior only reinforced his feelings of being unloved.
>
> As an adult, Keith makes it practically impossible for anyone to show him tenderness and affection. His untrusting behavior keeps others from giving him the love he so desperately needs.

**WHAT DO YOU THINK?**

- What methods did your parents use to rear you?
- How did they contribute to or detract from the development of your self-worth?
- What did your parents expect of you?
- How did you incorporate these expectations into your self-concept?
- How will you rear your children differently? similarly?
- Do you believe that we become the same type of parents as our parents, their parents, and so on?

Some parents may not want children, but have them because they believe it is expected of them. "Our parents are eager to be grandparents. We really can't disappoint them" or "All our friends have children" represent beliefs that compel many couples to have children. Other parents who do want children often want them for reasons detrimental to the development of the child. Bernard Berelson (1972) lists several reasons why some parents choose to have children. The following reasons reflect selfish elements:

- *Personal power*: Parents have nearly absolute power during the early years of childhood. Fathers or mothers may have little power over their authority figures (employers) or peers, but they have power over their children.

Children may be used to bind one parent to another ("You can't leave me, what about the children?"). Children also are used to increase political and economic power where marriage alliances are arranged.

- *Personal competence*: The ability to produce a child demonstrates personal competence and virility. "See what I made. She looks just like me."
- *Personal status*: "It is good for business to have a beautiful wife and well-behaved children."
- *Personal extension*: Children represent a form of immortality. "I am going to live on through my children. After all, someone must carry on the family name."
- *Personal experience*: Parents may live through their children. "My child is going to have all the opportunities I never had" (we might add, "whether he likes it or not"). A parent may be challenged by the possibility of shaping another human being into "perfection."
- *Personal pleasure*: There can be much pleasure in loving, caring for, and enjoying children. It can be a tremendously fulfilling experience for a parent. Unfortunately, some parents tend to smother their children with love and overprotectiveness.

People have children for many other reasons besides these. As further evidence, you might want to conduct the survey outlined in the following case in point.

Understanding our reasons for having children is a step in the direction of healthy child-rearing. Understanding that children are individuals in their own right, with no responsibility to fulfill our needs, is another step in the right direction. Further, we must understand that children need a secure, cohesive, and loving environment in which to grow and develop.

■ *Teachers* School teachers, too, have an impact on children's development. However, too often teachers are not fully aware of and responsive to children. Much like the child, the teacher is caught in a system of external and extraneous purposes and goals, a system of authorities, and a canned curriculum that defines

**WHAT DO YOU THINK?**
- How can adults show respect for children?
- Why do some adults fail to do so?
- What labels did adults use for you when you were growing up?
- How did these labels influence your self-esteem?

*See the discussion of unconditional positive regard in Chapter 2.*

## CASE IN POINT
## A Survey on Why Parents Decide to Have Children

This survey should be conducted with a variety of parents—both fathers and mothers—from different ethnic, cultural, and economic groups. You may want to use the following questions as a guide:

1. How many children do you have?
2. Did you plan the birth of each of your children?
3. Why did you decide to have each of your children?
4. Were you and your mate in agreement about having children?
5. What has been your greatest joy in having children?
6. What has been your greatest disappointment?
7. If you could live your life over again, would you have children?

■ The chances of developing a positive self-worth are greater in a healthy, loving environment.

appropriate behavior, success, and failure. The teacher is often guided by experts and authorities who remain anonymous and invisible and who are seldom in contact with a classroom or a child.

> Erica, who is brighter than most of her classmates, has become quite bored with the slow pace at which she and the other children are being taught. The teacher only notices that Erica is either looking out the window, apparently daydreaming, or getting out of her seat to sharpen her pencil. Annoyed with this lack of attention, the teacher tells Erica that she will have to sit in the principal's office until she decides she "wants to learn."

### WHAT DO YOU THINK?

■ What types of school activities help children develop self-esteem?

■ What school activities impede the development of self-esteem?

■ Did you enjoy school? Why or why not? Do you enjoy it now?

■ What specific things do you think a teacher can do to encourage children to feel important and to value themselves and their achievements?

Moustakas (1969) believes that in many cases, such as Erica's, it is the child who suffers when he or she comes into conflict with rules that interfere with his or her development and growth; it is the child who is belittled and shamed, and inevitably frightened and defeated. The child sees himself or herself as unimportant. The irony is that such children pay a double penalty by being told that the rules exist for their own good.

There are teachers, however, who seem to be able to work with or around the system and who never lose sight of children's needs. Even though they teach hundreds of children, they make each child feel important and special, even without reference to achievement and "good" behavior.

> The teacher, noticing that Roberto appears bored, discovers that he has some special interest in the terrarium. The teacher asks him if he would like to be in charge of its operation and also finds several books on terrarium animals for him that are written at his reading level. This special concern for Roberto teaches him that he is important, and learning continues to be rewarding.

## CASE IN POINT
### Shaping Influences

Perhaps you have been thinking about the effect people have had on you. Describe how you believe each of the following people affected the development of your self-esteem, both positively and negatively.

Father
Positive influence: _____

_____

_____

Negative influence: _____

_____

_____

Mother
Positive influence: _____

_____

_____

Relative (grandparent, aunt, uncle, etc.)
Positive influence: _____

_____

_____

Negative influence: _____

_____

_____

Teacher
Positive influence: _____

_____

_____

Negative influence: _____

_____

_____

## ■ Idealistic Expectations

■ *Perfectionism*  The unrealistic expectations of some adults are actually idealistic, perfectionistic demands on children's behavior. As young children, our behavior models typically are limited to some fictional heroes described to us at bedtime or to fragmentary glimpses of our parents (for example, we may seldom see our parents naked, or see them cry or exhibit fear). Later we may have as models a few historical figures, the descriptions of whom are totally unrealistic (for example, George Washington, who never told a lie). Our goal seems to be perfection, something we rarely see demonstrated but something for which we are told to strive. Striving for perfection is a self-defeating process, though. As human beings we are destined to fail, although as children (and even as adults) we try to succeed. Some common notions of perfection taught to us as children are:

- Not crying when we feel the need.
- Accepting the fact that our parents are always right even if what they tell us today is the opposite of what they told us yesterday.
- Always doing what we are told even if it is unreasonable and detrimental to our self-esteem.
- Guarding what we say so as not to embarrass our parents, even if what we say is true.
- Giving in to others at the expense of our own needs and wants.

- Knowing what mother and father expect of us even if they do not tell us.
- Always being kind and loving, never angry.
- Getting all A+'s in school.

See the discussion of conditions of worth in Chapter 2 and the discussion of irrational beliefs in Chapter 5.

■ *Conflict between Ideal Self and Real Self*   These idealistic expectations result in a conflict between our **ideal self**, the self we should be, and our **real self**, the self we actually are (Rogers, 1959). The wide chasm that exists between the real self and the ideal self presents an impossible obstacle that leaves us with bewildering feelings of helplessness. This perplexing problem we view as a failure to achieve what is expected by others and, consequently, ourselves.

■ *Denial of Self*   Unfortunately, the child can only believe that he or she is in some way morally and intellectually deficient when his or her performance is inadequate. This often robs the child of the opportunity to learn new things for fear of not being able to do them perfectly from the start. "I don't want to play softball" means "What if I can't hit the ball?" "I don't like to bowl" means "I've never bowled before, and I'm afraid I will look stupid." Even as adults we continue to strive toward the unrealistic and impossible goals of perfection.

## CASE IN POINT
## Assessment of Perfectionism

Some people are not sure if they suffer from the unrealistic demands of perfectionism. Perfectionism may have become so much a part of their motivation that they no longer notice its effects.

The following assessment may help you become more aware of how perfectionism may be affecting your life. Use the following scale to measure your agreement or disagreement with the assessment statements. Try to respond to the way *you* usually think, feel, and behave.

$$+2 = \text{Very much like me}$$
$$+1 = \text{Sometimes like me}$$
$$0 = \text{Neutral}$$
$$-1 = \text{Usually not like me}$$
$$-2 = \text{Definitely not like me}$$

_____ I should be able to excel at anything I attempt.
_____ If I cannot do something really well, there is no point in doing it at all.
_____ People will think less of me if I make mistakes.

_____ If I do not set very high standards for myself, I will never be successful.
_____ An average performance is unsatisfying to me.
_____ If I get angry with myself for failing to live up to high standards, it will help me to do better in the future.
_____ I should be upset when I make a mistake.
_____ It is wrong to make the same mistakes several times.
_____ I am less of a person when I fail at something important.
_____ It is shameful when I display weakness or foolish behavior.

Add up your score. My score is _____.

If your score is +20, you possess a very high degree of perfectionism. If your score is −20, you are relatively unaffected by perfectionism. This assessment has been used with several classes of college students. The results indicate that many of us tend to be affected, to varying degrees, by perfectionistic demands.

*1.* The value we place on ourselves is called our self-image. T  F

*2.* Our attitudes, behaviors, and feelings are indicators of our level of self-esteem. T  F

*3.* Canfield and Wells believe that our highest value is the enhancement and preservation of our relationship to others. T  F

*4.* Children who grow up believing they are unacceptable to others may develop a malevolent attitude. T  F

*5.* Parents are the only ones influential in shaping us as adults. T  F

*6.* Our educational system is solely to blame for problems relating to children's self-esteem. T  F

*7.* The basic reasons parents decide to have children can greatly affect the children's self-worth. T  F

*8.* By the time the child is old enough to attend school, the development of self-esteem is complete. T  F

*9.* The ideal self is the self that we believe we should be. T  F

*10.* The self that describes who we believe we really are is called the actual self. T  F

*The answers to these review questions are on page 84.*

## DISCUSSION: CHARACTERISTICS OF NEGATIVE SELF-ESTEEM

All kinds of things happen to us that result in our feeling bad about ourselves. Sometimes, thoughtless people affect our feelings of worth, at least temporarily. We may feel worthless because of our race, sex, creed, religious beliefs, political beliefs, aptitudes, or income. Failure also can be very damaging to our self-esteem, whether it is a failure at school, failure as a spouse, failure as a parent, failure at work, or a feeling of not being able to live down a past mistake.

It appears that many people suffer from low self-esteem, probably as a result of growing up with some of the problems discussed in the preceding section. The best evidence of low self-esteem comes from behavior.

■ Behaviors

*1.* People who experience low self-esteem have little self-respect. Their insistence on degrading themselves clearly demonstrates this lack. We hear people say, "I can never do anything right," or "I'm stupid," or "I'm no good," and on and on. These frequent devaluations do nothing to enhance self-respect and often drive away others who could meet the need for friendship.

*2.* These individuals also frequently blame others for their condition, which leads us to a second behavioral problem: they often behave irresponsibly. For example, they may be late for appointments, yet invariably blame something or someone else for their tardiness, or they may seldom follow through on tasks they have agreed to do. With a defeatest attitude and a lack of self-confidence, they seem to arrange for failure by producing low-quality work; this further verifies their belief that they can seldom do anything well. These beliefs become a **self-fulfilling prophecy**, which severely limits their future achievements and further supports their negative views about themselves. Robert Merton (1957) defines *self-fulfilling prophecy* as a "false definition of a situation evoking a new behavior which makes the originally false conception come true" (p. 423). (Self-fulfilling prophecies can also be positive, as when we do surprisingly well at something and so develop confidence that we can do it.)

3. People with low self-esteem often appear to be guarded and withdrawn. When their friends try to help by offering praise or constructive criticism, they behave defensively by negating the feedback or attacking the people who offer them help. These attacks may be projections directed at behaviors in the other people that the attackers dislike in themselves. They may say, "Well, you are like that too" or "You're not perfect either." They see others' attempts to help as ego-threatening. Hence, they not only reject themselves, they also reject others.

4. People with low self-esteem are often unable or unwilling to be open with others, to give important personal information about themselves. Sidney Jourard (1974) refers to the process of letting oneself be known to others as **self-disclosure**. Self-disclosure is one means by which the healthy personality is achieved and maintained (Jourard, 1964)—but only if the self-disclosure meets the condition of **authenticity**, a term used by Jourard (1968) to mean honest self-disclosure. People with low self-esteem, if they self-disclose at all, tend to say things about themselves that they do not mean. Their disclosures seem to have been chosen more for cosmetic value than for truth.

The consequence of a lifetime of lying about themselves is the loss of contact with their real selves—what Karen Horney (1950) refers to as **self-alienation**. She describes self-alienated people as having:

■ An inability to recognize themselves as they really are, without minimizing or exaggerating.
■ An inability or unwillingness to accept the consequences of their actions and decisions.
■ An inability or unwillingness to realize it is up to them to do something about their difficulties.

People who are self-alienated believe that others, fate, or time will solve these difficulties. This is a further indication of their irresponsible behavior: they do not see themselves as directing their own lives.

5. People with low self-esteem usually resist change. They seem to prefer the safety of stagnant and unfulfilling patterns of behavior over the risk of trying new behaviors, environments, and relationships. If they continue to avoid such risks, their lives may never be fulfilling and they may continually suffer from low self-esteem.

People with low self-esteem have many regrets. We may wonder why they behave as they do. This question is often difficult to answer, for as we mentioned earlier, people with low self-esteem are usually guarded about themselves. However, they appear to have a fear of failure that results from feelings of inadequacy. They attempt to present a false image of themselves as a means of preserving their self-esteem; however, this facade results in a confused and distorted self-image, further contributing to their low self-worth. In addition, they often try to diminish the self-esteem of those they really admire in an attempt to lessen the imagined gap between the self they see and the self they would like to be.

*See Chapter 6 to learn about depression.*

## ■ Attitudes

Clearly, then, people suffering from low self-esteem have a dim and murky view of themselves. This negative self-image stems from a general attitude: "I am not worthwhile, hence I do not count for much in the world." They believe themselves neither useful nor necessary. Many believe that it is wrong to think positively about themselves—that they should only think positively about others. Even a suggestion that they should feel good about themselves leads to a response like, "That would be conceited."

People with this self-diminishing attitude see no clear purpose for their existence and often question their reason for being. Unable to trust their own judgments, they believe there is little they can do to change and continue to search desperately for answers outside themselves. Therefore, they are easily persuaded by the beliefs and values of others. This vulnerable position causes them to talk and act in ways suited more to others' needs and desires than to their own. This further confuses their organization of values and attitudes.

The confusion and frustration of not having found self-satisfaction often results in their "giving up." They accept the notion that the world is a miserable place and that there is not much anyone can do about it, least of all themselves. It follows that people with low self-esteem see the world through the same eyes as they view themselves and adopt the same untrusting attitude toward others as they have toward themselves. Sullivan (1953) believes that for some this untrusting attitude develops early. A child may learn to deal with apparent contradictions by concealing what he or she is thinking or feeling. For example, a mother may tell a child that being honest is the most important quality, then punish the child for telling the truth. The resulting lack of trust may greatly reduce the child's chances for achieving satisfying relationships.

## ■ Feelings

Fear has much to do with our untrusting attitude toward others. The fear of being known and of being rejected, and the fear of knowing ourselves and rejecting ourselves, leads to another cause of low self-esteem: the feelings we have about ourselves. These negative feelings seem to lend support to the attitudes we hold and the behaviors we exhibit. However, it is often difficult to know what the person with low self-esteem is feeling. Many of us are more aware of our thoughts than our feelings. That may be because many of us have difficulty expressing our feelings honestly. Hence, we have learned to place little importance on them. Psychotherapists find that helping people to feel and to feel good about feeling is a major task. Simple human emotions are still disapproved by many of us (Brennecke and Amick, 1978).

People experiencing low self-esteem feel unloved even when others express or show love for them. They often perceive such demonstrations as insincere, because they believe they are unlovable. They ask, "Why would anyone want to love me?" They see themselves as unlovable because they do not love themselves. Moreover, they reject the concept of self-love because they believe it is an expression of conceit. While they raise no objection about applying the concept of love to various objects (I love my shoes, I love my diamond, I love nature, and so on), and while they believe it is virtuous to love others, they consider it sinful to love themselves. They further believe that the greater their self-love, the less their capacity to love others. On the contrary, the author of *The Art of Loving*, Erich Fromm (1956), believes that if people are to love productively, they must love themselves first; if they can love only others, they cannot love at all.

If our basic need for love and belonging is not met, deep hurt and resentment often result; these feelings are, in turn, directed back onto ourselves. If there is no apparent outlet for these feelings of self-rejection, an even greater problem develops—the problem of depression. Deep, negative feelings that are not expressed in a healthy way but are kept inside will continue to erode self-esteem, resulting eventually in self-pity and self-hatred. The belief that asking for help from others or sharing concerns with others is an admission of weakness leaves the person with low self-esteem even more vulnerable. This denial of need may cause negative, self-destructive feelings—the person may become purposeless, indifferent, helpless, and, eventually, hopeless. Suicide may seem a reasonable alternative.

*See Chapter 6 for a discussion of depression.*

Figure 3.1 shows low self-esteem as a circular self-defeating process in which negative feelings cause negative attitudes, negative attitudes cause negative behaviors, negative behaviors support the negative feelings, and on and on, each part affecting and being affected by self-esteem. In effect, a person with low self-esteem becomes a psychological prisoner of his or her own negative self-image (Branden, 1969). At this point, it may appear that there is little hope for such a person. On the contrary, there is hope. Later in this chapter, we will discuss how to overcome negative self-esteem and how to acquire and sustain a more positive self-esteem.

FIGURE 3.1
The development of self-esteem may be seen as a circular process.

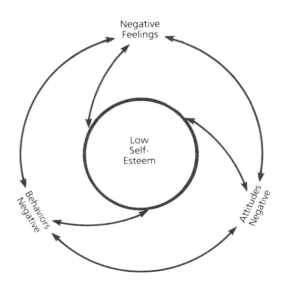

*11.* Robert Merton defines _____ _____ as a
false definition of a situation that results in a new behavior that makes the previously
false conception come true.

*12.* _____ is the process of letting one's self be known to
others.

*13.* _____ is only healthy and useful if it meets the
condition of authenticity.

*14.* Karen Horney believes that _____ is a consequence of a
lifetime of lying about oneself to others.

*15.* The person experiencing low self-esteem often suffers from feelings of _____ ,
_____ , and _____ .

*16.* Rejecting, blaming, and attacking are characteristic behaviors associated with
_____ _____ .

*The answers to these review questions are on page 84.*

## DISCUSSION: CHARACTERISTICS OF POSITIVE SELF-ESTEEM

### ■ Behaviors

People with positive self-esteem are responsible for themselves and behave in responsible ways. When they commit themselves to do things, they usually follow through. This sense of responsibility contributes to their feelings of worth as persons. They realize they can be counted on by others. Honesty and integrity are the foundations for their interactions. These values permit them to trust themselves with others. Thus, they are able to say "no" to things they do not want to do without fearing rejection.

They relish experiences in which they can grow and learn more about themselves, and they use their creativity in constructive ways. We can say that persons with high self-esteem strive for congruence; that is, they want their behavior to be consistent with their feelings, thoughts, attitudes, and experiences. They are free to act on their feelings and express their love for others by demonstrating affection, encouragement, and support.

People with high self-esteem are able to take a greater variety of risks—the more chips they have, the more they can afford to lose. They are free to be open to new experiences and to others because they are capable of accepting failure and rejection as part of growing. They seldom see failure and rejection as a reflection of their self-worth. When they excel, they are able to accept praise for their accomplishments without pretense or false modesty. In so doing, they allow themselves to continue to build their self-esteem. Another quality they have is trust in themselves. This trust frees them to be spontaneous and live fully at the moment of experiencing, rather than in the past or future. It is no wonder that people enjoy being with those who exhibit positive levels of self-esteem—they are exciting and comfortable to be around. Their behavior indi-

TABLE 3.1
Characteristics of People with Positive Self-Esteem

**Responsibility**: They can be depended on to do what they have agreed to do.

**Honesty, integrity, and congruence**: They are accountable for their values, beliefs, and opinions.

**Personal growth**: They search for opportunities to grow, learn, and realize their potential and creativity.

**Positive attitude**: They are optimistic about themselves, others, and the world.

**Expression of feelings**: They express feelings openly without fear of rejection.

**Risk-taking**: They are open to new and challenging experiences.

**Acceptance of failure and rejection**: They view failure and rejection as part of growing.

**Acceptance of praise**: They can accept compliments without negating responses.

**Trust in themselves and others**: They trust their own and others' competency.

cates to others that they possess positive and healthy attitudes about themselves and the world around them. Table 3.1 lists several characteristics of people with positive self-esteem.

### ■ Attitudes

The most important attitude of people with high self-esteem is their belief that they are worthwhile and valuable. They need no particular credentials to support this feeling; they believe they are worthwhile because they belong to the society of human life. It is not necessary for them always to be important to others, for they are important to themselves. They do not have to strive continuously

■ The person with a healthy self-esteem has a positive influence on others.

---

## CASE IN POINT
## Believing in Yourself or One's Self

Mary Hudson Vandegrift was born in Texas and went to elementary school and high school in Texas and Oklahoma. In 1933, she was widowed at twenty with a six-month-old daughter. She borrowed $200 and established $600 credit to buy a gas station and went on to become the first woman to found an oil trade group (Society of Independent Gasoline Marketers). Today, she is the president of Hudson Oil Company. During an address at Wichita State University in 1979, she stated, "the genius of living is to carry the spirit of a child into old age. What is the spirit of a child? That of wide-eyed open wonder, excitement and zest; the optimistic attitude that nothing is too good to be true and that the world literally is a wonderful place!" (Schwartz, 1980, p. 7).

---

for perfection to prove themselves but can function productively within their presently known limitations. If they do accomplish extraordinary things and become important to others, they experience even greater feelings of worth.

People with positive self-esteem also have the attitude that it is important to continue to learn and grow psychologically. Therefore, they are open to what they can learn from others as well as what they can learn from more fully knowing themselves. They continually seek out and involve themselves in activities and relationships that have the potential for enhancing their self-esteem, even though involvement may mean conflict and disappointment.

This involvement stems from their belief that people are the sum of all their experiences. Since they like who they have become, they value all the experiences that helped make them the people they are today. Therefore, they continue to use their experiences to grow, and they also encourage others to grow and learn from their life experiences. Knowingly and unknowingly, they become models for others. Though they may not be teachers, they often teach.

People who feel worthwhile experience a personal freedom that is seldom controlled by guilt. In other words, they do not allow regrets to get in the way of their experiencing *now* in a positive and growing way. Many people spend too much time and energy fretting over the past; each tomorrow is spent worrying about what should have been done better today. People with high self-esteem do not accept responsibility for events beyond their control—especially the actions of others. They do accept responsibility for their own choices. They believe that "life is what you make it" and that, within reason, we can be whatever we choose to be. In this way, we are all free.

As you might expect, people who experience a high degree of self-worth usually have very positive feelings about themselves and others. These positive feelings set the stage for them to live full, productive, and rewarding lives.

### ■ Feelings

Generally, people whose self-esteem is high feel happy and contented with themselves and their life styles. They feel loved and appreciated by others and can share feelings of warmth and affection with others. Although they experience positive feelings most of the time, however, they also are able to feel, accept, and express a wide range of feelings, from sorrow to anger to joy. They do not attempt to avoid unpleasant feelings but accept all their feelings as natural and human.

*17.* The positive person demonstrates his or her worth to others by sharing responsibility for their behavior. T  F
*18.* The only way a person can reach a high level of self-esteem is through achievements and accomplishments. T  F
*19.* Congruence and integrity are qualities characteristic of a person with high self-esteem. T  F
*20.* The only problem faced by people with positive self-esteem is that they often feel guilty about negative behaviors from the past. T  F
*21.* The positive person's feelings are demonstrated by the love and respect shown for self and for others. T  F

*The answers to these review questions are on page 84.*

## DISCUSSION: MAINTAINING SELF-ESTEEM

Two of our most time-consuming and important tasks are developing and maintaining self-esteem. Perhaps the greatest challenge in life is maintaining self-esteem in healthy and growth-encouraging ways that are beneficial both to ourselves and to others.

Although it is theoretically possible, maintaining positive self-esteem continuously may seem a difficult task. However, even if we have grown up in a negative environment, we can, if we choose, achieve a satisfying level of self-esteem. For most of us, high self-esteem may serve as a goal toward which to work. It is important to realize that personal growth is a lifelong process in which we proceed slowly, experience after experience, decision after decision, toward becoming the person we have the potential to be. Each of us, no matter how young or how old, has time to grow toward becoming the person he or she would like to be. Each new day presents opportunities to try healthier behaviors and grow through new experiences.

Each day also may bring things that get us down. As we confront the hassles of everyday life, we must realize that the world is a less-than-ideal place to live. We must also realize that the way we view the world is greatly affected by our past interpretations of our life experiences. These interpretations become the basis for our present level of self-esteem. Influenced by this present level of self-esteem, we have at least two ways to view the experiences of everyday life—positively and negatively.

> Marie is pretty and has always attracted male attention. In high school, she did more dating and cheerleading than studying. Her first job was as a typist in a posh insurance office. During the first six months, she came to realize how inadequate her skills and background were. She began to think of herself as stupid and to feel that her good looks were the only reason she had been hired. Consequently, she began to resent the man who had hired her and other people in the office. She assumed that others saw her as she saw herself.

■ The experiences of life daily affect us positively and negatively.

Whenever a male coworker stopped to chat, she cut him off or insulted him. Soon, she had the reputation of being a bad-tempered snob.

When an executive assistant position was created, Marie asked her boss if she could have it and was told she was not ready for the job yet. Her boss thought her sometimes offensive behavior toward others could create problems in this new position. However, she assumed he did not think she was smart enough, so she quit her job.

It may be that in Marie's past, her beauty and femininity were emphasized at the expense of her intellectual development. She may have had little chance of knowing which qualities were important or of realizing other possibilities for growth. Marie may have been partially correct in her assessment of how some people see attractive women, but it dominated her thinking.

## ■ Understanding Irrational Beliefs

Ellis and Harper (1975), Beck (1976), Meichenbaum (1977), and other cognitive therapists view negative interpretations of experiences as problems in our thinking. They also believe that our perceptions of our worth result from the collection of expectations and beliefs we have acquired during our development. The effect is determined by what we say to ourselves about a particular experience. According to Ellis and Harper, those of us who are greatly disturbed by the behavior of others toward us may make such negative self-statements as the following:

- I must be loved and approved of by every significant person in my life; if not, that is awful.
- I must not make errors or do poorly; if I do, that is terrible.
- People and events should always be the way I want them to be.

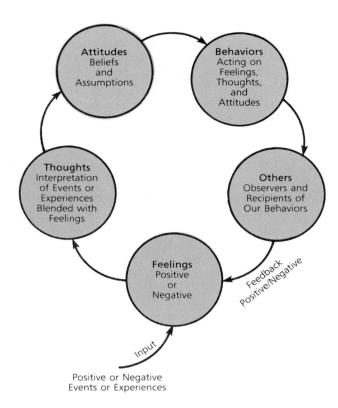

FIGURE 3.2
The way we feel,
think, and behave is
influenced by others
and influences others'
responses to us.

Marie assumed she was unintelligent. She also assumed her boss hired her for her good looks and refused her the new position because he thought she did not have the ability to do the job. In Marie's mind, this confirmed her beliefs about herself. Her feelings, thoughts, and attitudes influenced her behavior. Her behavior resulted in negative responses from others, and these responses, though misinterpreted, confirmed her beliefs. This process, diagramed in Figure 3.2, may severely limit our chances for success in trying new esteem-building behaviors.

Marie could have handled this situation in a healthier way by asking her boss why he believed she was not ready to take the executive assistant position. She would have found his reasons quite different from her assumptions. Marie also might have been able to work on changing her offensive behavior. Instead of quitting, for example, she could have taken some courses to help her improve. Marie's feelings, thoughts, attitudes, and behaviors were unhealthy and kept her from viewing her job as an opportunity for growth.

The negative beliefs described by Ellis and Harper are quite common. Many of us were taught unrealistic beliefs such as these. That is why we have such terrible feelings when someone does not like us or when we fail. In spite of their commonness, though, these beliefs are *irrational*. They are based on the belief that our self-worth is solely determined by the approval of others and by continual strivings for perfection. According to Ellis and Harper, the negative

**WHAT DO YOU THINK?**

■ What have you changed about yourself recently?
■ How do people change their attitudes?
■ What ways of interpreting unpleasant events do you have that enhance your self-esteem? that damage it?

self-statements based on this belief must be replaced by positive self-statements such as the following:

- It is definitely nice to have people's love and approval, but even without them, I can still accept and enjoy myself.
- Doing things well is satisfying, but it is human to make mistakes.
- People are going to act the way they want, not the way I want.

*See Chapter 5 for a discussion of Ellis and other cognitive therapists.*

Many of us have had negative interpersonal experiences and may be somewhat sensitive to the judgments of others. Most of us want to be well thought of and, consequently, may be too concerned with what others are thinking about us. Sherod Miller (1983), a communication specialist, responds to this concern by noting that most of the time, no one is thinking about us—other people are too busy thinking about themselves. If on occasion people say things about us that sound derogatory, we can find out whether we have cause for concern by asking them what they meant by what they said.

*See Chapter 10 for more about communication.*

## ■ Developing Significant Relationships

We can begin to develop significant relationships by more positively communicating about ourselves to others. We constantly give clues about how we value ourselves. These clues influence how others value us, which in turn reinforces the value we place on ourselves, and on and on. Let's look at an example. A group discussion is taking place. Bob, in a vibrant voice, exclaims, "I just had a great idea. Let me tell you about it!" Paul, in a quiet monotone, says, "I had an idea a little while ago, but it really wasn't very good. Let me see if I can

■ Our feelings about our self-worth are evident to others.

remember it." You can easily see who values himself more. Chances are the group will be more interested in Bob's idea.

■ Appreciating Ourselves

Another way we can positively influence our relationships is by showing more genuine appreciation for ourselves and for others. By doing this, we build our own and others' self-esteem.

Problems in relationships usually develop when people feel unappreciated by each other. They tend to forget their purpose for being together, and soon their

---

## CASE IN POINT
## Appreciations

Take a few moments to think about some of the things you appreciate about yourself. List them in the spaces below. These appreciations need not reflect what you think others appreciate about you, just what *you* appreciate about yourself.

I appreciate the following things about myself:

_____

_____

_____

_____

_____

_____

_____

_____

_____

_____

_____

_____

When was the last time you expressed these appreciations?

Now spend a few moments thinking of what you appreciate about another significant person in your life.

I appreciate the following things:

_____

_____

_____

_____

_____

_____

_____

_____

_____

_____

_____

_____

When was the last time you shared your appreciations with this person?

Would you be able and willing to share your appreciations with three people?

positive feelings for themselves and for each other are obscured. The self-esteem of each begins to suffer, and the relationship gradually loses its value. The possibility of our maintaining high-quality relationships is greatly increased when we regularly express our appreciations to ourselves and our significant others. Then, our need for mutual nurturing and supportive relationships in which we learn and grow will be satisfied.

*See Chapter 11 for a discussion of intimacy.*

■ *Changing Our Behavior*   It seems as though many of the negative experiences in life are associated with people's attempts to develop relationships. Previously, we stated that negative interpretations of experiences often involve a problem with thinking. However, they also may involve a problem with behavior. When we discover that repeated negative experiences have affected our self-worth, we certainly need to examine what we may be doing to contribute to these experiences. Such examinations may indicate that we are punishing ourselves as a way of emphasizing our lack of self-appreciation and self-respect. We may also feel trapped by the way we have approached our problems in the past—our behavior.

Aaron Beck (1976) suggests that if we change our behavior with regard to a particular situation, the outcome of the change may allow us to examine and eventually change our thinking.

> Marty, a twenty-five-year-old man, had had only one date in his life, and that had been seven years earlier, in high school, when a friend had "fixed him up." The evening had turned out to be a disaster, at least for Marty. At the encouragement of a friend, Marty finally sought professional counseling from a qualified psychologist. Several sessions passed before Marty reluctantly agreed to do one of the things he feared most—ask a woman for a date. When Marty appeared for his next session, he happily reported that he had asked a young lady to go out with him. She had, and they both had had a great time. They had planned another date for the following weekend, and he no longer believed he was an undesirable creature.

By risking a change in his behavior, Marty not only changed his thinking about his behavior, he also changed, at least partly, his outlook on life. Marty took the first step toward achieving a more positive self-esteem.

■ *Developing Realistic Expectations*   There is nothing wrong with having an ideal self-image as a source of motivation for personal goals and personal growth. But when we believe we *must* be perfect to feel good about ourselves, we destroy our sense of worth. Perfectionistic expectations rob us of the ability to accept ourselves as fallible but worthwhile human beings. When we judge ourselves by perfectionistic standards, our appreciation of our actions and achievements is replaced by frustration, compulsiveness, and defeat.

*See "Conclusion: Goal Setting and Decision Making."*

**WHAT DO YOU THINK?**

■ How can you determine when your expectations are too high?
■ How can people change their expectations?
■ Shouldn't we maintain high expectations in order for society to progress?

> Holly, having become aware of how her perfectionistic standards had been affecting her, remarked, "I've been trying to be bright, witty, popular, pretty, and successful at everything I do. I've been trying very hard to be all these things to please others and feel better about myself instead of just being me. It's no wonder I've been feeling so little joy in my life."

The irony is that in trying to be all these things, Holly missed the very thing she hoped to gain—more joy in her life. Certainly, recognition of our achievements contributes to our self-esteem. But when the drive to achieve and accomplish becomes excessive, it can detract from our joy and satisfaction.

### ■ Activities and Experiences

Many activities we often treat as essential to our lives may actually detract from our self-worth. Some examples are participating in the latest fads and socializing with the "in" people. A closer look at the real importance of some of these involvements may reveal that they not only are unimportant in relation to our values but actually diminish our self-worth.

> Six months had passed since Jim's acceptance into the most prestigious fraternity on campus. The feeling of excitement at having survived the initiation process had died months ago. His experience so far had been quite unlike what he had expected. Instead of providing a warm, friendly environment with the goal of brotherhood, the fraternity was plagued with cliques one entered by wearing the most expensive clothes and knowing the most influential people. Jim realized that to remain a "brother" would mean denying his needs and values and diminishing his feelings of self-esteem. He decided to leave the fraternity.

Everyday experiences may test our self-esteem. Picture yourself riding along in your car on an uncrowded highway. It is a sunny autumn afternoon and you are feeling happy and alive. You look into the rear view mirror expecting to see an empty stretch of highway behind you. Instead, you see a black and white car with a blue flashing light on top; the person inside is motioning for you to pull over and stop. Your training tells you to obey immediately. In the few moments (which seem like hours) it takes for the police officer to get out of

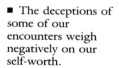
■ The deceptions of some of our encounters weigh negatively on our self-worth.

■ The consequences of being human often affect our worth temporarily.

his car and appear at your side window, you notice several things happening to you. First, your legs begin to shake and your heart begins to beat rapidly. Second, you notice that your entire body feels both hot and cold. When the officer arrives and asks to see your driver's license, you notice that your hands are shaking so much that you can hardly remove your license from your wallet. This is truly a stressful event. Soon you are on your way, traveling at a slower speed and in possession of a speeding citation. You are no longer aware that it is a beautiful day; and even though you are alive, you certainly do not feel happy. Your self-esteem appears to have taken a temporary plunge. Quietly, you berate yourself for the "stupid" thing you did.

*See Chapter 7 for more about stress.*

If your self-esteem is generally positive, you will soon be able to admit: "Yes I was going over the speed limit, and yes, occasionally I am careless and break the law." You will be able to view this experience as an unfortunate happening from which you have learned something. If your self-esteem is generally negative, you may deny your responsibility by making excuses and blaming the officer. You may also use the experience to confirm your low self-esteem.

*See Chapter 5's discussion of cognitive dissonance theory.*

## ■ Dealing with People

We have to deal with all kinds of people every day: store clerks, supervisors, car mechanics, teachers, lawyers, and medical doctors, to name a few. The confrontation that comes with dealing with others can present problems. Public embarrassment caused by an instructor or boss who singles us out in the presence of others as an example of what not to do or say can be devastating. Sometimes, others may attempt to put us down to make themselves feel more important. Of course, the degree to which these interactions affect our self-esteem depends

*For related discussions, see Chapter 9, "Group Dynamics and Leadership," and Chapter 10, "Assertive Communication" and "The Shared Meaning Process."*

on how high our self-esteem was in the first place. Someone who already feels negative about himself or herself will either lash out or withdraw when a conflict arises. This person may also attempt to avoid most conflicts, even though it is difficult and even unhealthy to do so. On the other hand, a person who generally feels positive will confront the conflict in assertive ways and not interpret the outcome as a reflection on his or her self-esteem.

### ■ Our Environment

Our environment, though safe and secure, may be so unstimulating that it begins to affect us in negative ways. This may be the case when we become bored with the familiarity or the routine associated with our surroundings: a feeling of stagnation often develops. The work or school environment can affect us in this way, as can the room, apartment, or house we live in. Although the way we feel about our environment may actually be a reflection of how we feel about

---

## CASE IN POINT
## Analysis of a Recent Conflict with Another Person

Briefly describe a recent conflict in which you were involved:

_____

_____

_____

_____

_____

_____

_____

What regrets do you have about how you handled your part in the conflict?

How might you handle a similar conflict differently in the future?

_____

_____

_____

_____

_____

_____

_____

_____

_____

What satisfactions do you feel about how you handled the conflict?

_____

ourselves, it is important not to allow our surroundings to produce feelings of stagnation. For some of us, a good place to start positive change in our lives is to change something in our environment. That does not necessarily mean we should quit our jobs, drop out of school, or move into a new apartment or house. Making drastic changes without first considering other factors may cause further problems with self-esteem.

We can assess our environment by first analyzing our situation to discover what conditions are affecting our feelings. A few minor changes (asking for a change in responsibilities at work, involving ourselves in more stimulating activities at school, or redecorating our surroundings at home) may create a more desirable atmosphere. In addition, such simple changes as taking a new, more scenic route to school or work may add zest to our lives. The important thing is that we use our creativity to change our negative feelings.

## ■ Physical Health

Our physical health and how we feel about the condition of our bodies greatly affect our feelings about ourselves. Conversely, the value we place on physical well-being is often a reflection of our self-worth in general. A person who does not value himself or herself often places little value on physical upkeep. Leaving the care of the body to chance often results in its not receiving the proper nutrition, exercise, stress management, and monitoring (McCamy and Presley, 1972). This lack of care may result in the body's losing its resistance to ever-present attackers (viruses and so on). Unable to defend itself, the body gives in, and we become ill.

*See Chapter 4 for more about the physical self and Chapter 7 for more about stress.*

When we are ill, we usually feel miserable and defeated. If illness occurs often or becomes chronic, the feelings of misery are prolonged, and our self-esteem often suffers. Even if we do not become seriously ill, a lack of appreciation for our bodies becomes evident in a lessening of energy and stamina. This may severely limit our actions and performance in many ways, further lowering our self-esteem.

If we wish to grow and to enhance our self-esteem, we must place equal value on emotional, intellectual, and physical well-being. We will discuss more about the physical self in the next chapter.

22. It is important to realize that we maintain our self-esteem by engaging in the \_\_\_\_ _____ process of personal _____ .

23. Ellis and other cognitive therapists view negative interpretations of experiences as a problem with _____ .

24. Our behavior usually results from our beliefs, or _____ , about ourselves.

25. The statement "People are going to act the way they want, not the way I want" is an example of a _____ self-statement.

26. Our _____ with _____ probably affect our self-esteem more than any other factor.

*27.* Ellis and Harper suggest that the belief that our self-worth is solely determined by the approval of others is _____.

*28.* Our _____ expectations often rob us of the ability to accept ourselves as fallible but worthwhile human beings.

*29.* Aaron Beck suggests that we can often change our way of thinking by risking a change in our _____ .

*30.* If we begin to feel stagnant and unstimulated, it may be important to analyze the quality of our relationships and our _____ .

*The answers to these review questions are on page 84.*

## SUMMARY

■ One of the most important factors determining our feelings, attitudes, values, behaviors, and life goals is self-esteem—the degree to which we value ourselves and feel useful and necessary in the world.

■ Various levels of self-esteem may be experienced. Some people may be described as having high, or positive, self-esteem, while others are described as having low, or negative, self-esteem.

■ Three major factors affect and are affected by self-esteem: attitudes, behaviors, and feelings.

■ The way we develop as children greatly affects our self-esteem in later life.

■ Parents are the greatest influence on the development of their children's self-esteem; teachers, relatives, and peers are other shaping influences.

■ A child who grows up feeling loved, accepted, and valued will probably enjoy a higher level of self-esteem and live a happier life. On the other hand, a child who grows up without these feelings may suffer from low self-esteem and live an unhappy and unfulfilled life.

■ The malevolent attitude—the belief that everyone is an enemy—severely affects personality development and the ability to live a satisfying life.

■ The development of self-esteem is a lifelong process in which the level of self-esteem tends to rise or fall as the discrepancy between the real self (actual self) and the ideal self (desired self) narrows or expands.

■ We can achieve a satisfying level of self-esteem even if our personality development was influenced by a negative environment.

■ People with low self-esteem are usually characterized by such behaviors as putting themselves down in the presence of others, blaming themselves and others, acting irresponsibly, being guarded and withdrawn, acting defensively, attacking others, rejecting themselves and others, being unable to disclose themselves to others, and resisting desirable change.

■ The following attitudes characterize low self-esteem: I do not count for much; the world is a miserable place; it is dangerous to reveal myself to others; my ideal self is so far removed from reality that there is no use trying to achieve it.

■ Low self-esteem is characterized by such feelings as fear, hurt, rejection, depression, anger, self-hatred, and the feeling of being unloved.

■ People with positive self-esteem are usually characterized by such behaviors as enjoying being with themselves and with others, showing love and respect for themselves and for others, behaving responsibly, demonstrating honesty and integrity, demonstrating assertiveness and congruence, taking risks, trusting themselves and others, accepting praise and criticism, and being spontaneous and free.

■ The attitudes that characterize people with positive self-esteem include beliefs in the worth and value of themselves and others, the importance of learning and growing, the importance of seeking out and developing significant interpersonal relationships, the importance of viewing all life experiences in terms of their contribution to growth, the necessity of taking responsibility for their own decisions and behaviors, and the freedom to become whatever they desire.

■ The feelings that characterize people with positive self-esteem include love and appreciation for themselves and others. They can express and accept a wide range of feelings, from sorrow to anger to joy. A general feeling of happiness and contentment prevails.

■ We can maintain our self-esteem by increasing our awareness of ourselves and of the effects of our relationships and surroundings on our self-esteem.

■ The way we have interpreted our experiences dramatically affects the way experiences presently influence our self-esteem.

■ The achievement of high self-esteem should serve as a lifelong goal for each of us to work toward.

## SELECTED READINGS

Branden, N. *The Psychology of Self-Esteem: A New Concept of Man's Psychological Nature*. Los Angeles: Nash, 1969. A book that focuses on the role self-esteem plays in life (values, responses, and goals).

Buscaglia, L. *Living, Loving, and Learning*. New York: Ballantine Books, 1982. A popular writer and speaker's view that learning to love ourselves and others is a way to grow and realize more of our human potential.

Cooper, J. E.; Holman, J.; and Braithwaite, V. A. "Self-Esteem and Family Cohesion: The Child's Perspective and Adjustment." *Journal of Marriage and the Family* (February 1983): 153–158. An investigation of the relationship between children's self-esteem and their perceptions of family cohesion.

Jourard, S. *Disclosing Man to Himself*. Princeton, N.J.: D. Van Nostrand, 1968. An important contribution to the humanistic psychology movement and the worth and integrity of the individual.

Murphy, G. *Outgrowing Self-Deception*. New York: Basic Books, 1975. A book that suggests many ways in which we can stop lying to ourselves and thus form a more realistic impression of ourselves.

Shostrom, E. *Freedom to Be*. Englewood Cliffs, N.J.: Prentice-Hall, 1972. A discussion of how we can overcome manipulation by others, begin to emphasize our own dynamic individuality, and appreciate the individuality of others.

## GLOSSARY

**authenticity:** honest self-disclosure.

**ideal self:** a set of beliefs that result in self-expectations concerning what one should be or could be, or the optimal self.

**malevolent attitude:** the belief that everyone, to a greater or lesser degree, is an enemy.

**real self:** that which a person identifies honestly as being his or her actual self.

**self-alienation:** detachment from self and from others.

**self-disclosure:** letting oneself be known honestly to others.

**self-esteem:** the degree to which one values oneself and feels useful and necessary in the world.

**self-fulfilling prophecy:** an originally false prediction of the future that comes true because of the influence of the prediction itself.

## REFERENCES

Beck, A. *Cognitive Therapy and Emotional Disorders.* New York: International Universities Press, 1976.

Berelson, B. *The Population Council Annual Report.* New York: Population Council, 1972.

Branden, N. *The Psychology of Self-Esteem: A New Concept of Man's Psychological Nature.* Los Angeles: Nash, 1969.

Brennecke, J. H., and Amick, R. G. *Psychology and Human Experience,* 2d ed. Encino, Calif.: Glencoe, 1978.

Canfield, J. T., and Wells, H. C. "Self-Concept: A Critical Dimension in Teaching and Learning." In *Humanistic Education Source Book,* edited by D. A. Read and S. B. Simon. Englewood Cliffs, N.J.: Prentice-Hall, 1975.

Cooper, J. E.; Holman, J.; and Braithwaite, V. A. "Self-Esteem and Family Cohesion: The Child's Perspective and Adjustment." *Journal of Marriage and the Family* (February 1983): 153–158.

Ellis, A., and Harper, R. A. *A New Guide to Rational Living.* Englewood Cliffs, N.J.: Prentice-Hall, 1975.

Fromm, E. *The Art of Loving.* New York: Harper & Row, 1956.

Horney, K. "The Search for Glory." In *Self-Explorations in Personal Growth,* edited by C. Moustakas. New York: Harper Colophan Books, 1956.

Horney, K. *Neurosis and Human Growth: The Struggle Toward Self-Realization.* New York: Norton, 1950.

Jourard, S. M. *Disclosing Man to Himself.* Princeton, N.J.: D. Van Nostrand, 1968.

———. *Healthy Personality: An Approach from the Viewpoint of Humanistic Psychology.* New York: Macmillan, 1974.

———. *The Transparent Self.* New York: Van Nostrand, Reinhold, 1971.

McCamy, J., and Presley, J. *Human Lifestyling: Keeping Whole in the Twentieth Century.* New York: Harper & Row, 1972.

Maslow, A. H. *Motivation and Personality,* 2d ed. New York: Harper & Row, 1970.

Meichenbaum, D. *Cognitive-Behavior Modification: An Integrative Approach.* New York: Plenum Press, 1977.

Merton, R.K. *Social Theory and Structure.* New York: Free Press, 1957.

Miller, S. "Worry About What Others Think of You?" *New Relationships* 1 (October 1983): 1.

Moustakas, C. *Personal Growth: The Struggle for Identity and Human Values.* Cambridge, Mass.: Howard A. Doyle, 1969.

O'Connell, V., and O'Connell, A. *Choice and Change: An Approach to the Psychology of Growth.* Englewood Cliffs, N.J.: Prentice-Hall, 1974.

Rogers, C.R. "A Theory of Therapy, Personality and Interpersonal Relationships as Developed in the Client-Centered Framework." In *Psychology: A Study of a Science,* vol.3, edited by S. Koch. New York: McGraw-Hill, 1959.

Schwartz, D. *Introduction to Management: Principles, Practices, and Processes.* New York: Harcourt Brace Jovanovich, 1980.

Sullivan, H.S. *The Interpersonal Theory of Psychiatry.* New York: Norton, 1953.

## ANSWERS TO REVIEW QUESTIONS

**Page 65.**    *1.* F   *2.* T   *3.* F   *4.* T   *5.* F   *6.* F   *7.* T   *8.* F   *9.* T   *10.* F

**Page 69.**    *11.* self-fulfilling prophecy   *12.* self-disclosure   *13.* self-disclosure   *14.* self-alienation   *15.* rejection, fear, hurt   *16.* low self-esteem

**Page 72.**    *17.* F   *18.* F   *19.* T   *20.* F   *21.* T

**Page 81.**    *22.* lifelong, growth   *23.* thinking   *24.* attitudes   *25.* positive   *26.* relationships, people   *27.* irrational   *28.* perfectionistic   *29.* behavior   *30.* environment

Part II gives information that will enable you to assess and perhaps modify three aspects of your total self—your physical self, your mental self, and your emotional self.

Chapter 4 explores the physical self. It begins by describing the effects of body type and stereotype on human social behavior. Attributions of others, which may be based on our physical attractiveness, also are given attention, along with proper nutrition, weight control, strength, aerobic fitness, health, and life extension. We continue the exploration of our physical self by concentrating on the psychological impact of our sex on our identity and future social prospects.

Chapter 5, which discusses the cognitive self, relates information on how the mind functions to new techniques for altering both thinking styles and specific thoughts. The purpose of such intervention is to reduce irrational thinking and increase possibilities for emotional and behavioral growth. Special attention is given to applying this new understanding of how the mind works to improving study skills.

In Chapter 6, we investigate a necessary and precious aspect of our existence—our feeling self. Internal bodily changes, unconscious mental evaluations, and external physical expressions are described in terms of their adaptation and survival value. Two contrasting emotions—love and depression—are described in some detail to increase your understanding of the depth of human emotion.

# ASPECTS
# OF
# IDENTITY

# PHYSICAL SELF

FOCUS

It's fun to let our minds run free, allowing streams of thought to flow. Ideas cascade about us, complete with rich images. Read to the end of this paragraph; then close your eyes and relax. As you relax, permit moving portraits of yourself to flood your mind. Do not be selective, just let your relaxed mind turn out image after image. Enjoy a few moments of this soothing mental exercise.

Were you able to see yourself? Could you watch without evaluating yourself? Do you believe your size, sex, shade, or shape give others reliable clues to your personality? Has your personality been shaped by others' reactions to one or more aspects of your physical self? Finally, do you believe that your anatomy seems to control a large part of your destiny?

**4**

PHYSICAL
SELF

## DISCUSSION:  BODY TYPE AND BEHAVIOR

The notion that there are distinct personality types based on physique and the related notion that one can judge a person's character at first sight have a long history in literature and in scientific writing. Most people pride themselves on their ability to "size up" a person at a glance. The **physical self** and its effect on our behavior and on the behavior of others are the subjects of this chapter.

The chapter is divided into three parts. The first introduces the possibility that parts of our personal and social adjustment are shaped or limited by our genes and the expression of those genes in our body type. The second discusses the extent to which our physical image influences adjustment by affecting our self-perception and the perceptions and reactions of others. The third explores potential physical and mental adjustments to ensure physical attractiveness, health, and long life.

### ■ The Physical Self and Adjustment

On the most basic level, we are physical organisms that function in an environment to which we must adjust. One basic physical need is to maintain equilibrium. When conditions change, our physiological processes respond in order to counterbalance the effects of the change and reestablish harmony. For example, when the outside temperature drops, we consume more energy to regulate our body heat. The term for this continuous adjustment process is **homeostasis**.

Homeostasis, like many physical responses, can be profoundly influenced by our psychological state (Carroll, 1969). For instance, fear may stop or reverse our digestive processes. Our physical state can have equally profound effects on our psychological behavior. Irritability, fear, excitability, and insomnia, all symptoms of acute anxiety, can be caused by an overactive thyroid gland. *There is a constant interaction between psychological and physiological mechanisms in adjustment.* In addition, many of our physical responses are learned, and learning is never automatic.

### ■ Personality and Physique

Many observers have come to the conclusion that our physical selves come in three **phenotypes**: the broad, heavy person; the narrow, tall person; and the person in between (Eysenck, 1973). Further, for over 2,500 years of recorded history, physicians, poets, and philosophers have noted a **correlation** between physique and character. We may note, for example, that Cassius has a lean and hungry look, and therefore is untrustworthy. Santa Claus is fat, and by design a jolly, and therefore trustworthy, fellow. (One should not, however, confuse correlation with *causation*. Just because two things occur together, it does not follow that one causes the other to occur.)

Over forty years ago Sheldon and Stevens (1942) found correlations between body type and temperament. As late as 1978, Montemayor, after an exhaustive review of the research literature, reported modest but consistent support for these early findings. The body types are illustrated in Figure 4.1. An **endomorph**, the broad, heavy person, is likely to love comfort, talking, and social

Endomorphy
7–1–1

Mesomorphy
1–7–1

Ectomorphy
1–1–7

A balanced physique
4–4–4

*FIGURE 4.1
Sheldon's Somatotypes. The first number represents soft roundness, the second hard muscularity, and the third fragile thinness. Personality traits have been associated with each of these types.*

dining. Sheldon termed this personality type **viscerotonic**. The **ectomorph**, a narrow, tall person, likely loves privacy, subtle humor, and social restraint. Sheldon's name for this personality type is **cerebrotonic**. The person in between, the muscular **mesomorph**, loves adventure, exercise, and physical courage. This personality is called **somatotonic**.

*See Chapter 1 for a discussion of personality types.*

> Bill is mad. Mad at himself, and mad at his friends. He is especially mad at the parents of his best friends. Big boned and somewhat overweight, Bill projects what he hopes is a powerful image. He wants to be large, but hard and muscular, not fat. He trains regularly. The problem is that everyone offers him food and then stands back to watch him eat.
> If Bill doesn't oblige, he can see the confusion and disappointment in their eyes and sense the awkward drop in conversation. So Bill eats, and resents himself for being so vulnerable. Bill's image is endomorphic and his behavior is typically viscerotonic.

## ■ Biological Determination

For the most part, our phenotype is a function of our genes. While nutrition, exercise, and our general style of life can affect our physique; such dimensions as bone structure, fat-cell distribution, hormone levels, and height are largely inherited. The apparent connection between phenotype and personality type could be an indication that part of our personality is determined by genes.

Sheldon (1942) said as much during World War II (Sheldon and Stevens, 1942), and was attacked as being a Nazi! Such an idea seemed to support the racist policies of the Third Reich. Sheldon was no Nazi, but the idea that at least 10 percent of our behavior is genetically controlled is still attacked as racist, sexist, and socially dangerous. It is also attacked as speculative and overly simplistic.

## ■ Sociobiology

**Sociobiology** is a discipline that is attempting to discover the extent to which our behavior is genetically determined. The existence of biological foundations for social behavior is well accepted with reference to the social insects and the social animals below man (Hamilton, 1972). The concept is meeting fierce resistance from humanistic and behavioral psychologists (as well as from political Marxists and liberal Democrats and Republicans) when it is applied to modern humans, however.[1]

The field of sociobiology came to national attention in 1975 with the publication by a Harvard zoologist, Edward O. Wilson, of the book *Sociobiology: The New Synthesis*. This fusion of **genetics** and population biology extended neo-Darwinian evolutionary theory into the study of social behavior among insect and animal societies. The last chapter applied the same general principles to our species, **Homo sapiens**. The notion that our behavior could be theoretically linked to that of Old World monkeys and apes, for instance, unleashed a fury from some elements within the social sciences.

What are the bases for believing human behavior is affected by human biology? To the biologist, adjustment is termed **adaptation**. Our physical selves represent a successful adaptation to a wide variety of environments. As humans, we are basically like all other living organisms. The kind of body we have is an indication of the kind of behavior of which we are capable. Each species has a unique **morphogenotype**, or basic biological structure, and a bioengineer can examine the physical properties of each organism and describe the limits of its performance (Lenihan, 1974). *Our capacity to adjust is thus limited.* There are sounds we cannot hear, frequencies of light we cannot see, and topical features we cannot feel. Most important, the construction of our brain sets limits and perhaps gives direction to the ways we mentally solve problems of everyday living.

*For more on this topic, see Chapter 5, on the cognitive self, and Chapter 7, on stress.*

David Barash (1977) maintains that behavior arises from the structure and function of the nervous system and is inherited. In higher species, behavior does not mean specific acts but rather predispositions that may be expressed in diverse and complex behavior patterns.

Our human body is an ancient structure, millions of years old, that has been constantly shaped by its interaction with the physical world, even as it has more recently begun to shape the world. However, the idea that our genes may give direction to our behavior is disturbing to many. Most can accept the idea that there are physical limits on their potential for behavior. The related idea that their bodies may partly direct their thoughts and actions is more foreign, and more frightening.

■ *Procreative Proficiency*    You are familiar with the idea of "survival of the fittest." In Darwin's original formulation, fitness meant the superiority of certain individuals within groups of competing members of the same species occupying the same territory. Survival fitness now means **procreative proficiency**—the ability to reproduce the most of one's own kind. The unit of survival has shifted from the individual to the genes that carry the code for reproducing similar individuals.

Such a shift provides an explanation of some otherwise perplexing behavior observed among all social creatures. For example, wasps sting attacking enemies at the cost of their own lives; birds risk death to warn other birds of an impending

---

1. Marxists do not want to believe that noneconomic factors shape power relationships, and American liberals are fearful that sociobiology could lead to a reduction in social opportunities for the disadvantaged.

FIGURE 4.2
Procreative
Proficiency, the new
standard for physical
fitness?

threat; and sterile soldier ants die to protect a reproductive queen. Such **altruism**, or self-sacrifice, does not make sense in terms of individual survival. Why then does it exist? Darwin had no answer.

Sociobiologists believe individuals act not only on the basis of individual fitness but also on the basis of **inclusive fitness**, which involves the genetic representations of individuals through their close relatives. **Kin selection**, rather than natural selection, becomes the key for survival. Organisms are motivated by a tendency to protect their own genes (Dawkins, 1976). Thus you protect yourself so you may pass on your genes through reproduction. You also protect your relatives, because they share your gene pool, and they too may pass it on. Your chance for immortality is thus enhanced, because "Genes are forever" (Dawkins, 1976, p. 37).

■ *Kin Selection and Protective Behavior*   A fascinating deduction from the theory of kin selection states that self-sacrificial acts will occur in a specific order based on the greatest good for the greatest number—of shared genes! This means you will help parents before spouses, brothers and sisters before parents, and an identical twin before anyone else.

Kinship theory has received substantial empirical verification from studies of the animal kingdom (Barash, 1977). However, Alper (1978) states that "there is no direct evidence for the genetic basis of human behavioral traits, and in fact it is probably impossible to find evidence either for or against the principle" (p. 200). One hint of at least verbal verification has come from American adolescents. Freedman (1979) described perilous situations involving various persons to young adults and asked if they would be willing to be hurt in order to help those at risk. Brothers were helped before cousins, sisters before girl friends, and, in general, family members before strangers.

---

## CASE IN POINT
## Altruism among the Eskimos

During the harsh winters, Eskimo family groups must move constantly in order to survive. Aged grandparents of some groups willingly stay behind on ice floes when it becomes apparent that the long and dangerous journey might be slowed down by their infirmities. They die so that their families might live.

According to sociobiologists, this is a clear case of sociobiological evolution. The altruistic gesture increases the inclusive fitness of those who die. Family groups with less altruistic genes, slowed down by their old members, may not live to reproduce. (Read further for an alternate explanation of why an ancient Eskimo may choose self-sacrifice.)

---

**WHAT DO YOU THINK?**

■ If nepotism has genetic causes, how can we preserve democracy and the institution of the family while at the same time ensuring the economic and political equality of opportunity upon which democracy rests?

*See Chapter 8 for more about socialization.*

*See the Selected Readings (Rubinstein and Slife) for a fine discussion of the ethical and social implications of sociobiology.*

Wilson (1975, 1978) cites research indicating that genes establish predispositions, set emotional curbs, and direct hormonal messages that act upon such human behaviors as learning modes, mental and neuromuscular abilities, and personality traits. Differential sex roles and such specific practices as aggression, **nepotism** (showing favoritism to relatives in hiring practices and the like), and reciprocity (giving help in the expectation of receiving help) are seen as examples of genetic effects on human behavior patterns.

### ■ Critics of Sociobiology

Critics of sociobiology, such as Harvard's Sociobiology Study Group, maintain that cultural evolution, individual experience, and socialization are far better vehicles for understanding human behavior. All of these depend on our capacity to learn. In this view, we learn the roles we are to play, the rules that shape these roles, and the ways we are expected to relate to the world and to each other. The behavior of the Eskimo elders is seen as having cultural roots. Perhaps there are no genetic differences between the Eskimo families, and the gift of the grandparents is adaptive. It may well be offered because offering it is the thing to do, a learned cultural trait. The honor and glory of giving such gifts to loved ones may be taught from childhood, to be acted on in old age. The Harvard Study Group, and most psychologists, believe that to try to reduce the richness of human behavior to an elaboration of a limited set of biologically determined dispositions is absurd and dangerous.

REVIEW
QUESTIONS

---

*1.* One basic physical need is to maintain internal equilibrium, or h_____ .

*2.* There is constant interaction between our ps_____ and our ph_____ mechanisms of adjustment.

*3.* The physical characteristics we inherit from our ph_____ .

*4.* Sheldon termed the tall, narrow person an E_____ .

*5.* Viscerotonia is associated with the En_____ phenotype.

*6.* The discipline that attempts to determine the extent to which genes direct our social behavior is called S_____ .

*7.* The reproductive proficiency of you and your close relatives comprise your

In_____ fitness.

*8.* Such behaviors as altruism, nepotism, and reciprocity are examples of k_____

selection.

*The answers to these review questions are on page 131.*

---

## DISCUSSION: THE SEXUAL SELF

David Barash (1977) flatly states that "Sociobiology relies heavily upon the biology of male-female differences and upon the adaptive behavioral differences that have evolved accordingly. Ironically, Mother Nature appears to be a sexist" (p. 283). Read the following *Case in Point.*

If you can imagine such an experience, how would you complete this tale of sexual transformation—first woman, then man? Would you project future happiness and success for this new man, or a life of confusion, frustration, and despair?

Angelica–Angelo is a fictitious name, but not a fictional character. Angelo and at least sixteen others like him live in Santo Domingo. A local Spanish term, "penis-at-twelve," describes the essence of their shared genetic disorder. Angelo was conceived a male, with the XY male chromosome, but the hormones necessary for the formation of male genitals were not present when he was a six-week-old developing fetus (a critical period of development, as you will see later). At birth, he looked like a girl. He was christened Angelica and raised as a girl. At puberty, male hormones rushed through his body and initiated the completion of his sexual self as directed by his original genetic code.

Julianne Imperato-McGinley (1980) wrote about eight children from the United States with the same genetic disorder. Now, as young adults, these

---

## CASE IN POINT
## Angelica–Angelo

Imagine yourself to be a beautiful, slim, brown-eyed little girl. You live in a remote village in Santo Domingo and you are dreaming of your fifteenth birthday, your Quince! This magic day, still a few years away, marks the end of childhood and the beginning of young womanhood, and you have been preparing for it since the moment of birth when your parents knew they had been graced with a little girl.

You visualize yourself in a lovely white gown, a symbol of the virtue and purity that has been so carefully taught to you by your grandmothers and protected by your father and brothers. All eyes are upon you as you glide across the floor in the arms of your proud father. You shyly catch the eye of a handsome. . . .

Now imagine that you enter puberty and your dreams are shattered as your slim, little-girl body takes on its adult proportions. Instead of the beautiful breasts, narrow waist, and rounded hips of your dreams, you watch in horror as your body becomes muscular, your shoulders widen, and your hips and waist form into a straight line. Dreams of feminine romance and the fulfillment of motherhood vanish as you observe your genitals change from those of a female to those of a male.

North Americans all consider themselves to be women, even though they must receive injections to maintain their feminine forms.

In the United States, there is a greater opportunity for medical intervention in response to sexual disorders. The eight Americans were given no chance to allow their genitals to become masculinized at puberty. They were all castrated shortly after birth and a functional vagina was constructed for each of them. In this way, female **coitus** and orgasm, if not conception and biological mother-hood, were retained as possibilities. In Santo Domingo, nature was allowed to run its course.

Apparently, mother nature knows best. Five of the eight U.S. women are reported to have serious psychological problems, while all of the seventeen men from Santo Domingo made a relatively smooth transition from the female to the male sexual identity and role. None of them need injections to maintain their new status.

## ■ Gender Identity

**WHAT DO YOU THINK?**

■ Would you prefer to be a senorita or a senor?

Although socialized to femininity, the Santo Domingo youths readily adopted the culturally accepted male sex role. Their **gender identity** is now male as well. Their occupational aspirations, sexual orientation, and sexual activity are those of the traditional Hispanic male. As the sociobiologists suggest, perhaps their male genes helped direct them in overcoming their earlier gender training. Perhaps the less restricted life style of the Hispanic male meant a new threshold of opportunity for these former girls, which they readily accepted. Their local culture was supportive, with several parents proud that their daughter was, in reality, their son.

**WHAT DO YOU THINK?**

■ If the way we intereact with other humans is even partially determined by our genes, what does that do to the notion of free will?

The difficulties of the Americans may be due to their awareness of their castration. While the six-week fetal mishap went unnoticed by them, they were conscious of the events of puberty. Also, their inability to bear children and their need for constant injections to keep them physically feminine may also be psychologically stressful. Another possibility is that their original genetic and hormonal codes created in each of them a *male brain* (see page 98), which predisposes them to male, rather than female, imagery, temperament, and activity.

■ *Becoming Sexually Human*    Figure 4.3 gives an overview of the long process of becoming a masculinized or feminized human being. As you can see, neither genes and hormones nor labeling and socializing are sufficient by themselves to produce a stable gender identification, preference, and role. Also notice how important timing is to our sexuality. The presence or absence of hormones during our fetal period and again at puberty makes an enormous difference. So does the manner in which others relate to us during infancy and adolescence.

> Carol and Robert are best friends. Best friends are life-savers in junior high. "Jack and Jill" is what their other friends call them. "Jack" is Carol Stevens, a husky, square-built girl of thirteen who is head and broad shoulders above her classmates. "Jill" is Bob Carmichael, a slightly built, fine-featured young man of fourteen, without the shadow of a chin whisker.
>
> Jack and Jill are friends in mutual suffering and self-defense. Each knows how bad it feels to display physical traits that everyone "knows" belong to the opposite sex and to be in junior high.

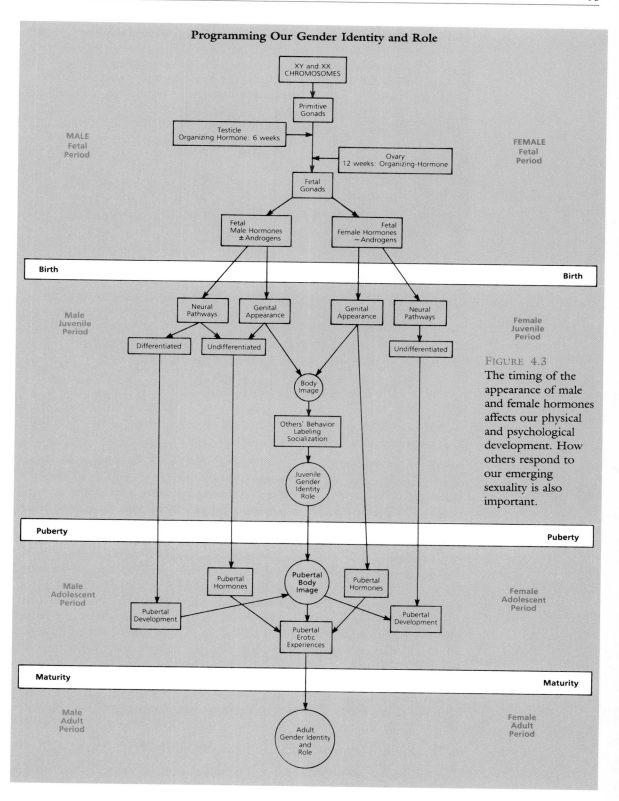

**Programming Our Gender Identity and Role**

FIGURE 4.3
The timing of the appearance of male and female hormones affects our physical and psychological development. How others respond to our emerging sexuality is also important.

■ Sexuality—a way of seeing ourselves and relating to others.

## ■ Sex-Linked Differences in Human Behavior

Sexuality can be viewed as a way of seeing ourselves and a way of relating to others. These change as we progress through our life cycle. The single most salient factor in shaping the nature of our interpersonal relations is our sex. Grady (1977) finds that sex is a social label associated with widespread ideas of sex differences. (See **attribution theory**, page 105.) Maccoby and Jacklin (1974) hold that there are few natural male or female differences in behavior. Not all agree.

Many think that the behavioral differences between the sexes are not illusory. It is certain that females, and not males, menstruate, **gestate**, and **lactate**. It is equally certain that males, and not females, impregnate. In line with these adaptive functions, aggressive behavior seems to be a more intense and stable trait for males from birth (Moyer, 1974). Aggression contributes to inclusive fitness; it protects relatives and ensures that the stronger male will reproduce. **Nurturing** behavior is found to be more stable among females (Kagan and Moss, 1962). However, there are wide variations in aggression and nurturance within each sex, and at present it is impossible to attribute real differences observed to the exclusive influence of biology, socialization, or imitation.

## ■ The Brain, Hormones, and Sexual Differentiation

The role of hormones and sex-linked behavior is under intensive study at the moment. John Money and Anke Ehrhardt (1972) report the effect of **androgens** (a class of male hormones) on the behavior of females. In the 1940s several women were given shots of an androgen to help prevent miscarriage. Some gave birth to girls with malformed genitals. These organs were surgically corrected and the *androgenized* girls were raised from birth as females. Their behavior as children was tomboyish—they were much more energetic and competitive than a matched set of normal girls. When young they were less interested in dolls and infants; when adolescent they were less interested in romance and dating. Today, only two-thirds want to have children, and the majority value a career above marriage and family. Such behavior is, at present, atypical among American girls and suggests to some a link between prenatal hormones and sexual nature.

Wilson (1978) reports just such a link. A single recessive gene can produce the early (fetal) introduction of a substance that mimics the male hormone and appears to masculinize girls. In a related study, boys and girls who were exposed to additional male hormones before birth later had significantly higher scores than their brothers or sisters on tests of potential aggressiveness (Reinisch, 1981).

In the first six weeks after conception, the sex organs of all embryos are identical; they have the capacity to develop either way, regardless of the makeup of the sex chromosomes (Gorski, 1979). The embryonic sexual glands begin to develop into testicles at six weeks *if instructed to do so by the male (XY) chromosome*. In females, at about twelve weeks, the female (XX) chromosomes order the gonads to take the form of ovaries. After the development of either testicles or ovaries, the powerful gonadotropic hormones take over and control the development of the external sex organs. A surplus of androgen causes the external structure to form a penis. Without this surplus, the same structure forms into a clitoris. Another fetal structure, the labioscrotal swelling, either remains open to form the vaginal opening and labia or, under the influence of androgens, fuses in males to form the scrotum. (See Figure 4.4.)

Under normal conditions, an inhibiting agent excreted by the testes or ovaries will cause the unused, opposite-sex structures present in the fetus to wither away. We are thus born with internal and external sex organs that correspond to our genetic sex. Later, at puberty, further hormone secretions control the

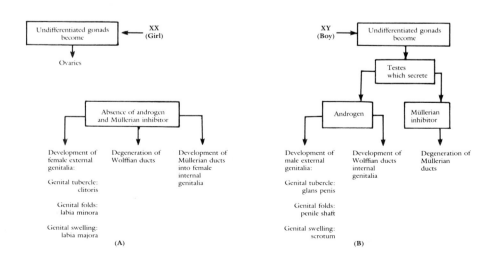

FIGURE 4.4
Pathways for differentiation of the A) female genital system B) male genital system.

appropriate secondary sexual characteristics such as facial hair and a deeper voice in males and enlarged breasts and wider hips in females.

In the first weeks after conception, the brains of males and females are thought to be identical. If the brain receives a surplus of androgen from the newly forming testes in a male, a region of one brain center, the hypothalamus, will be altered and a male brain will develop (Reinisch, 1981). This brain directs the adrenal glands and the testes to produce larger amounts of the hormones epinephrine and testosterone in the male. These hormones in turn produce a higher energy output and a greater tendency to act on the environment, to force changes. You will remember that a more active, more competitive nature has been ascribed to males. The behavior aroused by female hormones (estrogens) seems to involve tendencies toward maternal responses (Money and Ehrhardt, 1972). Males are typically more sexually active than females. This nonillusionary difference is under the control of androgens (Reichlin, 1971). The sexual activity levels of females are also regulated by androgens. This is possible because the adrenal glands produce small amounts of the male hormones. Similarly, the testes produce small amounts of the female hormones. Thus in all of us male and female traits are under at least partial control of estrogens (feminizing hormones) and androgens (masculinizing hormones), as well as progesterone (pregnancy hormones). Our sexuality appears to be regulated by the amount of these three hormone groups present within our systems from day to day, as well as at critical periods in the development of our physical selves.

## ■ Sex Hormones versus Socialization

See Chapter 8 for more about socialization.

The masculine behavior of the androgenized girls appears to be due to changes in their fetal brains plus the constant, brain-regulated production of higher levels of androgens as their bodies grew and changed. These powerful physical effects seem to have more than offset the effects of social learning about appropriate sex roles.

A dramatic example of social versus physical effects on sex differences is unfolding at present. In 1972, Money and Ehrhardt reported the case of an infant boy whose genitals were mutilated by accident. It would have been impossible for him to function as a normal male, so surgery was performed and the child was raised as a girl. At four the child behaved like a typical girl. At the same time, her identical twin brother was behaving like a typical boy! Upbringing appeared more powerful than genetics in shaping gender identity and gender role. In 1982, however, Diamond reported that by thirteen years of age, the child had developed a manly gait, wanted to become an automobile mechanic, and was not happy with her female role. Neighborhood and school mates began calling her "cave woman." By sixteen she was under the care of a psychiatrist, trying to adjust to life as a female.

See Chapter 11, on intimacy, for more about sexual expectations.

Conflict between the physical self and social learning can arise for all of us. We inherit a physical structure that predisposes us to precocious sexual activity. At puberty, pleasure centers in the brain are sensitized by sex hormones. This makes us more receptive to erotic stimuli—visual stimuli in males, tactile stimuli in females (Wolman and Money, 1980). Once sensitized, these centers are stimulated by androgens from the adrenal as well as from the sexual glands. (This is thought to be the reason why female humans are sexually receptive throughout their menstrual cycle, rather than only during **estrus**, the fertile period, as is the general case among mammals.) Social rules govern our sexual activity, and it can be comforting to know what is expected of us in terms of sexual values, attitudes, and actions. On the other hand, it can be distressing to find ourselves unable or unwilling to conform to these expectations.

REVIEW QUESTIONS

*9.* David Barash believes Mother Nature is a sexist. T F

*10.* At puberty, powerful sex hormones overcame the sex genes and changed the girls of Santo Domingo into boys. T F

*11.* Maccoby and Jacklin hold that there are few natural differences between male and female behavior. T F

*12.* The androgenized girls were no more energetic or competitive than other girls their age. T F

*13.* The majority of androgenized girls valued marriage and family more than a career. T F

*14.* In the first six weeks after conception, the sex organs of males and females are identical. T F

*15.* Our secondary sex characteristics (hips and facial hair, for example) are shaped by sex hormones at puberty. T F

*16.* While external genitals may differ by sex, there is no difference between the male and female brain. T F

*17.* It is an illusion that males are more sexually active than females. T F

*18.* Our sexuality is regulated by the amount of sex hormones present in our bodies daily and at critical periods in our development. T F

*The answers to these review questions are on page 131.*

# DISCUSSION: ATTRIBUTION

The association of body type and behavior has had its greatest impact on theories of childhood development. Dr. Ilg and Dr. Ames (1961) of the famed Gesell Institute believe that babies act as they do largely because of their phenotypes and that parents should not try to make them over.

## ■ The Looking-Glass Self

Many psychologists do not agree with Ilg and Ames. As early as 1905 Charles Horton Cooley (1864–1929) argued that the human mind is actually a product of a person's interaction with the world. Cooley believed that our sense of self is a mirror reflection of how we think others judge the way we look and act. This **looking-glass self** is made up of (1) what we think others see in us, (2) how we think others react to what they see, and (3) how we evaluate ourselves in response to these perceived reactions from others.

## ■ Stereotypes and Self-Image

What sort of person do you see when you look in the mirror? How is such a person expected to act? Very clear and consistent **stereotypes** exist in the minds

## CASE IN POINT
## Mirror, Mirror, on the Wall . . .

Look at yourself in a full-length mirror and describe your reflection.

When I view my face I see _____

_____

I see my body as _____

_____

My best physical attribute is _____

_____

The part of my physical self I hate the most is _____

_____

People who look as I look are expected to be

_____

_____

People who look as I look are expected to act

_____

_____

I believe the stereotypes about the way I look are _____

_____

of most people concerning phenotypes and expected behavior. These stereotypes develop early and are held to be true for individuals of different races, classes, and cultures (Montemayor, 1978). For example, we all "know" that endomorphs eat and drink more; mesomorphs are the best soldiers; ectomorphs smoke more and are nervous; females are soft and delicate; and males are strong and silent. You may see yourself, and be seen by others, as being fat and jolly precisely because everyone "knows" all fat people are jolly.

Stereotyping also changes how we act toward other people. Bandura and Walters (1963) attribute much of our personalities to the effects of social learning. People positively reinforce our behavior *when we act as we are expected to act*. If you are thin, being shy is expected and rewarded. If you are male and muscular, being sensitive is unexpected and less likely to be rewarded. By such continuous shaping, our personalities come to mirror our body types. In other words, *perception* of sex and body type, not the type itself, may be what is correlated with observed behavior patterns.

### ■ The "Bodily Me"

We come to see ourselves as we think others see us. Zastro (1979) believes that our sense of identity is the key element of our personality. A central part of this sense of identity is achieved through recognition and exploration of our physical selves, our bodies. "The child, the adolescent, the adult—each observes his own body and the bodies of others in order to compare and evaluate himself" (Diamond, 1957). For example, the onset of puberty produces rapid changes in height, weight, musculature, sex organs, and voice. People view us differently. We become obsessed with what others think of us and spend hours in front of a mirror (the looking-glass self). We must revise our body image in recognition

■ How is a person
who looks like I look
expected to act?

and acceptance of these changed perceptions and reactions. Pregnancy alters the self-image of the young woman, and so often does male pattern baldness in the young man. Both require acceptance if self-esteem is to be maintained. The passing years demand that we adjust our idea of a healthy body to the realities of advancing age. The despair of the sixty-year-old who clings to a twenty-year-old body image is real, and ridiculous. Gordon W. Allport (1960) believes that the "**bodily me**" is made up of the many sensations that exist within us and that this "bodily sense remains a lifelong anchor for our self-awareness" (p. 42).

### ■ Self-Fulfilling Prophecy

Finally, our perception of other people's reaction to our physical attributes, or lack of them, can influence our subsequent behavior, thus creating a self-fulfilling prophecy. For example, the mesomorphic male, who is expected to be an athlete, or the ectomorphic female, who is expected to be a scholar, find general support for their efforts in these areas and thrive in spite of perhaps only ordinary abilities. Such persons do well precisely because others think well of them.

*See Chapter 3, on self-esteem.*

### ■ Physical Beauty and Positive Perceptions

Physical attractiveness is the most important factor in producing positive expectations concerning the character of persons we do not know. Appearance leads quickly to conclusions about a person's traits and attitudes. An attractive physical self is important at all ages. Dion, Berscheid, and Walster (1972) find that unattractive children are liked less by their nursery school classmates. College students, acting as jurors in mock trials, find attractive defendants not guilty more often than unattractive ones. When damages are awarded, the attractive defendant receives significantly more money (Stephan and Tully, 1977). Police are less likely to ticket an attractive female for a moving violation.

Physical attractiveness is also important in old age. Kuhlen and Thompson (1970) have found that the changes in gross physical structure that accompany the aging process are in large measure responsible for determining the reactions of others to the elderly. The changes in weight and height and the generally lessened resiliency associated with **senescence** (aging) usually have a negative effect on how well the elderly are expected to perform and on whether they are included in ongoing activities. This *disengagement*—a process in which society and the aging individual withdraw from each other—is not in the best interests of either the individual or the society.

### ▪ The Eye of the Beholder

There are no universal standards for the measurement of physical attractiveness. Each age and every culture defines itself by redefining beauty. Being tall is often valued (Feldman, 1971). Kagan (1966) reports a height anxiety developing in children as early as the third grade. Individuals classified as dwarfs or midgets are so stigmatized that they tend to associate primarily with each other (Wineberg, 1968). In a study of women's preferences concerning chests, breasts, buttocks, and legs, Beck, Ward-Hull, and McClear (1976) concluded that women preferred both males and females to be of a moderate thickness (the lean mesomorph) with small buttocks. Large female breasts were preferred, but a large male chest was not. No clear leg preferences emerged from this study. Another study found that in selecting prospective dates and/or mates, males consistently ranked physical attractiveness higher than did females. There seems to be some empirical support for the commonly held belief that it is more important for a woman to be good-looking than it is for a man (Berscheid, Walster, and Bohrnstedt, 1971).

Being attractive may not attract the one you wish to attract. Extroverts tend to prefer mates who are larger in the chest, breast, and buttocks than the ideal; introverts do not. When we feel good about ourselves we tend to be attracted to a more physically imposing mate. When we fell insecure about ourselves, the physically unattractive mate actually makes us more sexually aroused (Kielser and Baral, 1970). Early-maturing girls become too attractive too soon and seem to incur such ambivalent responses from teachers as well as from classmates that their attitudes toward school and learning suffer (Davis, 1977).

### ▪ The Matching Hypothesis

We can't all be handsome or beautiful. Fortunately, when we select friends, dates, and mates, we realistically take into consideration our own perceived level of attractiveness. The **matching hypothesis** suggests that people of similar levels of physical attractiveness gravitate toward each other (Riedal and McKillip, 1979).

■ People of equal attractiveness seem attracted to each other.

Being perceived as attractive depends on more than height, color, or size of breast. The body image we project to others includes physical features, voice patterns, dress, grooming, and impressions of health and energy. We are seldom seen as a still life, posed against an appropriate backdrop. We are observed in motion, acting within a situation. The way we move and communicate also creates first impressions, as does the role we play. A man was introduced to one college class as a student, to another as a senior lecturer, and to a third as a professor. Each class gave written estimates of his height. As he grew in academic status, he also grew in estimated physical stature (Wilson, 1978). Competence and intelligence, warmth and sincerity, and similar nonphysical dimensions of self become increasingly important as we come to know each other.

## ■ Stereotypes and Stigmas

Evaluation by physique is seen by many psychologists as just another form of **prejudice**. As you know, stereotypes are attitudes held toward a whole group of people. They may be positive or negative. Some are so negative that they are termed **stigma** and result in their victims' being avoided or unnaturally treated. The physically handicapped are at times stigmatized, and such prejudice can become an important factor in the develeopment of emotional disturbances among them. It is possible to stigmatize yourself. Loss of control or of function of bowel, bladder, or sexual organs is often accompanied by deep shame and a loss of self-confidence. If such a handicap is accepted by those who are important to the afflicted individual, however, that handicapped person is *not* more likely than others to be maladjusted.

Race, sex, age, health, occupation, education, accent, and so on are used to classify people. We then respond to the classification, not to the person. We are surprised when someone does not meet our stereotype of him or her. We are then caught off guard and do not know how to respond.

Not all stereotypes are untrue, but all are unjust. Rosenthal (1970) found criminals as a group to be lower in IQ, more muscular, and more frequently brain damaged as measured by the electroencephalograph. But to respond to any former prison inmate as if he or she were an irrational, brutish idiot is unwarranted, because a given individual *may fall anywhere within the range used to compute the average*. In addition, your stereotyped response just might produce the behavior you fear.

■ *Discrimination*   Negative behavior that reflects stereotypical thinking about the physical self is all too frequently observed in America. Such unwarranted behavior is termed **discrimination** and extracts an enormous cost in lost performance and unfulfilled lives. Simply being left-handed used to be considered a physical handicap of such severity that children were beaten or bound to force them to become normal—that is, right-handed.[2]

The impact of being stigmatized because of characteristics of our physical self was perhaps best demonstrated recently by Jane Elliott. In order to teach her third-graders the "irrationality, the mindless brutality of racism," she had her students participate in an extended role-playing experiment in which part of her class was deemed superior and privileged and the rest were stigmatized as inferior and deprived. The basis for the assignment was a minor part of the physical self: eye color! For one day brown-eyed children were the master race; the following day, the blue-eyed children reigned supreme. The result was "anger, despair, frustration, and misery when they are the victims; with classic signs of racism when they are labeled 'superior.'"(Elliott, 1977, p. 599)

■ *The Brain and Social Labels*   We label people because we are verbal, conceptual animals. After experiencing an object (for example, a knife) in its many forms we develop a mental image (concept) of a knife. Our culture usually provides us with a word or phrase to identify the concepts we form. From then on, we respond to the concept knife, rather than constructing a novel response for each knife with which we come in contact. It is a matter of economy. We grant to that conceptual knife the characteristics or traits that were associated with the knives we have experienced in our past. A knife is sharp, hard, pointed, and so on. Any object that we perceive as "knife" we expect to be sharp, and we react to it accordingly. Life is more easily managed when we can toss people, too, into label boxes when deciding whom to approach or avoid. Concepts (stereotypes) can also be vicariously learned. We do not have to be cut to know that a knife is sharp. In the same way, we can "know" that skinny people are nervous or that females are passive.

## ■ Naive Psychology

We make character judgments with relative ease and with little proof. For example, 323 British men and women were quite willing to attribute character disorders based on the conformation of female buttocks. White (1979) reports that women with thin bottoms and small waists were labeled "neurotic"; those with large, lumpy bottoms and heavy thighs earned the label "alcoholic"; and those with fat bottoms and thick waists were labeled "lazy." These naive psychologists were quick to attribute positive personality traits to those bearing

---

2. The term sinister is from the Latin *sinisteri*, or left-handed.

buttocks that reflected the current ideal. The women with small waists, slightly full buttocks, and slim thighs were granted the culturally valued traits of being "sexy," "nice," and "liberal."

American attributionists seem to focus on the breasts. Kleinke and Staneski (1980) observe that American women with small breasts are seen as being more modest and moral. Medium-sized breasts appear to make a woman more likable and appealing, and, amazingly, large breasts seem to be associated with small IQs.

Such blatant, sexist judgments are associated with the fact that women have a more highly differentiated body image than men do (Jourard and Remy, 1957). That is, women tend to evaluate themselves part by part. Jourard and Landsman (1980) note that people who like their bodies appear to be less anxious, more secure, and have higher self-esteem. People with low self-esteem find more fault with their bodies. The "pear shape" is currently out of style; therefore today's women are most dissatisfied with their bellies, buttocks, and thighs. The short, upturned nose is "in," as is wrinkle-free, ageless skin. It is easy to understand why plastic surgery is so popular today.

## ■ Why We Make Attributions

**Attribution theory** is the formal body of information pertaining to the use of inferences and implied causality under conditions of minimal information. Fritz Heider (1958) holds that we use attributions so as to understand and control the world we live in. It is not enough that we observe the behavior of ourselves or others. We need to figure out why the behavior occurs. We especially need to know if something was done because of force or because of choice. For example, your friend does not show up for a date. Was this action **dispositional**—that is, caused by internal, personality factors? Or was it **situational**—that is, due to circumstances beyond the friend's control? Your feelings and reactions will depend on your answer to this question. Kelly and Michel (1980) reviewed current studies of this **locus of control** question and concluded that we test others and ourselves in three ways before making a decision.

The first test involves **consistency**. Does the act being judged display a stable trait? Does your friend regularly miss dates? The second test involves **consensus**. Is the trait in conformity with the norm? In your crowd, is it common not to show up for dates? The third test involves **distinctiveness**. Is this a global trait? Does your friend only miss dates, or are classes, tests, and appointments also missed? Table 4.1 gives the most likely attributions for three different sets of answers to these questions.

The table indicates that the first set of answers adds up to a situational attribution—your friend was just following tradition. The second attribution is dispositional, because missing the date is seen as constant, but it violates the social norm. The third attribution is situational and unique. Something must have come up unexpectedly.

Another central factor in making attributions is what Kelly terms the **discounting principle**. We tend to discount, or give less importance to, one factor if other likely factors are present. For example, you would discount the possibility that your friend had deliberately missed the date if you remembered that the time and place had not been firmly agreed upon in advance.

TABLE 4.1

Why Did Your Friend Stand You Up?

| INFORMATION | | | ATTRIBUTION |
|---|---|---|---|
| *Consistency*[a] | *Consensus*[a] | *Distinctiveness*[a] | |
| 1. High—always misses dates | High—everyone misses dates | High—doesn't miss other appointments | (External) SITUATIONAL |
| 2. High—always misses dates | Low—few miss dates | Low—misses other appointments | (Internal) DISPOSITIONAL |
| 3. Low—seldom misses dates | Low—few miss dates | High—doesn't miss other appointments | (External) SITUATIONAL |

[a]In practice, we do not give equal *intensity* to each of these factors. Therefore we do not simply average the answers in making our decision.

An attribution is a perception, and may not always be fair, impartial, or just. Perception is basically self-serving. Consider the following four statements:

*1.* There is a pervasive tendency for us to attribute our actions to situational requirements if our behavior is unacceptable.

*2.* There is a similar tendency for us to attribute the same unacceptable behavior to a stable personal disposition when we see someone else doing it.

*3.* If we catch ourselves doing something praiseworthy, we attribute it to the positive values we hold and the intelligent strategies we use.

*4.* If we observe others doing something exceptional, we tend to attribute their action to the demands of the situation (Jones and Nisbett, 1972).

In short, we tend to believe our bad behavior is situationally determined and our good behavior is dispositionally determined; and we hold just the reverse to be true for others. Kammer (1982) confirmed the notion that we see our actions as less consistent (more situationally determined) than the behaviors of even close friends. Such distortions do much to enhance and preserve our self-esteem.

*See Chapter 5, on the cognitive self, and Chapter 6, on the emotional self, for a better understanding of our use of internal dialogue as a defense mechanism.*

Storms (1973) believes that we may not be so hypocritical. He video-taped students from two perspectives: the view others would have of them, and the view they would have of themselves. When shown the tape of themselves as seen by others, the students made fewer situational and more dispositional explanations for their own less-than-perfect behavior! Storms concluded that we normally are simply unable to see ourselves as we see others.

### ■ Attribution Theory and Physical Attractiveness

*See Chapter 11, on Intimacy, for the roles played by similarity and propinquity in romantic love.*

We have spent a great deal of time discussing attribution in a chapter on the physical self. We have done so because it is on the basis of physical appearance that we first judge others and are judged by them. Physical appearance is more important than similarity or propinquity (physical nearness) in determining interpersonal attraction (Kleck and Rubinstein, 1975). Looking good and being good are associated in our minds; thus, we attribute to the beautiful person other traits we consider good. We take for granted that the beautiful person is intelligent, successful, competent, and pleasant, for example.

When photographs of the supposed authors of several essays were shown, both male and female judges rated essays attributed to highly attractive females more positively than they rated the same essays attributed to less attractive females (Fugita et al., 1977). Even among the mentally ill, the beautiful are more often diagnosed as being less disturbed and are given a better prognosis with more personal suggestions for improvement (Cash et al., 1977). If physically unattractive, such patients are more likely to be placed on drug therapy. If attractive, greater opportunity for personal counseling is offered. Incidentally, if a counselor is female, clients will be more likely to perceive her as being effective if she is physically attractive (Lewis and Walsh, 1978).

On the other hand, at times being physically attractive can be a handicap. If you are found guilty of using your physical assets to cheat an innocent victim, your exceptional beauty will likely earn you a more severe sentence. Similarly, if you act immorally, you will be judged more harshly if you are attractive. A beautiful woman who has intercourse on a first date is more likely to be seen as immoral than a homely woman who acts in the same way.

Attractive people are often seen as vain and egotistical (Dermer and Thiel, 1975). This negative attribution, plus the tendency of plain people to seek out equally plain partners, reduces the opportunity for beautiful people to develop relationships. Finally, the discounting principle, mentioned earlier, works against the peace of mind of attractive individuals. Good-looking people, like wealthy, successful, or socially prominent people, can never be sure why others are attracted to them: "Am I loved for myself, or is it my body (or wealth , or position, or fame, or the like)?" There is always a plausible reason for attractive people to discount attention and affection when it comes their way. At least one counseling couple, Jerry Lipkin and Bliss Kalet, stand ready to help such unfortunates. They run a "stress and trauma clinic" open only to exceptionally attractive people. They report that such people "often suffer guilt and anxiety syndromes related to their being better looking than anybody else and they need to get together and talk about it" (Maeder, 1983, p. 2A).

> Gary seems to have everything going for him. Tall and handsome, intelligent and well educated, he is considered a "sure bet" for success. But another six months have passed, and again Gary has been passed over for promotion.
>   It isn't his job performance. That is excellent. The problem is that Gary is too good-looking! His movie-star profile and exquisite taste in clothing have produced envy among his coworkers and in his immediate superior.
>   Gary feels confused and excluded. Higher-level managers are confused as well. "Gary certainly makes a great first impression. It's a shame his evaluations are so ordinary. Well, I guess nobody has everything."

You can see that attribution theory is revealing; but attribution research is limited by the fact that it is largely confined to first encounters. We can manage first impressions.

"I am me, the me I am right now." This is the motto of a person who monitors his or her projected self constantly and "becomes" the person the situation seems to call for (Snyder, 1980). While such constant self-monitoring is exceptional, **impression management**—presenting ourselves so as to shape the attributions of others—is commonplace during first encounters. How successful is impression management? Schwibbe (1981) succeeded in manipulating information about "attractiveness." Highly attractive persons were seen as having positive qualities. The same people, differently presented, were seen as unattractive and as having negative qualities.

FIGURE 4.5
Monitor Your Self

If you would like to test your self-monitoring tendencies, follow the instructions and then consult the scoring key.

These statements concern personal reactions to a number of different situations. No two statements are exactly alike, so consider each statement carefully before answering. If a statement is true, or mostly true, as applied to you, circle the T. If a statement is false, or not usually true, as applied to you, circle the F.

1. I find it hard to imitate the behavior of other people.                                      T    F
2. I guess I put on a show to impress or entertain people.                                  T    F
3. I would probably make a good actor.                                                             T    F
4. I sometimes appear to others to be experiencing deeper emotions than I actually am.                                                                                            T    F
5. In a group of people I am rarely the center of attention.                                 T    F
6. In different situations, and with different people, I often act like very different persons.                                                                                              T    F
7. I can only argue for ideas I already believe.                                                  T    F
8. In order to get along and be liked, I tend to be what people expect me to be rather than anything else.                                                                        T    F
9. I may deceive people by being friendly when I really dislike them.                  T    F
10. I'm not always the person I appear to be.                                                     T    F

SCORING: Give yourself one point for each question 1, 5 and 7 that you answered F. Give yourself one point for each of the remaining questions that you answered T. Add up your points. If you are a good judge of yourself and scored 7 or above, you are probably a high self-monitoring individual; 3 or below, you are probably a low self-monitoring individual.

*The Self-Monitoring Scale measures how concerned we are with the impressions we make on others, and our ability to control and modify our behavior to fit the situation of the moment.*
Mark Snyder, Psychology Today, March 1980

Women may have some difficulty managing impressions, however. Sex-typing seems more powerful than physical attractiveness in determining positive or negative attributions. Cash and Smith (1982) reported that men who on first impression were seen as attractive were evaluated as having more self-determination. They were also expected to achieve more and to suffer less anxiety and depression. However, such qualities as success, emotional stability, and internal locus of control were *not* projected as being significantly higher for attractive *women* than for their less attractive male counterparts.

■ *The Job Interview*    Looking attractive while interviewing for a job is a form of impression management. The results of Cash and Smith's study imply that, for a woman, looking strikingly attractive may not create a favorable impression during an interview for a responsible job, however. The stereotyped impression that women are weak and passive hurts them during job interviews.

Impression management during a job interview is tricky for men as well as women. If you present yourself in formal dress, appear unresponsive, and confine yourself to the use of professional terms, you will probably receive high ratings and be considered an expert in your field. If you dress casually, are responsive, and use a good deal of jargon in your speech, you will be rated as less of an expert, but as warmer and more attractive (Dell and Patkin, 1982). The difficulty lies in the fact that in order to be hired you must appear both expert and attractive—no small feat of impression management.

REVIEW
QUESTIONS

*19.* Our looking-glass self refers to a self-concept based on how others see us. T F

*20.* If we act in accordance with our phenotype, age, sex, race, and so on, our actions will usually be *rewarded / ignored / punished.*

*21.* Gordon W. Allport anchors our self-awareness in the *oral stage* / *"bodily me"* / *reactions of others.*

*22.* The most important factor in producing positive expectations about people we do not know is *positive thinking* / *helpful acts* / *physical attractiveness.*

*23.* When we feel insecure about ourselves, the *attractive* / *less attractive* prospective mate makes us more sexually aroused.

*24.* The matching hypothesis states that people of *similar* / *different* levels of physical attractiveness gravitate toward each other.

*25.* Negative stereotypes that result in their victims' being avoided or unnaturally treated are *prejudices* / *stigmas* / *labels.*

*26.* The formal body of information pertaining to the ways in which we make inferences based on limited information is termed _____ theory.

*27.* Attributing our exemplary behavior to our own good character is known as a *dispositional* / *situational* attribution.

*28.* The tendency, when making attributions, to give less importance to one factor if other likely factors are present is known as the _____ principle.

*29.* Attributing our poor behavior to situational demands *helps* / *hurts* us to enhance our self-esteem.

*30.* Storms used video-tapes to support the idea that we *do* / *do not* see ourselves as others see us.

*31.* Impression management is *rare* / *commonplace* during first encounters.

*32.* During a job interview, it is important to produce an impression that we are *attractive* / *expert* / *both attractive and expert.*

*33.* It is quite *possible* / *impossible* to overcome the negative effects of a poor first impression.

*The answers to these review questions are on page 131.*

## DISCUSSION: PHYSICAL FITNESS AND SELF-ESTEEM

Body image is critical to our concept of physical self. If we see our bodily self as being healthy, well proportioned, and active, anxiety is reduced and self-esteem is elevated. If others perceive us in the same way, they will attribute many positive characteristics to us.

The primary physical attraction between men and women is sexual in nature, and a strong, flexible, healthy body is a definite plus in terms of our sexuality. Physical fitness also enables and encourages us to join in social and work activities that allow us to be perceived as an active and involved individual—a most significant positive attribution.

■ Physical Fitness

A comprehensive notion of physical fitness includes body weight, posture, musculature, and endurance. Most people consider a lean, erect, and well-proportioned

■ Most people consider a lean, erect, and well-proportioned body to be physically fit.

body to be fit. Fitness also includes muscle strength, muscle endurance, flexibility, and perhaps most important in the long run, cardiovascular and respiratory fitness. These last dimensions of fitness are not self-evident. They are, however, associated with youth and vigor, traits our culture values highly. They are also associated with an increased capacity to cope with stress and to resist the infirmities and illnesses of old age. We all value health and vigor at any age.

There are standards for each of these dimensions of fitness. Strength, endurance, flexibility, and air transport estimates can be obtained by following the suggestions in the Personal Action Plan section of your Study Guide. Your decisions should be made in terms of your age, sex, body type, and medical history rather than in terms of a glamorized Hollywood ideal.

■ *Work, Study, and Physical Fitness*   If your job keeps you physically active for prolonged periods of time, it might keep you fit. Few jobs do. Study is difficult but not strenuous. The same might be said of most sedentary jobs that the majority of college students train for and hold after graduation. For most Americans, *the job fails us* when it comes to maintaining our fitness. Our leisure activities fail us as well. In order to have a physical self that is fit, we must train.

Van Huss, Niemeyer, Olson, and Friedrich (1969) give the following goals for physical training: (1) to develop physique; (2) to improve general physical condition; (3) to increase our skill in sports; (4) to control weight; (5) to rehabilitate ourselves; and (6) to protect ourselves from disease or injury. We might add to this list the following goal: to increase stress tolerance.

The physical self responds very specifically to stimuli. That means that *each muscle group* must be worked if it is to be improved. Instead of listing the innumerable exercises available for the more than six hundred muscle groupings, we will mention four areas that can be exercised with the expectation of positive results—posture, flexibility, strength, and aerobic fitness.

## ■ Improving Posture

*Posture* is the alignment of our body. Our posture is a result of genetics, early experiences, and long-established habits. Kurtz and Prestera (1976) believe that rigid muscular patterns reflect emotional blocks. We create muscle tensions to deaden impulsive wishes or to block fear and pain. These *defensive postures* become unconscious and habitual. For example, our jaws may become set to help us stop crying. For some of us, active intervention by trained body therapists may be called for. For most of us, awareness and continuous attention to and practice of correct posture is all that is required for a relaxed, flexible, and balanced bodily state to become habitual as we stand, sit, and walk. If you are dissatisfied with your posture, a program of daily posture checks and possible realignment is necessary until your muscle re-education becomes habitual. Periodic checks are then called for. Be sure to check yourself while you are under tension. How do you sit while studying for an exam or while writing a term paper?

*For "Rolfing" and similar approaches, see the Selected Readings.*

## ■ Improving Flexibility

*Flexibility* is the capacity to move the joints of the body through their full range without excessive strain or pain. Age, size, sex, diet, and medical history are related to flexibility. The extent and range of our daily physical activity is most important in this regard. We must move every joint through its full range *several times a day* if we are to maintain maximum flexibility (Miller and Allen, 1979).

Flexibility training consists of gently and slowly stretching (extending), and holding and then turning each joint. Swimming and cross-country skiing are good general exercises for flexibility because they require total bodily movement. Our rear upper leg muscles and our neck, shoulder, and back muscles tighten in response to general stress and respond well to systematic exercise. The payoff is less fatigue, less stiffness and soreness, greater mobility, and greater protection

---

## CASE IN POINT
## Posture Improvement and Health

Do you suffer from headaches? If you do, improving your posture may be a cure. Dr. Samuel Razook (1983) offers simple advice and prescribes home exercises to counteract headaches, stiff necks, and tired jaws. (Of course, these symptoms may have other causes.)

When standing or walking, check to see that your ears are kept in an even line with your shoulders, hips, and ankles. Don't let your head slump in front of that line.

When sitting, check your position. Be sure that you are not automatically leaning forward to do your work. Change positions every ten minutes.

against injury. The psychological payoff is more positive attributions' being made about our physical self by us and by others.

## ■ Improving Strength

*Strength* refers to the size and contractile force of our muscle system, including its tendons, ligaments, and bony structures. Strength is a powerful label. People tend to attribute positive character traits to those who possess obvious strength and vigor. A person labeled as weak is seen as less attractive and is less trusted. To label ourselves as weak reduces our ability to cope as well.

In addition to improvement in strength, muscle work increases *definition,* or the form of specific muscle groupings. A firm, well-defined torso is considered youthful and attractive for both men and women. Women who train need not fear excessive growth in size or definition of muscles; they will remain feminine looking, but more trim and with a finer-toned body. The fit, active look is now popular for both men and women in America.

Miller and Allen (1979) suggest you follow these steps in a muscle training program:

1. *Consult your doctor* before starting on any exercise program.
2. Select the specific muscle groups you wish to work on. Select more than one group so you may vary your training.
3. Consult an authority to determine the appropriate "lifts" to use in stimulating these muscles.
4. Use the maximum weight you can handle and do a set consisting of five or six repetitions of the lift.
5. Do three sets for each lift, varying the lifts.
6. When you are able to do three sets, and exceed the number of repetitions on the third set, *increase* the weight for that lift at the beginning of the next training session.
7. Train three times a week on nonconsecutive days.

## ■ Improving Aerobic Fitness

**Aerobics** refers to a variety of exercises beneficial to our oxygen and blood transportation systems—our heart, lungs, and blood vessels. This portion of our physical self is largely invisible to others, so few attributions are made in terms of aerobic fitness. However, our aerobic capacity "is the best index of overall physical fitness" (Cooper, 1970, p. 16).

Aerobic fitness is the ability to breath large amounts of air, to deliver large volumes of blood, and thus to be able to transport oxygen to all parts of the body. If you are dissatisfied with your aerobic power, a program of strenuous exercise that involves your large muscle groups in *continuous, rhythmic contractions* will result in increased cardiovascular and respiratory efficiency. We recommend that you see a doctor prior to entering an aerobic program.

Each of us is unique, and the exercise program one ultimately chooses should recognize and reflect this uniqueness. Because fitness requires almost daily activity, the best exercise is one you love or can become positively addicted to. Any number of exercises will produce the desired physical effect. The *intensity,*

■ Strenuous exercise that involves large muscle groups in continuous, rhythmic activity will result increased heart-lung efficiency.

*frequency,* and *duration* of the exercise are as important as the type of exercise. Naturally, a physical activity that requires less energy to perform (such as slow walking) will require more duration and greater frequency to produce practical results. A level of intensity necessary to produce measurable gains in aerobic capacity is approximately *60 percent of your maximum heart rate change.* This should be your minimum target heart rate for training. This rate will increase as you progress toward fitness.

*See the Personal Action Plan section on physical fitness for a simple procedure to determine your training heart rate.*

A *frequency* of three times a week, evenly spaced, seems desirable. *Duration* depends on intensity, but an exercise period consisting of five to ten minutes of warm-up exercises (including stretching and flexing), twenty minutes of sustained aerobic exercise, and five to ten minutes of cool-down exercises (walking, stretching) is considered normal. Cycling, jogging, cross-country skiing, swimming, and walking are well-researched methods of aerobic exercise, and group aerobic dancing is very popular at the moment.

*See the Selected Readings for additional information on fitness testing, exercise programs, and medical cautions.*

## ■ Exercise and Your Heart

The exact role of exercise in the prevention and rehabilitation of heart disorders is still under study. A sedentary life style, under conditions of increased stress and inappropriate diet, is considered to be a factor in the high incidence of early heart attacks in this country.

*See Chapter 7 for more about stress.*

REVIEW
QUESTIONS

*34.* Musculature, w_____ , and p_____ make up highly visible components of physical fitness.

*35.* Endurance, f_____ , and s_____ make up less visible components of physical fitness.

*36.* In terms of keeping us fit, our jobs and leisure activities f_____ us.

37. List any three of the six goals of physical exercise: _____ , _____ ,

_____ .

38. Unconscious emotional blocks may account for some habitual muscle tension and

poor p_____ .

39. If we are to maintain f_____ , every joint must be put through its full

range of motion each day.

40. Women should shy away from weight training if they wish to retain a feminine

body image. T F

41. The best index of overall physical fitness is ae_____ c_____ .

42. The level of intensity needed to produce measurable gains in aerobic capacity is

approximately _____ percent of maximum heart rate change.

43. Our sedentary life style *increases / decreases* our chances of living a long and

healthy life.

*The answers to these review questions are on page 131.*

## DISCUSSION: REGULATION OF BODY WEIGHT

America is a nation on a diet. This is not the eternal fast of the developing country, but the result of eating patterns that turn our bountiful harvests into a national health problem. We eat too much, so we are too fat. At the same time, weight is considered a crucial variable in our assessment of our physical self. To be obese, or to be considered obese, profoundly affects our perception of our self-worth and provokes largely negative expectations from those around us.

### ■ Obesity and Health

"Overweight people die younger, contract diabetes, cardiovascular disease, gall bladder disease, and gout more readily and suffer greater risks in surgery than

## CASE IN POINT
## A Super Achiever

Jane Collins is fat. There is no way around it. But Jane is also sparkling. She radiates charm and has a vibrant personality. Always well groomed and always on the go, Jane stands in proud defiance of the notion that fat represents failure. On the job, she is a super-achiever.

Jane represents the ideal of NAAFA (the National Association to Assist Fat Americans) support group. Jane accepts herself and doesn't worry about gaining or losing weight. She is not alone. Over 3,000 members of NAAFA agree that you don't have to be skinny to have self-esteem. Headquartered in Bellerose, New York, the group helps members to build self-confidence for their never-ending struggle to combat the belief that fat people are poor workers and poor employment risks.

their thinner counterparts" (Whitney and Hamilton, 1977). Obese people also have less muscular proficiency on some measures, such as dynamic strength, gross body coordination, and stamina (Brady, Knight, and Berghage, 1977). In recent years, a psychological burden has been added. Those who are obese and happen to fall ill are expected to accept personal blame for their misfortune and to view their suffering as a sign of nature's retribution for their history of overindulgence. Being stout has changed from a sign of power and affluence to a sign of a flawed character. During the 1984 presidential primaries, the majority of American voters said they would not vote for a presidential candidate who was overweight.

## ■ Women and Obesity

Nature and culture have conspired to make it doubly difficult for women to deal with overweight. "The cultural prescriptions for ideal weight . . . have an obsessional nature that have made women's lives miserable. . . . Evidence is beginning to appear that moderately overweight women are not at greater risk than so-called 'normal women' and that they do not have shorter life spans, as do over-weight men. However, it remains significant that the prevalence of obesity among women is 70% higher than men." (Haremustin, 1983, pp. 597–598).

The sociobiologist would say that the theory of inclusive fitness and our culture's "ideal woman" are incompatible. Fashion modeling, for example, actually requires women to maintain weights at **anorexic** levels. At the same time, a critical ratio of body fat is necessary for successful child bearing, and nature promotes its reproductive efficiency by defending women against losing weight.

■ Modeling requires women to maintain weights at levels that may be too low for optimum health.

(The metabolic rate is lowered, so fewer calories are burned.) Physical pressure to maintain weight and cultural pressure to lose weight add up to a real problem for many overweight women. No wonder diet books are perennial best sellers!

## ■ Ideal Weight

In 1983, insurance companies published updated tables of height and weight (see Table 4.2). These new guidelines reflect the weights that result in the *lowest mortality,* rather than some cultural notion of an "ideal." The tables are computed from average weights of insured persons, grouped by sex, height, and frame size. Age, health, phenotype, and ethnic origin, though important, are not included. The figures in the tables are therefore estimates.

Overweight or underweight is defined as a variance of 10 percent or more from the figures for your sex and height. Overweight is not necessarily the same as overfatness. Whether the weight comes from fat or from lean muscle tissue is more important than the weight itself. Athletes can be overweight without being fat, while older, less active people can be at the "low-mortality" weight while carrying too much fat. Excess body fat accumulates under the skin, so lifting a fold of skin and measuring its thickness is one way of identifying overweight due to overfatness.

## ■ Causes of Obesity

The chief cause of obesity is an imbalance of calories. Excessive intake of any or all of the three energy nutrients—carbohydrates, fats, or proteins—causes obesity. When energy intake exceeds the body's needs, the extra is stored as body fat. This is a survival mechanism that is, in America, a threat to survival.

TABLE 4.2
1983 Height and Weight Tables

| MEN | | | | | WOMEN | | | | |
|---|---|---|---|---|---|---|---|---|---|
| *Height* Feet | *Inches* | *Small Frame* | *Medium Frame* | *Large Frame* | *Height* Feet | *Inches* | *Small Frame* | *Medium Frame* | *Large Frame* |
| 5 | 2 | 128–134 | 131–141 | 138–150 | 4 | 10 | 102–111 | 109–121 | 118–131 |
| 5 | 3 | 130–136 | 133–143 | 140–153 | 4 | 11 | 103–113 | 111–123 | 120–134 |
| 5 | 4 | 132–138 | 135–145 | 142–156 | 5 | 0 | 104–115 | 113–126 | 122–137 |
| 5 | 5 | 134–140 | 137–148 | 144–160 | 5 | 1 | 106–118 | 115–129 | 125–140 |
| 5 | 6 | 136–142 | 139–151 | 146–164 | 5 | 2 | 108–121 | 118–132 | 128–143 |
| 5 | 7 | 138–145 | 142–154 | 149–168 | 5 | 3 | 111–124 | 121–135 | 131–147 |
| 5 | 8 | 140–148 | 145–157 | 152–172 | 5 | 4 | 114–127 | 124–138 | 134–151 |
| 5 | 9 | 142–151 | 148–160 | 155–176 | 5 | 5 | 117–130 | 127–141 | 137–155 |
| 5 | 10 | 144–154 | 151–163 | 158–180 | 5 | 6 | 120–133 | 130–144 | 140–159 |
| 5 | 11 | 146–157 | 154–166 | 161–184 | 5 | 7 | 123–136 | 133–147 | 143–163 |
| 6 | 0 | 149–160 | 157–170 | 164–188 | 5 | 8 | 126–139 | 136–150 | 146–167 |
| 6 | 1 | 152–164 | 160–174 | 168–192 | 5 | 9 | 129–142 | 139–153 | 149–170 |
| 6 | 2 | 155–168 | 164–178 | 172–197 | 5 | 10 | 132–145 | 142–156 | 152–173 |
| 6 | 3 | 158–172 | 167–182 | 176–202 | 5 | 11 | 135–148 | 145–159 | 155–176 |
| 6 | 4 | 162–176 | 171–187 | 181–207 | 6 | 0 | 138–151 | 148–162 | 158–179 |

*Weights at Ages 25–59 Based on Lowest Moratality.*
*Weight in Pounds According to Frame (in indoor clothing weighing 5 lbs., shoes with1" heels).*

*Weights at Ages 25–59 Based on Lowest Mortality.*
*Weight in Pounds According to Frame (in indoor clothing weighing 3 lbs., shoes with 1" heels).*

Source of basic data: *1979 Build Study,* Society of Actuaries and Association of Life Insurance Medical Directors of America, 1980.

TABLE 4.3

Figuring Out the Size of Your Frame

- Extend arm and raise forearm to 90-degree angle.
- Hold fingers straight, turn palm away from body.
- Put other thumb and index finger on protruding bones on either side of elbow, then measure the distance between thumb and forefinger.
- Find your height (with 1-inch heels) in the tables below. If your elbow measurement falls within the corresponding range, you have a medium frame. If it is larger, you have a large frame. If it is smaller, you have a small frame.

| MEN | | WOMEN | |
|---|---|---|---|
| *Height* | *Measurement* | *Height* | *Measurement* |
| 5'2"–5'3" | 2½–2⅞ | 4'10"–5'3" | 2¼–2½ |
| 5'4"–5'7" | 2⅝–2⅞ | 5'4"–5'11" | 2⅜–2⅝ |
| 5'8"–5'11" | 2¾–3 | 6' | 2½–2¾ |
| 6'–6'3" | 2¾–3⅛ | | |
| 6'4" | 2⅞–3¼ | | |

Source: Metropolitan Life Insurance Co.

Obese people, then, eat more than they need and have done so consistently for a long time. Some indirect causes are rooted in feelings; others are rooted in eating habits and activity patterns. Obese people tend to be less active. They are more likely to be influenced by external stimuli (colors, smells, unfinished portions) than by internal stimuli (hunger, tension, or satiety). Thin people are found to be just the reverse (Schachter and Freeman, 1974). Some researchers say obesity may also be due to genetic factors or to early feeding patterns that produce a permanent excess of fat cells that the body defends by maintaining a constant, moderately strong degree of hunger (Nisbett, 1972). If these researchers are correct, people may be no more directly responsible for their weight than they are for their height.

■ *Internal Weight Regulation and Obesity* As millions of dieting Americans know, the problem with weight control is not only losing weight but keeping the lost weight from being regained. Most of us keep within a few pounds of our normal weight each year despite great variation in the foods we eat and the exercise we do (Keesey and Powley, 1975). We manage to do this by unconsciously monitoring our food intake. Receptor cells in our brains monitor substances in the blood that fluctuate with food consumption. This information, in turn, allows part of the brain to act as a thermostat—or *appestat*—for our appetite.

Apparently, in obese people, the appestat is set too high, demanding more food than is needed. When this demand is met by overeating, other physiological changes take place that compound the problem. As fat cells increase in size, they also increase in ability to store fat. These fatter fat cells are associated with high insulin levels. Insulin helps convert sugar into fat, again making the obese able to store fat better. Diabetic patients say that when their insulin levels are too high, they "feel hungry," even if they have just eaten. Obese patients often report the same distressing urge.

WHAT DO YOU THINK?

- Do you think people are thin because they are less stimulated by food or less stimulated by food because they are thin?
- What could make them both unstimulated and thin?

When overweight people try to lose weight, they find that fat cells give up their stores with great reluctance. Muscle cells may be weakened by diets to reduce fat cells. When people feel fat, weak, and hungry, they are less likely to be physically active. But physical activity, along with diet, is the key to weight loss.

## ■ Weight Loss Programs

There is no magic way to lose weight. Quick weight loss diets are **not** recommended, as they do not rest on a base of sound nutrition, do not teach altered eating patterns or altered attitudes toward food and eating, and often present medical risk. In the long run, they do not work. Medical supervision is recommended if you are contemplating an extensive loss of weight. To achieve weight loss, it is necessary to: (1) know how much energy you spend in work, rest, and play (energy out); (2) know how much energy you consume in a day (calories in); and (3) adjust this balance until you achieve the desired level of stored energy (body fat). In brief, the best way to lose body fat is to cut calories while increasing bodily activity. We'll talk about activity first, then turn to diet.

## ■ Expending Energy

We spend energy in three ways: *basal (resting) metabolism, digestive metabolism,* and *voluntary activity*. The human body is very efficient; it expends its energy wisely and throws nothing away. Therefore, voluntary activity offers the best prospect for adjusting our energy balance through energy output. Theoretically, one hour of swimming a day should reduce the weight of a 150-pound man by one-tenth pound a day *if his calorie consumption stays the same*. Ten days of such activity should produce a weight loss of one pound. This may appear to be too little and too slow. However, in the long run, regular exercise can contribute to substantial reduction in body weight. As we have seen, improved muscle tone and blood transport systems are also products of regular aerobic exercise. Stern (1983) reports that if you are about to start a weigh-reducing program, success can depend on whether or not you exercise.

Exercise can increase the long-term success of your diet. Stern (1983) reports a comparison of three groups of dieters. The first reduced daily intake by 500 calories; the second actively "burned up" 500 extra calories daily; and the third reduced intake by 250 calories and burned up 250 more calories each day. Weight loss was similar in all three groups, but the diet-only group lost muscle tissue as well as fat, while the exercise groups lost mostly fat. Thirty minutes of exercise a day reportedly stimulated metabolism for hours after the workouts were complete, thus burning more calories. If we exercise while dieting, then, we may not have to diet forever. We may have the pleasure of eating, the pleasure of exercise, and the pleasure of being slim.

## ■ The Great All-American Diet

*For information on fad diets, see S. K. Fineberg's article, listed in the Selected Readings.*

"The only proven way to lose weight successfully and permanently is to adopt an eating plan that provides balanced nutrition at the appropriate energy level and to stay with such a plan for life" (Whitney and Hamilton, 1977, p. 252). "Balanced nutrition" means avoiding fad diets. The Great All-American Diet (GAD) is no fad. It is one that you can live with for the rest of your life. The United States Senate Select Commission on Nutrition and Human Needs included this diet in its 1980 report. The commission recommended that the average American lose weight and keep it off. In addition, it suggested that we set personal goals to regulate our salt, sugar, and fat intake.

Specific dietary goals include:

1. Eating less fat (no more than 30 percent of our daily intake.)
2. Eating no more than five grams of table salt a day.
3. Balancing the type of fats we eat between saturated (such as butterfat) and unsaturated (such as corn oil).
4. Eating less refined sugars (no more than 10 percent of our daily intake).
5. Keeping our cholesterol (fatty protein) intake low (less than the amount in the yoke of one egg a day).
6. Increasing complex carbohydrates (starch) and naturally occurring sugars (such as in fruit) until they comprise a full 48 percent of our daily intake.

In everyday terms, these goals require us to eat more fruits, vegetables, and whole grains and less refined sugars, red meats, high-fat dairy products, and salt. We should consume more potatoes and fewer potato chips, more whole-wheat bread and less white bread, more plain breakfast cereals and less bacon and eggs or sugar-coated cereals, and more skim milk and less whole milk.

The commission suggests that we divide the three energy nutrients as follows: each day our diet should consist of 12 percent protein, 58 percent carbohydrate, and 30 percent fat. This is quite a bit less protein and fat than we now consume. It is not easy to change something so basic as eating habits. However, the care, work, and expense required to stay on the GAD appears to be repaid in the prospect of a longer and more robust life.[3]

**WHAT DO YOU THINK?**

■ Which of the following offers the best solution to the problem presented in GAD and Weight Loss:
1. raise your calories to 1675 a day?
2. eat more fatty, red meat?
3. eat more legumes (beans, peas, seeds)?

---

3. Not all experts agree with GAD; many believe the restriction on dairy products is unwarranted and excessive.

## CASE IN POINT
## GAD and Weight Loss

The Great All-American Diet's prescription of 12 percent protein, 30 percent fat, and 58 percent carbohydrate each day is no problem *if you are at your desired weight.* However, if you are on a weight-loss diet of 1,200 calories or less a day, your protein needs as an adult will not be met under the rules of the diet.

Whitney and Hamilton (1977) report that a normal adult needs approximately 50 grams of protein a day for optimal health. Twelve percent of 1,200 calories is 144 cal-ories. As there are 4 calories per gram of protein, 144 calories can produce no more than 36 grams—not enough to meet your daily needs. You need more protein than 12 percent of your 1,200-calories per day.

44. The stereotype of the unhealthy fat person is *true / untrue / partially true*.

45. The 1983 guidelines of height and weight are based on *ideal / lowest mortality* figures.

46. Measuring a fold of skin is a *valid / invalid* way of estimating excess body fat.

47. Name the three energy nutrients: _____ _____ _____ .

48. The direct cause of obesity is that obese people eat _____ _____ .

49. Nisbett believes obesity is the result of *genetic factors / infant feeding patterns / both*.

50. In order to lose weight, you must use *more / less* energy than you take in.

51. Voluntary physical activity offers the *best / worst* prospect for achieving weight loss through energy output.

52. Despite great variation in eating and exercise, most people keep within a few pounds of their normal weight each year. T  F

53. Moderately overweight women *are / are not* at greater risk than normal women.

54. Exercise and diet together are *equal to / better than* diet or exercise alone.

55. Permanent weight loss requires an eating plan that will provide balanced nutrition for a lifetime. T  F

56. The Great American Diet consists of 58 percent _____ 30 percent ____ and 12 percent _____ .

*The answers to these review questions are on page 131.*

## DISCUSSION: LIFE EXTENSION

Ponce de Leon is said to have discovered Florida while searching for the legendary fountain of youth. The search goes on. We have been discussing diet and exercise in terms of looks and fitness; now we turn our attention to increasing the length of our life as well as its quality.

Many believe there is no adjustment they can make to prolong their "allotted" number of years. Recent research may turn that "truth" into a myth. According to Richard Walford (1983), a professor of pathology at the University of California, laboratory animals are routinely raised to increase their maximum life span by 50 to 100 percent, and "biologists agree that there's a very high order of probability—about 98 per cent—that [similar methods] will work on human beings."

Another myth is the assumption that our life span is largely determined by fate in the form of accidents, disease, war, or other catastrophes beyond our control. For the most part, we are born healthy and made sick as a result of misbehavior and environmental conditions. Lifestyles that increase personal risk, occupational and recreational conditions that ignore public health and safety, and environmental contaminants that plague us all—these, and a medical delivery system that demands illness before intervention, are the major contributors to illness and early death. As Pogo said, "We have met the enemy, and it is us."

## ■ Accepting Responsibility for Personal Longevity

We all can begin defeating our common enemy by accepting responsibility for our own style of life, what we do and don't do to ourselves. For example, we can increase the nutritional value of our meals, and we can exercise more. We can increase the pleasure of living and working while reducing stress, calories, stimulant abuse, smoking, excessive drinking, and overexposure to direct sunlight. Each of these good habits is associated with expanded longevity (Pearson and Shaw, 1980).

Psychologists are now beginning to study wonderfully healthy men and women as vigorously as they once studied the sick. These thriving people routinely report that the joy of living is to be found in the vigorous use of a healthy mind and body, working toward valued goals with people they love or respect. The importance of work to mental and emotional health has been dramatically illustrated during recent years, when unemployment has been high. Work, and the income derived from work, seem essential for carrying out the roles contemporary America expects from its citizens, male or female. Playing such valued roles helps prolong life and make life worth living.

## ■ Lifestyle and Disease

Lifestyle can affect the incidence of cancer and heart disease, major causes of premature death in America. Diet is believed to be the major environmental cause of cancer; smoking, the second (Doll, 1983). Quayle (1983) reports that "alcoholism is gaining on heart disease, cancer, and diabetes, and in a decade may become America's number one killer." Bruce Ames, a cancer specialist, writes that "there are large numbers of mutagens and carcinogens in every meal, all perfectly natural. . . . Foods naturally contain a range of cancer-preventing chemicals, or 'anti-carcinogens' as well" (1983). High-fat foods may increase the risk of cancer and such foods as fruits and vegetables may confer protection. Our job is to identify carcinogenic (cancer-causing) foods and determine if they present a major health risk. The National Cancer Institute has established the *Chemoprevention Program* to explore the use of natural and synthetic agents in preventing cancer.

Diet is also correlated with heart disorders. "At least 25 to 30 percent of American five- to 18-year-olds have 'dangerously high' cholesterol levels caused mainly by eating too many fats," reports the American Health Foundation (Cohn, 1984, p. 14A). Lowering cholesterol by the use of drugs has resulted in lowered heart attack rates. It is assumed that lowering cholesterol levels by diet will have a similar effect. The Foundation believes that heart attack prevention should begin early, with low-fat diets introduced when children first begin to eat regular foods.

Dr. Dean Ornish has documented the benefits of a vegetarian diet and stress-reduction techniques for people with heart disease (1983). Low-fat diets and low stress levels are associated with heart attack prevention as well. Exercise makes the heart stronger, more efficient, and less at risk (Hockey, 1973). Moderate exercise can increase high-density lipoprotein (HDL) levels and decrease low-density lipoprotein (LDL) levels in men who have had heart attacks (Ballantyne, 1983). HDLs are substances in the bloodstream associated with lowered risk of artery disease, which can cause stroke or heart attack; LDLs are associated

**WHAT DO YOU THINK?**

■ If you could extend your life span, what length would you choose?

■ Why?

## CASE IN POINT
## An Experiment in Life Extension

Sandy and Durk live well. Basically they read and write for a living. They exercise regularly, but not for long. No aerobic exercises are included in their brief routines. They are childless and are in their mid-thirties.

Such a sedentary lifestyle may appear common; however, Sandy and Durk are not your ordinary next-door neighbors. They have committed themselves to living younger longer and are using themselves as human guinea pigs to test diet and exercise routines suggested by several contemporary theories of aging.

They read the latest literature on aging, select potentially helpful programs, and, with the help of a friendly physician, program themselves for a maximum life span. Their routine consists of preparing and consuming, at regular intervals during the day, dietary supplements that may offer protection or relief from the ravages of daily living.

They write and intend to keep writing about their attempts and the results they obtain as measured by exhaustive medical tests. While the medical profession considers them profoundly unscientific, their dramatic adventure has sparked national interest in extending the quality and quantity of our "allotted years." Hopefully, we will be hearing from them both for a long time.

---

*See Pearson and Shaw's book* Life Extension *in the Selected Readings for more about this experiment.*

with increased risk.[4] Finally, eliminating the use of stimulants and depressants can help increase our ability to ward off disease and repair tissue damage.

■ *Growing Old*   Generally, research doesn't indicate that we can rejuvenate the body or reverse the aging process. There is support for the idea that we can slow aging and prolong the youthful portions of our lives, however.

■ *DECO*   Why do we grow old? The sociobiologists would say: to maximize "inclusive fitness." The gene seeks immortality; the genetic container is disposable. This theory holds that our brain monitors the number of harmful gene mutations within our system. When the mutants present a danger to the gene pool (the possibility of too many defective infants' being produced by the aging parents), then the brain may program the pituitary gland to release a death hormone, **DECO** (for "decreased oxygen consumption hormone"). According to the theory, the gradual loss of oxygen produced by the effects of DECO causes a deterioration of the body.

■ *Free Radicals*   Oxygen also figures in a related theory of aging. **Free radicals** are chemicals produced by radiation and by normal metabolism that react with oxygen and that can disrupt and destroy living cells. Gout and arthritis are thought by some to be products of free radical damage, as is normal aging (Harman, 1962). Excessive free radicals are associated with oxygen imbalance. The average life span of animals has been extended by giving them special nutrients (antioxidants) that protect against free radical damage.

---

4. "It takes several months to increase the HDL level but only a short time to lower it. So exercise should not be used as a handy medication, to be taken only when needed. It should be a lifelong habit." (J. Patsch, 1983).

■ Can we prolong
the youthful portion
of our lives?

■ *Autoimmune Reactions*  Part of aging may involve our **immune system's** failing to recognize our own cells and acting to defend against them (called an autoimmune reaction). Or, as we get older, our system may fail to recognize foreign organisms (such as cancers) and thus fail to reject or destroy them. If we can assist our immune system, we can prolong life.

*See Chapter 7, on stress.*

■ *DNA Repair*  Our immune system defends us. We also have a **DNA** repair mechanism. As our cells divide, strands of DNA (which carries genetic information) often break, and enzymes rush in to repair them. As we age, repair work falls behind, and like computer disks with too many error tracks our cells can no longer make accurate copies of themselves.

■ *Hormones*  When we are young (under thirty-five), our **thymus** gland, located behind our breastbone, produces a hormone that instructs our immune system to attack foreign targets. After thirty-five, the thymus shrinks, its hormones decline, and our defense system suffers. To the extent that we can prevent or reverse this shrinkage we can prolong life.

Another gland, the **pituitary**, also plays a role in aging. When we are young it produces and releases a growth hormone (GH) that allows us to eat more and stay lean, increases the benefits of exercise, and stimulates our immune system. An "aging clock" may be located in the pituitary. Menopause, male pattern baldness, and similar signs of aging appear to be the result of a built-in mechanism. If we can prolong the production of GH, we can prolong youth. That is the theory.

**WHAT DO YOU THINK?**

■ Would you commit yourself to an extremely low-calorie diet if it might extend your life span?

### ■ A Plan for Life Extension

Nature does seem to have a plan for us to age and die. Is it possible for us to have other plans, and to make them stick? Many believe we can slow the aging process. Walford (1983) claims that if we reduce our caloric intake by 60 percent over a number of years, while being sure we get superior nutrients, we can prolong life. That seems drastic. There are less extreme measures that may be effective. Reducing intake of polyunsaturated fats (fats susceptible to free radicals) and increasing use of *quenchers* (nutrients found in fruits and vegetables that quench, or terminate, certain chemical reactions) may slow free radical damage and prolong life. Using sun-blocking ointments reduces risk of skin cancer, and following a higher-fiber diet may protect against certain cancers as well.[5] Good sleeping patterns promote growth hormone production. Low stress levels also help. Since drug abuse and smoking are associated with reduced immune system effectiveness, lower growth hormone production, and impaired tissue repair, the elimination of these habits can increase our life span. There is much we can do. But there is no guarantee.

*See the Selected Readings for more information on life extension.*

### ■ The Quality of Extended Life

Would life extension be worth the effort that appears necessary? The best prediction is, "Yes, it would." The over-eighty age bracket is proportionally the fastest-growing population subgroup in our nation (Briley, 1983). One study found more than 90 percent of a representative group of seventy-five- to eighty-four-year-old Americans fully independent. The vast majority were self-sufficient and satisfied with life. The study reported that "Persons with a positive attitude and high morale tend to be those whose health and physical function are best" (p. 97).

At age seventy-nine, the very practical B. F. Skinner, along with his associate M. E. Vaughn, bring us insight into the many things we can do to shape our environment so that we can enjoy old age. How to keep in touch with the world, think clearly, keep busy, get along with others, and feel good are some of the areas explored (Skinner and Vaughn, 1983). They make a strong case for a well-planned old age. The payoff seems to be worth the investment.

In this chapter we have discussed the importance of a fit and attractive physical self. In the next chapter, the mental or cognitive self will be explored. Both a positive mental attitude and a positive lifestyle seem necessary for a full and flourishing life.

---

5. The *Dietary Guidelines* recommend we raise consumption of polyunsaturated fatty acids to lower risk of artery disease. There is so much conflicting evidence and opinions in this area it is risky to give specific advice at this time.

---

**REVIEW QUESTIONS**

*57.* According to Walford, biologists agree that there is little chance a diet that extends the life span of animals will work on humans. T  F

*58.* Pearson and Shaw report that good living habits can contribute to a longer life. T  F

*59.* Al_____ may become America's number-one killer within the next decade.

60. Foods without additives never contain cancer-producing chemicals. T F

61. There *is* / *is not* support for the idea that we can slow down aging and prolong life. T F

62. If we can assist our immune system we may prolong life. T  F

63. The p_____ releases a growth hormone (GH) that increases the benefits of exercise.

64. The vast majority of a representative sample of older Americans *were* / *were not* self-sufficient and satisfied with life.

*The answers to these review questions are on page 131.*

## SUMMARY

■ We are physical organisms that adjust to a changing environment. There is a constant interaction between psychological and physiological adjustment.

■ There appears to be a small, positive correlation between phenotype and temperament. The endomorph tends toward viscerotonia, the mesomorph toward somatotonia, and the ectomorph toward cerebrotonia.

■ Sociobiology is a discipline that attempts to discover the biological foundations of human social behavior. It includes such central concepts as altruism, inclusive fitness, and kin selection.

■ Sexuality is a way of seeing ourselves and relating to others.

■ Chromosomes combine at conception to form the genetic male or female. Differentiation begins during the prenatal period, when antigens program the gonads to form testes or ovaries. Later, the external genitals differentiate under the control of prenatal hormones.

■ Sex-linked behavioral differences are largely illusions, but levels of sexual and aggressive activity seem higher in the male, and nurturing levels appear higher in the female.

■ The theory of the "looking-glass self" offers an alternate explanation of the phenotype–temperament relationship. This theory is based on the notion of shared stereotypes. Social learning theory adds the idea that social reinforcement of expected behaviors shapes temperament to conform with phenotype.

■ Our physical self is made up of bodily images and sensations and remains a lifelong anchor for our self-awareness.

■ We regularly associate character traits with physical characteristics. Attribution theory studies this phenomenon.

■ Physical attractiveness is the most important factor in first impressions. A good appearance leads others to think well of us. We are most attracted to highly attractive people when our own self-esteem is high.

■ A positive body image is associated with low anxiety and increased self-esteem.

■ Negative stereotypes, or stigma, cause psychological pain. Discrimination arising from negative stereotypes extracts an enormous cost in lost performance and unfulfilled lives.

■ We tend to attribute our good behavior to dispositional determinants and our bad behavior to situational determinants.

■ We generally make just the opposite attributions about the behavior of strangers. Mental tests of consistency, consensus, and distinctiveness help us confirm these attributions.

■ Physical fitness includes posture, strength, flexibility, and endurance. Appropriate tests and exercises are available to allow each of us to become fit.

■ Aerobic fitness is the single best index of physical fitness and can be obtained through a pattern of sustained, rhythmic muscle contractions.

■ Intensity, frequency, and duration of exercise have to be coordinated with specific muscle stimulation if muscle fitness is to be achieved.

■ Obese people are seen as being less attractive, and they have more medical complications. Obesity is directly caused by an imbalance between energy-in (calories) and energy-out (activity).

■ The way to lose body fat is to cut calories while increasing activity levels. An eating plan that provides balanced nutrition at an appropriate energy level is needed to maintain healthful living. This plan should be followed for life.

■ There are several theories of aging, including those related to DNA repair, immune system failure, free radicals, and thymus and pituitary gland secretions. Some scientists believe aging is programmed by changes in the brain.

■ Diet, exercise, a positive attitude, and good lifestyle habits can extend the healthful, pleasurable portion of our lives.

## SELECTED READINGS

Cooper, Kenneth. A name synonymous with aerobic exercise. Any of his works is recommended. His charts of exercise programs for various age groups, covering several exercises, are especially helpful.

*Dietary Goals for the United States,* 2nd ed., is obtainable from the U.S. Government Printing Office, Washington, D.C. 20402. This book contains the Great All-American Diet.

Durden-Smith, J., and Desimone, D. *Sex and the Brain.* New York: Arbor House, 1983. A controversial yet thoroughly researched study of how and why sexual pleasure evolved.

Feldenkrais, M. *Awareness through Movement.* New York: Harper & Row, 1972. An exploration of the psychological impact of body shape, size, and energy flow.

Fineberg, S. K. "The Realities of Obesity and Fad Diets." *Nutrition Today* (July/August 1972): 23–26. A help in understanding the problem of obesity and the reasons some diets do not contribute to permanent weight loss.

Knox, D. *Human Sexuality: The Search for Understanding.* St. Paul, Minn., West, 1984. A work that captures the fascinating and complex topic that so permeates our lives and our society.

Kugler, H. *Doctor Kugler's Seven Keys to a Longer Life.* New York: Fawcett Crest, 1978. A collection of practical suggestions for increasing our life span while enjoying life.

Larrance, D. T., and Twentyman, C. T. "Maternal Attributions and Child Abuse." *Journal of Abnormal Psychology* 92 (November 1983): 449.

Money, J., and Ehrhardt, A. *Man and Woman, Boy and Girl.* Baltimore: John Hopkins University Press, 1972. A good work on sexual differences.

Pearson, D., and Shaw, S. *Life Extension.* New York: Warner Brooks, 1983. A popular and captivating account of an ongoing self-experiment in life span increase. The text, while selective in its coverage, contains an extensive source listing.

Pelletier, K. *Longevity.* New York: Delacorte, 1981. An interesting account of communities in which many members live past the century mark. The conditions of life within these communities are examined with an eye toward application in contemporary America.

Rubinstein, J., and Slife, B. (Eds)"Issue 1: Is Human Behavior Genetically Determined?" In *Taking Sides: Clashing Views on Controversial Psychological Issues,* 2nd ed. Guilford, Conn.: Dushkin Publishing Group, 1982. Sociobiology's conflict with conventional wisdom in contemporary psychology. Contrasting points of view are well presented.

Rolf, I. *Structural Integration,* New York: Viking/Esalen, 1975. An easy-to-read book that includes a description of "Rolfing," a deep body massage.

Sheldon, W. H.; Stevens, S. S.; and Tucker, W. B. *The Varieties of Human Physique.* Darien, Conn.: Hafner, 1970. A work that will give you an appreciation of the diversity of human anatomy.

Skinner, B. F., and Vaughn, M. E. *Enjoy Old Age.* New York: Norton, 1983. An authoritative guide to changing our environment so that we can be joyful and productive in our old age.

Snyder, M. "The Many Me's of the Self-Monitor." *Psychology Today,* March 1980.

Whitney, E. N., and Hamilton, E. M. N. *Understanding Nutrition,* 3d ed. St. Paul: West, 1984. A brilliant book on nutrition with illustrations and exercises that make this difficult subject comprehensible. The book also contains informa-tion that will protect you against the questionable claims of fad diet proponents.

Wood, P. *The California Diet and Exercise Program.* Mountain View, Calif.: Anderson World, 1983. A good expression of the idea that one can self-manage health and physical fitness through nutrition and aerobic exercise.

## GLOSSARY

**adaptation:** a change in structure, function, or form that makes an organism better able to survive in its environment.

**aerobic fitness:** the capacity of the heart, lungs, and blood vessels to deliver oxygen to working muscles.

**altruism:** performance of acts intended to help another. Such acts may stem from emotional distress or intellectual understanding of another's needs, or a desire to protect one's gene pool.

**androgen:** a hormone with masculinizing influence.

**anorexia:** a dangerous condition of self-imposed, perpetual fasting.

**attribution theory:** the formal body of information pertaining to the use of inferences and implied causality under conditions of minimal information.

**bodily me:** one's perception of one's physical self.

**cerebrotonia:** the personality type associated with the ectomorph. Characteristically shy, with a subtle sense of humor.

**coitus:** sexual intercourse.

**consensus:** in attribution theory, the degree to which the behavior in question is shared by others.

**consistency:** in attribution theory, the degree to which a person is seen to act similarly under similar conditions.

**correlation:** a reciprocal relationship between two measures (for example, the height of fathers and sons).

**DECO:** in theory, a pituitary hormone that causes decreased oxygen consumption and a deterioration of the body.

**discounting principle:** a principle that states that people tend to have less confidence in an explanation for an action if other plausible explanations exist.

**discrimination:** the showing of partiality or prejudice; negative distinctions in treatment.

**dispositional:** stemming from stable personality traits.

**distinctiveness:** in attribution theory, the degree to which actions are peculiar to a given set of circumstances.

**DNA:** deoxyribonucleic acid; the chemical substance of which genes are composed.

**ectomorph:** a body type characterized by linearity and not much muscularity or subcutaneous fat.

**endomorph:** a body type characterized by roundness and the ability to put on fat.

**estrus:** a period of sexual excitement in female mammals, corresponding to changes in sex organs at the time of ovulation.

**free radicals:** a class of chemicals that damage tissue by combining with other molecules to form harmful mutations.

**gender identity:** one's perception of one's own sexuality.

**genetics:** the biological study of heredity.

**gestate:** carry in the uterus during pregnancy.

**homeostasis:** stability between the internal and external environment.

**Homo sapiens:** the only living species of the genus Homo; humans.

**immune system:** the system by which the body protects itself against disease.

**impression management:** self-presentation meant to shape the attributions of others.

**inclusive fitness:** the genetic representation of the individual through surviving relatives; emphasis is on survival of the gene pool rather than the gene-bearing individual.

**kin selection:** the tendency to protect most those persons with whom one shares the most genes.

**lactate:** give milk; suckle young.

**locus of control:** responsibility for success or failure; may be seen to reside within or outside the self.

**looking-glass self:**   the socially constructed self; self-image based on the perceived reactions of others.

**matching hypothesis:**   the idea that persons of approximately equal physical beauty are attracted to one another.

**mesomorph:**   a body type characterized by squareness and heavy musculature.

**morphogenotype:**   the structural genotype for a species; the stable qualities in appearance that are common within a species.

**nepotism:**   the practice of favoring relatives, as by appointing them to office regardless of their qualifications.

**nurture:**   feed; cherish.

**phenotype:**   the body type displayed by an individual.

**physical self:**   the essential qualities of a person as indicated by sex, body type, height, and general health.

**pituitary:**   the "master gland" of the endocrine system. It secretes hormones that influence other tissue or glands. It also produces a growth and perhaps a death hormone.

**prejudice:**   an unreasonable or hostile attitude based on little or no evidence.

**procreative proficiency:**   adept at producing large numbers of offspring, which share a common gene pool.

**senescence:**   the process of growing old; the onset of old age.

**situational:**   based on the assessment that environmental forces caused the behavior observed to occur.

**sociobiology:**   a controversial school of thought that holds that approximately 10 percent of human social behavior is genetically determined.

**somatotonia:**   the personality type associated with the mesomorph. Characteristically a courageous lover of adventure and exercise.

**stereotype:**   a fixed idea of the nature of members of a group.

**stigma:**   a mark of disgrace or reproach.

**thymus:**   a ductless gland situated in the upper thorax near the throat; part of the immune system.

**viscerotonia:**   the personality type associated with the endomorph. Characteristically a lover of comfort and good conversation.

# REFERENCES

Allport, G. W. *Becoming*. New Haven, Conn.: Yale University Press, 1960.

Alper, J.; Beckwith, J.; and Miller, L. "Sociobiology Is a Political Issue." In *The Sociobiology Debate*. Edited by A. L. Caplan. New York: Harper & Row, 1978.

Ames, B. N. Quoted by P. Hilts. In "Foods Naturally Contain Cancer-Causing Chemicals." *Miami Herald* (September 22, 1983): 14E.

Ballantyne, F. Quoted by Dr. Neil Solomon in "Ask the Doctor." *Miami Herald* (February 2, 1983): 10C.

Bandura, A., and Walters, R. H. *Social Learning and Personality Development*. New York: Holt, Rinehart and Winston, 1963.

Barash, D. P. *Sociobiology and Behavior*. New York: Elsevier, 1977.

Beck, S. B.; Ward-Hull, C. I.; and McLear, P. M. "Variables Related to Women's Somatic Preferences of the Male and Female Body." *Journal of Personal and Social Psychology* 34 (December 1976): 1200–1210.

Berscheid, E.; Walster, E.; and Bohrnstedt, G. "The Happy American Body: A Survey Report." *Psychology Today* (November 1973): 119–123.

Brady, J. I.; Knight, D. R.; and Berghage, T. E. "Relationship between Measures of Body Fat and Gross Motor Proficiency." *Journal of Applied Psychology* (April 1977): 224–229.

Briley, M. "Over 80—and Doing Fine." *Modern Maturity* (October–November 1983): 96–97.

Carroll, H. A. *Mental Hygiene: The Dynamics of Adjustment*. Englewood Cliffs, N.J.: Prentice-Hall, 1969.

Cash, T. F.; Kehr, J. A.; Polyson, J.; and Freeman, V. "Role of Physical Attraction in Peer Attribution of Psychological Disturbances." *Journal of Counseling and Clinical Psychology* 45 (December 1977): 87–93.

Cash, T. F., and Smith, E. "Physical Attractiveness and Personality among American College Students." *Journal of Psychology* 3 (1982): 183–191.

Cohn, V. "Doctors Urge Low-Cholesterol Diet for Kids to Prevent Heart Disease." *Miami Herald* (March 15, 1984): 14A.

Cooley, C. H. *Human Nature and the Social Order.* New York: Scribner's, 1920.

Cooper, K. H. *The New Aerobics.* New York: Bantam Books, 1970.

Davis, B. L. "Attitudes towards School among Early and Late Maturing Adolescent Girls." *Journal of Genetic Psychology* 131 (December 1977): 261–266.

Dawkins, R. *The Selfish Gene.* New York: Oxford University Press, 1976.

Dell, D. M., and Patkin, J. "Effects of Certain Behaviors on Perceived Expertness and Attractiveness." *Journal of Counseling Psychology* 29 (May 1982): 261–267.

Dermer, M., and Thiel, D. "When Beauty May Fail." *Journal of Personality and Social Psychology* 31 (1975): 1168–1176.

Diamond, M. "Sexual Identity, Monozygotic Twins Reared in Discordant Sex Roles and a BBC Follow-up." *Archives of Sexual Behavior* 11 (April 1982): 181–186.

Diamond, S. *Personality and Temperament.* New York: Harper & Row, 1957.

Dion, K. K.; Berscheid, E.; and Walster, E. "What Is Beautiful Is Good." *Journal of Personality and Social Psychology* 24 (1972): 285–290.

Doll, R., a British epidemiologist. Quoted in "Food's Link to Cancer: Cause and Protection." *Miami Herald* (August 31, 1983): 1E.

Elliot, J. "The Power and Pathology of Prejudice." In *Psychology and Life.* Edited by P. G. Zimbardo and F. L. Ruch. Glenview, Ill.: Scott-Foresman, 1977.

Eysenck, H. L. *Eysenck on Extroversion.* London: Crosby Lockwood Staples, 1973.

Feldman, S. D. "The Presentation of Shortness in Everyday Life—Height and Heightism in American Society: Toward a Sociology of Stature." Paper presented to the American Sociology Association meeting, 1971.

Freedman, D. G. *Human Sociobiology: A Holistic Approach.* New York: Free Press, 1979.

Fugita, S. S.; Panek, P. E.; Balascoe, L. L.; and Newman, I. "Attractiveness, Level of Accomplishment, Sex of Rater, and the Evaluation of Female Competence." *Representative Research in Social Psychology* 8 (1977): 1–11.

Gorski, R. A. Quoted by R. Kotulak in "Gender: What Makes You Male or Female?" *Miami Herald* (March 9, 1979).

Grady, K. E. "Sex as a Social Label: The Illusion of Sex Differences." *Dissertation Abstracts* 38 (June 1977): 416.

Gregory, M. S.; Silvers, A.; and Sutch, D., eds. *Sociobiology and Human Nature.* San Francisco: Jossey-Bass, 1978.

Hamilton, W. D. "Altruism and Related Phenomena, Mainly in Social Insects." *Annual Review of Ecology and Systematics* 3 (1972): 193–232.

Haremustin, R. "Problems Associated with Eating." *Journal of the American Psychological Association* 38 (May 1983): 597–598.

Harmon, D. "Role of Free Radicals in Mutation, Cancer, Aging, and the Maintenance of Life." *Radiation Research* 16 (1962): 753–764.

Heider, F. *The Psychology of Interpersonal Relations.* New York: Wiley, 1958.

Hockey, R. V. *Physical Fitness: The Pathway to Healthful Living.* St. Louis: Mosby, 1973.

Ilg, F. L., and Ames, L. B. *The Gesell Institutes' Child Behavior.* New York: Dell, 1961.

Imperato-McGinley, J. "Sex Hormone Overrides Upbringing." *Science News* 117 (June 28, 1980): 406.

Jones, E. E., and Nisbett, R. E. "The Actor and the Observer: Divergent Perceptions of the Causes of Behavior." In *Attribution: Perceiving the Causes of Behavior.* Edited by E. E. Jones, D. E. Kanouse, H. H. Kelly, R. E. Nisbett, S. Valins, and B. Weiner. Morristown, N.J.: General Learning Press, 1972.

Jourard, S. M., and Landsman, T. *Healthy Personality.* New York: Macmillan, 1980.

Jourard, S. M., and Remy, R. M. "Individual Variance Score: An Index of the Degree of Differentiation of the Self and the Body Image." *Journal of Clinical Psychology* 13 (1957): 62–63.

Kagan, J. "Body Build and Conceptual Impulsivity in Children." *Journal of Personality* 34 (1966): 118–128.

Kagan, J., and Moss, H. A. "Birth to Maturity: A Study in Psychological Development. N.Y.: Wiley, 1962.

Kammer, D. "Differences in Trait Ascriptions to Self and Friend: Unconfounding Intensity from Variability." *Psychological Reports* 51 (1982): 99–102.

Keesey, R. E., and Powley, T. L. "Hypothalamic Regulation of Body Weight." *American Scientist* 63 (September–October 1975): 558–565.

Kelly, H. H., and Michel, J. L. "Attribution Theory and Research." *Annual Review of Psychology* 31 (1980): 457–501.

Kielser, S. B., and Baral, R. L. "The Search for a Romantic Partner: The Effects of Self-Esteem and Physical Attractiveness on Romantic Behavior." In *Personality and Social Behavior*. Edited by K. Gergen and D. Marlowe. Reading, Mass.: Addison-Wesley, 1970.

Kleck, R. E., and Rubinstein, C. "Physical Attractiveness, Perceived Attitude Similarity, and Interpersonal Attraction in an Opposite Sex Encounter." *Journal of Personality and Social Psychology* 31 (1975): 107–114.

Kleinke, C. L., and Staneski, R. A. "First Impressions of Female Bust Size." *Journal of Social Psychology* 110 (1980): 123–134.

Kuhlen, R. G., and Thompson, G. G. *Psychological Studies of Human Development*. New York: Appleton-Century-Crofts, 1970.

Kurtz, R., and Prestera, H. *The Body Reveals*. New York: Harper & Row/Quicksilver Books, 1976.

Lenihan, J. *Human Engineering: The Body Re-Examined*. New York: Braziller, 1974.

Lewis, K. N., and Walsh, W. B. "Physical Attractiveness: Its Impact on the Perception of a Female Counselor." *Journal of Counseling Psychology* 25 (May 1978): 210–216.

Maccoby, E., and Jacklin, C. *The Psychology of Sex Differences*. Stanford, Calif.: Stanford University Press, 1974.

Maeder, J. "The Jay Maeder Column." *Miami Herald* (November 19, 1983): 2A.

Miller, D. K., and Allen, T. E. *Fitness: A Lifetime Commitment*. Minneapolis: Burgess, 1979.

Money, J., and Ehrhardt, A. A. *Man and Woman, Boy and Girl*. Baltimore: Johns Hopkins University Press, 1972.

Montemayor, R. "Men and Their Bodies: The Relationship between Body Type and Behavior." *Journal of Social Issues* 34 (1978): 48–64.

Moyer, K. E. "Sex Differences in Aggression." In *Sex Differences in Behavior*. Edited by R. C. Friedman, R. M. Richart, and R. L. Vande Wiele. New York: Wiley, 1974. Chapter 18.

Nisbett, R. E. "Hunger, Obesity, and the Ventromedial Hypothalamus." *Psychological Review* 79 (1972): 433-453.

Ornish, D. *Stress, Diet, and Your Heart*. New York: Holt, Rinehart and Winston, 1983.

Patsch, J. "Exercise and Hardy Hearts." *Science Digest* 11 (July 1983): 87.

Pearson, D., and Shaw, S. *Life Extension*. New York: Warner Brooks, 1980.

Quayle, D. "Why We Can't Prevent the Devastating Effect of Alcoholism and Drug Abuse." *American Psychologist* 38 (April 1983): 11–15.

Razook, S. "Improving Posture May Cure Headaches." *Miami Herald* (October 9, 1983): 3G.

Reichlin, S. "Relationships of the Pituitary Gland to Human Sexual Behavior." *Medical Aspects of Human Sexuality* 5 (February 1971).

Reinisch, J. M. "Fetal Hormones, the Brain and Human Sex Differences: A Heuristic, Integrative Review of Human Sexuality." *Archives of Sexual Behavior* 3 (1981): 51–90.

Reinisch, J. M. "Prenatal Exposure to Synthetic Progestins Increases Potential for Aggression in Humans." *Science* March 13, 81. 1171–3.

Riedal, S., and McKillip, J. "Friends, Lovers, and Physical Attractiveness." Paper presented at the meeting of the Midwestern Psychological Association, Chicago, May 1979.

Rosenthal, D. *Genetic Theory and Abnormal Behavior*. New York: McGraw-Hill, 1970.

Schachter, S., and Freeman, J., "Effects of Work and Cue Prominence." In *Obese Humans and Rats*. Edited by S. Schachter and J. Rodin. Potomac, Md.: Erlbaum Associates, 1974.

Schwibbe, G., and Schwibbe, M. "Judgement and Treatment of People of Varied Attractiveness." *Psychological Reports* 48 (February–June 1981): 11–15.

Sheldon, W. H., and Stevens, S. S. *The Varieties of Temperament*. New York: Harper, 1942.

Skinner, B. F., and Vaughn, M. E. *Enjoy Old Age.* New York: W. W. Norton, 1983.

Snyder, M. "The Many Me's of the Self-Monitor." *Psychology Today* (March 1980): 97–101.

Stephan, C., and Tully, J. C. "The Influence of Physical Attractiveness of a Plaintiff on the Decisions of Simulated Jurors." *Journal of Social Psychology* 101 (1977): 149–150.

Stern, J. S. "Movement Makes the Difference." *Vogue* (October 1983): 400.

Storms, M. D. "Videotape and the Attribution Process: Reversing Actor's and Observers' Points of View." *Journal of Personality and Social Psychology* 27 (1973): 165–175.

Van Huss, W. D.; Niemeyer, R. K.; Olson, H. W.; and Friedrich, J. A. *Physical Activity in Modern Living,* 2nd ed. Englewood Cliffs, N.J.: Prentice-Hall, 1969.

Walford, R. Quoted in "Beyond the Fountain of Youth: Life after Your 100th Birthday." *Miami Daily News* (July 27, 1983): 1C.

White, D. "The Bottom Line." *Psychology Today* (July 1979): 88–89.

Whitney, E. N., and Hamilton, E. M. N. *Understanding Nutrition.* St. Paul, Minn.: West, 1977.

Wilson, E. O. *Sociobiology: The New Synthesis.* Cambridge, Mass.: Harvard University Press, 1975.

———. *On Human Nature.* Cambridge, Mass.: Harvard University Press, 1978.

Wineberg, M. S. "The Problem of Midgets and Dwarfs and Organizational Remedies: A Study of the Little People of America." *Journal of Social Psychology* 74 (1968): 97–102.

Wolman, B. B., and Money, J., eds. *Handbook of Human Sexuality.* Englewood Cliffs, N.J.: Prentice-Hall, 1980.

Zastro, C. *Talk To Yourself: Using the Power of Self-Talk.* Englewood Cliffs, N.J.: Prentice-Hall, 1979.

## ANSWERS TO REVIEW QUESTIONS

**Page 93**. *1*. homeostasis  *2*. physiological, psychological  *3*. phenotypes  *4*. ectomorph  *5*. endomorph  *6*. sociobiology  *7*. inclusive fitness  *8*. kin selection

**Page 99**. *9*. T  *10*. F  *11*. T  *12*. F  *13*. F  *14*. T  *15*. T  *16*. F  *17*. F  *18*. T

**Page 108**. *19*. F  *20*. rewarded  *21*. "bodily me"  *22*. physical attractiveness  *23*. less attractive  *24*. similar  *25*. stigmas  *26*. attribution  *27*. dispositional  *28*. discounting  *29*. helps  *30*. not  *31*. commonplace  *32*. both  *33*. possible

**Page 113**. *34*. weight, posture  *35*. flexibility, strength  *36*. fail  *37*. develop physique, improve physical condition, increase sports skills, control weight, rehabilitate, protect from disease or injury  *38*. posture  *39*. flexibility  *40*. F  *41*. aerobic capacity  *42*. 60  *43*. decreases

**Page 120**. *44*. partially true  *45*. lowest mortality  *46*. valid  *47*. protein, fat, carbohydrate  *48*. too much  *49*. both  *50*. more  *51*. best  *52*. T  *53*. are not  *54*. better than  *55*. T  *56*. carbohydrate, fat, protein

**Page 124**. *57*. will  *58*. T  *59*. Alcohol  *60*. F  *61*. is  *62*. T  *63*. pituitary  *64*. were

# 5

# COGNITIVE SELF

## Focus

As you read this, become aware of the amount of information bombarding your senses. From this page comes knowledge carried in the light that strikes your eyes. Additional visual data comes to you from rays reflected from all the other objects, including your own body, that are within your view. Look around. Be aware of the many colors, forms, textures, and perhaps patterns of motion that are converging on you.

As you handle this book, you receive information concerning its size, texture, weight, and configuration. Can you feel the information flowing to you from the table, chair, and floor? What is the temperature of the air around you? Is it still or in motion? What aromas are being brought to you on the air?

The real world outside us continuously supplies data for us. So does our inner world. Do your feet hurt? Are any muscles tense and uncomfortable? Can you hear gurglings from within? Is your heartbeat strong and regular? What about your breathing? Are your legs crossed, or is one hand in contact with your face? What information about yourself is being transmitted and received at the same time?

Have stray thoughts entered your consciousness during this reading? Information bombardment also comes from mental stimulation. Become aware of your feelings. Where does the information come from that lets us know how we feel? We are all engulfed in a sea of information all the time. Over one million messages make contact with us each second. What enables us to make sense of this buzzing confusion? How are we able to make use of it?

**COGNITIVE
SELF**

## DISCUSSION:  COGNITIVE CONTROL

This chapter will focus on the psychological aspects of our attempts to make sense of our world and to bring regularity to the stream of communication it sends. We must do this as we constantly make adjustments to our changing world.

**Cognition** is the act of making sense of experience. It is the acquisition, organization, and use of knowledge. Such cognitive activities as comparing, planning, and predicting are characterized by the use of mental skills acquired through living.

We are born with limited skill for receiving information. A loud noise will produce a reflexive start in a newborn, but most complex stimuli simply pass by. On the other hand, there appears to be no limit to the capacity of a fully developed human brain to pick up information (Neisser, 1976). And since we do not forget an old fact each time we learn a new one, the limits of human cognition are not to be found in our ability to learn. Rather they appear to be found in our capacity to *control the flow of information* that we absorb.

### ■ Avenues to Cognitive Control

There are two avenues to **cognitive control**. The first is *the ability to focus on a single item of experience* out of the hundred million experiences of each moment. Our ability to learn is sharply limited by our ability to attend to or notice relevant cues. Robin Barr (1981) notes that we focus our attention by dividing incoming stimuli into two groupings, the message and the background noise.

■ What our mind needs is a good traffic cop.

We use notions of what we think is important and what we predict will occur to help us distinguish the two groups. Divided attention destroys our concentration.

> Maxwell doesn't really like college. What he doesn't like most is having to conform to all the expectations associated with being a college student. He isn't happy here and his poor attendance reflects his discontent. Max leaves the campus as quickly as possible after each class—no extracurricular activities for him.
>
> His professors say he's bright enough, but he gets very little work done, and even less work done well. Following directions seems to be his academic Waterloo. Max never quite gets his assignments, never quite remembers deadlines or test days, and never quite gets the point of a lecture or discussion.
>
> The first of his family to attend college, Max tells his dad that he didn't miss much. The mind of Max is always a million miles off campus, and it is embarrassing for him when he's called on in class and doesn't know the topic, much less the answer! Maxwell can't or won't concentrate hard or long enough to get a sharp focus on the material he is expected to learn. His grades reflect this divided attention.
>
> Cognitively, Max dropped out of college long ago. His friends don't expect him to finish this term.

The second avenue to cognitive control is *the ability to search meaningfully for connections* between what we are attending to and appropriate information that we have in memory from past experience. An infant can be expected *not* to notice a clear glass plate positioned in front of an attractive toy. He can be expected to react with surprise and rage when he crawls headlong into its hard surface. A toddler *will* notice the glass and effectively waddle around it to reach the toy. This increased capacity in attending to and receiving information, and in directing subsequent responses, represents quite a growth in cognitive control.

## ■ Adjustment Problems and Cognitive Control

The toddler is more able than the infant to cope with the real world. This is because good cognition is closely associated with good adjustment. Just as the toddler was able to reach his goal without frustration or emotional upset because he could see more selectively, interpret more accurately, and behave more flexibly, so many of our adult adjustment problems are grounded in faulty perceptions, irrational assumptions, negative emotions, and dysfunctional actions.

**Cognitive-behavioral therapy** attempts to help people regain the ability to see the world as it is, to rationally assess the present, and to respond with greater flexibility to its demands. To do this, therapists attempt to help clients change both their style of thinking and some of their specific thoughts. We will discuss cognitive-behavioral therapy in more detail later in this chapter.

**WHAT DO YOU THINK?**

■ Can you think of times when you would *not* want to see the world as it really is?

*See Chapter 14 for a discussion of psychotherapy.*

## ■ Scientific Psychology and the Mind

Using measures of time and concepts of space, it is possible to treat aspects of mental operations with scientific precision and to formulate laws describing their basic nature (Blumenthal, 1977). For example, remembering and thinking are mental acts that take time. They also occupy space in our central, psychological processing system, our mind. Memory and thinking seem to interfere with each other. We have trouble holding items in memory while we think about them, and vice versa. To experience this interference, try adding pairs of two-digit numbers in your head. It is easy. Now try adding pairs of seven-digit numbers in your head. The increased difficulty does not lie in your mental arithmetic, which is the same in both cases. The problem is in time-space limitations of your mind—we cannot hold the larger numbers in our "working memory" while we process them.

### ■ Adjustment as a Change in Cognitive Behavior

The cognitive processes of receiving, organizing, storing, and retrieving information shed light on our problems of adjustment. Adjustment means a change in behavior, and a change in behavior is the very definition of learning. Cognitive processes such as listening, focusing attention, and remembering are the most important neurophysiological processes in learning. If we understand them, we can better understand adjustment.

We will begin with the theoretical. The process of cognition will be outlined first. We will then turn our attention to the practical—our rational and irrational thoughts. What specific thoughts occupy us during times of decision? What are the effects of certain patterns of thought on subsequent feelings and adjustments?

**WHAT DO YOU THINK?**

■ Can you recall a specific example of learning something new that helped you to understand, appreciate, or apply old knowledge in new and better ways?

**REVIEW QUESTIONS**

1. The amount of information bombarding our senses at any moment is <u>small / large / virtually unlimited</u>.

2. The processes that lend stability and regularity to this information are termed _____ processes.

3. We have <u>limited / unlimited</u> capacity to control the information we absorb.

4. One of the two ways in which our cognitive control is limited involves our limited ability _____ .

5. Cognitive skills <u>remain static / develop</u> as we live and act in the world.

6. Psychological adjustment <u>is / is not</u> greatly affected by our developing cognitive skills.

7. Today the scientific study of the mind is considered by psychologists to be <u>possible / impossible</u>.

8. The difficulty in mentally solving the addition of seven-digit numbers lies in _____ and _____ limits of our mind.

9. This chapter will stress the <u>physiological / psychological</u> aspects of cognition.

10. Listening, _____ , and remembering are the most important neurophysical processes in learning.

*The answers to these review questions are on page 172.*

*The answers to these review questions are on page 172.*

## DISCUSSION: COGNITIVE DEVELOPMENT

Sigmund Freud gave us tremendous insight into the workings of the unconscious mind and John B. Watson made us aware that our behaviors can be shaped by experiences we cannot recall. The writer of the twentieth century who has had the greatest impact on our understanding of cognition is Jean Piaget, a Swiss psychologist. His notions on the nature of mental development and the effect of mental operations on adjusting to a changing environment are inspiring new avenues of research and application every day.

## ■ The Cognitive Theories of Jean Piaget

Piaget published observations, based on the development of cognitive processes in children, from 1927 until his death in 1980. Trained as a zoologist, Piaget was interested in logic, **epistemology** (the study of the nature of knowledge), and children. He was fascinated with the wrong answers children give to every-day questions because he could learn from them how young minds work. After years of observing his own and other people's children, he concluded that intellectual development follows a definite pattern in all normal children.

To Piaget, *cognition is action* (Phillips, 1975). The mind is a dynamic system that constructs itself in order to take information from the environment. Each new input must filter through an existing **brain structure**. At the same time, each new input will strengthen or produce changes in that structure. Jean-Pierre Changeux, a neuroscientist, believes that "up to 80% of the early synaptic contacts between cells [in the brain] are eliminated during development, while a few are selected and strengthened. The changes occur only as a result of activity (Pines, 1983, p. 51)." Our brain is thus the property of *actions*. In childhood, these actions are largely physical interactions with real objects. Later the actions involve simple, mental representations of real objects encountered in the past. Finally, a complex network of mental representations can become free of specific experiences and form the logical thinking structures of the adult. (See the Case in Point entitled "The Growth of the Mind.")

## ■ The Emergence of Mental Representations

Cristy is three months old, and beautiful. Her sparkling eyes and radiant health make everyone want to reach out to her. Today it is Cristy who is reaching out. Her doting father has just presented her with a gift—her first rubber ball! It is small, soft, and colorful, just the toy for daddy's little girl.

Cristy's eyes widen as she stretches for the ball, fumbles it, and gets it in her grasp. Squeezing mightily, she succeeds in getting the ball to her mouth where she happily chews and drools for her proud parents.

The ball was something new for Cristy. Now consider what takes place later when she is presented the ball again. When she sees it, she makes motions with her fingers, arms, and mouth. To her *ball* means "hold, squeeze, and chew." It is so defined in her mind and body by her previous actions on it. Thus, cognition is action. Later, during play, she discovers that the ball rolls, bounces, and returns to its original shape when squeezed. Her further cognitive growth is explained by Piaget as the development, via interactions, of an increasingly complex **schema** for recognizing and directing subsequent interactions with the ball. (A schema is a mental outline or diagram of an object or process. More than one schema are *schemata*.)

## ■ *Assimilation and Accommodation*    What if the infant is given a ball that is different—too big to fit into her mouth or to be grasped by her hand? How

■ Cristy is learning by doing.

will she react? Her schema for *ball* will compel her to try to act on the new ball in exactly the same way as she did the original. This pattern Piaget calls **assimilation**, or the changing of the input to fit an existing brain structure.

With the larger ball, though, assimilation will not work. To interact successfully with the new ball, adjustments are required. This adjustment in brain pattern is termed **accommodation**.

A variety of experiences with balls of varying sizes, colors, and resiliencies will allow Cristy to develop a wide range of specific motor responses to objects seen as balls. It will also produce a transformation of the schema for *ball* that is part of her new cognitive structure. *Ball* will change from a specific set of attributes to a general class of attributes. This new mental structure, or *concept*, will not relate specifically to any particular ball, and it will allow Cristy to be quite flexible in her capacity to recognize balls and to respond differently to them. In the future, she will react to any new ball in a generalized way—that is, in terms of her abstract schema rather than in terms of any specific ball that she has experienced in the past. Schemata are thus seen as generalized mental patterns that are the result of interactions between (1) prior expectations and (2) currently available situational information (Alloy and Tabachnik, 1984).

## ■ Surviving in a Changing World

Our minds, then, have evolved to store generalizations rather than specifics as memories. Piaget believed that this helps us to survive in a changing world. It allows us to profit from experience even though no experience exactly repeats itself. We "both make sense and impose sense upon the world, simultaneously!"

(Alloy and Tabachnik, 1984, p. 141). When we "impose sense" we assimilate new information into our existing thought patterns, and when we "make sense" we accommodate, or change, these patterns. Lower animals, Cristy, and you and I use the joint influence of prior expectations and current sensations to direct our thoughts, emotions, and actions. You can see the importance of the idea of schemata formulation in understanding the psychology of adjustment.

A simple example of adult schema formulation is to be found in learning to drive. At first we learn to apply previously mastered motor responses, such as grasping and pushing, to the steering wheel, brakes, and so on. Next we learn to make specific coordinated responses under limited driving conditions. Later we are able to drive a variety of automobiles under vastly different circumstances. Finally we are able to **automatize** driving and perform better when not thinking of the mechanics of driving. (Automatized thinking is the use of unconscious, automatic thought.) We are thus free to focus on the goals of driving, a more complex mental task. The more routines we have automated, the greater brain capacity we have free to focus on relevant, new information.

■ *Automatized Thinking and Problem Solving*   Blumenthal (1977) believes that "our ability to learn may thus be limited to the degree that our attention is free and to the degree that it can be directed to the events to be learned" (p. 150). In terms of adjustment this suggests that if a problem occupies all our mental energy, it is most difficult for us to notice novel aspects of the situation that might provide useful cues in solving the problem. Rigid, compulsive behavior may result.

**WHAT DO YOU THINK?**

■ Can you think of a problem that you solved while doing anything other than concentrating on its solution?

## ■ Becoming More Effective in Adjusting to a Changing World

If you equate poor adjustment with poor information processing, the work of Richard Feuerstein (1979) in helping train poor learners to improve their reasoning and problem-solving skills provides helpful suggestions for increasing effectiveness in adjusting. Feuerstein finds the cognitive deficits of poor learners to include:

*1. A passive approach to the environment.* They readily say "I don't know" rather than search for a plausible answer. This is like saying "I can't cope." Adjustment, like learning, requires us to be active and persistent in seeking solutions.

*2. Impulsivity.* Good adjustment requires, not acting impulsively but exercising patience and care in searching for meaningful connections.

*3. Failure to recognize problems or to notice that discrepancies are important.* These cognitive deficits in attending to relevant cues can cause poor adjustment in all areas of life.

*4. Failure to make comparisons.* The meaningful search problem in cognitive control is concerned with making connections between old and new information. Failure to make such appropriate connections is associated frequently with failures to find workable solutions to problems of adjustment.

**WHAT DO YOU THINK?**

■ Do you recognize any of these deficits in your cognitive style?
■ Would being more persistent and less impulsive help you to better adjust?

The importance of Feuerstein's work is that he has demonstrated that these deficits in cognitive skill can be identified in poor learners and remedial programs initiated with the expectation of good results.

## CASE IN POINT
# The Growth of the Mind

Piaget's research on the thinking processes of children has led to changes in the way children are being taught at home and in school. He believed that the intellectual skills of all children progress through a series of distinct, orderly, and logical stages of development: the sensorimotor stage, preoperational stage, concrete operational stage, and formal operations stage.

### The Sensorimotor Stage

From birth to approximately two years, a child progresses from reflex actions to the ability to form a mental construct, or model, of objects encountered during play. Until the child is about a year old, prior to the development of such constructs, an object that is out of sight is literally out of mind. It simply ceases to exist. A child will again and again respond with surprise as it reappears. At the end of the sensorimotor period a child will search for a missing object—a sign that an image is being retained to help direct the search. Such *object permanence*, said Piaget, allows the child to think in mental images and enter the symbolic world of language. Once children learn that their existing knowledge is imperfect—that it won't work for them—their **encoding** (the way they code and store new information for later use) plays a large role in their constructing more advanced knowledge (Siegler, 1983).

### The Preoperational Stage

With language abilities, two- to seven-year-olds possess a new instrument with which to solve problems and come to terms with the environment. They will increasingly manipulate objects through mental acts rather than motor acts. Toward the end of the preoperational stage, a child will pause when presented a problem, think about it, and only then respond physically. This pause to reflect signals the emergence of intelligence. Preoperational children are quite *egocentric*—they can hold but one point of view, their own. This inability to grasp the perspective of the other accounts for much of the frustration for both child and caretaker that abound during this period. The child's selfishness arises from limited awareness rather than from a character disorder.

### The Concrete Operational Stage

The seven-to-eleven age span marks a dramatic unfolding of the child's intellectual capacities. In this stage is developed the ability to *conserve*, or to understand that objects can be transformed and then changed back into their original shape. A ball of clay can be stretched. A child of four will typically report that the stretched ball has more clay. A child of nine can reverse the stretching process in his mind and so is not fooled by the apparent increase in size. This age also marks the emergence of the ability to classify objects in terms of their properties—to be able to discern that there are more yellow crayons than red crayons, for example. This is the beginning of abstract rational thought, the foundation of logic and science.

Interestingly, there is growing evidence that we act as scientists almost from birth. New research with children as young as two years old indicates that they have a remarkable understanding of "cause and effect" relationships, given their limited experience. Both physical and social causation (rather than magical causation) are explored by five- to eight-month-old babies as they turn on light switches, drop food, and watch for the reactions of both people and things around them. The search for cause-and-effect relationships appears to be built into our genetic code (Pines, 1983).

### The Formal Operations Stage

Between the ages of twelve and fifteen, the final stage of mental growth occurs, according to Piaget. Formal operations include conserving, reversing, and decentering (shifting focus on) abstract ideas. These allow adolescents to explore hypotheticals—problems that exist only in the mind. Thus they can reflect on possibilities, evaluate outcomes, and plan and direct future events with greater precision. Idealism flourishes as all things become possible. Piaget believes that giving challenging tasks that are appropriate to each child's stage of development will result in the construction of minds that are at the same time critical and creative. These minds are capable of leading us toward novel and improved responses to the world as it is. Such minds can change the world.

■ Experiences with puzzles of varying size, color, and complexity will allow this young girl to develop a wide range of specific motor responses to individual "pieces" of the future.

*11.* According to Piaget, intellectual development <u>is complete at birth / is unique / follows an orderly pattern.</u>

*12.* The infant primarily learns through <u>physical activity / emotional reactivity / mental insight.</u>

*13.* New information must <u>filter through / change</u> existing schemata.

*14.* The meaning of *ball* to an infant is contained in his or her physical responses to a particular ball. T F

*15.* Piaget's term for mental diagrams or outlines is sc_____.

*16.* Piaget called the function of changing incoming data to fit existing cognitive structures as _____.

*17.* The function of ac_____ is the changing of existing schemata to better fit incoming data.

*18.* According to Piaget, our minds have evolved to reconstruct experience in terms of <u>generalizations / exact copies</u> of the original event.

*19.* When we can concentrate on the goals of driving rather than the mechanics of driving, we can be said to have au_____ our driving skills.

*20.* Reducing a large number of daily activities to automatized routines <u>prevents us from / frees us for</u> concentrating on novel aspects of our environment.

*21.* Cognitive deficits can be isolated and specific training given to remedy them so as to improve our ability to change our behavior. T F

*22.* Children appear to have an early understanding of cause and effect. T F

*The answers to these review questions are on p. 172.*

## DISCUSSION: THE PERCEPTUAL CYCLE

A single schema, in Piaget's theory, represents many things. It may be as simple as a grasping reflex or as complex as a plan to obtain a university degree. The point to be emphasized is that schemata are formed via transactions with the real world. These schemata then direct the nature of future transactions. If we do not have an appropriate schema, we will have no pattern to recognize and will not be able to integrate information that is present in our environment. *This is the focusing of attention problem in cognitive control.* If our schema is not rich with relevant connections, we will not be able to make best use of the information that is received. *This is the meaningful search problem in cognitive control.*

*Focusing of attention and meaningful search were discussed at the beginning of this chapter.*

### ■ Individual, Schema, and Environment

Ulric Neisser (1976) beautifully illustrates the interaction among the environment, the person, and the schema by contrasting the ability of an infant, an amateur chess player, and a chess master to obtain information from a glance at a chess board.

> This is the story of three wise men at play. The first wise man is very young, only an infant really. He is enthusiastic and impatient to begin. The second wise man is a novice at the game. However, he is fascinated by chess and eager to improve his performance. The third wise man is an expert. His years of top-level competition have honed his considerable skill to the level of a champion.
>
> And now for the performance. A large chess board is set up in the center of the room. A carefully conceived problem is presented by the exact arrangement of the chess pieces on the board. The players enter blindfolded, are led to the center of the room, and are unmasked. The audience leans forward as each player, in turn, approaches the problem in terms of his own unique cognitive style.
>
> The first wise man crawls onto the board, scattering the careful array. He quickly grasps the Bishop with both tiny hands and thrusts it into his mouth.
>
> The second wise man's eyes dance anxiously over the reassemble pieces. First one sector and then another comes under painful scrutiny. With a deep sigh, the second wise man moves a pawn.
>
> The third wise man glances intently at the whole board, turns away momentarily as if in deep thought, and then decisively makes his move.

All three of these "wise men" began on even terms. Each could see the board with its array of carved and colored pieces. They received exactly the same physical messages carried in the light (Gibson, 1966). The three differed in the anticipatory schemes each brought to that information and the way these schemes directed further search. The infant saw colors and shapes and was directed toward pieces that could be grasped and placed in his mouth. Such behavior is said to be "stimulus bound," because the external environment alone directs it.

The amateur player and the chess master possessed the capability to go beyond the data contained in the optic array. First of all, they held in memory the rules of chess. This enabled them to perceive the board and its pieces within a cultural system of roles, rules, and goals. This knowledge of the role of each piece, the rules that govern its movement, and the object of the game of chess *freed* both of them to look beyond the physical properties of each piece toward its relative

**WHAT DO YOU THINK?**

■ Do you think you can purchase cognitive freedom by accepting the rules of society?

position on the board. Here the amateur and the master parted company. A more limited perceptual schema directed the search of the amateur—the more limited the schema, the more likely a crucial aspect of a position was missed. Chase and Simon (1973) report that an expert player may have in memory as many schemata pertaining to chess positions as we have words in our vocabulary. The chess master is not necessarily brighter than the amateur, just richer in terms of perceptual schemata.

## ■ Information Storage and Retrieval

The chess master has stored in his memory more chess-related information than the novice. But his mastery over the novice is not the result of superior information alone; it also results from the way the information has been stored. It has been stored for optimal retrieval from long-term memory. The ability to organize information in a way that makes it readily accessible for a variety of situations is the mark of a champion. Information must be encoded so that it is flexible and available for transfer to new problem situations.

The infant paid attention to the surface features of the chess pieces—their color, taste, weight, and texture. That is how he would code and store the elements of his chess experience. The amateur and the expert tended to pay attention to deeper, structural features of the chess problem as it was presented to them. The chess novice would tend to store the experience as a specific series of moves to make if the situation came up again. The chess master would tend to recognize the experience as an illustration of, or a variant of, a principal or rule that might be of use in several future situations. As you can see, it is the expert who would profit most from the experience.

## ■ Adjustment and the Perceptual Cycle

In terms of cognitive control, the game of chess is similar to the game of life. To be able to profit from experience is the key to good adjustment. Chess is a continuous series of moves and countermoves, an adjustment problem. Successful adjustment is determined by what Neisser terms the *perceptual cycle* (see Figure 5.1). In this cycle, our original schema directs our sensory receptors (eyes, ears, and so on) and so influences what information we will pick up. This information modifies the original schema and so influences further search and subsequent responses. Our decisions (like moves in chess) can be no better than our information; our information can be no better than the schema that permits its reception. This complex relationship is known as the **encoding specificity principle**. Crocker (1982, p. 81) states it as follows: "what is stored is determined by what is perceived and how it is encoded, and what is stored determines what retrieval cues are effective in providing access to what is stored." All adaptive behavior, in life as in chess, is thus seen as beginning with a continuing set of skilled cognitive transactions.

## ■ The Rules of Life

Piaget also viewed the rules of life as being much like the rules of chess—part natural, part arbitrary. The arbitrary rules are imposed by society. Other rules

FIGURE 5.1
Our mental schema directs what objects we search for, and the nature of the objects we find influences both our future search and our mental schema.

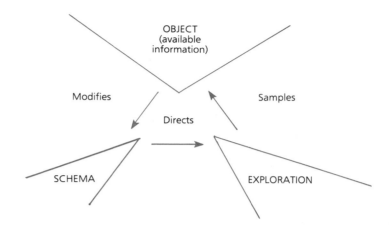

**PERCEPTUAL CYCLE**

are laws of logic, or *logico-mathematical knowledge*, that accurately reflect the laws of nature. These can be learned only by individual *invention*. (An invention, in Piaget's formulations, is anything conceived of through insight from an experimental manipulation of objects.) He believed that teachers who tell young children something only prevent them from inventing it themselves and thus hinder their development. He preferred problems to solutions and structured play to formal instruction.

■ *Inventing Mental Abstractions*    Just as actions on physical objects, such as balls, can produce an abstract concept of *ball*, so actions on several objects can produce abstract concepts that relate these objects to one another. Piaget (1964) has told the story of a child playing with pebbles. He lays them in a row and counts them from left to right. Next he arranges them in a circle and counts them once more. His count is always the same—ten. This concept—*ten*—was not to be discovered in any pebble; it existed only in the relations among the

## CASE IN POINT
## Learning from Play

In 1982, Emler and Valiant studied the use of pretending and play in the learning of cognitive skills. They concluded that play-training is successful to the extent that it does the following things:

1. Enhances involvement in play (because cognition is action).
2. Encourages reflection on pretending activities (which involves practice in focus and meaningful search).

3. Induces a verbal account of the rules that govern play (which provides encoding and retrieval practice).

**WHAT DO YOU THINK?**

■ *Can you apply these pretending and play rules to make your studying more effective?*
■ *Do you ever play-act in preparing for an exam?*

■ Playing with pebbles allows a child to become aware of (or invent) such concepts as size, weight, number, and pattern. Such concrete notions form the beginnings of both art and science.

pebbles. It had to be *invented* by the young child. Such rules relating objects to each other are found only in the mind. They are mental **operations**, or transformations of information received through action. To Piaget, such logico-mathematical experience is possible only because we live in an orderly universe.

At first, you remember, the child lives in a mystical, magical universe. Objects appear and disappear, events happen without cause, and time does not exist. As mental schemes develop through experience and maturation, a rich cognitive network becomes available for recall and association with each new experience. This creates more richness. Finally, by the time the child reaches puberty, his or her mind is capable of relating abstract concepts to other, equally abstract concepts. You may recall that Piaget termed this stage **formal operations**.

Young adults ponder the relationships between time and space, truth and beauty, and so forth. Such motivated inquiry, based on real-world experience but now free of its particularities, enables each of us to form conceptions of the laws of nature. Piaget believed that our collective cognitive structures can closely approximate the laws of nature as they exist because knowledge is cumulative. Long-term memory allows each generation to build on the past. Our very survival depends on our ability to discover properties of objects, to invent relationships among them, and to accept conventional wisdom.

■ *Social Information*  Social information, the conventional wisdom that makes up the other part of the rules of life, pertains to accepted ways of looking at or relating to objects or events. Such social information is learned in a less physically active manner. By telling or modeling a culture's collective folklore, older members transmit conventions to younger ones. This enhances the meaning and continuity of their lives. Examples of social information are: "That is a TV set" (labeling objects), "Polite boys open doors for their mothers" (folkways), and "Love America; it is the land of the free" (accepted feelings and beliefs).

According to Piaget, discoveries and inventions reflect reality and are constantly being restructured to resemble it more closely. Social information also reshapes cognition; but it does not reflect the realities of the laws of nature. Such social realities are important to adjustment, however; we live in two worlds, one dictated by nature, the other dictated by custom and tradition.

**WHAT DO YOU THINK?**

■ Which world places most demands on you at this time, the natural or social world?

REVIEW
QUESTIONS

*23.* Neisser's perceptual cycle represents the notion that mental activity is a (an) action / reaction / interaction between the organism and its environment.

*24.* Piaget believes that simple reflex schemata and highly complex schemata are alike in that both / neither are (is) formed via transactions with the real world and both / neither direct(s) the nature of subsequent transactions.

*25.* Part of our cognition of the real world is shaped by information contained in the _____ that strikes our eyes.

*26.* Superior intelligence / An extensive vocabulary of chess moves separates the chess master from the amateur.

*27.* The expert encodes / decodes information so that it is flexible and available for transfer to new problem situations.

*28.* Our adjustment decisions can only be as good as / be far better than our schemata for focusing on relevant data.

*29.* Crocker states that perception and information encoding determine what retrieval cues will be effective in gaining access to what is stored. T F

*30.* Knowledge of relationships, or logico-mathematical rules, exist only in the minds of people / in the properties of the objects themselves.

*31.* We dis_____ information about the nature of objects. We inv_____ information about the relationships among objects. We acc_____ information about cultural conventions.

*32.* It is important to know both the laws of nature and the laws of society if we are to make optimal adjustments to life. T F

*The answers to these review questions are on p. 172.*

## DISCUSSION: TIME, MEMORY, AND REALITY

Cognition can be viewed as a movement away from confusion toward order and stability. To be stimulus-bound, like the infant chess player, is to be controlled by the moment. Immediate experience must be integrated into large conceptual schemes if a meaningful, purposeful life is to be possible. Purpose implies desired movement toward a goal. Goal-directed behavior implies the cognition of time—in this case, future time.

## ■ The Time Factor in Cognition

Mental processes take time. A useful approach to understanding mental processes is to separate short-term activity from long-term activity for purposes of study. Our senses receive information (are stimulated) in temporal order. This time-ordered sequence must be transformed into simultaneous happenings if we are to make sense of our sensations. If all input faded as quickly as it was received, we would be paralyzed or reduced to spasms of uncoordinated motion. Survival demands that we be able to hold information in store while we process it in order to respond in a resourceful manner.

■ *The Psychological Present*   Our psychological present is made up of impressions that we rapidly integrate into a single unit of attention. Stimuli bombard us, but we can attend to only one event at a time. Thus, many inputs produce but one impression (Blumenthal, 1977). This rapid integration of experience takes place at intervals of approximately one-tenth of a second (White, 1963). Within each interval, all information, regardless of its source, is perceived as a unit. Sensations from our internal and external environments must compete with our recollections and new thoughts for attention. Stimuli not attended to disappear without a trace.

## ■ The Buffer Delay

When two events happen together, they are fused into one, or one is masked from consciousness. At times this is a great advantage, as when the parts of a puzzle are seen as one and the solution appears as a flash of insight. At other times it is a great disadvantage, as when the light turns green just as another car enters the intersection.

Fortunately, we are capable of rapid shifts of attention. Our mind does not normally shut down when it is overloaded—that is, when it receives more information than it can process. It can briefly retain the surplus information it receives. This retention is known as **buffer delay**—a short (about three-quarter-second) interval during which impressions are held as direct representations of the events of the past moment. These impressions are available for scanning if our perceptual schemata direct us to search them for additional information. Otherwise they fade forever without our being aware of their existence.

We must first attend to something if we hope to retain it. If eight-week-old infants noticed the connection between moving their feet and the movement of a mobile hanging above their heads (it was attached to their feet), they gave evidence of remembering it two weeks later. If they didn't notice it at the time, they gave no indication of recalling it later (Davis and Rovee-Collier, 1983).

> Sometimes dormitory life at college can be exasperating. Jackie wanted her roommates to be impressed with the beautiful, carved figurine that she had brought back from her Spring break in Fort Lauderdale. She didn't want them to ignore it and force her to draw attention to it herself.
>
> Jackie had a plan. First she casually placed the carving on the coffee table. Then she placed herself so that she could observe her friends as they entered the room. Sure enough, Jackie saw one girl glance at her "object d'art." No one said a word about it. Jackie quietly removed the piece and hid it in her room.

Two weeks later, not one person had mentioned the missing figurine! "OK, you win," thought Jackie. "Listen," she announced to her assembled roommates. "Two weeks ago, I hid something that had been in plain sight in this room. If any or all of you can tell me what it was, I'll take your next turn at cleaning the bathroom!"

To Jackie's surprise, only one girl stepped forward.

## ■ Short-Term Memory

We also have the capacity for a much longer delay, or buffer, involving information that was attended to but incompletely processed. This buffer is called **short-term memory**. We are able to hold information in our awareness after we have focused on it for ten seconds or longer. It is this capacity that makes us masters of our planet. Here is where intelligence, the ability to make adaptive choices, is to be found. Intentions may be recalled or generated, and information from our past may be combined with impressions of the moment and recent past. In these ten seconds, our past, present, and future are suspended in the same attentional *integration* (the same mental time and space) and can be scanned in order that we may give direction to our actions.

■ *Rehearsing Items in Short-Term Memory*   This glorious opportunity rapidly fades. In ten seconds or less we are reduced to the lower primate level—perhaps capable of brilliant insight, but limited to immediate reactions. We can overcome this mental limitation by *rehearsing*, or repeating information to keep it in short-term memory. Look up a telephone number at random. Do not repeat the number to yourself or write it down. After thirty seconds try to dial it without error. It is difficult not to rehearse such information, because this cognitive strategy has become so much a part of our everyday adjustment pattern.

It is also very difficult to retain complex information in short-term memory and at the same time perform complex operations on it. (Remember when we asked you, earlier in the chapter, to try adding seven-digit numbers in your head.) Both processes seem to occupy the same central psychological space. Perhaps it is difficult for you to retain specific statements you are reading while trying to relate them to cognition and adjustment. Stray thoughts, cognitions having absolutely nothing to do with psychology, may also intrude into your awareness, competing for the same mental time and space.

## ■ Long-Term Memory

Perhaps you also daydream while you study. Daydreaming is universal. In this way, we bring together, in short-term memory, separate impressions from events that happened at quite different times. This ability to reconstruct past events and fuse them with present integrations is included in what is termed **long-term memory**, or knowledge.

While impressions (rapid mental integrations) and immediate recall (short-term memory) are considered to be the product of electrochemical activities in the brain (Harter, 1968), long-term memory is considered to be a product of our own internal reconstruction (Neisser, 1967). The greater the time delay between exposure and recall, the greater the proportion of reconstruction found

■ Daydreaming is universal.

in the retrieved material (Singer, 1982). Konorski (1967) finds the neural processes that produce mental images to be widely distributed across the entire brain. Such processes direct the formation of Piaget's schemata and your daydreams. Your dream fantasy may represent a close approximation of events of your past, or it may be an original composition. Combinations of fact and fancy are equally possible.

## CASE IN POINT
# Cognitive Styles and School Performance

In general, schools reward a particular cognitive style (Shade, 1983)—an *analytical* style that requires focusing on external stimuli and categorizing abstract events in terms of certain features. The typical high achiever tends to process information using the analytical, hypothesis-testing approach. He or she is self-motivated, self-directed, and task oriented.

Another style is displayed by the intuitive thinker. Students who trust their intuition more than they trust "scientific fact," who require more motivation and direction, who are more people-centered and prefer global thinking, class discussions, student presentations and "hands-on" class activities find college much more difficult because they do not profit as much from lectures, textbooks, and handouts.

If you are an intuitive thinker, you can master the analytical cognitive style, now that you know what professors and most professions expect. Alternatively, you can shop for that occasional professor who uses student presentations, review sessions, study questions, and other means of motivating students by giving them a clear understanding of what they are to know. You can also profit from knowing that it is your right to obtain whatever structure and cues you need in order to learn. In short, you can change your cognitive style or take the trouble to get the help your natural cognitive style demands. We strongly recommend the latter.

### Study Aids

The findings of cognitive psychology support the notion that active study is most helpful. Encoding processes, such as the passive scanning of a text, are sufficient for immediate retrieval but are not usually sufficient for optimal long-term retention. You have to organize the information for future recognition or recall. Recognition and recall depend on similar information processing. In recognition, we quickly match our sensations with our perceptions by using cues from our past history, the environment, and the content of our problem. We use the same process in recall, with the difference that the matching takes longer. The term *search for associative meaning* (SAM) describes both recognition and recall (Gillund and Shiffrin, 1984).

Professors help you learn when they give you specific instructions to learn and inform you that you will be tested on the assigned material. In trying to anticipate what will be asked, you *organize* the information in a meaningful fashion; this encoding benefits long-term more than short-term retention. Without such organization, long-term recall is poor (Masson and McDaniel, 1981; Halpin and Halpin, 1982). Students who study for and take a test have been found not only to achieve more but to retain their learning longer than students who "study to learn" rather than study for a test (Singer, 1982).

If speed of recall is your problem and you can't complete tests on time, night classes may be for you. Tilley and Warren (1983) find that information retrieval is faster at night because of generally increased levels of mental arousal. Errors also increase, though; so if you are "quick but sloppy," an early morning class seems in order.

Many college classes demand the mastery of a great number of vocabulary terms. If the word you are to learn refers to a concrete object, something that occurs in nature and can be seen, the use of *vivid imagery* as an encoding device improves retention and retrieval. The

■ Cognition and Reality

From what has been said about cognition, you may have concluded that our world is largely of our own choosing (through perceptual schemata) *and of our own making* (through internal construction). It follows that at times it is difficult for us to be sure that what we are experiencing is really there. However, our original schemata are grounded in concrete actions on the real world, and our

■ Matching mood and memory: Is this person studying for a test on depression?

generation of similar images at both encoding and retrieval is a helpful strategy.

When encoding abstractions, words without concrete referents, the use of *verbal coding* produces significant improvement in retention. Memorizing definitions helps in these special cases. Finally, if you are mastering material that has a definite mood, such as a poem, painting, or period of history or culture, your retrieval will improve if you get yourself into a *similar mood* during both encoding and retrieval—while studying and again while being tested (Bower, 1981).

Cognitive psychology helps us adjust to the demands of learning by pointing to the importance of organizing new information into meaningful clusters *while studying* and connecting the new information with what is already known. The use of such **mnemonic** devices is supported by research (Camp, Markley, and Kramer, 1983). When we use mnemonic memory aids, we tie new information to letters of the alphabet, vivid images from our past, familiar story lines, and the like. The new information is recalled as the familiar story unfolds, for example. The introduction to this text gives additional aids for learning and remembering the material from this textbook.

### WHAT DO YOU THINK?

■ *What portion of class time do you think should be devoted to testing and review of test results?*

original mental constructions are immediately acted on or tested for reality. Thought and action in infancy are simultaneous events. Such stable, well-grounded knowledge forms a hard core of reality from which to distinguish fact from fancy. A part of this hard core of reality is our stable mental construction or schema for ourselves—our self-concept. Bower (1972) believes that we use self as a monitor of experience. Judgments of *self–not self* and *real–not real* flow from

*See Chapter 4 for more about body images.*

**WHAT DO YOU THINK?**

■ How do you go about separating fact from fancy?

thoughts, actions, and images that have become automatized through constant attention and repetition. Our body image, for example, is based on such continuous observations and comparisons. See Chapter 4 for more about body image. When impressions or mental constructs do not correspond to these stable mental models, we tend to reject their reality. We are even capable of training ourselves to monitor our dreams and alter the endings or awaken ourselves if they become disturbing.

## ■ Cognitive Dissonance Theory

Much interesting work is being done in investigating how our psyche works to bring its cognitions, feelings, and actions into harmony. **Cognitive dissonance theory** (Festinger, 1957) holds that we tend to reconstruct knowledge of our actions, beliefs, or feelings in order to balance them with each other. We seem to prefer a predictable world and a positive self-image. If, for example, we hear ourselves say one thing and then see ourselves do just the opposite, or if we discover that our best friend loves our worst enemy, we feel uneasy, guilty, or insecure. In order to reduce this psychological discomfort, or cognitive dissonance, we unconsciously reconstruct reality. We may manufacture a justification for our action, or fail to notice obvious but disturbing facts. We may deny our thoughts, feelings, or actions and be surprised to find that our attitude toward both our friend and our enemy has subtly changed.

We reduce mental contact by changing our perceptions of what really happened to us. As interesting as this is, it is more interesting to learn that Festinger finds that we consistently make the adjustment that is psychologically easier. If our beliefs are well-grounded in experience, for example, we will change our feelings or actions in order to preserve our beliefs. Because our behavior is often public, and thus more difficult to deny, we most often change our beliefs or attitudes to make them accord with our actual behaviors. Thus basic contact with reality is maintained even in the face of psychological adjustment.

In 1979, Festinger and Carlsmith directed college students to complete about thirty minutes of very tedious and boring work. As they were about to leave, each student was asked to tell the next subject what an exciting and thrilling task it had been! Some students were given twenty dollars for telling this white lie; others were given one dollar. After the lie had been told and the fee collected, the subjects were asked to rate for themselves the interest level of the original task. Which group of students do you think rated the dull task most interesting?

Most people predict that the ones who received the twenty dollars would change their opinion on the basis that "money talks." Money does talk. In this instance, what it said—through the students—was "I did it for the twenty dollars." Somehow this sounds more acceptable than "I'm an honest person but I just lied to my fellow classmate for one dollar." The group membrs who received a dollar couldn't deny what they had told the next subjects, so they convinced themselves that the task was really interesting. They were the ones who rated it higher. The twenty-dollar group could justify their lie, so they didn't need to change their attitude.

Cognitive dissonance acts as a drive state. If we are hungry or thirsty, we take action to find food or drink. In the same way, if we sense an inconsistency between our behavior and our attitude, we do something to reduce the tension produced by that knowledge. Each time we make a decision, we feel such dissonance.

> Parents are painful. If my parents knew I'd dropped Biology, they'd probably tell me to, "Get back into that lab or get yourself home!" I can't go back, either to the lab or home. I can't tell them.
>
> I'll have to tell them sometime. This is killing me. I know they can't afford for me to be dropping classes they've paid for. I also know I can't go back to that class. Maybe I'll write them a letter. No, I'll call Mom. She'll let me talk long enough to explain. On the other hand, Dad gets made quick, but gets over it just as quick. That's it, I'll call Dad and get it over with.
>
> The trouble is, no matter what I decide, I'll think I did something stupid. I'll feel bad no matter what I do.

■ *Postdecisional Depression*    Something like the anecdote above happens whenever we have to make a difficult choice. Immediately afterward we believe we've made the wrong choice and feel sad. Such postdecisional depression is quite common. We reevaluate the factors involved and elevate the importance of those that point toward the correctness of the choice we didn't take. The resulting anguish is usually short-lived. Because we cannot easily undo our choice, we quickly increase the importance of the factors that are consonant with our choice, and thus reduce our pain. We avidly read brochures extolling the virtues of the automobile we have just purchased, for example.

■ *Cognitive Dissonance and Foreseeable Negative Consequences*    College students demonstrated an interesting limiting aspect of cognitive dissonance. Students from Princeton, a small and exclusive university, were induced to record speeches favoring the increase of the next freshman class to twice the size of the traditional one. Some were told that their recorded message would not be used, others were told it might be used, and still others were told that it would be used to influence the college board of admissions to change its admissions policy.

■ Smoking demands beliefs in support of smoking in order to reduce cognitive dissonance.

All were told afterward that their message had been so used. They were then asked to evaluate the prospect of the next freshman class's being doubled. Since admitting a larger class was inconsistent with their narrow self-interest, a negative view was expected. This was what was recorded—from those students who had been told beforehand that their recorded message would or might be presented to the board. These Princetonians responded more favorably to the idea of a less exclusive university because it made them feel less guilty for what they had recorded earlier. Gothals, Cooper, and Naficy (1979) report that cognitive dissonance is produced only when negative consequences were or could have been foreseen prior to an inconsistent action.

Those who smoke and know smoking is dangerous to their health and obnoxious to those around them can obviously see negative consequences may result from their behavior. They are in daily mental conflict and must add beliefs consonant with their actions to support their repeated smoking behavior. "The link between cigarettes and lung cancer is only statistical." "My uncle smokes and he is seventy-five years old." "Smoking keeps me slim; fat people die of heart attacks." "Smoking relaxes me. Stress kills." "Have a cigarette." Dissonance is reduced if they can say, "Everybody I know smokes."

## ■ Cognitive Limits on Our Ability to Cope

The process of cognitive dissonance reduction helped the Uruguayan survivors cope with stark reality. At times, however, the physical bases of our mental processes place limits on our ability to cope with complex human problems. For example, as you recall, we can retain in short-term memory only a limited number of impressions (about six to eight) at one time. This places a limit on the complexity of problems we can successfully attack. Human adjustment problems are typically quite complex. They must be reconstructed into a series of simpler problems if they are to be resolved. Mental processes provide for such restructuring by making it possible to:

1. Focus our attention on relevant cues.
2. Delay processing of overload information until later.

## CASE IN POINT
## Living with Survival

On October 13, 1972, a Uruguayan Air Force plane crashed in the Chilean Andes. Sixteen people survived sixty-nine days of subzero temperatures and the constant threat of starvation. They were trapped in the wreckage with twenty-nine others who had died in the crash or shortly afterward. The survivors later revealed that they had stayed alive by eating the flesh of the dead.

They all held that cannibalism was horrible. In order to survive the awful knowledge of their actions, each survivor tried to reduce the gap between his beliefs and his behavior. One compared the cannibalism to a heart transplant, in which human organs are taken in by others so that they might live. Others found support in the tenets of their religious faith: They found a parallel between their actions and the ceremony of holy communion, in which each individual symbolically drinks the blood and eats the flesh of Christ so that he might live (Reed, 1974).

3. Bring together information from our past and present.
4. Transform impressions into long-term knowledge.
5. Scan these new constructions for meaningful cues.

These impressive capabilities enable us to select a potential solution and act on it or direct our actions toward further search.

33. If two or more events happen at the same time, we sense them as <u>one / more than one</u> impression.

34. A short, three-quarter-second delay in which incoming stimuli may be held for later processing is called a b_____ delay.

35. A longer delay after information has been focused on but not yet placed in long-term memory is called s_____ m_____ .

36. Reconstructed experiences, present stimulation, logical and social laws, and even present motivation may be held in one complex impression in short-term memory. T F

37. It is <u>easy / difficult</u> to hold information in short-term memory and process it at the same time.

38. Neisser believes that long-term memory is <u>a direct recording of past experience / a new, internal construction.</u>

39. Encoding processes sufficient for immediate retrieval <u>are / are not</u> usually sufficient for long-term retention.

40. The nature and function of long-term memory implies that our cognitive world is <u>of our own choosing / chosen for us.</u>

41. The cognitive style of the high achiever in college is usually <u>analytical / intuitive</u>.

42. Studying for a test produces <u>better / poorer</u> achievement and <u>more / less</u> retention than studying to learn.

43. When cognitions become unconscious and automatic habits, they are said to be au_____ .

44. Bower believes that we use our firm concept of self as a monitor of the reality of our impressions. T F

45. If we find that our best friend loves our worst enemy, our feelings toward <u>our friend / our enemy / both</u> may undergo cognitive and affective change.

46. Princeton students who had foreseen the consequences of their recorded messages felt the <u>most / least</u> cognitive dissonance.

*The answers to these review questions are on page 172.*

## DISCUSSION: COGNITION AND EMOTION

Long-term memory is a mental reconstruction of past events. When we directly experience an event, it evokes an emotional reaction is us; we are pleased, afraid,

*Chapter 6 discusses the emotional self.*

or angry, for example. Information from these affective reactions becomes a part of any later reconstruction or memory of that event. Emotion, then, forms a common background for all of our experiences and all of our knowledge.

Emotion is centered in areas of the brain that are ancient in origin. It is thought by some that cognition evolved in order to direct emotional reactions toward biologically significant events (Plutchik, 1980). Incoming stimuli must pass through these areas en route to higher cognitive centers. These primitive areas mature during our fetal and neonatal periods and are dominant during our infancy. Thus they shape and are shaped by our earliest experiences. Our first actions are emotional reactions. We cry in hunger or suck in joy. Pain and pleasure, sex and aggression are all experienced in the same region of our brain. Our earliest cognitions are thus intensely emotional in composition.

## ■ Affective Dispositions

If our first experiences are primarily positive, we tend to have positive **affective dispositions**, or habitual emotional reactions to present events. Many things make us happy. If our past was largely painful, current stimuli evoke painful associations, and we may develop negative emotional habits. These learned emotional predispositions form a basic portion of our self-concept and cognitive style of responding to life's events. Gordon Bower (1981) induced happy or sad moods in college students through hypnotic suggestions, sad movies, comedy tapes, and so forth. He found that when sad, subjects generated unhappy associations, were pessimistic, and often saw themselves as failures. Their thinking and acting were influenced by their mood.

**WHAT DO YOU THINK?**

■ Do you think a teacher must generate excitement in order to be a good teacher? Why or why not?

■ *Mood and Memory*    The cognitive process of retrieval or recall of information is strongly influenced by the emotional climate in which the information was learned. Bower had his subjects try to recall events from their past that they had recorded in a daily diary. Recall of childhood events and personal experiences were better when the material they were attempting to remember fit the mood induced during the experiment. This is why teachers, preachers, politicians, and all good salespeople try to stimulate you emotionally before presenting their message. Emotion plays a basic role in all our cognitive processes.

■ *Mood and Information Processing*    Schafer and Murphy (1943) found that emotional information reaches our brain and helps determine what we will attend to or integrate into our experience. As emotion links our needs and habitual dispositions to present happenings, it motivates us and directs our further activities. If we are thirsty, we attend to cues that have an association with quenching thirst, for example. In the language of Piaget, emotion restructures our schemata and thus is basic to cognitive control. Amnesia, repression, and Freudian slips all attest to the link between emotion and central cognitive processing. *Freudian slips* are slips of the tongue in which we inadvertently say just what we unconsciously wanted to say but were reluctant to say because of social conventions.

■ *Pain Perception*    The curious link between pain and ongoing mental activity demonstrates the central role **affect** plays in cognition and adjustment. Have

■ Soldiers from all wars often reported relief, not pain, from serious injuries sustained on the battlefield.

you suffered injury while totally involved in an activity and been unaware of the pain? Soldiers often report relief, not pain, from severe injuries sustained on the battlefield (Beecher, 1959).

Acupuncture, placebos, and such pain-reducing practices as the **directed focusing** and **controlled breathing** used in natural childbirth classes are thought to owe their degree of success to the fact that our minds have a limited capacity for central processing, and the perception of pain requires some of this capacity. Just as most of us cannot hold twelve numerals in our head and process them arithmetically, so we cannot maintain the perception of pain while our mind is otherwise fully engaged.

Betty is ready. For more than six of the last nine months, Betty and her husband have been training for this moment. It is two in the morning and everything is going well. The x-rays were normal, and the fetal heartbeat is strong and regular, perhaps a bit fast. Just like they were taught to expect.

"Awake and Aware" seems to be a much better way to have a baby than either the saddle block or the general anesthesia Betty received in delivering her previous children. This third delivery should be over quickly.

Just as her baby is making its first presentation in this world, a loud and terribly profane wail is heard from the next room. *"Kill me. I can't stand this. I want to die!"* Alone, ignorant, and afraid, the tension and pain is too much for the young expectant mother next door. Her terror is heightened by the fact that her doctor is not present.

"You seem to be under control, Betty. See if you can slow things down a bit. I'd better take care of the next room or you're baby's first word will be a curse!"

With that, Betty's doctor leaves. Betty and her husband, alone with their almost newborn child, begin to earnestly apply the breathing and pain-control techniques that they had practiced almost in jest. Hold that tiger.

*47.* Plutchik believes that cognition evolved to direct emotional reactions toward biologically significant events. T F

*48.* Emotion / Cognition / Attribution forms a common background for all our personal knowledge.

*49.* Another name for our habitual emotional reactions is our af_____

dis_____ .

*50.* According to Schafer and Murphy, behavioral / cognitive / emotional information motivates and helps direct our search for new information.

*51.* If our first experiences were largely happy, we will be likely to develop positive / negative / neutral emotional habits.

*52.* Amnesia, repression, and Freudian slips attest to a link between emotion and central cognitive processing. T F

*53.* Emotional information helps in determining which stimuli we will attend to or search for. T F

*54.* No matter how fully our minds are engaged, we will always be able to sense the pain of a serious injury. T F

*The answers to these review questions are on page 173.*

## DISCUSSION: SELF-TALK

The great contribution that cognitive theorists have made to adjustment psychology is the notion that a great deal of what we feel and do is directed and controlled by what we think. We do not have to accept the primacy of cognition to make use of its insights in helping ourselves and others. Many clinical psychologists believe that thinking (intellectualizing) acts to prevent our getting at the heart of an adjustment problem. They hold the problem to be deficient or excessive emotionality. They place emotions first. Some behavioral psychologists believe that gaining cognitive insight, or verbally knowing the roots of a problem, is of little value in appropriately altering behavior. They place behavior first. Most clinical psychologists are **eclectic** (they choose their ideas from many sources) and **pragmatic** (they are practical). They tend to use what works in attempting to help their clients. There is growing evidence that a combination of interventions—that is, altering thoughts, feelings, and behaviors—is superior to a more pure form of insight, sensitivity, or behavioral therapy alone (Meichenbaum, 1977).

**WHAT DO YOU THINK?**

■ Is it possible for a teacher or parent to be consistently warm, relaxed, and rewarding with a hyperactive child?

### ■ Reciprocal Causation

Our behavior does not seem to be determined by external events alone. Our cognitive makeup is also important. **Reciprocal causation**, or the interaction of multiple factors to produce a single effect, is illustrated by Albert Bandura's observation that "If a child realizes that misbehavior will get him nowhere, he stops." The behavior of stopping is not merely a function of external punishment but also of new cognitions, new understandings, on the part of the child (Orton and Phillips, 1983).

Even hyperactive children, who seem to overreact to the slightest stimulation, are chiefly directed by an interaction of sensations, perceptions, and emotions. If such children perceive that they are accepted and that the demands placed on them by others are reasonable, their episodes of hyperactivity are significantly reduced (Peter, Allen, and Horvath, 1983).

## ■ Internal Dialogue and Self-Control

**Internal dialogue**, the flow of conscious events that goes on in our heads, is important in guiding all types of behavior. Donald Meichenbaum (1969) has been successful in training hospitalized schizophrenic patients to emit "healthy talk" while being interviewed by teaching them to instruct themselves to do so during the course of an interview session. He believes that self-talk aids us in attending to the task at hand. It also prevents distracting stimuli from hurting our performance. A number of his trained subjects actually repeated aloud the verbal instruction: "Give healthy talk; be coherent and relevant" while they were being interviewed. Vygotsky (1962) defines *intelligence* as the ability to benefit from instructions, including self-instructions.

As adults, we do not usually repeat out loud the speech that is directing our behavior. However, this was not always so. Luria (1961) proposes a three-stage process by which voluntary motor acts come under verbal self-control in humans. At first, the speech and gestures of significant others direct a child's behavior: "That's a good girl; put your toys in the toy box." The next step involves the child's talking out loud while regulating her own behavior: "Toys—box—good

■ Self-talk can control our feelings and actions.

## CASE IN POINT
## Crippled Children

Billy and Lori are quiet children. They are well behaved but not really thoughtful. They do what they are told. In school, the teachers say that they are no trouble, but they seem to be slowly falling behind the other children in classroom performance. As school work becomes more complicated and the children are asked to plan and complete increasingly complex tasks, Billy and Lori seem more and more lost.

Their parents use a "no-nonsense" approach to raising hard-working, God-fearing young-sters. Their father lays down the law and backs it up if he has to. Their mother says little; she just expects her children to mind. "Don't ask

why, just do it—and don't try to talk me into anything, either."

Such authoritarian parental attitudes are often expressed in the liberal use of external punishments and the restricted use of verbal reasoning in producing home discipline. Children from such homes are handicapped be-cause they have had little practice in using spon-taneous speech to obtain help and little training in using internal speech to direct and control their own behavior. They enter school with this handicap, and it becomes more damaging as the years roll by (Camp, Swift, and Swift, 1982).

**WHAT DO YOU THINK?**

■ Do you think you silently talk to yourself as you go about your daily routines?

girl." Finally, the child will be governed by covert, or inner, speech while putting the toys away and feeling good about herself.

Inner speech is not always silent. When you are performing a task you have mastered, and all is well, you are not aware of your inner dialogue. It is un-conscious. Under stress, however, speech fragments appear in consciousness or are actually uttered aloud (Gal'perin, 1969). You may be driving your car, performing all the requisite motor tasks unconsciously and efficiently, when the image of a police car appears in your rear-view mirror. At once you become painfully aware of your every driving act. You may well hear yourself saying aloud, "slow down, left turn signal," and so on.

■ *A Positive Mental Image*   By the way, when a skill is mastered and regulated by silent internal dialogue, the conscious stating of the governing instructions hinders performance. In bowling, for example, it is beneficial to rehearse mentally prior to each shot. You go over what you intend to do and how you intend to do it. It is important to focus on the intended outcome, to create a positive mental image of success in attaining the goal (a strike or spare). While making the shot, however, it is beneficial to eliminate everything from your mind except the spot or line you intend to roll the ball over. Repeating instructions to yourself while bowling interferes with the body-mind coordination that all your practice has built up.

■ Inappropriate Self-Talk

People who have adjustment problems frequently engage in inappropriate self-talk. For example, both aggressive and impulsive children tend to emit immature verbalizations while engaged in problem-solving tasks (Camp, 1975; Meichen-baum, 1977).

■ For a strike, concentrate on the image of yourself making a strike.

In an interesting study of male university students who rarely dated and who had high anxiety concerning interpersonal relations, it was found that while they rated their own social performance as ineffective, an objective rating indicated that they actually had as many social skills as men who dated often (Glasgow and Arkowits, 1975). Their difficulty lay in their cognitive deficits, not their physical attractiveness or social skills. Twentyman, Boland, and McFall (1981) found infrequent daters to be victims of a low level of interaction with members of the opposite sex. They were less knowledgeble about social cues and less skillful in interpreting their effect on others. Added to these mental handicaps was a cognitive style that labeled social setbacks, such as being turned down, as catastrophic. This caused them to avoid initiating interactions with attractive females.

"Apparently, a fear of failure is less of a problem to high frequency daters, some of whom reported making many unsuccessful overtures toward women for every instance of success—with little effect on their self-confidence" (Twentyman, Boland, and McFall; 1981, p. 544.). Negative self-talk, rather than real success or failure, seems to have controlled the feelings and actions of the infrequent daters.

*Noncreative* people are also prone to engage in negative self-statements, verbal attacks on themselves (Patrick, 1937). They tend to label themselves as noncreative and to put down their own efforts and probability of success.

All of us have had some experience with negative self-talk. When we notice something unusual concerning our own behavior, some sign that our efforts are not working, we usually respond with an internal dialogue "comprised of negative self-statements and images, which likely have deleterious effects" (Meichenbaum, 1977, p. 217). Meichenbaum goes on to say that we rarely consider the role our own thinking plays as a source of our poor performance.

■ Negative self-talk may stand between Jim and his desire to interact in this social situation.

## ■ Irrational Beliefs

The basic premise of cognitive therapists is that emotional suffering and inappropriate behavior are due to irrational mental constructions of events and faulty assumptions about the reactions demanded by these events. These assumptions lead to an internal dialogue that, in turn, gives rise to negative emotions and faulty behavior (Ellis, 1962). For example, if you enter a crowded room thinking everyone is staring at you and making remarks about you, you may feel anxious, or depressed, or infuriated and may as a result walk with an air of bogus superiority, or resignation, or animosity. Your feelings and actions are the direct result of your thinking process and the specific content of your thoughts.

*For a more complete list, see Chapter 3.*

Albert Ellis, the founder of **rational-emotive therapy**, lists the following as common sources of misconceptions about the true nature of everyday events:

1. I must be loved or approved of by everyone.
2. I must not make errors or ever do poorly on anything I undertake.
3. People and events should always be the way I want them to be.

Another, more fundamental irrational belief is that a person's worth as a human being is solely dependent on, and determined by, the opinions of other people. The specific cognitive beliefs outlined above lead to a rigid self-evaluation. "I must be perfect to be loved. I must be loved by all." They also lead to a rigid evaluation of others. "Everyone should think and act as I believe they should." To a person who has internalized such a belief system, the world is composed of people and events that are forever disillusioning, tragic, or threatening.

## ■ An Irrational Cognitive Style

Such irrational beliefs lead, it is believed, to an irrational cognitive style. This habitual style of thinking is variously termed "catastrophising," "awfulizing,"

## CASE IN POINT
## Destructive Beliefs

Each of us learns a system of verbal rules that we come to accept as true. This network of assumptions acts as the filter for our experiences. Automatically it guides our attention and directs our responses. Unfortunately not all of these beliefs are literally true; not all will stand up to objective analysis and reflective reasoning. The untrue portion of our belief system accounts for many of our problems of adjustment.

Below you will find two listings of destructive beliefs. The first is associated with general emotional discomfort; the second is more specifically related to emotional depression.

*List 1.* Beliefs associated with general emotional discomfort (Ellis, 1973, p. 37):

a. It is an absolute necessity for an adult human to be loved or approved of by virtually every significant other person.

b. One should be thoroughly competent, adequate, and achieving in all possible respects to consider oneself worthwhile.

c. Certain people are bad, wicked, or villainous, and they should be severely blamed and punished for their villainy.

d. It is catastrophic when things are not the way one would like them to be.

e. It is easier to avoid than to face life's difficulties and self-responsibilities.

f. Human unhappiness is externally caused, and people have little or no ability to control their terrors and disturbances.

g. One's past history is an all-important determiner of one's present behavior; and, if somethng once strongly affected one's life, it should definitely continue to do so.

*List 2.* Four common misconceptions of the genuinely depressed (Raimy, 1975):

a. I will be depressed forever.

b. No one understands the depth of my misery.

c. If I get any more depressed, I will lose my mind.

d. If I recover at all, recovery will take a long time and will be incomplete.

and "musterbating" (Ellis and Harper, 1976). Every nonperfect event is viewed as being catastrophic and as demanding that something be done. The irrational cognitive style involves making a series of *contingency statements* (*if, then* statements), with the "then" always a tragedy or a must. An extreme example of this thinking style is the following progression:

- *If* I do not make a perfect score on this exam, *then* I will fail the course.
- *If* I fail the course, *then* I will not be admitted to graduate school.
- *If* I am not admitted to graduate school, *then* I cannot train for my profession.
- *If* I cannot train for my profession, *then* I will be a failure in life.
- *If* I fail in life, *then* no one will want me or love me.
- *If* one is unwanted and unloved, *then* life is not worth living.
- Therefore, *if* I do not make a perfect score on this exam, *then* I might as well end my worthless life.

**WHAT DO YOU THINK?**

- Do you think showing a bit of charity toward your own mistakes would help or hinder your growth?

Although this example is extreme, the increasing suicide rate among young, healthy, intelligent college students testifies to the presence of such tortured internal dialogue.

## ■ Catastrophic Fantasy

We are typically not quite so dramatic in the presentation of our private fears. However, we all engage in some catastrophising. Fritz Perls (1969) uses a similar concept, called **catastrophic fantasy,** to describe the tendency to rob ourselves of present joy because of a largely unconscious fear of being unmasked—of being revealed to all as a fake, unworthy of the respect and love of those we admire.

*See the discussion of self-fulfilling prophecy, p. 65.*

Our negative expectations, or irrational beliefs, can also become automatized. These beliefs then apear spontaneous and compelling. Such cognitions may lead to maladaptive actions that produce the very effect the irrational belief predicted, thus confirming and reinforcing the cognitive style. While we all entertain irrational expectations at times, we usually manage to contain or repress such dysfunctional thoughts and act on more realistic assessments of the events that confront us (Meichenbaum, 1977).

## ■ Cognitive-Behavioral Interventions

Beck (1976), a cognitive-behavioral therapist, teaches his clients to recognize and monitor their own cognitions. Largely by keeping careful records, his clients learn to use specific examples of their own behavior to test the validity of their cognitions and to become aware of the negative effect of irrational beliefs on their emotions and subsequent actions. With the help of therapy, distortions in thinking and dysfunctional thinking styles are uncovered, examined, and made more realistic. For example, the statement "My whole week was a disaster" might be examined in terms of the assignments given and accepted for the week and in terms of any accomplishments made during the week and recorded on the mandatory activity record. Alternative and less catastrophic interpretations are encouraged, and changed cognitions and behaviors are elicited and reinforced. Beck finds such an approach superior to nondirective and supportive procedures in the treatment of emotional disorders, especially depression.

R. L. Ownby (1983) reports an interesting application of cognitive-behavioral intervention in helping a thirteen-year-old boy overcome compulsive hand washing. The boy became anxious about being accepted in a new school, and resorted to washing his hands over forty times a day in an attempt to control this dreadful anxiety. The strategy was simple and effective. First the boy was instructed to count and record each instance of hand washing. When he was painfully aware of the extent of his washing behavior, rational-emotive discussions of fears and compulsions were begun.

The technique of *thought stopping* was then introduced. First the boy would be asked to *ruminate,* to think again and again of his fears concerning the new school. While he was so engrossed, the therapist would shout "Stop!" Of course, this halted the stress of anxious thoughts. The boy was then taught to monitor his own thoughts and to silently shout "Stop" to himself when they were leading him toward a strong need to wash his hands. He was then instructed to focus his attention on visualizing a pleasant scene in which there was no need for fear or compulsion. By employing this simple series of interventions, the child was able to regain control of his thoughts and emotions and to become better adjusted to his new environment.

### ■ Cures for Addictions

It is in youth and childhood that many of the "bad habits" are formed that continue to plague us throughout our adult lives. For example, the attitudes and expectations that lead the adolescent to begin smoking soon vanish, but the addiction to cigarettes is not so quickly lost.

Stanton Peele, a social psychologist, finds that four components have to be present if a person is to cure himself or herself of an addiction:

*1.* An urge to quit, an unhappiness with the addiction that cannot be rationalized away.

*2.* A moment of truth, a belief that you must quit, that no one can quit for you, and that you can quit.

*3.* A change of identity, an image of self in which the rewards of living become greater than the pleasures of addiction.

*4.* The sure knowledge that one slip does not mean a return to permanent addiction (Peele, 1983).

### ■ *Losing Weight*  Constructing rational alternative beliefs is a determining factor in overcoming an addiction. Compulsive eating, leading to obesity, is another bad habit often grounded in childhood experiences. Baker-Strauch (1982) has identified some good predictors of a client's responsiveness to treatment. If you

■ Image yourself as a beautiful, slim person just before starting to eat.

take responsibility for your fatness, believe that you can change, and do not believe that society is victimizing you because you are fat, then your chances of losing weight and keeping it off are improved. Using mental imagery to picture yourself as a beautiful, slim person just prior to sitting down to eat is also an effective weight-reducing cognitive technique.

### ■ Cognitive Deficits of Clinical Patients

Larry, having failed a college algebra exam, is afraid that he is terrible in math, can never pass college algebra, and therefore must give up his dream of becoming an accountant. The situation appears hopeless.

In near desperation, Larry meets with his algebra professor. He learns from her that his mathematical reasoning, as demonstrated in class discussions, is excellent. The professor asks a few questions and then tells Larry there are several glaring gaps in his high school training in algebra. She offers Larry the use of a programmed text in algebra, a self-paced book that will allow Larry to catch up on his preparation for college work. She notes that Larry views math as an endless series of steps to memorized and emphasizes that math is instead a language, a tool for precise thought.

Larry begins to reconceptualize his problem. He is weak in math skills, but thinks well in mathematical terms. He now knows that math is a tool for thought. His deficits are not overwhelming, and he has access to both text and teacher to help him overcome them. He wants to be an accountant, and an extra semester of study, or the use of a math tutor, does not seem too high a price to pay for a chance at a life-long career.

Nothing, and everything, has changed. Larry has still failed his college algebra exam, but somehow now that does not seem to be so terrifying.

Beck (1970) finds that his clinical populations, like Larry, tend to:

1. Make faulty inferences (draw conclusions inconsistent with available evidence).
2. Exaggerate the negative meaning of events.
3. Ignore important data that disconfirm a belief.
4. Oversimplify events as being all good or bad, right or wrong.
5. Overgeneralize the importance of a single event—for example, view a poor test score as a sign of a worthless life.

Imagine, for example, that you find yourself playing golf in a foursome with three strangers. They know each other and, after giving you a courtesy greeting, stick pretty much to themselves. If you (1) inferred that their lack of involvement with you signified that they did not respect you, you could (2) feel insulted and resentful, and (3) not be aware of the little courtesies of the course that *were* being extended to you during the round, and (4) conclude that they were deliberately insulting you. If you saw this as confirmation that you lacked worth as a person, you could (5) view the entire round as a catastrophe.

**WHAT DO YOU THINK?**

■ Do you think you can change your self-talk and improve the quality of your life?

### ■ Post-Treatment Changes in Cognitive Style

After successful therapy, Beck's clients are reportedly more aware of what they fail to say to themselves that would help (cognitive deficiencies) and what thoughts or thought patterns interfere with adaptive responses (cognitive excesses). Such clients become more capable of viewing negative events as disappointing rather than tragic and *unfortunate* rather than catastrophic.

Cognitive-behavioral therapists also teach new beliefs, such as: (1) that it is irrational to expect others to act as you think they should act; (2) that it is not necessary to be loved or approved of by everyone; and (3) that the disapproval of others is not proof of inadequacy. As a result of such rethinking, clients' assessments of themselves and others become more positive and supportive. In their work "Mistakes That Can Ruin Your Life, and How to Avoid Them" Lazarus and Fay (1975) list the most common mistaken beliefs, explain them, and give instructions on how to rethink and change to avoid making them in the future.

When we learn to view cognitions as behaviors that can be modified, *learned helplessness* (the belief that we are powerless to change life's circumstances) can be restructured to become *learned resourcefulness* (the belief that we can systematically improve existing conditions.) Goldfried and Goldfried (1975) train their clients to generate a series of statements that instruct them to:

1. Identify problems.
2. Produce alternative solutions.
3. Subject each to logical and/or empirical tests.
4. Repeat this sequence until a satisfactory adjustment is made.

*See the discussion of goal setting and decision making on p. 473.*

Recently, a comprehensive cognitive–social learning model for social skill training was tested and found to be effective (Ladd and Mize, 1983). The model featured three basic training objectives:

1. *Enhancing social skill concepts.* This means building concrete images of what skillful behavior looks like.
2. *Promoting skillful performance.* This means giving opportunities for the practice of correct mental and behavioral responses.
3. *Fostering skill maintenance and generalization.* This means providing opportunities for follow-up training and for appropriate application of the new skills in a variety of social situations. "This requires training in self-evaluation and self-adjustment" (p. 156).

## ■ Mastery of the Cognitive Self

In brief, by modifying our understanding of our cognitive selves, we can learn to:

1. Attend to important events.
2. Focus on relevant cues within each event.
3. Rationally reappraise problem situations.
4. Flexibly scan long-term memory stores for appropriate meanings and associations.
5. Modulate excessive, deficient, or inappropriate emotionality.
6. Initiate a problem-solving series of behaviors leading to an increased probability that we will arrive at an adaptive response and act on it.

In short, by becoming aware of our cognitive selves, we can learn to reconstruct our self-talk so that it becomes an automatized pattern of resourceful thinking rather than a considerable part of our adjustment problems.

55. According to cognitive-behavioral theory, cognitions are behaviors that <u>cannot / can</u> be modified.

56. Self-talk, including silent and unconscious inner speech, is termed <u>in_____</u> dia_____ by cognitive theorists.

57. Luria believes children's internal dialogue is developed in three stages: (A) using silent speech, (B) using speech fragments, (C) acting on adult speech. The correct developmental sequence is: (A,B,C), (B,C,A), (C,B,A).

58. Immature verbalizations <u>were / were not</u> found to be typical of aggressive and impulsive children.

59. Meichenbaum believes that <u>rarely do we / we often</u> give adequate consideration to the role our negative self-statements play in influencing our emotions and actions.

60. Beliefs have little or nothing to do with success in changing diet and smoking habits. T F

61. We all have irrational beliefs, but clinical populations have difficulty repressing or compartmentalizing them and acting on more rational cognitions. T F

62. List two irrational cognitive processes that Beck reports to be typical of his clients

_____ .

63. After successful treatment, cognitive therapy clients tend to label negative events as <u>unfortunate / catastrophic.</u>

64. Goldfried and Goldfried replace negative self-talk with self-instructions to engage in problem-solving. T F

*The answers to these review questions are on page 173.*

## SUMMARY

■ It is possible to treat aspects of mental operations with scientific precision and formulate laws describing the basic nature of cognition.

■ *Cognition* is the act of making sense of experience. It is the acquisition, organization, and use of knowledge.

■ Our control of cognition is limited by our ability to focus on important events and search our memory for meaningful connections to apply to adjustment problems or to direct further search.

■ The process of cognition includes attending to, organizing, storing, and retrieving information.

■ Jean Piaget believed cognition to be a product of action that grows from interactions between the mind and the environment.

■ A *schema* is a mental outline or diagram as simple as a grasping reflex or as complicated as a plan for college graduation. Schemata allow us to move away from confusion and rigidity and toward order and flexibility.

■ Mental processes, such as those used in buffer delays and short-term memory, allow us to perceive life as a stream of information and to hold information in store long enough to process it further.

■ Long-term memory, or knowledge, is a product of internal mental reconstruction. It represents choice and change and is not an exact replica of past events. Our cognitive world is grounded in reality but is largely of our own choosing and our own making.

■ Our mental processes place a limit on our ability to cope with the demands of reality. Human adjustment problems typically must be recast into a series of simpler problems.

■ Emotion forms a common background for all our knowledge. It strongly influences our search for and acquisition of information. It also affects the meaning we give to events we perceive.

■ A great deal of what we feel and do is directed by what we think—our internal dialogue.

■ Irrational beliefs form the content of inappropriate cognition. Such beliefs, when automatized, appear spontaneous and compelling, but are in fact learned dysfunctional behaviors.

■ Faulty cognitive beliefs and styles of thinking are considered behaviors that can be modified.

■ Learned resourcefulness can replace learned helplessness when we use functional self-talk to cope with problems of adjustment.

## Selected Readings

Blumenthal, A. *The Process of Cognition*. Englewood Cliffs, N.J.: Prentice-Hall, 1977. Basic notions of how the mind works and how to control its workings.

Greenspoon, J., and Lamal, P. A. "Cognitive Behavior Modification—Who Needs It?" *Psychological Record* 28 (Summer 1978) 343–351. A biting critique of this general approach to adjustment.

McMullin, R. E., and Giles, T. R. *Cognitive-Behavioral Therapy: A Restructuring Approach*. New York: Grune & Stratton, 1981. A brief, step-by-step outline of specific techniques.

Meichenbaum, D. *Cognitive-Behavior Modification: An Integrative Approach*. New York: Plenum Press, 1977. A book that beautifully describes cognitive change through client-therapist interaction.

Morowitz, H. J. "Rediscovering the Mind." *Psychology Today* (August 1980): 12–18. Reflective thought seen as a major change in our physical universe.

Phillips, L., Jr. *The Origins of Intellect: Piaget's Theory*, 2nd ed. San Francisco: W. H. Freeman, 1975. Piaget and his ideas of cognitive methods of inquiry related to American psychology and education.

Posner, M. *Cognition: An Introduction*. Glenview, Ill.: Scott, Foresman, 1973. A fascinating history of the study of memory and thought.

Rubenstein, C., "Regional States of Mind," *Psychology Today* (February 1982): 22–30. Patterns of emotional life in nine parts of America.

Scarf, M. "Images That Heal." *Psychology Today* (September 1980): 32–46. An exploration of the growing faith in the mind's powers to heal.

Stark, E. "Hypnosis on Trial." *Psychology Today* (February 1984): 345–346. How accurate is memory produced via hypnotic suggestion?

## Glossary

**accept:** demonstrate a willingness to receive something as true, right, or proper; to Piaget, a passive behavior.

**accommodation:** adaptation of mental schemata to better fit incoming data.

**affect:** emotion, feeling, or mood.

**affective disposition:** a customary frame of mind, nature, mood, or temperament.

**analytical thinker:** one who uses the self-motivating, self-directing, rational cognitive style associated with high college achievement.

**assimiliation:** absorption of new data into existing mental structures; involves responding to something novel as if it were familiar.

**automatize:** perceive and respond without conscious attention or deliberation.

**brain structure:** the arrangement of the various parts that comprise the brain.

**buffer delay:** a brief absorption of sensory input. Information is held in its original form for 0.05 to 2.0 seconds.

**catastrophic fantasy:** an unreal image that depicts an impending calamity, disaster, or misfortune.

**cognition:** the process of acquiring, storing, retrieving, and revising knowledge.

**cognitive-behavioral therapy:** an integration of the techniques of behavior therapy with the insights of semantic (speech) theorists.

**cognitive control:** the act of choosing what to attend to and what response to formulate and act on so as to maintain a coherent path toward a goal.

**cognitive dissonance theory:** theory relating to the effects of perceived inconsistencies between beliefs or between beliefs and feelings or actions.

**controlled breathing:** the voluntary regulation of breathing so as to reduce the perception of pain and the urge to contract the uterus during the last stages of delivery.

**directed focusing:** fixing of attention on an object for an unbroken period of time so as to reduce anxiety, tension, or the perception of pain.

**discover:** act on objects in order to uncover the properties of these objects, according to Piaget.

**eclectic:** choosing fragments from among varying doctrines without regard for the internal consistency or possible contradiction arising from an analysis of the choices.

**encoding:** transforming information to make it easy to store in long-term memory and retrieve as needed.

**encoding specificity principle:** The relationship among perception, long-term memory, and recall of stored information.

**epistemology:** the investigation of the origin, nature, methods, and limits of knowledge.

**formal operations:** the fourth and last of Piaget's stages of cognitive development; characterized by manipulation of abstractions.

**internal dialogue:** the soundless speech that makes up much of what goes on in our heads, our private verbal worlds.

**long-term memory:** knowledge. This part of memory involves persistent, organized, and often automatic ways of cognitive processing. Terms for mental structures related to long-term memory are *symbol, schema, concept,* and *attentional set.*

**mnemonics:** systems for improving memory.

**operations:** internal transformations of information from one form to another, producing new structures that modify the object of knowledge.

**pragmatic:** in philosophy, relating to a system that tests the validity of concepts or procedures by their practical results.

**rational-emotive therapy:** a technique for (1) determining the properties of upsetting events, (2) identifying specific beliefs that give rise to negative emotions, and (3) helping clients to alter these beliefs so as to improve behavior.

**reciprocal causation:** the interaction of multiple factors to produce a single effect.

**schema:** Piaget's term for a mental construct we generate to organize experience (the plural is *schemata*).

**short-term memory:** the part of memory that holds impressions for five to twenty seconds for monitoring or restructuring.

## REFERENCES

Alloy, L. B., and Tabachnik, N. "Assessment of Covariation of Humans and Animals: The Joint Influence of Prior Expectations and Current Situational Information." *Psychological Review* 91 (1984): 112–149.

Baker-Strauch, D.; Hartigan, K. J.; and Morris, G. W. "Perceptions of the Causes of Obesity and Responsiveness to Treatment." *Journal of Counseling Psychology* (September 1982): 478–484.

Barr, R. A. "How Do We Focus Our Attention?" *American Journal of Psychology* 94 (December, 1981): 591–603.

Beck, A. *Cognitive Therapy and Emotional Disorders.* New York: International University Press, 1976.

———. "Nature and Relation to Behavior Therapy." *Behavior Therapy* 1 (1970) 184–200.

Beecher, H. *Measurement of Subjective Responses.* New York: Oxford University Press, 1959.

Blumenthal, A. L. *The Process of Cognition*. Englewood Cliffs, N.J.: Prentice-Hall, 1977.

Bower, G. H. "Mood and Memory." *American Psychologist* 36 (February 1981): 129–148.

———. *"A Selective Review of Organizational Factors in Memory."* In *Organization of Memory*. Edited by E. Tulving and W. Donaldson. New York: Academic Press, 1972.

Camp, B. "Verbal Mediation in Young Aggressive Boys." Unpublished manuscript, University of Colorado School of Medicine, 1975.

Camp, B. W.; Swift, W. J.; and Swift, E. W. "Authoritarian Parental Attitudes and Cognitive Functioning in Preschool Children." *Psychological Reports* 50 (1982): 1023–1026.

Camp, C. J.; Markley, R. P.; and Kramer, J. J. "Naive Mnemonics: What the 'do-nothing' control group does." *American Journal of Psychology* 96 (Winter 1983): 503–507.

Chase, W. C., and Simon, H. A. "The Mind's Eye in Chess." In *Visual Information Processing*. Edited by W. G. Chase, New York: Academic Press, 1973.

Crocker, P. R. E. "Encoding Specificity in Short-Term Memory for Movement Information: A Comment on Lee and Hirota (1980)." *Journal of Motor Behavior* 14 (1982): 81–85.

Davis, J., and Rovee-Collier, C. K. "Alleviated Forgetting of a Learned Contingency in 8 Week Old Infants." *Developmental Psychology* 19 (October 1983): 353–365.

Ellis, A. *Humanistic Psychotherapy*. New York: McGraw-Hill, 1973.

———. *Reason and Emotion in Psychotherapy*. New York: Lyle Stuart Press, 1962.

Ellis, A., and Harper, R. A. *A New Guide to Rational Living*. Hollywood, Calif.: Wilshire Book Co., 1976.

Emler, N., and Valiant, G. L. "Play and Cognition: Studies of Pretense, Play, and Conservation of Quantity." *Journal of Experimental Child Psychology* 33 (February–June 1982): 257–265.

Festinger, L. A. *A Theory of Cognitive Dissonance*. Stanford, Calif.: Stanford University Press, 1957.

Feuerstein, R. *Instrumental Enrichment: An Intervention Program for Cognitive Modifiability*. Baltimore, Md.: University Park Press, 1979.

Gal'perin, P. "Stages in the Development of Mental Acts." In *A Handbook of Contemporary Soviet Psychology*. Edited by M. Cole and I. Maltzman. New York: Basic Books, 1969.

Gibson, J. J. *The Senses Considered as Perceptual System*. Boston: Houghton Mifflin, 1966.

Gillund, G., and Shiffrin, R. M. "A Retrieval Model for Both Recognition and Recall." *Psychological Review* 91 (January 1984): 1–67.

Glasgow, R. E., and Arkowits, H. "The Behavioral Assessment of Male and Female Social Competence in Dyadic Heterosexual Interactions." *Behavior Therapy* 6 (1975): 488–498.

Goldfried, M., and Goldfried, A. "Cognitive Change Methods." In *Helping People Change*. Edited by F. Kanfer and A. Goldfried. New York: Pergamon Press, 1975.

Gothals, G. R.; Cooper, J.; and Naficy, A. "Role of Foreseen, Foreseeable and Unforeseeable Behavioral Consequences in the Arousal of Cognitive Dissonance." *Journal of Personality and Social Psychology* 37 (1979) 1179–1185.

Halpin, G., and Halpin, G. "Experimental Investigation of the Effects of Study and Testing on Student Learning, Retention, and Ratings of Instruction." *Journal of Educational Psychology* 74 (February 1982): 32–37.

Harter, M. R. "Excitability Cycles and Cortical Scanning: A Review of Two Hypotheses of Central Intermittency in Perception." *Psychological Bulletin* (1968): 47–58.

Konorski, J. *Integrative Activity of the Brain: An Interdisciplinary Approach*. Chicago: University of Chicago Press, 1967.

Ladd, W., and Mize, J. "A Cognitive–Social Learning Model of Social-Skill Training." *Psychological Review* 90 (April 1983): 127–157.

Lazarus, A., and Fay, A. "Mistakes That Can Ruin Your Life, and How to Avoid Them." *Good Housekeeping* (October 1975): 64–76.

Luria, A. *The Role of Speech in the Regulation of Normal and Abnormal Behaviors*. New York: Liveright, 1961.

Masson, M. E. J., and McDaniel, M. A. "The Role of Organizational Processes in Long-Term Retention." *Journal of Experimental Psychology* 7 (Summer 1981): 100–101.

Meichenbaum, D. *Cognitive-Behavior Modification: An Integrative Approach*. New York: Plenum Press, 1977.

_____. "The Effects of Instructions and Reinforcement on Thinking and Language Behaviors of Schizophrenics." *Behavior Research and Therapy* 7 (1969): 101–114.

Melton, G. B. "Toward 'Personhood' for Adolescents: Autonomy and Privacy as Values in Public Policy." *American Psychologist* 36 (January 1983): 99–103.

Neisser, U. *Cognition and Reality: Principles and Implications of Cognitive Psychology.* San Francisco: W. H. Freeman, 1976.

_____. *Cognitive Psychology.* New York: Appleton-Century-Crofts, 1967.

Orton, R., and Phillips, D. C. "The New Causal Principle of Cognitive Learning Theory: Perspectives on Bandura's Reciprocal Determinism." *Psychological Review* 90 (April 1983): 158–165.

Ownby, R. L. "A Cognitive Behavioral Intervention for Compulsive Handwashing with a Thirteen-Year-Old Boy." *Psychology in the Schools* 20 (April 1983): 8–12.

Patrick, C. "Creative Thought in Artists." *Journal of Psychology* 4 (1937): 35–73.

Peele, S. Reported in, "One Approach to Addiction: Cure Yourself." *Miami Herald* (September 29, 1983): 1B.

Perls, F. *Gestalt Psychology Verbatim.* Lafayette, Calif.: Real People Press, 1969.

Peter, D.; Allan, J.; and Horvath, A. "Hyperactive Children's Perceptions of Teachers' Classroom Behavior." *Psychology in the Schools* 20 (April 1983): 234–240.

Phillips, J. L., Jr. *The Origins of Intellect: Piaget's Theory,* 2nd ed. San Francisco: W. H. Freeman, 1975.

Piaget, J. "Development and Learning." *Journal of Research in Science Teaching* 2 (1964): 176–186.

Pines, M. "Baby, You're Incredible." *Psychology Today* (February 1982): 51.

_____. "Can a Rock Walk?" *Psychology Today* (November 1983): 46–54.

Plutchik, R. *Emotion: A Psychoevolutionary Synthesis.* New York: Harper & Row, 1980.

Raimy, V. *Misunderstandings of the Self.* San Francisco: Jossey-Bass, 1975.

Reed, P. P. *Alive.* New York: Lippincott, 1974.

Schafer, R., and Murphy, C. "The Role of Autism in Visual Figure-Ground Relationship." *Journal of Experimental Psychology* 32 (1943): 335–343.

Schwartz, R., and Gottman, J. "A Task Analysis Approach to Clinical Problems: A Study of Assertive Behavior." Unpublished manuscript, Indiana University, 1974.

Shade, B. J. "Cognitive Strategies as Determinants of School Achievement." *Psychology in the Schools* 20 (October 1983): 488–493.

Siegler, R. S. "Five Generalizations about Cognitive Development." *American Psychologist* 38 (March 1983): 263–277.

Singer, M. "Comparing Memory for Natural and Laboratory Reading." *Journal of Experimental Psychology* 3 (September 1982): 331–346.

Tilley, A., and Warren, P. "Retrieval from Semantic Memory at Different Times of Day." *Journal of Abnormal Psychology* 92 (August 1983): 718–723.

Twentyman, C.; Boland, T.; and McFall, R. M. "Heterosocial Avoidance in College Males." *Behavior Modification* 5 (October 1981): 523–552.

Vygotsky, L. S. *Thought and Language.* Cambridge, Mass.: MIT Press, 1962.

White, C. T. "Temporal Numerosity and the Psychological Unit of Duration." *Psychological Monographs* 77 (1963): 12.

## ANSWERS TO REVIEW QUESTIONS

**Page 136.**  *1.* virtually unlimited  *2.* cognitive  *3.* limited  *4.* to notice relevant cues, to search meaningfully  *5.* develop  *6.* is  *7.* possible  *8.* time, space  *9.* psychological  *10.* focusing attention

**Page 141.**  *11.* follows an orderly pattern  *12.* physical activity  *13.* filter through  *14.* T  *15.* schemata  *16.* assimilation  *17.* accommodation  *18.* generalizations

*19.* automatized  *20.* frees us for  *21.* T  *22.* T

**Page 146.**  *23.* interaction  *24.* both, both  *25.* light  *26.* An extensive vocabulary of chess moves  *27.* encodes  *28.* only be as good as  *29.* T  *30.* in the minds of people  *31.* discover, invent, accept  *32.* T

**Page 155.**  *33.* one  *34.* buffer  *35.* short-term memory  *36.* T  *37.* difficult  *38.* a new, internal construction   *39.* are not   *40.* of our own choosing   *41.* analytical   *42.* better, more   *43.* automatized   *44.* T   *45.* both   *46.* most

**Page 158.**   *47.* T   *48.* Emotion   *49.* affective dispositions   *50.* emotional   *51.* positive   *52.* T   *53.* T   *54.* F

**Page 168.**   *55.* can   *56.* internal dialogue   *57.* (C,B,A)   *58.* were   *59.* rarely do we   *60.* F   *61.* T   *62.* They make faulty inferences, exaggerate the negative meaning of events, ignore important data, oversimplify events, and overgeneralize the importance of a single event.   *63.* unfortunate   *64.* T

# EMOTIONAL SELF

## FOCUS

How do you feel? Close your eyes and relive a moment when you were keenly alive. Allow the memory to fill your consciousness. Do not rush, but experience again the special occasion.

What dominated your recollection? Was it vivid images? Did smells, sensations, or actions come most clearly to mind? For most of us, our richest memories bring forth a rush of emotion. The joy, anger, fear, or embarrassment associated with the occasion never fades, while other details recede from memory.

In all its many forms, emotion constitutes a necessary and precious part of our lives. It is emotion that makes living worthwhile, for without the richness and even the disruptions of our emotions, our lives would be barren and robot-like. Joy, empathy, love, and happiness are the wellsprings of optimism and hope. Even grief, fear, and anger, when they are not overwhelming, add texture and fullness to human existence. Positive emotions can spur and direct our growth, and negative ones can alert us to the need for change in our lives.

**6**

EMOTIONAL
SELF

## DISCUSSION: EMOTION AND SURVIVAL

Each of us has experienced strong emotion. We think we can recognize a strong emotional state in ourselves and in others. But the very concept of emotion becomes fuzzy when psychologists try to define it for study. Sometimes emotions are treated as a cause for behavior: "He hit me because he was angry." At other times, they are viewed as a result of behavior: "He was angry at himself for hitting me." Whether cause or effect, emotions need definition.

### ■ Defining Emotion

An **emotion** is an intense, relatively uncontrollable feeling that affects, and is affected by, our thoughts and actions. Emotions have been defined in terms of motivational states, subjective feelings, internal changes, facial expressions, and overt acts. Emotions can involve all of these, but only one is always a component of any aroused state. Emotions always involve internal bodily changes. We may cry in sadness, frustration, or joy. Our faces may remain placid while we fume. We are even capable of being completely unaware of the rage or hurt being expressed in our voices. No matter how we fool ourselves or others, we cannot experience an emotion without having changes take place in our nervous systems, internal organs, muscles, and glands. It is emotion defined *as an internal bodily change* that has received the greatest attention in modern times.

### ■ The Seat of Emotion

If Elizabeth Barrett Browning had been writing in the time of William Shakespeare, her famous question, "How do I love thee? Let me count the ways," might have been answered: "with all my liver." In biblical times in the Near East, the answer might have been: "with all my genitals." In ancient Rome and in our own time, it is answered: "with all my heart." For the last three hundred years, however, scientists, if not the general public, have known that the brain is the source of our emotional behavior. (In ancient Greece, Aristotle thought the brain could *not* be the center of emotion because the brain was insensitive to pain. He believed the brain was the radiator of the blood.) Only within the last ninety years have scientists begun the process of pinpointing the precise neural structures involved in the cognitive, skeletal, and **visceral** (internal organ) activity necessary for us to feel and express emotion. Thus, a modern, scientific answer to the question "How do I love thee?" might be as follows:

> *How do I love thee?*
> *Let me count the ways:*
> *I love thee with my cerebellum and cerebral cortex.*
> *I love thee with my neurotransmitter substances.*
> *I love thee with my hypothalamus.*
> *I love thee with my DNA molecules.*
> *But most of all,*
> *I love thee with my pituitary excretions.*

### ■ Evolution and Emotion

Charles Darwin published *The Expression of the Emotions in Man and Animals* in 1872. He held that emotions are the products of evolutionary history and are therefore innate. Darwin reported that basic emotions are the same across all human races, and that neither age nor culture seriously distorts emotional expression. Plutchik's research (1980) supports the contention that emotions are innate. He believes there are but eight **basic emotions**: fear, anger, disgust, sadness, acceptance, anticipation, surprise, and joy (see Table 6.1).

Moreover, Izard (1977) found that most students from nine cultures agreed about the basic emotion being expressed in posed photographs presented to them. Natives of Borneo and New Guinea also agreed on the emotions thus displayed.

### ■ Learned Emotional Expression

While basic emotions may be innate, elaborate emotional expression is learned. The radio and television comedian Jack Benny would place his hands on his hips, open his eyes wide, and puff one word—"Well!"—to express strong emotion. The audience had learned to anticipate this funny emotional message.

### ■ Emotion and Physical Survival

To Darwin, basic emotions are universal among humans because they have *survival value*. Emotions represent a successful adjustment, or adaptation, to specific environmental demands—an example of the survival of the fittest. Emotions may be classified as either **prosocial** or **antisocial**.

■ *Antisocial Emotions*   The bared fangs and claws of a threatened cat are recognizably antisocial. They ready the cat for defense or attack. This mobilization

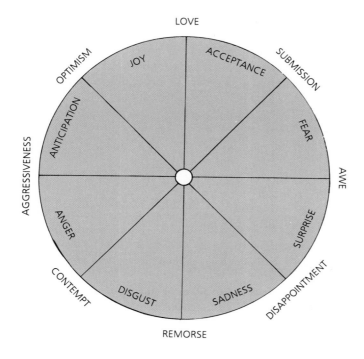

TABLE 6.1
Plutchik's emotion "wheel," showing the eight primary emotions and "dyads" resulting from mixtures of adjacent primaries. The wheel plots the similarities among emotions—and what they produce when mixed—as described by lab subjects. Thus, the primaries fear and surprise, when combined, yield the dyad awe, and joy mixed with acceptance leads to love. (From Plutchik, 1980b. Reprinted from *Psychology Today Magazine*. Copyright © 1980. Ziff-Davis Publishing Company.)

## CASE IN POINT
# Computer Smiles

Facial expressions provide crucial information about an individual's internal mood state, but are difficult to quantify. We report . . . a mathematical method for measuring facial expressions, using photographs and a specially designed computer programme. (Thornton and Pilowsky, 1982)

It is difficult to base hard science on soft evidence. Ekman and Friesen (1976) have attempted to use a *Facial Action Coding System* to reduce facial expressions to numerical values to answer the question "are there universally recognized emotional expressions?" The movements of specific facial muscles can help answer that question, if they can be measured with precision. Ekman and Friesen use trained raters to assess visible muscle differences. The difficulty is that human raters differ in their evaluation of what muscle action is present in a given photograph. If humans can't agree on what is being presented, how can they measure the degree to which other humans recognize what emotion that specific presentation communicates?

Using a photograph of a neutral expression as a starting point, Mark Thornton and Issy Pilowsky have constructed a computer model of a face that can change with mathematical precision (see Figure 6.1). Perhaps now we will be able to measure with accuracy the degree to which people of different ages and cultures can estimate the mood of a subject when viewing a standard image on a computer screen. This, in turn, may help us finally determine if Darwin was correct.

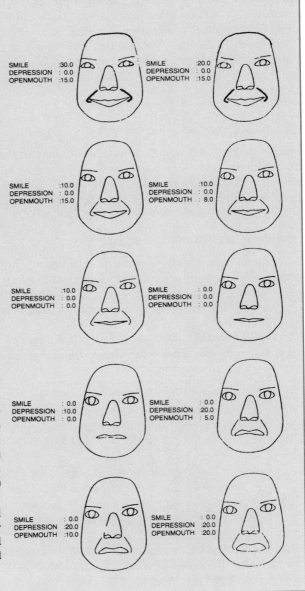

FIGURE 6.1 Mathemathically modelled facial expressions as presented on graphics display screen. (The expressions have been combined for convenience. They are normally displayed individually).

**WHAT DO YOU THINK?**

■ Make a sneering face. Do your fangs (incisors) show? Why?

of energy either to fight or to flee is one of the chief products of emotion (Cannon, 1929).

In addition to direct survival value, Darwin saw *signal value* in the physical expression of anger. Antisocial postures, sounds, and gestures signal to a foe an impression of the sender's size, strength, and willingness to fight. Such displays have indirect survival value because they lead to the dominance within a species of certain individuals and reduce actual combat.

■ *Prosocial Emotions*   Emotional signals that represent submission also facilitate survival; the successful attacker will seldom kill the submissive rival. These submissive signals may be considered prosocial. In aggressive animals, the prosocial emotions of courtship (acceptance, anticipation, surprise, joy, love, passion, affection) also have survival and signal value. Courtship rituals suppress aggression, ready the organism for mating, and signal a willingness to mate (the sociobiologists would add, "and to protect").

■ *Of Frogs and Men*   Darwin observed that facial expressions, gestures, and reflexive acts such as elimination are associated with fear in a continuous series of higher forms of life. If you pick up a frightened frog, you run the risk of a wet hand. Have you noticed that you frequently go to the bathroom just before an exam? These antisocial emotional responses are similar, although millions of years of evolution separate you from the frog. If an animal meets a dangerous predator and does not feel fear, it may not flee, and may not live to reproduce. Sociobiologists propose that every emotion has some survival value (Chance, 1980).

REVIEW QUESTIONS

*1.* An emotion is a feeling state / an internal change / a tendency to act / all of these.

*2.* The response that is a part of all emotional experience is facial expression / subjective feeling / internal change.

*3.* Emotions have been described as the cause / an effect / both cause and effect of behavior.

*4.* Darwin held that emotions can best be understood in terms of evolutionary history / special creation / inclusive fitness.

*5.* To Darwin, emotions have _____ value and _____ value.

*The answers to these review questions are on page 215.*

## DISCUSSION: THE DEVELOPMENT OF EMOTIONAL EXPRESSION

The emergence of emotions, especially love, in young children has fascinated parents for generations. The development of emotional potential has recently received a good deal of research.

■ First Emotions in Infancy

Children cannot feel or express all emotions at birth, but they are born with the capacity to develop an ability to sense and express a wide range of emotions freely and appropriately. It is the greatest challenge of parenthood to provide the infant and toddler with the warmth, acceptance, stimulation, patience, firmness, and freedom necessary for these innate potentialities to unfold.

   Newborn infants display few emotions. They are either asleep, quiet and alert, mildly distressed, or very upset. With great sensitivity they shift in and out of these few moods quickly. It is not unusual to find a newborn irritable one moment and contented the next.

WHAT DO YOU THINK?

■ Why do you think responding does not encourage the infant to cry more?

*See page 167 for a discussion of learned helplessness.*

■ *First Cry*  The first cry is a defensive emotional expression, a message that something is wrong. Bowlby (1969) sees this cry as an instinctive signal that releases maternal behavior. A mother can distinguish her child's cry from that of other children within hours of its birth and can interpret her child's cries within days. For example, a cry of pain is unmistakable and impels a mentally healthy caretaker to respond immediately. A baby's cry will elevate blood pressure and perspiration levels in normal adults (Frodi, 1978).

According to Ainsworth (1967), "letting the baby cry it out" may well be the first conflict between mother and child, a conflict producing the first steps toward emotional tension in the infant. Regular, prompt responding to an infant's cries leads both to a closer bond between caretaker and baby and to less frequent and more appropriate crying by the baby. In extreme cases, when a baby stops crying because crying brings only fatigue and never help, the beginnings of **depression** may have been initiated (Seligman, 1975). Knowledge that nothing we might do can possibly improve our condition is related to depression in animals and in humans.

■ *First Fear*  The cry of fear does not appear until about seven months (Scarr and Salapatek, 1970). The expression of fear is a function of mental growth. This can be seen in the progression of factors that trigger the fear response. At first, physical sensations, such as a sudden noise or a loss of support, are necessary. Later, the perception of heights or strangers will suffice. Finally, the dark, now filled with imagined creatures, can elicit fear.

■ *First Smile*  The first smile, so precious to parents, does not display the emotion of love. The newborn is not yet capable of experiencing joy, love, or hate. General excitement and, later, delight or distress may be the first felt

■ By three months, smiling is a common response in a healthy baby. Smiling helps reassure loving caretakers close at hand.

emotions (Bridges, 1932). The first smile is a response to random firing of neurons in the primitive areas of the brain and not an adjustment to any outside stimulation (including hugs and kisses). The intriguing fact is that the infant's facial muscles are, at birth, capable of giving expression to any emotion. A smile, however caused, is the most easily recognized emotional expression and has the effect of building an attachment with the parent. A ready smile is thus an important adjustment in infant survival and remains a social asset throughout life.

■ *First Love*   Love seems to be born between two and five months after birth (Mahler, Pine, and Bergman, 1975). This first love is a perfect union between the mother and the infant, because the two-month-old cannot yet distinguish between self and caretaker. The first sign of infant love is the spontaneous social smile. By three months, this is common in a healthy, developing baby. The fact that this beautiful smile is generously offered to any sight that resembles a mother's face is important to survival. It keeps a caretaker close by and responsive because of its reinforcing properties.

■ *First Anger*   You will hear no laughter from a two-month-old, but you may witness rage. This stormy emotion is generalized in the infant; it is produced by physical discomfort or frustration and is not social rage. The two-month-old may be extremely angry, but not at you.

## ■ Intellectual Growth and Emotion

The development of emotional responses is linked to the infant's intellectual growth. In a four-month-old, a gentle tickle may produce a laugh. This was not possible earlier. It is evidence of the first appearance of a sense of self, an awareness of a selfhood distinct and apart from others. Have you ever tried to tickle yourself? You cannot do it, nor can you successfully tickle an infant until he or she has gained a sense of independent existence. Growing independence and ample opportunity to express it seem to be necessary parts of the development of **emotional maturity**, the appropriate and effective use of emotion.

Our range and selectivity of emotional expression grow as we mature intellectually. A growing memory gives the baby the ability to differentiate between friends and strangers, and the generous social smile becomes restricted to friends. **Stranger anxiety**, a protective antisocial emotion, appears in the seven-month-old. Fretting, crying, and clinging may be produced even by people who are not total strangers. However, the fact that the seven-month-old may swing from grief to contentment in a matter of seconds indicates that this memory is still primitive.

## ■ Physical Development and Emotion

Physical development and emotions also are linked. Between eight and fourteen months, when infants become toddlers, an entire range of new emotions comes into focus. Now able to move at will, toddlers often place themselves in physical danger. They then observe fear, anger, and worry in their caretakers while feeling arousal in themselves. They do damage, and again grief and anger are displayed for them to observe. Toddlers demand much of their mothers' time, and the jealousy of the fathers and older children is often conveyed to them in subtle and not-so-subtle terms. Their attempts to explore and manipulate their expanding world lead to repeated frustrations. Frustration in infants quickly turns to aggression. The mother, in an attempt to curb this disturbing, emotionally driven activity, may employ the dubious strategy of introducing guilt into the emotional world of the toddler.

> Little Terry has energy to burn. From the moment he opens his eyes in the morning, to the last battle to stay awake at night, he is constantly on the go. Thank God for the playpen.
>
> The playpen keeps him safe and within bounds. It allows Nancy, his mother, to enjoy the relative luxury of picking up after him in peace. It is usually a short-lived peace. No matter how many attractive toys Nancy keeps in the playpen, no matter how often she changes them, within minutes of being plunked down, Terry wants out. The devil with the playpen.
>
> It is difficult to tell who is more frustrated, Nancy or the toddler. Cries, shouts, and threats fill the air as reason gives way to raw emotion.

Because of their physical growth, toddlers daily come into direct and vicarious contact with frustration, grief, anger, and anxiety, as well as pride, joy, and love. Their lives become emotionally enriched. This physical and mental growth also gives toddlers occasion to hear the names associated with these subjective feelings. Later they will use these names to label their own emotional sensations.

*See Chapter 2 for a discussion of conditioning.*

### ■ Negativism

At about two and a half years of age another stage of emotional development arrives. A two-year-old who causes damage, heartache, or anxiety does it in innocence. Two-year-olds are absorbed in exploring and manipulating. If things get broken, it is the result of a friendly accident, not planned malevolence. At two and a half, this may not be the case. By this time, children have learned to say "no."

**Negativism** is actually another sign of a developing sense of self. That you have a choice, that you *can* say "no" and act in defiance of rules, is a powerful discovery to a child not yet three years old. A sense of mastery, of control, is awakened in this blossoming mind. However, if these early assertions are completely indulged, temper tantrums and prolonged emotional infancy will likely result. Such children can become immature adults, forever crying, yelling, or moping in order to get their own way.

**WHAT DO YOU THINK?**

■ Can you say "no" without feeling guilty?
■ If not, why not?

■ *Physical Punishment and Reduced Emotional Capacity*   If, at the other extreme, these assertions are physically crushed in the toddler, especially if rejection and coldness accompany the punitive countermeasures, repression, excessive shyness, and an inability to respond emotionally can become part of the child's personality. Severe punishment, especially physical spanking, reaches its peak against the two-and-a-half-year-old. Those spanked often and harshly are found, on the average, to be "quieter, less articulate, and more sullen" later in life (Gilmartin, 1979). In our culture, boys receive three times as much physical punishment as girls. This may be one factor responsible for the fact that our men cannot express their feelings as well as our women. Many suffer social and physical consequences because of this reduced emotional capacity.

*See Chapter 7, on stress.*

■ *The Importance of Negative Feelings*   Burton White, in *The First Three Years of Life* (1975), stresses the importance of negative feelings in the development of emotional stability. At three, the child's vocabulary includes the phrase "I hate you." This is usually said in frank honesty and, if taken as a valid expression of the moment, is quickly replaced by other emotions. Such honesty is too often intolerable to parents, however, and the children are taught to deny or repress their own feelings: "You don't really feel that way. Only bad children hate their Mommies!"

*See Chapter 7, on stress.*

> "I hate you! I hate you! I hate you, Mommy!"
> No one told Cindy that being a mother would always be fun. But no one told her that the little bundle she nursed and rocked so lovingly would, just three years later, scream and yell and kick at her, either. And all because Cindy wouldn't let her little girl pour the milk for daddy at dinner.

The expression of negative feelings may include a predisposition to kick, swing, or bite. Refusing to accept this antisocial behavior will *not* blunt the child emotionally. With firmness, gentleness, and a sense of humor, parents can teach the child to distinguish among feelings, the acknowledgment of them, and the hurtful expression of them. In general, it is best if parents allow their toddler the greatest freedom of negative expression that they can tolerate. In any case, children have a right to be taught not to deny or reject their feelings, but rather to accept and express them in ways that are within the bounds of group living. Thus spontaneity and openness and consideration and thoughtfulness may be combined in healthful ways in our children.

If the toddler is treated with gentle firmness and allowed to win at times, an emotionally strong, assertive, and affectionate young child will emerge. Only when you know that you can choose to say "no" and survive, only when you know that you have the right of opposition, can you freely express the right to

■ Spontaneity, openness, consideration and thoughtfulness are hallmarks of emotionally healthy children.

*See Chapter 3, on self-esteem, for related topics.*

say "yes," to cooperate by choice. By the age of three, the emotionally healthy child has developed his range of emotional responding and has learned to leave negativism largely behind (White, 1975).

The ability to feel deeply and to express pleasures and pains appropriately to love ones, workmates, and friends alike constitutes a hallmark of emotional health. The biological expression of emotion, necessary for survival in animals, finds its greatest expression in humans if, during their first years, they learn self-acceptance and the ability to get along with others.

REVIEW
QUESTIONS

*6.* Newborn infants shift emotional states <u>quickly</u> / <u>slowly</u>.

*7.* Letting a child "cry it out" <u>strengthens</u> / <u>weakens</u> the bond between caretaker and child and leads to <u>more / less</u> crying.

*8.* The first sign of positive emotional expression associated with love is <u>following with the eyes</u> / <u>smiling</u> / <u>the social smile</u>.

*9.* The child will laugh at a gentle tickle at <u>birth / four months</u>.

*10.* The anger, grief, and anxiety caused by the two-year-old is <u>deliberate / willful / incidental</u>.

*11.* Physical punishment is associated with quiet, sullen, and inarticulate older children. T F

*12.* During the first three years, children should be allowed the <u>greatest / least</u> amount of negative emotional expression that is tolerable to the parents.

*The answers to these review questions are on page 215.*

## DISCUSSION: A THEORY OF EMOTION

The infant is delightful because its emotional expression is quick, complete, and honest. You know just where you stand with an infant. This is not so with an adult. We mask our feelings. To understand emotions, then, we must examine internal sensations as well as external expressions.

**WHAT DO YOU THINK?**

■ Do you believe that an employer owns your smile during your working hours?

> Gina, the airline flight attendant, was tired. Her feet were tired. Her shoulders were tired. But most of all, her face was tired. As she worked in the rear of the plane, cleaning up after the in-flight meal, Gina heard the dreaded words "Why aren't you smiling?" "You smile first," she answered without looking up and without emotion. The traveler broke into a big grin. "Fine," said Gina, "Now freeze, and hold that expression until we land in Miami."
>
> Contrast the tyranny of the frozen professional smile with the exultation of an infants's quick, spontaneous smile. What effect do you believe forced smiling has on our emotions?

### ■ Three Dimensions of Emotion

*See Plutchik, 1980, for an example of such a theory.*

Internal sensations are often used in explanations of **motivation**, the purpose behind our actions. Common sense says that emotions initiate action. "You see a bear, feel afraid, and run." This vivid example, cited a century ago (James, 1884), can be used to illustrate the three dimensions of an emotion that must be addressed by any comprehensive theory—the cognitive, motor, and visceral responses associated with the emotion.

Today, an emotion is often thought of as an "action set" (Lang, 1983) or as "a patterned bodily reaction" (Plutchik, 1980) brought about by a stimulus. This complex state of arousal is assumed to have a survival potential. In modern humans, this affective state is thought to be the product of both biology and social learning (Averill, 1983).

## ■ Emotion as a Bodily Reaction

To analyze an emotion, let us start with the bear in "You see a bear." First there must be an appropriate stimulus event, the bear. Second, it must receive our attention.[1] Next this stimulus must be seen as a bear. We must discriminate the bear from a tree trunk, for example. At the same time, a cognitive appraisal of the meaning or significance of the presence of a bear must be made. (We do not have to have complete information to react emotionally to this meaning.) We are stimulated to gain access from long-term memory to our conceptual information about bears, the danger of bears, and the social norms pertaining to expected responses to the presence of a bear in the context in which we find ourselves (Schachter, 1962; Lang, 1983; Averill, 1983). Every society has such norms—"feeling rules" about how people should feel and act in various situations (Hochschild, 1979).

*See Chapter 5 for more on cognition.*

Now we come to the next phase of our story. You "feel afraid and run." The cognitive process mentioned above releases a *response set* that involves at least three patterns of behavior: (1) affective language behavior to describe the event and our feelings toward it (our subjective state of feeling fear); (2) overt motor behavior to act out the reactions expected of us under the perceived circumstances (our running); and (3) visceral support for these motor behaviors (our hearts' pounding).

Finally, our description of emotion as a set of patterned bodily reactions would not be complete without repeating that current theory holds that the cognitive, motor, and visceral responses stimulated by the bear have survival value. In this case, we run to protect our life.

## ■ The Social Purpose of Emotion

Remember that our whole body and mind respond as one to an emotion-provoking event. Also remember that humans respond within a set of learned social rules that organize the emotion, and that these rules serve a social purpose, what sociobiologists would call the inclusive fitness of the group (Averill, 1983). For example, if you saw a bear, and were in charge of young children, you might organize your emotion as anger and find a means of attacking the bear or at least keeping it at bay. An antisocial emotion may be prosocial with respect to the protection of one's own family.

## ■ The Many Facets of an Emotion

Emotions are complex; they have many facets. They can be seen as dispositions to approach or avoid a stimulus object (the bear). This is why we can feel the

---

1. However, we do not have to be consciously aware that we are attending to the bear (Lazarus, 1982), nor must the bear be really there.

emotion (fear) even if we do not carry out the motor response (running). Emotions can be classified as being either pleasant (like happiness) or unpleasant (like sadness). Another facet of emotions is that they can dispose us to attend to a stimulus object (through acceptance, joy, anticipation) or reject it (through disgust or loathing). If we are in conflict as to how to respond to a stimulus, our emotions may dispose us to disorganization (anxiety, dread). Finally, an important facet of any emotion is its intensity. Fear and terror differ only in intensity, as do joy and ecstasy.

Table 6.2 shows Plutchik's formulation of the complex events involved in the development of an emotion. It is interesting to note that Plutchik believes that the effects in the table represent universal patterns of behavior that are emitted by all complex organisms. The emotions associated with each of the eight effects are the basic emotions (see Table 6.1), and all our other emotional sensations are complex combinations of these eight.

**WHAT DO YOU THINK?**

• Can all that you feel be derived from eight emotions?

REVIEW
QUESTIONS

13. Today an emotion is seen as a complex bodily reaction. T F

14. We no longer believe that emotions serve purposes of survival. T F

15. We cannot cognitively process information that we are unaware of. T F

16. An emotional stimulus can release language responses, motor responses, and visceral responses within us. T F

17. Human emotional response follows a pattern of social norms that are learned and shared among group members. T F

18. Emotions are unidimensional. Each may be classified in one and only one way. T F

19. Our emotions help organize us for action; they are never a force for disorganization. T F

20. Plutchik believes that each of the eight basic emotions is associated with an effect that represents a universal pattern of behavior for all complex organisms. T F

*The answers to these review questions are on page 215.*

TABLE 6.2

Sequence of Events Involved in the Development of an Emotion

| STIMULUS EVENT | INFERRED COGNITION | FEELING | BEHAVIOR | EFFECT |
|---|---|---|---|---|
| Threat | "Danger" | Fear, terror | Running | Protection |
| Obstacle | "Enemy" | Anger, rage | Hitting | Destruction |
| Potential mate | "Possess" | Joy, ecstasy | Courting, mating | Reproduction |
| Loss of object | "Isolation" | Sadness, grief | Crying for help | Reintegration |
| Group member | "Friend" | Acceptance, trust | Grooming, sharing | Affiliation |
| Gruesome object | "Poison" | Disgust, loathing | Vomiting, pushing away | Rejection |
| New territory | "What's out there?" | Anticipation | Examining, mapping | Exploration |
| Novel object | "What is it?" | Surprise | Stopping | Orientation |

Source: Adapted from R. Plutchik, "A General Psychoevolutionary Theory of Emotion," in *Emotion: Theory, Research, and Experience,* vol. 1, edited by R. Plutckik and H. Kellerman (New York: Academic Press, 1980), Table 1–2, p. 16.

## DISCUSSION: THE PHYSIOLOGY OF EMOTION

When we are in the grip of a strong emotion, we are aware that changes are taking place within our bodies. Psychologists that view emotion as primarily a biological event tend to focus on these agitated or depressed bodily states (Cannon, 1929).

### ■ The Nervous System

Understanding the physiology of emotion requires some understanding of the nervous system. When you see a bear, it is represented in your brain, your **central nervous system (CNS)**. But the CNS by itself is senseless and helpless. It cannot feel or act. It requires that information be brought to it by neural subsystems, and it must direct neural subsystems to initiate and coordinate action. These information-action subsystems comprise our **peripheral nervous system**. (Study Figures 6.2 and 6.3 as you read on.)

The peripheral nervous system is divided into two parts, the somatic nervous system and the autonomic nervous system. The **somatic nervous system** innervates the muscles attached to our bones and so enables us to move (to run, for example). The **autonomic nervous system** innervates the muscles of our internal organs and glands, our viscera.

The autonomic nervous system (ANS) is itself divided into the **sympathetic nervous system (SNS)** and the **parasympathetic nervous system (PNS)**. The SNS and the PNS have evolved to mobilize and conserve energy for survival. The heart, lungs, pancreas, kidneys, stomach, intestines, genitalia, and adrenals are examples of visceral organs and glands innervated by the ANS (see Figure 6.3).

### ■ How the Nervous System Works in Emotional Responses

Let's return to the bear. If you see a bear and wish to run, it is apparent that first the ANS must become activated. Your muscles need energy to work, so the heart must beat faster, the lungs expand more rapidly, and so on. Your brain (CNS) receives impulses from these glands as they change, and it is these internal sensations of visceral changes that we perceive as emotion. Have you ever "whistled in the dark" to divert your attention from your visceral changes and so not feel afraid?

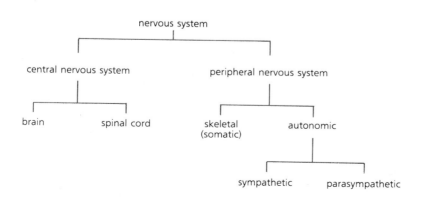

FIGURE 6.2
The Nervous System

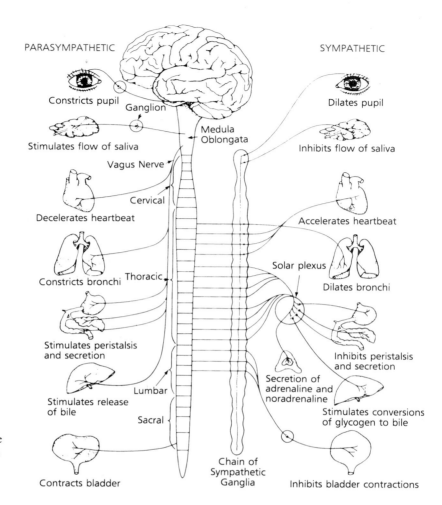

FIGURE 6.3
The autonomic nervous system. Observe how the two systems work in opposition to one another.

Notice in Figure 6.3 that the SNS mobilizes energy and the PNS conserves energy. Both functions are necessary for adequate adjustment. It is the SNS that accelerates heartbeat and prepares us to run. The PNS comes into play when the danger is past. Increased activity in the PNS is associated with a slower heartbeat, lower blood pressure, and so on. We conserve or restore our energy after the emergency. The two systems work cooperatively and jointly to maintain an appropriate response to the demands of life. From the biological viewpoint, emotion is adaptive. It helps us survive. As we will see in the next chapter, on stress, emotion can also constitute a danger to our health.

REVIEW
QUESTIONS

21. The peripheral nervous system is divided into two parts, the s_____
and the a_____ nervous systems.

22. The somatic nervous system enables us to run. T F

*23.* The a_____ nervous system innervates for the muscles of our visceral organs and glands.

*24.* Activity in the s_____ nervous system mobilizes energy for an emergency.

*25.* "Whistling in the dark" helps us <u>focus our attention on / divert our attention from</u> visceral changes and so reduce our fear.

*26.* Increased activity in the parasympathetic nervous system is related to <u>increased / decreased</u> activity in the heart.

*The answers to these review questions are on page 215.*

## DISCUSSION: DIMENSIONS OF EMOTIONAL FAILURE

■ **Dysfunctional Emotional Reactions**

As mentioned earlier, emotions can be seen as adaptive reactions used by living organisms in their quest for survival. However, not all aspects of emotion are positive for humans. The evolutionary notion that emotions work for us, derived from animal studies, seems to ignore the fact that for millions of humans, emotion constitutes a problem in living, not a successful adaptation to life. Antisocial emotions, mentioned earlier in the chapter, include fear, anger, jealousy, and depression. These "negative" emotions can be functional, as when we feel fear when endangered, anger when frustrated, and anxiety when in conflict. But sometimes they are dysfunctional. Emotions become dysfunctional when they incapacitate us or rob us of personal fulfillment or the good company of our friends.

Emotions may have been a survival mechanism for our species, but they can be the cause of severe problems of adjustment if they fail in one or more of three dimensions: (1) appropriateness, (2) level of intensity, and (3) effectiveness of expression.

■ Appropriateness of Feelings

The first dimension of emotion is *appropriateness*. Is the emotion felt and expressed suitably in terms of the psychological situation? This is a matter of judgment. Others (including our conscience, acting as an internalized other) judge the appropriateness of our emotions.

■ *Cognitive Appraisal and Emotional Appropriateness*   Richard Lazarus (1982) speaks of *cognitive appraisal*, the sometimes rational and sometimes irrational assessment of emotionally arousing stimuli. (For example, is the bear dangerous?) Spiesman (1965) investigated cognitive appraisal by giving subjects different appraisals of the meaning of a very gory film and then monitoring their emotional reactions while they viewed it. A control group saw the film without sound. One experimental group heard a factual description of the filmed events. Another heard a distant, overly intellectualized account, and still another was presented with a dialogue that tended to deny or gloss over the bloody incidents being shown on the screen. All groups were tested for emotional levels during and after the movie. Those who were led to deny or intellectualize what they were seeing were significantly less affected than the controls or those watching the straightforward presentation. Clearly our emotional responses are affected by the way we interpret a situation.

If your cognitive appraisal agrees with that of people around you, your emotion is likely to be deemed appropriate. If their assessment calls for laughter and you feel terror, you may have a problem. Even if your assessment agrees with the others, your response may be deemed inappropriate if it is not the one expected under the circumstances. You may place different emphasis or different meanings on the same sensations. Your social class or cultural background may influence you to conclude that a different emotional response is called for (Douvan and Adeson, 1966). For whatever reason, if your emotional expression is judged inappropriate, an adjustment becomes necessary, because those others serve as jury and executioner as well as judge.

■ *Social Pressure to Conform to Standards of Appropriateness*  You may well ask what business it is of others how you feel. In truth, others make it their business because all of us depend on the emotional expressions of others to serve as *cues* to help us judge what a situation means and what response is called for. If you are unreliable or habitually respond in a unique way, the security and togetherness of those around you are undermined. Their world becomes less ordered and less sane. Pressure is typically applied to bring the errant member into line—hence, the adjustment problem.

> George loves to please: He loves to entertain. If he wants something from someone, he will appeal to pity or to debt for past favors. George loves affection and is uncomfortable around people who are angry or aggressive. He loves those who help and hates those who hurt.
> According to Richard Wallen (1972), George's emotional style is that of a "friendly helper" who embraces the tender emotions and will attempt to use them even when they are inappropriate—that is, when stronger emotions are clearly called for.

**WHAT DO YOU THINK?**

■ Do you identify with George? Are you uncomfortable around anger or aggression?

**WHAT DO YOU THINK?**

■ What should you do when you do not know what others expect but you believe an emotional expression is called for?

This does not mean we can never use our own values to judge the appropriateness of an emotion or its expression. We have a perfect right to do so. It does mean, however, that we should be ready to take responsibility for the consequences of such judgments. To feel and express outrage at an injustice that is tolerated by those around you may reflect personal growth and mark the beginning of social progress for your school, town, or nation.

**WHAT DO YOU THINK?**

■ Are your emotions accepted by those around you?
■ If not, what do you do when your strong feelings are ignored, rebuffed, or ridiculed?

■ *Accepting Our Feelings as a Legitimate Part of Ourselves*  A common failure related to emotional appropriateness occurs when our emotional reaction does not fit our self-image. To others, our appraisal and reaction may seem perfectly justified, even necessary. We become furious or grief-stricken when our home is broken into, for example. But to us, public displays of such strong emotion may be totally unacceptable. Such self-talk as "Anger is for the weak" or "Never cry over spilled milk" can cause us to reject our own feelings and their honest expression (Ellis, 1973). The irrational but common belief that we must always be perfect rules out negative emotions and forces us into inappropriate emotional assessments or expressions.

While we do not have to be perfect, it is interesting to note that research has shown that expressing anger can (1) make us angrier, (2) solidify an angry attitude, and (3) establish an angry habit (Tavris, 1982). People who display such actions, attitudes, and habits find it difficult to maintain close, warm personal relationships.

*See the discussion of assertiveness, page 335, for suggestions on appropriate expression of negative emotions.*

## ■ Levels of Emotional Intensity

The second dimension of emotion involves *emotional intensity*. Remember that many hold that the only thing that differentiates emotions from one another is their level of intensity (Duffy, 1941; Lindsley, 1951). Consider this example. While you are walking alone through a dark alley, the silence is broken by a sudden noise! Your reaction may be apprehension, fear, or terror. Except for their intensity, these emotions are indistinguishable. If you were feeling very powerful at that moment, and not inclined to be fearful, the noise might have made you annoyed, angered, or outraged. Again, these emotions fall along a continuous line of increasing intensity; Plutchik (1980) looks at them as being separated only by intensity.

Intensity becomes an adjustment problem when it is either so deficient or so excessive that it interferes with our ability to communicate. Persons with high spinal cord injuries, for example, cannot transmit sensations to the brain for intensity coding. They can still respond emotionally; they know what emotion is called for; but because they cannot feel intensity, their response is often inappropriate and misunderstood (Schachter, 1971).

**WHAT DO YOU THINK?**

■ Under what conditions has the intensity of your emotions been dysfunctional for you?

> Kurt is tough as nails! He walks tough, talks tough, looks tough, and loves it. You can get mad around Kurt, and you can fight. Kurt's comfortable around a fight. It's when you get warm and affectionate that Kurt shies away. He

■ Being a "sturdy battler" restricts our range of emotional expression.

WHAT DO YOU
THINK?

■ Do you identify with
Kurt? Do you mistrust
people who appear too
affectionate and warm?

doesn't like losers. If he wants something from you, he'll tell you just what you'll get if you don't come across. Kurt can take as good as he gives, too.
    Richard Wallen (1972) says Kurt is a "sturdy battler" whose explosive emotional style is always excessively intense.

■ *Excessive Emotionality*   We typically associate emotional adjustment problems with excessive intensities of emotion—rage rather than anger, terror rather than apprehension. These states involve a loss of control, a disintegration of the capacity to respond appropriately. Brain mechanisms control the intensity of emotional states. The wide range and rapid changes in infant emotion are largely due to the immaturity of these structures at birth. Neurochemical imbalances in these areas due to genetic deficiency, drug abuse, injury, or disease can provoke intense rage and terror reactions. A familiar example is the drunken rage, a drug-abuse reaction; a drug-induced rage that has more recently become common is the cocaine explosion. Both illustrate failures to regulate emotional intensity due to brain disorders.

    Surprisingly, behavioral disorders characterized by apathy, withdrawal, and unresponsiveness are also examples of excessive emotional arousal. Forbes and Chaney (1978) monitored the heart rate, blood pressure, and other skeletal and visceral activity of neurotic patients undergoing group therapy. They reported that arousal is just as high in depressed patients as in those recognizably tense, angry, or anxious. Extremes of depression are associated with excesses of emotional intensity.

■ *The Yerkes-Dodson Law*   "Test anxiety" illustrates a relationship between emotional intensity and task complexity known as the Yerkes-Dodson Law (Morris, 1979). Simply stated, the law says that the more complex a task, the lower the level of emotion that can be tolerated without impairment of performance. Your exam is a complex task that requires a low level of arousal. The skill of cultivating low levels of arousal can be learned and used to improve test performances.

*See Chapter 7, on stress.*

■ *Minimal Levels of Arousal and Emotional Control*   The brain needs a minimal level of sensory arousal to maintain emotional control. In 1960, Shurley found a way to reduce the level of outside stimulation dramatically. Volunteers were suspended in liquid in a dark, quiet isolation tank. The masks that allowed them to breathe and speak were weighted so that the volunteers were suspended in the water without even the sensation of gravity. No one could endure this sightless, soundless, weightless state for more than six hours. Giggles, cries, angry outbursts, and hallucinations were recorded. Lack of stimulation led to loss of emotional control. Low levels of stimulation to the brain, whether the cause is internal or external, are associated with adjustment problems.

■ *Sensory Deprivation*   D. O. Hebb (1958) used this concept of **sensory deprivation** in his studies of *brainwashing*, a technique developed by the Chinese and used for altering the political consciousness of U.S. soldiers during the Korean War. Brainwashing includes breaking down trust and emotional ties among prisoners so that each feels alone and helpless. In this state, the prisoner becomes absolutely dependent on the guards for survival. This dependence, together with fear, isolation, and endless, dull routine (which, incidentally, did not include brutalization), produced the sensory deprivation that led to depression and easier manipulation.

■ *Optimal Levels of Emotional Arousal*   Mild levels of emotional arousal appear to be both functional and fun. When mildly aroused, we are more alert and more attentive and feel more alive. We learn and remember better. That is why good teachers are forever trying to stimulate the class.

The relationship between mood and memory is now being explored (Bower, 1981; Laird, 1982). In general, if we can match the mood of what we are learning, or if we can recapture the mood we were in at the time of learning, we can recall more. The facts of a melancholy tale can be recalled better if we are melancholy while hearing it and while retelling it. Events are coded for emotion, and the activation of similar emotions aids in information retrieval.

*See the discussion of memory in Chapter 5.*

Do you frequent amusement parks or football stadiums? Those who do seek mild levels of *aversive stimuli* (such as danger, injustice, or the threat of loss) so that they may feel and express negative emotions, such as fear and anger, for the pleasure such emotions bring when they are experienced under conditions of security and social acceptance.

**WHAT DO YOU THINK?**

■ Do you gain pleasure from yelling at umpires?

■ *High Intensity, Strong Emotion, and Good Adjustment*   Even high emotional intensity is not always associated with an adjustment problem. Sexual pleasure, for example, is associated with intense levels of arousal and strong emotional expression. (But even here, performance suffers under conditions of overstimulation.) We are, at other times, called upon to produce extreme bursts of energy. Fleeing from danger or attacking a foe demands excessive energy mobilization and release. Herculean feats of strength and endurance seem impossible without the accompaniment of intense motion. For example, a mother who lifts the front end of an automobile to free her trapped child will later find the feat impossible.

■ *Type A Personality and Emotional Tension*   Adjustment problems do arise when people remain emotionally tense for long periods of time. Friedman and Rosenman (1974), who conducted a ten-year study of 3,500 male Californians, reported a strong link between emotional intensity and heart attacks. They identified a distinctive *Type A personality*, a man marked by excessive drive, impatience, aggressiveness, and a pressing sense of urgency. Such men were found to be almost three times more likely than less intense (Type B) men to get coronary heart disease. The Type B men also smoked less, ate less rich food, and exercised more. A combination of prolonged emotional intensity and physical self-abuse seems to work against health.

**WHAT DO YOU THINK?**

■ Which do you think is more critical, the physical abuse or the chronic stress?
■ Why?

*More about Type A personalities in Chapter 7.*

■ Effectiveness of Emotional Expression

The third dimension of emotion involves *emotional expression*. We can also fail in this social dimension. Emotions are "underlying feelings associated with our actions and thoughts" (Nikelly, 1977). Other people cannot directly sense our feelings or thoughts. They must infer our emotions from our actions.

I never see him laugh. I never see him cry. Looking at Tom, you never know if he is winning or losing. He is the coolest man I've ever seen. That's ok by me,

**WHAT DO YOU THINK?**

■ Do you identify with Tom? Is it easy for you to suffer fools?

but his poor wife and kids seem kind of forlorn. Tom takes great pride in his knowledge, always tries to get what he wants by overwhelming you with facts and quotes. He always makes me feel uncomfortably stupid and awkward.

Richard Wallen (1972) terms Tom a "logical thinker." People with this emotional style are reluctant to express any emotion.

■ *The Language of Emotion: Facial and Vocal Expression*    Facial expressions constitute the basic vocabulary of our emotional language (Ekman and Friesen, 1975). The muscles of the face have evolved so as to give vivid expression to our feelings. Mehrabian (1971) found that only a small amount of a communication (Mehrabian specified 7 percent) is transmitted in what we say, the verbal message. A greater amount (38 percent) is carried in how we say it, the vocal message. But most of our meaning (55 percent, according to Mehrabian) is conveyed in our facial expressions. The facial muscles work together to produce the smiling, frowning, laughing, crying face that gives others insight into our inner lives.

The ability to interpret correctly the emotion contained in a facial expression increases with age (Izard, 1977). This means that maturation and experience, as well as physical evolution, play a part in this survival skill.

Facial expressions may be misinterpreted. We rarely depend on the face alone to carry our messages. The 38 percent of our meaning that is carried by how we say something is to be found in the volume, pitch, rate, and fluidity of our speech (Rosenthal, 1974). An angry message is usually high in volume, pitch, and rate. Depression is reflected in low volume, rate, and pitch. Lack of fluidity—broken-up speech—is associated with repressed anger and also depression. We also reveal anxiety by a break in the flow of our speech. (See the Case in Point "Let Him Talk. He'll Hang Himself.")

## CASE IN POINT
## Let Him Talk. He'll Hang Himself

The ancients used the mouth to determine the guilt or innocence of an accused person. If seeds, forced into the mouth, came out dry, the accused was guilty. If the accused could not spit on command, she was guilty. Saliva, under the control of our autonomic nervous system, stops when we are under stress. An innocent person who has nothing to fear should be able to let the saliva flow while being interrogated, or this was the assumption behind the tests.

A new lie detector that uses the voice has been developed on the principle that all muscles, when in use, have a slight tremor or vibration. This tremor is dampened by the autonomic nervous system when the person is under stress. When we are innocent or truthful (relaxed), our voices should include this tremor.

When we are guilty or lying (tense), our voices should not include the tremor.

A machine, the *voice stress analyzer*, can detect and record the presence or absence of our tremors and convict us "out of our own mouths." It can be attached to a telephone. No connections to the person are needed. It can be used without the knowledge or consent of the accused, who may not even know he is accused or suspected of anything.

The validity of the technique (many variables other than guilt cause tremor reduction) and the ethics of using it (because of violation of privacy and so on) are under question. If you are interested in finding out more about it, see B. Rice "The New Truth Machine," *Psychology Today* 12 (1978): 67–78.

■ *The Language of Emotion: Body Expression*    Our bodies as well as our faces and voices help us communicate emotion. Specific acts, like slamming doors, are expressive. More subtly, we use **body language.** You may not be able to describe a silent sexual "come-on," but after experiencing one, you can never forget it. Birdwhistell (1952) has developed a science of **kinesics** to explore the human body as a language system. Posture and gesture combine to produce body language. Body language gives a dimension to our emotional expression that facial and vocal muscles are incapable of communicating.

Our posture usually indicates our emotional state quite clearly. The forward-thrusting, assertive stance of anger can hardly be confused with the apathetic slump of depression or the recoiled cringe of terror. When depressed patients improve, they spend increased time in motion, they initiate and terminte motion more quickly, and they make more complex bodily motions than when they were deeply depressed (Fisch, Frey, and Hirsbrunner, 1983). Even distance can be expressive. The amount of distance we establish and maintain between ourselves and those with whom we communicate reveals the degree of trust, warmth, and intimacy we are prepared to extend.

Using his Profile of Nonverbal Sensitivity Scale (PONS), Rosenthal (1974) concluded that women are more sensitive and accurate than men in reading body language. However, an interesting form of body language that men do respond to is the size of a woman's pupils. Our pupils widen with sexual stimulation and general interest (a prosocial predisposition), and men find women with widened pupils much more attractive than those with narrowed pupils (Hess, 1975). (Some women report the "wide-eyed, innocent look" to be attractive in young men, as well.)

■ *The Cultural Basis of Poor Emotional Expression*    We often suffer problems in adjustment because we have been carefully taught not to trust our own emotions. The muscles that contract to form our postures, gestures, facial expressions, and vocal patterns are voluntary muscles. Even our visceral muscles can come under a degree of voluntary control. Muscles can contract automatically, as in an infant's smile; but they can also be directed to contract, as in the smile of the used car salesman. Our culture values the strong, undemonstrative type who places reason above emotion. The sensitive, expressive person is often seen as handicapped in this business-oriented civilization. The poker face is prized in a game in which deception counts. Children learn to manipulate their emotional expressions in order to keep their parents' love and support. Under these conditions, spontaneity is lost and certain emotions become taboo. According to Fritz Perls (1969), the open and honest expression of emotion is essential to mental health. Much of his therapy was devoted to helping clients relearn this lost skill.

The difficulty for many of us in expressing negative emotions without guilt or anxiety pinpoints a unique problem of human adaptation: We can *feel about how we feel*. We can be taught to feel guilty for feeling anger toward one we love, or ashamed at feeling grief over the loss of a prized possession. "Don't cry. Its only a toy," translates into, "You're silly or selfish for having such feelings. Don't allow yourself to have them. Never express them."

As honest feelings become associated with negative outcomes, children learn to mistrust feelings and restrict their expression. Izard (1977) finds that our

**WHAT DO YOU THINK?**

■ How do you express anger, fear, and happiness?
■ When at home?
■ When with friends?

facial muscles trigger an automatic reaction within our brains. He believes that this reaction tells us which emotion we are feeling. If your face is formed into a smile, for example, you should feel happiness. (Try it yourself.) This may mean that to learn not to *show* feelings may actually lessen our capacity to *have* feelings. A failure in expression becomes a failure in intensity and appropriateness as well.

### ■ A Failure in Emotional Expression: Aggression

*See Chapter 13, on maladjustment, for related discussions.*

Losing the capacity to feel deeply is the greatest personal failure in emotional expression. On a group level, the greatest failure in emotional expression occurs when we express anger, hostility, or rage through **aggression**—behavior intended to injure another person or to destroy property. Hostile aggression, rather than instrumental aggression, represents a failure in emotional expression. *Instrumental aggression*, the calculated use of violence to achieve some desired end, can be devoid of emotion. The end (noble or ignoble) is thought to justify the means. We may show aggression to protect ourselves, for example. *Hostile aggression* is the venting of anger on a victim. It is violence carried out for the sole purpose of inflicting injury.

*See Chapter 2, on personality, for an explanation of Freudian theory.*

■ *Aggression as an Instinctive Response*    Freud believed that aggression was instinctive, an expression of the *death wish* that could be directed against others or against oneself. Prosocial emotions (such as love), substitute victims (such as bowling pins), and vicarious forms of aggression (such as watching sports contests) were seen by Freud as the only way humans could reduce the carnage of aggressive behavior.

■ *Aggression as a Response to Frustration*    In the 1930s, the idea that aggression was an emotional response to frustration was introduced (Dollard, 1939). This **frustration-aggression hypothesis** offered another avenue toward reducing aggression—the reduction of frustration. Aggression was seen as an instinctive release of pent-up pain, psychological or physical. The idea that this release of aggression had a biological basis was buttressed by the finding that humans, as well as lower animals, had neurological mechanisms in the brain that released aggressive behavior (Papez, 1937). Chemical imbalances within these mechanisms, increasing or inhibiting the flow of excitement within the brain, have been associated with abnormal childhood aggression and impulsive violence (Rogers, 1983). "Unpleasant events tend to evoke aggression in humans, as in other animals" (Berkowitz, 1983, p. 1135). For normal people, however, neither brain structure nor brain chemistry alone is believed to be the *cause* of aggression.

*See Chapter 4 for a discussion of prejudice and discrimination.*

■ *Aggression as a Socially Learned Response*    Human aggression is considered by many today to be a product of our social lives. The frequency, the form, and the function of aggression are determined by learning and the influence of others (Bandura, 1977). In other words, we learn the when, how, and what for of aggression. We also learn when not to be aggressive and which people are appropriate or inappropriate victims of aggression.

We learn to be aggressive in the same manner we learn other social skills—by direct instruction, by imitating others, and by receiving incentives or rewards

■ Professional boxers display aggression. The murder rate in the United States rises after major televised fights.

for being aggressive. Parental admonitions such as "to be strong, you have to fight for what you get" can be overlearned. Observing models acting aggressively (as on TV) teaches aggression. Learning (directly or indirectly) that "violence pays" also increases aggressive behavior.

See Chapter 8, on socialization, for more about social learning.

Social learning theorists believe that two conditions must be present for aggressive responses to occur in adults: (1) an arousing stimulus—something, such as frustration, sexual attraction, or competition, that causes our hearts to pound, our blood pressure to rise, and so on—and (2) a stimulus that elicits an aggressive response—previous pain, a traditional victim, something to be gained or avoided, and so on. If you have been previously annoyed by someone, and then been aroused *by whatever means*, and then given a chance to act aggressively against the annoying party, you are more likely to show an ag-

## CASE IN POINT
## TV Violence and Aggression

There is a growing body of evidence that TV violence increases the number of Americans who use violence as an adjustment alternative. However, TV violence does not affect all of us the same way. Children who believe television reflects real life and who identify with aggressive characters (heroes or villians) display more aggressive actions at home and school. Such children are less popular at school and watch more and more violent television (Eron, 1982). Unpopularity is painful, and pain stimulates aggression. Such children become caught in a cycle of aggression, rejection, and more aggression. Adults also are influenced by real violence on TV. After a highly promoted prize fight, the number of murders committed increases. The victim is likely to be of the same race as the loser of the televised fight (Phillips, 1983).

**WHAT DO YOU THINK?**

■ Are we as individuals and as groups responsible for our own aggression?
■ Can we control aggression enough to make our homes, streets, nation, and planet safe?

gressive response, and the response is more likely to be intense. You will be more likely to be more hostile. However, simple arousal, including sexual arousal, without prior aversive exposure does *not* produce increased aggression (Zillman and Sapolsky, 1977).

■ *The Outlook for Curbing Violence in America*    Because of our increased awareness and knowledge of the causes of aggression, it may now be possible to keep violence within bounds. Indeed, in these days of atomic violence, it is mandatory. Reducing frustration and competition, teaching nonaggressive ways of responding, and being careful to avoid reinforcing aggression when it occurs can reduce the stimuli that trigger aggression.

■ Assertiveness: An Alternative to Aggression

Cooperation, negotiation, problem solving, and assertiveness are all social skills that have been found to reduce the need for violence. A behavioral approach that helps reduce both anxiety and hostility is **assertiveness training**. The training occurs in small support groups in which shy or hostile people practice firm but controlled assertive responses under the direction of a therapist. They then are encouraged to try them in real life.

Those in training practice insisting on their rights *without abusing the other person*. Real-life situations are drawn from the group members and presented to the support group. The members act out assigned roles in which they behave shyly, assertively, or aggressively. Postures, gestures, voice levels, and specific dialogues are enacted and constructively criticized. Assertive alternatives are suggested. Group members act together and help one another. The effective expression of negative emotions, such as fear or anger, is often the objective of a group session. In addition to gaining specific skills another desired outcome is increased awareness of freedom and social responsibility.

> Betty and her family are eating out at a nice restaurant. Always mindful of her diet, she orders a salad and requests that the dressing be delivered ''on the side.'' A short while later the waiter presents the salad, *with the dressing piled on top.*
> **Shy Betty**: Says nothing to the waiter, but grumbles to her husband and vows never to eat there again. Her husband, Jim, feels bad because he didn't take action for his wife. The kids just feel bad.
> **Aggressive Betty**: Loudly calls the waiter back and gives him hell for not having brains enough to remember a simple order. Betty demands, and gets, another salad. She also gets embarrassed looks and a prolonged silence from her family. The meal is ruined.
> **Assertive Betty**: Motions the waiter to her table and notes that she had ordered her dressing on the side. Betty asks politely but firmly that the salad be returned and her original request be honored. The waiter soon returns with the order corrected. Jim nods pleasantly, and tips the waiter generously after a satisfying meal.

*See Chapter 10 for more about various styles of communication.*

REVIEW
QUESTIONS

*27.* To feel fear when endangered and anger when frustrated is <u>functional</u> / <u>dysfunctional</u>.

28. Others / We and others judge the appropriateness of our emotional expressions.

29. Our emotional responses are / are not affected by how we interpret a situation.

30. Apprehension, fear, and terror differ most in terms of emotional appropriateness / intensity / expression.

31. You should try to stimulate / relax yourself just before attempting a complex task.

32. Most information in a message is carried by the verbal / vocal / facial transmission.

33. Depressed patients are as aroused as / less aroused than tense, anxious, or angry patients.

34. Our brain needs a minimal / constant level of sensory arousal.

35. The facts of a hilarious tale are better recalled if we are happy / sad while learning it.

36. It is at times / never functional to be intensely emotional.

37. The science of kinesics explores the human body as a chemistry / language / energy system.

38. Our emotional expression tends to become more / less spontaneous and authentic over time.

39. Hostile / Instrumental aggression is the venting of anger on a victim.

40. Freud believed that aggression is instinctive / caused by frustration / cognitively controlled.

41. Social learning theorists believe human aggression is caused by arousing stimuli / eliciting stimuli / both arousing and eliciting stimuli.

42. Assertiveness training includes practice in insisting on individual rights while / without abusing the other person.

*The answers to these review questions are on page 215.*

# DISCUSSION: DEPRESSION

As we mentioned, a useful scheme for classifying human emotions is to divide them into prosocial and antisocial emotions. Under this system, for example, fear and anger are antisocial and joy is prosocial. In this section and the next one, we will explore two emotions that are not emergency reactions like fear or anger. Rather, these emotions represent the complexity of our emotional lives. We will begin with an antisocial emotion, depression, and end on a high note with the most prosocial of all human emotions, love.

## ■ Characteristics of Depressed People

Termed the "common cold of psychopathology" by Martin Seligman, depression has replaced anxiety as the disease of the decade. The profile of depression as seen in alcoholic men (Steer, 1982) is, in many ways, a typical profile of depression. Such men exhibit the following characteristics:

*1.* Negative attitudes (pessimism, a sense of failure, self-accusation, and self-dislike),

■ Painful activities such as worrying, complaining, and crying are maintained at unusually high levels by those suffering from depression.

2. Physiological disorders (anorexia, weight loss, sleep loss), and

3. Performance deficiencies (work impairment, general fatigue).

Serious depression thus illustrates a failure in the three dimensions of emotion. Physiologically, depressives maintain high levels of internal arousal. Behaviorally, the emit inappropriate and excessively low levels of expression and outward activity. The dejected mood, sad face, and slumped posture of depressed persons stand in stark contrast to their high energy mobilization. Prosocial emotions and pleasurable activities such as sexual activities, sleeping, and eating are maintained at low levels, while antisocial emotions and painful activities such as worrying, complaining, crying, and withdrawing are more constantly exhibited. With high energy mobilization accompanied by only low-energy activities, it might be reasonable to expect depressed people to be agitated. On the contrary, fatigue is the most common ailment they report.

**WHAT DO YOU THINK?**

■ Is Susan's depression psychological, or could it be due to the social role she is forced to play because she is a woman?

Susan appears tired and strangely quiet, not at all like the energetic and articulate "young aspiring professional" image she wants to project. The problem is that Susan's part-time job just doesn't seem to be leading anywhere. The income is poor and the opportunity not much better. There aren't many attractive men at work, either. Susan often regrets that her formal education was interrupted by an early and brief marriage.

Susan wants to appear bright and enthusiastic so that she can get full-time work. A full-time job will pay enough for the university and professional training she dreams of. But it's so hard to pretend, and so hard to fight fatigue.

## ■ Psychophysiological View of Depression

The psychophysiological view of depression explains the origins of this disorder in physiological terms and the outcomes of it in behavioral terms (Akiskal and McKinney, 1973). A malfunctioning thyroid gland causes sluggishness, for example, and certain cortical mechanisms of reinforcement (pleasure centers in the brain) may not receive appropriate stimulation because of a shortage of various neurotransmitters (substances that carry messages between nerve cells). Small proteins known as peptides seem to regulate our neurotransmitter substances. Thus chemical imbalances can make us incapable of receiving pleasure from ordinary stimuli, so normal rewards are not adequate to shape and maintain prosocial responding. A smile, a pat, and an admonition to "cheer up" will not suffice.

Coppen (1967) found depression to be associated with low potassium and high sodium levels. He theorized that this state results in reduced neurological activity. The use of enzymes to regulate the amount of this brain activity resulted in the first antidepressant drug—**lithium**, a carbonated salt solution that is often dramatically effective in the treatment of depression. A promising treatment routine is to provide for regular psychotherapy sessions that include weekly medical checkups for lithium carbonate levels (Volkmar et al., 1982).

**WHAT DO YOU THINK?**
■ Are your low periods associated with physical problems?
■ How might they be related?

## ■ Psychotherapeutic View of Depression

The psychotherapeutic approach to depression (Arieti and Bemporad, 1979) defines depression as "an unresolved state of sorrow or sadness." It appears that the chief risk factor for depression in both men and women is the early loss of a parent (Roy, 1981). A person who learns to ease the pain of such early losses by denying them rather than working them through may not be prepared later to respond to other severe losses by the usual process of grief work, or mourning.

In young children, the pain of losing something or someone they love is often made worse by the pain of guilt. Parents at times engage in *moralistic blaming* ("Don't lie to me. Only bad people lie!") and in *threats of abandonment* ("If you lie again, I am going to go off and just leave you"). They do this to control their children. Children so abused can come to accept the chilling "fact" that they are evil or bad. Blaming themselves for a loss, and being too young to bear the double pain of guilt and loss, they short-circuit their agony by the use of denial.

This unresolved guilt and loss can be successfully repressed as long as such people can depend on a strong person or a strong goal to provide them with constant reassurance that they are worthy of existing. When the person or the goal is removed (by death, separation, or repeated failure), the guilt returns and depression is precipitated.

**WHAT DO YOU THINK?**
■ How do you work through your sorrows?

**WHAT DO YOU THINK?**
■ How can we get children to do what is right without causing them to feel guilt or shame?

### ■ *Steps in Normal Grieving*

Parkes (1972) traces the following steps in normal grieving: an initial shock followed by denial of the loss; severe pangs of bereavement coupled with hopes of recovery of the loss; an acceptance of the permanence of the loss; and finally, the slow beginnings of readjustment. Kubler-Ross (1969) identifies similar steps in people who are grieving in anticipation of the loss of their own lives. First, there is *denial*: "Not me!" This is followed by *anger*: "Why me!" The third stage is *bargaining* with God for more time. *Depression* follows, finally to be replaced by *acceptance*.

Not everyone goes through all five stages (Kastenbaum, 1977). Notice, however, that the knowledge of a significant loss generally produces anger, which is followed by depression. In psychoanalytic theory, depression is related to loss by way of *introjected* anger. For example, you are frustrated or provoked but do not feel capable of directly expressing your anger in aggression. You may cope with this emotional tension by turning it inward, on yourself. This is introjection. "Anger turned inward" is one definition of depression. Newman and Hirt (1983) find that those who typically cope by introjecting are typically swayed by external influences, rather than trusting their internal sensations; these people display more depression.

## ■ Behavioral View of Depression

The behaviorists' view of depression (Lazarus, 1982; Lewinsohn, 1982) centers on the effects of insufficient rates of positive reinforcement. It holds that a deficiency in reinforcing stimuli extinguishes prosocial responses in the depressed. For example, when the neglected infant's cries or coos for attention are ignored, the child may give up, slip into depression, and die (Spitz, 1945).

A lack of social skills can result in a person's receiving low levels of positive reinforcement. Depressed responses can also elicit certain kinds of reinforcement from others and so be strengthened. Consider the businessman whose depression acts both as an excuse for failure (his work problems are due to sickness, not incompetence; this involves negative reinforcement) and as a releaser of help (anyone would help a sick man; this involves positive reinforcement). The long-term problem with depressive responses is that the depressed person's low frequency of prosocial behavior is aversive, not reinforcing, to others. People tend to avoid those who habitually are sad and withdrawn. This, of course, only reduces further the level of positive reinforcement received by the depressed and extinguishes the social skills they still employ. Thus they drive away the very reinforcement they need to end this downward cycle.

**WHAT DO YOU THINK?**

■ Do you sense a lack of support during your low moods?

## ■ Cognitive-Behavioral View of Depression

While telling a depressed client "Cheer up! Think positively" is seldom effective, cognitive-behaviorists view depression as primarily a thought disorder. A particular style of thinking, *negative overgeneralization*, is an excellent predictor of depression (Carver and Ganellen, 1983). Depressed people generally:

1. Set standards for themselves that are too high.
2. Are intolerant of their failure to meet the standards.
3. Interpret a single failure as an indication that they have little self-worth.

This tendency to be critical and punitive toward themselves becomes a morbid preoccupation. The gloom of the depressed accurately reflects their morbid thoughts. They tend to have a rigid self-image that is distorted downward. This gives rise to negative expectations and hopeless projections for themselves and often for those they love. Beck (1967) reports three important irrational thoughts of the depressed.

*1.* They believe that they are responsible for their misfortunes, that they are worthless, inferior, and bad.

*2.* They see their lives as a continuous encounter with tragic misfortunes and failures.

*3.* They believe that the future will be much like the past and present, that there is little hope for improvement. Suicide becomes a possibility.

Whether these conclusions represent cognitive distortions or relatively accurate judgments of personal deficiencies is now under study (Kanfer and Zeiss, 1983). Lewinsohn and Hoberman (1982) believe that depressing thoughts and feelings are responses to reduced rates of positive reinforcement caused by actual deficiencies in social skills.

■ *Learned Helplessness*   Martin Seligman (1977) was able to produce behavior similar to human depression in laboratory animals by placing them in situations in which they suffered pain and could not escape or reduce the pain. Such animals experienced *learned helplessness.* Later they responded helplessly in situations in which it was possible to escape or to reduce pain. For example, a dog trained in helplessness failed to learn to leap a barrier to avoid an electric shock, while untrained fellow dogs learned without difficulty.

Feelings of being helpless and without hope are expressed frequently by humans who are depressed and suicidal. In an attempt to demonstrate learned helplessness in humans, Miller and Seligman (1975) subjected groups of student subjects to loud, unpleasant noises through earphones. One group was able to escape the noise, another was not. Later the groups were tested with simple problems and puzzles. The "no-escape" subjects, like their canine counterparts, performed poorly. Perhaps they had temporarily learned helplessness. Already-depressed subjects in both groups also performed poorly. They had long ago mastered helplessness, according to Miller and Seligman. Learned helplessness can be reversed through reeducation (Fowler and Peterson, 1981). Children with a history of failure in reading were given direct attribution retraining. They were taught new ways to look at failure and were given partial reinforcement for persistence in the face of frustration. Their reading improvement was attributed to a new respect for effort and an improved sense of self-esteem.

**WHAT DO YOU THINK?**

■ What do you say to yourself when you are feeling blue?

## ■ Depression: A Complex, Antisocial Emotion

It is not unusual for a sad person to be cranky at the same time. Depression, an antisocial emotion, is complicated by the fact that it includes at least two additional antisocial emotions—guilt and anger. ("Anger turned inward," you recall, is one definition of depression.) The depressed, feeling powerless, often believe that expression of anger is evil and dangerous. They learn to turn it inward by blaming themselves for all their difficulties. As mentioned, self-blame produces guilt feelings, perhaps the most complex and painful of emotions. Guilt is so painful that we will do almost anything to reduce it. The idea that certain values are absolute, and that violating them brings punishment from parents, peers, or police, becomes well established. That retribution will also come from God is also carefully taught to many children.

Internalized guilt, repressed anger, and high anxiety account for that sad, cranky feeling in the temporarily depressed and for the high arousal levels of the chronic depressive. As noted earlier, pain tends to instigate aggressive responses, and depressed people are often cranky and hurtful to those they love. Depression meets the criteria of an antisocial emotion.

*43.* Depressed people exhibit high / low levels of arousal and high / low levels of activity and expression.

*44.* The flexible / rigid self-image of the depressed person is distorted upward / downward.

*45.* The psychotherapeutic concept of depression stresses an earlier pattern of doing / not doing grief work.

*46.* Depressives, according to Arieti and Bemporad, look outside / to themselves for reassurance that they are worthy of living.

*47.* In psychoanalytic theory, introjected anger / fear leads to depression.

*48.* The behavioral view of depression suggests that high / low rates of prosocial responding result in high / low rates of positive reinforcement.

*49.* Beck believes that the thought patterns of depressed people are mature / immature and realistic / irrational.

*50.* A promising therapy routine for depressed patients involves regular psychotherapy / regular checkups for lithium carbonate levels / both.

*51.* Depressed people tend to make negative / positive / neutral generalizations about the meaning of single events.

*52.* A dog trained in helplessness will fail to / learn to leap a barrier to avoid an electric shock.

*53.* Depressed people tend to blame themselves / others for their failures.

*The answers to these review questions are on page 215.*

## DISCUSSION: LOVE

Love is the antithesis of depression. It enhances our self-esteem and makes all things seem possible. All of us have, at some time in our lives, given love; such attachment is universal in surviving infants. We may, however, have survived without having received love. This is a human tragedy. To be both loved and loving is a delightful experience.

### ■ Defining Love

Love is almost impossible to define for study. A "strong feeling," an "ardent affection," a "passionate attachment," a "commercial commodity," or merely a "four-letter word"—love is all these and more. It is sad that most psychology texts do not include the term in their indexes. This omission is perhaps due to several factors. Those who come to psychological clinics for emotional help often lack the capacity to love deeply, and research animals do not exhibit love in human form. Denied the laboratory and the clinic for research data, the clinical or laboratory psychologist is at a disadvantage in observing love, and the professional literature reflects this fact.

## CASE IN POINT
## You Love Me, But Do You Really Like Me?

Think of a person you love, or think you love. Answer the following questions with that person in mind. Respond to each question below with a number from one to nine, with nine being the most positive answer.

_____ 1. I think that he/she is unusually well-adjusted. It seems to me that it is very easy for him/her to gain admiration.

_____ 2. If I could never be with him/her, I would feel miserable. It would be hard for me to get along without him/her.

_____ 3. I have great confidence in his/her good judgment. I would vote for him/her in a class or group election.

_____ 4. If he/she were feeling bad, my first duty would be to cheer him/her up. I would do almost anything for him/her.

_____ 5. I think that he/she and I are quite similar to each other. When I am with him/her, we are almost always in the same mood.

_____ 6. I feel that I can confide in him/her about almost anything. When I am with him/her, I spend a good deal of time just looking at him/her.

_____ 7. He/She is the sort of person I would like to be.

_____ 8. I would forgive him/her for practically anything.

See page 215 for scoring and an interpretation of your score.

Source: Adapted from Z. Rubin, "Measurement of Romantic Love," *Journal of Personality and Social Psychology* 16 (1970): 267–268.

## ■ Social-Psychological View of Love

Some **social psychologists**, freed from the clinic and not restricted to the laboratory, believe they have identified certain elements of love. You may or may not embrace their notions. To Erich Fromm (1956), love is a giving of oneself to another. "He does not give in order to receive; giving is in itself exquisite joy" (p. 20). Fromm finds four elements common to all forms of love: *caring, responsibility, respect,* and *knowledge.* If we love someone or something we care for it. Response-ability means the ability to be responsive to the one you love. Respect includes acceptance, and knowledge means we understand and appreciate the special qualities of our loved ones.

To Walster and Walster (1978), romantic love is simply an agitated state of physiological arousal that individuals come to *define* as love. The source of arousal may be sex, gratitude, anxiety, joy, fear, and so on. What makes these differentiated reactions love is that the individuals involved *label* them as love. Ovid, the first-century Roman poet, noted in *Ars Amatoria (The Art of Love)* that sexual passion was often aroused during gladiator fights but was labeled as affection.

A modern social psychologist, Zick Rubin (1973), excludes passion as a valid criterion of love. He believes love is an *attitude* that contains dimensions of: (1) attachment, wanting to be with and be approved of by the loved one; (2) caring, giving equal importance to self and loved one; and (3) intimacy, wanting to have close and confidential communication with the loved one.

*See Chapter 11 for more about love.*

## ■ Chemical View of Love

Do these notions of love excite you? Perhaps the idea of Libbowitz and Klien (1981) will help explain why. They hold that love is similar to an amphetamine high. They say the loving brain produces its own chemical intoxicant, *phenylethylamine.* Chocolate contains phenylethylamine; perhaps this is why we mold it into the shape of a heart and present it to our loved ones. In the same chemical vein, John Money finds love "rooted in neural pathways and hormones emanating from the pituitary gland" (1983, p. 53).

## ■ Psychotherapeutic View of Love

*See Chapter 2, on personality, for more about these phenomena.*

The psychotherapeutic school views love as a mixture of sexual instinct, dependency needs, ego-ideal strivings, and emotional displacement. We fall in love to be pleased, cared for, and reunited with our primal loves, our mothers. We also fall in love to be made whole. In this view we seek a mate who complements our strengths and thus completes our ideal self. Conflicts among love, fear, and hate complicate our adjustment to life.

## ■ Humanistic View of Love

The humanists view love as an essential part of human potential. It is seen as a critical aspect of human existence, important throughout life and necessary for self-actualization. Humanists view the capacity to love as an emotional expression of the wholesome personality. They see self-hate as rendering us unable to give or accept love (but in need of seeking it). These theorists tend to agree with Harlow (1971) that human love, like primate love, must pass successfully through a series of developmental stages if it is to reach its highest expression. Harlow lists the necessary stages as (1) infant love, (2) peer love, (3) age-mate passion, (4) maternal love, and (5) paternal love.

## ■ Behavioral View of Love

The behaviorists view love as a set of conditioned responses, including emotional responses. Viewing emotions as drive states (motives) rather than as states of being, they look at love as an instrument, a tool to be used to attain pleasure or avoid pain. Bodily states are felt, but "it is the conditions rather than the feelings which enable us to explain behavior" (Skinner, 1974, p. 245). Love is thus a predisposition, under specific stimulus conditions, to emit a given set of loving operants. In this definition, the term *predisposition* means a high probability of responding in a certain way. The term *specific stimulus conditions* means persons, objects, or events that are naturally reinforcing or have become so through conditioning. The term *set of loving operants* means loving acts. In short, love is loving acts.

**WHAT DO YOU THINK?**
■ Do you agree with Skinner?

Loving acts are seen as being learned (therefore love is learned), either by direct experience or observation. Our loved one can become a generalized positive reinforcer to us (Miller and Siegel, 1972). We then receive pleasure as we reinforce the behavior of the loved one. Giving love becomes a loving act toward ourselves.

Some conditions, such as seeing a beautiful body, can elicit respondent emotional behavior such as increased heart rate, blood pressure, and blood flow. Such forms of arousal, when associated with pleasure in the presence of an appropriate partner, can become discriminative stimuli for the emotion of love. This is why we try to surround our dates with flowers, chocolate, and excitement. The resultant high arousal, in association with us, may be interpreted by the date as a sign of being in love. As you may know, we often get caught in our own scheme.

## ■ Cognitive View of Love

Cognitive theorists add the dimension of beliefs to the arousing stimuli, the subjective feelings, and the loving acts of the behaviorists. Irrational beliefs abound. In the cognitive view, whispering "I love you" influences *both* partners, because our beliefs, expressed in self-talk, mediate our responses to incoming stimuli.

*See Chapter 12, "Barriers to Intimacy."*

When in love we tend to think affirmatively. Love gives rise to perceptual distortions (romantic illusions) that enable us to accept as real the generous assessment of ourselves that is reflected in the behavior of our loved ones. We return this generosity and attribute good qualities and intentions to both ourselves and our loved ones. Charity and love embrace one another.

## ■ Love As a Complex Emotion

**WHAT DO YOU THINK?**
■ What are some of the feelings you associate with love?

Emotionally, love is associated with peace, acceptance, happiness, joy, and ecstasy on the one hand and agitation, jealousy, depression, and vengeance on the other. Love is considered a prosocial emotion, with tender feelings predominating. When in love, we sense strong feelings of attraction and an emotional closeness with our loved one. Our postures and gestures give us the "look of love," and we try to maximize contact with our beloved. We touch, or at least make eye contact, as frequently as possible. When love is returned, we feel warm and alive, even when we are not sexually aroused. We feel special. Basking in the luxury of being wanted and unconditionally accepted, we tend to act in supporting ways that encourage our loved ones to grow.

■ *Other Emotions Embedded in Love*    Acceptance and empathy are two prosocial emotions embedded in the larger emotion love. *Acceptance* means unconditional positive regards; you do not have to prove yourself to one who loves you. *Empathy* is the vicarious sharing of the emotional state of your loved one; to share joy or pain without jealousy or sympathy is a sign of love. Brenner (1971) demonstrated the existence of empathy within love by having college students recite in public in the presence of their romantic partners or watch their partners recite in public. They were then asked to recall events just before, during, and after the recitations of strangers, lovers, and self. They remembered what was recited, but not what came just before or after their own or their lovers' recitations. No such empathetic stress affected the recall of events surrounding the recitations of strangers. Acceptance and empathy are the cornerstones of a helping relationship. Carl Rogers (1970) believes these are the essential ingredients in establishing a therapeutic (loving) relationship with another human being.

■ The Social Utility of Love

People differ on just how useful love is. Evolutionists, noting that love does not appear in nonaggressive species, maintain that love inhibits aggression within a species and makes both mating and caring for the young possible. Thus, love makes species survival possible. Bowlby (1969) suggests that the loving acts of the newborn make individual survival more probable.

Love is accepted in almost all of psychiatry and psychology as the antidote for fear, hate, and depression. It is thus the therapy of choice. To be able to give and to accept love are seen as signs of mental health. Thus, love helps us survive the long and arduous journey through life. *Brotherly love* (Fromm, 1956) is looked on as the one force capable of opposing greed and violence and saving civilization. And many religions regard love as a source of salvation for the immortal soul.

**WHAT DO YOU THINK?**

■ Do you think the "caring" dimension of real love will protect it from improper use?
■ Do you think it is better to have loved and lost than never to have loved at all?

■ The Costs of Love

Love is not without cost, however. Lost love, or the loss of a loved one, can result in grief, depression, and even death (Wilkerson, 1978). Loving someone can also impair emotional and mental health (Fischer, 1983). Great anxiety and stress are often found in individuals attempting to cope with the problems of those they love. Many wives report themselves exhausted by the alcoholism and

## CASE IN POINT
## The Language of Love

Perhaps the educator who best speaks the language of love is Leo Buscaglia, professor of education at the University of Southern California. Leo believes that "love is life" [and] becoming all that you can be." Let us end this chapter on emotion with some wisdom from his book *Living, Loving, and Learning*.

**Love**

We need to be loved. We need to be felt, we need to be touched, we need some sort of manifestation of love.

Happiness comes only when we push our brains and hearts to the farthest reaches of which we are capable. The purpose of life is to matter—to count, to stand for something, to have it make some difference that we lived at all.

To love is to risk not being loved in return. And that's all right too. You love to love, not to get something back, or it isn't love.

Don't miss love. It's an incredible gift.

abuse of their husbands, for example. The care of invalid parents and the delinquency of adolescent children can test the depths of love. Finally, the lasting commitment to another person that is part of a loving relationship is difficult to keep through poverty or poor health. The marriage vow "For richer or poorer, for better or worse, in sickness and in health, until death us do part" can seldom be fulfilled without personal sacrifice.

Love has other negative aspects. It can be used to exploit others. In excess, it can blind us to the need for change in ourselves, our loved ones, and even our nation. Mixed with scorn, it can produce vengeance. Mixed with insecurity, it can produce jealousy. Mixed with inadequacy, it can produce overpossessiveness. Mixed with false pride, it can produce prejudice and discrimination. Mixed with dogma, it can produce suicide and murder. Finally, mixed with national politics, it can produce war and the potential destruction of life on our planet.

**WHAT DO YOU THINK?**

- Do you think the potential of love has been oversold?
- Why or why not?

REVIEW QUESTIONS

54. Which of the following is rejected by social psychologists as an essential ingredient of love: passion / caring / intimacy.
55. Love is considered to be a prosocial / antisocial emotion.
56. Love is conducive to high / low self-esteem.
57. While love is pleasurable, most psychologists see it as being trivial in terms of human growth and change. T F
58. Fromm sees brotherly / self / mother love as a force capable of saving civilization.
59. Walster and Walster view love as a(an) agitated / euphoric / blissful state of physiological arousal.
60. John Money views love as flowing from the heart / liver / pituitary.
61. Giving love can / cannot become a loving act toward oneself.

*62.* In excess, love can <u>alert / blind</u> us to needed changes in ourselves and in those we love.

*63.* To feel empathy is to <u>accept / share the feeling of / feel sorry for</u> another person.

*The answers to these review questions are on page 215.*

## SUMMARY

■ In all its forms, emotion is a necessary and precious part of human existence.

■ Emotion is a subjective feeling state accompanied by internal changes and a predisposition to act so as to enhance survival.

■ Charles Darwin holds that emotions are innate, a product of evolution that have signal and survival value.

■ Pro-social emotions, such as love, facilitate human interaction. Anti-social emotions, such as fear, hinder such interaction.

■ Children are born with a potential for full, deep emotional sensation and expression. They require opportunity to be expressive and a degree of freedom to express negative emotions if they are to reach their full potential.

■ Cognitive growth affects emotional development in the infant. The social smile, negativism, and fear of the dark illustrate the connection between growing cognitions and emotional predispositions.

■ Physical growth affects emotional development. Increased size and strength makes possible a wide range of behaviors that bring forth strong emotional reactions from both the toddler and others.

■ Contemporary theories of emotion stress an associational network among thoughts, action impulses, and somatic disturbances.

■ The Yerkes-Dodson law states that the more complex a task, the lower the level of arousal that can be tolerated without impairing performance.

■ Emotions become dysfunctional when they are: (1) inappropriate, (2) deficient or excessive, and/or (3) expressed in nonconventional or aggressive ways.

■ Every society has "feeling rules" governing how people should feel and act under specific circumstances.

■ Aggression is seen as the result of (1) instincts, (2) frustrations, and (3) social-learning experiences.

■ Negotiation, compromise, and assertive behavior are seen as healthy and helpful alternatives to the aggressive response.

■ Emotional expression is communicated by (1) facial expressions, (2) verbal and vocal language, and (3) body language.

■ Appropriateness of emotional expression is determined by both self and others.

■ Emotional adjustment is complicated by the fact that we pass judgment on our own feelings.

■ Depression is seen as an unresolved state of sorrow or sadness that is accompanied by low self-esteem, a low rate of prosocial responding, feelings of helplessness, negative self-talk, and perhaps malfunctioning pleasure centers in the brain.

■ Guilt and anger, often repressed, are associated with depression and help account for its resistance to change.

■ Love is a powerful, prosocial emotion that is accompanied by high self-esteem, a high frequency of tender, loving acts, feelings of pleasant arousal, and a sense of being unconditionally accepted. Attachment, caring, and intimacy form the central core of this emotion.

■ Acceptance and empathy are additional emotional components of love that allow for individual growth and fulfillment.

■ The paradox of emotional freedom lies in the fact that our potential for emotional growth cannot be reached without a great deal of freedom and a judicious amount of control.

## SELECTED READINGS

Briggs, D. C. *Your Child's Self-Esteem.* Garden City N.Y.: Doubleday, 1970. A wealth of information on the foundations of healthy emotions in children.

Grings, W. W. and Dawson, M. E., *Emotions and Bodily Responses: A Psychophysiological Approach.* N.Y.: Academic Press, 1978. An updated and well documented account of emotion as internal bodily changes.

Harlow, H. F. *Learning to Love.* San Francisco: Albion, 1971. A detailed and fascinating account of the emergence of love in primates.

Montagu, A. *Learning Non-Aggression; The Experience of Non-Literate Societies.* New York: Academic Press, 1980. Our very survival would seem to depend on our rapid understanding and control of aggression.

Plutchik, R. and Kellerman, H., *Emotion: Theory, Research, and Experience.* New York: Academic Press, 1980. The sociobiological, physiological, and cognitive-behavioral approaches to emotion are explored with great care in this work.

Tavris, C. "Anger Defused," *Psychology Today.* Nov. 1982, Vol.18, No.11, 25–35. Expressing anger makes you angrier, solidifies an angry attitude, and establishes a hostile habit.

Walster, E. and Walster, W. *A New Look At Love.* Reading, Mass.: Addison-Wesley, 1978. Good facts and good theory concerning passionate love.

Wood, J. *How Do You Feel?* Englewood Cliffs, N.J.: Prentice-Hall, 1974. A short paperback text that presents an excellent overview of emotions.

Wood, J. *What Are You Afraid Of?* Englewood Cliffs, N.J.: Prentice-Hall, 1976. A guide to dealing with your fears.

## GLOSSARY

**aggression:** instrumental or hostile action intended to injure people or property or to gain specific outcomes.

**anti-social emotion:** a feeling state that has the effect of impairing social relationships.

**assertiveness:** a style of responding in which individual rights are protected without abusing others.

**assertiveness training:** the formal teaching and modeling of assertive behavior.

**basic emotions:** eight emotions which augment the fundamental behaviors of all living organisms.

**central nervous system (CNS):** the brain and spinal cord.

**depression:** a feeling of personal worthlessness, apathy, and hopelessness.

**emotion:** feelings, internal changes, and overt acts that have a survival function.

**emotional maturity:** a developed capacity for the full and appropriate expression of feelings.

**frustration-aggression:** a theory in which aggressive responses are said to be the direct result of painful personal experiences.

**kinesics:** the science of body language.

**limbic system:** primitive brain structures forming a border between the cortex and the thalamus. The limbic system is involved in motivation, emotion, and memory.

**lithium:** simple, inorganic salts used to decrease the severity of both manic and depressive episodes in some bipolar depressives.

**love:** a complex, undefinable, prosocial emotion.

**motivation:** internal states that activate and direct behavior.

**negativism:** defiant behavior, common in early childhood, but present in all age groups.

**parasympathetic nervous system:** a neural subsystem that conserves bodily energy during times of rest and security.

**peripheral nervous system:** that part of the nervous system outside the brain and the spinal cord.

**posture:** the relation of each part of the body with all other parts; the general bearing.

**pro-social emotion:** a feeling state that has the effect of facilitating social relations.

**sensory deprivation:** a profound absence of external stimuli resulting in cognitive, perceptual, and emotional distortions.

**social psychology:**   the study of the effect of others and of environments on an individual's responses.

**stranger anxiety:**   an infant's fear response to unfamiliar people.

**sympathetic nervous system:**   the neural subsystem that mobilizes the body for action during times of stress.

**viscera:**   the internal organs of the body, such as the heart.

## REFERENCES

Ainsworth, M. D. *Infancy in Uganda: Infant Care and the Growth of Attachment*. Baltimore: Johns Hopkins University Press, 1967.

Akiskal, H. S., and McKinney, W. T., Jr. "Depressive Disorders: Toward a Uniform Hypothesis." *Science* 182 (1973): 20–29.

Arieti, S., and Bemporad, J. *Severe and Mild Depression*. New York: Basic Books, 1979.

Averill, J. R. "Studies on Anger and Aggression: Implications for Theories of Emotion." *American Psychologist* 38 (November 1983): 1145–1160.

Bandura, A. *Social Learning Theory*. Englewood Cliffs, N.J.: Prentice-Hall, 1977.

Beck, A. T. *Depression*. New York: Harper & Row, 1967.

Beier, E. G. "Nonverbal Communication: How We Send Emotional Messages." *Psychology Today* (October 1974): 53–56.

Berkowitz, L. "Aversively Stimulated Aggression." *American Psychologist* 38 (November 1983): 1135–1144.

Birdwhistell, R. L. *Introduction to Kinesics*. Louisville, Ky.: University of Louisville Press, 1952.

Bloomberg, M. L. "Depression in Abused and Neglected Children." *American Journal of Psychotherapy* 35 (July 1981): 342.

Bower, G. H. "Mood and Memory." *American Psychologist* 36 (February 1981): 129–148.

Bowlby, S. *Attachment and Loss*. New York: Basic Books, 1969.

Brenner, M. "Caring, Love, and Selective Memory." Paper presented at the Annual Convention of the American Psychological Association, Washington, D.C., 1971.

Bridges, K. M. B. "Emotional Development in Early Infancy." *Child Development* 3 (1932): 324–334.

Buscaglia, L. F. *Living, Loving, and Learning*. New York: Holt, Rinehart and Winston, 1982.

Cannon, W. B. *Bodily Changes in Pain, Hunger, Fear, and Rage*, 2nd ed. New York: Appleton-Century-Crofts, 1929.

Carver, C. S., and Ganellen, R. J. "Depression and Components of Self-Punitiveness." *Journal of Abnormal Psychology* 92 (August 1983): 330–337.

Chance, M. R. A. "An Ethological Assessment of Emotion." In *Emotion: Theory, Research, and Experience*, vol. 1. Edited by R. Plutchik and H. Kellerman. New York: Academic Press, 1980.

Condon, W. S., and Sander, L. "Neonate Movement Is Synchronized with Adult Speech: International Participation and Language Acquisition." *Science* 183 (1974): 99–101.

Coppen, A. "The Biochemistry of Affective Disorders." *British Journal of Psychiatry* 113 (1967): 1237–1264.

Darwin, C. *The Expression of the Emotions in Man and Animals*. London: Murray, 1872.

Dollard, J.; Doob, L. W.; Miller, N. E.; Mowrer, O. H.; and Sears, R. R. *Frustration and Aggression*. New Haven, Conn.: Yale University Press, 1939.

Douvan, E., and Adeson, J. *The Adolescent Experience*. New York: Wiley, 1966.

Duffy, E. "An Explanation of 'Emotional' Phenomena without the Use of the Concept 'Emotion'." *Journal of General Psychology* 25 (1941): 283–293.

Ekman, P., and Friesen, W. V. *Unmasking the Face*. New York: Prentice-Hall, 1975.

Ellis, A. *Humanistic Psychotherapy: The Rational Emotive Approach*. New York: Julian Press, 1973.

Eron, L. D. "Parent-Child Interaction, Television Violence, and Aggression of Children." *American Psychologist* 37 (February 1982): 197–211.

Fisch, H.; Frey, S.; and Hirsbrunner, H. "Analyzing Nonverbal Behavior in Depression." *Journal of*

*Abnormal Psychology* 92 (August 1983): 307–318.

Fischer, C. "The Friendship Cure-All." *Psychology Today* 17 (March 1983): 74–78.

Forbes, L. M., and Chaney, R. H. "Physical Arousal Concealed during Emotional Stress." *Psychological Reports* (1978): 35.

Fowler, J., and Peterson, P. "Increasing Reading Persistence and Altering Attributional Style of Learned Helpless Children." *Journal of Educational Psychology* 73 (1981): 251–260.

Friedman, M., and Rosenman, R. F. *Type A Behavior and Your Heart*. New York: Knopf, 1974.

Frodi, A. N.; Lamb, M. E.; Leavitt, L. A.; Donovan, W. L.; Neff, C.; and Sherry, D. "Fathers' and Mothers' Responses to the Faces and Cries of Normal and Premature Infants." *Developmental Psychology* 14 (1978): 190–198.

Fromm, E. *The Art of Loving*. New York: Harper & Row, 1956.

Gilmartin, B. G. "The Case against Spanking." *Human Behavior* 8 (February 1979).

Harlow, H. F. *Learning to Love*. San Francisco: Albion, 1971.

Hebb, D. O. *A Textbook of Psychology*. Philadelphia: Saunders, 1958.

Hess, E. H. "The Role of Pupil Size in Communication." *Scientific American* 233 (1975): 110–119.

Hochschild, A. R. "Emotion Work, Feeling Rules, and Social Structure." *American Journal of Sociology* 85 (1979): 551–575.

Izard, C. E. *Human Emotions*. New York: Plenum Press, 1977.

James, W. "What Is an Emotion?" *Mind* 9 (1884):188–205.

Kanfer, R., and Zeiss, A. M. "Depression, Interpersonal Standard Setting, and Judgments of Self-Efficacy." *Journal of Abnormal Psychology* 92 (August 1983): 319–329.

Kastenbaum, R. *Death, Society, and Human Behavior*. St. Louis: Mosby, 1977.

Kubler-Ross, E. *On Death and Dying*. New York: Macmillan, 1969.

Laird, J. D.; Wagner, J. J.; Halal, M.; and Szegda, M. "Remembering What You Feel: Effects of Emotion on Memory." *Journal of Personality and Social Psychology* 42 (1982): 646–657.

Lang, P. J.; Levin, D. N.; Miller, G. A.; and Kozak, M. J. "Fear Behavior, Fear Imagery, and the Psychophysiology of Emotion: The Problem of Affective Response Integration." *Journal of Abnormal Psychology* 92 (August 1983): 276–306.

Lazarus, R. "Thoughts on the Relations between Emotion and Cognition." *American Psychologist* 37 (September 1982): 1019–1024.

Lewinsohn, P. M., and Hoberman, H. M. "Depression." In *International Handbook of Behavior Modification and Therapy*. Edited by A. S. Bellak, M. Hersen, and A. E. Kazdin. New York: Plenum Press, 1982.

Libbowitz, M., and Klien, D. "Love at First Sight? Or Chemistry?" In an article by Michael Hinds, *Miami News* (March 2, 1981): 3C.

Lindsley, D. B. "Emotion." In *Handbook of Experimental Psychology*. Edited by S. S. Stevens. New York: Wiley, 1951.

Mahler, M. S.; Pine, F.; and Bergman, A. *The Psychological Birth of the Infant*. New York: Basic Books, 1975.

Mehrabian, A. *Strangers in a Waiting Station*. Belmont, Calif.: Wadsworth, 1971.

Miller, W. R., and Seligman, M. E. P. "Depression and Learned Helplessness in Man." *Journal of Abnormal Psychology* 84 (1975): 228–238.

Miller, W. R., and Siegel, P. S. *Loving: A Psychological Approach*. New York: Wiley, 1972.

Money, J. "Pituitary Love." *Omni* 6 (November 1983): 53.

Morris, C. G. *Psychology: An Introduction*. Englewood Cliffs, N.J.: Prentice-Hall, 1979.

Mowrer, O. H., and Sears, R. R. *Frustration and Aggression*. New Haven, Conn.: Yale University Press, 1939.

Newman, R. S., and Hirt, M. "The Psychoanalytic Theory of Depression: Symptoms as a Function of Aggressive Wishes and Level of Field Articulation." *Journal of Abnormal Psychology* 92 (January 1983): 42–47.

Nikelly, A. G. *Achieving Competence and Fulfillment*. Monterey, Calif.: Brooks/Cole, 1977.

Papez, J. W. "A Proposed Mechanism of Emotion." *Archives of Neurology and Psychiatry* 38 (1937): 725–743.

Parkes, C. M. *Bereavement: Studies of Grief in Adult Life*. New York: International University Press, 1972.

Perls, F. S. *Gestalt Therapy Verbatim*. Lafayette, Calif.: Real People Press, 1969.

Peterson, C.; Seligman, M. E. P.; and Luborsky, L. "Attributions and Depressive Mood Shifts: A Case Study Using the Symptom-Context Method." *Journal of Abnormal Psychology* 92 (1983): 96–103.

Phillips, D. P. "The Impact of Mass Media Violence on U.S. Homicides." *American Sociological Review* 48 (August 1983): 560–568.

Plutchik, R. *Emotion: A Psychoevolutionary Synthesis*. New York: Harper & Row, 1980.

Plutchik, R., and Kellerman, H. *Emotion: Theory, Research, and Experience*. New York: Academic Press, 1980.

Rice, B. "The New Truth Machine." *Psychology Today* 12 (June, 1978): 61–78.

Rogers, C. *On Becoming a Person: A Therapist's View of Psychotherapy*. Boston: Houghton Mifflin, 1970.

Rogers, J. E. "Brain Triggers: Biochemistry and Behavior." *Science Digest* 1 (1983): 60–65.

Rosenthal, R.; Archer, D.; DiMatteo, M. R.; Koivumaki, J. H.; and Rogers, P. L. "Body Talk and Tone of Voice: The Language without Words." *Psychology Today* (September 1974): 64–68.

Roy, A. "Specificity of Risk Factors for Depression." *American Journal of Psychiatry* 138 (July 1981): 959–961.

Rubin, Z. *Liking and Loving: An Invitation to Social Psychology*. New York: Holt, Rinehart and Winston, 1973.

———. "Measurement of Romantic Love." *Journal of Personality and Social Psychology* 16 (1970): 267–268.

Scarr, S., and Salapatek, P. "Patterns of Fear Development during Infancy." *Merrill-Palmer Quarterly of Behavior Development* 16 (1970): 53–90.

Schachter, S. *Emotion, Obesity, and Crime*. New York: Academic Press, 1971.

Schachter, S., and Singer, J. E. "Cognitive, Social and Physiological Determinants of Emotional State." *Psychological Review* 69 (1962): 379–399.

Seligman, M. E. P. *Helplessness*. San Francisco: W. H. Freeman, 1975.

———. "Reversing Depression and Learned Helplessness." In *Psychology and Life*. Edited by P. G. Zimbardo and F. L. Ruch. Glenview, Ill.: Scott, Foresman, 1977.

Shurley, J. T. "Profound Experimental Sensory Isolation." *American Journal of Psychiatry* 117 (1960): 539–545.

Skinner, B. F. *About Behaviorism*. New York: Knopf, 1974: 245.

———. *Verbal Behavior*. New York: Appleton-Century-Crofts, 1957.

Spiesman, J. C. "Autonomic Monitoring of Ego Defense Process." In *Psychoanalysis and Current Biological Thought*. Edited by N. S. Greenfield and W. C. Lewis. Madison: University of Wisconsin Press, 1965.

Spitz, R. A. "Hospitalism: An Inquiry into the Genesis of Psychiatric Conditions in Early Childhood." In *The Psychoanalytic Study of the Child*. Edited by A. Freud. New York: International University Press, 1945.

Steer, R. A.; McElroy, M. E.; and Beck, A. T. "Structure of Depression in Alcoholic Men." *Psychological Reports* 50 (February–June 1982): 724–731.

Tavris, C. "Anger Defused." *Psychology Today* 18 (November 1982): 25–35.

Thornton, S., and Pilowsky, I. "Facial Expressions Can be Modelled Mathematically." *British Journal of Psychiatry* 140 (1982): 61–63.

Volkmar, F.; Bacon, S.; Shakir, S.; and Pfefferbaum, A. "Group Therapy in the Management of Manic-Depressive." *American Journal of Psychotherapy* 35 (April 1982): 226–234.

Wallen, R. "Emotional Styles Typology." In *An Expanding Repertoire of Behavior*. Edited by C. Mill and L. Porter. Washington, D.C.: NTL Institute for Applied Behavioral Science, 1972.

Walster, E., and Walster, W. *A New Look at Love*. Reading, Mass.: Addison-Wesley, 1978.

White, B. L. *The First Three Years of Life*. Englewood Cliffs, N.J.: Prentice-Hall, 1975.

Wilkerson, D. R. *Suicide*. Old Tapan, N.J.: Spire Books, 1978.

Zillmann, D., and Sapolsky, B. S. "What Mediates the Effect of Mild Erotica on Annoyance and Hostile Behavior in Males?" *Journal of Personality and Social Psychology* 35 (1977): 587–595.

## ANSWERS TO REVIEW QUESTIONS

**Page 179.** *1*. all of these  *2*. internal change  *3*. both cause and effect  *4*. evolutionary history  *5*. survival, signal

**Page 184.** *6*. quickly  *7*. weakens, more  *8*. the social smile  *9*. four months  *10*. incidental  *11*. T  *12*. greatest

**Page 186.** *13*. T  *14*. F  *15*. F  *16*. T  *17*. T  *18*. F  *19*. F  *20*. T

**Page 188.** *21*. somatic, autonomic  *22*. T  *23*. autonomic  *24*. sympathetic  *25*. divert our attention from  *26*. decreased

**Page 198.** *27*. functional  *28*. We and others  *29*. are  *30*. intensity  *31*. relax  *32*. facial  *33*. as aroused as  *34*. minimal  *35*. happy  *36*. at times  *37*. language  *38*. less  *39*. Hostile  *40*. instinctive  *41*. both arousing and eliciting stimuli  *42*. without

**Page 204.** *43*. high, low  *44*. rigid, downward  *45*. not doing  *46*. outside  *47*. anger  *48*. low, low  *49*. immature, irrational  *50*. both  *51*. negative  *52*. fail to  *53*. themselves

**Page 209.** *54*. passion  *55*. prosocial  *56*. high  *57*. F  *58*. brotherly  *59*. agitated  *60*. pituitary  *61*. can  *62*. blind  *63*. share the feeling of

**Interpretation of responses to quiz on page 205.**

Total your score for the even-numbered questions. This is the *love scale*. The odd-numbered questions comprise the *liking scale*. Do you both love and like your chosen partner? Loving and liking are qualitatively different. Women generally like and love their partners about the same, while men generally score higher on their reported love for their partner.

This is an interesting exercise to have your partner complete. Compare differences between loving and liking, not total scores. If you complete the scale a second time, using the name of a friend, you can test the sensitivity of the quiz in differentiating between love and liking.

Part III, Chapter 7, focuses on the process of adjustment by discussing stress. The chapter describes the demands that are placed on us and our mental, emotional, and physical responses to those demands. It explores the strain on our mental and physical health caused by the constant need to adjust to or make changes in our complex and changing world.

Major life events, such as marriage, and daily concerns, such as getting to class on time, produce changes in our bodies that may make us more vulnerable to disease and more susceptible to injury and death. Much is being learned of the complex relationship between stress and physical and mental illness, and Chapter 7 reviews some of this interesting new information.

How we view life, how we see our role in it, how effectively we see ourselves filling that role, and how many internal and outside resources we can call on in times of trouble all have been found to be good predictors of successful coping. Chapter 7 includes an exploration of direct and defensive coping methods along with its analysis of stress.

# STRESS

# 7

# STRESS

The human being is the only animal that is forever unfinished. All of us have the burden of completing ourselves during our lifetime. This is an awesome task. Our genes and our families are necessary but insufficient factors in our development. At any moment our emerging selves reflect choice and chance far more than a grand design. Our unique responses to life are not determined for us at birth or at maturity. We must forever change to meet the ever changing demands or strains of living.

Fortunately, we are constituted to do just that. Our central nervous system and our immune system can perceive minute changes in our environment and change their cellular structures to better meet the demands of the new reality. This coordinated bodily response to any perceived demand is termed **stress**. Stress makes it more likely that we will be able to cope successfully with whatever life has to offer.

**STRESS**

## DISCUSSION: THE STRESS RESPONSE

**Stress** is a nonspecific response of our bodies to any demand placed on them. We change so as to reduce the level of tension or stress. *Distress* results from our being either understimulated or overstimulated—by boredom or by anxiety, for example. This chapter will examine some causes and effects of stress and tell how we cope with it.

### ■ Human Stressors

Anything that humans can sense can be stress provoking. We can divide the possible human stressors into four categories, as shown in Table 7.1.

*Unlearned physical stressors* are those that can damage or overload our senses—for example, a sudden noise, scalding water, or an internal hemorrhage. *Unlearned psychological stressors* are painful or pleasurable psychological events, such as losing a loved one, getting or not getting a promotion, or winning at cards. Frustration, competition, and conflict are sources of unlearned psychological stress found in contemporary America.

*Learned physical stressors* require conditioning to become stressful: a touch by someone we despise, the sound of our boss approaching, or the touch of someone we love. *Learned psychological stressors* also must be conditioned. They are limited only by our ability to learn. We can, for instance, learn to swell with pride or cringe in terror at the sight of a colored cloth (a flag). We can learn to respond with stress to almost anything, including ideas, such as divorce, sex, or final exams.

Stress has a bad reputation, but remember, it is a nonspecific response to any demand, whether that demand is pleasant or unpleasant. Hans Selye, who has spent a lifetime studying stress, terms pleasant stress *eustress*. For unknown reasons, eustress has less damaging effects than the same amount of distress would have. Your heart may pound and your temperature may rise at your lover's touch—definite signs of stress—but you need have no fear.

**WHAT DO YOU THINK?**

■ Is what you fear the most physical, psychological, learned, or unlearned?

### ■ The Human Stress Response

According to Selye's *The Stress of Life* (1976), while the number and types of stressors are infinite, we give a single response to all of them.[1] When we are stressed, a host of internal changes take place to enable us to react with anger,

---

1. Specific bodily responses to specific stressors are now under investigation. A conservation–withdrawal response to stress has also been demonstrated. It will be discussed later.

TABLE 7.1
Stressors

|  | PHYSICAL | PSYCHOLOGICAL |
|---|---|---|
| Unlearned | Example: a loud noise | Example: frustration |
| Learned | Example: a raised eyebrow | Example: a Nazi flag |

fear, or lust and so be ready either to confront our stressor or to flee from it. This *flight or fight response* (Cannon, 1929) mobilizes energy so that we may survive by confrontation or escape. The amount of electrical activity in our brain increases, our vision and hearing improve, our blood clots faster, and we become less sensitive to pain. All of these factors and more are helpful in combat.

This remarkable adaptive response worked well for us when our enemies were lions, tigers, and bears. We could use our anger to direct our attack or our fear to effect our escape. Having done so, we could return to a calm and restful state until the next crisis.

Today, our lions have turned into freeways, gas lines, and urban sprawls; our tigers are now corporations, taxes, and regulations; our bears have become inflation, recession, and radiation. All place demands on us, but now they appear in phantom forms seemingly impossible to escape or to physically attack. Do our bodies grasp this fact? No. They keep responding as if our enemies still bore their ancient forms.

A great fear of many modern Americans is to be called on to speak to a large group of strangers, a modern version of bracing the lion in its den. Imagine yourself in such a situation.

> You approach the platform, notes in hand, and hear no applause following your introduction. As you are deciding whether to glance at your notes or at the audience, what physical sensations flood your consciousness? If you are terrified by the very idea of public speaking, you can hear the deadly silence and feel your eyes bulging. Your hands are cold and sweaty and the trembling in your legs reaches your hands, causing the notes to shake in front of you. Suddenly you have the urge to go to the bathroom.

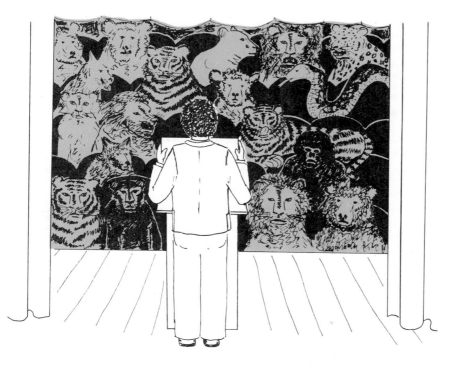

■ Lions and tigers and bears.

As you stand firm and are about to recite your well rehearsed opening lines, the lump in your throat, your dry mouth, and your rapid, shallow breathing make it impossible for you to deliver them. It does not matter, for you are certain your words could not be heard above the loud thumping of your heart, the pounding in your head, and the gurgling in your stomach.

You feel your face drain of color. Your knees give way, and consciousness leaves you....

Your emotions do not seem to be helping. But consider your situation. You are in an artificial environment, engaged in a stressful encounter in which it is inappropriate to either flee or fight. But your brain and viscera are preparing your body to do just that. Every symptom you have felt is useful from the standpoint of physical defense or attack.

Sweat is our cooling mechanism, and sweaty palms provide a better grip. Cold hands and trembling legs reflect a massive blood shift toward the body's vital centers—its brain, heart, and large muscles. Some muscle groups tighten, other relax so that you can move and breathe with greater capacity. The blood flows away from your digestive tract and genitals. You do not need to waste energy while in combat; thus you experience the lump in the throat, the dry mouth, and nausea. Nor do you need to carry excess baggage into battle, so your bladder and bowels automatically empty when you are under extreme stress. Even fainting may be seen as a physical defense mechanism, for it prevents further pain and brings a stillness that might help avoid detection.

Many additional, unfelt changes are also taking place. For example, your spleen is increasing its production of red corpuscles to improve blood clotting, fat is increasing in your bloodstream for ready energy where needed, and your liver is supplying glycogen for energy. This massive mobilization and redirection of energy, termed **catabolism** takes place unconsciously. You do not have to will your heart to beat faster or your breathing to quicken.

It is unfortunate that few of these changes aid us in public speaking. It is a price we pay for leaving the cave.

REVIEW
QUESTIONS

*1.* People are the only <u>unfinished / finished</u> animals.

*2.* The number of stressors is limited <u>by our ability to sense changes / to physical</u>

<u>dangers or threats of danger</u>.

*3.* Our bodies respond in <u>specific ways to each demand / the same way to all</u>

<u>demands</u>.

*4.* Hans Selye terms this nonspecific response _____ .

*5.* The mobilization of energy for confrontation or escape is termed <u>c_____</u> .

*6.* Our bodies respond to traffic jams and income taxes <u>differently than / the same</u>

<u>way</u> our ancestors responded to lions and bears.

*The answers to these review questions are on page 262.*

## DISCUSSION: PROLONGED STRESS

The dry throat and other symptoms of distress are not the only price we pay for our civilized existence. In ancient times when danger passed, a deep calm descended on us. The relief that slowed our breathing also reduced the amount of oxygen we consumed and the carbon dioxide we produced. Our brain activity also slowed and our sweating ceased. Blood pressure and heart rate decreased, and even the chemistry of our blood altered. These changes had a profound restorative effect on our minds and bodies. The stress response, necessary for survival, was balanced by the **restorative response,** equally necessary.

When speaking before a group of strangers, we cannot run away or fight them, even though we are well prepared to do so. We therefore cannot directly and completely discharge the energy we have mobilized. We cannot experience the deep calm of the restorative response. Stress remains within us in the form of glandular secretions, muscle contractions, and neural discharges. We feel these states as anxiety, anger, or depression.

## ■ When Stress Is Harmful

Stress is harmful when we respond to it by becoming nervous and withdrawn, or irritable and antagonistic. These behaviors hinder our growth, our potential for becoming a finished animal, a complete human being. Bad feelings and unproductive behavior are a high price to pay for civilization, but the total price is higher still. Hans Selye describes many of our modern ills as **diseases of adaptation**. We are being injured or destroyed by our own defense systems, which have not been able to keep up with the times. Selye, having studied the general effect on an organism of any demand placed on it, reports that prolonged, unremitted stress will produce a great variety of **psychosomatic** disorders from headaches to heart attacks.

■ *The Body's Responses to Persistent Stress*   Selye describes our responses as a group of changes that occur in sequence, a **general adaptation syndrome** (GAS). These involve the entire body and are intended to help the body survive. the GAS can be divided into three stages—the alarm reaction, the stage of resistance, and the stage of exhaustion.

The *alarm reaction* is the flight or fight response. If we are unsuccessful in warding off an illness, for example, we display general symptoms such as a loss of sleep, aching joints, loss of appetite, headaches, and low-grade fevers. All these occur in response to any illness.

The *stage of resistance* occurs if the stressor continues. Our bodies then develop a resistance to that specific stress, and the earlier symptoms disappear. We may regain our sleep and eating patterns, for example, but still feel tired and not interested in eating. Our neural and glandular systems remain hyperactive, and we remain overstimulated and constantly mobilized for defense.

The *stage of exhaustion* occurs when the stressor continues despite our best defenses. Glands must rest and restore their balance. If they cannot rest, they overtax themselves, resistance stops, and symptoms reappear; if the stressor persists, we may die. After such a death, an autopsy usually reveals enlarged adrenal glands, a wasted **lymphatic system** (part of the system that defends against disease) and peptic ulcers. All this is found in addition to the failed organ, such as the heart, that is officially listed as the cause of death.

■ *Adaptive Responses That Can Kill*   We can die of grief, fear, frustration, or triumph. Walter Cannon (1942) and George Engel (1977) write of **emotional**

**death**. Cannon was fascinated by reports of voodoo death, a form of execution in which one who has violated a sacred taboo is placed under a fatal spell. Cannon writes of a young healthy man who died seemingly without reason after a witchdoctor pointed a bone at him. The young man was an Australian Aborigine, a member of a tribe that believes in voodoo.

"Death by bonepoint" is a rarity in our modern world. But is emotional death as rare as it would first appear? Engel discusses 275 cases in which death occurred in persons not thought to be in danger of dying. For example, a healthy fifty-seven-year-old school teacher died of a heart attack on the day he learned of the death of his beloved father in-law. These recent, civilized victims seem vastly different in culture and socialization from the superstitious Aborigine. What factors link both to psychological death? Cannon emphasizes two factors that may apply to Engel's cases as well. The first is *cognitive appraisal*. The victim and his or her family must firmly believe that to be cursed means to die. The second factor is the sudden *removal of all social supports*. This occurs when the family and tribe act as if the victim were already dead. Engel reports a third factor, a sense of *loss of control,* a feeling of helplessness and hopelessness. Both groups share extreme excitement, a sense of powerlessness, and a lack of social supports. Under these severe conditions, psychological trauma can be transformed into physical exhaustion and actual death.

### ■ The Stress of Loneliness

**WHAT DO YOU THINK?**

■ Is there a difference between being alone and being lonely?

Our culture emphasizes independence, freedom, and the joys of the single life. We seem immune to being injured when we are cut off from our social supports. However, James Lynch, in *The Broken Heart* (1977), cites overwhelming data to support the notion that loneliness is associated today with increased death due to heart attacks, cancer, and strokes. He also finds that social conditions that lead to a life without family or close friends are related to increased psychosomatic disorders. A tendency toward increased hospitalization, work loss, accidents, injuries, debilitating diseases, and suicides accompanies loneliness. The common element in these cases of death, illness, accidents, and injuries is the physiological response to the prolonged stress of loneliness.

■ *At Home Alone*   The Case in Point tells how Japanese who leave Japan can encounter stress resulting in part from loneliness. People who stay at home can suffer loneliness too. Young women may find the isolation associated with motherhood very stressful. At times, the mother's stress may be taken out on the helpless infant. Salzinger and associates (1983) find that a mother's personal social network is closely associated with whether she mistreats her child. Child-abusing mothers are more isolated from their families, have fewer peer connections, and are more insulated as well (*insulation* means a lack of skill in reaching out and interacting with others). Stress and social ignorance combine to endanger the children of such mothers.

Interestingly, mother's tears may protect her child. An analysis of the chemical composition of human tears produced by emotion, and not irritation, shows that they contain prolactin, a pain-killing neurotransmitter. "The reason people feel better after crying is because tears remove chemicals that build up as a result of stress. . . . People who get ulcers, colitis and similar disorders cry less than people who don't" (Kotulak, 1984).

## CASE IN POINT
## Becoming American

It is difficult to be alone in Japan. It is a small, crowded, busy country that stresses loyalty to one's family, one's neighborhood (Japanese typically buy one house, near their relatives and job, and live in it for life), and one's company. The Japanese love social rituals and are, as individuals, less mobile and competitive than their American counterparts. They also suffer fewer heart attacks.

it has been proposed that the diet of the Japanese (more fish, less fatty meat, more vegetables and complex cereals) accounts for their lower incidence of heart disease. Now it appears that stress levels may play a vital role. Blakeslee (1975) reports that a study of Japanese-Americans indicates stress can be a major factor in heart disease. Japanese immigrants face a choice. They can live within a Japanese-American community and maintain close ties to their homeland's traditions, or they can rapidly adopt the customs and traditions of their new land. This choice appears to affect their health.

Neither diet nor smoking separates the behavior of heart-attack-prone Japanese-Americans from their more protected fellow Japanese immigrants. What separates them, it seems, is their adoption of a nontraditional lifestyle. As a group, they are more competitive and more aggressive; they are also more isolated and establish and maintain fewer social supports. In short, the more vulnerable new Japanese-American is one who strives to emulate the style of the rugged American individualist. (See Friedman and Rosenman, 1974.)

■ Stress and Life Events

The link between critical life events and physical and mental health has been carefully charted by Adolf Meyer of Johns Hopkins University since the 1930s. His anecdotal records were systematized into a **social readjustment rating scale** by Thomas Holmes and Richard Rahe in the 1960s. Using the stress of one's wedding day as a midpoint of stress, ranked 50, the instrument ranks each of forty-three critical life changes on a scale ranging from 0 to 100. "Death of a spouse" ranks at the top of the scale. Holmes and Rahe term these values *life-change units (LCUs)*. They conducted studies relating total LCUs of an individual in a given year with subsequent changes in health. When LCUs totaled between 150 and 199 (mild life crisis), 37 percent of those studied were found to have undergone an appreciable deterioration in health. Between 200 and 299 LCUs (moderate life crisis), the figure rose to over 51 percent; and among those suffering major life crisis, 79 percent fell ill within the following year (Holmes and Rahe, 1967). These figures may be conservative estimates, because Rahe now reports that the crucial variable is not the change itself, but how change is seen by the affected individuals.

■ Stress and Other Variables

Harris and Landreth (1981), in a study of college freshmen, found that several cognitive variables provided valuable additional information concerning the relationship between stress and health. For example, in addition to total life-change units, three other factors seem to play a role. The seriousness of an illness increases as an individual's (1) self-concept decreases, (2) trait anxiety increases (high trait anxiety is a general tendency to see life as threatening), and

(3) subjective evaluation of stress increases. College students with positive self-concepts feel less anxious, interpret events as less threatening, and experience healthier lives than their anxious, negative fellow students. This occurs even when both groups experience the same number of life-change units.

Orth-Gomer and Ahlbom (1980) confirm that people's perception of the amount and severity of the stress they are experiencing alters the impact of the stress on their health. Biersner, McHugh and Rahe (1981) find that a *perception of control*—a belief that what we do can make a difference—increases the impact of stressors on us. If, for example, we attribute the cause of a failure to uncontrollable internal factors (we were ill that day) or uncontrollable external factors, then it has few implications for our future performance, and it produces little stress within us (Foushee, Davis, Stephan, and Bernstein 1980).

Perceived supports are related to stress and illness in complex ways. If we see that we have support available to help us meet a demand, that knowledge *adds* stress because it increases our perception of personal control and responsibility. However, it also increases our tolerance of stress, because it makes it appear more likely that we can directly act on the stressor with good results (Biersner, 1981). In general, increased supports, especially social supports, are seen as a defense against the dangers of excessive stress.

Lazarus (1981) makes the sensible point that stress related illness is the result of having to make too much adaptation in too brief a time. It is often the small, daily stressors that take their toll. He reports that for college students at least, it is minor hassles, rather than major life events, that tend to maintain stress at unhealthy levels. The little hassles of college life revolve around three themes: (1) wasting time, (2) meeting high standards, and (3) experiencing personal loneliness.

Because college students differ from the general population, a special version of Holmes and Rahe's Social Adjustment Scale has been prepared for them and tested on college freshmen. The amount of stress reported by them was found to directly relate to their general health. The scale is reproduced in Table 7.2. See how you compare with your fellow scholars.

How stressful life has been for you seems to predict how well you will do academically in college (Lloyd, Alexander, Rice, Greenfield 1980): The higher the LCUs, the lower the GPAs (grade point averages) for the next two years. There is a "threshhold effect." When you experience fewer than twelve life-change events in one year, your grades are not likely to suffer. But twelve or more may hurt your GPA. Brown and Rosenbaum (1983) found a similar threshold effect for stressful events and IQ scores for children. The occurrence of more than fifteen events in one year was related to a drop in IQ from 105 to 91.

Results from Lloyd's study shed light on a value system that might explain why some students do poorly in college. It seems that play and a job mean more to the poorer student than to the better one. At least, changes in work (either new responsibilities or a new job) and changes in recreation are the two factors that produce the greatest negative effect on the grades of the already poor student. Many of you may have friends who have chosen a car and play over college itself. They work to support a car that they see as necessary for the good life; and have no time left for their classes.

**WHAT DO YOU THINK?**

■ Does your stress come from minor hassles, or major life changes?

■ Do you think it is the stressors or your perception of them that is most important in how stress affects your health?

TABLE 7.2

The College Schedule of Recent Experience

You can get an idea of how much stress you have experienced lately by (1) multiplying the value for each event by the number of times it happened to you during the past year (maximum of four times) and (2) totaling your results. Scores below 347 are considered to fall in the low stress catagory, and scores above 1,435 are classified as representing high stress.

| EVENT | NUMERICAL VALUE |
|---|---|
| (1) Entered College | 50 |
| (2) Married | 77 |
| (3) Trouble with your boss | 38 |
| (4) Held a job while attending school | 43 |
| (5) Experienced the death of a spouse | 87 |
| (6) Major change in sleeping habits | 34 |
| (7) Experienced the death of a close family member | 77 |
| (8) Major change in eating habits | 30 |
| (9) Change in or choice of major field of study | 41 |
| (10) Revision of personal habits | 45 |
| (11) Experienced the death of a close friend | 68 |
| (12) Found guilty of minor violations of the law | 22 |
| (13) Had an outstanding personal achievement | 40 |
| (14) Experienced pregnancy or fathered a pregnancy | 68 |
| (15) Major change in health or behavior of family member | 56 |
| (16) Had sexual difficulties | 58 |
| (17) Had trouble with in-laws | 42 |
| (18) Major change in number of family get-togethers | 26 |
| (19) Major change in financial state | 53 |
| (20) Gained a new family member | 50 |
| (21) Change in residence or living conditions | 42 |
| (22) Major conflict or change in values | 50 |
| (23) Major change in church activities | 36 |
| (24) Marital reconciliation with your mate | 58 |
| (25) Fired from work | 62 |
| (26) Were divorced | 76 |
| (27) Changed to a different line of work | 50 |
| (28) Major change in number of arguments with spouse | 50 |
| (29) Major change in responsibilities at work | 47 |
| (30) Had your spouse begin or cease work outside the home | 41 |
| (31) Major change in working hours or conditions | 42 |
| (32) Marital separation from mate | 74 |
| (33) Major change in type and/or amount of recreation | 37 |
| (34) Major change in use of drugs | 52 |
| (35) Took on a mortage or loan of less than $10,000 | 52 |
| (36) Major personal injury or illness | 65 |
| (37) Major change in use of alcohol | 46 |
| (38) Major change in social activities | 43 |
| (39) Major change in amount of participation in school activities | 38 |
| (40) Major change in amount of independence and responsibility | 49 |
| (41) Took a trip or a vacation | 33 |
| (42) Engaged to be married | 54 |
| (43) Changed to a new school | 50 |
| (44) Changed dating habits | 41 |
| (45) Trouble with school administration | 44 |
| (46) Broke or had broken a marital engagement or a steady relationship | 60 |
| (47) Major change in self-concept or self-awareness | 57 |

Source: Marx, M. B.; Garrity, T. F.; and Bowers, F. R. "The Influence of Recent Life Experiences on the Health of College Freshmen," *Journal of Psychosomatic Research* 19 (1975): 97.

## ■ The Physical Basis of Emotional Death

We can relate the stress from life changes to Selye's idea of the general adaptation syndrome and to Cannon's and Engel's work on emotional death. Cannon and Engel explain emotional death in terms of a breakdown in the brain's capacity to oversee the complex rhythm of the cardiovascular system under conditions of extreme stress. The sympathetic nervous system (SNS) increases heartbeat.

FIGURE 7.1
Stress and Disease

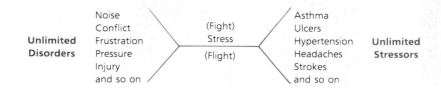

The parasympathetic nervous system (PNS) decreases heartbeat. The two must be working in harmony to maintain life. If exhaustion occurs because of extreme and conflicting signals (from SNS overstimulation), the coordinated firing of the neural pacemakers of the heart is disrupted; the heart quivers but does not pump. Blood pressure drops, and vital organs, deprived of oxygen and nutrients, cease to function. The consequence is emotional death. The heart can also slow down so much (from PNS overstimulation) that it is flooded, and the same sequence follows, again resulting in emotional death.

Richard Rahe is currently researching psychophysiological mechanisms that connect life change experiences with the onset of illness. He reports (1977) that cholesterol and epinephrine are positively related to life changes. If CLUs rise, so do these two chemicals in our system. Both are associated with stress-related disorders.

### ■ Physical Illnesses That Are Stress Related

Selye (1976) holds that *all* diseases are related to stress. Others believe at least some illnesses are stress related—various authorities have suggested links between arthritis and repressed anger, cancer and depression/anxiety, and heart attacks and power conflicts. (Fried, 1980; Pines, 1980). High blood pressure, headaches, muscle pains, allergies, sleep disorders, sexual disorders, bone disorders, digestive tract problems, respiratory problems, and heart problems have all been associated with stress. Kringlen (1977) studied identical twins whose lifestyles as adults were significantly different. The twin who lived with more pressure (more stress) was more likely to suffer a heart attack. As you recall, the number of potential stressors is unlimited and the stress response is limited. To extend the picture, the number of stress-related disorders also appears to be unlimited. The situation is diagramed in Figure 7.1.

Unresolved stress can be dangerous to your health.

REVIEW
QUESTIONS

*7.* A deep calm that follows a stressful episode is known as the r_____

r_____ .

*8.* When we can neither flee nor fight a stressor, we can / cannot fully enjoy the benefits of the restorative response.

*9.* Hans Selye describes many of our modern ills as diseases of a_____ .

factors as *10.* The alarm reaction of the GAS is characterized by a reduction of symptoms / a mobilization of energy.

*11.* The stage of exhaustion is characterized by <u>enlarged adrenal glands / a reduction of symptoms</u>.

*12.* James Lynch, in *The Broken Heart,* relates psychosomatic disorders with _____ .

*13.* Both the primitives of Cannon and the moderns of Engel shares <u>social support / hope / excitement</u>.

*14.* According to Selye, stress can be produced by <u>unlimited / limited</u> stressors, and, in turn, can produce <u>unlimited / limited</u> disorders.

*15.* Such cognitive factors as perception of control and perception of social support <u>can / cannot</u> influence the impact a stressor will have on our subsequent health.

*The answers to these review questions are on page 262.*

## DISCUSSION: STRESS AND PHYSICAL AND MENTAL ILLNESS

In spite of the theories mentioned in the last section, no biomedical sequence connecting a specific stressor with a specific illness has yet been demonstrated. The search is complicated first by the fact that there are great individual differences in the way we respond to given stressors. Some of us raise our blood pressure, others raise the heart rate. The identical stressor may produce different intensities of response in different subjects. A second complication is our differing genetic makeup. Psychosomatic illnesses are thought to attack the weakest link in our chain of organs, muscles, and glands. For some it is the heart; with others it is the pancreas. Under stress, the first group may develop heart trouble, the second may develop diabetes. A third complication is the profound effects learning has on visceral responding. If you received attention for stomachaches as a child, while your friend received more response for headaches, under stress you might develop ulcers while your friend might complain of migraine. Profiles of personality types related to stress disorders are included in the Selected Readings at the end of this chapter.

### ■ Stress and Physical Illness

Let's consider an example of how stress may lead to physical illness. Imagine yourself in an aversive situation. You hold a dirty, boring job that you cannot afford to give up. Let us further assume that you choose to respond with anger toward those you hold responsible for the frustrations, responsibilities, and conflicts built into your work situation. You cannot discharge that anger directly by attacking your boss, nor can you eliminate the source by leaving the job. The scene is set.

When anger is directed towards others, the acids in our digestive system may remain at high levels, and ulcers and other gastric disorders may result (Brady, Porter, Conrad, and Mason, 1958; Weiss, 1972). In addition, small blood vessels may contract, redirecting blood flow and producing prolonged high blood pressure.

This high blood pressure is the silent killer of our age. Elevated pressure, combined with serum cholesterol (blood fats) and small blood clots, may lead to **atherosclerosis.** The fats and clots are forced into the arterial walls, clogging and stretching them and bringing about hardening of the arteries (Benson, 1975). When arteries become clogged, the blood supply to vital organs decreases, and **angina** and heart attacks may result. If a clot breaks loose, it may circulate and block blood flow to any part of the body, resulting in disability and even death. If a vessel breaks in the brain, or if a vessel leading to the brain breaks, the loss of mental and physical functions associated with a **cerebral stroke** occurs.

Stress may also be related to bacterial or viral disorders. Germs are not the cause but simply a necessary condition for disease to occur (Pelletier, 1979). Our response to these invaders is also important, and it depends on our immune system. When an invader enters our bodies, our immune system identifies it as foreign and produces cells that surround, limit, and finally kill it. The activities of the immune system are suppressed when we fight or flee. In addition to the fight or flight response to stress, we also manifest a **conservation–withdrawal** response when we are unable to fight or flee. When we feel helpless like this, our bodies release opiate-like substances that decrease our perception of pain but that also suppress the ability of our immune systems to produce T-lymphocytes, white blood cells that fight invaders. This reduction in the effectiveness of the immune system makes us more vulnerable to disease (Anderson, 1982). Colds and other viral disorders may then take command.

Disorders such as diabetes, arthritis, and allergies may also result from a malfunctioning immune system. If we identify an organism incorrectly, we may attack our own tissue (arthritis), fail to attack a foe (cancer), or maintain a level

**WHAT DO YOU THINK?**

- When do you usually get colds and/or headaches?
- Could they be stress-related?

---

## CASE IN POINT
## First Things First

Mother nature knows best—or does she? When our brain senses that we are under attack, messages sent to our pituitary gland cause it to stimulate our adrenal cortex (the outer portion of our adrenal gland) to secrete hormones throughout our body. These hormones help release sugars, which provide quick energy for responding to the attack. However, the same hormones delay growth of new tissue around a wound, inhibit formation of antibodies, and decrease the formation of white blood cells. We suppress more than our immune system while under attack. Our reproductive systems, male and female, are also suppressed. Both menstrual cycle and sperm production are curtailed while we are under stress, and we lose interest in sex.

Obviously, mother nature is taking care of first things first. She is conserving our energy

and directing it to the front lines for either attack or retreat. Later, when we are safe, will be time enough to heal wounds, repair injuries, ward off disease germs, and rekindle our sexual flames.

If stress is prolonged—if we are constantly under attack—Mother Nature works against us. During this time, we are increasingly susceptible to disease and injury. A good example of this period of susceptibility is during *bereavement,* the period of mourning following the death of a loved one. The feelings of helplessness and loneliness that characterize bereavement are perhaps the most stressful experiences for humans and are accompanied by a markedly depressed immune response on the part of the bereaved for a period of from two to four months (Anderson, 1982). Surviving loved ones are themselves at great risk during this period.

## CASE IN POINT
## Cancer in College

Steven Locke (1978) found a way to conduct an experiment on college student volunteers without directly exposing them to either prolonged stress or to cancer cells. He studied the efficiency of the immune system under conditions of increasing stress as measured in LCUs. College students, identified by a questionnaire as being under high or low levels of life changes, were rated on their ability to cope. Blood samples containing approximately equal numbers of white blood cells were drawn from each subject. These white cells, which fight infection, were then exposed to human leukemia cells. Each leukemia cell was tagged with radioactive chromium. Each time a leukemia cell was killed by the action of the white cells, a bit of chromium was automatically released into a test tube. These bits were counted. The number of bits of chromium became a measure of the *natural killer cell activity* (NKCA) within each blood sample. The study showed that the NKCA was best for the groups that coped well with stress even when they had a high level of life changes.

of attack out of proportion to the threat (asthma). Such diseases, unlike the common cold, are not self-limiting.

Cancer, in animals, at least, has also been experimentally linked to prolonged stress. Healthy rats exposed to cancer cells rarely contract cancer. Healthy rats placed under prolonged stress, then exposed to cancer cells, frequently contract cancer (Locke, 1978).

Headaches, too, can be related to stress, but not through immune system responses. Muscle tension and altered blood flow combine to produce the pain and nausea associated with migraine headaches. Skeletal muscles in spasm account for the nonthrobbing, dull band of pain known as the tension headache (Stoyva, 1977). A headache is almost always psychosomatic, a habitual response to stress rather than a response to disease or injury.

### ■ Stress and Mental Illness

Distortions of mood, thought, and/or activity are largely attempts by us to eliminate, relieve, control, organize, or understand painful conditions of intolerable stress. Vinokur and Selzer (1975) find higher instances of perceived stress reported by populations designated as suffering from a range of mental problems, from paranoia through depression. People under stress are less able to concentrate, withstand pain, endure fatigue, or make sense of the important events happening around them. Hans Selye has theorized that chronic unresolved stress can result in emotional and physical exhaustion. Fatigue, apathy, and a loss of curiosity and the capacity for joy may result from stress. We may remain forever unfinished, operating on a more primitive, less fully human, plane of existence.

REVIEW
QUESTIONS

*16.* At present, it is <u>easy / difficult</u> to trace a specific type of stress to a specific medical problem.

*17.* Bodily responses to <u>fear / anger / fear or anger</u> can produce high blood pressure.

*18.* Heart attacks and strokes are disorders that can result from h_____

b_____ p_____.

*19.* Hormones released during stress hinder the working of our i_____ system and leave us vulnerable to disease.

*20.* According to Locke, good copers produce <u>more / less</u> NKCA than poor copers even under conditions of high stress.

*21.* <u>Arthritis / Cancer / Headache</u> is more clearly associated with stress than with disease or injury.

*22.* People under intense stress are <u>more / less</u> able to concentrate, endure pain and fatigue, and make sense of events.

*The answers to these review questions are on page 262.*

---

## DISCUSSION: JOB STRESS

With the possible exception of the home, no institution shapes our personality as much as does our job. Our daily work and the rewards we derive from that work affect our self-esteem, our social relations, and our physical and mental health.

### ■ The Basis of Job Stress

While Selye maintains that we were made to work, the design and location of work can have serious effects on our well-being. If job-related health disorders were given consideration by our legislatures, we would all be able to depreciate ourselves during our work life for income tax benefits. Some could qualify for greater deductions than others. In addition to such pollutants as chemicals, asbestos, tobacco, coal, and similar noxious materials, noise itself is a pollutant of great significance. Glass and Singer (1971) found that a measurable amount of stress occurs every time noise is introduced into a workplace. Loud, soft, predictable or not, *all noise causes stress,* even when the workers think themselves adapted to it. After one half hour of noise, work output suffers and workers become less tolerant of frustration. German, Italian, and Russian studies (Tanner, 1976) all link noise to worker illness and, in general, extend the findings of Glass and Singer (1972).

How far you have to travel each day to and from work is also an indication of the amount of stress you will absorb. If you drive, the longer trip over the more congested route is more stressful. If you leave the driving to others, the longer trip appears to be less provoking. Using stress hormones taken from urine samples, Freedman (1975) found that stress was less for commuters who got on at the beginning of the train line than for those who got on near its central terminus. This was explained in terms of freedom of choice and sense of personal control. The early riders could select seats and companions and make similar choices denied later travelers. Here, psychological rather than physical factors appear to regulate the amount of stress.

On the job, anxiety and the number of health-related problems have been found to vary with the frequency at which stressful events are encountered. The number of jobs held at the same time and the hours and conditions of work are related to stress. Dr. Mark Russek, professor of cardiovascular disease at New York Medical Center, reports that ninety-one of a hundred heart attack victims he studied were holding two or more jobs and working more than sixty hours a week, or they were experiencing unusual job insecurity, discomfort, or frustration. Long hours, low pay, routine tasks, pollution, insecurity, and little opportunity for increased responsibility or advancement are stressors common to low-level jobs.

## ■ Stress Related to Types of Jobs

Dr. Michael Smith (1977) of the National Institute of Occupational Safety and Health reports that rank-and-file workers get just as sick as, if not sicker than, industry tycoons and professional overachievers as a result of on-the-job stress. The "simple" jobs are not stress free, and the rich and powerful do not pay for their success by having stress-linked breakdowns, as was once thought to be the case (Tanner, 1976).

Women and poor people, who hold a disproportionate number of undesirable jobs and are less able to use anger to their advantage, report more stress and more health problems. In fact, women in general report more perceived stress at work. Those who report high job stress and high life-change units experience a greater number of symptoms of stress-related health disorders. This holds true for high- or low-salaried women in positions of high or low responsibility (Pepitone-Arreola-Rockwell et al., 1981).

According to Robert Karasek (1983), "The greatest stress occurs in jobs where the individual faces heavy psychological demands, yet has little control over how to get the work done" (p. 45). Over 25 percent of all jobs fall in this "high-demand, low-control" category. Jobs in which people have to work at a pace set by a piece of machinery are among today's most stressful jobs. Karasek maintains that low-level service jobs, where company rules strictly dictate how the worker must relate to the client, also are very stress provoking. Stressful common jobs are held by inspectors, health technicians, clinical laboratory technicians (but not doctors), miners, industrial workers, warehouse personnel, and office managers. Librarians, professional technicians (who do research and non-routine work), stock handlers, store checkout workers, repairmen, and college professors were found to be in the least stressful occupations.

### ■ Stress in Jobs Open to College Graduates

College graduates expect fulfilling and rewarding careers. Such positions are not plentiful, and much stress is experienced in training for and obtaining them. People with a high need to achieve are often torn between being aggressive and being liked. Both these attributes are thought necessary in top management. People who believe it necessary to hide their anger during this drive for power are prime candidates for stress disorders (McClelland, 1976).

Glamorous jobs in the communications and entertainment industries are chained to time (deadlines, air times, and so on). Friedman and Rosenman (1974) report that it is better to work twelve or fourteen hours a day without

**WHAT DO YOU THINK?**

■ Are you in or do you anticipate entering a high- or low-stress occupation?

■ What are the trade-offs?

■ Leaders are often torn between a need to be aggressive and a need to be liked.

time pressure than four hours with time pressure. For the young executive, too much responsibility, too heavy a workload, and decisions that affect the lives of others are particularly stressful (Burke, 1976). Not enough information to get the job done, not being able to influence superiors, and too slow personal progress on the job all create occupational stress without increasing performance or profits.

## ■ Type A Individuals and Job Stress

Some straining young workers are known as **Type A** individuals. They are characterized as impatient, impulsive, competitive, aggressive, and hostile. They display a high drive to achieve, a sense of time urgency, and an elevated devotion to the job (Waldron, et al, 1980). These characteristics seem to benefit the organization (at least in the short run)—at the expense of the individual. Such workers have an elevated risk of coronary heart disease.

The tempestuous Type A person sometimes seems to be acting out of anger and hostility, but is also functioning from a base of repressed anxiety grounded in a fear of failure. Suzanne Kobasa (1979) finds that the equally hard-driving competitor of the Type A person, one who loves challenge and change and is fully involved in social as well as work relationships, does not suffer as much from job-related psychosomatic disorders (Selye and Cherry, 1978; Kobasa, Maddi, and Kahn, 1982).

As a group, Type A personalities attain higher education in greater numbers, receive more honors and awards, hold higher professional status, and achieve higher social class standing. More Type A women are employed, and they are more aggressive, active, and angry, than their Type B female counterparts.

■ *Type A Individuals in College*   Colleges have more than their share of Type A students. Waldron, et al, (1980) finds that Type A students spend more time studying, earn higher grade point averages, and seem to possess the attitudes and habits that contribute to career success. They are superior in academic performance. However, their social performance suffers by comparison. They are not more successful in opposite-sex relations nor in social relationships in general.

High academic pressure and high social insecurity seem to be associated with high stress among college students (Suls, Becker, and Mullen, 1981). The sad fact is that the generally successful Type A students find little joy in superior academic performance. They are interested in social comparisons, and their occasional episodes of poor school performance, combined with their lack of social supports, make them vulnerable to stress. They exhibit longer and stronger reactions to everyday life stressors. They feel bad when they do badly, but typically do not feel great when they do well.

■ *Home Environments of Type A Individuals*   Type A personalities may be produced by certain home environments. Waldron, et al (1980) finds Type A men to have had more severe fathers and to have received more severe punishment as a child. The punishment seems to have produced resentment and hostility, not guilt. Similarly, Type A women are found to have had mothers who physically punished their little girls. Again, anger and aggression, rather than guilt or remorse, was produced by this treatment.

Coming from such severe home conditions, it is not surprising that Type A personalities report that they receive the greatest satisfaction in life from their jobs. Even though they note that their school or work responsibilities cause them excessive stress in their home life, their recreation, and their social relations, they don't become disenchanted with work, for it is there that they truly live (Burke and Weir, 1980).

## ■ Signs of Job Stress

How can we tell if job stress is present? From the standpoint of the worker, a pattern of tiredness, nervousness, sleeping difficulties, loss of appetite, depression, general dissatisfaction with the job or with life—any or all of these can signal job-related stress. If you find yourself taking tranquilizers, alcohol, or other mood changing drugs to stay on—or on top of—the job, you can suspect job stress.

From the standpoint of management, figures indicating increases in absenteeism, on-site accidents (especially where employee substance abuse is suspected), compensation claims, and personnel turnover are signs of job distress. Decreases in productivity, quality control, and profit margins are bottom-line indicators of stressful working conditions.

## ■ What to Do About Job Stress

If you think your job is causing you stress, the first thing to do is to talk to your fellow workers. Many people consider it a sign of weakness to speak of being under stress. It is a weakness not to. If your coworkers report similar

## CASE IN POINT
## Compensation

The well-being of transferred employees, their husbands or wives, and their children was the subject of a recent study (Brett, 1982). Researchers examined the impact of the transfer on the individual and his or her work, family life, marriage, and social relationships. Workers who were more mobile—who changed jobs and job locations more often—were found to be more satisfied with their families and marriages and less satisfied with their general social rela-tionships than those who were more committed to one job or one location.

Leaving old friends and making new ones is stressful. Highly mobile families appear to protect themselves against such recurring pain and anxiety by investing their interests and energies in family relationships. They compensate for their limited social life by placing more value on their enriched personal life.

*See the discussion of cognitive dissonance in Chapter 5 for more about our need to balance our actions with our beliefs and values.*

distress, it is important to work with management to redesign the workplace and/or the nature of the task itself so that stress is reduced. Stress is cumulative—that is, it builds up over time. Constantly complaining to fellow workers will not reduce stress nor increase your ability to tolerate it. If changes can't be worked out, job transfer or job change should be given careful consideration.

But many people believe they can't afford to leave their jobs. You might think that the well-paid, well-trained professional would have the greatest opportunity to flexibly change jobs if conditions were stressful. McKenna, Oritt, and Wolff (1981) find this not to be the case. They do find that job satisfaction and company commitment are negatively correlated to occupational stress—that is, the more stress, the less satisfaction and commitment. The surprising finding is that extensive education and training lead to a *lessened* probability of leaving a job, even under severe stress and dissatisfaction.

REVIEW
QUESTIONS

23. Prolonged noise can increase <u>work output / tolerance of frustration / stress</u> .

24. If you travel to work via a crowded commuter train, the longer your trip, the <u>more / less</u> stress you will experience.

25. The most stressful jobs are related to <u>m</u>          -paced operations.

26. Holding two or more jobs, working more than sixty hours a week, and experiencing job insecurity <u>are / are not</u> factors associated with heart attacks.

27. Trying to be aggressive and well liked at the same time results in high stress for power-seeking executives.  T  F

28. Young executives <u>are stressed by / thrive on</u> making decisions that affect the lives of others.

29. Type A students study <u>more / less</u> and make <u>better / worse</u> grades than their Type B fellow students.

*The answers to these review questions are on page 262.*

## DISCUSSION: THE UTILITY OF STRESS

Our unfinished nature seems to indicate that we have not survived by finding an unchanging niche and conforming to it. We do not seem content to remain idle until hunger forces us to attack or to hide until forced to forage for food. Nor are we content to graze continuously in large, protective bands. We seem to have a need for new experiences, mild uncertainties, and moderate risk taking. We need stress.

The complete absence of stress in childhood results in poor development (Levine, 1959). Both moderate distress and stimulating eustress produce more competent offspring. Adult volunteers who attempt to remain in a completely stress-free environment (a sightless, soundless, weightless, motionless body of liquid heated to body temperature) soon begin to have disturbances of mood, thought and action. They ask to be released.

*See the discussion of sensory deprivation in Chapter 6.*

Stress can facilitate our behavior as well as distort it. Optimum stress levels can improve concentration, prolong endurance, build strength, and reduce errors (Hebb, 1958). Have you waited just the correct amount of time before studying for an exam and been amazed at how much you accomplished in a short time without undue worry or guilt? A mobilization of energy was working for you.

**WHAT DO YOU THINK?**
- Can you study well just before exams?
- What does your answer say about your optimum stress level?

Writers, poets, inventors, and musicians speak of stress as an intensity of feeling that accompanies the times they are at their creative best. They long for a quiet retreat but generally do their best work in places like Los Angeles and New York City, where they are surrounded by stressors.

### ■ "Race Horses"

Hans Selye speaks of "race horses," men and women whose natural pace is hard-driving and who search for constant stimulation without apparent distress. Samuel Klausner (1968) calls people such as race car drivers "stress seekers" and reports their being drugged on their own visceral reactions to stress. That is, they need that charged-up feeling at regular intervals to feel alive. As a group, such stimulus addicts are high in intelligence, ambition, emotional stability, and leadership skills (Ogilvie, 1974). These traits are shown in their careful planning and preparation for their adventures. (Their painstaking exercise of control contrasts with the impulsive risk taker who acts out his or her fantasies or

## CASE IN POINT
## What Makes Johnny Jump?

"When the mixture becomes 51 percent excitement and 49 percent fear, that's when you can go out the door." The person speaking is no teenager, but Gordon Riner, a veteran parachutist who operates Parachutes Are Fun, Inc. near Easton, Maryland. His unusual customers need varied, novel, and complex experiences to get high on life.

Such sensation seekers are, in a sense, ad-

dicts. They crave constant high levels of stimulation and seem to thrive on levels of stress that would crush most of us. Interestingly, each develops his or her own area of adventure. Other people's thrilling avocations seem to them to be unduly stressful. It is unlikely that Gordon would voluntarily spend his time exploring underwater caves, for example.

frustrations on our freeways.) Contrary to the general rule, stimulus seekers show little relationship between life changes and physical disorders (Cooley and Keesey, 1981).

Most of us may not need high levels of sensation, but we do need some stress in our lives. Most of all, we need positive stress. Giving and receiving love, a state of arousal, is thought to be necessary for emotional well-being (Rogers, 1971; Glasser, 1965). Recognition and moderate responsibility, forms of eustress, are believed to be necessary for reducing anxiety and for building self-esteem (Erikson, 1968; Selye and Cherry, 1978).

## ■ Stress and Change

Stress is an adjustment demand. Adjustment can mean growth, as when we learn more effective ways of gaining the support of others. A lack of response, or the wrong kind of response, can alert us to the possibility that we may need to redirect our energies.

Albert Bandura (1977) states that four sources of information are needed for the successful change of human behavior. Accepting and acting on each source of information involve a degree of stress. The first involves *performance accomplishment*—confronting a stressor successfully. The second involves *sensitization to one's physiological state*—being aware of the body's response to stress. The third involves *vicarious experience*—working through painful situations under conditions of minimal stress. The fourth involves *persuasion*—accepting a message that at first was resisted. Change implies a prior state of disequilibrium or strain.

> Jim had to undergo stress in order to reduce stress. No matter what Jim was asked to do, he would always agree, but feel anger rather than joy at being so helpful.
>
> Jim finally sought help for his constant feelings of resentment. At first he resisted the notion that the source of his anger was his inability to say no. However, when he agreed to relive anger-provoking situations, he became painfully aware that his tense physical state typically involved unreasonable demands made upon him by people he did not want to risk losing.
>
> With the help of role playing, Jim learned to overcome the stress of standing up for his rights. He practiced saying no in a friendly but firm manner. It was hard, but Jim persisted. After several of these vicarious experiences, Jim felt skilled enough to confront his friends and fellow students when they made unreasonable demands upon him. Jim could now say no and not feel threatened. His reason for feeling angry had been reduced, and he felt much more at ease with himself.

**WHAT DO YOU THINK?**

■ Do you believe Selye is correct in his contentions about "deeper" adaptive energy? If he is correct, will your current life style serve you well?

We might note that gaining strength through overcoming a stressor can be overdone. The lives of death-camp and death-march survivors were generally shortened, not prolonged, by their successful coping experience (Bettelheim, 1943). Selye (1974) speaks of fixed amount of "deeper" adaptive energy, which, when exhausted, leaves us without resources to continue living. He believes we can replenish "superficial" adaptive energy by eating, but can only preserve our original store of survival energy. Tolerable levels of stress preserve this vital store by helping to immunize us against future, more traumatic experiences.

**REVIEW QUESTIONS**

*30.* We seem to require an unchanging environment/constant stimulation/a frantic existence.

*31.* Infants who receive some negative stress do better/worse than those who receive no stress, positive or negative.

*32.* "Race horses," or stimulus addicts, are thought to be more/less intelligent than the average person.

*33.* It is sometimes/always/never good for a person to feel stress.

*34.* List two of the four sources of information necessary if a person is to make positive changes in behavior: _____ _____ .

*35.* Tolerable stress can help to _____ us against future shocks.

*36.* Selye believes our deeper adaptive energy can/cannot be replenished by eating.
*The answers to these review questions are on page 262.*

## DISCUSSION: CONSTRUCTIVE AND DEFENSIVE COPING

A reasonable position regarding stress is to recognize that it is natural, an inevitable part of our lives. We have no choice but to respond to the strain of living. We do have a number of choices with respect to how we will respond to stressors and to stress. There is no one best way to cope. Each person and situation is different. Stress is a complex interaction between the specific nature of the demand, the emotional and mental state of the individual, and the strength of the coping resources that individual can bring together to combat the stressor. What we can benefit from accepting is that we do not have to be passive recipients of stress. There is much we can do to reduce its noxious effects and to take advantage of its potentials.

■ Stress is an inevitable part of our lives.

## CASE IN POINT
## Stages of a Stress Encounter:
## Life Change to Physical Illness

Richard Rahe (1974) suggests that a person experiencing life changes must pass through six *transformations* (stages) before physical illness, if it occurs, is medically recognized. Let us say you are fired from your job, a relatively strong stressor. The first transformation is your cognitive appraisal—in this case, your interpretation of the fact that you have been fired. This appraisal acts as a filter that will either reduce or exaggerate the effects of the stressor. Being fired may be a major disgrace, a minor annoyance, or a great relief, depending on your perception of the meaning of being fired.

The second transformation is your use of ego-defense mechanisms. You may be able to rationalize being fired: "the best thing that has ever happened to me." (Defense mechanisms will be discussed shortly.) If the stress of being fired overwhelms your psychological defenses, a third transformation takes place. It comprises the physiological reactions of the alarm and resistance stages of the general adaptation syndrome. Some reactions are conscious (moodiness, muscle tension, and so on); some are unconscious (high blood pressure, high blood fats, and so on). This mobilization of energy gives rise to the fourth transformation—direct coping responses that can vary from using simple relaxation exercises to complex strategies for gaining reemployment.

If physiological activation continues despite your coping efforts, symptoms reappear (Selye's exhaustion stage) and you decide to play the role of sick person and report your symptoms to a doctor. This is the fifth transformation. The final transformation takes place when your doctor diagnoses your symptoms as an illness. While doctors are trained to treat causes, not symptoms, the "illness" may consist of a label for the symptom rather than the cause. If you report a burning sensation in your stomach, you may be diagnosed as having stomach ulcers. To Hans Selye, the ulcers are a symptom of the disease "being fired."

### ■ Types of Coping

Coping can be divided into two types. **Direct coping** is acting to alter the environment that caused the stress (for example, after being fired, you find a better job). These active coping efforts activate the fight or flight response. **Indirect coping** is acting on yourself to alter the significance of the stressor. (You intellectualize your firing as a statistical certainty given the current state of the economy.) This indirect style makes use of defense mechanisms. Defensive coping efforts, triggered by a perception of helplessness, activate the conservation—withdrawal response (Ursin, Boode and Levine, 1978).

Taking some direct action is generally better than changing ideas of reality. (But some forms of direct action may be harmful—you might attack the boss after he has fired you or rob a bank to recover your lost income.) Indirect coping acts are not always mental. Smoking, getting drunk, overeating, and abusing drugs are all defensive coping strategies. They reduce the symptoms of stress in the short run but do not act directly on the stressor.

Gary Schwartz (1977) calls such actions *disregulators* because they interfere with the function of the brain as a natural health-care regulator. Negative information from our peripheral organs concerning the effects of stress is used by our brain to regulate our behavior to maximize health. Successful defensive coping—through drugs or denial, for example—is dysfunctional because it perpetuates our stressful lifestyle and continues the accumulation of stress that will eventually produce exhaustion, breakdown, and premature death. Dr. Schwartz finds little comfort in the fact that chemical coping, the use of drug therapy, is the method of choice for most doctors today for handling diseases of adaptation. Fortunately, this picture is changing. Just as stress-related disorders make up 50 to 80 percent of a typical medical practice, major and minor tranquilizers still make up the major portion of patients' prescription drugs. Ninety percent of the prescriptions for minor tranquilizers are written by general practitioneers.

Doctors often administer such drugs because it is less time consuming than helping a patient to work out a more healthful life style. (Doctors are not trained to do this.) Drugs do offer symptom relief, and that is what we expect when we go to the doctor. They lower blood pressure, reduce heart rate, neutralize acidity, produce a calming effect, and relax muscles. Drugs may have some other positive effects. If we stay on the medication, the chance of a more serious disorder is lessened. More important, drug therapy at times makes possible a tolerance of stressful reactions while more permanent behavioral adjustments are being incorporated and a natural restoration of healthy functioning is being returned to us (Wolpe, 1978).

In light of the apparent disadvantages of defensive coping, you may wonder why people use it. Defensive coping is less complex, more accessible, and promises quicker results than direct coping. The function of defensive coping, a Freudian concept, is to defend the self against threats to self-esteem. Such coping also serves to protect against feelings of anxiety. Anxiety itself is a defense against anger, the trigger for the direct but dangerous coping tactic of aggression. Anxiety attacks are seen as a result of dangerous impulses to destroy a stressor. Anxiety inhibits this response, but at the cost of constant nervous arousal (Cameron, 1963). In our modern world, it is almost never prudent to attack whoever is pressuring us, frustrating us, or causing us injury. That is why our times have been termed the "age of anxiety." We will examine anxiety more closely later in the chapter.

**WHAT DO YOU THINK?**

- Do you like change?
- Do you believe more in luck or effort?
- Are you deeply involved in work, play, and people?
- What do these questions have to do with successful coping?

## CASE IN POINT
## Risk Reduction

Burt was both unlucky and lucky. He was unlucky to find himself eligible to be included in a scientific medical experiment. To be included, he had to be in the top 5 percent of the U.S. population in terms of blood cholesterol level—and he was aware of the connection between high blood fats and increased heart disease. He was lucky because, when he volunteered to participate in the long-term study of the possible benefits of a new anti-cholesterol drug, he was placed in the diet-plus-drug-therapy group. Loving life and wanting to prolong his good health, Burt faithfully adhered to his prescribed diet and faithfully took his prescription drug.

Ten years later, Dr. Basil Rifkind, director of the study, reports that anti-cholesterol drug therapy, combined with a low-calorie, low-fat, low-salt, high-complex-carbohydrate diet, can lower the risk of coronary heart disease by as much as 50 percent (Schorr, 1984). Burt is lucky indeed. This report is the first to demonstrate conclusively that the risk of coronary heart disease can be reduced by diet plus **cholestyramine,** a cholesterol-lowering drug.

Joe is a friendly and outgoing person. He seems to have a good sense of humor, and he likes to help people. Because he is a hard worker, Joe is able to combine a part-time job with a full schedule of college classes.

But Joe is not so friendly when things aren't going well. When complications set in, the ready smile and helpful demeanor turn quickly to rage. Today is one of those complicated days. Just after Joe is "chewed out" by his supervisor at work, his parole supervisor arrives and wants to "chat." Joe is upset and embarrassed. The people he works with don't even know he is on parole. Joe sullenly agrees to talk in the back room. Soon talk turns to shouts and curses:

"Leave me alone! Get off my back or I'll kill you!" screams Joe.

Joe doesn't "kill" the parole supervisor, but he does smash him in the face.

With surprising calm, the parole supervisor holds his reddened cheek. "That's enough. That's direct assault. Call the police."

Joe seems quite calm when the police arrive. He tells them how well he is doing in college, and how his parole supervisor just won't leave him alone. "Yes," Joe said "I know what assaulting a parole officer means. I didn't have any choice. I had to hit him." The same lack of normal anxiety that lets Joe be so outgoing and friendly during good times lets him explode impulsively during bad times.

### ■ Defensive Coping Techniques

More than thirty specific techniques of defensive coping appear in the literature. We will describe a few of the basic mechanisms. All of these are substitutes for direct forms of behavior aimed at reducing distress by gaining love, security, esteem, or recognition. When direct means appear threatening, inaccessible, or unproductive, alternative approaches are used to reduce, direct, or control the energy mobilized to respond to stress. We also use defensive coping when we are faced with intangible foes, and cannot tell who or what is threatening us. The aim is always the same: to reduce stress by maintaining self-esteem and controlling dangerous impulses.

When under stress, people tend to fall back on approaches that have worked for them in the past. Fighters fight, fleers flee. Defensive coping can be divided into these fight or flight response patterns. People who tend to fight—to acknowledge stress so as to control it—are called **sensitizers.** More will be said about them later. People who tend to avoid or flee from stress are knows as **repressors** (Byrne, Darry, and Nelson, 1963). Such people appear emotionally stable, behave conventionally, give high reports of self-esteem, and tend to seek simplicity and order in their lives (Tucker, 1970). They appear beautifully adjusted. However, they also display little humor, sexuality, or self-assertion, and they have extremely high levels of physiological arousal. Several types of defensive mechanisms are commonly used by repressors. Other types are more often used by sensitizers.

### ■ *Defensive Mechanisms Used by Repressors*   **Repression** is a pattern (automatic and unconscious) of avoiding anxiety-producing thoughts and feelings by not allowing them into awareness. A student may "forget" that a term paper is due on Thursday, for example. Repression may be a response to a sudden overwhelming event, such as experiencing combat, or it may evolve slowly as punished thoughts and feelings are **suppressed**—deliberately forgotten—again and again until the forgetting gradually becomes uncounscious and automatic.

■ This "repressor" held back his anger toward his boss while at work. Now he is safely at home.

Repression becomes an overlearned habit (Dollard and Miller, 1950). The process of repression inhibits recall of impulsive or traumatic events and thereby reduces anxiety.

**Denial** is a refusal to acknowledge painful or threatening circumstances. It is a way of blocking out stressful situations. Burke and Weir (1980) found that Type A men have an unusual ability to deny feelings of fatigue while at work. Denial allows them to work through pain, a short-term benefit with long-term costs in terms of health. Lazarus (1977) regards denial as adaptive in cases in which no adequate response is possible—when a person is suffering from an incurable disease, for example. Such denial is not play acting; it is a real failure to internalize reality. Usually denial is dysfunctional, as when we fail to acknowledge the need to study before an important exam or to accept our drinking as a problem when in fact it is.

Repression and denial are two of the more common defensive coping mechanisms. The generalization of this response style leads to the negative personality traits mentioned for repressors. Repressors have difficulty with complexity, and because thinking may give rise to uncomfortable associations, they tend to lead nonreflective lives. Their lack of a sense of humor and lessened sexuality come from the fact that both require a capacity for impulsive behavior, if only in fantasy. Assertion requires a challenge to the status quo, a threatening idea to repressors, thus, they are not assertive.

Another defensive mechanism, **reaction-formation**, involves thinking and acting in a manner opposite one's anxiety-producing desires. This is a denial of one's true thinking, feeling self. Reaction-formation offers a safe way to express

**WHAT DO YOU THINK?**

■ Do you think a life without reflection is worth living?

sexual energies, and at the same time deny their existence. A person may wage war on the exploitation of sexual themes in literature, advertising, and the arts and never have to come to terms with his or her own sexuality. And what better way could one deny feeling any hostility toward loved ones than to use reaction–formation to be forever loving, caring, forgiving, and understanding? The key to identifying reaction–formation is to be found in its compulsive and excessive nature. The response is overdone.

Repression, denial, and reaction-formation are maintained at considerable psychic cost. We can discharge little of the energy mobilized for defense if we do not acknowledge that a threat is present. Such energy must be discharged.

Repressors generally use another defense mechanism to get rid of excess psychic energy. **Displacement** is the shifting of an impulse or feeling that has been punished (for example, anger) away from the original object or person to other, less threatening objects or persons (from father to little brother, and so on). This is the courage of the coward, but at times it may be necessary. How often we hear, "Don't take it out on me."

Counting is an example of another form of diversionary activity that uses energy and keeps our minds away from threatening subjects. We may find ourselves counting walls, cracks, or light poles while under stress. Any *escape into activity* discharges energy via displacement. Have you noticed how many little things have to be done just prior to final exams?

**WHAT DO YOU THINK?**

■ What effect would losing the Superbowl have on a repressor?
■ How would he or she handle it?

*For more about modeling see Chapter 3.*

You may have noticed that for the most part repressors deny or repress their true selves. **Identification** is a process by which they may build their egos by symbolically becoming another person. We reduce feelings of helplessness by becoming just like a feared person. A boy need not fear his father, for example, when he becomes "the spitting image of dad!" The sports fan role allows us to express triumph and hostility without anxiety—another example of defensive identification. Of course, identification can be a positive act of adjustment, too. We often model ourselves after the positive character traits we observe in others.

**Sublimation** is the unconscious channeling of impulsive and anxiety-producing energies into socially and morally acceptable patterns of action. It is a positive form of displacement. Frustration can be sublimated into aggression in sports, competition in business, or explosive expression in the arts. Freud believed sublimation to be the foundation of civilization. He saw great public and private enterprise as resting on the sublimation of sexual and hostile energies.

**Rationalization** is a form of self-deception in which the justification given for our actions is not the real cause of the behavior. Both repressors and sensitizers rationalize, but repressors use a less common form, termed "sweet lemon," which turns something "sour" into something "sweet." Elliot Liebow's "theory of manly flaws" (1967) is an example. Men whose jobs do not pay enough to allow them to support a family do not blame society or the job. They blame themselves and are torn and humiliated by their inability to care for their loved ones. Rather than face this failure daily, they abandon their wives and children. The rationalization they employ for leaving is, "There is too much of the dog in me." They present themselves as being too strong sexually ever to be faithful to one woman, so they move on. Thus, a weakness is converted into an imagined strength. The bitter loss of wife and children is denied, and the sweetness of the lonely life is compulsively acted out. A more mundane example of "sweet lemon" rationalization is presented by the student who says he likes a class he expected to hate but was forced to take.

**Regression** is a return to behaviors that were appropriate and successful at an earlier age. A three-year-old toddler who has been toilet trained for months may wet and cry during the first weeks of nursery school. These were the very acts that guaranteed attention and parental care at an earlier age. Repressors as a group tend to maintain regressive cognitive patterns that are simple, childlike, and without the complexities that threaten adult life. Unfortunately, the cute matron or the pouting patriarch is seldom effective in resolving the intricacies of modern living.

■ *Defense Mechanisms Used by Sensitizers* **Sensitizers** defend by absorbing and manipulating stressors. They embrace threatening stimuli and exaggerate their intensity. They report more anxiety, admit hostility and sexual arousal, and recall past failures and inadequacies to a greater extent than repressors (Byrne and Sheffield, 1965). This acknowledgement of stress results in less residual stress as measured by physical indicators. Sensitizers display exaggerated openness and honesty; they also have a negative self-concept, are less frequently chosen as partners, and report more physical and psychological disorders than others (Tucker, 1970).

The major tactic of sensitizers is to admit anxiety and anger in order to direct and control it. They exhibit a fight response. But this still shows indirect coping, for they center their efforts on controlling the symptoms, not the cause. Sensitizers often use the fighting technique of *divide and conquer*—they divide and conquer themselves. Feelings, ideas, and actions are often separated and kept divorced from each other so that control over them can be maintained. This makes potentially threatening situations tolerable. The division of self is practiced in three ways—through emotional insulation, through isolation, and through intellectualization.

**Emotional insulation** is the separation of feelings from ideas and actions. Sensitizers block honest emotional expression to protect themselves. An example is presented by the "tough" person. The tough is emotionally blunted, less human, because he or she will not form close relationships, share uncertainties, or express feelings other than sullen distaste. In this way, he or she defends against possible hurt.

Physical **isolation** is the separation of action from feelings and ideas. By controlling their very presence (by absenting themselves from awkward situations) sensitizers can reduce the possibility of losing control. The reduction of anxiety negatively reinforces this coping mechanism. By admitting anxiety, but refusing to allow people or events to place them at a disadvantage, sensitizers maintain a sense of power. The price is loneliness and less power. Such persons do not flee, but choose their battleground.

**WHAT DO YOU THINK?**

■ How does isolation produce less power?

**Intellectualization** is the separation of ideas from feelings or actions. Sensitizers use thinking to avoid the threat of feeling or acting. This divorce makes them insensitive to the emotional tone being expressed by themselves or others. *Worrying* is an art form that admits and exaggerates selected concerns, and by constantly analyzing all possible ramifications, keeps out higher levels of anxiety. Allowing in feelings and taking action are beyond the comprehension of intellectualizers. What they practice is a complex way of counting cracks.

**Projection** is a defense mechanism in which perceptions or impulses that threaten our self-esteem are disowned and forced outside ourselves. It is an attacking defense. We accept the existence of what we fear, but only in others.

When environmental actions prevent our acting out our impulses, and our superego prevents our even thinking of them, the energy finds partial release in a preoccupation with the presence of such traits in others. Internal tension is converted into tension between us and the outside world. For example, people who constantly complain about the sexual activity of the younger generation may be projecting fears of their own sexual urges onto others.

**Compensation** is the application of defensive energy to the development of a skill or trait that will make up for a real or imagined defect. A short person may adopt impressive clothing, an assertive posture, and a combative style, for example. The poor athlete may invest time and money in developing the athletic skills of his or her children. Compensation, unlike sublimation, is not always socially approved. You may compensate for a lack of love or esteem by over-indulging in drugs, food, or sex.

While other defense mechanisms are indirect coping responses, compensation, in the form of *overcompensation,* is a direct response to an inadequacy. The marginal student who, through compulsive study, becomes the honor graduate is exemplifying overcompensation. The fringe member of the street gang who, although frightened, volunteers to be the trigger man in a "war" is another example.

**Fantasizing** is engaging in imaginary exploits in which threatening impulses are acted out. Some fantasizing is normal. A rich imagination is associated with mental health. The repressor does not fantasize much. Such people distrust complexity and attempt to stay in the simple, never-ending here and now. Repressors must forget the past, distort the present, and never anticipate the future. Sensitizers, on the other hand, tend to live more in the future and reject both past and present. Fantasy becomes a major mode of adjustment. Movies, TV, sports, reading, and daydreaming occupy disproportionate amounts of time for those who suffer feelings of inadequacy or lack of fulfillment in their daily lives.

**Rationalization**, already mentioned in relation to repressors, is used by sensitizers in its more common form—"sour grapes." After striving for something and not getting it, the sensitizer will declare, "I never wanted it in the first place." "The exam was unfair. The professor is jealous of me. I have no time for study." All are examples of rationalizations for poor test performances. Self-serving excuses for daily failures can reduce anxiety and maintain self-esteem at the expense of personal growth.

**Conversion** is a dramatic defense against guilt in which energy is redirected into physical channels and disorders of **hysteria** develop. Such patients suffer real pain, but the source of the pain does not lie in bodily injury or disease. The pain and incapacity are always associated with a solution to a psychologically threatening situation. A combat pilot who develops blurred vision cannot go back into battle. A sore throat just before a theater performance or a headache or cold just before an exam are examples of conversion, a physical rationalization for nonperformance of a fear-provoking activity.

Among the numerous ways to cope with stress, which do people most often use? In one study, (Llfeld, 1980) three coping styles dominated subjects' responses to perceived stress. They most often coped by taking direct action.

Second, they used *rationalization* in conjunction with attempts to avoid the stressor. Third, they coped by employing the conservation–withdrawal device of accepting the stressor without attempting any alteration in their conditions of living.

REVIEW
QUESTIONS

*37.* Rahe's first transformation involves the use of <u>cognitive appraisal/ego defenses / coping skills</u>.

*38.* Taking action to alter the cause of stress is termed <u>d</u>         <u>c</u>          .

*39.* Schwartz terms "successful" indirect coping mechanisms *disregulators* because they interfere with <u>negative/positive</u> information used by the brain to regulate healthy responses.

*40.* A function of defensive coping is to protect against a loss of <u>s</u>            <u>e</u>          .

*41.* Learning to avoid awareness of anxiety-producing thoughts or feelings is termed <u>r</u>          .

*42.* Thinking and acting in ways opposite of our true inclinations is termed <u>r</u>       <u>f</u>          .

*43.* "Don't take it out on me" means "Don't use <u>d</u>           on me."

*44.* <u>S</u>           is the channeling of impulsive sexual or aggressive urges into socially valued enterprises.

*45.* "Sour grapes" is a term pertaining to the defensive mechanism <u>r</u>     .

*46.* Separating our thoughts from our feelings and actions so as to control them all is termed <u>i</u>          .

*The answers to these review questions are on page 262.*

## DISCUSSION:  ANXIETY AND ITS CONTROL

**Anxiety,** is a vague, unpleasant feelings accompanied by a premonition that something bad is about to happen, is a major component of most adjustment problems. When people are anxious, blood leaves their digestive system, and they may experience nausea, vomiting, or loss of appetite. Breathing, heart rate, and blood pressure all rise, causing, at times, hyperventilation or hypertension. Kidney problems, sleep onset disorders, speech pathologies, and even hyper-activity can result from prolonged anxiety. An understanding and control of anxiety, therefore, is central to successful adjustment. We will conclude this chapter on stress with a description of anxiety and a look at some old and new methods of gaining personal control of anxiety. Gaining control will allow us to tolerate stressful situations so as to confront the stressor and successfully adapt to or change this situation. Table 7.3 presents a scale that measures roughly the amount of anxiety you are currently experiencing. On the average, college students score 14 to 15 on this scale.

TABLE 7.3

Taylor Manifest Anxiety Scale

Score one point each time your response corresponds with the answer—True or False—keyed at the end of a statement.

1.  I do not tire quickly.  (F)
2.  I am troubled by attacks of nausea.  (T)
3.  I believe I am no more nervous than most others.  (F)
4.  I have very few headaches.  (F)
5.  I work under a great deal of tension.  (T)
6.  I cannot keep my mind on one thing.  (T)
7.  I worry over money and business.  (T)
8.  I frequently notice my hand shakes when I try to do something.  (T)
9.  I blush no more often than others.  (F)
10. I have diarrhea once a month or more.  (T)
11. I worry quite a bit over possible misfortunes.  (T)
12. I practically never blush.  (F)
13. I am often afraid that I am going to blush.  (T)
14. I have nightmares every few nights.  (T)
15. My hands and feet are usually warm enough.  (F)
16. I sweat very easily even on cool days.  (T)
17. Sometimes when embarrassed, I break out in a sweat which annoys me greatly.  (T)
18. I hardly ever notice my heart pounding and I am seldom short of breath.  (F)
19. I feel hungry almost all the time.  (T)
20. I am very seldom troubled by constipation.  (F)
21. I have a great deal of stomach trouble.  (T)
22. I have had periods in which I lost sleep over worry.  (T)
23. My sleep is fitful and disturbed.  (T)
24. I dream frequently about things that are best kept to myself.  (T)
25. I am easily embarrassed.  (T)
26. I am more sensitive than most other people.  (T)
27. I frequently find myself worrying about something.  (T)
28. I wish I could be as happy as others seem to be.  (T)
29. I am usually calm and not easily upset.  (F)
30. I cry easily.  (T)
31. I feel anxiety about something or someone almost all the time.  (T)
32. I am happy most of the time.  (F)
33. It makes me nervous to have to wait.  (T)
34. I have periods of such great restlessness that I cannot sit long in a chair.  (T)
35. Sometimes I become so excited that I find it hard to get to sleep.  (T)
36. I have sometimes felt that difficulties were piling up so high that I could not overcome them.  (T)
37. I must admit that I have at times been worried beyond reason over something that really did not matter.  (T)
38. I have very few fears compared with my friends.  (F)
39. I have been afraid of things or people that I know could not hurt me.  (T)
40. I certainly feel useless at times.  (T)
41. I find it hard to keep my mind on a task or job.  (T)
42. I am usually self-conscious.  (T)
43. I am inclined to take things hard.  (T)
44. I am a high-strung person.  (T)
45. Life is a strain for me much of the time.  (T)
46. At times I think I am no good at all.  (T)
47. I am certainly lacking in self confidence.  (T)
48. I sometimes feel that I am about to go to pieces.  (T)
49. I shrink from facing a crises or difficulty.  (T)
50. I am entirely self confident.  (F)

College students, on average, score 14 to 15 on this scale.

## ■ The Roots of Anxiety

The physical symptoms of anxiety are associated with the activity of a small part of our brain called the locus coeruleus (Henry and Stevens, 1978). Pearson and Shaw (1980) report that taking thirty to forty milligrams of propranolol, a drug that blocks receptor cells in the locus coeruleus from being stimulated by sympathetic nervous system activity, can reduce the amount of anxiety we feel prior to performing in public. Physical symptoms aside, many believe that anxiety is rooted in our basic human condition. Freud believed anxiety to be a product of unresolved conflicts between the id and superego. Garre (1962) sees anxiety arising from each infant's sensitivity to parental neglect or reluctance. Any such behavior is interpreted by the infant as a threat to his or her existence. Basic anxiety results. Karen Horney (1950) postulates an inadequate or unworthy self-concept as the root of anxiety. She holds that we construct an *ego ideal* designed to gain the unconditional approval of our parents. Comparing ourselves with this too-perfect, too-rigid, ideal self results in a constantly poor self-evaluation. Self-censure is the worst form of stress, for it is the most difficult to avoid, escape, or satisfy.

According to existential philosophy, anxiety springs from our growing awareness that we exist (which implies a nonexistence, or death, anxiety) and from the fact that we must make choices and be responsible for them. This view absolves parents and society of any blame but leaves us nervous nonetheless. Social learning theory holds that anxiety can be taught to the infant by the environment and by significant others as well as by the parents. Constant verbal instructions to "watch out" and premature exposure to adult problems are sources of learned anxiety. We can model anxiety by worrying constantly in front of our children.

Worry can be seen as a wish for a magical solution. Since most of what we worry about never takes place, worry appears to be an effective control device (though it is not) and can become a conditioned response that is transmitted to others. Once learned, worry and other forms of anxiety can become generalized and elicited by a wide range of conditions.

The same situations that threaten self-esteem produce anxiety. These are typically social situations in which competition, hostility, rejection, and guilt are part of the expected pattern of interaction. The singles bar is such a social situation.

> "My emotions are running wild," Jane said to her girlfriend as she sat in the singles bar trying to casually sip her free drink. "I don't know if I'm excited, frightened, disgusted, or bored."
>
> "Well, I know how I feel," her friend replied without trying to hide the anger in her voice, "I'm damn mad at having to be here at all. I feel like a commodity. This 'free drink' just adds insult to injury."
>
> "Mine is almost gone," Jane said quietly as she began to glance around without appearing to be concerned. "Look at Harry over there, posing by the piano. He looks like a fish in the moonlight—he shines, and stinks!"
>
> "That's good. Let's get out of here," said her friend. "All I see around this place are strumpets, or I guess I should say trollops. I feel guilty just being here."
>
> "The music's good. OK. I guess it's not working out," sighed Jane. Then, frozen in sudden interest, she anxiously whispers, "Don't look up. Here come those two fellows we were noticing last night. They're coming right toward us . . ."

As you can see, anxiety can be caused by conflicting motives, such as a desire to leave the bar and a desire to stay. It can also be produced by a conflict between a motive (to find companionship or excitement) and an inner standard (not to be a "trollop"). Finally anxiety can alter our social behavior. Apprehension concerning possible rape can prevent a woman from seeking recreation outside

WHAT DO YOU THINK?

■ Do you worry a great deal?

■ Why or why not?

See Chapter 3 for more about self-esteem.

the home. Apprehension concerning possible rejection can prevent a man from initiating contact with an attractive female.

## ■ Anxiety and Fear

The body responds to anxiety and fear in the same way. A fear response is associated with a real and present danger, however, and we quiet down after the danger has passed. Anxiety is dread of the unknown, and the danger may never pass. An *anxiety attack* is a panic response that often begins with spasms or weakness in the abdomen, then affects the entire visceral system. Heart palpitations, rapid breathing, nausea, and even fever rush together during an attack. A victim, trying to make sense of this extreme response in the absence of a clear stressor often fears a mysterious illness or experiences the more terrifying fear of "going crazy."

The fear of fear itself, known as **secondary anxiety** (Cameron, 1963), conditions people to go to any lengths to avoid the pain of another anxiety attack. They are often left with a sense of insecurity and unreality about themselves and their world. Their anxiety is so severe, so out of proportion to any visible danger, that they feel as if they are in the midst of a bad dream.

Anxiety is not pathologic; we all experience it at times. We tend to forget (repress) the moments of panic from childhood. Highly anxious people are not going crazy, but they do tend to live in a constant state of tension with restless, irritable activity during the day and poor sleep patterns at night. Speilberger (1966) differentiates between trait and state anxiety. **Trait anxiety** is a constant facet of a personality. Each of us is characteristically highly, minimally, or moderately anxious. People do not move from highly anxious to mentally ill. However, highly anxious individuals are less communicative, less optimistic, and make poorer grades than their less anxious counterparts. Anxiety hurts their chances for intimacy, concentration, and flexibility in responding to a crisis. **State anxiety** is a response to a specific event—a vague fear of the pending final exam, for example. A growing number of researchers (Jacobson, 1978) feel that most forms of disruptive behavior are rooted in anxiety.

*Chapter 12 talks about intimacy.*

## ■ Anxiety Related to Anger and Hostility

In Freudian theory, anxiety is a defense against the danger of impulsively responding to anger with hostility. It serves to suppress hostility. However, each time we hold back a hostile act, we feel frustrated and build up latent hostility. This is thought to account for the irritability and constant criticism displayed by very anxious people toward themselves and "safe" others. Such defensive reactions are unsuccessful in reducing the original conflicts or frustrations, so many people feel at the mercy of their anxieties.

## ■ Modulation of Anxiety

**WHAT DO YOU THINK?**

■ Do you believe you could learn to relax in the face of fear or frustration?

Personal control of anxiety can be achieved through learning or relearning ancient capabilities—specifically, the capacity for producing the restorative response at will, in appropriate circumstances, for maximum health and effectiveness. A stressor becomes a signal for deep relaxation. The difficulty does not lie in learning the restorative response. Several techniques have been developed to master deep relaxation. It is the application of such learning prior to or just at the appropriate moment of a stressful encounter that constitutes the learning problem. Because anxiety can be partially controlled via escape and avoidance behavior, learning to approach anxious situations to develop skill in responding with relaxation is most difficult to do. Ironically, what is needed is new learning in the face of strong incentives to avoid new learning.

Because anxiety is an asset as well as a curse, it is wise to approach changing our response patterns with caution. Words such as *control, eliminate,* and *regulate* suggest a finality and rigidity that can be dysfunctional. We have elected to talk about *modulation* of anxiety in an attempt to express the flexibility and sensitivity in responding that is needed to handle stressful situations.

We can modulate anxiety by bringing it into our consciousness and directing its course. The term *altered states of consciousness* is popular today. The idea of getting into a different state of awareness is intriguing, and humankind has sought such an experience in a thousand ways—through religion, philosophy, drugs and physical exhaustion, for example. We will discuss ways to achieve and maintain an altered state of consciousness that is incompatible with anxiety and that blocks the ravaging effects of prolonged stress or allows restoration.

This altered consciousness is based on a new awareness that we can modulate the workings of our autonomic nervous system. In the 1960s, Dr. Neil Miller and his associates (Di Cara and Miller, 1968) were successful in training a rat to direct and control the functioning of its autonomic nervous system. In striving to receive positive reinforcement in the form of electrical stimulation of the pleasure centers of its brain, the rat was able to change its heart rate, its blood pressure, and its blood flow (Miller, 1974). This demonstration was exciting, for these functions are the very ones implicated in stress-related disorders in humans. Within months of these pioneering experiments, humans were successfully taught to alter their brain wave patterns, heart rates, blood pressure, blood flow, and skin resistance.

A new awareness of the unity of body and mind and a new technology of electronic sensors, amplifiers, computers, and display devices were soon developed. New awareness and new technology were combined with a renewed belief in preventive medicine to open up novel approaches to the reduction of stress-related mental and physical ills. These new approaches differ from older methods of stress management in three respects. First, they do not depend on medication, surgery, or faith to produce a cure. Second, they depend on the active involvement of the person in directing and being responsible for his or her own improvement. The third difference is found in the radical assumption that the symptom is the problem and that symptom removal is a cure. This new field has been named behavioral medicine.

How do these new approaches relate to anxiety modulation? If you assume anxiety is a symptom of unresolved conflict, of childhood separation, or of existential fear, then successful therapy is directed toward identifying specific causes and structuring potentially cathartic experiences. However, you may view anxiety as being a learned response, conditioned by direct or vicarious experiences to many stimuli. You may also believe that the autonomic nervous system functions that characterize anxiety responses can be altered via voluntary control. These beliefs suggest directly attacking and modulating the *symptom* (the anxiety response) to cure anxiety. One way to do this is through biofeedback training.

*Chapter 14 discusses psychotherapy.*

## CASE IN POINT
## Biofeedback: An Answer to Anxiety?

Can you control your internal bodily activity? Up until the 1960s, most psychologists believed that our systems for regulating temperature and blood pressure, for example, were involuntary—beyond conscious control. Now several electronic devices have been developed that provide external linkages from our neurons, muscles, and glands to our higher brain centers, the voluntary control devices of our minds.

Training on any or all of the devices listed below can increase your awareness of your body's internal functions and, in most cases, allow you to increase control over them. Such awareness and control are now part of many health-related programs, including the modulation of anxiety.

The four devices that have received the most research application to date measure:

■ Electrical activity on the surface of the brain (electroencephalograph, or EEG).
■ Electrical activity associated with the contraction of muscles (electromiograph, or EMG).
■ Resistance to electrical activity associated with sweat gland activity (electrodermal resistence, or EDR).
■ Electrical activity that reflects thermal (temperature) changes due to alterations in surface blood flow (thermister).

The text tells about the effects of biofeedback training on selected physical and emotional disorders. See the *Journal of Biofeedback and Self-Regulation* for additional information.

### ■ Biofeedback

After a review of a decade of research on **biofeedback**, George Fuller, of the Biofeedback Institute of San Francisco, reported (1978) on its effectiveness. Electromiograph (EMG) training in forehead muscle relaxation is effective in alleviating anxiety symptoms and conditions such as tension headaches and *bruxism*, the gnashing of teeth.

We can learn to relax our minds as well as our bodies. Electroencephalograph (EEG) training is effective in insomnia cases in which muscle tension is not a problem. Such training enables insomniacs to allow sleep to come rather than encouraging them to drug themselves into a sleep-like state. EEG is also effective in enhancing concentration and attention—problems of cognition often suffered by the highly anxious. Obsessive-compulsive worriers are also helped.

Many stress-related disorders, from hemorrhoids to menstrual cramps, are related to blood volume changes. **Vasomotor** activity—the expanding and contracting of blood vessels—can be modulated by the aid of the thermister, or temperature trainer. Migraine headaches, asthma, and high blood pressure are conditions in which skin-temperature training is useful.

The EDR, or electrodermal response, has application in the treatment of hypertension and hyperhydrosis (excessive sweating in anxiety or arousal) and indirectly in the treatment of many fear disorders when used as part of **systematic desensitization** training (Wolpe, 1973). Heart-rate feedback, along with desensitization, is applicable to reducing anxiety concerning heartbeat irregularity that is not medically dangerous.

Physical pain, in many cases, is reduced by biofeedback training. Anxious, tense people are less tolerant of pain. We are all more sensitive to pain while under moderately high stress. Sexuality and anxiety are incompatible. Biofeedback equipment is useful in monitoring genital muscle contractions and blood flow in both men and women and is thus helpful in treating sexual dysfunctions such as impotence in men and low genital arousal in women. Finally, Fuller reports that closed circuit television and videotape recorders are feedback devices helpful in the development of social skill training. Such behavioral feedback is helpful to highly anxious individuals.

Biofeedback training is brief and inexpensive when compared with more traditional forms of therapy for anxiety. It is best used in conjunction with a trained counselor, and so it does cost something, however. The training is necessary until you have learned (1) to produce deep relaxation at will and (2) to become sensitized to internal and external cues that signal a need for your antianxiety response.

Biofeedback is not the only way to modulate anxiety. Ancient forms of self-modulation, such as yoga and Zen Buddhism and newer forms such as transcendental meditation can also be paths to the restorative response. Meditational techniques such as yoga and Zen follow different roads toward unity of body and mind. Physical exercise, rhythmic exercise, mental activity and its absence, restful postures, and direct breathing and thought control are all to be found among the Eastern approaches. None of these depend on the technology of biofeedback.

A careful review of contemporary research on the effects of meditation on somatic arousal—heartbeat, blood pressure, skin resistance, and so forth—reveals a surprising pattern. Those who meditate show no lower somatic arousal while they are meditating than others who are simply resting (Homes, 1984). It may be that simply resting, doing nothing, is enough to reduce muscle tension, calm the mind, and generate the restorative response. It is difficult to simply "do nothing," but it can be learned.

All these techniques—from biofeedback to "doing nothing"—involve a state of mind quite foreign to the value system of the West. The common element is *passive attention*, a process of doing without effort or final goal (Peper, 1977). But attending to the means, not the outcome, and not striving go against all our value training. "Letting it flow" and "allowing it to happen" are phrases attempting to capture this noncompetitive, process-focused approach to the cultivation of low arousal. Anticipation and evaluation kill progress in learning deep emotional calm. A restful, relaxed body and an alert but passively attentive mind form the base for the restorative response.

**WHAT DO YOU THINK?**

- How have you attempted to modulate anxiety?
- How well have you done?

## ■ Four Methods for Training in Low Arousal

The West has produced several meditational methods that are promising for training in low arousal. Below is a very brief description of four of them. If a particular method appears promising to you, details may be obtained by reading the works cited at the end of this chapter.

The four methods are the following:

*1. The Relaxation Response* Herbert Benson (1975) found no significant difference between the metabolic benefits to be derived from transcendental meditation, the popular yoga style, and this simple procedure. All that is necessary to produce the relaxation response is a few minutes, twice a day, in which you experience:

a. A quiet environment (no unexpected noises).
b. A passive attitude (the most important factor).
c. A comfortable position (not so comfortable as to produce sleep).
d. An object to dwell on (the number 1, for example).

Now, while remaining passive, breathe slowly in and out. Repeat the number 1 or its equivalent on each "out" breath. Benson reports this procedure to be associated with reduced drug and alcohol use, both of which are costly coping techniques often used to reduce anxiety.

2. *Progressive Relaxation*  In over seventy years of clinical testing, Edmund Jacobson (1978) found that every thought is accompanied by muscle tension, and that the path to deep calm lies in emptying your mind of thoughts and systematically relaxing your voluntary muscles. He believes the involuntary muscles will then follow, involuntarily. A brief version of progressive relaxation includes these steps:

a. Lie quietly on your back with your eyes gradually closing.
b. Recognize contraction (tension) in a muscle group by bending or tightening the appropriate muscles.
c. Observe the sensation of tension in the selected muscle. Learn to distinguish muscle tension from other sensations.
d. Realize that what you are feeling is the result of *doing*. What you want to accomplish is *not doing*—"going negative."
e. Relax. Let muscles go limp. Do not gradually release tension.
f. Permit yourself a half hour of continuous relaxation without movement, but also without rigidity.
g. On the days to follow, learn to recognize tension in your body in the following order:

1. Right arm.
2. Left arm.
3. Right leg.
4. Left leg.
5. Trunk.
6. Shoulders.
7. Neck.
8. Brow.
9. Eyes.
10. Forehead.
11. Cheeks.
12. Jaws.
13. Lips.
14. Tongue.
15. Throat.
16. Muscles associated with visual imagery.
17. Muscles associated with negative self-talk.

You can sense tension and let it go while you are active as well as while you are lying down. Fear and worry are modulated when you relax the tensions you sense while engaged in fear and worry. "If you relax these particular tensions, you cease to imagine or recall or reflect about the matter in question" (Jacobson, 1978, p. 251).

3. *Autogenic Training*  While Jacobson wants you to let your mind go negative, Luthe and Schultz (1970) want you to use your mind, or at least that portion

that controls voluntary speech, to achieve the opposite of stress, the *neutral autogenic state*. Again, regular training in a tranquil atmosphere without disturbance is considered essential. While in this restful environment, passively concentrate on following the suggestions contained in these six phrases.

   *a.* My arms and legs are heavy.
   *b.* My arms and legs are warm.
   *c.* My heartbeat is calm and regular.
   *d.* My body breathes itself.
   *e.* My abdomen is warm and regular.
   *f.* My forehead is cool.

The reference to a cool forehead is important, because blood rushes to and warms the forehead in times of worry. During these mental exercises, your skeletal and visceral muscles begin to relax in response to your passive concentration on the sensations of being heavy and warm.

*4. Self-Hypnosis*   Reports of subjects who have been successfully hypnotized describe the following: a sense of deep relaxation, a narrowing of attention, and an increased level of suggestibility (Hilgard and Hilgard, 1975). These are identical to the passive concentration or passive attention considered essential to success in biofeedback, progressive relaxation, and autogenic training. Relaxing self-talk forms the basis for self-hypnosis, as this example demonstrates:

> *In a comfortable sitting or lying position, say to yourself: "I am becoming more and more relaxed. I let my whole body relax. I let my muscles go limp. I feel my arms (and legs, and so on) relaxing even more. Now I direct my attention to my forehead (and shoulders, and so on). I let it relax more and more. My body is beginning to feel rather heavy. I feel myself sinking into the chair (or bed, or floor). My shoulders, neck, and head are more and more relaxed. My mind is relaxing along with my body. I set all worries aside. My mind is calm and peaceful. As I count from twenty backwards toward one, I will feel myself going down further and further into this deeply relaxed hypnotic state." After the backward count, make a suggestion to yourself concerning your worry or fear. Example: "When I awake I will be able to concentrate on my studies" or "I am going to awake very calm and refreshed and able to control my worries." Before ending the experience, say to yourself, "Now I am going to count backward from five to one. At the count of one I will awake relaxed, alert, and beautifully refreshed."*

Herb Benson in a recent comparison of hypnosis with the relaxation response, reports that individual differences in gaining beneficial effects from the relaxation response in the treatment of anxiety might be related to responsiveness to hypnosis. That is, anxious people who can be easily and deeply hypnotized derive substantial relief from anxiety when they practice the relaxation response without hypnosis. The state of being hypnotized is considered identical to the state of being deeply relaxed in both mind and body (Benson, Arns, and Hoffman, 1981).

## ■ Combining Methods for Anxiety Modulation

The various methods described above may be combined. Biofeedback stresses an experimental approach in which you may try any combination of techniques. The equipment will inform you instantly what works for you. Empirical data, rather than faith in an authority, helps you to improve your ability to combat anxiety.

The mastery of any of these techniques to the extent necessary for modulating anxiety requires a great deal of disciplined work. Some positive results usually occur with your initial attempts, however, and encourage you to practice. The function of this increasing skill is to allow you to use your increased tolerance for stress to cope directly with the situation that produced the stress in the first place. Its major benefit is that it allows a clear mind and a calm body to consider and put into action some rational coping techniques.

**WHAT DO YOU THINK?**

- Can you improve your performance by not striving?
- Can you relax and concentrate at the same time?

**REVIEW QUESTIONS**

47. Anx_____ is considered a major component of most adjustment problems.

48. Which of these is not a cause of basic anxiety? Fear of choice / Fear of death / Fear of airplanes.

49. W_____ is an indirect coping mechanism, a wish for a magical solution to a problem.

50. Anxiety that is part of the personality is trait / state anxiety.

51. The fear of fear itself is known as s_____ anxiety.

52. Irritability is / is not usually a personality trait of anxious people.

53. The authors of this text prefer the term m_____ to either control or regulation when they discuss changing anxiety responses.

54. Biofeedback instruments reduce / give information about the anxiety responses of the moment.

55. Deep relaxation appears to demand personal striving / goal setting and evaluation / passive concentration.

56. The function of the restorative response is to allow you to escape / avoid / cope with stressful situations in your life.

*The answers to these review questions are on page 262.*

# SUMMARY

- We have survived by being able to change our behavior to meet the changing demands placed on us.

- These demands are termed *stressors* and are present without limit in our environment.

- Our response to any demand is termed *stress*. Our body changes in order to energize us and to direct that energy towards confrontation or escape.

- Excessive stress or a failure to cope with stress leads to "diseases of adaptation." Selye describes the stress sequence in terms of a general adaptation syndrome consisting of three stages: alarm, resistance, and exhaustion.

- Richard Rahe lists six transformations that take place before the presence of a stressor can become a psychological or physical illness.

■ Herbert Benson emphasizes the link between stress and high blood pressure, strokes, and heart attacks.

■ Engel, Lynch, and others report loneliness and other extreme stressors to be linked to disease, injury, and emotional death.

■ A failure of the immune system, related to prolonged stress, results in reduced ability to defend against disease cells.

■ Vinokur and Selzer report a link between high stress and emotional and mental illness.

■ Albert Bandura finds that certain forms of stress are necessary for personal growth and change.

■ Eustress also requires adjustment but is less damaging physically and is not emotionally damaging at all.

■ Jobs are among the chief stressors in modern America.

■ Stress is best viewed as a natural, inevitable part of daily living, and we are capable of modulating stress so that it works for us, not against us.

■ Defensive coping mechanisms are indirect methods of regulating stress. They serve to protect the ego and reduce the probability of destructive aggression.

■ Drugs, from alcohol and valium to cocaine and heroin, are termed *disregulators* because they hinder the functioning of the brain's coping mechanisms.

■ Anxiety is a response to perceived threat that produces chronic fear and irritability.

■ Anxiety has roots in early childhood experiences and in the realities of human existence. It may become a conditioned response and be transmitted to others.

■ The restorative response, a profound state of low arousal, is incompatible with anxiety. It has been produced by both Eastern and Western approaches, from yoga to biofeedback.

■ An attitude of passive attention appears to be central to both Eastern and Western approaches that have been successful in producing a prolonged state of low arousal.

■ The restorative response reduces the ravages of stress and allows us to use a clear mind in a calm body to select and use rational, direct coping techniques in response to stress.

## SELECTED READINGS

Antonovsky, A. *Health, Stress, and Coping*. San Francisco: Jossey-Bass, 1979. A good review of the types of persons, groups, and environments that encourage more effective tension management.

Benson, H. *The Relaxation Response*. New York: Morrow Press, 1975. A beautiful book that describes behavior patterns that provoke premature heart attacks and offers a simple relaxation technique for combating stress.

*Biofeedback and Self-Regulation* (published by Plenum Press). A quarterly journal; a good way to keep abreast of the latest findings in the field of biofeedback research and application.

Friedman, M., and Rosenman, R. F. *Type A Behavior and Your Heart*. New York: Knopf, 1974. A book that describes a personality type associated with increased risk of heart attacks and suggests methods for changing to a less risky personal outlook.

Jacobson, E. *Progressive Relaxation*. Chicago: University of Chicago Press, 1974. Tested techniques for muscle relaxation to produce a deep, restorative calm.

*Journal of Human Stress* (published by Opinion Publications, Inc.). Reports of continuing investigations of environmental influences on both health and human behavior.

Kobasa, S. C.; Hilker, R. R.; and Maddi, S. R. "Who Stays Healthy under Stress?" *Journal of Occupational Medicine* 21 (1979): 595–598. A proposal that basic character structures must be changed if effective coping styles are to be learned. See what you think.

Lazarus, R. S. "Positive Denial: The Case for Not Facing Reality." *Psychology Today* (November 1979); 44–60. An interview in which Lazarus states that refusing to face facts and holding false beliefs about reality can at times be useful in coping with stress.

Lecron, L. *Self-Hypnotism*. Englewood Cliffs, N.J.: Prentice-Hall, 1964. A lively and professional description of relaxation through self-suggestion.

Luthe, W., and Schultz, J. *Autogenic Therapy*, Vols. 1, 2, and 3. New York: Grune and Stratton, 1969 and 1970. A description of the systematic use of verbal phrases to induce a deep, restorative calm.

Pelletier, K. *Holistic Medicine: From Stress to Optimum Health*. New York: Dell, 1979.

Selye, H. *The Stress of Life*, rev. ed. New York: McGraw-Hill, 1976. The book that has done more than any other to popularize the idea of a relationship between a stressful lifestyle and subsequent illness.

Selye, H. *Stress Without Distress*. Philadelphia: Lippincott, 1976. A philosophical work that contains the wisdom gained by Dr. Selye in a lifetime of studying stress.

# GLOSSARY

**angina:** pain in the chest, not caused by heart muscle damage.

**anxiety:** a fear response to a perceived future threat.

**atherosclerosis:** thickening of the interior walls of the arteries.

**biofeedback:** a method of getting information from our own bodies.

**catabolism:** changes in living cells that provide energy for vital processes.

**cerebral stroke:** a sudden trauma with the brain itself.

**cholestyramine:** a chemical that lowers blood fats and thus the probability of heart disease.

**compensation:** efforts to gain success to make up for real or imagined failures.

**conservation–withdrawal response:** a response to stress characterized by feelings of helplessness and a suppression of the immune system.

**conversion:** production of bodily infirmities that block threatening responsibilities or desires.

**denial:** a refusal to accept the reality of a threat.

**direct coping:** attempts to change the conditions that produce stress.

**diseases of adaptation:** bodily disease or injury brought on by attempts to combat stress.

**displacement:** the discharge of threatening feelings against a safe substitute.

**emotional death:** death initiated by psychological, rather than physical, trauma.

**emotional insulation:** blocking of emotional expression to protect against future hurt.

**fantasize:** gain imaginary satisfaction through daydreaming.

**general adaptation syndrome:** the body's pattern of reaction under continued stress.

**hysteria:** paralysis and/or memory loss due to mental conflicts.

**identification:** taking on of the characteristics of a significant other.

**indirect coping:** altering of oneself to reduce stress.

**intellectualization:** the use of thinking to avoid the threat of feeling or acting.

**isolation:** deliberate regulation of stress by retreat from stressful situation.

**locus coeruleus:** a sector of the limbic system of the brain; stimulation of this sector is associated with feelings of anxiety.

**lymphatic system:** body system that includes the ducts that discharge white blood cells to protect against infection.

**projection:** attribution of one's undesirable traits to others.

**psychosomatic:** relating to physical symptoms attributable to psychological disturbances.

**rationalization:** a socially acceptable excuse.

**reaction-formation:** an act in opposition to unconscious wishes.

**regression:** a return to a more primitive, infantile response.

**repression:** exclusion of uncomfortable thoughts or feelings from awareness (largely unconscious forgetting).

**repressors:** people who reduce their awareness of stress or stressors.

**restorative response:** a state of profound calm.

**secondary anxiety:** a fear of the bodily changes associated with fear.

**sensitizers:** persons who acknowledge stress so as to control it.

**social readjustment rating scale:** a method of measuring the relative amount of stress experienced by a person.

**state anxiety:** fear produced by an identifiable stressor.

**stress:** reaction to any demand placed on a person.

**sublimation:** substitution of acceptable for nonacceptable forms of activity.

**suppression:** the deliberate forgetting of disturbing thoughts, feelings, or actions.

**systematic desensitization:** a process of reconditioning.

**trait anxiety:** chronic fear that is part of the makeup of an individual.

**Type A:** a personality type characterized by impatience and work addiction; thought susceptible to premature heart disorders.

**vasomotor:** relating to blood vessel expansion or contraction.

## REFERENCES

Anderson, A. "How the Mind Heals." *Psychology Today* 16 (December 1982): 51–56.

Bandura, A. "Self-Efficacy: Toward a Unifying Theory of Behavioral Change." *Psychological Review* 84 (March 1977): 191–215.

———. *Social Learning Theory.* Englewood Cliffs, N.J.: Prentice-Hall, 1977.

Benson, H. *The Relaxation Response.* New York: Morrow, 1975.

Benson, H.; Arns, A. A.; and Hoffman, J. W. "The Relaxation Response and Hypnosis." *International Journal of Clinical and Experimental Hypnosis* 29 (1981): 259–270.

Bettelheim, B. "Individual and Mass Behavior in Extreme Situations." *Abnormal and Social Psychology* 38 (1943): 417–452.

Biersner, R. J.; McHugh, W. B.; and Rahe, R. H. "Biochemical Variability in a Team Sports Situation." *Journal of Human Stress* 7 (September 1981): 12–18.

Blakeslee, S. "Study of Japanese-Americans Indicates Stress Can Be a Major Factor in Heart Disease." *New York Times* (August 5, 1975): 8.

Brady, J. V.; Porter, R. W.; Conrad, D. G.; and Mason, J. W. "Avoidance Behavior and the Development of Gastroduedenal Ulcers." *Journal of Experimental Analysis of Behavior* 1 (1958): 69–73.

Brett, M. J. "Job Transfer and Well Being." *Journal of Applied Psychology* (August 1982): 450–460.

Brown, B., and Rosenbaum, L. "High Stress Lowers IQ Scores." *Science Digest* (October 1983): 78.

Burke, R. J. "Occupational Stress." *Journal of Social Psychology* 100 (1976): 235–244.

Burke, R. J., and Weir, T. "The Type A Experience: Occupational and Life Demands, Satisfaction and Well-Being." *Journal of Human Stress* 6 (December 1980): 28–38.

Byrne, R. J.; Darry, J.; and Nelson, D. "Relation of the Revised Repression-Sensitization Scale to Measures of Self-Description." *Psychological Reports* 13 (1963): 323–334.

Byrne, R. J., and Sheffield, J. "Response to Sexually Arousing Stimuli as a Function of Repressing and Sensitizing Defenses." *Journal of Abnormal Social Psychology* 70 (1965): 114–118.

Cameron, N. *Personality Development and Psychopathology: A Dynamic Approach.* Boston: Houghton Mifflin, 1963.

Cannon, W. B. *Bodily Changes in Pain, Hunger, Fear and Rage,* 2nd ed. New York: Appleton-Century-Crofts, 1929.

———. "Voodoo Death." *American Anthropologist* 44 (1942): 169–181.

Cooley, E. J., and Keesey, J. C. "Moderator Variables in Life Stress and Illness Relationship." *Journal of Human Stress* 7 (September 1981): 35–40.

Di Cara, L. V., and Miller, N. E. "Instrumental Learning of Vasomotor Responses by Rats: Learning to Respond Differentially in the Two Ears." *Science* 159 (1968): 1485–1486.

Dollard, J., and Miller, N. E. *Personality and Psychotherapy.* New York: McGraw-Hill, 1950.

Engel, G. "Emotional Death and Sudden Death." *Psychology Today,* (November 1977): 114–115.

Erikson, E. H. *Identity: Youth in Crisis.* New York: Norton, 1968.

Foushee, H. C.; Davis, M. H.; Stephan, W. G.; and Bernstein, W. M. "The Effects of Cognitive and Behavioral Control on Post-Stress Performance." *Journal of Human Stress* 6 (June 1980): 41–48.

Freedman, J. J. *Crowding and Behavior*. New York: Viking Press, 1975.

Fried, J. J. "Mind and Body: The Inseparable Link." *Science Digest Special* (Spring 1980): 50–53.

Friedman, M., and Rosenman, R. F. *Type A Behavior and Your Heart*. New York: Knopf, 1974.

Fuller, G. D. "Current Status of Biofeedback in Clinical Practice." *American Psychologist* (January 1978): 39–48.

Garre, W. J. *Basic Anxiety: A New Psycho-Biological Concept*. New York: Philosophical Library, 1962.

Glass, D. C., and Singer, J. E. "Behavioral Consequences of Adaptation to Controllable and Uncontrollable Noise." *Journal of Experimental Social Psychology* 7 (1971): 244–257.

———. *Urban Stress: Experiments on Noise and Social Stressors*. New York: Academic Press, 1972.

Glasser, W. *Reality Therapy*. New York: Harper & Row, 1965.

Harris, J. L., and Landreth, G. L. "Predicting Seriousness of Illness Using External Stress, Imagery, and Other Cognitive Mediating Variables." *Journal of Human Stress* 7 (December 1981) 28–35.

Hebb, D. O. *A Textbook of Psychology*. Philadelphia: Saunders, 1958.

Henry, P. J, and Stevens, P. M. *Stress, Health and the Social Environment: A Sociobiological Approach to Medicine*. New York: Springer, 1978.

Hilgard, E. R., and Hilgard, J. R. *Hypnosis in the Relief of Pain*. Los Altos, Calif.: William Kaufmann, 1975.

Holmes, T. H., and Rahe, R. H. "The Social Readjustment Rating Scale." *Journal of Psychosomatic Research* 11 (1967): 213–218.

Homes, D. S. "Meditation and Somatic Arousal Reduction." *American Psychologist* 39 (January 1984): 1.–10.

Horney, K. *Neurosis and Human Growth*. New York: Norton, 1950.

Jacobson, E. *You Must Relax*. New York: McGraw-Hill, 1978.

Karasek, R. "Jobs Where Stress Is Most Severe." *U.S. News & World Report* (September 5, 1983): 45–46.

Klausner, S. Z., ed. *Why Man Takes Chances: Studies in Stress-Seeking*. New York: Doubleday, 1968.

Kobasa, S. C. "Stressful Life Events, Personality, and Health. An Inquiry into Hardiness." *Personality and Social Psychology* 37 (1979): 1–11.

Kobasa, S. C.; Maddi, S. R.; and Kahn, S. "Hardiness and Health: A Prospective Study." *Journal of Personality and Social Psychology* 42 (1982): 168–177.

Kotulak, R. "What's Behind Those Tears? Chemistry." *Miami Herald* (January 4, 1984): 1F.

Kringlen, E. "Heart Disease and Life Stress." *Science News* 112 (1977): 166.

Lazarus, R. S. "Coping with Stress: Effects on Somatic Illness, Morale, and Social Functioning." Presented at Stress and Behavioral Medicine Symposium sponsored by BioMonitoring Applications, New York, 1977.

———. "Little Hassles Can Be Dangerous to Health." *Psychology Today* 15 (July 1981): 58–62.

Levine, S. "The Effects of Differential Infantile Stimulation on Emotionality at Weaning." *Canadian Journal of Psychology* 13 (1959): 243–247.

Liebow, E. *Tally's Corner*. Boston: Little Brown, 1967.

Llfeld, S. W., Jr. "Coping Styles." *Journal of Human Stress* 6 (June 1980): 2–10.

Lloyd, C.; Alexander, A. A.; Rice, D. G.; and Greenfield, N. S. "Life Events as Predictors of Academic Performance." *Journal of Human Stress* 6 (September 1980): 15–26.

Locke, S. "Stress May Damage Cell Immunity." *Science News* 113 (March 1978): 151.

Luthe, E., and Schultz, J. *Autogenic Therapy*. Vols. 1, 2, and 3. New York: Grune and Stratton, 1969, 1970.

Lynch, J. J. *The Broken Heart: The Medical Consequences of Loneliness*. New York: Basic Books, 1977.

Marx, M. B.; Garrity, T. F.; and Bowers, F. R. "The Influence of Recent Life Experiences on the Health of College Freshmen." *Journal of Psychosomatic Research* (1975): 87–98.

McClelland, D. C. "Sources of Stress in the Drive for Power." In *Psychopathology of Human Adaptation*. Edited by George Serban. New York: Plenum Press, 1976.

McKenna, J. F.; Oritt, P. L.; and Wolff, H. K. "Occupational Stress as a Predictor in the Turnover Decision." *Journal of Human Stress* 7 (December 1981): 12–18.

Miller, N. E. "Applications of Learning and Biofeedback to Psychiatry and Medicine." In *Compre-*

*hensive Textbook of Psychiatry,* 2nd ed. Edited by A. M. Freedman, H. I. Kaplan, and B. J. Sadock. Baltimore: Williams & Williams, 1974.

Ogilvie, B. C. "Stimulus Addiction: The Sweet Psychic Jolt of Danger." *Psychology Today* (October 1974): 88–94.

Orth-Gomer, K., and Ahlbom, A. "Impact of Psychological Stress on Ischemic Heart Disease when Controlling for Conventional Risk Indicators." *Journal of Human Stress* 6 (March 1980): 7–15.

Pearson, D. and Shaw, S. *Life Extension.* New York: Warner Books, 1980.

Pelletier, K. R. *Holistic Medicine: From Stress to Optimum Health.* New York: Dell, 1979.

Peper, E. "Passive Attention: The Gateway to Consciousness and Autonomic Control." In *Psychology and Life,* 9th ed. Edited by P. G. Zimbardo and F. L. Ruch. Glenview, Ill.: Scott, Foresman, 1977.

Pepitone-Arreola-Rockwell, F.; Sommer, B.; Sassenrath, E. N.; Rozee-Koker, J.; and Stringer-Moore, D. "Job Stress and Health in Working Women." *Journal of Human Stress* 7 (December 1981): 19–26.

Pines, M. "Psychological Hardiness: The Role of Challenge in Health." *Psychology Today* 14 (December 1980): 34–36.

Rahe, R. "Life Stress Events and Illness." Presented at Stress and Behavioral Medicine Symposium sponsored by BioMonitoring Applications, New York, 1977.

———. "The Pathway between Subjects' Recent Life Changes and Their Near-Future Illness Reports: Representative Results and Methodological Issues." In *Stressful Life Events: Their Nature and Effects.* Edited by B. S. Dohrenwend and B. P. Dohrenwend. New York: Wiley, 1974.

Rogers, C. R. "A Theory of Personality." In *Perspectives on Personality.* Edited by S. Maddi. Boston: Little Brown, 1971.

Salzinger, S.; Kaplan, S.; and Artemyeff, C. "Mother's Personal Social Networks and Child Maltreatment." *Journal of Abnormal Psychology* 92 (1983) 68–73.

Schorr, B. "Anti-Cholesterol Treatment Can Cut Risk of Heart Disease Up to 50%, a Study Shows." *Wall Street Journal* (January 13, 1984): 4.

Schwartz, G. E. "Behavioral Approaches to Stress Management and Correction of Disregulation."

Presented at Stress and Behavioral Medicine Symposium sponsored by BioMonitoring Applications, New York, 1977.

Selye, H. *The Stress of Life,* rev. ed. New York: McGraw-Hill, 1976.

———. *Stress Without Distress.* New York: Lippincott, 1974.

Selye, H., and Cherry, L. "On the Real Benefits of Eustress." *Psychology Today* 11 (March 1978): 60–63, 69–70.

Smith, M. J. "Occupational Stress." *Proceedings of the Conference on Occupational Stress* 3, Los Angeles, 1977.

Spielberger, C. D., ed. *Anxiety and Behavior.* New York: Academic Press, 1966.

Stoyva, J. "Cultivated Low Arousal through Biofeedback: A Learned-Anti-Stress Response?" Presented at Stress and Behavioral Medicine Symposium sponsored by BioMonitoring Applications, New York, 1977.

Suls, J.; Becker, M. A.; and Mullen, B. "Coronary-Prone Behavior, Social Insecurity and Stress Among College-Aged Adults." *Journal of Human Stress* 7 (September 1981): 27–34.

Tanner, O. *Stress.* New York: Time-Life Books, 1976.

Tucker, I. F. *Adjustment: Models and Mechanisms.* New York: Academic Press, 1970.

Ursin, H.; Boode, E.; and Levine, S. *Psychobiology of Stress: A Study of Coping Men.* New York: Academic Press, 1978.

Vinokur, A., and Selzer, M. L. "Desirable versus Undesirable Life Events: Their Relationship to Stress and Mental Distress." *Journal of Personality and Social Psychology* 32 (1975): 329–337.

Waldron, I.; Hickey, A.; McPherson, C.; Butensky, A.; Gruss, L.; Overall, K.; Schmader, A.; and Wohlmuth, D. "Type A Behavior Pattern: Relationship to Variation in Blood Pressure, Parental Characteristics, and Academic and Social Activities of Students." *Journal of Human Stress* 6 (March 1980): 8–16.

Weiss, J. M. "Psychological Factors in Stress and Disease." *Scientific American* 226 (1972): 106.

Wolpe, J. *The Practice of Behavioral Therapy,* 2nd ed. New York: Pergamon Press, 1973.

———. "The Training Programs of the Behavioral Therapy Unit at Temple University." *Journal of Behavior Therapy and Experimental Psychiatry* 9 (December 1978): 295–300.

# ANSWERS TO REVIEW QUESTIONS

**Page 222.** *1.* unfinished   *2.* by our ability to sense changes   *3.* the same way   *4.* stress   *5.* catabolism   *6.* the same way

**Page 228.** *7.* restorative response   *8.* cannot   *9.* adaptation   *10.* a mobilization of energy   *11.* enlarged adrenal glands   *12.* loneliness   *13.* excitement   *14.* unlimited, unlimited   *15.* can

**Page 231.** *16.* difficult   *17.* fear or anger   *18.* high blood pressure   *19.* immune   *20.* more   *21.* Headache   *22.* less

**Page 236.** *23.* stress   *24.* less   *25.* machine   *26.* are   *27.* T   *28.* are stressed by   *29.* more, better

**Page 238.** *30.* constant stimulation   *31.* better   *32.* more   *33.* sometimes   *34.* performance accomplishment, senstization to stress, vicarious experience, persuasion   *35.* immunize   *36.* cannot

**Page 247.** *37.* cognitive appraisal   *38.* direct coping   *39.* negative   *40.* self-esteem   *41.* repression   *42.* reaction-formation   *43.* displacement   *44.* Sublimation   *45.* rationalization   *46.* intellectualization

**Page 256.** *47.* Anxiety   *48.* Fear of airplanes   *49.* Worry   *50.* trait   *51.* secondary   *52.* is   *53.* *modulation*   *54.* give information about   *55.* passive concentration   *56.* cope with

We adjust and grow within the context of our relationships with others. It is through our interaction with others that we come to know ourselves. Consequently, without the aid of others, we would have great difficulty surviving. Part IV focuses on this interpersonal aspect of adjustment and growth.

Chapter 8 deals with socialization—the process by which human culture is transmitted. It includes considerations of individual capacities and needs, the acquisition of beliefs and values, the formation of a self-concept, and stages of self-development throughout the life cycle.

In Chapter 9, we explore the relationship between each of us as individuals and the numerous groups to which we belong throughout our lives. Although this type of material is seldom found in adjustment texts, we believe it is important when studying personal adjustment to understand the power of group influence on each of us and, more important, the influence each of us has on the various groups to which he or she belongs.

# SELF
# AND
# OTHERS

# 8

# SOCIALIZATION

We are born human beings, yet at birth
our vast human potential is largely
untapped. What human society would
recognize us as one of their own? We
neither speak nor understand any
language. We have no beliefs, values, or
attitudes. We know no customs or
standards for behavior. Indeed, at birth we
appear to know nothing. We survive only
through the aid of others; ultimately, we
adjust and fulfill our human potential only
through our interaction with them.

In this chapter we will briefly survey the
unfolding of human potential. We will
consider the physical, mental and social
development of the individual, including
stages of development throughout the life
cycle, and the formation of beliefs, values,
attitudes and the self-concept.

**8**

SOCIALIZATION

## DISCUSSION: SOCIALIZATION

Human potential unfolds as part of a larger process called **socialization**. This is the critically important process in which human **culture** is transmitted. It involves the interplay of hereditary and environmental factors in the physical, mental, and social development of the individual.

### ■ The Importance of Culture

Without culture, the human species would perish. Like all other living species, we survive because of our ability to adapt to the environment. But our adaptation is significantly different from that of other life forms in at least two major respects. First, we have not evolved specific physical adaptive characteristics equal to those of other species. The polar bear, for example, can thrive in an extremely cold environment because of its heavy fur, while human skin alone will not permit survival in such frigid temperatures. Second, we do not exhibit forms of complex, unlearned activity comparable to those of other species. Experimentation has shown, for instance, that South African weaver birds completely isolated from their natural environment and from others of their species for a period of six generations were able to build nests in the typical pattern of their wild ancestors when supplied with appropriate materials (Williams, 1972). We, on the other hand, must learn to build our shelters. Indeed, as a species, we must learn our social heritage or culture to survive, for culture is our unique adaptive mechanism. Thus, socialization is indispensable to human existence.

### ■ Heredity versus Environment

**WHAT DO YOU THINK?**

■ Can you think of any ways in which your genetic inheritance may affect your behavior?

■ How has your environment affected your behavior?

■ Which has been the stronger influence on your own development—heredity or environment?

■ In what ways might you have been a different person if either your heredity or environment had been different?

No one really knows whether heredity or environment has a stronger influence on our development. Some of our characteristics are obviously products of genetic inheritance. A male, for example, cannot conceive and give birth to a child. Just as certainly, other characteristics are produced by environmental factors. You could not speak English if you had never been exposed to the English language. Still other characteristics such as intelligence seem to be products of the interaction of hereditary and environmental factors. At present, perhaps the only statement regarding this issue that researchers can agree on is that "We are born with certain genetic limitations and potentials, and environmental factors determine the extent to which we realize our potentials" (Babbie, 1977, p. 104). Both heredity and environment, then, are important factors in our development.

### ■ Physical Development

**Physical development** refers to the person's progression from simple to more complex levels of bodily organization. At the moment of your conception, you were a single-celled organism that measured only about 0.14 millimeters in diameter (McNeil, 1966). During the *embryonic stage* (the first two months following conception, your size increased to about one and one-half inches and your cells multiplied and began to differentiate into layers that formed your nervous, circulatory, skeletal, muscular, digestive, and glandular systems. Through

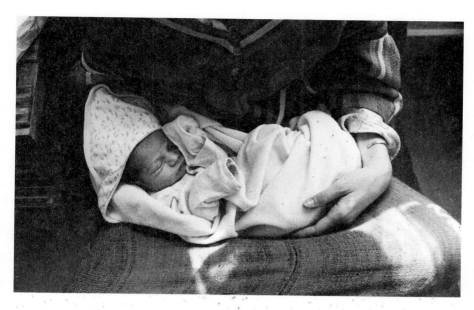

■ The newborn human cannot survive without the aid of others.

the *fetal stage* (the third month following conception until birth), you continued to develop so that at birth you measured approximately twenty inches in length, weighed approximately seven pounds, and consisted of billions of cells organized in a manner that made it possible for you to survive with the aid of other people.

You were completely dependent on others to feed and protect you. However, when you were born, you did possess several biological structures that contributed to your survival. **Reflexes** such as digesting food and eliminating wastes were automatic and required no previous learning experiences. But, as already mentioned, someone had to feed you.

During the *neonatal stage* (the first month following birth), you broke in your biological equipment. You breathed air, eliminated wastes, controlled your temperature, circulated your blood, and maintained the acid-alkaline balance in your body for the first time (McNeil, 1966). Throughout the rest of your *infancy* (approximately the first two years following birth), you continued to **mature** and **grow** in a sequential pattern that included staying awake longer, controlling voluntary muscles, sitting, standing, crawling, walking, feeding yourself, and talking (Elkind and Weiner, 1978). During this period, you were also maturing in a cognitive sense.

## ■ Cognitive Maturation

**Cognition** refers to the process of knowing. Cognitive maturation, then, is the unfolding of our potential to know. At the moment of your birth, you appeared to know nothing. You were relatively unaware of yourself as an object in the environment and of what was happening around you. Soon, however, you began to discriminate among objects in your environment and to display problem-solving and reasoning abilities.

Over time, your **perception** became more acute. Your eyes and ears began to make more finely tuned discriminations. You began to orient yourself and

*See Chapter 5 for a more complete consideration of cognition.*

to get used to the constant presence of stimuli within your environment. Through both respondent and operant conditioning, you learned a variety of responses to environmental stimuli. You also conceived some strategies for *problem solving,* a kind of learning that involves overcoming an obstacle to reach a desired goal. You began to *reason* (to obtain new information by applying rules to existing information) and to comprehend and speak a language. Thus, by the end of infancy, you had made significant strides in cognitive maturation. In addition, you had begun your social development.

## ■ Social Development

**Social development** refers to the person's movement from simple to more complex social statuses and roles. A **status** is a social position and a **role** is a pattern of expected behavior associated with a status. At present, for instance, you occupy the status of student and, at this very moment, you are playing the role of a student (that is, reading this textbook). People hold many statuses simultaneously but tend to play only one role at a time. In addition to being a student, you may be son or daughter, mother or father, brother or sister, male or female, laborer or manager, Protestant or Jew, Polish-American or Irish-American, eighteen years old or fifty-eight years old. But, at this moment, you are playing only the role of student. In essence, society is a set of interrelated statuses, and culture determines the content of social roles.

In all societies social development is correlated with physical and mental development, so that people are not expected to fill statuses and play roles that are beyond their physical and mental capabilities at any given time. When you were three years old, no one expected you to be relatively self-sufficient (that is, to play an adult role). On the other hand, physically and mentally mature people are not expected to display behavior associated with simple statuses and roles. Imagine how people would respond to you now if you started crying because you had spilled your milk at the dinner table.

Socialization progresses through a general sequence of social development in which the individual proceeds from dependent to independent to interdependent statuses and roles (Mendoza and Napoli, 1982). During infancy and early childhood, the person is primarily in a state of dependency, and expectations for independent behavior are not very high. Although the first instances of independent social behavior may appear early (for example, when the infant refuses to eat food that is given to him or her), general expectations for independent and responsible social behavior usually do not emerge until middle childhood, somewhere between the ages of five and twelve. In adolescence, when the person is usually held more responsible for his or her social behavior, expectations for independent behavior become particularly acute. Indeed, many adolescents are expected (or at least told) by their parents to act grown up. By this time, the person has had the opportunity to learn the basic requirements of interdependent relationships through family contacts, student-teacher interactions, and the give-and-take of friendships. However, interdependency is most closely associated with adulthood, when people are expected to enter into interdependent relationships such as those of the adult working world, marriage, parenthood, grandparenthood, and so on (Thompson and Van Houten, 1970).

## ■ Social Maturity

Although marriage and the bearing and rearing of children is a social expectation in virtually all human societies (Goode, 1964), people who do not marry are not necessarily considered socially immature. Social maturity is determined more by willingness to accept the interdependent nature of society and to behave in ways consistent with that interdependent nature than by playing any given adult role. Thus, it is possible for a person who does not marry to achieve social maturity. Conversely, an adult person who behaves selfishly and who fails to cooperate with others will be considered socially immature regardless of whether or not he or she is married.

> Marilyn is just about at her wit's end with David, her husband. She knew when she married him that he was somewhat selfish and uncooperative, but she thought he was going through a phase he would soon outgrow.
>
> Now, eight years later, David has not changed. As a result, he has lost several jobs and most of his friends. He has also failed to recognize the need for cooperation in his relationship with Marilyn, and she is seriously considering divorce.

REVIEW QUESTIONS

*1.* The fundamental survival mechanism of human beings is culture. T F

*2.* Heredity has a much stronger influence on the socialization process than does environment. T F

*3.* Human physical development begins at the moment of conception. T F

*4.* Humans display excellent reasoning abilities at birth. T F

*5.* Social development is not correlated in any way with either physical or mental development. T F

*6.* The general sequence of social development is from dependent to independent to interdependent statuses and roles. T F

*7.* Socialization is the process of transmitting human culture. T F

*8.* People who do not marry are socially immature. T F

*The answers to these review questions are on page 293.*

## DISCUSSION: INTERACTION WITH OTHERS

Socialization is largely a people process. It involves not only the unfolding of our physical and mental capacities, but the existence of an ongoing society and significant interaction among the people of that society. It is through our interaction with others that we acquire *human nature,* a critical prerequisite to becoming human.

### ■ Human Nature and Human Contact

Human nature means different things to different people. Freud viewed it as our tendency to seek pleasure while at the same time avoiding punishment and guilt; Skinner views it as our innate ability to respond to differential stimuli; and Rogers views it as our drive to actualize our potentialities. Here, however,

*See Chapter 2 for a discussion of the ideas of Freud, Skinner, and Rogers.*

we are using human nature in the sense that Frederick Elkin (1960) uses it: "the ability to establish emotional relationships with others and to experience such sentiments as love, sympathy, shame, envy, pity, and awe" (p. 7).

According to Elkin, human nature is not part of our biological inheritance; it is learned. It develops in **primary groups** such as the family, in which we have close, intimate, and intense face-to-face contacts frequently. It is through interaction in primary groups that we begin to empathize—to understand and share the feelings of others. Only when this happens are we prepared to become human within the context of our culture and society.

Hypothetically, children deprived of human contact cannot develop human nature. Although there are no known cases in which children have been totally deprived of human contact and have survived, there are some cases in which children have been reared in isolation or have suffered a severe lack of attention and affection as infants. In all cases, the children displayed a distinctive lack of human nature.

Two well-documented instances in which children were reared in isolation are the cases of Anna and Isabelle (Davis, 1949). Anna was an illegitimate child who was confined to an isolated existence in a single room. She had only minimal social contact and scarcely any instruction. Even her bedding and clothing were rarely changed. When, at age six, she was found and taken from the room, she could neither walk nor display any behavior that reflected human intelligence. She was emaciated, expressionless, and apparently indifferent to herself and her surroundings. She made no attempt to feed, dress, or care for herself. For the next four years, Anna was provided with human contact and the care and attention usually extended to a child, first in a county home and later in a foster home and a school for retarded children. By the time she died from hemorrhagic jaundice at age ten and a half, she had learned to follow verbal instructions, talk in phrases, wash her hands before and after meals, brush her teeth, walk, and

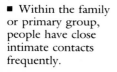

■ Within the family or primary group, people have close intimate contacts frequently.

run without falling. Generally, she had a pleasant disposition. At the time of her death, her social behavior approximated that of a normal two-and-a-half to three-year-old child. Anna probably was somewhat mentally deficient, but it is unclear whether her lack of social development was due primarily to mental deficiency, lack of human contacts in early life, or a combination of the two.

Isabelle was also illegitimate and was found at age six in circumstances similar to Anna's. Perhaps the most significant difference between Anna and Isabelle was the human contact provided Isabelle by her deaf-mute mother. Although their communication was restricted to gestures, Isabelle and her mother spent considerable time with each other in a darkened room. When found, Isabelle could make only a few croaking sounds. Because of her inadequate diet and a lack of sunlight, she suffered from rickets, and she responded to strangers with apparent fear and hostility. Initial testing revealed that her social development approximated that of a normal nineteen-month-old infant. Unlike Anna, Isabelle was given a systematic program of training by a variety of specialists. At first she responded slowly, but after a few months her development accelerated rapidly. Within two years, she achieved a social and cultural level typical of an American six-year-old, and by age fourteen her sixth-grade school teachers rated her as a well-adjusted and competent student. She was described as energetic, cheerful, and bright. Although the cases of Anna and Isabelle cannot be considered definitive, they do lend support to the argument that children deprived of primary relationships will not become fully human.

## ■ Critical Periods

Isabelle apparently was able to recover from early deprivation. Davis (1949) has estimated that children who suffer extreme social and cultural isolation must receive adquate human contact and treatment by the time they are fifteen years old or they will never become fully socialized. In a broader context, other scholars have formulated a critical periods hypothesis. Williams (1972) summarizes it as follows:

> *There are critical periods, or stages, in the development of animals, including man, during which the individual is most receptive to learning from particular kinds of experiences. These periods are of very limited duration. If an experience is to become a regular part of an individual's later behavior, it has to be acquired during the critical period when the individual is most ready to learn from that kind of experience. Earlier or later exposure to such experience will produce little or no effect on the individual's later actions (p. 116).*

Observation of and experimentation with Rhesus monkeys by Mason (1961) and Harlow and Harlow (1962) have demonstrated that the first year of life is a critical period in the normal social and sexual development of these animals. Generally, monkeys reared in isolation for their first year could not relate affectionally to other monkeys.

Observation of and experimentation with humans have not produced such clear-cut results, although they have pointed in the same direction. Spitz (1945, 1946), for example, observed the behavior of ninety-one orphaned and abandoned young children who were initially cared for in an understaffed hospital. During the first year, the infants received only minimal human contact. Their

**WHAT DO YOU THINK?**

■ Did your parents or others provide you with much physical contact when you were a child?

■ How did you respond to their contact?

■ Can you see any relationship between the amount and kind of contact they gave you and the amount and kind of contact you give to others today?

■ If you had been given either more or less contact as a child, how do you think you would be different today from the way you are?

average score on developmental tests fell considerably. Despite more favorable conditions in the second year, they failed to develop adequately. By the end of the third year, more than one-third of the original ninety-one had died, and those who remained were severely retarded. Many could not walk, all but one could not dress themselves, and all but two had vocabularies of five words or less.

More recently, Burton L. White (1975) has concluded "that the period that starts at eight months and ends at three years is a period of primary importance in the development of a human being. To begin to look at a child's educational development when he is two years of age is already too late, particularly in the area of social skills and attitudes" (p. 4).

### ■ Amount of Human Contact

No one knows exactly how much human contact is required for the normal development of a person, but it seems clear that some is necessary. Perhaps the meager contact between Isabelle and her mother was enough; perhaps it was not. Maybe Isabelle had potentialities she was unable to fulfill because of her isolation.

*See Chapter 11 for further consideration of the effects of touch.*

Eric Berne (1964) maintains that all people need to be touched and to be recognized by others.Our hunger for touch and recognition are satisfied by *strokes,* which Berne defines as "any act implying recognition of another's presence" (p. 15). Physical strokes involve physical contact such as touching or holding. Psychological strokes are symbolic acts such as words, gestures, or looks that imply recognition. According to Berne, physical stroking is absolutely essential to physical and mental growth. Infants who do not receive sufficient stroking suffer physical and mental deterioration. As children mature, they also develop a hunger for psychological strokes. They seek and need recognition that stimulates their growth and verifies their presence. Berne notes that, although even negative strokes such as hitting or scolding may serve as recognition of a child's presence, only positive strokes such as hugs or smiles lead to healthy emotional development. A lack of sufficient strokes always produces a negative effect on development. If Berne is correct, it certainly makes sense to give infants and children a great deal of positive stroking so that their needs for touch and recognition will be fulfilled and they will develop to their fullest potential. Of course, the same holds true for adults.

> Angela did not receive much recognition from her parents when she was a child. It's not that they treated her badly, but they almost never showed affection in a physical way through hugs or kisses. In fact, they rarely even complimented her achievements. Neither did anyone else.
>
> A young woman now, Angela tends to keep to herself. She has no great ambitions and lacks confidence in her ability to accomplish anything beyond the ordinary. Underassertive and lonely, she seems to have committed herself to an uneventful, unfulfilling, and sad life.

REVIEW
QUESTIONS

*9.* According to Elkin, human nature is learned. T F

*10.* Primary groups are those in which we have close, intimate, and intense face-to-face contacts frequently. T F

*11.* Hypothetically, children who are deprived of human contact will not become human. T F

*12.* It has been established beyond doubt that children who suffer extreme social and cultural isolation must receive adequate human contact and treatment by the time they are six years old or they will never become fully socialized. T F

*13.* According to Berne, lack of sufficient strokes always produces a negative effect on development. T F

*The answers to these review questions are on page 293.*

## DISCUSSION: PSYCHOLOGICAL DEVELOPMENT

As we proceed through physical, mental, and social development, we also develop psychologically. **Psychological development** refers to the progression from simple to more complex levels of awareness of **self** and the relationship between self and society.

### ■ The Self

As we saw in Chapter 2, the self is a person's conscious idea of who and what he or she is. It is sometimes referred to as the self-concept or self-image. It includes notions of who and what we are in a physical, mental, emotional, and social sense (often called the *real* self) and of who and what we would like to be (often called the *ideal self,* or what Freud referred to as the *ego-ideal.*).

We are born with a diffuse consciousness that, only over time and through our communicative contact with others, is transformed into a distinctive sense of who and what we are. In the beginning, our contacts take place on a physical level, and our sense of stability and continuity stem from three sources; "[our] body, which furnishes a constant flow of internal stimuli and has regularly recurring needs; [our] external surroundings, which constantly bombard [our]awakening senses and have a certain stability; [our] attendants, who observe a certain regularity in ministering to [us]" (Davis, 1949, p. 208). The regularity of the stimulation from these initial sources of physical contact leads to a sense of separateness that is necessary for self development.

It is important to realize that, although the basis for self-development originally issues from physical contact, self-development requires more than just physical contact, and the self is a psychological and not a physical entity. That is why, as Davis has said, "parts of the body [such as] tonsils—can be lost without any corresponding loss to the self. Only when the loss has a real social meaning . . . does the change make a difference for the self" (p. 209). Thus, although the loss of your tonsils would have virtually no psychological effect on you, the loss of an arm or a leg would. Tonsils have no social meaning, but arms and legs do. Why? In part because through communicative contact with others, we have learned to attach social meaning to our arms and legs.

### ■ Communicative Contact

G. H. Mead (1934) maintains that communicative contact with others is necessary for self development, because the reflexive character of the self can be developed only through such communication. By reflexive character Mead means the self's ability to be both subject and object to itself. At this moment, for example, you are reading this book, a subjective act in the sense that your self is the doer of the act. But it is also possible for you to pause and reflect on your act of reading the book. In this instance, your self is doing the reflecting; however, it is also the object of the reflection. You can think about and make judgments about your self. The self can "step outside its own skin" and view itself from another standpoint.

Only by learning to take the role of another can we begin to view our selves objectively as well as subjectively (see the Case in Point). Thus the communicative contact that allows us to attain this skill is necessary to our development. Communicative contact with others continues to be a necessity even after we have acquired the ability to talk with ourselves. In the long run, we must interact with others to check the accuracy of our responses and keep in tune with reality. In this view, it is virtually impossible to overstate the importance of others in the development of the self.

### ■ Development of the Self

According to Mead, the self develops in three stages. The first is the *preparatory* stage, in which the infant begins to imitate the behavior of others. Simple behaviors such as mimicking a frown or a gesture are critical first steps toward assuming others' attitudes. The second stage is the *play* stage, in which the child begins to play social roles such as "mommy," "daddy," and "doctor." As they play these roles, children begin to experience what it is like to see the world from another's point of view. The self, however, is still incomplete, because the child has not yet gained a unified conception of himself or herself. He or she has simply learned to play a number of unrelated roles.

The third stage is the *game* stage, in which the self becomes complete. To play an organized game is more complex than merely to play a role, for an

---

## CASE IN POINT
## Talking with Yourself

When you were born, you did not have the ability to view your own behavior objectively. Soon, however, you learned that the satisfaction of your wants depended to a great extent on others' attitudes toward you. You also learned that you could influence these attitudes and could thereby control the satisfaction of your wants only if you first understood the attitudes. Thus, you were motivated to view yourself from the standpoint of others. You learned symbols that could be used in imagining others' attitudes toward you and in communicating your own reactions to what you imagined their at-

titudes to be. Hence, you could carry on a conversation with yourself, with your self being both the subject and the object of your conversation. This practice of talking with yourself, which you acquired at an early age, continues today, most often in the form of an inner dialogue, although you may also talk out loud with yourself occasionally. You can, for example, ask yourself whether or not you are making your best effort to learn the concepts presented in this book. Then, on reflection, you can judge your own behavior and provide yourself with a reasonably objective answer.

organized game demands that the players act out several interrelated roles at the same time. To play a game such as baseball, for instance, the child must respond to the expectations of all the other players. "He must have the responses of each position involved in his own position. He must know what everyone else is going to do in order to carry out his own play" (Mead, 1934, pp. 140–141). In this manner, children begin to view and make judgments about themselves and others, not from the standpoint of a particular individual, but from the standpoint of several individuals who act as a group. Mead calls this group standpoint the *generalized other*. In the game of baseball, the generalized other is the team. In the game of life, the generalized other is the *normative structure* of society.

**Social norms** are standards for behavior within society. They are embodied in the rules that tell us what we should and should not do. Generally, informal norms that distinguish correct from incorrect behavior are calld **folkways** (for example, folkways define proper manners). Informal norms that distinguish good from evil behavior are called **mores** (for example, our mores prohibit cannibalism). Formalized norms, whether they distinguish correct from incorrect or good from evil behavior, are called **laws**. As children internalize social norms, they come to understand what their society expects of them and others in particular social situations. When this happens, they have acquired the ability to view themselves from an objective as well as from a subjective standpoint. In short, the self is complete, and it has become a social product in the fullest sense.

The self, however, comprises more than internalized social norms. It includes a conscious idea of who and what we are. As such, the self is a structure of attitudes. This structure develops from our subjective consciousness and our interaction with others who communicate their attitudes about us to us. Of course, social norms do tend to pattern our behavior and, in so doing, mold us into who and what we think we are. But particular individual experiences and reactions from others, whether or not they conform with or express social norms, also may contribute to the formation of the beliefs that are so much a part of the self.

### ■ Beliefs

**Beliefs** are perceived relationships between two things or between a thing and one of its characteristics (D. J. Bem, 1970). For example, you may believe that smoking causes cancer, that oil and water do not mix, and that watching TV is stimulating. Some beliefs result from direct sensory experience. If, for instance, someone asks you why you believe that watching TV is stimulating, you may answer that you have watched TV and felt stimulated. No further explanation is necessary. However, your belief that smoking causes cancer is somewhat more complicated and seems to rest on more than just direct sensory experience. Hence, when asked why you believe smoking causes cancer, you might reply by quoting from an article published in a medical journal. If asked why you believe the article, you may answer that it was written by a scientist whom your doctor says is a trustworthy expert. If asked why you believe your doctor, you may say that you believe your doctor because you simply do believe your doctor. In this case, your belief that smoking causes cancer ultimately rests on your faith in an external authority—your doctor.

**WHAT DO YOU THINK?**

■ Think about your typical, everyday behavior patterns. Are they consistent with society's expectations for behavior?

■ Which of your usual behaviors seem to be more related to interaction with particular people or situations than to general societal expectations?

■ Think about your self concept as it was ten years ago and as it is now. In what ways has it changed? What factors account for these changes?

*See Chapter 5 for additional information regarding the formation of beliefs.*

D. J. Bem (1970) argues that all our beliefs ultimately rest on one of two fundamental beliefs: a belief that our own sensory experience is correct or a belief that some external authority is correct. These fundamental beliefs are often formed in childhood and are continually validated by experiences throughout our lives. Consequently, we usually accept them without question. How many times, for example, have you seriously questioned your belief that you are alive or your belief that your religion preaches the truth? Many people may never seriously question such fundamental beliefs.

Most of our fundamental beliefs are not produced by a single experience. They are generalizations grounded in countless experiences. Suppose that when you were a child, your parents bought a used car from a salesperson who told them the car was in excellent working order when, in fact, it was in need of major repairs. Suppose further that the same experience happened to you when you bought your first car. These experiences might be generalized into the belief that *all* used car salespersons are untrustworthy.

### ■ Stereotypes

**Stereotypes** are generalizations treated as being universally true. All of us have many stereotypes. Collectively, they represent our conception of reality. To the degree that they allow us to interact with our social and physical environments in an effective manner, our stereotypes are functional. Sometimes, however, our stereotypes tend to interfere with effective interaction. For example, your belief that all used car salespersons are untrustworthy might prevent you from developing a friendship with a person who sells used cars. After all, who wants a friend who cannot be trusted? But suppose you meet a used car salesperson who is a very trustworthy person. In this case, it would be dysfunctional to

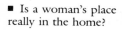
■ Is a woman's place really in the home?

retain your belief that all used car salespersons are untrustworthy, a belief that is clearly untrue. A more realistic action would be to rearrange your used car salesperson stereotype to include the possibility of trustworthiness as well as untrustworthiness. Thus, working stereotypes—those that are subject to modification whenever appropriate information is acquired—are functional. Rigid stereotypes—those that are not subject to change, even in the face of contradictory evidence—are dysfunctional.

> Ron is confused. Ever since he can remember, his parents have told him that Jews are stingy. In fact, just about everyone else in the small town in which he was reared, a town which, incidentally, has no Jewish residents, agrees that Jews are stingy.
>
> Thus, it was particularly confusing for Ron to learn that his college roommate, Al, one of the most generous persons he has ever known, is a Jew. Perhaps, Ron muses, Al is only *part* Jewish.

■ *Rigid Stereotypes*    Rigid stereotypes almost always lead to unrealistic behavior, and they often lead to conflict, confusion, and unhappiness. An understanding of the dysfunctionality of such stereotypes can be gained through an examination of traditional sex roles in contemporary American society. Of course, males are obviously different from females in a biological sense. But societies go beyond mere biology and assign behavioral differences to males and females. Below are lists of stereotypical American masculine and feminine traits (Chafetz, 1978).

| MASCULINE | FEMININE |
| --- | --- |
| Athletic, strong | Weak, nonathletic |
| Less worried about appearance and aging | Worried about appearance and aging |
| Unemotional, stoic | Emotional, sentimental |
| Logical, rational, objective, intellectual | Scatterbrained, inconsistent, intuitive |
| Tending to lead, dominating | Tending to follow, subservient |
| Independent, free | Dependent, overprotected |
| Aggressive | Passive |
| Success oriented, ambitious | Easily intimidated, shy |

Generally, Americans have tended to view masculinity and femininity as opposites. Thus, if we expect men to be strong, dominant, independent, and aggressive, we expect women to be weak, subservient, dependent, and passive. But how do these stereotypes square with reality? Are *all* men strong? Are *all* women passive? Chafetz has conducted research that indicates "that many, if not most, members of one sex will have some traits assigned stereotypically to the other" (p. 40). S. Bem (1977) has come to approximately the same conclusion. In addition, Bem has found that *androgynous* persons (those with a fairly even balance of masculine and feminine traits) are more adaptable and adjust better than those who represent extreme sex-role stereotypes. Constantinople (1973) argues that not only do significant numbers of the members of one sex have characteristics stereotypically associated with the other sex, but also that it is possible for the same individual either to be simultaneously very masculine *and* very feminine, or to be simultaneously marginally masculine *and* marginally feminine. In short, traditional American sex role stereotypes appear to be largely out of touch with reality.

Many Americans, however, continue to act on the basis of these inadequate stereotypes. They believe that any *real* man must be a good provider, an efficient decision-maker, and a mechanical wizard; and that any *real* woman must be patient, emotional, and above all else, a mother. Hence, the unmechanical male or the impatient female may conclude that there is something wrong with him or her. It is no wonder that rigid stereotypes often lead to conflict, confusion, and unhappiness.

**WHAT DO YOU THINK?**

■ What stereotypes do you associate with each of the following: Ku Klux Klan member; congressman; garbage collector; doctor; ballet dancer; professor?

■ Which of these stereotypes are functional? Which are rigid?

■ *The Perpetuation of Rigid Stereotypes*    As we saw in Chapter 2, reinforcement need not be continuous for a learned response to be repeated; intermittent reinforcement is extremely effective. With regard to sex role stereotypes, Maccoby and Jacklin (1974) conclude: "If a generalization about a group of people is believed, whenever a member of that group behaves in the expected way, the observer notes it and his belief is confirmed and strengthened. When a member of the group behaves in a way that is not consistent with the observer's expectations, the instance is likely to pass unnoticed" (p. 355).

Expectations for behavior seem to affect the ways we view behavior, then. If we expect someone to behave in a particular way, we often perceive the person as behaving that way, whether or not the person really does behave that way. For instance, Tavris (1977) points out that identical behavior displayed by a man and a woman in a work situation may be interpreted differently: "The man is competitive but the woman is aggressive; the man is aggressive but a woman is a castrating bitch. If a man gets angry and screams at his coworkers, they decide he is legitimately upset. . . .If a woman gets angry and screams at her coworkers, they decide it must be her time of the month, or that, like all women, she is hysterical. Same actions, different labels" (p. 182). Women may be as likely as men to use the labels cited above. *All* of us—old as well as young, rich as well as poor, black as well as white, boss as well as worker, and woman as well as man—are potential victims of rigid stereotyping.

■ *Gender Role Stereotypes and Values*    The emotional or evaluative meanings of the words used in any language are reflections of prevailing cultural values. In American society, words associated with masculinity are generally more positive than those associated with feminity. We stereotype men as being brave, practical, adventuresome, logical, confident, trustworthy, and experienced. However, women are stereotyped as being fickle, shallow, petty, frivolous, vain, coy, and sneaky. Chafetz (1978) points out that when we describe women, even the "positively charged words are innocuous compared with their masculine counterparts. Females are said to be 'idealistic, humanistic' rather than a 'contributor to society'; 'innocent' rather than 'adventurous'; 'patient' rather than 'ambitious'; 'gentle, tender, soft' rather than 'moral, trustworthy'" (p. 41). In other words, we value masculinity more than we do feminity.

## ■ Values and the Self

A **value** is an idea that something is intrinsically (in and of itself) desirable. Honesty is a typical American value. If you ask most Americans why they believe honesty is a desirable trait, they will tell you that it is desirable simply because it is desirable. It does not need anything else to justify its desirability. Notice, however, that some of the things we value *do* need something else to justify their desirability. For example, you might like to have a lot of money. But when asked why you would like to have money, you might reply that if you had money, you could use your time to do more fulfilling things than to work for a living. In this case, money is just a means to an end. Your belief that money is desirable is an *evaluative* belief that rests ultimately on the value of self-fulfillment. Of course, if you like money because you consider it intrinsically desirable, then having money would be one of your values. Thus, it is possible for one person's value to be another's evaluative belief.

It is also possible for a person to experience value conflict. Suppose you value both a job promotion and life in the city or town in which you currently live. Further, suppose that tomorrow your boss offers you a job promotion that requires you to move to a less desirable city. You want the promotion, but you do not want to move. What will you do? You will probably have to do much hard thinking to determine which is more valuable to you—getting the promotion or remaining in the same city. (If you conclude that the two are equally valuable, we suggest that you make a choice and adjust to it. In other words, do not second guess yourself. After all, either way you have chosen something you value. Be happy with it and do not waste your time thinking about what might have been.)

In any event, values, like beliefs, are integral parts of the self. And, like beliefs, values are learned from individual experiences and from interaction with others. Finally, many of our values, like many of our beliefs, are culturally determined.

*See the Conclusion to this text for a general discussion of decision making.*

*See the Conclusion to this text for a general discussion of decision making.*

REVIEW
QUESTIONS

*14.* The _____ is a person's conscious idea of who and what he or she is.

*15.* G. H. Mead speaks of the self as being reflexive in character. By this, he means that the self can be both _____ and _____ to itself.

*16.* Mead sees the self developing in three stages: the _____ stage, the ___ stage, and the _____ stage.

*17.* We refer to standards for behavior within society as _____ .

*18.* When a person perceives a relationship between two things or between a thing and one of its characteristics, the person is said to have a _____ .

*19.* A _____ is a generalized belief treated as being universally true.

*20.* An idea that something is intrinsically desirable is called a _____ .

*The answers to these review questions are on page 293.*

## DISCUSSION: AGENCIES OF SOCIALIZATION

At any given time, every society is only one generation removed from extinction. If the culture is not transmitted to the young, the society will no longer exist. Because socialization is such a critical process, societies are unwilling to allow people to act randomly to control it. Rather, to ensure that important beliefs, values, customs, and social norms are transmitted, societies channel their transmission through particular social structures, often referred to as **agencies of**

**socialization**. In virtually all societies, the family is the first agency to socialize the child, and its influence on the person's development tends to be powerful.

### ■ Family

The family's influence is powerful primarily for three reasons: (1) our initial conceptions of ourselves, other people, and the external environment are formed within the context of the family; (2) we have a tendency to maintain family contacts throughout our lives; and (3) our family places us in our society (that is, our initial placement on the social stratification scale is that of the family into which we are born), and we reflect that placement.

In most instances, the dominant cultural beliefs and values are transmitted through the family, although other particular beliefs and values peculiar to the individuals within our family may also be transmitted. Many societies have distinctive subcultures, and their general approaches to life may be different from one another. One would expect, for example, that the life styles of wealthy, sixth-generation Anglo-Americans would be different from the life styles of poor, first-generation Mexican-Americans. Families that are part of a strong subcultural tradition may teach beliefs and values that vary somewhat from those of the dominant culture. Therefore, although the family's influence on a person's development tends to be powerful, societies that contain a variety of subculutres cannot rely too heavily on the family to transmit the dominant culture.

### ■ Neighborhood and Peer Group

Closely related to the family and the subculture are the neighborhood and the peer group. In some instances, the neighborhood itself may have a strong subcultural flavor. Children who grow up in such a neighborhood will, no doubt, gain a wider exposure to the traditions they learn in their own homes. Even in mixed neighbborhoods in which no particular subcultural tradition dominates, the influence of socioeconomic class tends to produce a sameness in many of the beliefs and values expressed by the people. Children who live in a poor neighborhood are likely to learn to view the world differently from children who live in an affluent neighborhood.

The peer group comprises people of approximately the same age who share similar social statuses (Mendoza and Napoli, 1982). It becomes increasingly significant as an agency of socialization as the child moves away from his or her early dependence on family members and toward more independent behavior.

## CASE IN POINT
## Peer Group Influence

Think about your own social development and how you began to identify with and to rely on your friends more and more throughout your childhood and adolescence. It is probable that many of your beliefs, values, attitudes, and behaviors were shaped by your peer group. It is also probable that your peer group continues and will continue to be a significant influence on you throughout your adulthood.

The neighborhood and the peer group, then, are important agencies of socialization. However, like the family and the subculture, they may not transmit the dominant culture as completely and efficiently as the society demands. Clearly, a more reliable agency of socialization is needed.

## ■ School

This more reliable agency is the school. Some small, primitive societies do not have schools (Mendoza and Napoli, 1982), but in these societies the family is sufficiently strong to transmit the culture. In societies such as ours, schools are definitely needed. In fact, the major function of the school in modern societies is to transmit the dominant culture. Notice that in the public school system in the United States, for example, classes are taught in the English language, American history is emphasized, all students are exposed to the value of cleanliness, the virtues of a democratically based political system are extolled, and everyone learns about George Washington's tree-cutting escapade. It is not very likely that these are aspects of the typical curricula in French, Italian, Russian, or Chinese schools, It is also unlikely that you would be the person you are today if you had attended school in the Soviet Union rather than in the United States. Thus, the school affords us the opportunity to become a relatively complete social product.

Of course, the school cannot transmit *all* aspects of a culture. Indeed, it is virtually impossible for any one person to know the entire content of a given culture (Davis, 1949), and no one is expected to have this knowledge. But everyone is expected to know the essentials—the language; the basic social, political, and economic beliefs and values; the social norms; and the customary behaviors. Going to school ensures that we will be exposed to these aspects of culture, regardless of the provincialism of our family, subculture, neighborhood, or peer group.

## ■ Occupation and the Mass Media

Occupation and the mass media are also agencies of socialization. Beliefs, values, and behavior patterns acquired from occupation tend to be transmitted from parents to children in child-rearing practices. Kohn (1969), for example, argues that middle-class occupations stress the value of self-direction and tend to deal with the manipulation of interpersonal relations, ideas, and symbols. Conversely, working-class occupations stress the value of conformity to rules established by authority and tend to deal with the manipulation of material objects. Through their child-rearing practices, middle-class and working-class parents tend to transmit their own values to their children. In turn, the children grow up with a tendency to move into occupational statuses similar to those of their parents. Thus, occupation plays a role not only in the transmission of culture but in the perpetuation of the social class structure from one generation to the next.

Elements of the mass media may also serve as transmitters of culture. Although they do not offer the direct, person-to-person contact found within the other agencies of socialization, radio, television, newspapers, magazines, movies, and so on may teach aspects of the culture to vast audiences. A televised speech by the president of the United States may expose millions of viewers to democratic values as well as to the English language. Films such as *Patton* and comic books

**WHAT DO YOU THINK?**

■ What are some of the things you have learned in school that directly support what you have learned at home? That directly contradict what you have learned at home?

■ In what ways has your work experience contributed to your attitudes and behavior patterns?

■ Think about some of your favorite movies and TV programs. Have they affected your attitudes or behaviors?

■ Are there any films or TV programs you have expressly disliked? What values underlie these films or TV programs?

■ The mass media, such as television, may be a powerful transmitter of cultural beliefs and values.

such as *Batman* may teach the culturally determined qualities of heroism. And advertising may convince us of the values of bathing regularly, eating moderately, dressing appropriately, and keeping our breath fresh and our teeth clean. Since we are exposed to the mass media at an early age and since this exposure tends to continue indefinitely, components of the mass media are potentially significant agencies of socialization throughout our life cycle.

REVIEW
QUESTIONS

*21.* The <u>family / peer group</u> is the first agency of socialization for the person.

*22.* The peer group comprises people of approximately the same age who <u>have about the same amount of welath / share similar social statuses</u>.

*23.* The major function of the school in modern societies is to <u>transmit the dominant culture / teach people to be functional literates</u>.

*24.* <u>Everyone / No one</u> is expected to know the entire content of his or her culture.

*25.* The <u>peer group / occupation / mass media</u>, although impersonal, may teach aspects of the culture to vast audiences.

*The answers to these review questions are found on page 293.*

## DISCUSSION: LIFE CYCLE

The **life cycle** is the general sequence of events in our physical, psychological, and social development as we progress from infancy through old age. Many scholars have dealt with the life cycle. As we saw in Chapter 2, for example, both Freud and Erikson have commented extensively on it. Two other scholars worth noting here are Daniel J. Levinson and Roger L. Gould. Both have concentrated on adult development—Levinson on men's, Gould on both men's and women's.

## ■ Levinson's Seasons of Life

Levinson (1978), who studied male subjects, believes women pass through approximately the same stages as men do, but in a slightly different fashion. He identifies three adult "eras": *early adulthood* (ages seventeen to forty-five), *middle adulthood* (ages forty to sixty-five), and *late adulthood* (starting at about age sixty). Note that there is an area of overlap as one era ends and the next begins. This overlap is a transitition between eras.

Each era consists of an alternating series of stable (structure-building) periods and transitional (structure-changing) periods. The primary task of a stable period is to build a *life structure*—that is, to make choices and commitments to particular beliefs and values and to a particular lifestyle. In addition, each stable period has other unique tasks that reflect its place in the life cycle. The primary tasks of a transitional period are "to question and reappraise the existing structure, to explore various possibilities for change in self and world, and to move toward commitment to the crucial choices that form the basis for a new life structure in the ensuing stable period" (Levinson, 1978, p. 49). Like stable periods, each transitional period has additional unique tasks that reflect its place in the life cycle.

## ■ Early Adult Transition

Adult development begins with the *early adult transition* (ages seventeen to twenty two).[1] One of the two tasks here is to move out of the pre-adult world. This requires modification or even termination of existing relationships with important persons, groups, and institutions. The second task is to move into the adult world. This involves the creation and consolidation of an initial identity. By the end of the early adult transition the young person has begun to create a life within the adult world.

## ■ Entering the Adult World

The period from about age twenty-two to about age twenty eight is called *entering the adult world*. Within this period a variety of initial choices are made and tested with regard to occupation, love relationships (often including marriage and family), peer relationships, values, and lifestyle. There are two primary, yet antithetical, tasks: exploring the possibilities for adult living and creating a stable life structure. In order to complete these tasks, the young person must keep his options open while at the same time making something of his life.

---

1. The ages given for this and other periods are not to be taken as absolutes; however, most periods do not vary by more than a couple of years in either direction. Thus, the early adult transition could begin anywhere between fifteen and nineteen and could end anywhere between twenty and twenty-four.

## ■ Age-Thirty Transition

During the *age-thirty transition* (from about age twenty-eight to about age thirty three) there is a critical examination of the choices and commitments made in the preceding period. Adjustments made as a result of this examination may be used as the basis for the formation of a more satisfactory life structure in the next stable period. There is a sense of urgency connected with the age-thirty transition as a man becomes more serious, more "for real." He senses that if there are things he would like to change about his life, he had better get started, for soon it will be too late. For some people, the age-thirty transition is smooth, without great disruption or crisis. They make modifications but not fundamental changes in life structure. For most men, however, this transition takes a more severe and stressful form, the *age-thirty crisis*. A man may find, for example, that his present life structure is intolerable, but may have great difficulty forming a better one. Thus, considerable pain may be experienced during this period.

> Charles will celebrate his thirtieth birthday in two weeks. From his point of view, however, there will be little to celebrate. He has been working for the same company since he graduated from college at twenty-two. Although his first couple of promotions came relatively soon, he has not been promoted in almost four years, and he feels stuck in his current position. Charles believes that at this rate he will never reach the upper level of management to which he has long aspired. Thus, he is not happy with his present work situation. He has been thinking of looking for a position with another company.
>
> On the other hand, in just two more years Charles will be fully vested in the company's retirement plan. Furthermore, he likes the company and feels relatively comfortable working there. The company likes him, too, and it appears that the security of a long career with the company is most likely if Charles desires it. When he thinks of these factors, he becomes reluctant to begin the search for a position with another company.
>
> Charles is in the midst of a personal crisis.

## ■ Tasks of the Novice Phase

Levinson refers to the first three periods of adulthood (the early adult transition, entering the adult world, and the age-thirty transition) as the *novice phase* of adulthood (ages seventeen to thirty-three). During this time, a young person emerges from adolescence, finds his place in adult society, and commits himself to a more stable life.

While each of the periods in the novice phase has its own particular tasks, several tasks are common to all three periods and characteristic of the entire novice phase. Among these common tasks are relating to authorities, gaining greater authority oneself, and forming adult values with regard to community, ethnicity, politics, and religion. However, the most prominent of the common tasks in the novice phase are: (1) forming a "Dream" and giving it a place in the life structure; (2) forming mentor relationships; (3) forming an occupation; and (4) forming love relationships, marriage, and family.

■ *The Dream*    During the novice phase each man conceives a *Dream*, a vision, "an imagined possibility that generates excitement and vitality" (Levinson, 1978, p. 91). The Dream is initially vague and only loosely connected to reality, although it may include concrete images such as being a highly respected community member, a great artist, or an athletic superstar. The developmental task of the young person is to give the Dream greater definition and find ways to live it out. So the Dream takes shape in the early adult transition and is gradually integrated within an emerging adult life structure in the novice phase. Failure to achieve this integration may lead to the death of the Dream, and with it the young person's sense of purpose in life.

■ *The Mentor*   At some point during the novice phase the young man forms a relationship with a *mentor*, a person (almost always a male) who is usually about eight to fifteen years older than his protege. The mentor serves a variety of functions: teacher, sponsor, host and guide, exemplar, and counselor. The mentoring relationship is often found within a work setting, with the mentoring functions being performed by a boss, senior colleague, or teacher. Sometimes the relationship evolves informally, with the mentor being a friend, neighbor, or relative.

The most crucial developmental function of the mentor is to support and facilitate the realization of the Dream. He accomplishes this by believing in his protege, by giving the Dream his blessing, and by helping to define and accepting his protege's newly emerging adult self.

■ Advice, acceptance, and emotional support from a mentor at some time in the novice phase is critical to the social and psychological development of a young person.

Over time this relationship between apprentice and expert evolves into a relationship in which the balance of giving and receiving is more equal. This critical shift is part of an ongoing process by which the young man will ultimately transcend the father-son, man-boy division of his childhood, a process that continues throughout the novice phase.

The mentoring relationship is relatively short-lived, usually lasting two to three years and never more than ten. It may end completely, perhaps with a gradual loss of involvement, or may end with the formation of a modest friendship; it may end when one man dies, changes jobs, or moves. Often, intense mentor relationships become embroiled in strong conflicts and end with bad feelings on both sides. Still, however, the young man has learned and will continue to learn from the mentor as he incorporates the mentor's admired qualities into himself. This internalization of the qualities of significant people is a primary source of adult development.

■ *Occupation*    The process of forming an occupation takes place throughout the often beyond the novice phase. The first serious occupational choice is usually made sometime between ages seventeen and twenty-nine, during the early adult transition or the entering the adult world stage. Having made an initial choice, the young man must then acquire skills, values, and credentials as he attempts to establish himself within the occupational world. Some men commit themselves to a particular occupation relatively soon, while others may struggle for years to sort out their interests and to discover what occupations may help them to live out those interests. By the end of the age-thirty transition, when the novice phase has been completed, the early phase of occupational choice has been concluded. The formation of an occupation continues throughout early adulthood, but usually within the pattern already established by the end of the novice phase.

■ *Love Relationships*    Like his occupation, a man's marriage and family life are formed and continue to develop throughout the novice phase and often beyond. Developmental tasks include forming the capability of having adult peer relationships with women and accepting the responsibilities of marriage and parenthood. Approximately 80 percent of the men in Levinson's study entered into first marriage by age twenty-eight. Unfortunately, according to Levinson, "Most men in their twenties are not ready to make an enduring inner commitment to wife and family, and they are not capable of a highly loving, sexually free and emotionally intimate relationship" (p. 107). Men who marry for the first time between twenty-eight and thirty-three, during the age-thirty transition (as did approximately 20 percent of Levinson's sample), have the advantages of having gained greater self-knowledge and of having resolved some of the conflicts that might have prevented them from making an appropriate commitment to marriage and family. However, they may also have the disadvantage of marrying under pressure. The sense of urgency typically experienced during the age-thirty transition may motivate them to marry more to "normalize" their lives than to fulfill deep love relationships.

A love relationship that has particularly great impact on a young man during the novice phase is his relationship with the *special woman,* who may or may not be his wife. It is a unique relationship that goes beyond loving, tender, romantic, and sexual feelings. The unique quality of the special woman is found in her connection to the man's Dream. Like his mentor, she "helps him to shape and live out the Dream: she shares it, believes in him as its hero, gives it her blessing, joins him on the journey and creates a 'boundary space' within which his aspirations can be imagined and his hopes nourished" (Levinson, 1978, p. 109).

Also like the mentor, the special woman is the transitional figure. Early, as he struggles to become an autonomous adult, she fosters the young man's adult aspirations while accepting his dependency. Later, he will develop into a more complete adult and will have less need of her sometimes actual and sometimes illusory contributions.

By end of the age-thirty transition, a man's life is remarkably different from what it was when he entered the novice phase at seventeen. Adolescence has long since past, and he is well on his way to becoming a member of the adult world. Now, he will move toward major new choices or recommit himself to those already made as he attempts to work out a relatively satisfactory life structure. Choices consistent with his Dream, values, and talents will provide the basis for satisfactions; choices inconsistent with these factors will lead to considerable pain in the second structure-building period.

## ■ Settling Down

The second life structure, which is the vehicle for the culmination of early adulthood, takes shape at the end of the age-thirty transition and lasts until age forty; it called *settling down*. This period involves two major developmental tasks: establishing a niche in society (anchoring oneself more firmly in one's occupation and in society generally) and "making it" (striving to advance, to build a better life, and to be affirmed by others). In short, this period is characterized by attempts to advance in virtually all areas of life: social rank, power, fame, creativity, quality of family life, and so on.

Progress in the settling down period brings new rewards but also produces greater responsibilities and pressures. As each man becomes "more his own man," he must give up even more of the little boy within himself, an internal figure he never completely outgrows.

## ■ Midlife Transition

Early adulthood ends in the late thirties, and middle adulthood begins at about age forty-five. The *midlife transition* (ages forty to forty-five) is a bridge between these two eras. This structure-changing period brings a new set of developmental tasks as the life structure again comes into question. Men ask themselves: "What have I really accomplished? What do I really want for myself and others? What do I really get from and give to my family, my work, my community, and myself?"

Although some men are relatively untroubled by these questions, most experience the midlife transition as a period of moderate or severe crisis. They believe they cannot go on as before. They need at least a few years to form new directions or to modify old ones.

## ■ Entering Middle Adulthood

By about age forty-five, the time for reappraisal and exploration is over and the process of forming a new life structure begins. The life structure that emerges in the first middle adulthood period, *entering middle adulthood* (ages forty-five to fifty), varies greatly in satisfactoriness from one man to the next. Some men seem unable to overcome their failure to handle the developmental tasks of earlier periods. For these men, middle adulthood will be an era of frustration and decline. Others form life structures that appear workable in the world but are poor reflections of their true selves. For them, life lacks inner excitement and meaning. Still other men form life structures that build on the successes and self-knowledge gained in the past. For them, middle adulthood is often the most creative and fulfilling era of the life cycle.

## ■ Other Periods

Levinson's study does not focus on men beyond forty-five or fifty; however, he suggests that there is evidence that the sequence of alternating structure-building and structure-changing periods continues throughout the life cycle. The age-fifty transition (ages fifty to fifty-five), for example, is the time in which changes can be made so that a man can settle into middle adulthood. The *culmination of middle adulthood* (ages fifty-five to sixty) is the structure-building period that completes middle adulthood, and the *late adult transition* (ages sixty to sixty-five) ends middle adulthood and establishes the basis for entering late adulthood. Figure 8.1 summarizes Levinson's stages of development.

## ■ Gould's Transformations

Roger L. Gould (1978), who studied both men and women, presents a view of the life cycle that is strikingly similar to Levinson's in several respects but, of course, different in others. According to Gould, four major phases of adulthood occur between the ages of sixteen and fifty. The developmental task in each of these phases is to challenge and resolve one of four false assumptions, formed during childhood, that tend to keep us in a state of dependency. Each of these assumptions is related to our childhood desire to obtain absolute safety from harm by following the dictates of our parents. The resolution of each false assumption signifies a change in consciousness from more childlike to more adult ways of interpreting life events. Over time, we relinquish our childish desire for absolute safety and with it, our reliance on our parents to protect us from harm. Ultimately, we become our own persons.

■ *Ages Sixteen to Twenty-Two*   The first phase lasts from about sixteen to about twenty-two. The false assumption to be challenged and resolved is "I'll always belong to my parents and believe in their world." Even before completing high school, we begin to challenge this belief in minor ways. The challenge becomes stronger between the ages of eighteen and twenty-two, when events such as living away from home foster a questioning of the assumption. Leaving our parents' world is a critical first step in building an independent, adult identity.

■ *Ages Twenty-Two to Twenty-Eight*   The second phase takes place between ages twenty-two and twenty-eight, when we make decisions on major issues such as

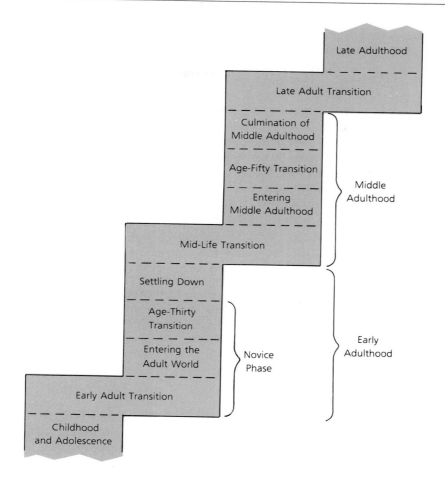

FIGURE 8.1
Developmental
Periods in Early and
Middle Adulthood

marriage, pregnancy, and careers. The false assumption here is "Doing things my parents' way, with will power and perseverance, will bring results. But if I become too frustrated, confused or tired or am simply unable to cope, they will step in and show me the right way." During this period we begin to realize that will power and perseverance alone do not always bring positive results and that we must live our own lives. We become more self-confident as we prove our competence by dealing effectively with major life issues.

■ *Ages Twenty-Eight to Thirty-Four*   By the end of the second phase, most of us have become self-reliant adults. Indeed, by this time "our adult consciousness is developed enough so that we feel able to turn inward and reexamine ourselves for something other than the narrow limits of independence and competence that seemed so all-important a few years earlier" (Gould, 1978, pp. 153–54). Thus, the major false assumption related to the third phase (ages twenty-eight to thirty-four) is "Life is simple and controllable. There are no significant co-existing contradictory forces within me." As we open up to what is inside us, we begin to understand the complexity of living and to realize that many of our simple rules about life do not work in the complicated real world. We begin to accept our limitations and the fact that life is not fair. With this acceptance, both our competence in the world and our adult consciousness are increased.

■ *Ages Thirty-Five to Forty-Five*   During the midlife decade (ages thirty-five to forty-five), we become aware of the pressure of time in our lives: "Whatever we do must be done now" (Gould, 1978, p. 217). The major false assumption of this fourth phase is "There is no evil or death in the world. The sinister has been destroyed." As we come to terms with our own mortality, we dig deep inside ourselves and begin to accept the ugly, demonic side of life, a part of us and of the world from which the immature mind tries to protect itself by creating the false illusion that absolute safety is possible. "Eventually we work our way deeper into our core, to form a new understanding of the meaning of our life uncontaminated by the need for magical solutions or protective devices (Gould, 1978, p. 218). By about age fifty we resolve the last major false assumption, and with its resolution, we complete the passage from childhood to adult consciousness, from "I am theirs" to "I own myself."

Levinson and Gould have extended and enhanced the work of Freud and Erikson on the life cycle. They have provided us with insights into adult development and a general understanding of how the process of socialization continues after childhood and adolescence. We are now ready to examine in more detail the relationship between the individual and the group, which we will do in Chapter 9.

REVIEW
QUESTIONS

26. Levinson identifies three adult eras: _____ adulthood (ages _____ to _____ ) , _____ adulthood (ages _____ to _____ ) and _____ adulthood (starting at about age _____ ).

27. The two developmental tasks of the early adult transition are to _____ and to _____ .

28. Two people who are especially important to a young man in the novice phase because they support and facilitate the realization of his Dream are the _____ and the _____   _____ .

29. A man's first serious occupational choice is usually made some time between the ages _____ and _____ .

30. Early adulthood ends in the late thirties; middle adulthood begins at about age forty-five. The bridge beween these two eras is called the _____  _____ .

31. Gould identifies _____ major phases of adulthood that occur between the ages of _____ and _____ .

32. The false assumption "Life is simple and controllable; there are no significant contradictory forces within me" is related to Gould's _____ phase (ages _____ to _____ ).

33. According to Gould, we resolve the last major false assumption by about age _____ .

*The answers to these review questions are on page 293.*

# SUMMARY

■ Socialization is the process of transmitting human culture. It is essential to human survival because culture is the mechanism through which humans adapt or adjust to their environment.

■ Both heredity and environment are important factors in the individual's development as a person.

■ It is probable that children deprived of primary relationships will be thwarted in their physical, psychological, and social development. If the deprivation is severe and prolonged, they will, in essence, fail to become human.

■ The self develops through social contact with others. Over time, we learn to view our own behavior from the standpoint of others. Eventually, we can experience the self both subjectively (from the inside looking out) and objectively (from the outside looking in).

■ All our beliefs ultimately rest on one of two fundamental beliefs; a belief that our own sensory experience is correct or a belief that some external authority is correct.

■ Collectively, our stereotypes represent our conception of reality. Working stereotypes (those subject to modification whenever appropriate information is acquired) are functional. They keep us in touch with reality. Rigid stereotypes (those not subject to change, even in the face of contradictory evidence) are dysfunctional. They keep us out of touch with reality.

■ A value is an idea that something is intrinsically desirable. It is an end rather than a means to an end. Thus, values are important integral components of the self.

■ To ensure that important cultural beliefs, values, customs, and social norms are transmitted ot the young, societies channel their transmission through particular social structures, often referred to as agencies of socialization.

■ Families, subcultures, neighborhoods, peer groups, schools, occupations, and mass media are all potentially important agencies of socialization in American society. The school is particularly important. Its major function is to transmit the dominant culture.

■ The life cycle is the general sequence of events in our physical, psychological, and social development as we progress from infancy through old age. Daniel J. Levinson, who has concentrated on adult male development, has identified a life cycle that consists of alternating series of stable (structure-building) periods and transitional (structure-changing) periods. Roger L. Gould, who has focused on the development of both male and female adults, believes there are four major phases of adulthood between ages sixteen and fifty, each with the developmental task of challenging and resolving one of four major false assumptions formed during childhood.

# SELECTED READINGS

Bem, D. J. *Beliefs, Attitudes, and Human Affairs*. Belmont, Calif.: Brooks/Cole, 1970. A brief examination of the formation of beliefs and attitudes.

Gould, R. L. *Transformations: Growth and Change in Adult Life*. New York: Simon and Schuster, 1978. Gould's study of adult development.

Levinson, D. J. *The Seasons of a Man's Life*. New York: Ballantine, 1978. Levinson's study of adult male development.

Mead, G. H. *Mind, Self, and Society*. Chicago: University of Chicago Press, 1934. Mead's classic on the development of the self.

Rubin, Z. "Does Personality Really Change after 20?" *Psychology Today* (May 1981): 18–27. An article that raises serious questions concerning how much our personalities change after age twenty.

Sargent, A. G., ed. *Beyond Sex Roles*. St. Paul, Minn.: West, 1977. An exploration of gender role stereotyping that contains 120 pages of exercises designed to help people to become more aware of and to change their gender role stereotypes.

Williams, T. R. *Introduction to Socialization: Human Culture Transmitted*. St. Louis: Mosby, 1972. A comprehensive and thorough overview of the process of socialization.

# GLOSSARY

**agencies of socialization:** social structures such as the family or the school that are extremely important in the transmission of culture.

**belief:** perceived relationship between two things or between a thing and one of its characteristics.

**cognition:** the mental process of knowing.

**culture:** the learned and shared way of life of a society, including its beliefs, its values, its group habits, its standards for behavior, and the material goods it makes and uses.

**folkways:** informal norm that distinguishes correct from incorrect behavior; for example, folkways define proper etiquette.

**growth:** biological changes that take place over time.

**law:** deliberately formulated or formalized norm that may distinguish correct from incorrect behavior (as in laws against disturbing the peace) or good from evil behavior (as in laws prohibiting murder).

**life cycle:** the general sequence of events in our physical, psychological, and social development as we progress from infancy through old age.

**maturation:** the unfolding of biological potential.

**mores:** informal norms that distinguishes good from evil behavior; for example, our mores prohibit cannibalism.

**perception:** awareness of the environment.

**physical development:** the person's progression from simple to more complex levels of bodily organization.

**primary group:** a group of people, such as a family, in which close, intimate, and intense face-to-face contacts are frequently shared.

**psychological development:** the progression from simple to more complex levels of awareness of self and the relationship between self and society.

**reflex:** a relatively fixed response to stimuli that emanates from the functioning of structures within the nervous system.

**role:** a pattern of expected behavior associated with a status; for example, playing the role of student requires taking notes in class, studying, writing papers, taking exams, and so on.

**self:** a conscious idea of who and what one is.

**social development:** the person's movement from simple to more complex statuses and roles.

**socialization:** the process of transmitting culture.

**social norms:** standards for behavior within society; societal rules.

**status:** a social position; for example, student.

**stereotype:** a generalized belief treated as being universally true.

**value:** an idea that something is intrinsically desirable.

# REFERENCES

Babbie, E. R. *Society by Agreement: An Introduction to Sociology.* Belmont, Calif.: Wadsworth, 1977.

Bem, D. J. *Beliefs, Attitudes and Human Affairs.* Belmont, Calif.: Brooks/Cole, 1970.

Bem, S. "Psychological Androgyny." In *Beyond Sex Roles.* Edited by A. Sargent. St. Paul, Minn.: West, 1977.

Berne, E. *Games People Play.* New York: Grove Press, 1964.

Chafetz, J. S. *Masculine, Feminine or Human? An Overview of the Sociology of the Gender Roles,* 2nd ed. Itasca, Ill.: F. E. Peacock, 1978.

Constantinople, A. "Masculinity-Feminity: An Exception to a Famous Dictum?" *Psychological Bulletin* 80 (1973): 389–407.

Davis, K. *Human Society.* New York: Macmillan, 1949.

Elkin, F. *The Child and Society: The Process of Socialization.* New York: Random House, 1960.

Elkind, D., and Weiner, I. B. *Development of the Child.* New York: Wiley, 1978.

Goode, W. J. *The Family.* Englewood Cliffs, M.J.: Prentice-Hall, 1964.

Gould, R. L. *Transformations: Growth and Change in Adult Life.* New York: Simon and Schuster, 1978.

Harlow, H., and Harlow, M. K. "Social Deprivation in Monkeys." *Scientific American* 207 (1962): 136–46.

Kohn, M. L. *Class and Conformity.* Homewood, Ill.: Dorsey Press, 1969.

Levinson, D. J. *The Seasons of a Man's Life*. New York: Ballantine, 1978.

Maccoby, E. E., and Jacklin, C. N. *The Psychology of Sex Differences*. Stanford, Calif.: Stanford University Press, 1974.

McNeil, E. B. *The Concept of Human Development*. Belmont, Calif.: Wadsworth, 1966.

Mason, W. A. "Social and Sexual Behavior" In *Critical Periods of Development: A Report on a Conference*. New York: Social Science Research Council, 1961. Item 15, pp. 15–17.

Mead, G. H. *Mind, Self, and Society*. Chicago: University of Chicago Press, 1934.

Mendoza, M. G., and Napoli, V. *Systems of Society: An Introduction to Social Science,* 3rd. ed. Lexington, Mass.: D. C. Heath, 1982.

Spitz, R. A. "Hospitalism." *Psychoanalytic Study of the Child* 1 (1945): 53–72.

———."Hospitalism: A Follow-Up Report." *Psychoanalytic Study of the Child* 2 (1946): 113–117.

Tavris, C. "Stereotypes, Socialization, and Sexism." In *Beyond Sex Roles*. Edited by A. Sargent. St. Paul, Minn.: West, 1977.

Thompson, J. D., and Van Houten, D. R. *The Behavioral Sciences: An Interpretation*. Reading, Mass.: Addison-Wesley, 1970.

White, B. L. *The First Three Years of Life*. Englewood Cliffs, N.J.: Prentice-Hall, 1975.

Williams, T. R. *Introduction to Socialization: Human Culture Transmitted*. St. Louis: Mosby, 1972.

## ANSWERS TO REVIEW QUESTIONS

**Page 269.** *1.* T  *2.* F  *3.* T  *4.* F  *5.* F  *6.* T  *7.* T  *8.* F

**Page 272.** *9.* T  *10.* T  *11.* T  *12.* F  *13.* T

**Page 279.** *14.* self  *15.* subject, object  *16.* preparatory, play, game  *17.* social norms  *18.* belief  *19.* stereotype  *20.* value

**Page 282.** *21.* family  *22.* share similar social statuses  *23.* transmit the dominant culture  *24.* No one  *25.* mass media

**Page 290.** *26.* early, seventeen, forty-five; middle, forty, sixty-five; late, sixty  *27.* move out of the pre-adult world, move into the adult world  *28.* mentor, special woman  *29.* seventeen, twenty-nine  *30.* midlife transition  *31.* four, sixteen, fifty  *32.* third, twenty-eight, thirty-four  *33.* fifty

# 9

# GROUP DYNAMICS AND LEADERSHIP

Perhaps one of our strongest desires, from
the time we enter school to the present, is
the desire to belong, to be identified with
a group or several groups. Group
membership contributes much to the
development of our self-worth. We belong
to certain ethnic groups. We are members
of families. We are Democrats,
Republicans, or independents. We belong
to a particular church and we attend a
particular college. We are on bowling
teams or belong to flying clubs. We may
find great satisfaction in gaining entrance
to particular fraternities or sororities. We
work for certain business firms and belong
to certain branches of the military service.
We work on special committees. We have
a support group of friends. Wherever we
go we identify ourselves as members of
these groups. In this chapter we are going
to explore two important aspects of the
process of social interaction—group
dynamics (the function of groups and how
they work) and leadership (the potential
influence each of us can have on the
groups to which we belong).

**9**

GROUP
DYNAMICS AND
LEADERSHIP

DISCUSSION: GROUP FORMATION

Understanding **groups** and our relationship to them is important for two reasons. First, it will help us to see the importance of groups to each of us in terms of our adjustment, our growth, and our survival. Second, it will help us to function better as group members.

### ■ Defining Groups

If each member of your class were to answer the question "What is a group?" you probably would hear as many different answers as there are different students. This would not be too surprising, because numerous definitions have been proposed by social psychologists. Generally, a *group* is defined as people working or playing together toward common goals.

### ■ Group Membership

Edgar H. Schein (1970) notes that people seek membership in groups for many reasons:

- *Fulfilling the need for affiliation* (belonging). We may find friendship, support, love, and affection.
- *Developing, enhancing, or confirming a sense of identity and maintaining self-esteem*. Our membership affords us status within the group and with outsiders.

---

## CASE IN POINT
## Group Memberships

List the important groups to which you belong and tell how you benefit from each.

Group 1 _____

_____

_____

_____

Group 2 _____

_____

_____

_____

Group 3 _____

_____

_____

_____

Group 4 _____

_____

_____

_____

Group 5 _____

_____

_____

_____

■ *Establishing and testing reality.* We validate our own perceptions of life by consulting with others.

■ *Increasing security and a sense of power.* We seek strength in the belief "United we stand, divided we fall."

■ *Getting a job done.* We seek help from members when we need their assistance to gather information and accomplish a task.

Thus, we join groups for many reasons. Some of us join groups simply because our friends belong to these groups, and enjoy interacting with those we like or find attractive. It does not matter what we are doing as long as we can be with our friends. Many students go to a particular college to be with their friends.

*For another description of why we choose certain people as friends, see Chapter 11's discussions of propinquity and characteristics of friendship.*

■ *Special Interest and Need Groups*   Have you ever joined a special interest group such as a foreign language club, a sailing club, a computer club, or an art club? It can be quite rewarding to meet other people with similar interests to learn and to share ideas.

People also form groups to share stress. During times of disaster (hurricanes, floods, fires, and so on), people often band together for emotional and physical support. They work together to find shelter and to rescue victims. Pepitone and Kleiner (1957) find that high threat increases the individual's attraction to the

■ These rescue workers trying to save two men buried under a collapsed dirt wall show how people join together in times of need.

*See Chapter 7 for more about stress.*

group. When people are under stress, it quickly becomes apparent that the best way to survive is to work with others so there can be collective support. Have you ever joined a study group to help you prepare for a final exam?

■ *Support Groups*   Throughout our lives, each of us belongs to at least one support group of close friends with whom we can share our problems, our concerns, and our happiness. For many, a particular support group may serve as a source of encouragement and nurturance for their entire lives. The cohesiveness of such groups is often stronger and more long lasting than the cohesiveness of the family to which each support group member belongs. This is perhaps because we are able to choose the members of our support groups, but not the members of our families.

■ *Making Contact*   Another reason people join particular groups may have little to do with the groups' goals. Instead, the motivation may involve external reward not always apparent to other group members. An insurance salesperson moves to a new community and immediately joins a church or civic club to establish contacts for future business. A college man joins a particular fraternity because he believes it will afford him the "necessary" status to meet women.

■ *Group Pressure*   Group membership certainly has advantages. However, it may also have disadvantages. Group pressure may negatively influence our need for independence in choosing our beliefs, values, and life goals. We may rely excessively on a group to help us make important life decisions. Consequently, our need to belong to groups may impede the realization of our potential as human beings. As individuals, it is important to recognize the difference between our responsibility to the group and our responsibility to ourselves.

When our initial motivation for joining a particular group is not fulfilled, we may lose interest and drop out. Have you ever noticed how in some of your classes the attendance at the beginning of the term is much better than at the end?

> Richard had met Carla two months before they were to begin their freshman year at the community college. He was fascinated by her for several reasons, especially by the fact that she spoke both English and Spanish. Hoping to get her to care more for him, he enrolled in a beginning Spanish course. Two months into the term, Carla decided to renew a relationship with someone she had dated previously, and Richard dropped his Spanish course.

## ■ Subgroups

In groups larger than eighteen to twenty members, **subgroups** often form to allow the warm and intimate human contact that is possible in groups of five or less (Theodorson, 1953). These groups are usually formed in the same way as the larger group. Subgroups may make the larger group more functional for its members by helping them achieve their common goals. It is interesting to observe the subgrouping phenomenon when attending large parties. To increase our chances for contact and perhaps remedy our discomfort, we tend to arrange ourselves into smaller, more manageable subgroups.

Membership in most groups is somewhat transitory in response to the changing needs of the members. The variables that influence group membership are quite numerous and not always easy to observe. In the next section, we will discuss one such variable that is relatively easily observed—the structure of the group.

1. The term *group* is defined as people working together toward _____ _____ .

2. Membership in groups often helps individuals provide for their _____ needs of friendship, support, love, and affection.

3. Group membership also provides for a sense of identity, helps us maintain our _____ , and may offer some _____ .

4. "United we stand, divided we fall" implies that a group may provide _____ for its members.

5. When a group becomes too large to satisfy some of its members' needs, _____ _____ may be formed to provide for these needs.

*The answers to these review questions are on page 326.*

## DISCUSSION: GROUP STRUCTURE

Perhaps you have observed that in certain groups a variety of behaviors differentiate members from each other. These differentiations are the basis for the **group structure**. Members act in different ways. Some talk more, some have more respect or influence, and all perform different tasks. This differentiation usually is determined by the *roles, status, norms,* and *cohesiveness* within each group. These factors determine the *group structure*, which is commonly defined as the observable pattern of relationships among the members within a group.

### ■ Roles

Each member of a group is expected to behave in certain ways during group interaction. Consider the college classroom, for example. The instructor has the expected role of preparing adequately each day to teach the class. The activities and topics, for the most part, are directed by this person. The interaction between the members of the class and the instructor is usually controlled by the person playing the role of instructor. In a highly structured class, the instructor controls the interaction among all the class members.

Students also have an expected role in the class. They are to ask questions, answer questions, do assignments, prepare for class discussions, and show evidence that learning has occurred.

Certain members begin to emerge early in the life of the class as individuals who interact more often with the instructor by answering and asking questions. These individuals often become the focus of attention, both of the instructor and of other class members. It is not long before they have the expected role of major responders in class activities and discussions.

*See Chapter 8 for a discussion of socialization.*

## ■ Status and Power

Each expected role is evaluated by the members of the group according to its importance and prestige. This evaluation results in each member's having some degree of social status within the group. The degree of social status a person enjoys usually corresponds to the amount of influence or power the person has in the group (see Figure 9.1).

Power and influence usually are also the key factors in determining who becomes the leader or leaders of any group. **Influence** is the capacity to have an impact on the course of events in a group or on the behavior of a group or a person. **Power** is the ability to require specified behavior of other group members. The presence of power implies the ability to apply sanctions in case of noncompliance.

Power is an emotion-laden term, particularly in cultures that emphasize individuality and equality. However, power can be a highly effective instrument for good (Mondy, Holmes, and Flippo, 1980). The degree and nature of power held by an individual or individuals within a group often depends on the group's goals. The power an individual has may be derived from the goal-related in-

FIGURE 9.1
Status within a
group or
organization.

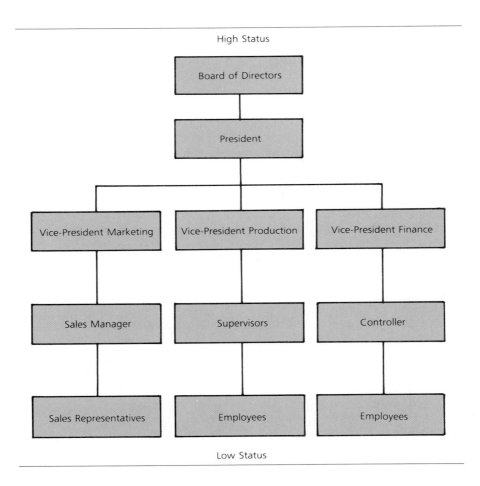

formation or resources he or she possesses. Each of us has power in a group at one time or another.

French and Raven (1960) define five different frameworks of power:

*1.* **Legitimate power** belongs to the president or elected leader of any group or organization. The person having legitimate power can influence or control group members and situations because of the role he or she is given, regardless of personality. *Legitimate power* is defined as the formal power given to any individual by right of the role or position held in the group.

*2.* **Reward power** is based on a person's ability to administer and control the rewards others will receive for complying with certain directives. Rewards come in many forms—pay raises, promotions, praise, and favors. *Reward power* is defined as the power an individual holds because he or she can give something to someone else.

*3.* **Coercive power** is based on a person's ability to administer and control punishments (the power to reprimand, demote, withhold, and fire) to group members who do not follow directives. "Since you came to class late, you will not be allowed to take the exam." "If you do not get this job done by next Tuesday, you will be fired!" *Coercive power* is defined as the power an individual holds because he or she can withhold or take away something another person desires.

*4.* **Expert power** is based on the special knowledge, skill, or expertise a person possesses. Connie is thought of as the real pro when it comes to her knowledge about surgical nursing, even though she is not the head nurse. Other nurses, even the head nurse, often come to her for advice.

■ Power belongs to more than the designated leader, as a television director guides the on-screen "star."

*Expert power* is defined as the power an individual holds because of his or her knowledge or expertise.

5. **Referent power** is the power a person may possess because of personal characteristics that make him or her attractive to others, in more than just the physical sense. Some people can lead others by their charisma. They may not hold any other power, but people listen to them and follow them. The result might be good (Martin Luther King, Jr.) or bad (Adolph Hitler). Another form of referent power is derived from association with a powerful leader. The wife of the president of the United States has this form of referent power. *Referent power* is defined as the power an individual holds because of his or her charm, personal magnetism, or association with others who hold power.

**WHAT DO YOU THINK?**

■ What kind of power do you have?
■ How do you use your power to get what you want?

We all have some form of power at various times in our lives. All of us have the potential to use our power effectively as members of various groups.

It may appear that many people strive for legitimate power, reward power, and coercive power. In most situations the person holding a position of authority, such as the president or supervisor of a business, does appear to have the power to do as he or she sees fit. However, the other forms of power are also very important.

> Eric is the most knowledgeable person in the computer center of a large corporation. He is instrumental in creating programs and systems that are helping his company become very competitive in the marketplace. On several occasions, he has been offered the position of manager, but he enjoys his present work so much, he always turns it down. He is admired by his peers, his supervisor, and the president of the company, and can do nearly anything he wants. In addition, he does not have the responsibility and the "headaches" that usually go with being the manager. Eric has expert power.

As members of a class, students may influence the interactions in the class and may also influence the behavior and decisions of the instructor. They may even have some of the kinds of power discussed above. However, in most cases, the ultimate power in the class is reserved for the instructor, who by the nature of his or her position and authority can apply sanctions in the form of grades to those members who comply or do not comply with the class's laws, or norms.

## ■ Norms

Norms are rules of behavior that usually emerge to increase the successful functioning of the group. All members are expected to obey the norms, and any deviations from the norms may result in punishment from other group members. Some examples of group norms are: being on time, waiting to be acknowledged by the chairperson before speaking at meetings, and respecting the dignity of other group members.

*Chapter 8, on socialization, discusses related matters.*

## ■ Cohesiveness

*Group cohesiveness* is the attraction the members feel toward the group. Members of a cohesive group usually are deeply involved with the group's goals, feel very

■ As group size increases, group cohesiveness decreases.

close to one another, and are loyal to the group. Groups vary in their degree of cohesiveness.

■ *Measuring Cohesiveness* We can measure the cohesiveness of groups by using a technique known as **sociometry** to measure the attraction group members feel toward each other. In one measurement technique, each person is asked to indicate the people he or she would most want as partners for various activities. Then the percentage of group members chosen is compared with the percentage of people chosen from outside the group. This comparison gives an indication of how cohesive the group is. Another sociometric measure asks group members to name the most and least preferred group members. Negative choices are subtracted from positive choices to obtain an estimate of cohesiveness. There is a controversy over the effectiveness of asking people to think of the least preferred group member, so this method is usually discouraged.

In addition to sociometry, other measures have been used that focus on the members' attraction to the whole group rather than the individuals in it. Some people are attracted to a particular group because of its reputation. For example, a person may not care for most of the members of a football cheerleading squad, but may feel good about belonging because of the overall popularity of the group.

Group cohesiveness is influenced by the same variables that initially determine the formation of the group. Attraction to other individuals in the group, enjoyment of group activities, and the belief that membership in the group will be beneficial in attaining one's goals in life all contribute to the cohesiveness of a group. Group size, the presence of outside threats, competition, and communication are other influences.

**WHAT DO YOU THINK?**

■ Think of groups you belong to now or belonged to in the past. Which groups do you think are (or were) cohesive?

■ What is it about these groups that make (or made) them attractive to the members?

■ *Group Size*    As the size of a group increases, its cohesiveness decreases (Porter and Lawler, 1965). Larger groups are more likely to have difficulty achieving adequate communication among members. Furthermore, as the size of a group increases, so do its inflexible, bureaucratic rules.

■ *Outside Threat*    Threat from natural disaster, war, or competition with another group often increases the cohesiveness of a group. Group cohesiveness has been observed to be higher in communities after they have been affected by natural disasters (Quarantelli and Dynes, 1972). Janis (1951) reports that, contrary to what military strategists thought would happen, light bombing of civilian populations during World War II sometimes increased the cohesiveness and morale of the populations.

■ *Competition*    In competitive situations, nothing is quite as attractive as being on a winning team or being associated with one. Yet, Wilson and Miller (1961) found that under some circumstances even the members of a losing team may be highly attracted to the group. Perhaps this is due to the time and effort put into the preparation for competition, or to the fact that "misery loves company."

■ *Communication*    The quantity and quality of communication may be a strong factor in group cohesiveness. It appears that highly cohesive groups communicate more than less cohesive groups (Lott and Lott, 1961). In terms of quality, the communication in highly cohesive groups is more cooperative and friendlier. It is also oriented toward coordinating the activities of the group members (Shaw, 1976).

Clearly, the factors that influence the success of a group and its members are numerous. In the next section, we will discuss another important variable—leadership—which affects members' satisfaction and the group's productivity.

REVIEW
QUESTIONS

6. The observable pattern of relationship, among the members in a group is referred to as _____ _____ .

7. _____ , _____ , _____ , and _____ are variables that determine group structure.

8. The importance and prestige a member enjoys in a group are called _____ _____ .

9. _____ is the capacity to have an impact on the course of events in a group or on members of a group.

10. A person with the ability to require specified behavior of other group members has _____ .

11. A person who holds a highly influential formal position within a group, such as the president of a college, is said to have _____ _____ .

12. Group members who have special knowledge or skills usually have _____ _____ within the group.

13. _____ are rules that emerge to govern the functioning of a group.

14. The attraction members have toward a group is called _____

_____ .

15. Social psychologists often use _____ to measure the attraction group members feel toward each other.

*The answers to these review questions are on page 326.*

# DISCUSSION: LEADERSHIP

Imagine attending your largest class and being told that your instructor had been seriously injured in an auto accident. Furthermore, you are told that there will be no replacement for the remainder of the term. You and the other students will have to make arrangements to learn the material on your own. Or imagine a championship football team playing in the Super Bowl with both the first-string and second-string quarterbacks injured and out of the game. The third-string quarterback may not be able to motivate the team, even if he is as skilled and as well trained as the first two.

The loss of a leader often has a demoralizing effect. The effects are well illustrated by the disbelief, shock, grief, and anger with which Americans reacted to President John Kennedy's assassination. An immediate response was a concern about the future of the country. Would the government be able to maintain the national security? **Leadership** is vital to the effective functioning of a group. Leadership is also a potential area of personal growth for each of us. To develop our potential for leadership and influence is part of healthy adjustment.

## ■ Defining Leadership

Most of us have a general idea about what is meant by the term *leadership*. When thinking about the definition of leadership, you may think of a friend who seems to be a leader. You may think of leadership in terms of definite characteristics such as dominant, aggressive, or in-charge behavior. A leader may be someone who holds an office, such as president. Or a leader may be someone who possesses the highest level of skill for accomplishing the task. Each of these examples emphasizes different aspects of leadership. Hersey and Blanchard (1977) define leadership as "the process of influencing the activities of an individual or a group in efforts toward goal achievement in a given situation" (p. 84). Plunkett (1975) defines leadership in a more specific and formal way as the ability to get work done with and through others while simultaneously winning their respect, confidence, loyalty, and willing cooperation.

All groups have leaders. Diverse organizations such as street gangs, parent-teacher associations, church groups, political parties, and prison populations generally have someone who emerges as the organizer or authority on what to do. Often the group leader does not have a title, but the person's position is nevertheless clear.

■ Everyone attempts leadership at one time or another.

## ■ Potential for Leadership

Many of us may not see ourselves as leaders or as having the potential to become leaders. However, in any situation in which someone is trying to influence the behavior of another individual or a group, leadership occurs. Thus, everyone attempts leadership at one time or another, whether his or her activities are centered around a business, educational institution, hospital, religious organization, political organization, social organization, college classroom, peer group, or family.

Any time you are attempting to influence the behavior of someone else, you are a *potential leader*. The person you are attempting to influence is the potential follower, whether the person is your boss (the designated leader), a peer, a subordinate, a friend, or a relative (Hersey and Blanchard, 1977). In groups and organizations, getting the task accomplished (goal achievement) is more important than who is the leader. Leadership often passes from one individual to another as each contributes to the plan or process. For example, the secretary of the senior partner in a law firm has a subordinate position in the firm but may have tremendous influence on some decisions.

## ■ Choosing a Leader

Leaders are necessary in both informal and formal groups. Most groups are informal, and their leaders are usually chosen in an informal way without an actual vote of the members. For example, in many working committees, the individual who speaks out, displays the most confidence, and has ideas that seem to be compatible with those of the other members usually ends up as the leader or chairperson. Unfortunately, in some informal groups the leader is selected through the process of exception. Those who do not want to be leaders identify themselves, and the person who resists the least ends up as the leader by default. Unfortunately, although peer pressure forces this person to do his or her best, this type of leader selection process often results in disaster. The person chosen may be the least likely to provide the group with the leadership it needs. Regardless of how the leader is chosen, choosing the right leader is critically important to a group's success.

> Joan had been working for the Richman Company for only six months. Starting out as a junior accountant, she had been so busy trying to make a good impression and learn everything that she met only a few people. One day, Joan's supervisor asked her if she would like to serve on a special committee to review various group insurance plans and to select the best one for all the employees. Even though the additional responsibility seemed overwhelming, it offered an opportunity to meet more people, so she agreed.
>
> At the first meeting, the group decided to choose a chairperson who would assume responsibility for securing policies from different insurance companies, dispensing information to all committee members between meetings, and monitoring each meeting. Unfortunately, no one seemed willing to volunteer for the task. Finally, one member suggested that the task go to Joan, the newest member of the company, as "you no doubt have some fresh new ideas about how to run an effective meeting." Joan, who wanted to please everyone and be liked, agreed to serve as chairperson. Because of Joan's lack of experience and leadership skill, though, her tenure as chairperson was a disaster for her and for the committee.

In formal democratic groups such as professional organizations, political parties, labor unions, and social clubs, leaders are elected. Unfortunately, some elected leaders are chosen for political reasons (because, for example, they favor certain interest groups) rather than for their effectiveness as leaders.

In formal groups (corporations, church groups, branches of the military, educational institutions, some government agencies, and so on), leaders are not chosen by the group but are appointed by someone outside the group. When appointed, even the most effective leaders often must work hard to win the group's support. Group members frequently do not readily accept an appointed leader. Feelings of resentment often exist as members question the leader's qualifications. This is especially true when the group, if given the opportunity, would have chosen a leader from among its members. To overcome this problem, some organizations form search committees composed of some of the group members to aid in the selection process. This type of selection process is becoming increasingly popular, especially in institutions of higher education.

## ■ Characteristics of a Leader

Leadership is a developed art; the skills it requires can be acquired by nearly anyone with the motivation and patience to learn. However, being an effective leader is not easy. The effective leader must be concerned with five major factors:

*1.* The leader must be able to use his or her knowledge and skills and possess a positive attitude toward the group's goals and members.

*2.* The leader must be knowledgeable about the members of the group—their experience levels, skills, proficiencies, and attitudes toward the task and each other. How the members perceive the leader and how they perceive the importance of their contributions is important, too.

*3.* The leader must be concerned about the environment within which the group is functioning. It must be as comfortable and conducive to the accomplishment of the task as possible.

*4.* The leader must be aware of the resources available to aid the group in accomplishing its goals.

*5.* All these factors are said to by dynamic—that is, they constantly change. Therefore, the leader must continually evaluate the process of the group to determine what is effective and what may be impeding the group's effectiveness.

The skills and styles of a leader are vitally important. We will discuss them in more detail later in the chapter.

**WHAT DO YOU THINK?**

■ What leadership potential do you think you have?

■ How does it feel to think of yourself as a leader?

**REVIEW QUESTIONS**

*16.* Leadership is the ability to get work done with and through others while winning their _____ , confidence, loyalty, and willing _____ .

*17.* Effective leadership may be provided by individuals other than the _____ _____ of a group.

*18.* Leadership is a _____ _____ ; leadership skills can be acquired by nearly anyone with the motivation to learn them.

*19.* Most democratic formal groups choose their leaders by _____ .

*20.* In most formal groups or organizations, leaders are _____ .

*21.* An effective leader must possess a _____ _____ toward the group's goals and members.

*22.* The effective leader must continually _____ the group process to determine how well the group is accomplishing its goals.

*23.* The leader must be knowledgeable about the members' _____ _____ , _____ , _____ , and _____ toward the task and each other.

*24.* Leaders in some informal groups are chosen by the process of exception and become leaders by _____ .

*25.* Any time you have an opportunity to influence the behavior of someone else, you are a _____ _____ .

*The answers to these review questions are on page 326.*

## DISCUSSION: LEADERSHIP STYLES

There are many different ways of leading and many different kinds of leaders. The kind of leadership required depends largely on the type of followers in the group, their interactions, and the group's climate. For effectiveness, the most important factor is to match the type of leadership with the type of group.

## ■ Types of Leaders

Experiments conducted by Robert F. Bales (1953) indicate that leaders fall into two main categories. His study attempted to discover why group members identified certain individuals as group leaders. This he accomplished by having small groups work on a task. When the task was finished, the members were asked to identify anonymously the person they thought was the leader in the group. Bales consistently found that the person who had the best ideas and offered the group the most guidance toward doing the task was identified as the leader.

Bales then asked the members to identify the person they liked the most. The groups tended to pick individuals other than the leader as most popular. Bales concluded that the groups naturally tended to have two leaders. He labeled the one who pushed the group to get the job done the *task leader* (formal leader) and the one best liked the *social leader* (informal leader).

■ *Task Leaders*    Task leaders are needed when special skills are required. The office manager charged with the responsibility of completing a report on time, the foreman on a construction site, and the chairperson of a policy-making committee are examples of task leaders. Task leaders control, direct, and organize a group to carry out a specific job. Generally, their influence is limited to the specific task being done. Task leaders traditionally and typically are firm, directive, and intense about getting the job done.

■ Opportunities exist for all leaders. The voice of 3M in St. Louis is Harriett Sinclair, a branch sales coordinator processing orders as liaison between maker and market.

■ *Social Leaders*     Social leaders, on the other hand, are needed when diplomatic and persuasive skills are necessary to accomplish a goal. Typically, they are more supportive, encouraging, and conciliatory and less directing than task leaders. They tend to concentrate on the social aspects of the situation and try to get the group to function smoothly and happily.

Even though there are two basic types of leaders, one person can function both as a task leader and as a social leader, depending on which is needed. Perhaps a goal of effective leadership is to know enough about the various theories of leadership so that when a specific type of leadership is desirable, it can be provided.

## ■ Theories of Leadership

There are many theories of leadership. Leadership theories differ in methodologies, explanations, and conclusions. Each has its advocates who offer their particular theory as the only right and proper one. However, although more is known about leadership today than ever before, we still do not have a complete and integrated theory that represents the totality of leadership. In short, there is no best way to lead people that is appropriate in every situation.

For comparison, we will discuss the leadership theories of Elton Mayo, Douglas McGregor, Chris Argyris, Frederick Herzberg, Rensis Likert, and Paul Hersey and Kenneth Blanchard. Even though these leadership theories were originally applied to job settings, the theories apply to all forms of groups.

■ *The Hawthorne Effect*     One of the first major leadership theories grew out of a study that began in 1924 at a Western Electric Company plant in Hawthorne, Illinois. Some efficiency experts wanted to study the effect of illumination on productivity. They assumed that increases in illumination would result in higher productivity from the workers. An experimental and a control group were selected, and illumination was increased for the experimental group and kept the same for the control group. As expected, the work output of the experimental group went up as the lighting power was increased. Unexpectedly, however, the output of the control group also went up—without any increase in light. Surprised by these results, the experimenters called in Elton Mayo of the Harvard Graduate School of Business Administration and his associates to see if they could determine why this had happened.

Mayo's research began with improving the working conditions of a group of women who assembled telephone relays. Such innovations as scheduled rest periods and shorter work weeks were implemented. As expected, productivity increased. Then the researchers took the innovations away and the workers returned to the working conditions that had existed before the experiment. This radical change was expected to have an extremely negative impact on productivity. Instead, the output jumped to a new high. Baffled by these results, the researchers set out to discover why.

They finally concluded that the workers' increase in productivity had come not from a change in working conditions, but from a change in the amount of human interaction! As a result of the attention lavished on them by the researchers, the women came to feel that they were an important part of the company. They no longer viewed themselves as isolated individuals, but as members of a congenial, cohesive work group. The relationships that developed as a result of the study elicited feelings of affiliation, competence, and achievement. The workers' needs for these feelings, which had previously gone unsatisfied, were now being fulfilled. As a result, the women worked harder and more effectively than they had before. This unexpected outcome became known as the *Hawthorne effect*.

From these Hawthorne studies, researchers learned that it was necessary for leaders and managers to understand the importance of relationships among people. The most significant factor affecting organizational productivity, they said, was the interpersonal relationships developed on the job, not just the pay and working conditions, as had been previously thought.

Mayo (1933) viewed his findings as an indictment of industrial society, which treated human beings as insensitive machines. According to Mayo, too many managers assumed that society consisted of a horde of unorganized people whose only concern was self-interest and self-preservation. Management's basic assumption was that workers, on the whole, were a contemptible lot who wanted as much money as they could get for as little work as possible. Mayo called this assumption the *rabble hypothesis*. This assumption resulted in workers' being taught to look at work only as money in exchange for labor, a view that still robs many of us of the joy and satisfaction that come with accomplishment.

■ *Theory X and Theory Y*    Some scholars believe that Mayo's work paved the way for Douglas McGregor's (1960) classic theories. McGregor believed that the traditional organization, with its centralized decision making, superior-subordinate pyramid, and external control of work, is based on false assumptions about human nature and human motivation. He calls these assumptions *Theory X*. Theory X is quite similar to Mayo's rabble hypothesis. It assumes that most people prefer to be told what to do, are not interested in assuming responsibility, and want security above all. This philosophy is accompanied by the belief that people are motivated only by money, other financial benefits, and threat of punishment.

McGregor believed that people in a democratic society, with their increasing level of education and standard of living, are capable of more mature behavior than they are credited with. Influenced by Maslow's hierarchy of needs, McGregor concluded that Theory X assumptions about human nature, when applied universally, are often inaccurate, and that management approaches based on these assumptions often fail to motivate individuals to work toward the organization's goals. People whose physiological and security needs have been met are seldom motivated by managers and leaders who use direction and control strategies.

As a result of his belief, McGregor developed an alternative theory of human behavior called *Theory Y*. This theory assumes that people are not, by nature, lazy and unreliable. They can be self-directed and creative at work when positively motivated. Properly motivated people can achieve their goals best by directing their own efforts toward the accomplishment of the organization's goals. This is encouraged by **integrative leadership**, which assumes that all the major kinds of human needs can be somewhat satisfied at work and that the very activity of contributing to organizational success can be highly rewarding to the worker. Thus, it is believed that the employee's needs can be tied to those of the organization (Torgersen and Weinstock, 1972). Table 9.1 compares McGregor's Theory X and Theory Y assumptions.

TABLE 9.1

McGregor's Theory X and Theory Y Assumptions

| THEORY X | THEORY Y |
|---|---|
| 1. Work is inherently distasteful to most people. | 1. Work is as natural as play, if the conditions are favorable. |
| 2. Most people are not ambitious, have little desire for responsibility, and prefer to be directed. | 2. Self-direction is often indispensable in the achievement of organizational goals. |
| 3. Most people have little capacity for creativity in solving organizational problems. | 3. The capacity for creative problem solving is widely distributed in the population. |
| 4. Motivation occurs only at the physiological and security levels. | 4. Motivation occurs at the social, esteem, and self-actualization levels, as well as the physiological and security levels. |
| 5. Most people must be closely controlled and often coerced to achieve organizational objectives. | 5. People can be self-directed and creative at work if properly motivated. |

In Theory X organizations, people are unable to satisfy social, esteem, and self-actualization needs. When a job does not provide need satisfaction at every level, today's employee will be forced to look elsewhere for significant need satisfaction. We often hear someone say, "Thank God it's Friday!" Many people work to live, but live for the weekends. This lack of need fulfillment on the job perhaps explains some of the current problems organizations are facing with high turnover and increasing absenteeism. McGregor argued that this does not have to be the case; Theory Y organizations can provide for greater need fulfillment.

From our discussion of Theory X and Theory Y, you may get the impression that Theory X is bad and Theory Y is good. We must offer a word of caution, though, about drawing these conclusions. Theory X and Theory Y are attitudes about human nature, and people sometimes behave in the immature ways suggested by Theory X.

Torgersen and Weinstock (1972) report that many people are not psychologically prepared for the higher levels of individual responsibility and freedom associated with integrative leadership. Some people are stuck at the security need level or the social need level. They neither desire nor feel ready to cope with a Theory Y system. Some feel generally inadequate or inferior. Such people, it is held, want strong leadership and routine, stable jobs. Their performance might suffer, as would their satisfaction levels, should they be expected to assume more responsibility. Other workers are so accustomed to autocratic leadership that they would question the sincerity, indeed the sanity, of a participative democratic approach. Thus, we can understand the difficulty a Theory Y manager might have with a group of Theory X workers.

**WHAT DO YOU THINK?**

- What types of leader models have you observed in the past?
- What type of leader models are available to you now?

■ *Bureaucratic/Pyramidal and Humanistic/Democratic Value Systems*   Chris Argyris (1962) has postulated that the individual's inability to visualize the possibility of a healthier and more productive work environment may stem from a lack of maturity in some areas of personal development. In many individuals, this lack of maturity may be perpetuated by the beliefs inherent in the **bureaucratic/pyramidal value system**. This hierarchical system incorporates the assumption that people are motivated by direction, authority, control, and rewards

*See Figure 9.1, p. 300, for a diagram of a pyramid structure.*

and penalties that emphasize rational behavior and achievement. The system typically functions with one-way communication, and decisions are made at the top of the management pyramid. Bureaucratic/pyramidal values lead to shallow and untrusting relationships that foster immaturity and a lack of growth. (Similarly, if parents continue to treat their children as though they were not able to behave in responsible ways, the children will continue to behave irresponsibly.) Argyris believes this value system produces many of our current organizational and productivity problems.

*See Chapter 10 for more about communication.*

While Argyris (1957) was at Yale, he studied industrial organizations to determine the effect management practices had on individual behavior and personal growth within the work environment. His study resulted in the belief that formal administrative structure tends to make employees feel dependent, submissive, and passive. In short, it keeps them from maturing. Widespread worker apathy and a lack of effort in the workforce are not always the result of individual laziness. Individuals are given minimal control over their environment and are encouraged and expected to behave immaturely. The power and authority rest in the hands of a few at the top, and those at the lower end of the chain of command are strictly controlled by their superiors.

Conversely, the **humanistic/democratic value system** includes the assumption that people are motivated through authentic relationships, internal commitment, shared decision making, and the process of confirmation (focusing on the strengths of self and others rather than on weaknesses). Along the continuum from immaturity to maturity, Argyris has identified seven potential growth opportunities that may be experienced by group members in a humanistic/democratic system. They tend to develop from:

- A passive state to an active state (self-determination).
- A state of dependency on others to a state of relative independence ("standing on one's own two feet").
- A limited number of behaviors to many behaviors.
- Erratic, casual, and short-term interests to deeper, higher-quality interests.
- A very short time perspective, involving only the present, to a time perspective that includes the past and the future.
- Subordination to everyone to equality with peers.
- A limited awareness of self to an awareness that includes a sense of integrity and self-worth.

Both McGregor and Argyris believe that even though many formal organizations tend to stifle the growth of their members, individuals have the potential to become mature and self-motivated. They challenge management to provide a work environment in which people have a chance to grow and mature, satisfying their own needs while working for the success of the organization. They believe that people can be self-directed and creative at work if positively motivated. The resulting relationship between the individual and the organization will be profitable for both.

■ *The Motivation/Hygiene Theory*   As people mature, esteem and self-actualization needs seem to become more important. With this in mind, Frederick Herzberg (1966) conducted a series of studies concentrating heavily on these areas of need fulfillment. From these studies, Herzberg inferred a theory of work motivation that seems to have broad implications for management and leadership and for the effective use of human resources. It is called the *motivation-hygiene theory*.

Herzberg collected data about job attitudes by interviewing some two hundred engineers and accountants from eleven industries in the Pittsburgh area. The participants were asked to identify what made them happy or satisfied and unhappy or unsatisfied at their jobs. From the results, Herzberg concluded that people have two different categories of needs that are essentially independent of each other and affect behavior in different ways. When people are dissatisfied with their jobs, they tend to be more concerned about factors such as the working environment (remember the Hawthorne studies conducted by Elton Mayo). On the other hand, when people are satisfied with their jobs, it is because they enjoy the work itself.

Herzberg called the first category of needs *hygiene factors*. Examples of hygiene factors are company policies, effective administration, effective supervision, good working conditions, interpersonal relationships, adequate monetary compensation, adequate fringe benefits, status, and security. Although hygiene factors produce little growth in workers' output, they do prevent losses in performance. In other words, when the hygiene factors are not adequate, workers are unhappy; but adequacy of hygiene factors does not necessarily produce happiness.

Workers tend to be happiest with their jobs when the hygiene factors are adequate and when Herzberg's *motivating factors* are present. These factors, which seem to be effective in motivating people to superior performance, include feelings of achievement, recognition for accomplishment, opportunity for professional growth, challenging work, and increased responsibility. When these factors are present, people are happier and more motivated to be productive. (See Figure 9.2).

FIGURE 9.2
Herzberg's
Hygiene-Motivation
Theory

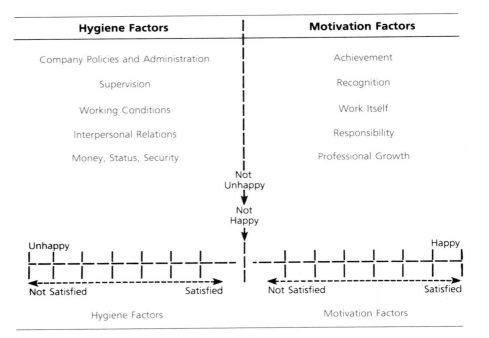

■ *Authoritative-Participative Theory*  Rensis Likert (1967) has developed a system for classifying the styles of leadership. According to Likert, leadership is a continuum ranging from the highly dictatorial or autocratic style to the democratic or participative style. Likert places leadership styles into four classifications:

■ *System I: Exploitative-authoritative.* Managers in this classification are autocratic—that is, they make all the decisions. They do not seek the opinions of subordinates; instead, they decide what is to be done, who will do it, and how and when it is to be completed. They motivate by fear and the threat of punishment. In this system, the manager demonstrates little confidence or trust in employees. The implied managerial response to the concerns of a subordinate are, "Do what you are told or you will be fired."

■ *System II: Benevolent-authoritative.* Managers in this classification still make all the decisions, but subordinates have some degree of freedom and flexibility in performing their tasks so long as they conform to the specified procedures. In this system, managers have a paternalistic ("big daddy") attitude: "I will treat you right if you play along and do what is expected of you." There is still a low level of trust, and the manager motivates with fear and rewards.

■ *System III: Consultative.* Consultative leaders have considerable confidence in their subordinates. They consult with subordinates before establishing goals and making decisions. Subordinates have considerable freedom to decide how to accomplish their tasks. A System III leader might say, "John, I have this decision to make, and I would like your opinion on the matter first." Such leaders rely on rewards instead of punishments for motivation.

■ *System IV: Participative-group.* This is Likert's preferred style of leadership. Leaders using this style include members of the group in the goal-setting and decision-making processes. Group members feel free to discuss

■ Participative leadership can provide numerous rewards.

TABLE 9.2
Comparison of Autocratic and Participative Leadership Styles

| AUTOCRATIC LEADER | PARTICIPATIVE LEADER |
|---|---|
| Depends on vested power and authority. "I'm in charge and I make all the decisions." | Depends on the abilities and contributions of all personnel in making and implementing decisions. "What are your ideas about how we can accomplish this goal?" |
| Thinks of work as drudgery. "You are paid to do this job, so do it!" | Helps make work enjoyable and satisfying to all. "If we all work together, we will also get to know each other better." |
| Threatens personnel. "If this is not done by tomorrow, a negative evaluation will be placed in your file." | Encourages personnel. "You have done a great job!" I will make a note of this for your evaluation." |
| Takes credit for the success of others. "It was my idea in the first place. Without my direction, they could not have done it." | Shares joy of success with others. "You have all done a great job. Your efforts made this project successful." |
| Blames others for failures. "It is all your fault. If you had listened to me, this wouldn't have happened." | Accepts responsibility for failures. "I am responsible. I should have gotten more information for you." |

Source: Schwartz, D. *Introduction To Management: Principles, Practices and Processes.* New York: Harcourt Brace Jovanovich, Inc. 1980.

matters of any kind. In this system, the power of knowledge (expert power) takes precedence over the power of authority (formal power and coercive power). Rewards and a high climate of trust prevail as motivators.

Much of Likert's research indicates that the subordinate-centered approach to leadership (System IV) is more effective in helping the group reach its goals. It is important to note, however, that the style of most leaders falls somewhere between the authoritative and participative extremes of the continuum. Leaders are seldom completely autocratic or completely participative. (For a brief comparison, see Table 9.2).

In this section, we have discussed several popular leadership theories. In the next section, we will discuss how we can use our knowledge of these theories to enhance our effectiveness as leaders and potential leaders.

REVIEW
QUESTIONS

26. Mayo's Hawthorne studies concluded that working conditions were the most important factor in increasing workers' productivity.   T   F   If false, the truth is: _____

_____

_____ .

27. McGregor's Theory Y organizations provide opportunities for the satisfaction of higher-level needs, such as self-esteem and self-actualization.   T   F   If false, the truth is: _____

_____

_____ .

28. Argyris believes that the formal organization has done more to aid the growth and maturity of individuals than any other phenomenon.   T   F   If false, the truth is:

_____

_____ .

*29.* McGregor and Argyris believe that people can be self-directed and creative in the work setting if positively motivated.   T  F   If false, the truth is: _____

_____

_____ .

*30.* Herzberg's theory of motivation demonstrates that money and fringe benefits are still the most motivating reasons to work.   T  F   If false, the truth is: _____

_____

_____ .

*31.* On Likert's authoritative-participative continuum, most managers are completely authoritarian.   T  F   If false, the truth is: _____

_____

_____ .

*32.* Fortunately, today, the prevalent humanistic/democratic value system is creating a more satisfying environment in which people can work and grow.   T  F   If false, the truth is: _____

_____

_____

_____ .

*The answers to these review questions are on page 326.*

## DISCUSSION: DEVELOPING EFFECTIVE LEADERSHIP

It is a fact that some people are able to obtain results far greater than expected by employing effective leadership. We said earlier that almost anyone could learn leadership skills. Unfortunately, however, great leadership ability seems rare in real-life situations. Some people cannot inspire others to achieve even minimal results. This is evidenced by daily reports of poor worker productivity, union walkouts and sickouts, and so on. Effective leadership is best measured by its results. In other words, leaders can best be judged by the behavior of those they lead, not by what they profess.

Personality or educational background does not necessarily make an effective leader. Some effective leaders are loud, aggressive, and gregarious, while others are soft-spoken and quiet. The most popular person often is not the most effective leader in a group. Effective leaders may or may not have college degrees. In fact, some very effective leaders in the past did not have even high school diplomas.

Although it is true that not all people want to lead, most people do enjoy a leadership role from time to time and may want to improve their leadership abilities. What makes a superior leader is often hard to pin down. Leadership practice and style constitute a web of factors that include such things as the leader's personality, skill, experience, confidence, and awareness of self. It is the intent of this section to help you identify leadership skills and explore ways in which you might become an effective leader in all areas of your life. Let's begin by looking at one more leadership style theory, the theory of Paul Hersey and Kenneth Blanchard (1977).

### ■ Maturity

Hersey and Blanchard have recently attracted the attention of many leaders and managers with their *situational leadership theory*. The theory is based on the notion that the effectiveness of a leadership style varies according to the level of maturity of the group members and according to the situation in which the group finds itself. "Maturity is defined in situational leadership theory as the capacity to set high but attainable goals (achievement-motivation), willingness and ability to take responsibility, and education and/or experience of an individual or a group" (p. 161). The concern, then, is more for psychological maturity than for chronological maturity.

Hersey and Blanchard believe an effective leader is the person who can diagnose the demands of the situation and the level of maturity of the group members and use the leadership style that is most suitable. Thus, the effective leader must have diagnostic skills, and, equally important, the ability to adapt his or her leadership style to the demands of the situation. This requires the effective leader to "have the personal flexibility and a range of skills necessary to vary his own behavior" (Shein, 1965, p. 61). One leadership style or behavior cannot be applied to every situation.

For example, imagine that you are a teacher. Most of your students generally turn in their assignments on time, but one or two students often turn in their work late, and when it is turned in, it is of poor quality. You may have to create some additional structure for these students and supervise them more closely until they are able to function more independently. Another student does high-quality work and gets assignments in on time, but you notice she is shy and appears to be insecure. You may need to be more supportive with this student and help facilitate her interaction with others in the class. Other students may be psychologically mature as well as competent in their schoolwork; you let them work independently. The effective teacher (leader) realizes that at times it is important to behave differently toward individual members of the class than toward the class as a whole.

Leaders who cannot differentiate in this way may cause problems. Perhaps you can recall the feelings you had when a teacher punished the entire class for the immature behavior of a few students. Consider a similar situation: imagine you work in an office in which you and other employees have the freedom of monitoring your own time schedule—when you come to work and leave work each day. The manager notices that one employee occasionally comes in late and leaves early. Lacking confrontation skills, the manager sends a memo informing all employees that from now on everyone will be on the same time schedule, from 8 A.M. to 4 P.M. with a half-hour for lunch. The final blow comes when the manager installs a time clock so that everyone can punch in and punch out.

**WHAT DO YOU THINK?**

■ How do you feel about decisions that punish the many for the behavior of the few?

■ What do you think the productivity level would be after such a decision?

■ How do you think the employees might behave in the future?

### ■ Leadership Skills

We are more likely to develop our leadership potential if we focus on developing specific leadership skills. Fritz Roethlisberger (1953) emphasizes three skill areas for consideration:

*1.* The skills of self-awareness and the realization of our impact on others.

## CASE IN POINT
## Leadership Strength/Skill Assessment

Each of us has some leadership strengths or potential leadership strengths, regardless of whether we have had leadership experience in the past. Identify as many strengths or potential strengths as you can for each category below. Remember, let your best self be known!

Knowledge areas:

_____

_____

Educational strengths:

_____

_____

Work experience strengths:

_____

_____

Group follower strengths:

_____

_____

Leadership experiences, past and present:

_____

_____

Leadership possibilities in the future:

_____

_____

Strengths in motivating self and others:

_____

_____

Observation strengths:

_____

_____

2. The skills of being able to diagnose a situation.
3. The skills of helping oneself and others to grow and develop.

■ *Self-Awareness*  An awareness of our strengths (capabilities) in all aspects of life (personal, interpersonal, organizational, recreational, and so on) and a continual updating of our recently developed strengths are essential to the development of our self-confidence and self-esteem. The acknowledgment of our strengths is an ongoing, lifelong process. Effective leaders, realizing the importance of self-confidence and a positive self-esteem, help others identify their strengths and capabilities by providing ongoing positive feedback. Leaders and group members should engage continually in the feedback process of building each other's self-esteem.

A knowledge of our values and value priorities is essential to our awareness of ourselves. Without knowing what is most important to us, we are severely handicapped when making personal decisions. The effective leader, knowing that values are the basis for what we do successfully in life, helps others identify what is most important to them. A leader also knows the importance of not judging the values of others and of discovering how differences of opinion when expressed in constructive ways can enhance the functioning of the group.

The effective use of power is another important ingredient of self-awareness. With self-confidence and self-esteem we are able to be assertive and confront individuals and situations when the time is appropriate. An effective leader is not afraid of the power of others and helps them find productive ways of using their power.

Leadership means modeling the behavior (setting an example) believed to be healthy for the effectively functioning group. Honesty and integrity are maintained in words and actions; that is, the effective leader does not say one thing and do another. Without integrity, we can earn little respect from others. Congruence of feelings, words, and actions is demonstrated by the effective leader.

Leadership also demands being open to the ideas and criticism of others. We cannot expect members of our group to view our ideas and criticisms as healthy possibilities for growth if we act in a closed and defensive manner ourselves. The effective leader is able to say honestly, "That is a great idea. I wish I had thought of it," or "Thanks for being assertive and offering me that criticism. I find it helpful." Remember that criticism is more easily heard when it is blended with positive feedback. "Your presentation this morning was very informative, and you presented it in a humorous and entertaining way. I noticed, though, that sometimes you lost your next thought. Perhaps if you used a short outline of the main points, it would make your presentation even better." Remember, too, that negative feedback is often more useful when it is solicited. "Tell me, how am I doing?" Through a continuous awareness of ourselves, we can make it possible for others to become more aware of themselves.

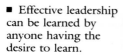

■ Effective leadership can be learned by anyone having the desire to learn.

■ *Diagnosing Situations*   As leaders, we must learn to be good observers, and to be good observers, we must be close to the functioning of the group. It is important to observe who contributes and who does not, who is being excluded and who is dominating, and what is getting in the way of the group's functioning effectively. Observation skills are developed over time. Through our own growing experience we begin to assign meaning to what we observe.

Effective listening skills are essential to the observation process. We must be able to listen without internal or external distractions. *Observation listening* requires that we hear both what is being said and what is *not* being said. The ability to interpret nonverbal behavior, and the skill to deal with feelings, are crucial to the diagnostic process. As leaders, we must be able to identify and express our own feelings and demonstrate empathy for the feelings of others. When we fail to include feelings as an integral part of the diagnostic process, feelings remain hidden, sapping the energy of the group and ultimately decreasing productivity.

The effective leader must have the ability to understand human behavior. There is no limit to the number and variety of interpersonal problems that occur within a group. "There seems to be excessive competition between Marie and Steve," or "It appears there is quite a bit of disagreement among us. Perhaps if we each shared more about our opinions and feelings, the additional information would help us understand the others' points of view and we could reach a consensus." Good observation skills require that we gather information about what is happening without judging it as good or bad. We must realize that whatever goes on in a group situation has cause and meaning.

■ *Developing as Leaders*   We can continue to learn, grow, and develop as individuals and as leaders in numerous ways, some of which were mentioned above. Referring to the growth and development of leaders and managers, George Terry (1972) states that emphasis has changed from "developing *learned* managers to *learning* managers" (p. 507). Because of this evolutionary change, the modern leader is becoming more of a group member, seeking answers rather than giving answers. New problems are viewed more as opportunities to learn and grow than as threats of failure. Therefore, we learn and grow as we accumulate more and more life experience.

Another way to learn about leadership is to read; there are hundreds of books about leadership and thousands of magazine articles. (See Selected Readings and References for a brief list.)

We can also observe others in leadership situations. We may see them demonstrating some of the leadership styles and skills mentioned in this chapter. Leadership theories begin to come alive when we see others implementing them. Try to determine which style they are using and whether it is appropriate to the situation. Sometimes, observing leaders and managers may provide models not of what leadership is but rather of what it is not.

Knowledge about why people do what they do can be gained from courses or readings in the behavioral sciences. Workshops and seminars offered at colleges and universities are extremely beneficial in learning effective leadership skills. Most programs, such as National Training Laboratories (NTL) in Bethel, Maine, provide the participants with a chance to try new, more effective leadership behaviors in a warm climate of acceptance and trust. Thousands of leaders around the world have been successfully trained in such seminars and workshops.

It is also important to keep up with the new and growing knowledge in the field in which we work. Leaders who demonstrate that they have not kept up with current knowledge in important areas lose power and respect in the group.

Being a growing and developing leader means being a risk taker. Taking risks to attempt new endeavors provides the excitement and life-blood of growth and development. We must be able to risk failure and defeat if we are to realize our potential as people and leaders. A leader who is not willing to do this cannot be effective.

As leaders, we must not only grow and develop ourselves but help others grow and develop. The best way to help group members in their own process of growing and developing, both individually and as a group, is to model the growth and development behavior mentioned earlier. Setting the example makes growth and development not only appropriate but desirable. People who work in a safe learning environment are more comfortable taking the risk to grow and change.

Well-trained and skilled business leaders often conduct in-service training sessions (training sessions provided on company time to learn new skills in specific areas, such as giving useful feedback) and thus expose their groups to numerous growth possibilities. Perhaps an even better plan is to hire consultants to conduct training sessions based on leader and group needs (such as training the group to be less competitive and more of a team). The time away from the actual task and the money spent on a competent consultant can be viewed as time and money well spent. Another possibility is to send one or several members of the group, other than the designated leader, to various organizational development training programs.

Earlier in this chapter, we stated that leadership is a learned art and that anyone who has the desire to learn can do so. We hope this chapter has helped you assess some of your own leadership capabilities and has given you the encouragement to use these capabilities as leadership opportunities become available to you.

REVIEW
QUESTIONS

33. Effective leadership is measured by the results it produces.   T  F   If false, the truth is: _____

_____

_____ .

34. The maturity component of Hersey's and Blanchard's situational leadership theory refers to the chronological maturity of the group members.   T  F   If false, the truth is: _____

_____

_____ .

35. As leaders, we must remember that it is more important to be concerned for others in the group than for ourselves.   T  F   If false, the truth is: _____

_____

_____ .

*36.* A leader should be more concerned with giving critical feedback to group members who need it than with giving positive feedback.   T  F   If false, the truth is:

_____

_____

_____ .

*37.* When value conflicts arise in a group, the leader should resolve the conflicts by imposing his or her values.   T  F   If false, the truth is: _____

_____

_____ .

*38.* In order to effectively diagnose a group problem, the leader must possess adequate observation skills.   T  F   If false, the truth is: _____

_____

_____ .

*39.* The goal of effective leadership training today is to become a learned leader.
T  F   If false, the truth is: _____

_____

_____ .

*40.* Observation skills require that a leader be an effective listener and have the ability to understand human behavior.   T  F   If false, the truth is: _____

_____

_____ .

*41.* The effective leader must set the example for personal and organizational growth and development.   T  F   If false, the truth is: _____

_____

_____ .

*The answers to these review questions are on page 326.*

## SUMMARY

■ We spend most of our lives interacting with numerous groups and organizations. Groups and organizations are basic to all life.

■ Membership in groups is a major part of our identity and of the development of our self-esteem. A *group* is defined as people working together toward common goals.

■ There are informal and formal groups and organizations, and most people belong to both types. *Informal groups* are formed by people having similar needs and are built on mutual interest and trust. *Formal groups,* such as corporations, are usually formed with a special goal or mission in mind.

■ *Group structure* is the observable pattern of relationships among the members within a group. It is influenced by such factors as roles, status, norms, and cohesiveness.

■ Most groups and organizations have *leaders*, people who attempt to influence the behavior or goal achievement of another individual or of a group. Almost anyone who aspires to be an effective leader can do so if he or she is willing to take risks and learn from available knowledge and experience.

■ Depending on the type of group or organization, leaders may be chosen by the group members through informal or formal democratic selection (voting) or appointed by someone in authority outside the group. Most groups more readily accept leaders whom they choose than leaders who are appointed by an outsider. How the leader is chosen often has much to do with the productivity of the group.

■ There are many different types of leaders and styles of leadership. The effective leader is the one who can adapt to the style most appropriate to the group and its goals.

■ Effective leaders possess or are willing to learn the necessary skills: They possess self-awareness and realize the impact of their awareness on others; they can diagnose group situations and provide leadership to resolve conflicts that may be impeding the group's functioning; and they take responsibility for their own personal and professional growth while encouraging and supporting the growth of others.

## SELECTED READINGS

Argyris, C. *Management and Organizational Development: The Path from XA to YB*. New York: McGraw-Hill, 1971. Case studies used as tools to study human behavior in organizations.

Blake, R. R., and Mouton, J. S. *The Grid for Supervisory Effectiveness*. Austin, Tex.: Scientific Methods, 1975. Descriptions of leadership styles used in the managerial grid theory, which analyzes the relationship between the needs of the individual (people concerns) and the needs of the organization (task concerns).

Blanchard, K., and Johnson, S. *The One Minute Manager*. New York: Berkley Books, 1982. Advice on how to save time and increase your productivity at work, at home, and with the family.

Likert, R. *The Human Organization: Its Management and Value*. New York: McGraw-Hill, 1967. A classic work in the field of human behavior in organizations that for many years has served as the guidebook for leaders and managers.

Molloy, J. T. *Molloy's Live for Success*. New York: Bantam Books, 1981. A book that tells how to develop effective leadership skills through effective communication.

Scheele, A. *Skills for Success*. New York: Ballantine Books, 1979. A book that discusses the effective use of power to get personal results; teaches the reader how to take risks and capitalize on opportunities.

## GLOSSARY

**bureaucratic/pyramidal value system:**   a system in which people are motivated by direction, control, rewards, and punishments.

**coercive power**:   power to withhold or take away something another person desires.

**expert power**:   power resulting from possession of knowledge or expertise needed by others.

**groups**:   people working together toward common goals.

**group structure**:   differentiation among group members, influenced by roles, status, norms, and cohesiveness.

**humanistic/democratic value system**:   a system in which people are encouraged to develop authentic relationships with others and to share in the decision-making process.

**influence**:   the capacity to affect the course of events in a group or the behavior of a group or a person.

**integrative leadership**:   leadership style that assumes that the needs of human beings can be integrated with the needs of organizations.

**leadership**:   the process of influencing the activities of an individual or a group in efforts toward goal achievement.

**legitimate power**:   formal power held by right of role or position in a group.

**maturity**:   according to Hersey and Blanchard (1977), the capacity to set high but attainable goals, willingness and ability to take responsibility, and education and/or experience of an individual or a group.

**power**:   the ability to require specified behavior of group members.

**referent power**: power resulting from charm, personal magnetism, or association with others holding power.

**reward power**: power to give someone else what he or she desires.

**sociometry**: a way to measure the attraction group members have toward each other.

**subgroups**: small groups within a larger group, formed to increase the warmth and intimate contact possible in groups of five or less.

## REFERENCES

Argyris, C. *Interpersonal Competence and Organization Effectiveness*. Homewood, Ill.: Dorsey Press, 1962.

———. *Personality and Organization: The Conflict between Systems and the Individual*. New York: Harper & Row, 1957.

Bales, R. F.; Parsons, T.; and Shils, E. A. *Working Papers in the Theory of Action*. New York: Free Press, 1953.

French, J. R. P., and Raven, B. "The Bases of Social Power." In *Group Dynamics*, edited by D. Cartwright and A. F. Zander. Evanston, Ill.: Row, Peterson, 1960.

Hersey, P., and Blanchard, K. *Management of Organizational Behavior: Utilizing Human Resources*, 3rd ed. Englewood Cliffs, N.J.: Prentice-Hall, 1977.

Herzberg, F. *Work and the Nature of Man*. New York: World, 1966.

Janis, I. *Air War and Emotional Stress*. New York: McGraw-Hill, 1951.

Likert, R. *The Human Organization: Its Management and Value*. New York: McGraw-Hill, 1967.

Lott, A., and Lott, B. "Group Cohesiveness, Communication Level, and Conformity." *Journal of Abnormal and Social Psychology* 62 (1961): 408–412.

McGregor, D. *The Human Side of Enterprise*. New York: McGraw-Hill, 1960.

Mayo, E. *The Human Problems of an Industrial Civilization*. New York: Macmillan, 1933.

Mondy, R. W.; Holmes, R. E.; and Flippo, E. B. *Management: Concepts and Practices*. Boston: Allyn & Bacon, 1980.

Pepitone, A., and Kleiner, R. "The Effects of Threat and Frustration on Group Cohesiveness." *Journal of Abnormal and Social Psychology* 54 (1957): 192–199.

Plunkett, W. R. *Supervision: The Direction of People at Work*. Dubuque, Iowa: Wm. C. Brown, 1975.

Porter, L., and Lawler, E., III. "Properties of Organization Structure in Relation to Job Attitudes and Job Behavior." *Psychological Bulletin* 64 (1965): 23–51.

Quarantelli, E., and Dynes, R. "When Disaster Strikes." *Psychology Today* 5, no. 9 (1972): 66–70.

Roethlisberger, F. J. "The Administrator's Skill." *Harvard Business Review*, December 1953, p. 61.

Schein, E. H. *Organizational Psychology*, Englewood Cliffs, N.J.: Prentice-Hall, 1965.

———. *Organizational Psychology*, 2nd ed. Englewood Cliffs, N.J.: Prentice-Hall, 1970.

Schwartz, D. *Introduction to Management: Principles, Practices, and Processes*. New York: Harcourt Brace Jovanovich, Inc. 1980.

Shaw, M. *Group Dynamics: The Psychology of Small Group Behavior*, 2nd ed. New York: McGraw-Hill, 1976.

Terry, G. R. *Principles of Management*. Homewood, Ill.: Richard D. Irwin, 1972.

Theodorson, G. "Elements in the Progressive Development of Small Groups." *Social Forces* 31 (1953): 311–320.

Torgersen, R. E., and Weinstock, I. T. *Management: An Integrated Approach*. Englewood Cliffs, N.J.: Prentice-Hall, 1972.

Wilson, W., and Miller, N. "Shifts in Evaluation of Participants Following Intergroup Competition." *Journal of Abnormal and Social Psychology* 63 (1961): 428–432.

## ANSWERS TO REVIEW QUESTIONS

**Page 299.**   *1.* common goals   *2.* affiliation or belonging   *3.* self-esteem, status   *4.* security   *5.* subgroups

**Page 304.**   *6.* group structure   *7.* Roles, norms, status, and cohesiveness   *8.* social status   *9.* influence   *10.* power   *11.* legitimate power   *12.* expert power   *13.* Norms   *14.* group cohesiveness   *15.* sociometry

**Page 308.**   *16.* respect, cooperation   *17.* designated leader   *18.* developed art   *19.* election   *20.* appointed   *21.* positive attitude   *22.* evaluate   *23.* experience levels, skills, proficiencies, attitudes   *24.* default   *25.* potential leader

**Page 316.**   *26.* F   *27.* T   *28.* F   *29.* T   *30.* F   *31.* F   *32.* F

**Page 322.**   *33.* T   *34.* F   *35.* F   *36.* F   *37.* F   *38.* T   *39.* F   *40.* T   *41.* T

Part V explores two of the most important factors affecting the adjustment of nearly everyone—communication and intimacy.

Chapter 10 explores the processes of communicating and understanding through verbal and nonverbal means. It discusses skills (sending and receiving messages) and styles of communication as well as barriers to communicating effectively. Many believe that ineffective communication is the major cause of interpersonal problems within relationships, within the family, at work, at school, and between nations.

Chapter 11 focuses on our need for intimacy and on how we can successfully meet this important need. It explores ways in which we can increase our capacity for finding satisfying intimacy.

In Chapter 12, we turn to some of the many problems people encounter in their search for intimacy. We discuss the effects of role conflicts, value conflicts, social pressures, loneliness, and romantic ideals on our success in establishing intimate relationships.

# INTERPERSONAL ADJUSTMENT

# 10

# COMMUNICATION

Take a few minutes to imagine that you
are the sole survivor of a nuclear attack.
Think for a moment of the consequences
of being deprived of the opportunity to
interact with others. What are you feeling?

Survival in a communication-free
environment would be difficult at best and
impossible at worst. We learn, grow, and
interact with others through
communication. It is essential to our
survival both individually and as a race. It
is almost as much a part of us as the air
we breathe. Through it we convey our
needs and desires; we resolve problems;
we govern nations; we are entertained; we
hurt one another; and we fall in love.

This chapter is about communicating
effectively. Learning the basics of effective
communication and practicing them as
part of our everyday lives should greatly
enhance our personal growth and our
relationships with others.

**10**

Communica-
tion

## DISCUSSION: Effective Communication

Communicating effectively can reduce the misunderstandings and unresolved conflicts that often result in the termination of intimate and working relationships. Each of us has some skills in communication. However, the results we hope for often are not realized.

### ■ Defining Communication

**Communication** is the process of sending and receiving messages through which we and others are known and understood. It may involve words (oral or written), symbols, or nonverbal language. It also involves careful receiving (listening) on the part of the person to whom the message is directed. That sounds like a simple process. However, a number of overt and subtle skills are essential for the communication process to be effective.

### ■ Defining Effective Communication

A parent who gives a child a look of approval and a pat on the shoulder, a bus company that distributes a simple and understandable timetable, and a teacher who asks students for feedback as to the effectiveness of his or her lectures are all practicing effective communication. Effective communication entails an *interchange*; a two-way contact in which information, ideas, and/or perspectives are exchanged with understanding as the primary goal. This means we need to know, first, what it is we want to communicate, and second, how to communicate it so that the person or persons receiving our message can understand it as accurately as possible.

Let's consider the communication process in Figure 10.1. The sender transmits a message to the receiver through a selected medium. The receiver acknowledges the message by responding through feedback to the sender indicating that the message is understood. Ideally, this is how effective communication takes place. However, problems may exist at each point in the process.

### ■ Sending a Message

First, the sender must know what his or her intentions are in sending the message. In other words, what is the desired outcome? Second, the sender must

FIGURE 10.1
Communication is a
two-way process.

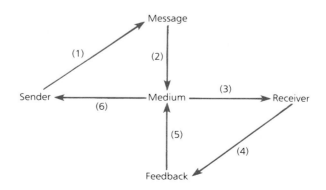

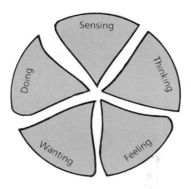

FIGURE 10.2
The Awareness wheel helps us send a message more accurately and effectively.

decide what information about himself or herself (feelings or thoughts) or about the topic (concepts or ideas) is most important. Third, the sender must have as much information as possible about the receiver or receivers. It may be important to understand the needs of the receiver as well as the importance of the information. Fourth, the sender must decide how to convey the message clearly and accurately and choose the best medium to do this.

To help us understand the sender's responsibility, Miller, Nunnally, and Wackman (1975) have developed a model for effective communication called the awareness wheel. The awareness wheel has five parts, as shown in Figure 10.2. The five parts, or dimensions, are designed to help the sender gather the information necessary to send the message accurately and effectively. Let's take a closer look at how it can help us communicate more effectively.

> Allen looks up from his magazine and says, "Penny, let's take a break now. We could ride our bikes over to Dino's for a pizza. Do you want to?" Without looking up from her accounting work, Penny responds, "Just a moment," and continues working. After a few minutes pass, Allen asks again, "Come on, Penny, are you ready to go now?" Penny mumbles and continues to work on her figures. Allen waits a few more minutes, then abruptly leaves the room, slamming the door on the way out. Penny looks up in shock and amazement at Allen's behavior. She runs to the door only to see Allen riding his bike out onto the street.

Let's analyze the interchange between Penny and Allen to discover how this breakdown in communication could have been avoided. Allen and Penny might have been able to convey their messages more effectively had they used the concepts in the awareness wheel. Allen could have used at least four of the five dimensions of the wheel to communicate more clearly his needs or wishes. Suppose he had chosen to use the *feeling* dimension. He could have said "I'm feeling left out," or "I'm feeling bored," or "I'm feeling lonely," or "I'm feeling angry." Sharing his feelings would have let Penny understand more accurately the basis for his wishes. He might have added statements from the *thinking* dimension, such as "I'm thinking you've been very busy with your work lately and we haven't done much together," or "It's such a beautiful day—I think it would be fun to go for a bike ride together." The message could have been further clarified by statements from the *wanting* dimension, such as: "I want us to pack a picnic lunch and ride our bikes to the beach for the afternoon" or "I want us to ride our bikes to Dino's for a pizza." He might have clarified his

WHAT DO YOU THINK?

■ How do you know what you want to communicate before you speak?
■ In what ways do you express your feelings?
■ What difficulty do you think some people have in expressing their feelings?

■ We spend much of
our lives trying to
make other people
understand us.

message even more by stating, "I'm going to ride my bike over to Dino's for a
pizza. Would you like to come with me?" This statement represents the *doing*,
or action, dimension of the awareness wheel.

The more dimensions used, the clearer the message. The more information
we can convey, the fewer the chances that we will be misunderstood. The more
we are understood, the greater the satisfaction we will experience in our relationships. By speaking for himself, Allen could have let Penny know what he
was feeling, thinking, wanting, and doing. Let's explore the ways Penny could
have used the awareness wheel to speak for herself and respond to Allen.

Suppose Penny had begun with the *sensing* dimension. Our senses help us
tune in to what is going on around us. Using this dimension, Penny might have
said "You've had a sad look on your face lately. I've seen you sit around the
house, and nothing seems to interest you. I've even heard you sigh while I do
my accounting." Sensing data only relays what has been observed with the
senses. Penny could have added interpretive meaning to her sense data by using
the *thinking* dimension. Her interpretation would have stemmed from her own
past learning experiences in connecting sensory information with meaning. She
might have said, "I think you are bored," or "I think you are lonely," or "I
think you are annoyed." By using these two dimensions, she could have let
Allen know that she was aware of him through his behavior.

By using the other three dimensions, she could have given Allen her response
to his statements. She might have begun by saying, "I'm feeling pressured to
complete this project I've been working on the past two weeks. I'm beginning
to feel bored with it and I'm quite annoyed with myself for agreeing to work
at home to complete it. When I agreed to do it, I thought we could use the
extra money, but I didn't know it would involve this much time. I, too, want
to spend time with you right now. I'm going to try to finish this within the

next hour, and even if I don't, we'll go for a bike ride to the beach or to Dino's, whichever you prefer."

Allen might well have responded, "That's great! I'll make the picnic lunch to take to the beach, and I'll make sure there's enough air in the bike tires."

With more information about their sensings, feelings, thoughts, wants, and actions, Penny and Allen could have achieved a satisfying solution to a situation that otherwise could result in a serious misunderstanding.

■ *Communicating Feelings and Thoughts*    Feeling and thinking are both essential to effective communication; however, saying "I feel" when we mean "I think" often muddles our messages. In general, *thinking* (head talk) involves an explanation of an interactive situation, while *feeling* (gut talk) leads to an understanding of it. Head talk is the prose of communication; gut talk is the poetry (Banet, 1973).

Most of us have learned to use *think* statements correctly—that is, we do not say "I think" when we mean "I feel." We are taught that *think* statements are important, as they represent attempts to define, opine, observe, infer, rationalize, categorize, generalize, and summarize, all of which are certainly important for survival in our interpersonal environment. *Think* statements are bound by the rules of logic and scientific inquiry, and they require words or symbols to be communicated. They may be true or untrue and may also be proven or disproven. Perhaps it is because the validity of our *think* statements can be tested that many of us hedge our statements by erroneously using "I feel" instead of "I think."

*Feel* statements report our affective, immediate, nonrational, emotional, gut responses to people and events. They are usually personal and idiosyncratic in that they refer to our inner states—that is, to what is happening inside of us. *Feel* statements are not true or false, good or bad, but are only communicated

■ We communicate more effectively when we use all of our personal resources (thoughts, feelings, and wants).

honestly or dishonestly. Unlike *think* statements, *feel* statements may not require words. Sometimes they are best communicated nonverbally, a process we will discuss later in this chapter.

To communicate our messages more effectively, we need to practice using "I feel" and "I think" accurately. For example, "I feel that Jane is responding irrationally" is not an expression of feeling but a statement of opinion based on an observation of Jane's behavior. If your intention is to share your feeling about Jane's behavior, it is more accurate to say, "I am uncomfortable (annoyed, angry, hurt, sad, frightened) with Jane's response." "I feel that all people are created equal" expresses adherence to an abstract principle that cannot really be felt. This is a statement of belief that may be more accurately stated: "I believe all people are created equal." Often, the presence of the word *that* after the words *I feel* is a clue that we are inaccurately using the word *feel* to make a *think* statement.

Following is a partial list of words that convey feeling and that may help us identify feeling statements.

| | | | |
|---|---|---|---|
| angry | confident | glad | sad |
| anxious | confused | grieved | satisfied |
| apathetic | content | hesitant | silly |
| bored | daring | jubilant | surprised |
| calm | elated | lonely | uneasy |
| cautious | excited | loved | uncomfortable |
| comfortable | fearful | proud | weary |

*Sharing our feelings* with others is important to effective communication. Many of us share our feelings so seldom that we may condition ourselves to screen out awareness of our internal reactions to people and events. By getting in touch with our innermost feelings and by communicating them along with our thoughts, we greatly enhance our communication and enrich our interpersonal relationships.

■ *Responsible Communication*    Effective communication occurs when we take responsibility for our thoughts, feelings, and behaviors. We do this by speaking only for ourselves and by letting others speak for themselves. How many times have you heard yourself or someone else say, "We all feel great." "She will be angry if you do that." "This would make most people happy, don't you think?" "It might be good for us to be more understanding with each other." You might ask, "What is wrong with these statements? I use them all the time." Perhaps you do, and so do many of us. This is one of the many reasons we may be ineffective as communicators. When you speak for anyone other than yourself, you make a glaring assumption—the assumption that you are either a mind reader or such an expert on the inner experience of others that you know what they think, feel, and want.

We can avoid this error by remembering to speak only for ourselves. Statements that include *I, me, my,* or *mine* help us communicate our feelings, thoughts, needs, and desires more clearly. Instead of the "speaking for others" statements used in the previous paragraph, we could say, "I feel great." "I would be angry if you did that to me." "This would make me happy." "I am going to be more understanding of your ideas." When we speak for others we are behaving ir-

**WHAT DO YOU THINK?**

■ How often do you hear people speaking for others?

■ Do you do this?

■ Why do you think some people find it difficult to speak for themselves?

responsibly. Only when we speak for ourselves and let others speak for themselves can we respond authentically to each other.

*1.* The process of sending and receiving messages, with understanding as the goal, is called *communication.* T  F

*2.* Ideally, if the sender of a message is certain of the information to be sent, knowledge of the receiver is unimportant. T  F

*3.* The awareness wheel was designed to help the sender gather important information to aid in effective communication. T  F

*4.* "I feel that the United States is the best country in the world" is an accurate statement from one dimension of the awareness wheel. T  F

*5.* It is important to differentiate between feeling statements and thinking statements when communicating. T  F

*6.* Feeling statements are neither good nor bad, true nor false, but are either honest or dishonest. T  F

*7.* Sharing our feelings as well as our thoughts is crucial to effective communication. T  F

*8.* When we assume that we know what someone is thinking, feeling, sensing, wanting, or doing and speak for them, we are behaving irresponsibly. T  F

*The answers to these review questions are on p. 355.*

## DISCUSSION: ASSERTIVE COMMUNICATION

When we speak for ourselves, we are more likely to demonstrate **assertive communication**. We also demonstrate that we are fully responsible for our intentions, thoughts, and feelings, thus further enhancing our personal power and self-esteem.

### ■ Defining Assertive Communication

Perhaps we can best define assertive communication by describing what it is not. First, it is not making passive statements, such as, "Uh, excuse me but I was wondering if you would be willing to tell me again how to do this." This need would be better expressed in an assertive way by simply saying, "I want you to explain again how you want me to do this." Second, it is not making aggressive statements, such as, "I am sick and tired of the way you tell me what to do." An assertive statement is, "I feel put down when you tell me what to do." Assertive communication, then, is communicating in such a way that we make our needs, feelings, thoughts, and desires known without decreasing our self-esteem and the self-esteem of others.

WHAT DO YOU
THINK?
■ How assertively do
you communicate?
■ How often do you
observe others using
assertive
communication?

### ■ *Self-Esteem and Assertiveness*   People who employ passive statements convey their timidity by asking permission to be heard ("If anyone is interested, I may have a solution to the problem" or "This may not be important to any of you, but . . ." or "This is probably not a good idea, but . . ."). They seem to assume that no one is interested in hearing what they have to say. Bower and Bower

(1976) describe them as *silent martyrs*. They often use martyr statements in an attempt to manipulate others into giving them what they want, hoping others will feel sorry for them. The use of passive statements results in a continual eroding of their self-confidence, self-respect, and self-esteem.

The self-esteem of people who use aggressive statements also suffers. These people attempt to get what they want by verbally attacking others, forcing a win/lose confrontation. They usually "have the last word" and walk away from a confrontation as "the winner." However, they make few friends, and their self-esteem suffers from feelings of guilt at having mistreated others.

*See Chapter 3 for more about self-esteem.*

### ■ Indirect Communication

■ *The Question*   The question is perhaps the most frequently used form of **indirect communication** (communication that approaches the issue in an ambiguous way). In fact, many questions are *pseudoquestions* (Pfeiffer and Jones, 1974). Here, the questioner may not be seeking information or even an answer from the receiver. Instead, the questioner is offering an opinion and hoping to force the other person to agree.

Our communication would be more effective if we eliminated many kinds of questions entirely. By replacing many questions with statements, we could come closer to honest communication with each other. Before we can achieve the goal of direct communication, however, we must be able to identify the various pseudoquestions that people use.

■ We often use questions to probe, expose, and intimidate.

According to Pfeiffer and Jones, there are eight basic types of pseudoquestions: co-optive questions, punitive questions, hypothetical questions, imperative questions, screened questions, set-up questions, rhetorical questions, and "got'cha" questions (see Table 10.1). *Co-optive questions* ("Don't you think . . . ?" "Isn't it true that . . . ?" "Wouldn't you rather . . . ?" "Don't you want to . . . ?" "You wouldn't want that, would you?") attempt to limit the responses of the other person. The sender limits the other's responses by building into the question certain restrictions.

Questions such as "What proof do you have for those statements?" are *punitive questions* used when the questioner wants to expose or punish the other person without appearing to do so. The goal of punitive questioning is to put the other person on the spot. The *hypothetical question* is often used by the sender to criticize or to probe for an answer he or she is reluctant or afraid to ask for directly. Hypothetical questions often begin with "If," "What if," or "How about."

A type of pseudoquestion that actually makes a demand is the *imperative question*. Questions such as, "Have you done anything about . . . ?" or "When are you going to . . . ?" are examples. This type of question implies a command: "Do what you said you were going to do." Like the punitive question, it is often used to put someone on the spot; it implies that they have been negligent.

TABLE 10.1
Pseudoquestions as Communication

| PSEUDOQUESTION | TYPICAL USE | EXAMPLE | ALTERNATIVE |
|---|---|---|---|
| Co-optive question | To limit the receiver's responses by building in restrictions | Wouldn't you rather go to the art museum than to the beach? | I would like to go to the art museum. |
| Punitive question | To expose or punish | What right do you have to be in this room? | I want you to leave this room. |
| Hypothetical question | To criticize or probe | What would you do if that happened to you? | I would be shocked if that happened to me. |
| Imperative question | To put someone on the spot by implying that they have been negligent | When are you going to turn in your project? | I would like you to turn in your project soon. |
| Screened question | To get the other person to assume responsibility for your preference | Where would you like to go for our vacation? | I would like to go to Canada for our vacation. |
| Set-up question | To maneuver the other person into a vulnerable position | May I assume that you were not prepared for this exam? | I feel sorry that you failed this exam. |
| Rhetorical question | To seek agreement | Isn't that right | I think that is correct. |
| Got'cha question | To trap | Aren't you the person I saw him with last night? | I believe I saw you with him last night. |

**WHAT DO YOU THINK?**

■ How often do you use questions as a communication style?
■ What do you think your life would be like if you eliminated pseudoquestions from your communication?

The *screened question* is a very common variety of pseudoquestion. Its use is most often to blame for misunderstandings in attempts to communicate. The sender, afraid of simply stating a choice or preference, asks the other person what he or she likes or what he or she wants to do, hoping the choice will be what the sender secretly wants. For example, suppose you and your partner decide to go out to dinner together. Afraid to take the risk of making a suggestion that you are not sure will be accepted, you resort to the use of a screened question by asking your partner, "What kind of food do you prefer?" You secretly hope the other person will name your favorite food, say Mexican. To your concealed disappointment, your partner names Chinese food, which you do not like. However, since you gave your partner the choice of naming the food of the evening, and since you once told your partner you liked all kinds of food, you suffer through a Chinese meal. Screened questions may also greatly frustrate your partner. Questions such as "What are you doing Friday night?" and "What do you think about our relationship?" ask the other person to reveal himself or herself at no expense to the sender. If the sender is intent on being responsible and communicating effectively, he or she might say, "I would like to go out to dinner and a movie Friday night, and I would like you to join me." "I think our relationship is a good one, but I think we can improve it by improving our communication."

"Would you agree that . . . .?" and "Is it fair to say that you . . . ?" are examples of the *set-up question.* This pseudoquestion attempts to maneuver the other person into a vulnerable position—to "lead the witness" as a skillful attorney might do in the courtroom. One of the simplest types of pseudoquestion is the *rhetorical question.* The sender may make a statement and immediately follow it with a phrase that assumes approval in advance: "Right?" or "OK?" or "You see?" or "You know?" The sender is not asking for a response and, in fact, hopes not to get one. When people are feeling insecure, they often use "Right?" as an attempted guarantee that their statements will meet agreement. The eighth type of pseudoquestion, *"got'cha" question,* is a more trapping form of the set-up question: "Didn't I see you . . . ?" "Didn't you say that . . . ?" "Weren't you the one who . . . ?" are examples. Here, the sender tries to trap the other person by digging a pit for the respondent to fall into.

A good rule to remember is that behind every pseudoquestion is a responsible and direct statement that will contribute to effective communication. By beginning our statements with: "I want . . . ," "I feel . . . ," "I think . . . ," "I heard . . . ," "I will . . . ," and so on we can achieve greater accuracy and less chance for misunderstanding.

Of course, we may legitimately use questions to gather information about various things we need or want to know. Questions such as "Do you have an interest in this project?" or "Would you like to join the organization?" are examples of questions that do not disguise our motives. Other legitimate questions ask for feedback ("How am I doing?") or request information about another person's needs ("How may I help you?"). Questions that are used to enhance effective communication are certainly permissible and are indeed necessary.

■ *Cliches*    When we use cliches, we do not communicate much of ourselves but use pat, standardized, and stylized ways of communicating. Examples of cliches are plentiful: "She's as cute as a button." (How many times have you thought of a button as being cute?) "Her mind is as sharp as a tack." "Better safe than sorry." "Better late than never." "It's an open and shut case." "He has us over a barrel." "She left no stone unturned." "The early bird catches the worm." "If you've seen one, you've seen them all." "He's beating around the bush."

We all have been taught numerous cliches, which we often use; and it may be difficult to avoid using them occasionally. But the frequent use of worn-out phrases greatly diminishes the effectiveness of our communication.

**WHAT DO YOU THINK?**
- What cliches do you use?
- Where did you learn to use these cliches?

■ *The Effects of Indirect Communication*   Indirect communication has several negative effects:

1. Indirect communication encourages people to make guesses about each other. Without direct, open communication, people cannot get to know each other successfully; and what they do not know, they will make guesses about. Guessing games inhibit and obstruct communication.
2. Indirect communication fosters inaccurate assumptions. If we are forced to guess about others, we may often be wrong. Yet we attempt to communicate with others based on our assumptions, even though we are unable to check their accuracy.
3. Indirect communication increases the probability that we will be forced to infer the motives of others. In other words, we try to psych each other out: "Why is she doing that?" "What does he hope to gain by that?"
4. Indirect communication encourages game playing, which is usually dishonest or deceptive. To deliberately choose not to be open and straightforward leads us away from the goal of understanding. Game playing is often contagious; one person starts, and others, for their own survival, join in. Game playing often includes sending **mixed messages**. Mixed messages

■ Many times we send mixed messages to hide our feelings.

# CASE IN POINT
## Practicing Assertive Communication

Each day we find ourselves attempting to deal with conflicts with others. Many of us often wish we had handled these conflicts differently as is evidenced by the frequency of such statements as, "I wish I had said this . . . ." or "I wish I had another chance to . . . .", etc.. Becoming assertive takes practice. Sometimes we need to rehearse our assertive communication ahead of time so that when situations arise that call for assertiveness, we are prepared.

Practice writing several assertive statements for each of the following situations. Discuss your statements with other classmates and encourage them to discuss their statements with you. You can learn from each other.

1. You are in a restaurant and have ordered a steak, medium rare. When the steak arrives you discover that it is very rare. The waiter leaves and does not return for quite some time. Finally the waiter arrives and asks if you are enjoying your meal? You respond,

_____

_____

_____

2. You have been working for a company for one month. Because you have wanted to be accepted and liked by your new boss, you have worked overtime on several occasions. You have made plans to go out with a friend immediately after work today. Just as it is time to leave, your boss asks you if you will stay and work two more hours. You respond,

_____

_____

_____

3. Your doctor prescribes medication for a current ailment. When you ask him what you have, he responds by telling you not to worry because it is nothing major. You respond,

_____

_____

_____

are the result of incongruent communication (changing the message, speaking inconsistently, or behaving in ways not aligned with our words), and they often cause misunderstanding and hurt feelings: "Thanks for not coming to my birthday party," or "Your're a nice jerk."

5. One of the surest effects of indirect communication is defensiveness. People tend to become defensive because there is often an implied threat behind indirect communication. Their need to defend themselves makes effective communication even less likely. Defensiveness can be recognized by such postures as denial and projection.

## ■ Self-Concept and Communication

The question may be asked "Why would anyone choose to communicate indirectly and irresponsibly on purpose?." One of the most important single factors affecting people's communication with others is their self-concept—how they see themselves and their situations (Chartier, 1974).

4. A salesperson approaches you and asks if she can be of assistance. You respond, "No thank you. I am just looking right now." The salesperson continues to follow you as you walk telling you that you would look nice in nearly everything you see. You begin to be annoyed and respond by saying,

_____

_____

_____

5. You are the parent of three children from age 5 to 11. One day you discover that you are yelling at them because they do not seem to be listening to you. The more you yell, the less they seem to listen. Deciding on another approach, you say to them,

_____

_____

_____

6. You have been married to your mate for nearly 8 years. In the beginning of your relationship, sex with each other was more frequent. The last time you attempted to discuss the infrequency of sex with your mate, he/she got angry and refused to talk about it. Realizing that the problem is continuing, you

decide to make an attempt to open communication again. You say,

_____

_____

_____

7. Your grandmother, that you have not talked to in 6 months, calls you on the telephone just as you are in the middle of discussing the recent infrequency of sex with your mate. You say,

_____

_____

_____

8. A friend invites you to a large party so you can meet some "influential people." When you arrive, everyone seems to be in small groups or paired off with someone. You begin to feel lonely and uncomfortable. As you gaze around the room you notice a person of the opposite sex standing by the punch bowl. You walk up and say,

_____

_____

_____

People have thousands of concepts about themselves: who they are, what they stand for, where they live, what they do and do not do, what they value, and what they believe. Perceptions of self vary in clarity and importance from person to person. We can think of our self-concepts as filters through which we see, hear, evaluate, and understand the world around us.

A weak or negative self-concept often distorts our perception of how others see us and generates feelings of insecurity and sometimes fear as we attempt to relate to others. Our negative view of ourselves causes us to have difficulty conversing with others (for example, difficulties in admitting we are wrong, expressing our feelings or wants, accepting constructive criticism from others, or voicing ideas or thoughts different from the ideas and thoughts of others). Our concern is that others may not like us if we are different or if we disagree with them. However, we soon realize that we are lying to others and deceiving ourselves. The result is that our self-esteem suffers; we feel devalued, unworthy, inadequate, and inferior. This lack of confidence causes us to believe that our

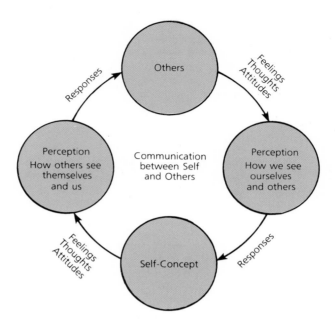

FIGURE 10.3
The relationship
between our self-
concepts and our
interactions with
others is circular.

ideas are uninteresting to others and not worthy of communicating. We may
become even more seclusive and guarded in our communication.

Even as our self-concepts affect our ability to communicate, so our communication with others shapes our self-concepts. Most of our perceptions are
derived from our experiences with other human beings. We learn who we are
from the ways we are treated by significant others in our lives. From verbal and
nonverbal communication with those important people, we learn whether or
not we are liked, accepted, worthy of respect, and successful as human beings.
If we are to have strong self-concepts, we need love, respect, and acceptance
from the significant others in our lives. We also need authentic and effective
communication with others. For a better understanding of how our communication with others affects the shaping of our self-concepts, see Figure 10.3.

REVIEW
QUESTIONS

9. People often purposely use indirect statements to confuse others. T F
10. Asking a question is always one of the most direct methods of
communicating. T F
11. Using words effectively to "put others in their place" is called assertive
communication. T F
12. Effective communication should never include the use of questions. T F
13. When we use indirect communication, others may become defensive because they
feel threatened. T F
14. Indirect communication often results in inaccurate assumptions. T F
15. Our self-concepts play an important part in our communication with others. T F
16. Our past experiences with communication have little to do with our self-
concepts. T F

*The answers to these review questions are on page 355.*

## DISCUSSION: LISTENING STYLES

Imagine the futility of a radio station's broadcasting programs to a community that has its radios either tuned to another station or turned off. The same futility exists when someone is attempting to communicate with you and you are either tuned in to something else or turned off.

### ■ A Society of Poor Listeners

In communication, careful **listening** is as important as careful sending. Unfortunately, many of us are poor listeners, for several interrelated reasons. First, much of our training in communicating focuses on the essential skills of expressing ourselves and persuading others to adopt our views. Until quite recently, little attention has been paid to the skill of listening. Although most of us agree that listening is important, the overemphasis on sending skills and the underemphasis on receiving skills cause many of us to devalue the importance of effective listening. A related problem is the assumption that if we can hear, we are listening. Listening involves much more than the physical process of hearing. Listening is an emotional and intellectual process integrating our past physical, emotional, and intellectual experiences, which help us interpret the message as we search for meaning and understanding.

The second reason we are poor listeners stems from the fact that the act of listening is less obvious to the observer than the act of sending a message. For example, perhaps someone is speaking to you about something of utmost importance to him or her, and by all appearances you are listening: your head is nodding, your posture appears accepting, and your eyes are fixed on the sender's face. Unfortunately for the sender and possibly for you, you are actually thinking about your activities for the upcoming weekend. This *deceptive listening* is one

■ The act of listening requires continual self-discipline.

of the cruelest ways we demonstrate our lack of positive regard and even our contempt for the sender. Occasionally, we are exposed by being so far removed from listening that we interrupt the sender with our own unrelated messages. We are also exposed when the sender asks us for a response, and our response is quite unassociated with the sender's message. Our apparent lack of interest and concern most often leaves the sender with feelings of not being important enough to be heard and understood. Think of a recent incident during which you were sharing something important to you and the person to whom you were speaking interrupted you in the middle of your message to interject something unrelated to what you were saying. Try to remember how you felt at that moment.

Such behavior on the part of the intended receiver leads us to the third reason we are poor listeners: we are often more concerned with what is important to us than with what is important to others. We would actually be more honest if we put our fingers in our ears when we stopped listening to alert others that we are no longer interested in what they are saying and are ready to interrupt them with tales of our own.

A fourth reason we are poor listeners is similar to the second reason, except for intent. Rather than acting on the assumption that what we have to say is more important than what others have to say, we continually interrupt their messages to demonstrate to them how much we understand their problem by citing numerous examples from our repertoire of similar experiences. The result is that we often demonstrate just the opposite of our intent. Although we attempt to show understanding, we do not allow others to communicate their thoughts or feelings.

A fifth reason for being poor listeners is that we often do not want to hear what others are saying, because their message may pertain to some behavior or statement from us that is disturbing to them. For example, a husband may often remind his wife that he feels put down by her remarks, and she may continue to ignore his message. We often *selectively listen* by tuning in and tuning out as we choose.

## ■ Effective Listening

The effective listener must be able to discern and understand the sender's meaning—the goal of communication. Reik (1972) refers to the process of effective listening as "listening with the third ear." This means that we not only listen to the words, but to the meanings behind the words—to what the speaker is feeling and thinking. Contrary to what many people think, effective listening is not a passive activity but an active one. The effective listener interacts with the sender to develop meaning and reach understanding.

Chartier (1974) suggests several principles that help us increase the effectiveness of our listening skills. A few follow:

*1.* The listener should have a purpose for listening: "What can I learn from this information? How can it improve my life?"
*2.* It is important that the listener withhold any judgment until the sender has completed the message. The information that we want or need may be coming later.

*3.* The listener should resist distractions (such as noises, views of others, extraneous thoughts, and so on).

*4.* The listener should digest what the sender has said before responding: "How does this apply to me? How do I feel about this?"

*5.* The listener should seek the important themes of what the sender says by listening through the words for additional meaning. We should listen to the tone of the voice and notice the nonverbal expressions.

■ *Listening for Meaning*  The assumption that others understand our meaning is one of the major barriers to successful communication. When we are in doubt, however, we can ask the receiver for feedback to help us gauge his or her understanding. Miller, Nunnally, and Wackman (1975) suggest an excellent method to evaluate the listener's understanding. They call it the *shared meaning process*, and it unfolds in the following manner (see Figure 10.4). First, the sender prefaces the message by saying, "I would like to share an important meaning with you. It is so important to me that I am going to ask you to reflect (send back) what you think I mean." After stating the message, the sender asks, "What do you hear me saying?" The receiver then reflects as accurately as possible his or her understanding of the message. The sender then either acknowledges that the receiver has understood the message or restates the message, asking again for a reflective response. This process continues until the sender is satisfied that the receiver has understood the meaning of the message. Let's use a dialogue to illustrate the use of the shared meaning process.

COLLEEN: "Bruce, I'd like to share something with you that is very important to me."

BRUCE: "Okay."

COLLEEN: "Lately, when we've been with Don and Connie, I've felt put down by the way you talk to me and about me. For example, last night you said that I wouldn't have the good job I have if it weren't for your pushing me. I think I

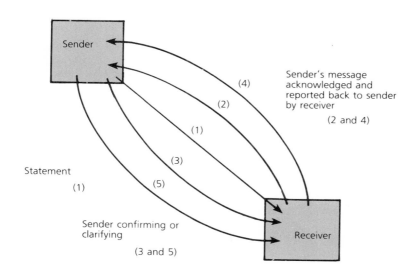

FIGURE 10.4
Shared meaning process.

got this job through my own efforts. I do appreciate your support, but I do not believe you pushed me to find this job. Sometimes, I think you exaggerate your part in some of my accomplishments. So, I'd appreciate it if you would be more considerate of me by being more accurate in what you say about me. What do you hear me saying?''

BRUCE: ''I hear you saying you always feel put down by me and I exaggerate when I talk about you.''

COLLEEN: ''No—that's not quite what I'm saying. I'm saying that I feel put down by you lately, when we're with Don and Connie, and sometimes I think you exaggerate your influence on my decisions and successes. What do you hear me saying?''

BRUCE: ''I hear you saying that lately, when we've been with Don and Connie, you've felt put down by some of the things I say about you and me. I also hear you saying that, at times, I exaggerate the influence I have on your decisions and accomplishments.''

COLLEEN: ''Yes. That's right.''

Bruce may now want to respond by sharing a meaning of his own. Colleen will then reflect her understanding of Bruce's message before she makes another response, if another response seems necessary, and so on until Bruce is satisfied that Colleen understands his message.

■ *Reflecting*   It is certainly not necessary to use the shared meaning process every time you talk. The process is useful when you have an important message for which a clear meaning is essential, or when you believe you are being misunderstood. The process is useful for several other reasons as well.

■ Resolving conflicts requires careful listening and honest responses.

- It is useful in helping the sender better understand his or her own message. Hearing our own messages reflected back may help us discover if we have left out any important parts and may help us better understand what we are trying to say. In this way, our partner acts as a consultant.
- The shared meaning process can be initiated by the listener as a way of letting the sender know he or she is listening and understanding.
- The process is useful if we want to use someone as a sounding board to clarify a personal concern. In this way, we may use another person to help us get in touch with our thoughts, feelings, and intentions.
- If we want to send an intimate positive message to someone who finds it difficult to receive compliments and who may negate such feedback, the shared meaning process will keep the message from being lost and will ensure that the receiver receives the message. For example, "I've been wanting to share something that I like about you for some time now, and I want to be certain you understand my meaning. I like your courage, strength, and tenderness. I've observed these qualities in you on many occasions, and I've admired them. What do you hear me saying?"
- The process is also useful and necessary when certain procedural steps to a situation need to be conveyed accurately. In cases where accurate communication is important, the use of the shared meaning process is essential.

If either the sender's or the receiver's intention is not to understand, the shared meaning process certainly will not work. For example, if the sender's intention is to prove to the receiver that he or she is not a good listener—if the sender is seeking to trap the receiver—the process is being used ineffectively and will not work. The process will not work when the receiver succumbs to the temptation to respond to the message by agreeing or disagreeing instead of reflecting the message to clarify understanding. This may be especially true if the issue is an emotional one. The process also may not work if the sender's message is too long and complicated. If the message is long, it may be better to break it into several small parts and several shared meanings. The process will not work if the sender forgets his or her original message and intent or changes the message when resending it.

In order for the process to work, it is important for the sender to remember: (1) to keep to the intent of the message, (2) to make brief statements, (3) to send the message clearly and directly, (4) to acknowledge the receiver's accurate reflection, and (5) not to change the original message. The receiver should remember: (1) to report back the message heard in his or her own words, (2) to refrain from responding to the message, and (3) to keep reporting back the message received until the sender confirms that it is correct.

## Common Styles

**Chit-Chat** There are several different styles of communication that we use each day (Miller, Nunnally, and Wackman, 1975). Sociable, friendly, and playful chit-chat is one style that adds lightness and cheerfulness to a complex and often serious world. This style of communication prevails in much of our everyday life—for example, with store clerks, waiters or waitresses, friends and acquaintances, fellow employees, and family members—where the absolute understanding of all our utterances is not crucial. A few examples of chit-chat are *passing time* ("How's your tennis game these days?"), *making simple observations* ("You look nice in your new dress"), *expressing amenities* ("I haven't seen you in a long time"), *joking, story telling, reporting information or events,* and *stating simple preferences and opinions.*

■ *Style for Effecting Change*    Another style is used when our intention is to effect a change in a particular situation, whether at work, at school, at home, or in organizations to which we belong. This style is used when we are *persuading* ("I know it is difficult but, let's try it again"), *directing* ("We've got to have this completed by 4:00 P.M."), *diagnosing* ("It appears that there is a problem in the accounting procedure"), and *evaluating* ("The results of our survey indicate that most of our members do not understand what we are hoping to accomplish"). This style also includes *selling, bargaining, promoting, advocating,* and *preaching.* This style of communication is quite useful and appropriate in our daily functioning. However, in attempts to resolve significant relationship issues, its use can be disastrous and usually results in misunderstandings and hurt feelings.

■ *Tentative and Speculative Style*    The intention of the first style we mentioned is to keep things light and smooth. The intention of the second style is to keep things smooth while attempting to effect change or gain control of a situation. A third style is quite useful when it is necessary to stop and deal carefully with an important and sensitive issue. This style works well in dealing with relationship issues. Its effectiveness results from its being a tentative and speculative style whereby we reflect on aspects surrounding the issue and explore possible alternative solutions. It is characterized by such statements as: "I'm wondering why you are so quiet today." "Perhaps one of the reasons our relationship works so well is that we have several common interests." "I guess you've been bored lately. Maybe we should make an effort to do more than sit around the house." This style is further enhanced when we speak for ourselves and use "I want" and "I feel" statements.

Communication is enhanced by the use of a variety of communication styles. People who use one style all the time may lose credibility. We become quite weary of the individual who is always joking, or reflecting, or serious.

REVIEW
QUESTIONS

Circle the correct italicized word for each of the following.

*17. Hearing/Listening* is the complex process of searching for meaning and understanding in a message.

*18.* When we appear to be listening but actually are thinking about something other than what the sender is sending, we are engaged in *passive/deceptive* listening.

*19.* Reik's reference to "listening with the third ear" refers to the importance of listening to the *meaning/voice* behind the words.

*20.* The *shared meaning/speculative* listening process is one of the best ways to check on the listener's understanding of the message.

*21.* The shared meaning process is essential in situations where *expedience/accuracy* in communication is crucial.

*22.* Conversation intended to *persuade/pass time* is associated with the style of communication termed chit-chat.

*23.* The style of communication designed to effect change is characterized by *bargaining and directing/speculating and joking.*

*24.* The style of communication that seems most effective for dealing with sensitive relationship issues is referred to as a *preaching/tentative* style.

*The answers to these review questions are on p. 355.*

## DISCUSSION: NONVERBAL COMMUNICATION

No discussion of effective communication would be complete without including **nonverbal communication** (Fast, 1970). Nonverbal communication has fascinated writers, sculptors, and painters for many centuries as they have attempted to describe the human condition. Often we communicate more of our messages nonverbally than verbally. An understanding of nonverbal communication may help us express ourselves more fully, and it certainly will help us become more effective listeners, as Reik suggests when he encourages us to seek greater understanding of the sender by "listening with the third ear."

### ■ Defining Nonverbal Communication

*Nonverbal communication* includes any means we may use to communicate other than spoken words. It is characterized by facial expressions, gestures, body position and movement, tone of voice, and general appearance. At times, nonverbal communication may be more effective than words—for example, in expressing despair at losing a loved one or the ecstasy of being in love. At these moments, the touch of a hand or an embrace may communicate what words cannot. Perhaps we have heard people say, "Words cannot describe the feelings I have at this moment." We know by the expression on their faces and the look in their eyes the genuineness of their feelings.

As babies, before we can use verbal language, we effectively use nonverbal communication to convey our desire for food, affection, warmth, and so on. It does not take parents long to learn to interpret this nonverbal behavior. As adults, we all use nonverbal means to let others know what we want and do not want. These nonverbal messages are often referred to as "good vibrations" or "bad vibrations." Strangers often find each other by nonverbal communication.

> A man and a woman are among the guests at a large party. Both are experiencing the loneliness of being in a crowd of strangers. As they look around the room for a familiar face, their eyes meet momentarily, then quickly move away. After a short time, their eyes meet again for a more prolonged look, then turn away again. She notices his neat appearance and the way he walks and stands. He notices the expressiveness of her eyes and her welcoming smile. As the evening progresses, they find it easier to establish eye contact. Having assigned meaning to each other's nonverbal messages, by evening's end, they make verbal contact.

### ■ *Nonverbal Meaning*
We learn the meaning of nonverbal communication from years of observing and modeling the behavior of others. Some nonverbal cues are quite obvious; others are subtle and go unnoticed by our conscious minds. Throughout our lives, we learn to attach verbal meaning to nonverbal behavior.

## ■ Kinesics

**WHAT DO YOU THINK?**

■ In what specific ways do you express yourself nonverbally?
■ What are some of the nonverbal behaviors that your parents used with you?
■ Do you use these same behaviors today?

The study of nonverbal communication was nearly nonexistent until early in this century. From 1914 to 1940, there was considerable interest in how people communicate by their facial expressions. Psychologists ran dozens of experiments. Similar interests were shown by anthropologists, who studied body movement. Edward Sapir (quoted in Davis, 1973, p. 2) wrote that, "We respond to gestures with an extreme alertness, and one might almost say, in accordance with an elaborate code that is written nowhere, known by none, and understood by all." Beginning in the 1950s, social scientists such as Edward T. Hall (1959) began to tackle the nonverbal phenomenon in a systematic way. The study of *kinesics* (see Chapter 6) has since become a popular topic for research among anthropologists, psychologists, sociologists, and psychiatrists.

*For another discussion of pupil dilation, see Chapter 6.*

### ■ *Communicating with the Eyes*

The eye has often been referred to as "the window to the soul." The eyes are easily observed and often very revealing. Physiologically the eye dilates in darkness to open its lens and receive more light. Psychological factors also affect the dilation of the eye. Hess (1965) contends that pupillary behavior accurately reflects differences in interests, emotions, and attitudes. His classic study reported that male homosexuals showed greater pupillary dilation in response to male pinups than to female pinups, and heterosexual males showed the opposite. Females showed pupillary dilation when looking at male pinups and even greater dilation when looking at pictures of mothers with babies. It was further found that heterosexual males showed much greater pupillary dilation when looking at female pinups with dilated eyes. It is interesting to note that for centuries women used the ancient drug belladonna to dilate their eyes, thus enhancing their attractiveness to members of the opposite sex.

### ■ *Communicating with Facial Expressions*

Harper, Weins, and Matarazzo (1978) believe that in many respects the face may be the single most important body area in the channeling of nonverbal communication. Other researchers have made the following comments about facial expression:

> *The face is rich in communicative potential. It is the primary site for communicating emotional states; it reflects interpersonal attitudes; it provides nonverbal feedback on the comments of others; and some say that, next to human speech, it is the primary source of giving information. For these reasons and because of its visibility, we pay a great deal of attention to what we see in the faces of others. (Knapp, 1972, pp. 68–69).*

> *Although there are only a few words to describe different facial behaviors (smile, frown, furrow, squint, and so on), man's facial muscles are sufficiently complex to allow more than a thousand different facial appearances; and the action of these muscles is so rapid, that these could all be shown in less than a few hours' time. (Ekman, Friesen, and Ellsworth, 1972, p. 1)*

> *Facial expression is perhaps the area in nonverbal communication research that comes closest to the more traditional concerns of psychology. The question of nature versus nurture as the origin of behavior is very much present here as is the issue of the components of human emotionality. (Weitz, 1974, p. 11).*

## CASE IN POINT
## Understanding Nonverbal Expression

Using Plutchik's (1962) categories, match the corresponding facial expression to each category from the following pictures:

Category _____    Category _____    Category _____

Well-documented research (Blurton-Jones, 1972; Eibl-Eibesfeldt, 1971) suggests that facial expressions may be an innate characteristic of humans that cuts across cultures, unlike most other aspects of human behavior, which are largely cultural.

Researchers have proposed several categories to describe the wide range of facial expressions. Plutchik (1962) has suggested the following categories: (1) coyness, happiness, joy; (2) surprise, amazement, astonishment; (3) apprehension, fear, terror; (4) pensiveness, sorrow, grief; (5) annoyance, anger, rage; (6) tiresomeness, disgust, loathing; (7) attentiveness, expectancy, anticipation; (8) acceptance, incorporation.

Take a few moments to look over this list of emotions. Make facial expressions that you believe communicate each emotion. Do your facial expressions accurately convey your feelings?

■ *Body Language*   In our society, certain gestures have agreed-on meanings—the hand wave (greeting), the hitchhiking thumb ("I want a ride"), the thumb up ("It looks good"), the thumb down ("It looks bad"), the salute ("Yes, sir"), the index finger and the thumb held to form an O ("It's okay"), the clenched fist (power or determination), and the open hand (welcoming acceptance). However, not all body signals are easy to interpret.

Fast (1970) suggests that when a woman sits with her legs parallel and slightly crossed at the ankles, it may indicate that she is an orderly person; but it is far more likely to be an affected positioning or the result of charm school training. Many believe that crossed legs or arms folded across the chest indicate rejection, discomfort, insecurity, or lack of trust. However, they may also mean that a person has simply changed position for the sake of comfort.

■ *Congruence*    In an earlier chapter, we used the term *congruence*, which also applies here. People often use *incongruent* body language, both consciously and unconsciously, so that their appearance is different from what they are thinking or feeling at the moment. How many times have you attempted to smile when you felt like crying, or stood rigid and erect to stop your knees from shaking, or frowned and shook your fist when you were actually frightened and felt like running away? If you are like most of us, you have probably exhibited incongruent behavior many times as a way of surviving situations in which you believed you could not allow your actual feelings or thoughts to be known.

Body language can be incongruent in other ways, as well. Many politicians adopt various body language generalities to achieve what we call *charisma*. John Kennedy had such charisma; no matter what he said, a few gestures, a correct posture, captivated his audience. Lyndon Johnson and Richard Nixon took lessons in effective body language to manipulate their audiences (Fast, 1970). Mimics such as David Frye and Rich Little have used the body language of many politicians and celebrities to entertain their audiences, who recognize each individual's specific mannerisms.

The real value of nonverbal communication is in the blending of all forms of communication—spoken words, tone of voice, eyes, facial expressions, hand movements, and body position. The message someone is conveying can most often be trusted when observations indicate that all methods of communication being used are congruent.

REVIEW
QUESTIONS

25. Any means used to communicate other than the spoken word is called _____ _____ .

26. Words may not be sufficient to describe our _____ _____ .

27. Much of our nonverbal communication is learned through observing and _____ _____ the behavior of others .

28. The _____ is often referred to as "the window to the soul."

29. Pupillary dilation may result from both _____ and _____ factors.

30. The _____ is thought to be the single most important body area for nonverbal communication.

31. Some people believe that crossed _____ and folded _____ are signs of uncomfortableness.

32. Communication is most effective when all levels are _____ _____ .

*The answers to these review questions are on page 355.*

# SUMMARY

- The process of sending and receiving messages is termed *communication*. Ineffective communication is the source of most misunderstandings and unresolved conflicts.

- Effective communication is an interchange of information, ideas, and perceptions with understanding as the goal.

- The awareness wheel is a five-dimensional communication aid that helps people send messages more accurately. The sender can focus on what he or she is doing, sensing, wanting, thinking, and/or feeling.

- It is important, when communicating, to differentiate between "I think" and "I feel" statements. Thinking statements refer to rational thoughts (head talk), while feeling statements refer to emotional sensations (gut talk).

- Assertive communication is more likely to take place when we take responsibility for our thoughts, feelings, and behaviors and speak only for ourselves. When we speak for ourselves, we are usually communicating more directly.

- Questions are often a form of indirect communication designed to expose, punish, criticize, probe, set up, trap, or disarm the other person.

- Cliches are another form of indirect communication that greatly diminish effective communication.

- Indirect and irresponsible communication is often used by people with weak or negative self-concepts. These people are afraid to own their thoughts or feelings for fear of being rejected or ridiculed by others. They also believe that what they have to say is of little value to others.

- Careful listening is as important as careful sending. Unfortunately, many of us are poor listeners because little attention has been given to the skill of listening. Pretending to listen when we are actually thinking about something else is often one of the cruelest ways we demonstrate our lack of respect for others.

- Effective listening is an active process. It includes not only carefully listening to the words, but "listening with the third ear"—that is, for the meaning behind the words or for what the sender is thinking and feeling.

- The shared meaning process is a reflective process designed to aid in the accurate understanding of important messages. It is especially useful in resolving relationship issues.

- There are various styles of communication: chit-chat is a light, everyday style mainly used to pass time; the style for effecting a change is used when our goal is to persuade, direct, diagnose, or evaluate a situation; and the tentative or speculative style is best used when we are seeking alternative solutions to a problem. It is important to use a variety of styles. We may lose our credibility with others if we always use the same one.

- Nonverbal communication often effectively communicates when words cannot. Facial expressions are believed by many to be the single most important body area for channeling nonverbal communication. We also use eyes, hands, and body positions to communicate many nonverbal signals to others.

- Communication is effective when all levels of communication, words and nonverbal behavior, are congruent. Understanding through congruence is the goal of communication.

## SELECTED READINGS

Goleman, D. "Can You Tell When Someone is Lying to You?" *Psychology Today* August, 1982, pp. 14–23. A provocative article that describes the verbal and nonverbal ways we might be able to determine whether someone is telling us the truth.

Harper, R. G.; Weins, A. N.; and Matarazzo, J. D. *Nonverbal Communication: The State of the Art.* New York: Wiley, 1978. One of the most scholarly and well-documented books on nonverbal communication; includes five major areas—facial expressions, nonverbal vocal behavior, kinesics, visual behavior, and proxemics.

Harrison, R. P. *Beyond Words: An Introduction to Nonverbal Communication*. Englewood Cliffs, N.J.: Prentice Hall, 1974. An introduction to the growing field of nonverbal communication. The focus is on the reader's own nonverbal behavior.

Lazarus, S. *Loud and Clear: A Guide to Effective Communication*. New York: Amacom, 1975. An entertaining guide to verbal and nonverbal communication. Included are ways to improve communication within the family and on the job.

Miller, S.; Nunnally, E. W.; and Wackman, D. B. *Alive and Aware: Improving Communication in Relationships*. Minneapolis: Interpersonal Communication Programs, 1975. A book to help you increase your awareness of how you communicate and relate to other significant people in your life. Included are specific skills for helping you express yourself to others.

Tubbs, S. L., and Moss, S. *Human Communication: An Interpersonal Perspective*. New York: Random House, 1974. An approach to communication that draws on existing knowledge from various sources, including anthropology, linguistics, psychology, sociology, and organizational theory.

Weisinger, H., and Lobsenz, N. M. *Nobody's Perfect: How to Give Criticism and Get Results*. New York: Warner Books, 1981. A book to help you learn how to give and take criticism in a way that does not diminish your self-esteem or the self-esteem of others.

## GLOSSARY

**assertive communication:** responsible communication that does not decrease our self-esteem or the self-esteem of others.

**communication:** the process of sending and receiving messages through which we and others are known and understood.

**indirect communications:** communication that involves ambiguous messages.

**mixed messages:** the result of incongruent communication.

**listening:** the process of integrating our past experience to help us interpret messages with meaning and understanding.

**nonverbal communication:** any means we use to communicate other than the spoken word.

## REFERENCES

Banet, A. G. "Thinking and Feeling." In *The 1973 Annual Handbook for Group Facilitators,* edited by J. E. Jones and J. W. Pfeiffer. Iowa City: University Associates, 1973.

Blurton-Jones, N. G., ed. *Ethological Studies of Child Behavior*. Cambridge, U. K.: Cambridge University Press, 1972.

Bower, S. A., and Bower, G. H. *Asserting Yourself: A Practical Guide for Positive Change*. Reading, Mass.: Addison-Wesley, 1976.

Chartier, M. R. "Five Components Contributing to Effective Interpersonal Communication." In *The 1974 Annual Handbook for Group Facilitators,* edited by J. E. Jones and J. W. Pfeiffer. Iowa City: University Associates, 1974.

Davis, F. *Inside Intuition: What We Know about Nonverbal Communication*. New York: McGraw-Hill, 1973.

Eibl-Eibesfeldt, I. "Transcultural Patterns of Ritualized Contact Behavior." In *Behavior and Environment: The Use of Space by Animals and Men,* edited by A. H. Esser. New York: Plenum Press, 1971.

Ekman, P.; Freisen, W. V.; and Ellsworth, P. *Emotion in the Human Face: Guidelines for Research and an Integration of the Findings*. New York: Pergamon Press, 1972.

Fast, J. *Body Language*. New York: M. Evans and Co., 1970.

Hall, E. T. *The Silent Language*. Greenwich, Conn.: Fawcett, 1959.

Harper, R. G.; Wiens, A. N.; and Matarazzo, J. D. *Nonverbal Communication: The State of the Art*. New York: Wiley, 1978.

Hess, E. H. "Attitude and Pupil Size." *Scientific American,* April 1965, pp. 46–54.

Knapp, M. L. "The Field of Nonverbal Communication: An Overview." In *On Speech Communication: An Anthropology of Contemporary Writings and Messages,* edited by C. J. Steward and B. Kendall. New York: Holt, Rinehart and Winston, 1972.

Miller, S.; Nunnally, E. W.; and Wackman, D. B. *Alive and Aware: Improving Communication in Relationships.* Minneapolis: Interpersonal Communication Programs, 1975.

Pfeiffer, J. W., and Jones, J. E. "Don't You Think That . . . ? An Experiential Lecture on Indirect and Direct Communication." In *The 1974 Annual Handbook for Group Facilitators,* edited by J. E. Jones and J. W. Pfeiffer. Iowa City: University Associates Publishers, 1974.

Plutchik, R. *The Emotions: Facts, Theories, and a New Model.* New York: Random House, 1962.

Reik, T. *Listening with the Third Ear.* New York: Pyramid, 1972.

Weitz, S., ed. *Nonverbal Communication: Readings with Commentary.* New York: Oxford University Press, 1974.

## ANSWERS TO REVIEW QUESTIONS

**Page 335.** *1.* T  *2.* F  *3.* T  *4.* F  *5.* T  *6.* T  *7.* T  *8.* T

**Page 342.** *9.* T  *10.* F  *11.* F  *12.* F  *13.* T  *14.* T *15.* T  *16.* F

**Page 348.** *17.* Listening  *18.* deceptive  *19.* meaning  *20.* shared meaning

*21.* accuracy  *22.* pass time  *23.* bargaining and directing  *24.* tentative

**Page 352.**  *25.* nonverbal communication  *26.* thoughts, feelings  *27.* modeling  *28.* eye  *29.* physiological, psychological  *30.* face  *31.* legs, arms  *32.* congruent

# 11

# INTIMACY

## FOCUS

Hi! How are you?
May I join you?
I am attracted to you.
I like you.
Share with me.
Accept me.
I care for you.
I want you.
I need you.
I love you.
Trust me.
Help me.
Want me.
Touch me.
Hold me.

These are phrases we often use to express our need for close human contact with others. This need for intimacy is one of our strongest needs. Maslow (1968) indicates that achieving deep intimacy is essential for us to become self-actualizing and fulfilled. Yet, psychotherapists believe that alienation is the most prevalent problem of our time.

The need for intimacy is recognized by TV, radio, magazine, and billboard advertisers. We are supposed to buy the toothpaste with "sex appeal" and our deodorant should make us smell like a "real" woman or a "real" man and should hold up under the stresses of everyday life. Perfumes and colognes are supposed to contain "secret formulas" intended to make us irresistible. Some of us even take ocean cruises or fly to exotic places where we expect to find, at last, that special person awaiting us with open arms.

The pursuit of intimacy is clearly one of our most important human undertakings. Because we place such great importance on intimacy, we often experience fear of failure when attempting to achieve it.

INTIMACY

## DISCUSSION:   EMOTIONAL INTIMACY

The need and desire for **intimacy** has been for centuries and continues to be a central theme in much of our poetry and literature. Movies and television programs nearly always portray some struggle concerning intimacy. Wars have been fought as a result of it. Without intimacy, it is doubtful that anyone can achieve a satisfying level of happiness. The potential each person has for achieving the rewards of intimacy is enormous. However, although essential for healthy adjustment, intimacy is extremely difficult to achieve.

### ■ Defining Intimacy

There are many definitions of intimacy. Some people think exclusively of the word *sex* when they hear the word *intimacy*. Others think that it is any significant interaction between two or more people. We like the definition proposed by Carolynne Kieffer (1977): "Intimacy is the experiencing of the essence of one's self in intense intellectual, physical, and/or emotional communion with another human being." We can qualify this definition further by adding Eric Berne's (1973) statement that intimacy is "the direct expression of meaningful emotions between individuals, without ulterior motives or reservations" (p. 322).

Achieving this degree of intimacy may seem quite difficult for many. We hope this chapter will help them. The most important thing to remember is that intimacy is a *process* that requires constant attention (Dahms, 1976). This means the expenditure of time and energy directed toward growth in the areas of **emotional intimacy** and **physical intimacy.** Emotional intimacy is never attained once and for all, just as we do not eat once and for all. Can you imagine what would happen to many of us if we ate food only as often as we are intimate with someone, or if the quality of food were only as good as the quality of our intimate relationships? We would either starve or die of malnutrition. The fact is that many are starving emotionally and some are literally dying (by suicide) because of a lack of intimacy.

*Emotional intimacy* is the highest level of intimacy and focuses on our feelings. It is evolved, maintained, and enhanced by constant evaluation and growth. Unless it is maintained by this process, it soon disappears. After emotional intimacy has been lost, physical intimacy will soon disappear as well.

> Two years to the day have passed since Sandra and Jerry were married. As they sit in the waiting area of the marriage counselor's office, both are thinking about what went wrong in their relationship. The thoughts are not new. They are often the topic of conversation, conversation that frequently ends in their blaming each other. The wedding seems like yesterday, and yet, so long ago. Both are wondering how the wonder and warmth of the first few months of their marriage could have disappeared from their lives. What should they have done to make their union more satisfying and more lasting?

### ■ Finding, Developing, and Maintaining Intimacy

Healthy emotional relationships are characterized by accessibility, naturalness, and nonpossessiveness. In order to find, develop, and maintain an intimate relationship, we must be available, available for daily contact with another person. If we make ourselves unavailable (through excessive privacy), we cannot develop an emotionally intimate relationship with anyone. Partners in satisfying intimate relationships are mutually accessible. Songs such as "I'll Be There" and "You've Got a Friend" describe this accessibility.

Finding the right person may seem difficult. The question is often asked, "How can we meet people who can and will help us fulfill our needs for intimacy?" The answer is that we must discard many of our beliefs and practices—the games we play, restrictive "shoulds" and "oughts," and superficial, one-line communication style—and risk the natural honest expression of our desire for intimate contact with the other person.

*See Chapter 10 for more about communication.*

Many believe it is quite risky to be honest with others, especially where intimate feelings are concerned. However, communicating naturally and honestly with a stranger is probably more frightening than risky. It may appear to be risky, though, because occasionally we have been rejected when we were natural and honest. Unfortunately, many of us tend to generalize our relatively few experiences of rejection to every new encounter. Consequently, we go through life concealing ourselves—a process that is ultimately self-defeating. Jourard and Whitman (1976) state, "We not only conceal ourselves; we also usually assume that the other person is in hiding. We are wary of him because we take it for granted that he too will frequently misrepresent his real feelings, his intentions or his past, since we so often are guilty of doing those very things ourselves" (p. 105). Because we believe the other person is also playing the game of "guess who I really am," we choose to be dishonest. It is no wonder that after a lifetime of hiding, many of us no longer know who we are.

**WHAT DO YOU THINK?**

■ What do you do when you suspect that someone you care about is being dishonest with you?

■ It is through the freedom of sharing our hopes, fears, joys, plans for the future, and memories of the past that we come to know each other intimately.

CASE IN POINT
## Experiencing Mutual Self-Disclosure

It is easier for some people to talk about mutual self-disclosure than to experience it. To experience it may involve some risk. We often overcome our uncomfortableness when we practice doing what we fear. So, let's practice some self-disclosure.

Find someone you care about and invite him or her to participate in the following mutual self-disclosure experience. Each of you should begin the experience by alternately sharing with each other your responses to the following:

- Some of my greatest joys have been...
- My saddest moment was...

- My hopes are...
- The most confusing time of my life was...
- My happiest moment was...
- My greatest fear is...
- I need...
- I want...
- I feel...

If you want, continue sharing more of yourself with your partner. Let your feelings take you where they want to go. Take the risk and enjoy yourself!

---

*For related discussions, see Chapter 3, on self-esteem, and Chapter 10, on communication.*

■ *Mutual Self-Disclosure*  Jourard (1974) believes that the only way people can come to know each other is through mutual self-disclosure. It is through the freedom of sharing our hopes, fears, joys, plans for the future, and memories of the past that we come to know each other intimately.

■ *Overcoming the Fear of Self-Disclosure*  The fear of not being loved is the main reason many of us are afraid of letting our "real selves" be known. It is here one of the problems with intimacy—fear of making contact—is connected with self-esteem. If our self-esteem is positive, we can realize that if someone knows who we really are and does not choose to become intimate with us, we would have been starved for intimacy in a relationship with that person anyway; the relationship would not have satisfied our needs. Thus, letting ourselves be known, even though it may result in rejection, is worth the apparent risk. Our efforts are not wasted, but rather are essential to finding a significant someone with whom we can grow naturally.

**WHAT DO YOU THINK?**

■ Have you been rejected by someone recently?

■ How do you respond to the feeling of rejection?

■ Growing Together Naturally

Growing together naturally means accepting one another as we are, not for our ability to change to meet the other's requirements (unless we wish to change) or to play expected roles. Rogers (1961) describes this naturalness by using the terms *acceptance, warmth, genuineness,* and *unconditional positive regard.*

■ *Acceptance*  Acceptance involves accepting all that we have become and all that the other person has become. This is essential to a relationship, because no one can change anything that has already happened. When we accept the sum of our combined experiences as having meaning and value, together we have life experience from which to grow and to become intimate with each other. Acceptance does not mean being attracted to another only until we find

out that there are differences between us (religion, family, status, goals, educational training, and so on).

■ *Warmth*   Warmth involves conveying our acceptance of another in a way
that encourages that person to feel comfortable enough to express his or her
innermost feelings. In natural relationships, feelings are of ultimate importance
and are highly respected. Feelings represent conscious, current, yet changing
sensations that are responses to what has happened, is happening, and will
happen in our lives. They usually are more accurate and personalized pieces of
information about ourselves than are our thoughts. Failure to express our feelings in a potentially intimate relationship usually means we will not achieve
intimacy.

*See Chapter 6 on the
emotional self.*

■ *Genuineness*   Genuineness means real, honest, and accurate expression of ourselves to the other in words and behavior. When we are genuine, other people
love us for being who we are instead of for matching some contrived image. It
is sad when we realize that we have allowed someone to love the person we
would like to be rather than the person we are. As much as we might like to,
we cannot maintain a facade indefinitely. Eventually, deception takes its toll on
us, our partner, and our potentially intimate relationship.

■ *Unconditional Positive Regard*   Unconditional positive regard means accepting, supporting, and respecting the worth of the other without reservation. Our
caring and concern do not change because the other person is not what we
would like him or her to be.

*For more about this
subject, see Chapter 3.*

To grow naturally in an intimate relationship, then, the individuals involved
must accept all of what they have been, what they are, and what they have the
potential to become, both separately and together. As you may see, there is no
room for possessiveness in an intimate relationship.

■ *The Absence of Possessiveness*   Caring on the highest level brings delight in the
independence of others, not in the possession of them (Dahms, 1976). To want
to possess another person usually means that we want to own, direct, and control
that person for our own needs and purposes, out of our own insecurity.

Our insecurity results in the fear of losing our hold on the other. However,
no healthy individual can stand to be suffocated, suppressed, and held back by
possessiveness. The irony is that in attempting to possess the other, we can drive
the other away, losing what we hoped to keep through our possessive behavior.
As one person put it, "I want to be loved and I want to be free. Give me the
freedom to breathe and grow and I probably will be with you for a long time,
even forever. Try to possess and control me and I will be gone." Buscaglia
(1972) states, "Love can only be given, expressed freely. It can't be captured
or held, for it's neither there to tie nor to hold. Love is trusting, accepting, and
believing, without guarantee" (p. 107).

Rick believed his relationship with Monique was a dream come true. Many
times he wondered what she saw in him. She was popular, attractive, and a
straight A student. Rick considered himself lucky indeed. Unfortunately, as time
passed, Rick began to behave in jealous and possessive ways. When Monique

wanted to spend time with some of her friends, Rick would become angry and resentful. Even though he felt badly about his behavior, he did not seem able to contain his feelings. Monique, realizing that her freedom was severely restricted by Rick's behavior, decided to end their relationship.

Emotional intimacy can only exist when we are nonpossessive. To share our lives with another significant person without possessiveness may be a big order for many of us. However, unless we can be secure enough in our own self-esteem to avoid attempting to possess other persons, we may destroy many potentially intimate relationships.

In summary, remembering two major points can significantly increase our chances and capacity for intimacy:

- First, we must trust our understanding of ourselves, our urges, desires, needs, wants, and so on and trust the humanness of the other person.
- Second, we must take the perceived risk of practicing honest and accurate self-disclosure with our potentially intimate partner. Taking this risk may ultimately invite our significant other to take a similar risk. In this way, we each let our needs be known to the other.

REVIEW
QUESTIONS

1. Maslow indicates that achieving deep intimacy is _____ in order to become _____ and fulfilled.

2. _____ is believed by some to be the most prevalent problem of our time.

3. Intimacy is the experiencing of intense _____ , _____ , and/or _____ communion with another person.

4. _____ _____ is the highest level of intimacy and focuses on our _____ .

5. Jourard believes that the only way people can become intimate is through mutual _____ .

6. Three characteristics of a healthy emotional relationship are_____ , _____ , and _____ .

7. Rogers describes naturalness in a relationship as _____ , _____ , _____ and _____ .

*The answers to these reveiw questions are found on page 381.*

## DISCUSSION: PHYSICAL INTIMACY

The need for physical intimacy is basic to all human beings. To be close, to be touched, to feel the warmth and life of another human being brings vibrant sensations into our awareness from deep inside. An organization concerned with parental effectiveness and child development distributes a bumper sticker that asks, "Have you hugged your kid today?" No one seems to object to hugging

■ To be close, to be touched, to feel the warmth and life of another human being . . .

children. Perhaps we need bumper stickers that ask, "Have you hugged your mate, your fellow worker, your boss, or anyone today?"

## ■ The Need to Touch

We have been taught verbally and through observation that touching is reserved, if it is to be done at all, for a select few and only under special circumstances such as greetings, good-byes, and comforting of the bereaved at funerals. Americans are known the world over as a reserved and no-touch society (Hartman, 1970). This is perhaps due in part to the taboos on touching that grew out of a fear closely associated with the various denominations of the Christian tradition—the fear of bodily pleasures. The anthropologist Ashley Montagu (1978) believes that "Two of the negative achievements of Christianity have been to make a sin of tactual pleasures, and by the repression of sex, to make it an obsession" (p. 249).

Physical intimacy draws strong reactions from some people. It is laden with taboos, guilt feelings, distortions of fact, myths, and so on. These impediments to intimacy, combined with fears concerning body image and rejection, cause some people to become so physically rigid that if someone touches them, they shudder in fear or embarrassment.

WHAT DO YOU THINK?
■ How do you feel about touching others?
■ How do you feel about being touched?
■ When is touching appropriate behavior for you?

A young college professor one day decided to use a touching exercise with his class in human relations. After having discussed the importance of touching in interpersonal relationships, he explained that the exercise would be conducted in the classroom, and that students who felt too uncomfortable to participate could move to the periphery of the room. To his surprise, over half the class moved to the outside of the room, giggling and embarrassed at the thought of touching some of their classmates.

The importance of physical intimacy (touching) begins before conscious memory, when the fetus is nestled in the mother's womb and the developing nervous system begins recording sensations of touch and movement.

> *These then, are our first real experiences of life—floating in a warm fluid, curling inside a total embrace, swaying to the undulations of the moving body and hearing the beat of the pulsing heart. Our prolonged exposure to these sensations in the absence of other competing stimuli leaves a lasting impression on our brains, an impression that spells security, comfort and passivity. (Morris, 1971, p. 15)*

These beginnings of intimacy are interrupted by the moment of birth as we experience for the first time a loss of intimate body contact. What happens from this point on in our lives determines many things, including our attitudes, behaviors, feelings, and capacity for experiencing physical intimacy. According to Montagu, the newborn looks forward to "a continuation of that life in the womb—to a womb with a view—before it was so catastrophically interrupted by the birth process" (p. 60). For most of us, the physical contact so important before birth continues to be important throughout our lives.

■ *Therapeutic Touch*    The healing potential of **therapeutic touch** has been known since ancient times, as in the ancient practice of laying on hands. Today, touching is proving to be a useful adjunct to orthodox nursing practice. It is taught as part of the Master's curriculum in nursing at New York University, is the subject of continuing education courses and workshops at universities throughout the United States, and is part of in-service programs for nurses at several hospitals around the country.

*See Chapter 7, on stress, for related topics.*

Basic to therapeutic touch is the concept that the body has an excess of energy (Krieger, Peper, and Ancoli, 1979). The person who administers therapeutic touch tries to direct his or her own excess energies for the use of the ill person, whose energy state can be thought of as less than optimal. This is accomplished

## CASE IN POINT
## Therapeutic Touch

The possible effects of therapeutic touch are illustrated by a report on three patient volunteers: a man in his sixties with severe neck and back pain who for several years had walked only with the aid of crutches; a thirty-year-old woman with a history of fibroid tumors; and a young woman in her twenties with a history of severe, chronic migraine headaches.

After each patient had received brief applications of therapeutic touch on two consecutive days, the man walked out of the laboratory, down the stairs, and out onto the street carrying his crutches under his arm. The thirty-year-old woman's fibroid tumors were no longer observable, and the woman in her twenties reported that her headaches had diminished. Each patient reported relaxation during therapeutic touch and physiological indices indicated that the subjects were indeed relaxed (Krieger, Peper, and Anconi, 1979).

■ In the process of touching, there appears to be a transfer of energy from one person to another.

by the therapist's lightly placing the palms of both hands over and around the area of illness. In the process of touching, it appears that a transfer of energy may take place that helps the patient to repattern his or her energy level to a state comparable to that of the healer.

■ *The Mutual Experience of Touch*   It appears that touching is as important as being touched. In fact, researchers in therapeutic touch are directing their attention to the effects on the therapist as well as the effects on the patient. Perhaps the effect is similar to the experience expressed by Walter Ong (1967), who writes, "touch involves my own subjectivity more than any other sense. When I feel this objective something 'out there,' beyond the bounds of my body, I also at the same instant experience my own self. I feel other and self simultaneously" (pp. 169–170). To demonstrate this phenomenon, place one of your hands in an open position in front of you. Do you feel your hand? Now touch the hand you are holding in front of you with your other hand. You feel both hands. In the same way, when you touch another person, you also feel yourself.

Sometimes you may feel awkward when touching another, especially if you really care about that person. Most of us have experienced this awkwardness. Perhaps you are not sure of the other person's response. Comfort usually comes from knowing the other person feels the same as you. One of the ways to test this is to risk disclosing your fear and awkwardness to your partner or potential partner. You may discover that your fear and awkwardness will soon diminish.

It is important to begin overcoming fear and awkwardness by slowly exposing yourself to the things you fear.

Sometimes our touching may be misinterpreted as an indication that we seek sexual contact. If that happens, we should let the other person know that physical intimacy and touching have benefits in addition to those related to sexual encounter. There is much to be experienced and learned about ourselves and others by touching, stroking, caressing, massaging, hugging, and holding without the contact's ending necessarily in sexual intercourse. When attempting to avoid sending erroneous messages, consider the appropriateness of the type of touch to the situation. For example, if our intention is to communicate that we have missed someone and are glad to see him or her, it would be inappropriate to demonstrate our intention by touching the other person on an area of the body heretofore designated as a zone of sexual arousal. It may be equally inappropriate, when engaged in the process of sexual arousal with another person, to avoid touching the areas of the body that bring about sexual pleasure and to continually pat the person on the arm instead.

*See Chapter 10 for more about mixed messages.*

### ■ Sexual Intimacy

Sex is an emotional necessity for some individuals, but not all. Martin Herbert (1970) suggests that sexual activity is associated with emotional meanings that may be different for some human beings than for others. In one person's formula, sex equals the ultimate expression of love and, in this way, is an emotional necessity. For others, it seems to be more a biological function expressed without emotional involvement. A lifetime of sexual abstinence may be the choice of others.

True sexual intimacy is the physical parallel of emotional intimacy. It is body conversation in which two people become part of each other, in a sense, both physically and psychologically. Their thinking, emotional expression, and sexual behavior are unified. Sexual intimacy can often give us the courage to disclose ourselves emotionally even more intimately to the other person. In this way, our emotionally intimate relationship continues to grow and have meaning for each of us.

**WHAT DO YOU THINK?**

■ What are some of your beliefs about sexuality?

■ How appropriate are these beliefs at this time in your life?

### ■ *Sexual Attitudes*

It did not take long for our society, founded primarily on commercial values, to discover the usefulness of a powerful motivator like sex for advertising. Advertisers equate sex appeal with personal success, happiness, and affluence. Countless films, magazine stories, and television programs associate love, particularly romantic love, with sexual attraction. While the Victorian morality treated sexual relations as nearly subhuman and sinful, the new fashionable sexual ideology creates taboos at the other extreme, focusing on the horrors of sexual abstinence and sexual inadequacy. Marin (1983) writes that the "commercialization of sex now destroys true feelings as badly as traditional taboos did."

One of the unfortunate by-products of the new sexual ideology is the creation of unrealistic standards governing sexual functioning. With this new set of standards, we are often unduly concerned about whether we are long enough, big enough, deep enough, tight enough, fast enough, slow enough, attractive enough, tall enough, or good enough. "For many people, sex has become a labor rather than an adventure: the immense cultural pressure to do—whether spontaneously or not—the 'right' thing can be exhausting and destructive" (Marin, 1983). Realizing our needs and our confusion, writers have offered sex manual after sex manual to teach "accurate" techniques. Often, the need for orgasm is made the priority in intimate relationships; and the achievement of simultaneous, mutual orgasm "the crowning glory." The other intimate aspects of a relationship frequently are omitted. Sexual expression may become a drudgery focused on achievement rather than on joyful pleasure.

We certainly need to know something about how to have sexual intercourse with another person. However, the overemphasis on technique in sexual intimacy can make for a mechanistic attitude toward lovemaking and can support feelings of alienation, feelings of loneliness, and the depersonalization—the feeling of being inadequate as a person—that is one of the fundamental problems of our time (May, 1967).

■ *Sexual Decision Making*    The decisions about when and with whom to have a sexual relationship are important ones. The current "sexual freedom" has made these decisions more difficult than in the past. This is due in part to the apparent need to decide earlier and more often than in previous generations. Adolescents and young adults are often under pressure to engage in sexual relations, even though they may not be ready. Choices concerning how and when to include sex in their lives are numerous. Wrightsman (1977) believes that the conflict that results from these numerous choices is often resolved in favor of having sexual relations, but within the context of a loving relationship. Most people continue to believe that genuine affection must be present for sex to be enjoyed. After sex without affection, they often feel cheapened and disgusted with themselves and their partners.

Whether to have sexual relations, and with whom, involve very personal decisions. Each person must make his or her own decisions about sex and assume responsibility for them. Of greatest consequence to all concerned is the responsibility for pregnancies that may result from sexual involvement.

> Kim, an eighteen-year-old college freshman, has not experienced sexual intercourse. Although she has not lacked opportunities, she has chosen to wait for this experience until she feels an emotional attachment to the other person. She has dated many males of varying degree of maturity, but none has stimulated her to want to pursue a physically intimate relationship. Unfortunately, most of the males she has dated appear by their actions to want a physical relationship as a prerequisite to an emotional relationship. This has resulted in her dating an individual one or two times at most, certainly not enough time to get to know anyone on an emotional level. Although disappointed with her experiences and at times uncertain about her own standards for intimacy, Kim still intends to wait until her feelings for someone can justify a sexual relationship.

■ The Decision about Birth Control

Abstinence, abortion, contraception, sterilization, and children constitute the range of choices available to those sexually active during their fertile years. Birth and birth control are the vital concerns of individuals, religious and racial com-

WHAT DO YOU THINK?

■ How do the present sexual standards affect your personal feelings and your sexuality?

*For more information about the physical aspects of sexuality, see Chapter 4.*

munities, and nation states. In the United States, until recently, religion and the state stood together to restrict the practice of birth control, limiting even the dissemination of information under obscenity laws. Today, the government, religious groups, and political parties are torn from within. Some advocate providing free information, contraception, and abortion on request. Others condemn the active role of religion or the state in such activity. They work for the restriction or abolition of these practices.

A landmark decision in this area came in 1973, when the U.S. Supreme Court ruled that up to the end of the third month, the decision whether to terminate a pregnancy is entirely up to the woman. Women's rights groups have organized in an attempt to broaden this legal position, while the other extreme, right-to-life groups attempt to see it overturned. After the third month, rape, incest, the mental or physical health of the mother, or a potential genetic abnormality of the fetus are factors that determine the legal possibility of abortion.

Since 1973, the Supreme Court has made additional rulings on abortion:

- 1975—All abortions must be performed by a licensed physician.
- 1979—Minors seeking abortion must have parental consent or the consent of a local court.
- 1980—Abortion is a medical procedure excluded from payment by medicaid.
- 1983—State and local laws that intimidate women who seek abortions and doctors who perform abortions are unconstitutional (Hunter, 1983).

■ *Methods of Contraception*    There is almost no controversy over the right of couples to prevent conception. Appropriate methods are still debated, though, with the Roman Catholic hierarchy supporting **abstinence.** This implies refraining from sexual intercourse outside marriage and periodically refraining from intercourse during marriage by use of the *rhythm method.* In 1965, the rhythm method was the leading contraceptive method among Catholic couples. By 1976, however, the leading contraceptive among Catholics was the pill (33 percent). The difference between percentages of Protestant and Catholic couples who used the pill had disappeared (Lederer, 1983).

Table 11.1 gives an overview of some common methods of contraception. Consultation with all concerned, including medical personnel, is highly recommended prior to selection of a method or combination of methods.

New contraceptive methods are becoming available.Researchers are testing different delivery systems for the pill. Incisions, injections, and vaginal insertions are being tried to produce longer effects with less introduction of hormones. A birth-control pill for males is under study but is not yet an acceptable alternative. New pills for use with the rhythm method are available that have very low amounts of hormones, and thus less noxious side effects and less danger to the user. The function of these pills is to make the menstrual cycle regular and predictable. This allows a few days of abstinence each month to be, in theory, a highly effective birth-control practice. Since it is not morally objectionable to take the pill for the purpose of regulating the menstrual cycle, some believe this method falls within the acceptable boundaries of the Roman Catholic Church's doctrines.

TABLE 11.1

Summary of Contraceptive Methods

| METHOD | USER | EFFECTIVENESS | ADVANTAGES | DISADVANTAGES |
|---|---|---|---|---|
| Birth-control pill | Female | 98%[a] | Easy to use | Side effects; daily attention required; continual cost |
| IUD | Female | 95%[a] | Requires little attention; no expense after initial insertion | Side effects, particularly increased bleeding; possible expulsion |
| Condom | Male | 88–92%[a] | Easy to use; helps prevent venereal disease | Interruption of sexual activity; possible impairment of gratification; repeated cost |
| Diaphragm with cream and jelly | Female | 82–90%[a] | Small initial cost | Repeated insertion and removal |
| Vaginal sponge | Female | 85%[a] | No prescription; allows spontaneity; effective for 24 hours | Repeated cost; absorbs vaginal secretions |
| Cervical cap | Female | [b] | Worn 2–3 weeks; no additional expense after initial fitting | Does not fit all women; potential insertion problems |
| Spermicidal foam, cream, and suppositories | Female | 84%[c] | Easy to use; no prescription | Messy; irritating to some; continual expense |
| Rhythm | Female | 75–88%[a,d] | No cost; acceptable to Roman Catholic Church | Requires motivation, cooperation, intelligence; useless with irregular cycles and during postpartum period |
| Withdrawal | Male | 8–40%[e,f] | No cost or preparation | Requires timing; interrupts sexual activity; causes frustration |
| Douche | Female | 30–36%[e] | Inexpensive | Inconvenient; possibly irritating |

[a] "Update on Contraceptives: What's Safe? Effective? Convenient?" Changing Times, October 1983, pp. 72–76.

[b] This method has not been used extensively in the United States but is used in Europe. No information is presently available on the degree of effectiveness.

[c] Planned Parenthood Federation of America, Guide to Birth Control Methods: Six Accepted Methods of Contraception Washington, D.C.: (Planned Parenthood Federation of America, 1983).

[d] The wide range in percentage of effectiveness may be due to uncontrolled variables.

[e] Life and Health, Del Mar, Calif.: CRM Books, 1972, pp. 256–257, Marriage, the Family, and Personal Fulfillment (Englewood Cliffs, N.J.: Prentice-Hall, 1975).

[f] The wide range of effectiveness may be due to the fact that a male may release semen that contains sperm before climax. Also, this method requires a great deal of self-control and timing, since natural impulse during the sex act is to thrust deeper. This method is very risky.

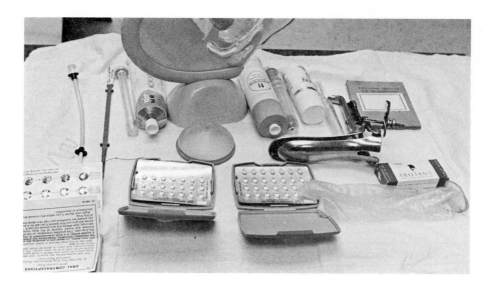

■ Contraceptive
devices.

**Sterilization** is another option available to both men and women. It is effective, safe, and has negligible short-term aftereffects. This may account for its being the favorite form of birth-control in the United States (Colen, 1983). In 1983, it was estimated that 14 percent of the male population and 15 percent of the female population chose sterilization as a birth-control method (Lederer, 1983).

In both the *vasectomy* (male procedure) and the *tubal ligation* (female procedure), the ducts in which the sperm or egg travels are tied, cut, plugged, or burned (cauterized), thus preventing conception. The vasectomy can be done in a physician's office (usually a urologist) in approximately fifteen minutes with relatively little pain or discomfort. An incision is made in the scrotum and the vas deferens (the tubes that carry the sperm) are cut and tied off. A tubal ligation, unless performed as part of a cesarean-section birth, is usually performed with the aid of a small, flexible, telescope-like instrument called a *laparoscope*. A small incision is made in the woman's abdomen. Using the laparoscope as a guide, the physician makes several burns in the fallopian tubes. This type of procedure is commonly referred to as "band-aid surgery." Attempts now are being made to block tubes with substances that can later be absorbed into the body or removed, to install valves that may later be opened, or through surgery to rejoin severed tubes so as to overcome the irreversibility of sterilization.

**Abortion**, the destruction of the fetus, is an ancient but radical method to prevent live birth after conception. It is considered a method of last resort, even by those who believe in abortion on demand. Recent Supreme Court decisions on abortion have already been discussed. Today the vast majority of legal abortions are performed under the mental health provisions of state statutes. Studies on the effect on mental health of having an abortion are not conclusive; however, in general, the vast majority of women who have abortions seem not to have severe, long-term psychological problems. According to one source, in the United States, approximately 6 percent seek psychological help (Guttmacher, 1973). Physical health is not at risk if the woman is young, the abortion is performed during the first twelve weeks, and the medical practitioner is trained and experienced. Abortion appears to be on the increase as a method of birth control. Studies conducted by the Alan Guttmacher Institute indicate that more than half of all the pregnancies in the United States are unintended and nearly half of these end in abortion (Cohen, 1983).

The question is often asked, "Why is abortion on the increase when contraceptive information and materials are so widely available?" According to the Guttmacher Institute, fear and confusion cause many women, especially under age twenty-five, to shun contraceptives or use them sporadically. Headlines slanted toward the harmful effects of some contraceptives have made many women stop using them. Unfortunately, a lack of information about contraceptives often leads to more dangerous solutions to the problem of unwanted pregnancy. In addition, the Guttmacher studies indicate that the pill "prevents more illness than it causes." The 500 deaths attributed to pill use are offset statistically by approximately 850 ovarian cancer deaths prevented by the pill (Cohen, 1983).

Contraception also may present a problem because of prevailing attitudes toward morality and sexuality. Today, the burden of contraception falls heavily on the woman. To be successful, women often are required to plan a deliberate routine prior to intercourse. This makes it necessary for women to recognize and accept their sexual impulses (and for men to be knowledgeable partners). Unfortunately, some find this psychologically difficult. Many unmarried couples are uninformed; others rationalize their sexual behavior by saying it results from loss of control, and this is incompatible with planning. Married couples (who have the majority of abortions) may have moral, economic, or aesthetic concerns about contraception, or they may believe that planning robs sex of its spontaneity.

In spite of these problems with contraception, most people want to use the best method of birth control. Unfortunately, there is no best method at present. Individual differences, including age, medical history, moral conviction, level of education, rate and range of sexual activity, and a host of similar variables must be taken into consideration in making the decision. Because this choice involves sensitivities and emotional components, it can seldom be made in isolation. Once a decision to limit conception is made, the legal, moral, and aesthetic responsibility for such a decision cannot be evaded by either partner. Such questions go far beyond the anatomy and physiology of sexuality and profoundly affect our psychological adjustment.

To accept our sexual self and to incorporate this aspect of our identity into a satisfying and responsible life style are two of the developmental tasks that confront each of us as we move into physical and social maturity. No tasks are more worthy of our best efforts.

REVIEW
QUESTIONS

8. Physical intimacy is essential only to some people. T F

9. Taboos surrounding touching often present problems for our expressions of physical intimacy. T F

10. There is evidence to support the belief that touch may have therapeutic healing potential. T F

11. Sex is an emotional necessity for everyone. T F

12. Orgasm is the goal each time we have sexual intercourse. T F

*13.* The only method of contraception that meets the moral code of the Catholic Church is sterilization.  T  F

*14.* Due to the emotional trauma of abortion, most women seek professional psychological assistance after having an abortion.  T  F

*15.* The development of satisfactory contraceptives has resulted in a rapid decline in the number of abortions in the United States.  T  F

*The answers to these review questions are on page 381.*

## DISCUSSION: SOURCES FOR INTIMACY

Our need for intimacy would go unmet if it were not for others. We are often the recipients of their expressions of intimacy, and we learn to model the behavior they use to find intimacy with others. Throughout life, our major sources are family, marriage or cohabitation, and friends.

### ■ Family Intimacy

Intimate contact ideally is found within the family unit. Newborn infants are totally dependent on adults (usually parents) for physical and emotional survival. Their physical needs are usually met with great care. Most children in our society grow up with proper nutrition and exercise. Monitoring the quality of this care is relatively easy for parents and others. Less obvious is the quality of care focused on emotional growth. Children need a warm, loving, touching, and

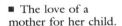

■ The love of a mother for her child.

stable environment. This means that the healthy, successful family provides opportunities for physical and emotional closeness for the infant.

### ■ Types of Intimacy

Harry F. Harlow (1971) describes five types of intimacy that can be provided by the family: **maternal love, infant love, peer love, heterosexual love,** and **paternal love.**

*See Erikson's psychosocial stages of development as described in Chapter 8.*

■ *Maternal Love*  The first of the intimacy systems is maternal love, the love of the mother for the child. The response of a mother to her newborn depends on many personality and cultural variables. Harlow suggests, "If the infant is one she wanted, she may view it with love and affection and even consider it beautiful—truly a triumph of mind over matter. However, if she has any doubts or conflicts about her anguished achievement, her response may be one of complete indifference" (p. 7). Many mothers have little maternal feeling until their infants have matured to the point where they begin to interact with their mothers. When the infant begins to coo and smile in response to maternal vocalizations or manipulations, the mother responds with maternal love.

During the first month of life, most mothers hold their babies in a close face-to-face position or cradled within their arms. This position provides maximum body contact between the mother and the infant. The maternal attachment to the infant usually continues to intensify as the infant becomes more responsive.

Freud concluded that motherhood was the ultimate—and the only—source of affection. However, it now appears that maternal affection, although extremely important, is only part of the process of finding intimacy.

*Read more about Freud in Chapter 2.*

■ The family is our greatest potential source of love and intimacy.

■ *Infant Love*    Infant love, which is the love of the baby for the mother, has often been confused with maternal love. These two types of intimacy operate simultaneously and often are difficult to separate. For example, when we consider a mother breastfeeding her newborn infant, it is impossible to determine the relative contribution of the nursing to each. The difference is that the mother is aware of the infant's existence and directs her affection to the infant. The infant, however, is entirely indiscriminate at birth and can form an attachment to any maternal figure. This beginning stage is characterized by physical sensations and satisfactions and is maintained by the pleasures of food and relief of organic tensions (hunger and physical discomfort).

The next stage of infant love is characterized by the comfort and attachment the infant feels toward the mother. In this stage, which lasts six months or longer, the infant is totally dependent on the mother. The next stage in infant love is the stage of solace and security. Here, the infant begins to explore the surroundings, but often returns to the mother for care and comfort. Assurances and reassurances are important to the infant as a bond of safety and security develops with the mother.

■ *Peer Love*    Peer love is probably the most important development provided and encouraged by the emotionally healthy and successful family. The development of peer love has long-range effects on our personal and social adjustment, for the ability to develop and maintain lasting friendships is important to the enhancement of our self-esteem and the esteem in which we hold others. This type of intimacy develops from interaction with other babies to social relationships with other children through preadolescence, adolescence, and adulthood. Peer relationships may exist between members of the same sex or opposite sexes. We can perhaps remember the importance of being asked to come out to play by other children. Our development during this stage is crucial to our preparation for the future requirements of heterosexual and adult attachments.

■ *Heterosexual Love*    Heterosexual intimacy typically emerges at puberty and reaches full expression by late adolescence. Many of our feelings, attitudes, and behaviors about heterosexual love develop from observation of other family members, as when we see our mothers and fathers expressing physical and emotional intimacy with each other. The related values, attitudes, and behaviors that comprise male and female roles and social status develop gradually from infancy onward. The teachings and experiences of the family that focus on heterosexual intimacy have far-reaching effects, therefore, the family must provide accurate information in both its teaching and its modeling of satisfying intimacy.

■ *Paternal Love*    *Paternal love* is the love of the father for the child. Typically, the father provides the growing child with experiential and cultural training. Think about what you learned from your father that may be of value to you today. Perhaps he taught you how to catch a ball, how to dance, or how to establish a savings account. Many of our survival skills are taught to us by our fathers.

There seems to be an increasing awareness of the importance of intimacy in the rearing of children. Organizations such as the Parent Effectiveness Training Program offer valuable assistance for parents and prospective parents. A school in California teaches parents and children together how to make their relationships more effective and fulfilling. Similar programs are being offered at YMCAs and YWCAs throughout the country.

The maintenance of close social bonds, the formation of gender identification, and the acceptance and adoption of sex roles are important provisions of the family. Our experiences in the family are extremely important to our future success with significant intimate relationships.

## ■ Marital Intimacy

Howard and Charlotte Clinebell (1970) believe that "intimacy in marriage can bring shared ecstasy, mutual satisfaction, well-being, joy, serenity, and peace" (p. ix). In short, marriage ideally can satisfy most of our needs for intimacy. Marriage has many untapped potentialities for those who are willing to learn and grow together toward the fulfillment of their individual and mutual needs. Each of us has a powerful longing for a meaningful relationship with at least one other person. This longing, either conscious or unconscious, is often felt as loneliness, which can only be relieved by the interpersonal satisfaction derived from an intimate relationship. Gibson Winter (1958) states, "Marriage is intended to be an intimate relationship. This is the one opportunity for sharing one's whole life with another person" (p. 71).

The permanency of marriage to one mate or the reliance on one mate for a lifetime, a belief inherited from Judeo-Christian tradition, appears for many to be rapidly becoming a thing of the past. To believe that one person can provide us with all we need for the development of self-esteem, intimacy, and personal growth may seem quite unrealistic to some. Further, to believe that every individual should stay attached emotionally and physically to another for a lifetime regardless of needs and growth may suggest that people are static and do not change. On the contrary, we know that people do change and have the capacity to do so throughout their lives. We also know that two people can choose to grow and change together for a lifetime and continue to meet each other's needs. Success in marriage greatly depends on the value we place on ourselves, our partners, and the concept of marriage. Those of us who view marriage as one of our highest-priority values will expend great effort in maintaining a satisfying union with our partners. Those of us who do not value marriage highly will tend to discard it and our partners, as we do many other things that lose their appeal or develop problems.

## ■ Alternatives to Marriage

There are several alternatives to marriage. **Cohabitation** (living together as mates without being legally married) is quite common in our society among all age groups. The acceptance of cohabitation has no doubt been aided by Robert H. Rimmer's novel *The Harrad Experiment* (1966). When it was published, this novel was the talk of sociologists, psychologists, and educators and a cause of

**WHAT DO YOU THINK?**

■ What experiences with intimacy do you remember from your childhood?
■ Why do you think these recollections are important to you?

**WHAT DO YOU THINK?**

■ What value do you place on marriage?
■ What beliefs do you hold about marriage?

concern for many parents. Rimmer advocated experimental cohabitation as part of the curriculum of higher education. He suggested that men and women could best learn about intimacy by experimentally living together.

Jennifer and Scott had been dating since their senior year in high school. Upon graduation, they applied for admission to the same colleges, hoping at least one college would accept both of them. Their hopes were realized, and they went away to college together. The college they attended required all freshman students to live on campus in dormitories. After the first year, students were permitted to live off campus and were even encouraged to do so because of limited campus housing. Scott and Jennifer often discussed their future living arrangements, and increasingly so as the freshman year came to a close. Many freshman couples had decided to live together the following year, a decision that Jennifer began to favor. Scott wanted to live with Jennifer but was afraid of what his parents might say. Jennifer thought her parents would understand, since she and Scott had been dating for over two years. The decision became a source of conflict between them.

Finally, Scott agreed, but only if neither would tell their parents about the arrangement. Although Jennifer wanted to tell her parents, Scott was afraid they might tell his parents. Before they left for summer break, Jennifer and Scott arranged to rent a small, one-bedroom apartment near campus. Scott decided he would tell his parents that he was going to live off-campus in an apartment with other men, and Jennifer agreed to tell her parents she was going to live off-campus with women friends.

In the Fall, Scott and Jennifer moved into the apartment, arriving a week before school to buy the necessary items to set up housekeeping. They found living together even better than they had imagined it would be. In fact, it was so satisfying, they had to remind themselves constantly that they were still students and had to force themselves to study.

One afternoon in November, while on a business trip, Scott's father made an unplanned four-hour stop in the city where Scott and Jennifer went to college. He decided to surprise Scott by dropping in unannounced and inviting him to dinner. Stunned at the sight of his father at his apartment door, Scott blurted out his secret. Fortunately, to the surprise of both Jennifer and Scott, his father intimated that he had wondered for some time why they had not decided to live together. In fact, it had been a topic of conversation at least once between him and Scott's mother. As they discussed it further, it became apparent to Scott that the thought of living with Jennifer without being married was more uncomfortable for him than for his parents.

Living together seldom is permanent. Most couples either break up or get married (Bower and Christopherson, 1977). Indeed, some couples view cohabiting as trial marriage. If it works out for a specified time, they get married (Danginger and Greenwald, 1973). Some couples, though, see cohabiting as a permanent alternative to marriage. They are extremely critical of the traditional and constraining laws regarding marriage. These couples often write their own unique contracts to ensure an equal relationship.

■ *Responsibility in Intimate Relationships*    For years it appeared that the only responsibility cohabiting people had toward each other was responsibility based on personal agreement. In the mid-1970s a few court cases broke tradition and awarded **meretricious spouses** (intentionally unmarried persons living together as if married) property at the termination of their relationship. One famous case, in April 1979, involved the actor Lee Marvin, who was sued for *palimony* (alimony granted to people not legally married) by Michelle Triola, the woman he had lived with for six and a half years. The court ruled that Triola should be paid $100,000 in alimony. Since that time, several other such suits have been brought with similar results. It would appear that although cohabitation does not have all the legal complexities of marriage, it does have some.

Even though cohabitation is a viable alternative for some couples, many believe that when a couple wants to have children, marriage is the best alternative. A survey of 1,191 college students showed that only 12 believed children should be reared outside of marriage (Bower and Christopherson, 1977).

Some couples may want to stay married and still have physically and emotionally intimate relationships with others outside the marriage. Whether this sort of relationship can be functional, however, depends on the couple that chooses it. Two anthropologists, Nena and George O'Neill (1972), suggest in their book *Open Marriage: A New Life Style for Couples* that each member of a married couple can have relationships—even sexual relationships—with other persons outside the marriage. Such relationships can be accepted and even encouraged as a normal part of a stable marriage. Unlike the traditional "closed marriage," the open marriage replaces "ownership of the mate with undependent living, denial of self with personal growth, possessiveness with individual freedom, rigid role behavior with flexible roles, absolute fidelity with mutual trust, and total exclusivity with expansion through openness." Contrary to the belief that love, sex, and jealousy go hand in hand, there is no place for the learned response of jealousy in the open marriage. While the O'Neills have put forth an intriguing concept of marriage, there is presently no evidence to substantiate the success of such marriages.

**WHAT DO YOU THINK?**

- Is it possible in our society to sustain emotional and physical intimacy with one person while at the same time engaging in emotional and physical intimacy with others?
- Have you ever attempted to manage more than one emotionally and physically intimate relationship at the same time?
- How successful were you?
- How did you feel?

## ■ Friendship

We have numerous opportunities to establish satisfying, need-fulfilling friendships. We would be overlooking a great source of interpersonal stimulation if we restricted our contact to the person to whom we are married or with whom we are living. Friendships offer us the opportunity to grow and share in the experiences and lifestyles of others. Friendships provide us with variety that may improve the quality of our lives in many respects. They also help us meet some of the needs that our partners may be unable or unwilling to fulfill.

Some people may even choose to have all their needs for intimacy met by friends. Many people neither marry nor cohabit; they are satisfied to live alone, yet interact daily with close frinds. This may be a satisfying alternative for meeting needs for intimacy.

■ *Attraction*   Psychologists have identified some general factors that influence most people's attraction to others. People tend to like others who:

- Are likable—are physically attractive, have pleasant personalities, and are competent.
- Live close to them and are available.
- Like them, do favors for them, and praise them.

■ Friendships offer us opportunities to grow and share in the experiences and lifestyles of others.

WHAT DO YOU THINK?

■ What do you have in common with those you refer to as your friends and acquaintances?
■ Why do you prefer to participate in activities with certain people more than others?

- Are similar in attitudes, interests, and personality.
- In many cases, are "complementary"—possess characteristics that seem to go nicely with theirs.

Living in the same neighborhood, enrolling in the same classes in college, working for the same company, participating in the same community project, and attending the same church are examples of the numerous conditions under which individuals come in contact. The friendships formed under such conditions illustrate the principle of **propinquity,** which holds that social ties tend to form among those who share a common physical location and who have had the opportunity to interact with each other over an extended period of time.

■ *Characteristics of Friendship*   In addition to the factors that cause people to be attracted to each other, other factors are involved in friendship. Friends support each other's full potential. That means they encourage the other to be what is best without envy or possessiveness. Friends are empathic with one another; a special bond of understanding and mutual support lives in their minds. Further, a friend can be counted on in time of joy, need, and sorrow. In a true friendship, the welfare of the other is of utmost importance.

REVIEW
QUESTIONS

*16.* Unfortunately, the family is no longer the greatest provider of intimate contact for children growing up.  T  F
*17.* Psychologists now believe maternal love and infant love are the same phenomenon.  T  F
*18.* The development that has probably the most important effect on children's future personal and social development is peer love.  T  F
*19.* Heterosexual love does not emerge until late adolescence.  T  F

20. Although the traditional concept of marriage is changing, traditional marriage still may be quite satisfying for those who choose to make it work. T F

21. Cohabitation is an alternative currently being practiced only by the young. T F

22. Cohabitation should be the choice of those couples who do not want to be materially and legally responsible to each other. T F

23. The principle of propinquity suggests that two people are more likely to form a lasting relationship if they were introduced to each other by mutual friends. T F

24. Studies have shown that physical attraction is the most important factor that draws potential friends together. T F

25. Mutual empathy is a major goal of true friendship. T F

*The answers to these review questions are on page 381.*

## SUMMARY

■ Intimacy is intense and meaningful communion between you and another person. It is focused on the expression of the intellectual, physical, and emotional aspects of self.

■ Emotional intimacy, the highest level of intimacy, is achieved and maintained through continual evaluation and growth. Emotional intimacy is characterized by accessibility, naturalness, and nonpossessiveness. *Accessibility* means being available for contact and communion with another. *Naturalness* means honestly expressing ourselves to others so we and they know who we are. We reveal our real selves through mutual and honest self-disclosure, stimulated by acceptance, warmth, genuineness, and unconditional positive regard for the other. *Nonpossessiveness* means not needing to own or possess another person.

■ Physical intimacy is the physical expression of emotional intimacy through touch. The quality of physical intimacy is determined more by the quality of emotional intimacy than by technique. Physical intimacy, unfortunately, is laden with taboos. Even though human beings all have the need to touch and be touched, people in the United States are known throughout the world as a no-touch society. Our intimate relationships can be greatly enhanced by allowing ourselves to risk acting on our need for touch.

■ Sexuality is one aspect of physical intimacy. Sex is a biological function for some and an emotional expression for others. The wide range of sexual attitudes stems partly from the commercial value of sex appeal on the one hand and the morality of the Victorians and Christianity on the other. Unfortunately, some of the new sexual standards of the past twenty years have further diminished the quality of our sexual expression. These standards have led to the depersonalization of the individuals involved, thus creating more alienation and loneliness.

■ Our major sources of intimacy are family, friends, and marriage or cohabitation.

■ The successful family provides opportunities for physical and emotional closeness. The family teaches the growing child about five types of intimacy: maternal love, infant love, peer love, heterosexual love, and paternal love.

■ Marriage is a source of intimacy chosen by many people. It has the potential of fulfilling most of our needs for intimacy.

■ Living together outside legal marriage is becoming an alternative for many. This type of lifestyle is chosen mainly to avoid the constraints assumed to be part of the traditional marriage. However, many believe that child rearing should take place within marriage.

■ Open marriage is another alternative being considered by some couples. In an open marriage, a couple may agree to have intimate involvements with individuals outside the marriage.

■ Friendships provide many with a satisfying intimacy. Friendships may complement the primary intimate relationship or may be the major source of intimacy.

## Selected Readings

Ford, E. E. *Permanent Love*. Minneapolis, Minn.: Winston Press, 1979. A book that develops realistic criteria for the healthy marriage and presents a four-step approach to maintaining a lasting relationship.

Fromm, E. *The Art of Loving*. New York: Harper & Row, 1956. A discussion of all aspects of love, from romantic love to self-love. This brief book is worth reading by anyone interested in understanding love.

Greenwald, J. *Creative Intimacy*. New York: Pyramid Books, 1977. An attempt to define the nature and meaning of intimate relationships and to outline the nourishing ways of relating that lead to the development of such relationships. The book includes checklists that help couples distinguish between the intimate and isolating aspects of their relationships.

Lamb, M. "Second Thoughts on First Touch." *Psychology Today* (April 1982): 9–11. An article that discusses evidence related to the effects of the maternal and infant bond that results from skin contact.

Marin, P. "A Revolution's Broken Promises." *Psychology Today* (July 1983): 50–57. An article that discusses some of the effects of the "sexual revolution" on interpersonal satisfaction.

Rainer, J., and Rainer, J. *Sexual Pleasure in Marriage*. New York: Pocket Books, 1969. A book that covers such topics as overcoming blocks to pleasure, courtship in marriage, and myths and facts about sexual compatibility.

## Glossary

**abortion:** the premature termination of pregnancy.

**abstinence:** the state in which a person voluntarily refrains from sexual activity.

**cohabitation:** an arrangement whereby persons of the opposite sex live together without being married.

**emotional intimacy:** the highest level of intimacy, characterized by accessibility, naturalness, and non-possessiveness and focused on feelings.

**heterosexual love:** love or passion expressed for a person of the opposite sex.

**infant love:** the love of the infant for the mother.

**intimacy:** meaningful intellectual, emotional, and physical interaction between two (or more) individuals.

**maternal love:** the love of the mother for the child.

**meretricious spouses:** intentionally unmarried persons living together as if married.

**paternal love:** the love of the father for the child.

**peer love:** the love of the child for age-mates.

**physical intimacy:** the expression of emotion through touch and sexual fulfillment.

**propinquity:** the principle that social ties tend to form among those who share a common physical location and who have had the opportunity to interact with each other over an extended period of time.

**sterilization:** the act of making a person unfruitful.

**therapeutic touch:** the act of giving energy to another through touch. For centuries, it has been known as "the laying on of hands."

## References

Berne, E. *The Structure and Dynamics of Organization and Groups*. New York: Ballantine Books, 1973.

Bower, D. W., and Christopherson, V. A. "University Student Cohabitation: A Regional Comparison of Selected Attitudes and Behaviors." *Journal of Marriage and Family* (August 1977): 447–452.

Buscaglia, L. F. *Love*. New York: Fawcett Crest, 1972.

Clinebell, H. J., and Clinebell, C. H. *The Intimate Marriage*. New York: Harper & Row, 1970.

Cohen, V. "Pregnancy Most Often Unplanned." *Washington Post Service, Miami Herald,* September 29, 1983, p. 3A.

Colen, B. D. "Sterilization: Favorite U. S. Birth Control." *Newsday Service, Miami Herald,* October 13, 1983, pp. 1B–3B.

Dahms, A. M. "Intimacy Hierarchy." In *Process in Relationships: Marriage and Family,* edited by E. A. Powers and M. W. Lees. St. Paul, Minn.: West, 1976.

Danginger, C., and Greenwald, M. *Alternatives: A Look at Unmarried Couples and Communes.* New York: Institute of Life Insurance Research Services, 1973.

Guttmacher, A. F. *Abortion: A Woman's Guide.* New York: Abelard-Schuman, 1973.

Harlow, H. F. *Learning to Love.* San Francisco: Albion, 1971.

Hartman, W. E.; Fithian, M.; and Johnson, D. *Nudist Society.* New York: Crown, 1970.

Herbert, M. "Is Sex an Emotional Necessity?" In *Man and Woman: The Encyclopedia of Adult Relationships.* London: Marshall Cavendish, 1970.

Hunter, N. "What Akron Does/Does Not Say." *The Nation* 237 (August 20–27, 1983): 137–139.

Jourard, S. M. *Healthy Personality.* New York: Macmillan, 1974.

Jourard, S. M., and Whitman, A. "The Fear That Cheats Us of Love." In *Process in Relationship.* Edited by Edward A. Powers and Mary W. Lees. St. Paul, Minn.: West, 1976.

Kieffer, C. "New Depths in Intimacy." In *Marriage and Alternatives: Exploring Intimate Relationships.* Edited by R. Libby and R. Whitehurst. Glenview, Ill.: Scott, Foresman, 1977.

Krieger, D.; Peper, E.; and Ancoli, A. "Therapeutic Touch: Searching for Evidence of Physiological Change." *American Journal of Nursing* (April 1979): 660–662.

Lederer, J. "Birth-Control Decisions: Hidden Factors in Contraceptive Choices." *Psychology Today* (June 1983): 32–38.

Marin, P. "A Revolution's Broken Promises." *Psychology Today* (July 1983): 50–57.

Maslow, A. H. *Toward a Psychology of Being,* 2nd ed. Princeton, N. J.: Van Nostrand, 1968.

May, R. *Love and Will.* New York: Norton, 1967.

Montagu, A. *Touching: The Human Significance of the Skin,* 2nd ed. New York: Harper & Row, 1978.

Morris, D. *Intimate Behavior.* New York: Random House, 1971.

Murstein, B. "A Theory of Marital Choice and Its Applicability to Marriage Adjustment." In *Theories of Attraction and Love.* Edited by B. Murstein. New York: Springer, 1971, 100–151.

O'Neill, N., and O'Neill, G. *Open Marriage: A New Life Style for Couples.* New York: Avon Books, 1972, p. 7.

Ong, W. *The Presence of the Word.* New Haven: Yale University Press, 1967.

Planned Parenthood Federation of America. *Guide to Birth Control Methods: Six Accepted Methods of Contraception.* Washington, D. C.: Planned Parenthood Federation of America, 1983.

Rimmer, R. H. *The Harrad Experiment.* Los Angeles: Sherbourne, 1966.

Rogers, C. R. *On Becoming a Person.* Boston: Houghton Mifflin, 1961.

Schulz, D. A., and Rodgers, S. F. *Marriage, the Family, and Personal Fulfillment.* Englewood Cliffs, N.J.: Prentice-Hall, 1975.

"Update on Contraceptives: What's Safe? Effective? Convenient?" *Changing Times.* (October 1983): 72–76.

Winter, G. *Love and Conflict.* Garden City, N.Y.: Doubleday, 1958.

Wrightsman, L. S. *Social Psychology,* 2nd ed. Monterey, Calif.: Brooks/Cole, 1977.

## ANSWERS TO REVIEW QUESTIONS

**Page 362.** *1.* essential, self-actualizing *2.* Alienation *3.* intellectual, physical, emotional *4.* Emotional intimacy, feelings *5.* self-disclosure *6.* accessibility, naturalness, nonpossessiveness *7.* acceptance, warmth, genuineness, unconditional positive regard

**Page 371.** *8.* F *9.* T *10.* T *11.* F *12.* F *13.* F *14.* F *15.* F
**Page 378.** *16.* F *17.* F *18.* T *19.* F *20.* T *21.* F *22.* F *23.* F *24.* F *25.* T

# BARRIERS TO INTIMACY

Terri and Phil had one important thing in common when they met. Neither had dated anyone longer than a year. The magic both felt when they first met led them to believe that they had finally met the "right" person. After they had dated just longer than a year, they decided to marry. They appeared to have similar values and goals. Each had a professional career; Terri was a physical therapist at a large metropolitan hospital, and Phil was an attorney with a prestigious law firm. They had good incomes and could afford nearly anything they wanted. They were the envy of their friends, who believed them an ideal couple in an ideal relationship. To their friends' surprise and dismay, however, Terri and Phil filed for a divorce just eighteen months after their wedding. What had happened?

See if you can speculate on how their relationship deteriorated as you read the following chapter.

**12**

BARRIERS
TO
INTIMACY

## DISCUSSION: MULTIPLE BARRIERS TO INTIMACY

Opportunities to develop a variety of significant intimate relationships seem nearly limitless. There are more people in the world than ever before. Through modern methods of travel, our chances to meet others who are capable of meeting our needs for intimacy are greatly increased. Yet many of us are unable to develop a satisfying and fulfilling relationship with anyone. "We can orbit the earth, we can touch the moon, but this society has not devised a way for two people to live together in harmony for seven straight days without wanting to strangle each other" (George Leonard, quoted in Buscaglia, 1982).

A variety of factors affect our ability to find and sustain satisfying intimate relationships. The demands of our rapidly growing, complex technological society leave little time for intimacy. These demands have greatly affected the quality of one of our greatest sources of intimacy, the family. Our search for intimacy also is hampered by certain social norms and stereotypes that have developed from societal beliefs and early religious teachings.

### ■ Social Norms and Role Stereotypes

Norms constitute a host of shoulds and should nots that greatly affect the roles of women and men in our society. As we discovered in an earlier chapter, role stereotypes are assumed differences between, say, men and women that are believed to be universally applicable by a social group. Fortunately, many of the traditional sex role stereotypes that have been allowed to govern our behavior are gradually changing for the better. Our purpose here is not generally to explore the effects of sexual discrimination, but to explore the effects of such discrimination on our capacity for intimacy.

*See Chapter 8, on socialization, for more about norms.*

Norms, though intended to ease social interaction, often conflict with our needs. Consider the beliefs described in the accompanying Case in Point. Such beliefs have serious and far-reaching consequences for intimacy. The male must suppress an important part of his humanness; in effect, he must bottle up the very feelings that are essential to tenderness and the development of a satisfying intimate relationship. He must always be on guard, and he becomes crippled by the stress of hiding his feelings.

*Chapter 7 discusses stress.*

Similarly, the role stereotype based on the traditional belief that the woman is inferior and must depend on the man is one that some believe greatly affects

---

## CASE IN POINT

Many American males believe that to be considered masculine (strong, aggressive, in control, and so on), they must suppress their tears when in public regardless of their feelings. Any suggestion of an emotional display reinforces the fear that they may lose control and demonstrate "weakness," as females are expected to do. If crying is a sign of weakness in men—and many men and women believe it is—then a man, when he feels the need to cry, must cry alone or not at all. In this way, he retains his masculine self-image.

## CASE IN POINT
## Another View

Not everyone believes sex role stereotypes restrict intimacy. Rubin, Peplau, and Hill (1976) studied attitudes toward sex roles by interviewing 231 couples who were college students. Ninety-five percent of the women and eighty-seven percent of the men stated they believed men and women should have "exactly equal say about their relationship." A follow-up study of these same couples indicated that even though they had liberal ideas about sex roles, very few of them managed to stay together in a lasting relationship. The reviewers concluded that if couples have similar values and beliefs, the sharing of these values and beliefs is more significant to their happiness than the contents of the beliefs. For example, couples who share the belief that the wife should stay at home, raise the children, and maintain the house are just as happy as couples who believe that each individual should be free to pursue a career in addition to the mutual obligations of caring for children and for the home.

our search for intimacy, even though this role limitation appears to be gradually diminishing. Constantina Safilios-Rothschild (1977) states:

> . . . when men and women are drastically unequal and women occupy a clearly inferior, disadvantaged sociological position, they necessarily become psychologically unequal; then men and women are unable to understand each other and to relate to each other as human beings. . . . Within this context, the development of a mature, fulfilling love has been almost impossible. . . . This has led not only to separation of love from marriage, but also to the separation of love from sexuality and to a profound alienation of men and women from their feelings and emotions. (p. 3)

Many other norms affect our attitudes, behaviors, and feelings toward intimacy. Most have come from the Middle Ages and from the Judeo-Christian heritage. Consider the following beliefs:

- A woman must be a virgin when she marries if the marriage is to be successful.
- Love, honor, and obey . . . until death do us part.
- Husbands and wives are one and belong to each other (possessiveness).
- The husband must provide for his wife and family and the wife must take care of her husband.
- Woman is cursed and will give birth in sorrow (her punishment for Eve's having sinned in the Garden of Eden).
- Sexual organs are unclean.
- Homosexuals are a menace to society.

Deeply felt needs for intimacy draw us together, yet carefully taught inhibitions laden with shoulds and oughts drive us apart.

Norms, then, particularly those that define roles, may create barriers to the fulfillment of intimacy. Harry Stack Sullivan (1953), the well-known author of books on modern psychiatry, has said that people are more alike than they are different. Specifically, people are more alike in being human than they are different in being male or female (Harper, 1971). Norms that define rigid role behaviors often limit our freedom in pursuing our needs for intimacy.

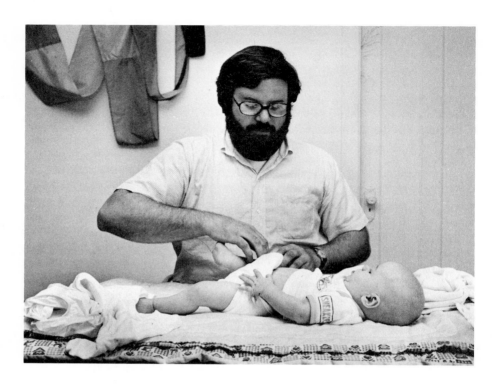

■ Male and female
roles are changing.

### ■ Demands of Society

"There are three things we cherish in particular—mobility, privacy, and convenience—which are the very sources of our lack of community" (Keyes, 1973, p. 15). These three things represent some of our most important freedoms. Consider for a few moments just how mobile our society has become. According to Alvin Toffler (1971), in 1914 the average American traveled 88,560 miles in his or her lifetime. Today, the average American travels 10,000 miles each year and perhaps 3,000,000 miles in a lifetime. The last seventy years have brought us the automobile (seven cars for every ten people, reports Information Please Almanac, 1983), the supersonic airplane, the super train, and millions of miles of highways. Airlines have special "million-mile clubs" for customers who frequently use air travel. People are constantly on the move—moving from town to town, and from one house to another—and that has drastically affected the formation of lasting friendships. Technological progress, which involves movement and change, has become as much a way of life as has intimacy. Someone is always saying, "Don't stand in the way of progress."

■ *Mobility*  As suggested above, mobility seemingly works against intimacy. The primary effect of Americans' constantly uprooting themselves is a detachment from enduring and significant relationships (Bennis and Slater, 1968). We move from job to job, town to town, and if we are materially "fortunate," we move from one social class up to another. Often, the result of such mobility is that we move from relationship to relationship. The rigorous pace of our modern

■ Increased mobility may result in more time away from intimacy.

life tends to permit only superficial attachments (Altman and Taylor, 1973). Many of us find ourselves developing temporary relationships as we travel about. Most of them last "only for the duration of the trip" as we fly from city to city. We may come in contact with more people in a single day than the feudal villager did in a lifetime.

Name, age, status, astrological sign, and availability for sex with "no strings attached" seem most important to some of us. We often can be more open with a stranger than someone close to us because the encounter will be brief and we expect no future evaluation or censure. We can choose to share as much or as little of ourselves as we want. Too often we share too little of ourselves with anyone. Because of our mobility, we may believe that it is useless to involve ourselves in intimate relationships that will soon end. To attempt a longer-lasting, higher-quality relationship may mean the loss of whatever intimacy we have developed. As a further consequence, we may learn eventually not to become too intimately involved with others. We experience drive-in relationships, disposable marriages, no-risk love affairs (Altman and Taylor, 1973). Our relationships become analogous to our popular convenience stores—they are open twenty-four hours, provide us with quick services, and their prices are usually high. The high price we pay for these relationships may be less intimacy and more loneliness.

■ *Privacy* Although privacy is essential to experiencing deep intimacy, too much privacy destroys many chances for intimacy to develop. Edward Hall

(1969) points out that not all cultures seem to have as great a need for privacy as ours; neither the Japanese nor the Arab language has a word for privacy, for example. In our society, there seems to be a correlation between wealth and privacy. The wealthier we are, the further we can move from each other. In an affluent society, to have privacy whenever we want is one measure of success.

Another reason we value privacy stems from the increasing problem of overcrowding in our nation's 285 metropolitan areas. As a result of increased mobility and the location of jobs in overcrowded cities and suburban areas, people have become, out of necessity, physically crowded together. Even in suburbia, single-family homes sometimes seem nearly on top of each other as lack of space has forced developers to build houses close together in giant housing developments. Whether they like it or not, many people can hear everything that goes on in their neighbor's residence, from domestic quarrels to flushing toilets. Most people's reaction to such overcrowding is probably summed up by a young couple's response to the question "How do you like your neighbors?" "Our neighbors are perfect. We don't know any of them." Vance Packard (1972) states:

> millions of Americans are now seeing their fellow men in general not as allies but as nuisance makers. We are so closely packed together—and walls often are so thin—that other people interrupt our solitude, clog our highways, and keep us from getting to work on time. They beat us to the parking space at the mall, they roar past our lakeside cottage with their 100 horsepower boats going full blast. In short, people in general are seen as problems to be coped with. (p. 190)

Advertisements for new homes reflect this growing need for privacy: "Come away from the crowd—hide out in the heart of town," or "A private and secluded home where you leave the crowds behind." However, some housing developments recognize that even though we value privacy we still have the need for human contact: "Come join us. We offer nice things to do and nice people to do them with."

■ *Safety and Security*    Safety and security appear to be of great importance to most people. A newspaper advertisement for a new condominium offers an example: "complete with intercom security system which screens visitors." Privacy affords us safety from the perils of our complex world. We look for safety from accidental injuries or death, from crowds, from many things we fear—including rejection, involvement, intimacy, and perhaps most of all, being known. Hence, although privacy can be a source of protection, it keeps us from the involvement that is necessary for the fulfillment of our need for intimacy.

■ *Convenience*    Convenience has affected intimacy in several ways, but perhaps most devastating is its effect on marriage. Marriages of convenience are not new. In the past, many marriages were arranged by parents to satisfy the economic or status requirements of the respective families. In recent times, marriages of convenience have served other purposes. When the selective service draft was in operation and marriage was a means for exemption, many people married to avoid military service. As Internal Revenue Service rules change and marriage becomes economically more or less desirable, people may marry or divorce to keep up with tax changes. For sexual convenience, some individuals may seek relationships that provide little more than sexual gratification.

Lederer and Jackson (1968) suggest that marriages of convenience are more common than we may think. They propose seven false assumptions about marriage, and among them are that people marry because they love each other, that most married people love each other, and that love is necessary for a satisfying marriage. However, Morris (1971) warns that loveless marriages may have long-term effects over generations. He refers to loveless mating as "economic rape." Children growing up in this situation seem to develop satisfactorily in a biological sense; however, they lack the ability to relate their biological features to a deep and lasting bond of intimate attachment. As a result, they "will find it difficult to make successful pair-bonds . . . and once again the next generation of children will suffer" (p. 80).

■ *Stress*  The capacity for experiencing intimacy is more greatly affected by excessive stress than most people are aware. Our response to stress is often characterized by intellectual, emotional, and physical withdrawal. When our physiological and security needs are threatened by an overcrowded, technological, and highly mobile society and our primary concerns are related to such mundane matters as whether we have enough fuel in our cars, we necessarily become preoccupied with satisfying those more basic survival needs at the expense of intimacy.

*For more on this subject, see Chapter 7, which deals with stress, and Chapter 8, on socialization.*

**WHAT DO YOU THINK?**
■ How successful was your family in providing opportunities for intimacy while you were growing up?
■ What opportunities for intimacy exist in your present family?

■ *Effects on the Family*  The family unit has perhaps suffered most of all. Social critics have had a field day speculating on the future of the family. Some believe it is near extinction, and others believe it is already dead, having outlived its usefulness. Still others, however, believe that, having existed all this time, the family will continue to exist, though modified, and will continue to serve an important function. "A healthy society requires a healthy family and the family will remain healthy only as it changes to meet the changing needs of society." (Alpenfels, 1970, p. 67).

The family has been called the "giant shock absorber" of society—the place to which the bruised and battered individual returns daily after having faced the everyday battles of life. But, as Alvin Toffler (1971) puts it, "As the super-industrial revolution unfolds, this 'shock absorber' will come in for some shocks of its own" (p. 238). A psychologist, Perry London (1978), notes that at one time, the family was the basic structural unit within the community; it implied intimacy because it was supposed to represent people's most significant aspirations. The basic unit today is the individual, who is able financially to live alone and also is able to find amiable companionship, sex, and other recreation without having to provide anything in return. He points out, though, that the individual may pay a price—the loss of dependability and familiarity in his or her personal life, the dependability and familiarity that can exist in the family unit.

If our needs for intimacy are not met within the family, we will begin to search elsewhere for substitutes; the wife takes a lover, the husband a mistress, and the children find companionship with peers and substitute parents—relatives, parents of friends, and so on. These substitutions for the intimacy tra-

**WHAT DO YOU THINK?**

■ What substitutes for family intimacy did you discover while growing up?

■ What substitutes do you have today?

ditionally provided by the family compete further with the family and often replace it altogether. The family's purpose then becomes the provision of only the basic needs of food and shelter for its individual members.

## ■ Substitutes for Intimacy

Just as family intimacy may be replaced by other forms of intimacy, human intimacy may be replaced by other attachments. Pets, work, and greed supply substitutes for intimacy for some people.

■ *Pets*     Pets of all kinds have become popular replacements for human intimacy. Pets provide us with unconditional love; they ask us no questions and tell us no lies. Morris (1971) sees our loving attachments to animals as encouraging:

> *If we are capable of tenderness toward animals it does at least reveal that we are capable of such tenderness. . . . It serves as a constant reminder that the human animal, when not warped by what must paradoxically be called the savageries of civilization, is fundamentally endowed with great potential for tenderness and intimacy. (p. 175)*

In their book *Between Pets and People*, two researchers, Aaron Katcher and Alan Beck, reported that 80 percent of the people interviewed said they believed their dogs were sensitive to their feelings. A third of those interviewed said that

■ For some, pets have become replacements for human intimacy.

they confided in their dogs, showing an unconscious belief that the animals could understand them. The authors went on to say that this relationship has a calming effect on the nervous system of the owner that reduces blood pressure. This "seems to help people live longer and apparently can reduce the number of deaths from heart attacks" (Pothier, 1984). The results of this study have prompted some operators of animal shelters to provide animals to homes for the elderly.

■ *Work*   Work is an acceptable substitute for intimacy in our society. Few people question the motives of someone who continually works long hours and appears to be productive. After all, the desire to "get ahead" is considered an admirable personal quality. Unfortunately, some people become "workaholics" to feel worthwhile and to provide a substitute for intimate personal relationships.

■ *Greed*   Many people believe greed is a motivating force in our society. The quest for material wealth in some ways may provide a replacement for intimacy. Horn (1976) points out that there is little relationship between a child's family income and how much he or she values money as an adult; regardless of the level of affluence, however, people who grow up in love-poor families seem to value money more than those who receive ample love as children. Horn further states that adults who are not receiving much love usually value material possessions very highly and that persons who place a high value on money and goods tend to avoid intimacy.

Grinker (1977) suggests that in some ways, the children of the rich resemble the children of the poor. Their awareness of themselves and others is limited, and they lack the capacity for tenderness. Their interaction with others is limited by their compulsiveness and their desire to exclude others who are unlike them. They are often left with feelings of being bored, depressed, and, most of all, unloved. It appears there is a high price to be paid for wealth.

REVIEW
QUESTIONS

*1.* Norms and stereotypes often produce shoulds and should nots that hamper our finding satisfying intimacy. T F

*2.* Mobility, privacy, and convenience represent three cherished freedoms that may severely limit our search for intimacy. T F

*3.* Superficiality in our attachments is one of the outcomes of our highly technical and mobile society. T F

*4.* Overcrowding in our cities and suburbs is resulting in an increased need for privacy and detachment. T F

*5.* Contrary to popular belief, stress has been found to have little effect on our capacity for intimacy. T F

*6.* Drug use has been referred to as the "great shock absorber of society." T F

*7.* Pets are one of the most popular substitutes for human intimacy in our society.  T F

*8.* As one might expect, the quest for money is the substitute for intimacy for those adults who grew up in wealthy families. T F

*The answers to these review questions are on page 401.*

## DISCUSSION: ROMANTIC LOVE

Many love songs of the past several decades continue to respond to attitudes from the Middle Ages and myths about love and intimacy. They portray the possessiveness, pain, and loneliness many of us associate with the search for love and allow us to sit for hours wallowing in self-pity. Songs such as "Lover Come Back to Me," "Can't Get Used to Losing You," "I'm So Lonesome I Could Cry," "You Belong to Me," "The Thrill Is Gone," "Breaking Up Is Hard to Do," "You Picked a Fine Time to Leave Me Lucille," and "Somebody Done Somebody Wrong" are just a few. Novelists and songwriters have grown wealthy writing about the ecstasy and agony of **romantic love.** The expectations associated with romantic love often contribute to our disappointment in relationships—disappointment that often leads to breaking up, estrangement, and divorce.

### ■ Characteristics of Romantic Love

Romantic love involves a set of idealized images by which we judge the other person and the quality of our relationship. The images of romantic love result in role expectations for each partner: The man is to be strong, confident, protective, and masterful at all times; the woman is to be always charming, loving, fragile, and dependent. We may hope to transform each other into the unreal heroes or heroines (princes or princesses) these images portray.

**WHAT DO YOU THINK?**

■ Do you have romantic feelings about someone?
■ What do you mean when you say "I love you"?
■ Are you satisfied with the love you are experiencing now?

In addition to promoting unrealistic role expectations, romantic love requires that each partner become the complete center of the universe for the other. The result is the belief that love, possessiveness, and jealousy are synonymous. Unfortunately, such romanticized standards bear little relationship to satisfying intimacy in the real world. In fact, we must hesitate when we refer to romantic love as love at all, for it is based on selfishness. This may be difficult for many of us to grasp, for romance is usually expressed by generous promises—"My love for you will last forever" or "I'll make you the best wife a man ever had." When we rationally analyze such guarantees of instant and enduring happiness, we can readily see how unrealistic they are for human beings, implying as they do that humans are unchanging. The selfishness of romantic love becomes more obvious when we think about romantic lovers' misery when separated. Each lover is sorry for himself or herself and is grieving over his or her personal loss of pleasure and intimacy (Lederer and Jackson, 1968).

■ *The Value of Romantic Love*    Romantic love does have some value in a relationship. It is important to visit our romantic fantasies from time to time to stimulate and add enjoyment to our lives. Romantic ceremony and ritual can provide much happiness in our relationships. However, attempting a fulfilling and lasting intimate relationship on the unrealistic ideals of romance seldom results in our meeting our needs and encourages disappointment and frustration when our expectations are not met.

■ *The Disappointment of Romantic Love*    People often have fallen in love with their romanticized expectations rather than with their mates. This tends to produce one of two actions. Either the spouse is rejected in search of the ideal

■ Romantic ceremony and ritual can provide stimulation in a relationship.

partner or an attempt is made to change the spouse to fit the romantic ideal. The course of events is described by John R. Clark (1961):

> *In learning how to love a plain human being today . . . what we usually want uncon-*
> *sciously is a fancy human being with no flaws. When the mental picture we have of*
> *someone we love is colored by wishes of childhood, we may love the picture rather than*
> *the real person behind it. Naturally, we are disappointed in the person we love if he [she]*
> *does not conform to our picture. Since this kind of disappointment has no doubt happened*
> *to us before, one might suppose we would tear up the picture and start over. On the*
> *contrary, we keep the picture and tear up the person. Small wonder that divorce courts*
> *are full of couples who never gave themselves a chance to know the real person behind*
> *the pictures in their lives. (p. 18)*

## ■ Divorce and Romantic Ideals

The high rate of divorce may be due, in part, to various ideals associated with marriage:

*1.* As we just discussed, people often get married with unrealistic expectations for both their mates and the marriage. They expect that the marriage will provide sexual fulfillment, intellectual stimulation, congeniality, shared recreation, mutual security, companionship, and a host of material satisfactions (Mead, 1970).

*2.* Some psychologists and sociologists believe current divorce statistics reflect, paradoxically, a frantic search for a more satisfying intimacy. According to Udry (1974), "High divorce rates do not indicate that marriage is no longer considered important by Americans. Rather, [they indicate] that marriage has become so important a source of emotional satisfaction that few people can endure a relationship that does not provide this" (p. 405). That a majority of divorced Americans remarry, and do so quickly, supports Udry's statements.

3. People often get married because they believe it is expected of them. Hugh Carter and Paul Glick (1970), in a government-supported research study, concluded that marriage is so well entrenched as the normal and approved status of adulthood that a considerable number of people will marry even if they are temperamentally unsuited to marriage and incompatible with their prospective partners. More than 90 percent of Americans marry at least once during their life (Murstein, 1971). For some, the appearance of marriage is perhaps more important than the success of it.

■ Finding the "Right" Mate

Ultimately, the process of dating and falling in love is part of the search for the "right person" to marry for most people. The ideals of romantic love, unfortunately, play an important part in this search. A man and woman meet, fall in love, and decide they cannot live without each other, no matter how impractical the match. Romantic love is not the only criterion in the search for the "right person," however.

Sexual compatibility is extremely important to many who are seeking a mate. Other factors include complementarity, proximity, and similarity. Other things being equal, people tend to date those whom they see most often and whose needs and characteristics seem to mesh with, or *complement*, their own or whose strengths match their weaknesses (Rubin, 1973). Perhaps the most important variable in mate selection is similarity. Byrne (1971) found that when both partners are measured on such variables as age, values, attitudes, education, religion, race, height, and socioeconomic standing, they resemble each other much more closely than chance would predict.

It is sometimes said that men tend to seek wives who resemble their mothers and women seek men who possess the traits of their fathers. An interesting study by Aron (Horn, 1974) examined the truth of these assumptions and discovered that we all tend to marry our mothers. While waiting for marriage licenses at Toronto City Hall, couples were asked to complete personality profiles on their fathers and mothers and their partners. Surprisingly, both men and women seemed to choose mates who had more in common with their mothers than with their fathers. The men tended to choose wives who were similar to their mothers in dominance and responsiveness, and the women chose husbands who were similar to their mothers in responsiveness and trust.

Many people, in the intense emotional involvement of courtship and marriage, are not aware of what they want in a marriage partner. Unfortunately, this ignorance often leads to unsatisfying relationships that eventually are terminated.

## DISCUSSION: THE EFFECTS OF FAILURE

Restrictive norms, a rapidly changing society, and other hindrances to intimacy produce numerous psychological problems. These problems create even more severe difficulties—lack of trust, loneliness, fear, and even suicide.

## ■ Lack of Trust

We place our trust in government, corporations, organizations, businessess of all kinds, doctors, lawyers, neighbors, and friends. They often disappoint us. We hear people say, "You just can't trust anyone anymore," or "I will never trust that person again." However, these are irrational statements and irrational beliefs. In the interest of our personal happiness, we must risk trusting again, for without trust, we can have no satisfying relationships. We doom ourselves to what one psychologist, Robert Weiss (1973), calls social loneliness and emotional loneliness—both resulting from the absence of intimacy.

## ■ Loneliness and Fear

**Social loneliness** is the lack of a social network of people to enjoy things with. When we change jobs or move to a new neighborhood—or when we begin a new term in a new class and do not know anyone—we often experience this loneliness. The obvious cure is to use our creativity to establish contact with others. **Emotional loneliness** is the lack of an intimate relationship. It cannot necessarily be remedied by just making contact, although that is certainly the first step. The cure for this painful loneliness is risking emotional intimacy with a significant other, as discussed previously.

Many of us become lonely for some of the same reasons we seek privacy: the fear of being known, the fear of exposure, and the fear of rejection. As in the progression of an undetected disease, the comfort and security of privacy may lead to the isolation of social loneliness and the anguish of emotional loneliness.

■ The fear of intimacy results in loneliness.

WHAT DO YOU
THINK?

■ Have you ever felt
lonely?
■ Do you feel lonely at
times now?
■ What do you do
about your loneliness?

Clark Moustakas (1961) states, "Many individuals long fervently to be with others and to find love, but they are held back by their own restraining fears" (p. 28). As a result of our fear of getting involved, of being known, of suffering rejection, and of sharing intimacy, we cut ourselves off from contact with others. We hide in a crowd; we sit alone; we ride alone. "Automobiles," says Hall (1969), "insulate man not only from the environment but from human contact as well. They permit only the most limited types of interaction, usually competitive, aggressive, and destructive" (p. 177).

> Patty lived in a suburb of Chicago nearly twenty miles from her workplace. Every day she drove for an hour or more each way. Even though it was expensive, she said, she was happy to have the freedom of owning her own car and not depending on anyone or anything. Then one day she received a notice that her apartment had been sold and the new owners were going to live in the apartment. She had six months to find a new home.
> Frantically, Patty searched every possible area, only to discover that the only apartment she could afford was over sixty miles from her workplace—at least a two-hour drive by car. A friend suggested that she give up driving to work and take the commuter train from her new community to her workplace. Reluctantly, she decided to try it. The first few days seemed strange, but she noticed that the ride was less than an hour long and that everyone seemed to be having a good time. It was not long before Patty met other commuters, and soon she was thoroughly enjoying the trip. She even began to look forward to seeing her new acquaintances each day. One day she phoned her friend to thank her for the suggestion. She had not known how lonely she had been driving to and from work until she began riding the train, she said.

*See Chapter 7, on stress, for related topics.*

Our fears of being known and of being rejected often compel us to disguise our loneliness and our need for intimacy from ourselves and from others. We are desperate to come together, to really know each other, yet we communicate in ways that guarantee we will stay apart. We deliver double messages—love me and leave me alone. Our concern for our emotional security has prompted Alan Dahms (1976) to write, "People exchange ideas in ways that tend to protect rather than expose their inner selves. Everyone stays safe in their emotional aloneness. They strive to be 'cool,' to appear unruffled, attractive, and invulnerable" (p. 86). Such interactions are common in discotheques and nightclubs—two of society's answers to our need for contact.

> Larry and Becky met at the beginning of their sophomore year in college. They believed there was a "certain chemistry" between them almost from their first meeting. They seemed to get along almost perfectly—at times, it seemed, too perfectly. As their relationship grew, they wished to communicate more of their needs to each other but were reluctant to do so, afraid to disturb the harmony they thought was the basis for their relationship. Ironically, protecting what they thought they had and avoiding the risk of growing together resulted in their eventual break-up.

## ■ Loneliness and Suicide

Loneliness is a major reason for suicides. Several researchers (Lowenthal and Haven, 1968; Jacobs, 1971) have demonstrated a correlation between loneliness and psychological problems such as depression and suicide. Suicide may result when prolonged loneliness pushes people to the point where no alternative seems hopeful.

The U.S. Public Health Service (*Hammond Almanac*, 1979) reports an alarming increase in the number of suicides each year. Suicides among young Americans between fifteen and twenty-four years old rose from 528 in 1966 to 4,747 in 1976, an increase of 900 percent in a single decade. The U.S. Public Health Service (*Hammond Almanac*, 1983) also reports that in 1978, murder claimed the lives of 15,580 males and 4,586 females, whereas suicide claimed the lives of 20,188 males and 7,106 females (nearly 30 percent more suicides than murders). From these statistics, it appears that we encounter a greater risk from ourselves than we do from each other. The statistics also show that loneliness is not peculiar to the very old and others we might suspect are suffering from it. The young suffer severely from loneliness because they often are caught between their unfulfilled need for intimacy and the overwhelming demands of modern society.

**WHAT DO YOU THINK?**

- Do you know anyone who has attempted suicide?
- Did they appear to be lonely?
- How did you feel about what they did?

## ■ Loneliness and Aloneness

It is the effect of *prolonged aloneness* that often takes its toll on us. "Loneliness is such as omnipotent and painful threat to many persons that they have little conception of the positive values of solitude, and even at times are frightened at the prospect of being alone" (May, 1953, p. 26). Being alone can have beneficial effects, however, and Moustakas (1961) refer to solitude as **existential loneliness.** Wolfe regards solitude as an intrinsic condition of existence. He believes that solitude is essential to creativity, that out of the depths of grief and despair springs the urge to create new forms and images and to discover unique ways of being aware and of expressing experience. Songwriters and poets often create their best works as the result of experiencing solitude. Thus, the aloneness of solitude can lead to creativity for some of us.

## ■ The Future for Love and Intimacy

Love, in its most loving sense, is appreciation and respect for another person for all that he or she has been in the past, is now, and has the potential to become. It is appreciation of the other person as someone with whom we can learn and grow. It is the belief that the other person complements us. As Leo Buscaglia defines it, it is "a process not of my wanting to make you over in my image as I would desire you, but my wanting to lead you back to yourself, to what you are, to your uniqueness, to your original beauty" (1982).

In our search for intimacy, we may be headed in as many directions as the mind can conceive. Old patterns of intimacy in friendships, love affairs, and marriage seem to have been undone in barely one generation (London, 1978). New ones are not yet well enough developed to be entirely clear. For both young and old, sexual values, housekeeping arrangements, and the means for coping are in transition. People of all ages are baffled by vague new demands and possibilities. Many seem to be using whatever means they can to find intimacy. They are living by new standards, defying the norms under which they were reared.

## CASE IN POINT

I should have told you
that love is more than being warm
in bed.
More than individuals seeking
an accomplice.
Even more than wanting to share.
I could have said
that love at best is giving what

you need to get.
But it was raining
and we had no place to go
and riding through the streets
in a cab
I remembered that words are only
necessary after love has gone.

Source: Rod McKuen, *Stanyan Street and Other Sorrows* (Random House 1970), p. 33.

It may seem that a miracle is necessary for intimacy to survive as the beginning of the twenty-first century approaches. We must remember, though, that we are flexible, capable of flowing with change and adjusting to nearly any situation to meet our needs. Even though our modern society appears to discourage intimacy in many ways, we are searching for it more fervently than ever. Carl Rogers (1970) believes that we are now probably much more aware of our inner loneliness than at any other time in history. As a result, we are more intensely seeking relationships that provide a higher quality of intimacy. Further, Buscaglia (1982) believes that our ability to form these meaningful and lasting intimate relationships is directly related to the condition of our mental health. Intimacy is more difficult to achieve when we are in a state of poor mental health.

Finally, we must unlearn much of what we have been taught in the past about love and intimacy and learn new attitudes that best fit each of our own sets of needs. By establishing our own norms for intimacy, we can grow toward becoming the healthy individuals we have the potential to become.

REVIEW
QUESTIONS

9. Romantic love is a set of unrealistic and idealized standards that some people use to judge the quality of a relationship. T F

10. Romance has no value whatsoever in a healthy intimate relationship. T F

11. The concept of romantic love may contribute to the dissatisfaction in relationships that end in divorce. T F

12. Udry suggests that the high divorce rate is an indication that intimacy is no longer valued by Americans. T F

13. A study conducted by Carter and Glick concluded that many people marry because they believe it is expected of them as part of adulthood. T F

14. Studies have shown that sexual compatibility is the primary reason why most people decide to marry a particular partner. T F

15. A study conducted in Toronto showed it is true that women tend to marry men who are similar to their fathers. T F

16. Contrary to what most believe, it has been found that how similar partners are to each other has little to do with their choosing each other as mates. T F

17. When we are able to find a remedy for our social loneliness, we will have few problems with emotional loneliness. T F

*18.* Psychologists believe there is actually little correlation between loneliness and psychological problems such as depression and suicide. T F
*19.* Social loneliness is the absence of a supportive social group. T F
*20.* The most terrifying loneliness anyone can experience is existential loneliness. T F
*The answers to these review questions are on page 401.*

## SUMMARY

■ Many factors affect our capacity to achieve satisfying intimate relationships. Norms, including role stereotypes, a rapidly changing mobile society, and the resulting problems of alienation, isolation, and loneliness are some of these factors. The expectations from role stereotypes severely limit our interactions with each other. Our crowded and mobile society greatly affects the quality and duration of our attempts at intimacy; the results are that we seek superficial and temporary attachments and excessive privacy to avoid the stressful pace of our daily lives. In an attempts to find safety and seclusion, many of us discover that we have escaped into loneliness.

■ The assumption that people marry only for love is false. Many marry for security, sex, self-esteem, or economic convenience, or because they think it is expected of them. The most important reason appears to be similarity between partners in values, education, religion, age, and many other factors.

■ Many of us have a limited and unrealistic concept of love. Our definition is based on selfishness, possessiveness, and the idealism of romantic love. These standards may cause us to have unrealistic expectations about intimate relationships.

■ The rising divorce rate may be due, in part, to our romanticized expectations of marriage. We expect our partners to live up to these expectations. When they do not, we want to change them or discard them. Some believe the divorce rate indicates that people marry because they believe it is expected of them, even though they may be unsuited to marriage or to their partners.

■ The absence of intimacy has resulted in a growing lack of trust between individuals. This further decreases our chances for achieving intimacy. Consequently, many people are experiencing social and emotional loneliness. Suicide has become a way for many to end their devastating feeling of loneliness. On the other hand, existential loneliness can result in creative and life-changing growth experiences.

■ It seems that we are searching for intimacy even more fervently than before. People of all ages seem confused but intrigued by a variety of possibilities. Each of us can find his or her own special ingredient for finding a satisfying intimate relationship.

## SELECTED READINGS

Adams, V. "Getting at the Heart of Jealous Love." *Psychology Today* (May 1980): 30–47. An examination of the effects of jealousy on the love relationship. The article also shows how men and women behave differently under the influence of jealousy.

Buscaglia, L. *Living, Loving, and Learning.* New York: Ballantine Books, 1982. One of the most practical and realistic discussions of love ever written. The book discusses learning to love yourself as a prerequisite to learning to love others.

Hopson, B., and Hopson, C. *Intimate Feedback: A Lover's Guide to Getting in Touch With Each Other.* New York: Signet Books, 1976. A presentation of some techniques for stimulating a more emotionally and sexually satisfying relationship. Included are exercises on touching, communication, conflict, and trust.

Rubin, Z. "Are Working Wives Hazardous to Their Husbands' Health?" *Psychology Today* (May 1983): 70–72. An article that discusses the effect that wives' working has on husbands' self-esteem, stress levels, and health.

Stapleton, J., and Bright, R. *Equal Marriage*. Nashville: Abingdon, 1976. A book that shows couples how to work out equality in nearly every aspect of marriage. The authors contend that equality is essential for a satisfying intimate relationship.

## Glossary

**emotional loneliness:** lack of an intimate relationship.

**existential loneliness:** the experience of loneliness from which we personally and creatively learn and grow. The creative use of time spent alone.

**loneliness:** a painful wish for meaningful human contact or intimacy.

**romantic love:** a set of idealized standards whereby we judge the quality of a relationship.

**social loneliness:** the absence of a supportive social network.

## References

Alpenfels, E. J. "Progressive Monogamy: An Alternative Pattern?" In *The Family in Search of a Future*. Edited by H. A. Otto. New York: Appleton-Century-Crofts, 1970.

Altman, I., and Taylor, D. *Social Penetration: The Development of Interpersonal Relationships*. New York: Holt, Rinehart, and Winston, 1973.

Bennis, W. G., and Slater, P. E. *The Temporary Society*. New York: Harper & Row, 1968.

Buscaglia, L. F. *Living, Loving, and Learning*. New York: Ballantine Books, 1982.

Byrne, D. *The Attraction Paradigm*. New York: Academic Press, 1971.

Carter, H., and Glick, P. *Marriage and Divorce: A Social and Economic Study*. Cambridge, Mass.: Harvard University Press, 1970.

Clark, J. R. *The Importance of Being Imperfect*. New York: McKay, 1961.

Dahms, A. M. "Intimacy Hierachy." In *Process in Relationship: Marriage and Family*. Edited by E. A. Powers and M. W. Lees. St. Paul, Minn.: West, 1976.

Grinker, R. R., Jr. "The Poor Rich." *Psychology Today* (October 1977): 74–81.

Hall, E. T. *The Hidden Dimension*. Garden City, N.Y.: Anchor Books, 1969.

Harper, R. A. "Sex and American Attitudes." In *The New Sexuality*. Edited by H. Otto. Palo Alto, Calif.: Science and Behavior Books, 1971.

Horn, J. "Love: The Most Important Ingredient in Happiness." *Psychology Today* (July 1976): 98, 102.

Horn, P., ed. "Newsline: We All Marry Our Mothers." *Psychology Today* (May 1974): 32.

Jacobs, J. *Adolescent Suicide*. New York: Wiley, 1971.

Keyes, R. *We, the Lonely People: Searching for Community*. New York: Harper & Row, 1973.

Lederer, W. J., and Jackson, D. D. *The Mirages of Marriage*. New York: Norton, 1968.

London, P. "The Intimacy Gap." *Psychology Today* (May 1978): 40–45.

Lowenthal, M. F., and Haven, C. "Interaction and Adaptation: Intimacy as a Critical Variable." *American Sociological Review* 33 (1968): 20–30.

May, R. *Man's Search for Himself*. New York: Dell, 1953.

Mead, M. "Anomalies in American Post-Divorce Relationships." in *Divorce and After*. Edited by P. Bohannan. Garden City, N.Y.: Doubleday, 1970.

Morris, D. *Intimate Behavior*. New York: Random House, 1971.

Moustakas, C. E. *Loneliness*. Englewood Cliffs, N.J.: Prentice-Hall, 1961.

Packard, V. *A Nation of Strangers*. New York: David McKay, 1972.

Pothier, D. "Pets Good for the Heart." *Knight-Ridder News Service, Miami Herald* (January 19, 1984).

Rogers, C. R. *Carl Rogers on Encounter Groups.* New York: Harper & Row, 1970.

Rubin, Z. *Liking and Loving.* New York: Holt, Rinehart and Winston, 1973.

Rubin, Z.; Peplau, L.; and Hill, C. T. "The Sexual Balance of Power." *Psychology Today,* (November 1976).

Safilios-Rothschild, C. *Love, Sex, and Sex Roles.* Englewood Cliffs, N.J.: Prentice-Hall, 1977.

Sullivan, H. S. *Conceptions of Modern Psychiatry.* New York: Norton, 1953.

Toffler, A. *Future Shock.* New York: Bantam Books, 1971.

Udry, J. R. *The Social Context of Marriage.* New York: Lippincott, 1974.

Weiss, R. S. *Loneliness: The Experience of Emotional and Social Isolation.* Cambridge, Mass.: M.I.T. Press, 1973.

Wolfe, T. *The Hills and Beyond.* New York: Harper & Bros., 1941.

## ANSWERS TO REVIEW QUESTIONS

**Page 391.** *1.* T *2.* T *3.* T *4.* T *5.* F *6.* F *7.* T *8.* F

**Page 398.** *9.* T *10.* F *11.* T *12.* F *13.* T *14.* F *15.* F *16.* F *17.* F *18.* F *19.* T *20.* F

In Part VI, we consider what happens to the individual when things go wrong and describe several direct coping strategies that may be used to help the person deal more effectively with life circumstances.

Chapter 13 introduces the concept of maladjustment and discusses several categories of maladjustments, including anxiety disorders, disorders of social concern, and psychotic disorders. These categories exemplify the broad range of categories of maladjustment and provide you with information about several maladjustments commonly suffered by people in our society. Some specific topics covered are irrational fears, substance abuse, psychosexual dysfunctions, and changing sexual mores, folkways, and customs.

Chapter 14 presents an overview of psychotherapy. It discusses a number of practical questions related to therapy, such as: When should a person consider entering therapy? What are some of the different types of therapists? How does one choose a therapist and a therapy? What does therapy cost? When should therapy end?

The bulk of the chapter comprises brief descriptions of over twenty different therapies or therapeutic approaches. Each description attempts to capture the characteristic flavor of the therapy. The descriptions of psychoanalysis, Rogerian therapy, behavior therapy, and cognitive therapy complement and round out earlier discussions of the corresponding schools of psychological thought.

# VI

# MALADJUSTMENT AND PSYCHOTHERAPY

# 13

# MALADJUSTMENT

*Dear Phoebe:*
*I can't tell you how shocked I was when I*
*came home early from my weekly bridge game*
*last Thursday night and found my husband*
*lounging in his favorite easy chair, dressed*
*only in my pantyhose! He says he is not a*
*homosexual and that he loves me very much.*
*It's just that he feels good when wearing the*
*pantyhose. Is he strange, or am I? What am*
*I to think?*

*Perplexed*


*Dear Perplexed:*
*Something's definitely going on! Contact your*
*local psychologist.*

*Phoebe*

**13**

MALADJUSTMENT

# DISCUSSION: MALADJUSTMENT

**Maladjustment** is the relative failure to meet adequately the psychological demands of oneself, the group, or the situation. There may be some instances in which usually well-adjusted people have a difficult time adjusting. Conversely, a few people may be very maladjusted in most instances, but able to adjust very well in others. Thus, *everyone* behaves in at least a slightly maladjusted way from time to time, and probably *no one* behaves in a maladjusted way all the time. Most of us, of course, seem to make fairly good adjustments most of the time.

## ■ Causes of Maladjustment

The answer to the question of what causes maladjustment has changed substantially over the years and continues to change. During the nineteenth century, the *medical* model came into wide acceptance.[1] This model holds that psychological maladjustment is caused by an underlying physical condition. Hence, brain damage may cause ineffective behavior, and lead poisoning may cause irritability or depression.

*See Chapter 14 for a consideration of electroconvulsive, or shock, therapy.*

The medical model has had a great influence on the treatment of maladjustment in the modern Western world. Generally, treatment has attempted to deal with the cause as well as the symptoms of the maladjustment, and medical procedures such as drug therapy and electroshock are used. The medical model has also influenced how people in general view those who suffer from severe maladjustment—as "sick" persons who suffer because of a condition beyond their control and who need professional help to be "cured."

*See Chapters 2 and 14 for discussions of Freud's approach to maladjustment.*

In the latter part of the nineteenth century, Freud introduced the *psychological model,* which holds that some maladjustments come from underlying psychological causes. Fixations, anxiety, and exaggerated ego defenses may cause the ineffective behavior.

*Chapter 7 covers Selye on stress.*

In the twentieth century, both the medical model and the psychological model have been extended. Selye's general adaptation syndrome depicts both biological and psychological decay as occurring under excessive stress. And the behaviorists view maladjustment as either the failure to learn effective behaviors or the efficient learning of maladjustment behaviors (that is, the maladjustive behaviors have been reinforced).

## ■ Types of Maladjustment

There are many types of maladjustment, each with its own set of symptoms and potential causes. It is important to realize, however, that mental health professionals often disagree concerning the types, symptoms, and causes of maladjustment. In an attempt to remedy this situation, the American Psychiatric Association published a *Diagnostic and Statistical Manual* (DSM) of mental disorders in 1952. The most recent edition (DSM-III) was published in 1980. Although DSM-III appears to be an improvement over its predecessors, it has

---

1. Prior to the nineteenth century, maladjustment was often assumed to be the work either of evil spirits or of God, who might punish people for sinning by inflicting maladjustment on them.

not yet received widespread acceptance among mental health professionals. Still, it is a useful and popular system. Therefore, we will rely primarily on DSM-III in the following discussion.

DSM-III specifies a large number of maladjustments (see Table 13.1 for a sample) and it is beyond the scope of this chapter to discuss every one of them. However, to give you an idea of the range of those maladjustments, we will briefly discuss three types: **anxiety disorders, disorders of social concern,** and **psychotic disorders.** It is perhaps important to reiterate that everyone displays maladjustment from time to time. Thus, if you begin to see a little of your own behavior in the following descriptions, do not become overly concerned.

## DISCUSSION: ANXIETY DISORDERS

Anxiety disorders are those in which **anxiety** is the predominant disturbance or the individual attempts to avoid anxiety by behaving in particular ways. Anxiety disorders are estimated to occur in 2 percent to 4 percent of the general population (DSM-III, p. 225). Specific anxiety disorders include panic disorder, generalized anxiety disorder, phobic disorders, and obsessive compulsive disorder.

TABLE 13.1
Sample of Disorders Listed in DSM-III

DISORDERS USUALLY FIRST EVIDENT IN INFANCY, CHILDHOOD, OR ADOLESCENCE

Separation anxiety
Identity disorder

ORGANIC MENTAL DISORDERS

Senile dementia, with delusions
Amnestic syndrome

SUBSTANCE USE DISORDERS

Alcohol abuse
Cocaine abuse

SCHIZOPHRENIC DISORDERS

Disorganized
Catatonic

PARANOID DISORDERS

Paranoia
Shared paranoid disorder

PSYCHOTIC DISORDERS NOT ELSE-WHERE CLASSIFIED

Schizophreniform disorder
Brief reactive psychosis

AFFECTIVE DISORDERS

Bipolar disorder, manic
Major depression, recurrent

ANXIETY DISORDERS

Phobic disorders
Obsessive compulsive disorder

SOMATOFORM DISORDERS

Psychogenic pain disorder
Hypochondriasis

DISSOCIATIVE DISORDERS

Psychogenic fugue
Multiple personality

PSYCHOSEXUAL DISORDERS

Gender identify disorders
Paraphilias

DISORDERS OF IMPULSE CONTROL NOT ELSEWHERE CLASSIFIED

Pathological gambling
Kleptomania

ADJUSTMENT DISORDER

With depressed mood
With anxious mood

PSYCHOLOGICAL FACTORS AFFECTING PHYSICAL CONDITION

PERSONALITY DISORDERS

Paranoid
Antisocial

Note: Neurotic disorders, which were grouped together as neuroses in DSM-II, are included in affective, anxiety, somatoform, dissociative, and psychosexual disorders in DSM-III.

■ Normal and Abnormal Anxiety

Anxiety is considered normal in many situations. Probably all students have experienced "butterflies" in their stomachs before taking an important final examination. Anxiety is considered abnormal when it repeatedly incapacitates the individual. Such anxiety is intense and may interfere with goals or relationships or cause great pain and consternation. Thus, anxiety disorders are characterized by anxiety that is more intense, frequent, and incapacitating than normal anxiety.

■ Causes and Development of Anxiety Disorders

As with all mental disorders, there is more than one theoretical explanation for the causes and development of anxiety disorders. In addition, there is evidence in the form of research, experimentation, and clinical data and experience to support all these various explanations. However, while each theoretical orientation—physiological, behavioral, cognitive, and psychoanalytic—has its own position, it appears that we may draw at least four tentative conclusions with regard to the causes and development of anxiety disorders (Mehr, 1983, pp. 169–170):

*1.* Individuals with anxiety disorders seem to be physically overreactive, an apparent predisposition in the development of anxiety disorders that may or may not be genetically transmitted.
*2.* Learning through both reinforcement and modeling seems to be a very significant factor.
*3.* Thoughts and self-perceptions are important.
*4.* Childhood experiences are important.

■ Panic Disorder

**Panic disorder** involves recurrent, short-term panic (anxiety) attacks. The attacks are unpredictable in that they are not usually associated with specific objects or situations and the individual usually does not know in advance when the next one will occur.

The anxiety in these attacks is experienced by the individual as particularly intense. A sudden onset of severe apprehension, fear, or terror, often linked with feelings of impending doom, virtually immobilize the person for the duration of the attack. Among the most common symptoms are palpitations, chest pain, choking or smothering sensations, feelings of unreality; hot and cold flashes, sweating, faintness, trembling or shaking, and fear of dying or going crazy. Attacks usually last only minutes but may last hours on rare occasions.

■ Generalized Anxiety Disorder

The primary feature of **generalized anxiety disorder** is a general anxiety that persists for at least a month. The individual feels a constant nervous tension that varies in intensity from uneasiness to anxiety but that does not reach the level of fear or terror associated with panic disorder.

Specific symptoms vary from one person to the next; however, manifestations of anxiety from each of the following four categories are usually present:

1. *Motor tension.* Examples: shakiness, trembling, muscle aches, eyelid twitch, strained face, easy startlement.

2. *Autonomic hyperactivity.* Examples: sweating, racing heart, clammy hands, dizziness, frequent urination, lump in the throat, flushing.

3. *Apprehensive expectation.* Examples: anxiousness, worry, anticipation that something bad will happen to oneself or others.

4. *Vigilance and scanning.* Examples: impatience, irritability, distractibility, difficulty in concentrating, insomnia, interrupted sleep, fatigue on awakening.

Jane has been encouraged to pursue a medical career since she can remember. In high school, she was able to get excellent marks in the tenth and eleventh grades. However, when she started to take more demanding honors courses in the twelfth grade, she was unable to perform as well. The worse the performance, the more anxious she became.

The following year she entered a pre-med program at college. By this time her level of anxiety had become so high she could get no grade higher than D. Physical manifestations of her anxiety included trembling, aching muscles, and dizziness. In addition, she was irritable, had difficulty concentrating, and couldn't sleep at night.

By the end of the second semester, she had become incapable of functioning in school, and her average was too low for her even to consider entrance into medical school. Unable to study, she dropped out of school and, at this time, is barely capable of holding a part-time job.

## ▪ Phobic Disorders

Phobic disorders involve intense and unrealistic fears, such as fear of being alone, of heights, or of harmless animals. Phobic disorders seem to be acquired either through conditioning ("I fell from a high place when I was young and, to this day, I still fear heights") or imitation ("My father always expressed fear when he saw a mouse in the house and I am afraid of them, too"). Typically, the person relieves the anxiety by avoiding the fear stimulus. The person who fears being alone, for instance, seeks the companionship of others rather than dealing directly with being alone. Being with others relieves the anxiety, encouraging the person to continue seeking the companionship of others. We can easily understand why it is often difficult to break a phobic pattern.

Clinicians have identified many specific phobias, from a fear of enclosed places *(claustrophobia)* to a fear of blood *(hematophobia)* to a fear of dirt or germs *(mysophobia)*. They have even identified a fear of irrational fear *(phobophobia)*! For purposes of classification, however, DSM-III divides phobic disorders into three categories: **agoraphobia, social phobia,** and **simple phobia**.

▪ *Agoraphobia*   Agoraphobia is a fear of either "being alone or being in public places from which escape might be difficult or help not available in case of sudden incapacitation" (DSM-III, p. 226). The initial phase of agoraphobia often consists of a series of panic attacks followed by the development of the

## CASE IN POINT
## A Sampling of Phobias

- Acaraphobia: fear of itching.
- Acrophobia: fear of heights.
- Ailurophobia: fear of cats.
- Anthrophobia: fear of human society.
- Aquaphobia (or hydrophobia): fear of water.
- Aviophobia: fear of flying.
- Brontophobia: fear of thunder.
- Dromophobia: fear of running.
- Erythrophobia: fear of blushing.

- Gamophobia: fear of marriage.
- Gephydrophobia: fear of bridges.
- Graphophobia: fear of writing.
- Mysophobia: fear of dirt or germs.
- Nyctophobia: fear of the dark.
- Phgonophobia: fear of beards.
- Triskaidekaphobia: fear of the number 13.
- Xenophobia: fear of strangers.
- Zoophobia: fear of animals.

fear that such an attack will occur when the person is without someone to help. Thus, the individual tends to seek constant companionship.

■ *Social Phobia*    Social phobia is a fear and avoidance of situations in which the person may be carefully observed by others. The person fears that he or she may behave in a humiliating or embarrassing way. Examples of social phobia are fears of speaking, performing, or eating in public; of using public lavatories; and of writing in the presence of others.

The person suffering from social phobia usually is concerned that others will detect his or her anxiety. For example, the person who fears speaking in public is concerned that others may detect a voice tremor. Thus, a vicious cycle may be created in which the fear of speaking in public leads to a trembling voice, which further intensifies the fear of speaking in public.

■ *Simple Phobia*    Simple phobia is a persistent, irrational fear and avoidance of objects and situations other than those included in agoraphobia and social phobia. This residual category of phobic disorders includes fears of many objects, the most common of which involve animals such as dogs, snakes, insects, and mice. Fear of heights and fear of enclosed spaces are examples of simple phobias related to situations rather than objects.

**WHAT DO YOU THINK?**

■ Can you remember any simple phobias from your childhood?
■ Which have disappeared and which remain?

Exposure to the phobic stimulus may produce an extreme panic attack, but direct exposure is not necessary for the individual to experience anxiety. Turmoil may be produced when the person thinks about the phobic object or situation.

Simple phobias often begin in childhood, and most disappear without treatment. However, those that remain with us in adulthood rarely disappear without treatment.

### ■ Obsessive Compulsive Disorder

As the name suggests, **obsessive compulsive disorder** involves obsessions and compulsions. **Obsessions** are recurrent, persistent ideas, thoughts, images, or

## CASE IN POINT
## Social Phobia

Have you ever suffered or do you now suffer from a social phobia—say, a fear of raising a question or challenging the teachers in your classes?
What were or are you afraid of?

_____

_____

What factors confirmed your fear?

_____

_____

Is or was your fear justified?

_____

_____

How did or how could you overcome your fear?

_____

_____

_____

impulses that are experienced as involuntary and as senseless or repugnant. In other words, senseless or repugnant thoughts keep coming into the person's mind. Common obsessions are thoughts of violence (for example, of killing one's child) of contamination (for example, of becoming infected by shaking hands with someone), and of doubt (for example, one may repeatedly wonder if one has performed some action, such as hurting someone in a traffic accident).

**Compulsions** are repetitive and seemingly purposeful behaviors performed according to certain rules or in a stereotyped fashion. The behavior is designed

■ A common simple phobia. Do you identify with this man?

to produce or prevent some future situation; however, the behavior is either unrealistic or clearly excessive and does not produce pleasure. In short, the person is driven to carry out some ritualized behavior that seems unrelated to his or her present circumstances. Common compulsions include hand-washing, counting, and touching.

Attempts to resist obsessions or compulsions produce anxiety that can be relieved by giving in to the obsessions or compulsions. After repeated failure at resistance, the individual may acquiesce and no longer experience a desire to resist.

REVIEW
QUESTIONS

1. Maladjustment is the relative failure to meet adequately the psychological demands of _____ , the _____ , or the _____ .

2. During the nineteenth and twentieth centuries, the two primary models for explaining the causes of maladjustment have been the _____ model and the _____ model.

3. Anxiety disorders are those in which anxiety is the predominant disturbance or the individual attempts to avoid anxiety by behaving in particular ways. T F

4. An individual suffering from panic disorder always knows when the next panic attack will occur. T F

5. Generalized anxiety disorder differs from panic disorder in that the level of fear is much greater in generalized anxiety disorder. T F

6. Three categories of phobic disorders are _____ , _____ , and _____ _____ .

7. Recurrent, persistent ideas, thoughts, images, or impulses experienced as involuntary and as senseless or repugnant are called _____ .

8. _____ are repetitive and seemingly purposeful behaviors performed according to certain rules or in a stereotyped fashion.

*The answers to these review questions are on page 437.*

## DISCUSSION: DISORDERS OF SOCIAL CONCERN

Some behaviors are at least as much a problem for other people as for the person who displays the behavior. Indeed, in some instances the individual may not perceive his or her behavior as a personal problem, although others directly affected by the behavior are concerned by it. In this section we will consider disorders of social concern in three areas: sexual behavior, substance use, and personality.

### ■ Sexual Behavior

Some aspects of sexual behavior may be intensely private (sexual fantasies, masturbation), while others are clearly of social concern (exhibitionism, sexual sadism). DSM-III divides the category of **psychosexual disorders** into four groups:

psychosexual dysfunctions, gender identity disorders, paraphilias, and a re-sidual class of other psychosexual disorders. Other sexual behaviors, such as homosexuality and bisexuality, are not classified as disorders but are matters of concern to some. Let us discuss these various behaviors, and then you may conclude for yourself which are primarily of private concern and which are of social concern.

■ *Psychosexual Dysfunctions*   Psychosexual dysfunctions involve inhibitions of sexual desire or psychophysiological functioning that prevent the individual from satisfactorily completing the cycle of sexual response. Good sex requires good nerves, blood vessels, and muscles. Disease or injury in any of these systems can cause sexual difficulties, as can poor nutrition or drug abuse. However, the vast majority of psychosexual dysfunctions are psychological in origin.

Our physiology predisposes us to be sexually active, but such activity requires an environment that provides a feeling of security for optimal expression. Pres-sure to be sexually active, creative, and orgasmic to prove masculinity or fem-ininity creates problems. A fear of failure, together with the additional concern that failure will result in the loss of the sexual partner, makes one less able to respond naturally and spontaneously. Power struggles, poor communication, and general tension in a relationship make sexuality difficult. Security and in-timacy support each other, and too little of either can destroy the other. Thus, psychosexual dysfunctions are born. The most common complaints today in-clude erectile dysfunction, premature ejaculation, inorgasmic dysfunction, and functional dyspareunia.

*Erectile dysfunction* is the inability to have or to maintain an erection during intercourse, and it is the most common dysfunction among males. A man's sexual self, his masculinity, is always in peril. If erection does not happen on cue, even once, his concept of himself may become clouded by doubts concerning his potency.

*Premature ejaculation* is the man's inability to control or delay ejaculation long enough to satisfy his own or his partner's desires, and it is the second most common dysfunction among males. The subjective evaluation of what is normal in this regard is a source of tension because of media-based expectations not grounded in reality. According to one source, most women reach orgasm from five to thirty minutes after the onset of foreplay (Wolfe, 1980). Hunt (1974) finds that the median duration of marital intercourse is ten minutes, quite a bit longer than the two-minute median of just a generation ago (Kinsey, Pomeroy, and Martin, 1948).

*Inorgasmic dysfunction* is the inability to experience an orgasm, and it is the most common dysfunction among females. A woman's sexual self is threatened if she is unresponsive or unable to respond orgasmically. The belief that "frigidity castrates the male" adds tension to this dysfunction.

*Functional dyspareunia*, painful intercourse, is the second most common dys-function among females. Lack of knowledge of or insensitivity to physiological cues related to readiness for intercourse accounts for much of this dysfunction. Infection and poorly healed lesions are major causes for pain that is not psy-chologically based. *Functional vaginismus* is the prevention of insertion of the penis by involuntary muscle spasms around the vaginal entrance; it was once one of the most common female disorders but is now relatively rare. Less fearful expectations of coitus appear to be the reason for the reduction of this disorder.

**WHAT DO YOU THINK?**

■ Have you ever suffered from a psychosexual dysfunction?

■ How did you feel? How did it affect you?

■ What did you do to correct the situation?

■ *Gender Identity Disorders*  In gender identity disorders, the individual has feelings of discomfort and inappropriateness about his or her anatomic sex and persistently behaves in ways generally associated with the other sex. In essence, the anatomical male feels like a female trapped in the body of a male, and the anatomical female feels like a male trapped in the body of a female. In adults this disorder is called *transsexualism;* in children it is called *gender identity disorder of childhood.*

At present, no one can be certain what causes transsexualism. Prenatal hormones could produce a male brain in a female body and vice versa. However, this has not yet been demonstrated to be a cause of the disorder. Mature transsexuals have the hormones of their physical, not mental, sex; and the problem does not follow lines of heredity. No established pattern of childhood experiences predicts transsexualism, although at times parents and child have secretly agreed on the child's disavowal of his or her anatomic sex.

Coping is extremely difficult for transsexuals. Those who desire gender transformation often are given hormone therapy, counseling, and similar reversible treatments for a two-year trial. At that time, surgical intervention may be considered. Castration (removal of ovaries or testes) and reconstruction (construction of vagina and breasts or penis) are possible but have not been perfected. Females who have been transformed to males are impotent, and males who have been transformed to females cannot conceive. The prognosis after surgery for those who have passed the two-year trial is reportedly good. The surgery confirms their life style, and they appear satisfied. However, the prognosis for those who demand surgery without the two-year trial is poor.

**WHAT DO YOU THINK?**

■ Should a two-year trial period preceding sex-change surgery be made mandatory?
■ Sould sex-change operations be outlawed?

■ *Paraphilias*  Paraphilias are sexual disorders in which the individual requires unusual or bizarre imagery or acts for sexual excitement. The imagery or acts tend to be involuntary and repetitive and generally involve (1) nonhuman objects, (2) real or simulated suffering or humiliation, or (3) nonconsenting partners.

Sexual imagery is common. It becomes a major disorder when the needed image demands a victim, as in *sadism* (in which pain is inflicted on another person), *masochism* (in which pain is inflicted on oneself), or *rape*. It is a minor disorder when it demands an unwilling partner, as in *voyeurism* (viewing of others without their knowledge or consent while they are undressing, nude, or involved in some sexual behavior) and *exhibitionism* (exposing of one's genitals to a nonconsenting person). It may be a minor nuisance (fetishism) or a major nuisance (transvestism) when the demand is for the image of an inanimate object.

*Fetishism* involves the use of certain objects (called *fetishes*) as the preferred or exclusive way to achieve sexual excitement. Fetishes are often articles of clothing, sometimes parts of the body, and, rarely, other, nonliving objects. Thus, the fetishist may become sexually excited by a pair of pantyhose, a pair of feet, or a pair of bookends.

**WHAT DO YOU THINK?**

■ What images arouse you?
■ Do you know why?

*Transvestism* is an obsession with dressing in the clothes of the opposite sex. Such dress is, at times, required for sexual arousal and for either heterosexual or homosexual performance. Early sexual experiences appear critical in the development of this disorder—for example, the person may have been punished by being dressed in the clothing associated with the opposite sex or may have worn or handled such apparel while masturbating.

■ Do you consider this man well-adjusted?

It must be pointed out that although there are several theoretical explanations for the origins and development of paraphilias in general, these explanations are supported primarily by generalizations from case histories. Thus, a great deal more research must be done to obtain a clear picture of why paraphilias develop.

■ *Other Psychosexual Disorders*   The primary disorder in the category "other psychosexual disorders" is **ego-dystonic homosexuality**. This occurs when the homosexual wants to change sexual preference to heterosexuality but has difficulty making this adjustment.

> Tim's parents reacted with disbelief and disgust when they found out he is homosexual. He loves them very much and had hoped they would be understanding and accepting when he revealed his long-standing secret to them, but they have not. Indeed, they have insisted that he enter into therapy with the goal of changing his sexual preference to heterosexual.
>    Tim has tried hard to please them. He has even attempted sexual intercourse with women on a couple of occasions. He dislikes this so much, however, that he is becoming more isolated and withdrawn. He is miserable and contemplates suicide more and more often.

■ *Homosexuality*   Homosexuality, sexual preference for members of the same sex, is no longer classified as a mental disorder, but it is still illegal in many states. In other states it is legal as long as it represents private choice between consenting adults. Of course, for many homosexuality is simply considered an alternative life style.

Personal choice, heredity, and prenatal and postnatal hormonal and environ-mental influences have all been proposed as the source of homosexuality. What-ever causes it to develop, a strong homosexual identity, once established, tends to resist later social influences that attempt to reshape sexual orientation.

Homosexuality may be considered a problem for the individual if he or she is having difficulty with a desired change in sexual preference, as described in the discussion of ego-dystonic homosexuality, or if the individual is having difficulty accepting himself or herself as a homosexual. Therapy may be useful under these conditions.

■ *Bisexuality*   Bisexuality is a pattern of performing sexually with persons of either sex. This orientation may result from social factors, or physiological predispositions, or both. Women seem more capable of being aroused by mem-bers of either sex. This may be because the female brain retains a bisexual potential, or because in women, being held and touched is more stimulating than mental imagery. Females are also allowed contact comfort from each other without being made anxious or guilty, as is the case with males in our culture.

Allowing a wide range of spontaneous sexual play during childhood does not produce bisexuality. On the contrary, such sexual permissiveness appears to encourage the development of a strong *heterosexual* identity and role for both males and females. Males emerge more emotional, less aggressive, less compet-itive, and more human, while females emerge with greater self-confidence, less fear of success, and greater independence (Pleck, 1976).

Bisexuality is not a disorder and requires treatment only for secondary symp-toms, should they occur. These are usually the result of a self-imposed or social stigma, and therapy should be directed toward restoring a sense of well-being and acceptance by the individual of whatever sexual preference he or she may desire.

*See Chapter 2 for Freud's view on instinct and sexuality.*

■ *What Constitutes Sexual Deviation?*   Aberration from statistical, legal, med-ical, psychological, or moral norms may constitute sexual abnormality or de-viation. Freud gave us a psychological perspective from which to judge the normality of sexual behavior. He considered sexual activity instinctive. Sexual instinct has a *source* (tension arising from internal or external stimulation), an *object* (an acceptable adult who can gratify the instinct by reducing the tension), and an *aim* (coitus, an act to reduce tension). "Normal" sexual behavior is represented by activities toward the reduction of sexual tension through inter-course with an appropriate adult member of the opposite sex. "Deviations" can be classified in terms of their relation to source, object, aim, or a combination of these. For example, prostitution is a deviation because the *source* of the activity for the prostitute is money or power, not sexual tension. Performing sexual acts with certain partners, such as members of same sex (homosexuality), children (pedophilia), relatives (incest), animals (zoophelia), and inanimate objects (fe-tishism), is a deviation because the *object* is not an appropriate adult member of the opposite sex. Voyeurism, exhibitionism, and sadomasochism are devia-tions because the *aim* is not coitus.

While Freud was interested in the discharge of tension as the product of sexual behavior, religion and even the state are sometimes interested in *procreation* as the product that justifies such pleasures of the flesh. Any practice that does not advance the production of legitimate children can thus be considered a deviation.

## CASE IN POINT
### Sexual Variations

What are some of the sexual behaviors you have experimented with?

_____

_____

_____

_____

Which, if any, do you think are regarded by others as abnormalities or deviations?

_____

_____

_____

What do you think and how do you feel when engaged in these behaviors?

_____

_____

_____

What would you think and how would you feel when engaged in these behaviors if you believed others regarded them as variations rather than deviations?

_____

_____

_____

Fetishism, fornication, adultery, homosexuality, incest, masturbation, oral sex, pedophilia, rape, sodomy, voyeurism, and others fail the test of high religious or state purpose.

In addition, every culture places restrictions even on sexual intercourse between married adults. For example, in some primitive societies coitus is either forbidden or mandated prior to important events such as planting, harvesting, hunting, or war. Failing to abstain during the entire baseball season (April through October) is a deviation for members of the Tokyo Giants.

Finally, anything expressly forbidden or mandated in law is a deviation if prosecution occurs. Marriages can be annulled if they are not consummated. Kinsey (1948) found that 95 percent of our male population had at some time violated one or more state or federal statutes pertaining to sexual behavior. Laws pertaining to masturbation, fornication, anal intercourse, and oral-genital contact (among others) are not regularly enforced but remain to make potential criminals of us all.

Sexual activity within human groups is extremely varied. One would be hard pressed to think of an activity that has not been attempted in the search for sexual gratification. The term *sexual variations,* rather than sexual abnormalities or deviations, captures this range without placing a stigma on the notion of being sexually experimental.

REVIEW
QUESTIONS

9. _____ _____ involve inhibitions of sexual desire or psychophysiological functioning that prevent the individual from satisfactorily completing the _____ of _____ _____.

*10.* The most common psychosexual dysfunction among males today is

_____ dysfunction.

*11.* The most common psychosexual dysfunction among females today is

_____ dysfunction.

*12.* At present, no one can be certain what causes transsexualism. T F

*13.* Paraphilias are sexual disorders in which the individual requires unusual or bizarre imagery or acts for sexual excitement. T F

*14.* Fetishism is an obsession with dressing in the clothes of the opposite sex. T F

*15.* _____ is sexual preference for members of the same sex.

*16.* A pattern of performing sexually with persons of either sex is called

_____ .

*17.* According to Freud, incest is a sexual deviation because the sexual object is not an appropriate adult member of the opposite sex. T F

*18.* Few cultures place restrictions on sexual intercourse between married adults. T F

*The answers to these review questions are on page 437.*

---

## ■ Substance Use

Throughout human history people have used certain substances (drugs) to alter their experiences. Such altered experiences usually contain initially pleasurable effects that involve changes in feelings, behavior, or physiological functioning and changes in perception of self and environment. At various times societies have accepted or rejected substance use for such purposes.

Contemporary American society has a decidedly mixed reaction to substance use. The recreational drinking of alcohol is legal in all fifty states, and it has been estimated that over 80 percent of adults (Engs, 1977) and 75 percent of high school seniors (Margulies, Viessler, and Kanded, 1977) drink alcoholic beverages. Although not supported by some groups within the society, alcohol use is widely accepted as normal and appropriate. The recreational use of heroin, on the other hand, is illegal in all fifty states and is considered abnormal and inappropriate by most Americans.

Substance use is considered a mental disorder when it is accompanied by certain behavioral changes such as impairment in social or occupational functioning, inability to control the use of or to stop taking the substance, and the development of serious withdrawal symptoms after cessation of or reduction in substance use (DSM-III, p. 163). These conditions are distinguished from "nonpathological substance use for recreational or medical purposes," which is not considered a disorder. In short, substance use in itself is not a mental disorder; but **substance abuse** and **physical substance dependence** are.

■ *Substance Abuse*    Substance abuse may be distinguished from nonpathological substance use by three factors.

> *1. A pattern of pathological use.* Examples: need for daily use of substance for adequate functioning; inability to stop or cut down use; intoxication throughout the day; complications of the intoxication (alcoholic blackouts, drug overdose)

*2. Impairment in social or occupational functioning caused by the pattern of pathological use.* Examples: inappropriate expression of aggressive feelings; erratic and impulsive behavior; failure to meet important obligations to friends and family; missed work or school; inability to function effectively because of intoxication.

*3. Duration.* The pattern of pathological use causing interference with social or occupational functioning must last at least *one month*.

■ *Physical Substance Dependence*  Physical substance dependence is generally a more severe form of substance use disorder than is substance abuse. Physical dependence requires only evidence of tolerance or withdrawal, although impairment in social or occupational functioning may also be present.[2] **Tolerance** means that there is a diminished effect with regular use of the same dose of the substance or that increased amounts of the substance are necessary to achieve the same effect. **Withdrawal** is a substance-specific syndrome that follows cessation or reduction in intake of a substance. For example, a chronic alcoholic who abruptly stops drinking experiences withdrawal symptoms—weakness, anxiety, perspiration, tremors, and nausea—within a few hours.

■ *Psychological Substance Dependence*  Some scholars speak of **psychological substance dependence** when referring to a situation in which "the individual needs the drug in order to cope, to function optimally from a subjective perspective" (Mehr, 1983, p. 229). For example, consistent cocaine use produces neither tolerance nor withdrawal, but it may be possible for the user to become psychologically "hooked" on the drug (Cohen, 1975). Mehr points out that psychological dependence "may be present without physical dependence, but is always present when physical dependence exists" (1983, p. 229). Thus, physical and psychological dependence are related terms, and each may be thought of as a type of **addiction**.

DSM-III lists nineteen categories of substance use disorders. In an attempt to provide a reasonable sampling of those categories, we will discuss disorders

---

2. For alcohol and cannabis, physical dependence requires a pattern of pathological use or impairment in social or occupational functioning.

## CASE IN POINT
## Tolerance to Alcohol

How much can you drink before you feel high?

_____

When you first began to drink, how much could you drink before you felt high?

_____

Do you think you are becoming physically dependent on alcohol?

_____

as they occur in six groupings: **alcohol, sedatives, opioids, stimulants, hallucinogens,** and **cannabis**.

■ *Alcohol* Alcohol is a central nervous system depressant that has both immediate and long-term effects on the user. It is rapidly absorbed into the bloodstream and carried to the brain, where it depresses the activity of cortical centers and allows unrestrained activity of other brain areas.

The initial *subjective* experience of the person who drinks alcohol is stimulation, although the opposite is really happening. For instance, subjective sexual interest may be increased, but the person's ability to be physiologically aroused in a sexual sense is decreased (Briddell & Wilson, 1976; Wilson and Lawson, 1978). Intoxication manifests itself in impaired motor coordination and judgment, poor self-control, impulsive behavior, and increased aggressiveness. Once intoxicated, the person who continues to drink in amounts large enough to raise the level of alcohol in his or her blood suffers gross impairment of motor coordination and cognition and ultimately falls asleep. Rapid drinking of large quantities by an individual who is already intoxicated may result in coma and even death.

Alcohol may be abused and may produce dependence. Long-term effects may include the development of tolerance, of an overwhelming sense of need for alcohol (craving), and of an inability to stop drinking after having had the first drink (loss of control). Craving and loss of control are often interpreted as signs of **alcoholism**. Other long-term effects may include withdrawal, Korsakoff's syndrome (a brain disorder that results from the destruction of brain cells caused by either the toxic effect of alcohol or a deficiency of vitamin $B_1$), cirrhosis (the destruction of liver cells), nutritional deficits, reduced effectiveness of white blood cells in fighting disease, and even chromosomal damage.

**WHAT DO YOU THINK?**

■ How much do you drink?
■ Are there any particular patterns to your drinking?

Alcohol abuse or dependence usually develops within the first five years after regular drinking is established and usually manifests itself in one of three patterns: (1) regular daily intake of large amounts; (2) regular, heavy drinking limited to weekends; and (3) long periods of sobriety interspersed with binges of daily heavy drinking lasting for weeks or months.

The causes and development of alcoholism, like those of all disorders, are open to debate. It appears that some alcoholics may have a genetic predisposition to drink. Goodwin (1979) suggests that many alcoholics may inherit a capacity to drink relatively large quantities of alcohol without becoming either sick or very intoxicated. In addition, they may inherit a capacity to experience more euphoria from alcohol than others do. Hence, a drinking pattern may emerge in which the individual drinks a lot because it produces pleasant feelings. But alcohol may also produce unpleasant effects—for example, a hangover. Thus, two reinforcers impinge upon drinkers who may have a genetic predisposition to drink: (1) they drink because it produces pleasant feelings, and (2) they drink because it relieves unpleasant feelings. Such reinforcement may ultimately transform a "social drinker" into an alcoholic.

Some alcoholics, however, seem to have no genetic predisposition to drink. Rather, they learn, either through imitation or from their own experience, to cope with stress and emotional problems through alcohol consumption. Emotional problems seem less severe because of alcohol's pain-reducing effect and its effect on the cognitive appraisal of stimuli.

Whether because of physiological or psychological factors or, perhaps, some combination of the two, alcoholics develop tolerance which, in turn, leads to heavier drinking. Heavier drinking leads to increased tolerance and so on until the person develops physical dependence and drinks to avoid the pain of withdrawal.

■ *Sedatives*  Sedatives are drugs such as barbiturates, tranquilizers, and hypnotics that can induce a relaxed state and sleep. They are usually taken orally in the form of pills or capsules, and they differ widely in rates of absorption, metabolism, distribution in the body, and likelihood of producing intoxication and withdrawal. They may be abused and may produce dependence.

The largest subcategory of sedatives is barbiturates, some of which are used medically for the control of epileptic seizure disorders; others are used to deal with sleeplessness. When abused, barbiturates produce effects similar to those of alcohol—impaired motor coordination and cognition, a release of inhibitions, and so on. Long-term abuse may produce chronic brain damage (Judd and Grant, 1975), and abrupt withdrawal may be fatal.

Barbiturates are more dangerous when combined with alcohol, as these two substances multiply each other's effects. Many accidental overdoses are attributed to this combination. Thus, barbiturates are considered extremely dangerous.

■ *Opioids*  Opioids are drugs such as opium, morphine, and heroin that produce a floating feeling and can reduce the perception of pain. Like alcohol and sedatives, opioids may be abused and may produce dependence.

The most abused opioid is heroin, which may be sniffed (snorted), smoked, taken orally, or injected either subcutaneously or intravenously. The most common form of initial use and long-term occasional use is snorting; intravenous injections are almost always preferred by those who have become physically dependent upon the drug.

Immediate effects are a euphoric "rush" that has been described as being similar in feeling to a sexual orgasm (although some users do not experience the rush) and a milder euphoric high that follows. The mild euphoria typically lasts four to six hours, during which the person is relaxed, withdrawn, and anxiety-free. This euphoria is followed by a slight letdown, a mildly depressed feeling, which tends to encourage the person to take another dose.

Long-term effects include tolerance that requires increasingly larger doses to produce a high equivalent to those obtained from the initial doses. Eventually the high disappears, regardless of the amount used. Users then take the drug to avoid the pain of withdrawal, which, like a severe case of the flu, is extremely unpleasant. Symptoms remain from seven to ten days. Heroin users may contract hepatitis or other infections from unsterile needles, and their resistance to physical diseases is lowered during withdrawal or between doses. In addition, both the individual and society suffer from the effects of crimes addicts often commit to get the money to support their heroin habits. Both may also suffer in other ways, as the Case In Point (see next page) illustrates.

■ *Stimulants*  Stimulants are substances that stimulate rather than depress the central nervous system. The commonly used major stimulants are cocaine and amphetamines. Both may be abused and may produce dependence; however, cocaine dependence is psychological, as tolerance and withdrawal do not develop with its use.

*Cocaine,* a white powder extracted from the coca shrub, is usually either snorted or injected intravenously, although it is sometimes taken in other ways

## CASE IN POINT
## "He Cheated Us All."

The theater world was shocked to learn in November 1983 that the actor James Hayden (see picture) had died in his New York apartment, the victim of what was almost certainly an overdose of heroin. Most of his friends and colleagues did not know that Hayden was a drug user. More ironic was the fact that, at the time of his death, Hayden was playing the role of Bobby, a junkie, in David Mamet's "American Buffalo." On hearing of his tragic death, one of his fellow actors commented "He cheated us all of the pleasure of knowing him as a human being." James Hayden had cheated himself and society as well.

■ James Hayden as Bobby.

when used simultaneously with other drugs. Immediate effects include a euphoria that lasts from four to six hours, lessened need for sleep, suppressed appetite, heightened alertness, increased intellectual functioning, and according to some reports, heightened sexual pleasure (Cohen, 1975; Post, 1975).

Long-term effects may include an ulcerated and perforated nasal septum (the wall that divides the inside of the nose), caused by constriction of blood vessels, and cocaine poisoning, which may result in death. In addition, long-term chronic use sometimes results in cocaine psychosis, a mental disorder in which the person loses touch with reality (Post, 1975).

*Amphetamines* may be taken orally or intravenously. Immediate effects include increased alertness and ability to concentrate, reduced fatigue and appetite, and elevated mood. Amphetamines have become popular with some people who need to overcome fatigue to complete a task (such as college students "cramming" for examinations). They are also popular as diet pills for people trying to lose weight.

Amphetamine abuse produces mental excitation, irritability, confusion, tremors, rapid speech, sleeplessness, and hypertension. Abrupt withdrawal may lead to convulsions (Kunnes, 1973). Taking large quantities within a short time may produce excitation for several days, followed by exhaustion and several days of sleep. Chronic abuse may lead to amphetamine psychosis, another mental disorder in which the person loses touch with reality (Snyder, 1973).

■ *Hallucinogens*   Hallucinogens are drugs that produce sensory distortion. Mescaline, psilocybin, and LSD are commonly used hallucinogens. These drugs may be abused, but they do not produce physical dependence.

Immediate effects include sensory distortion, such as seeing sounds or hearing colors; feelings of depersonalization and detachment from reality; and swift changes in emotions. Other immediate effects may include giddiness, weakness, nausea, increased body temperature and blood pressure (Barber, 1970), and a slight decrease in level of task performance (Pittel and Hofer, 1973). Individuals sometimes become violent while on a hallucinogenic "trip," committing acts such as mutilation and suicide (Cohen, 1970). Some individuals who have used hallucinogens have experienced *flashback,* a sudden, unexpected reexperiencing of parts of a drug trip from their past.

■ *Cannabis*   Cannabis is a preparation of resin taken from the *Cannabis sativa,* or Indian hemp plant. It is commonly called *marihuana* (sometimes spelled *marijuana*). It is usually smoked; sometimes it is mixed with food and eaten. Taken in large quantities, it has a mildly hallucinogenic effect. Cannabis may be abused and may produce tolerance (NIDA, 1977) and psychological dependence, but it does not produce withdrawal symptoms.

Immediate physical effects are virtually the same for all users: heart rate, blood pressure, appetite, and urination frequency increase; eyes become bloodshot; mouth becomes dry; respiratory passages widen (Tashkin, Shapiro, and Frank, 1974). Immediate psychological effects may be positive or negative. Positive effects include euphoria, relaxation, a sense of floating and well-being, and intensified perceptions. Negative effects include dysphoria (unpleasant, unhappy feelings), impaired judgment, and a feeling of going crazy or dying. Most regular users experience primarily positive psychological effects. An additional psychological effect, the slowing down of time, is common for all users.

Long-term effects are still in question. Some researchers contend that chronic use can produce a variety of devastating effects, from genetic damage to impotence to growth deficiencies (Nahas, 1975; Maugh, 1974a, 1974b). Others (Rubin and Comitas, 1975; Doughty et al., 1976) dispute these laims. Thus, additional research is needed. At present, it appears that chronic use may produce more asthma, bronchitis, pharyngitis, sinusitis, and emphysema than does heavy tobacco smoking (Mann, 1980). Chronic use also may lead to significant respiratory obstruction (Tashkin et al., 1976).

■ *General Factors in Substance Abuse*   When considering the question of whether or not a particular individual is likely to become a substance abuser, we should take into account several general factors (Mehr, 1983, p. 253):

1.  *Possible physiological predispositions.* This seems to be particularly important with regard to alcohol addiction. Do you experience a euphoric feeling when you drink? Are you able to consume relatively large quantities of alcohol without becoming sick or very intoxicated?

2.  *Social pressure.* This may be a very strong factor, particularly where drugs are readily available. Are you easily influenced by your peers?

3.  *Psychological vulnerability.* This seems to be a strong factor in individuals who experience great difficulty in coping effectively with anxiety, depression, and stress. Are you very anxious, depressed, or distressed? Have you developed or are you developing effective coping mechanisms?

*See Chapters 6 and 7 for discussions of anxiety, depression, stress, and coping mechanisms.*

*19.* One factor that distinguishes substance abuse from nonpathological substance use is a pattern of pathological use. T F

*20.* Physical substance dependence requires evidence of _____ or _____ .

*21.* The condition in which the individual needs a drug to cope or to function optimally from a psychological perspective is called _____ _____ _____ .

*22.* Alcohol abuse or dependence usually develops within the first five years after regular drinking is established. T F

*23.* Sedatives are drugs that have a stimulating effect on the central nervous system. T F

*24.* The most abused opioid is _____ .

*25.* Cocaine and amphetamines are stimulants. T F

*26.* Cocaine poisoning may result in death. T F

*27.* _____ are drugs that produce sensory distortion.

*28.* Cannabis, also known as marihuana, is a depressant. T F

*The answers to these review questions are on page 437.*

## ■ Personality Disorders

**Personality disorders** are maladjustments characterized by personality traits that deviate substantially from social norms and that prevent the person's achieving the satisfaction that comes with social acceptance. These personality traits are long-lasting patterns of thinking, perceiving, and behaving that are usually accepted by the person as part of himself or herself. Thus, the person suffering from a personality disorder tends to resist change and to rationalize the deeply ingrained problem personality traits as "the way I am."

■ *Origins and Development*   Personality disorders begin in childhood or adolescence and continue throughout most of the adult life of the individual. Often, relatives, friends, and coworkers are more disturbed by the individual's behavior than the individual is. In fact, the individual frequently is more bothered by others' reactions to the behavior than by the behavior itself. Therefore, people with personality disorders tend to have difficulty in their relationships with others and often blame others for their problems.

Two factors that seem important in the development of personality disorders are temperament and learning. It is possible that temperamental states (activity, boldness, timidity, quietness, and so on), which may be genetically transmitted, interact with learning experiences to produce deviant personality traits (Millon, 1981). For example, a shy and timid infant reared by emotionally cold and uncommunicative parents might develop into a *schizoid* personality (discussed later). It must be pointed out, however, that such an explanation is highly speculative for most personality disorders. The fact is that only one personality disorder, the *antisocial* personality, has been studied extensively, and much more research must be conducted before authoritative statements about origins and development can be made.

DSM-III specifies twelve categories of personality disorder and groups eleven of the twelve into three clusters: (1) odd or eccentric; (2) dramatic, emotional, or erratic; and (3) anxious or fearful. The twelfth category, "Atypical, Mixed, or Other Personality Disorder," is used for conditions that do not qualify as part of those previously specified.

■ *Odd or Eccentric Personalities*   Individuals with paranoid, schizoid, or schizotypal personality disorders frequently seem odd or eccentric. Those with **paranoid personality disorder** exhibit a pervasive, unwarranted suspiciousness and mistrust of others, as evidenced by guardedness, secretiveness, pathological jealousy, expectation of trickery or harm, and questioning of the loyalty of others. They are hypersensitive and appear to be cold and unemotional, lacking passive, soft, tender, and sentimental feelings and a true sense of humor. Individuals suffering from paranoid personality disorder are extremely difficult to live with.

**Schizoid personality disorder** is characterized by voluntary social isolation. People with this disorder have a defect in the capacity to form social relationships. They are reserved, withdrawn, seclusive, and have few, if any, close friends. In addition, they are usually humorless, dull, and indifferent to praise, criticism, and the feelings of others. Their social isolation is usually of more concern to others than to them.

People with **schizotypal personality disorder** display personality traits similar to those associated with schizoid personality disorder (social isolation, aloofness, and the like); however, in addition, they display various oddities of thought, perception, speech, and behavior. For example, they may exhibit *magical thinking*—belief that they have clairvoyance, telepathy, or a "sixth sense." *Ideas of reference*—beliefs or "feelings" that events are somehow related to them—are common (for example, they may believe others are talking about them behind their backs). *Odd speech* (such as vague, overelaborate, or metaphorical speech) is another common characteristic of individuals with schizotypal personality disorder.

■ *Dramatic, Emotional or Erratic Personalities*   Histrionic, narcissistic, borderline, and antisocial personality disorders are included in the dramatic, emotional, or erratic cluster. Individuals with **histrionic personality disorder** are overly dramatic and emotional. They exaggerate and constantly draw attention to themselves. They crave novelty and stimulation and are quickly bored with normal routines.

People with histrionic personality disorder tend to be perceived by others as superficially charming and appealing but shallow and without genuineness. They form friendships quickly but then may become demanding, inconsiderate, and manipulative. It is not unusual for them to make suicidal threats or even attempts in order to get their way.

Narcissus is an ancient Greek mythological figure who saw his own image reflected in a pool of water and fell in love with it. His fascination with his own image was so great that he could not pull himself away from the sight of it, and as a result, he starved to death. **Narcissistic personality disorder** is characterized by an exaggerated sense of self-importance, a preoccupation with fantasies of unlimited success, and an exhibitionistic need for constant attention and admiration. Individuals with this disorder have fragile self-esteem. They respond to criticism with either cool indifference or marked feelings of rage, inferiority, shame, humiliation, or emptiness. In addition, they tend to lack empathy for others and usually expect special favors without assuming reciprocal responsibilities.

Symptoms of **borderline personality disorder** include instability in various areas, including mood, self-concept, and interpersonal behavior, with no single feature invariably present. This is the most amorphous personality disorder and is frequently associated with other personality disorders. People with the disorder often display inappropriate, intense anger or lack of control of anger; intolerance of being alone; and marked shifts from normal mood to depression, irritability, or anxiety, and back to normal mood. In addition, they tend to be uncertain with regard to gender identity, career choice, friendship patterns, and values.

**Antisocial personality disorder** manifests itself in continuous and chronic antisocial behavior that violates the rights of others. The person with this disorder seems to lack a conscience and a concern for others. He or she apparently does not feel the anxiety that usually precedes the commission of an act perceived as immoral. In addition, the person seems to lack guilt and shame over transgressions, to lack loyalty to others, and to be unable to learn from experience. This disorder has been known in the past as *sociopathy* or *psychopathy*. It is the most extensively researched personality disorder.

The pattern of antisocial behavior begins before the age of fifteen and includes behaviors such as lying, stealing, fighting, truancy, and resisting authority. Of course, not all children who exhibit such behaviors become antisocial personalities. Those who do, however, frequently display early or aggressive sexual behavior, excessive drinking, and illicit drug use in adolescence. These behaviors continue into adulthood, when the person may also be unable to sustain con-

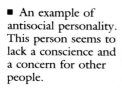

■ An example of antisocial personality. This person seems to lack a conscience and a concern for other people.

sistent work behavior, to function as a responsible parent, to accept social norms with regard to lawful behavior, or to maintain enduring attachment to a sexual partner. Some of these characteristics tend to diminish after the person has reached the age of thirty, but tension, depression, inability to tolerate boredom, and the belief that others are hostile toward them produce dysphoria and interpersonal difficulties for these people long after more flagrant antisocial behavior has diminished. Thus, it is particularly difficult for them to sustain lasting, close, warm, and responsible relationships with others.

Some researchers believe that the early relationship between parent and child is responsible for antisocial behavior. Children who do not receive adequate love and attention may become extremely self-centered and fail to learn to respect authority or to develop appropriate moral standards. Poor parent-child relationships are often found in the backgrounds of delinquent children (Redl and Wineman, 1962).

Other potential causes of antisocial behavior are related to insensitivity to pain and punishment. Experimentation has demonstrated that antisocial personalities are less sensitive to pain and punishment than ordinary subjects (Hare, 1970). This insensitivity may prevent the development of anxiety and guilt; and their absence may, in turn, lead to the antisocial behavior. It has not yet been determined whether the insensitivity to pain and punishment is caused by biological or environmental factors or by a combination of the two.

**WHAT DO YOU THINK?**
- Have you ever known anyone who displayed traits associated with the antisocial personality?
- Was (is) it difficult to maintain a relationship with this person?

■ *Anxious or Fearful Personalities*   The anxious or fearful cluster includes avoidant, dependent, compulsive, and passive-aggressive personality disorders. Individuals with **avoidant personality disorder** are hypersensitive to rejection, humiliation, or shame. The slightest hint of disapproval is devastating for these people; therefore, they withdraw socially and are unwilling to enter into relationships unless given unconditional approval and acceptance. People with avoidant personality disorders have a strong desire for personal relationships but lack the ability to relate comfortably to others. This leads to low self-esteem and its concomitant emotional structures: depression, anxiety, and anger.

Individuals with **dependent personality disorder** passively allow others to assume responsibility for major areas of their lives. Their inability to function independently is so great that they will subordinate their own needs to those of the people on whom they are dependent. People with this disorder not only leave major decisions to others, but they refuse to make demands on those they depend on, because they fear such demands might jeopardize the relationships and force them to rely on themselves. Individuals with dependent personality disorder lack self-confidence and tend to belittle themselves. Frequently, they suffer from another personality disorder, such as histrionic, schizotypal, narcissistic, or avoidant disorder.

**WHAT DO YOU THINK?**
- Do you allow or encourage others to make major decisions for you?

> None of their friends can understand why Donald continues to tolerate Evelyn's behavior. Throughout their sixteen-year marriage, she has been abusive to him in several ways, including belittling him in public, lying to him, and openly being unfaithful.
> What their friends do not know is that Donald relys on Evelyn to make every important decision for him and that he will accept almost any kind of abuse from her as long as she continues to make the decisions.

People with **compulsive personality disorder** have little ability to express warm and tender emotions. They are unduly conventional, formal, and serious in everyday relationships. They tend to be stingy with material possessions as well as with their emotions. Their preoccupation with and demand for perfection regarding trivial details, order, rules, organization, schedules, and lists interfere with their ability to take a broad view of things. People with this disorder often insist that others submit to their way of doing things but remain unaware of the negative feelings (such as resentment and hurt) that this behavior evokes in others. They are excessively devoted to work and productivity but tend to be indecisive, perhaps for fear of making a mistake.

Individuals with **passive-aggressive personality disorder** passively express covert aggression by resisting demands for adequate performance in both occupational and social functioning. The resistance is expressed indirectly through procrastination, dawdling, stubbornness, intentional inefficiency, or deliberate forgetfulness. As a result, these people display pervasive and persistent social or occupational ineffectiveness in situations in which more self-assertive and effective behavior is clearly possible. For example, a person who always is late to appointments, promises to complete certain tasks but never does, and continually forgets to bring important documents to meetings seems to be going out of his way to function ineffectively.

People who suffer from passive-aggressive personality disorder tend to fail in interpersonal relationships because of one of three patterns:

> 1. The *passive-dependent* pattern, in which the person attempts to manipulate others to do things for him or her by acting helpless or indecisive.
> 2. The *passive-aggressive* pattern, which involves a continuing but indirect hostility expressed through procrastination, stubbornness, pouting, inefficiency, and any kind of indirect obstructionism.
> 3. The *aggressive* pattern, which includes irritability, temper tantrums, and psychologically and physically destructive behavior.

It is believed that all three patterns rest on a core of dependency or passivity (Lazarus, 1976).

**WHAT DO YOU THINK?**

- Do you ever procrastinate or display intentional inefficiency?
- What causes you to do this?

**REVIEW QUESTIONS**

*29.* Personality disorders begin in childhood or adolescence. T F

*30.* Suspiciousness, guardedness, secretiveness, and jealousy are associated with _____ personality disorder.

*31.* _____ personality disorder is characterized by an exaggerated sense of self-importance and an exhibitionistic need for constant attention and admiration.

*32.* The person with antisocial personality disorder seems to lack a conscience and a concern for others. T F

*33.* In the past, the person with borderline personality disorder was referred to as a sociopathic personality. T F

*34.* Included within the anxious or fearful cluster of personality disorders are the compulsive and passive-aggressive personality disorders. T F

*The answers to these review questions are on page 437.*

# DISCUSSION: PSYCHOTIC DISORDERS

Psychotic disorders are maladjustments characterized by disturbances in thinking, feeling, and behaving that are so severe the person loses contact with reality. **Organic psychotic disorders** are associated with brain damage; **functional (nonorganic) psychotic disorders** are not associated with brain pathology, although chemical abnormalities have been found in the brains of some people suffering from functional psychotic disorders.

## ■ Characteristics of Psychotic Disorders

Specific characteristics of psychotic disorders vary somewhat from one type to another; however, there are many common factors. One is *inappropriateness of emotional response*. The individual's loss of contact with reality may be manifested in a seemingly total lack of emotional response. Or the emotional response may not fit the situation, as when a person laughs on hearing that a loved one has just been killed in a car accident.

Another characteristic common to most psychotic disorders is *personality disorganization,* in which the person may become disoriented or display grossly inappropriate behavior. The loss of contact with reality may manifest itself in the individual's not knowing who or where he or she is, as in the case of the person holding the proverbial "smoking gun" but not realizing that she has committed the murder. Or the person may behave in a totally unacceptable way, perhaps physically attacking another person for no apparent reason.

Two other common psychotic characteristics showing loss of contact with reality are hallucinations and delusions. **Hallucinations** are inappropriate perceptions of sensory phenomena. The person might hear someone talking to him when, in fact, no one is there. Or the person might feel the death grip of an imaginary evil spirit. **Delusions** are false beliefs the individual refuses to let go of, despite a wealth of information showing them to be false. Thus, the person might become convinced that she has some terrible, incurable disease, even though ten medical doctors certify that she is in excellent physical health. Or the person may become convinced that enemies are plotting to kill him when, in reality, no such threat exists.

## ■ Insanity

*Psychotic disorder* is a clinical term referring to the characteristics just discussed. **Insanity** is a legal term. It often is used in reference to psychotic disorders but means specifically the state of being unable to be held accountable for one's actions, to manage one's affairs, or to carry out one's social responsibilities. Thus, the individual who has become a threat to himself by continually attempting suicide might be declared insane. The judgment of insanity, however, is made by a judge rather than by a psychiatrist, although the judge might weigh carefully the psychiatrist's assessment of the person's psychological state before rendering the judgment.

## ■ Organic Psychotic Disorders

Brain damage may be caused by a variety of factors, from accidental injury to deterioration associated with excessive drinking or old age. Whatever the cause, the result may be some type of psychological disorder. These disorders are usually referred to as either *acute* or *chronic,* depending on whether they are permanent. Acute disorders are temporary; for example, persons with certain types of tumors or injuries may become disoriented and behave strangely until the tumor or injury has received appropriate treatment. Chronic disorders are permanent, as in the case of primary degenerative dementia, a disorder associated with old age. The condition is not reversible and will worsen with time, although the severity of the condition and the speed of its progression may vary tremendously from one person to the next, depending on biological, personality, and situational factors.

■ Functional Psychotic Disorders

■ *Schizophrenic Disorders*    One type of functional psychotic disorder is the **schizophrenic disorders**. These are characterized by a split between cognition and emotion and by the disorientation and confusion one would expect to accompany such a split. People with schizophrenic disorders, for example, may not know where or even who they are at any given time. Sometimes they may not be able to put thoughts together in a logical sequence. They tend to be secretive and unresponsive to other people and to external events. It should be pointed out, however, that symptoms may occur in a variety of combinations and with various intensities.

■ Schizophrenia: losing contact with reality.

Schizophrenic disorders have been subdivided into varying categories by different researchers. Some make a distinction between (1) *process,* or *nuclear,* schizophrenia, which is thought to be based on organic factors; and (2) *reactive* schizophrenia, which is believed to be precipitated by traumatic events in the person's life, such as the sudden loss of a loved one.

DSM-III divides schizophrenic disorders into five types based on their specific symptoms. The *disorganized* type, for example, is characterized by frequent incoherence, absence of systematized delusions, and blunted, inappropriate, or silly affect (feelings). Indeed, the person seems disorganized. The *catatonic* type involves physical immobility, often including mutism (inability to talk) and the absence of most voluntary actions. The person may remain absolutely still for hours, looking more like a statue than a living being. Sometimes this physical immobility is preceded or interrupted by a flurry of movement and excitement. The *paranoid* type involves unrealistic and illogical thinking, including delusions of persecution and/or grandeur, hallucinations, and personality disorganization. The person may become obsessed with the notion that he or she is destined to play some great role in history. The *undifferentiated* type does not meet the criteria for any of the previously listed types or meets the criteria for more than one. Generally, undifferentiated schizophrenia includes prominent delusions, hallucinations, incoherence, or grossly disorganized behavior. The *residual* type often involves emotional blunting, social withdrawal, eccentric behavior, illogical thinking, and loosening of associations, although the psychotic symptoms that occasioned the initial evaluation or admission to clinical care are no longer prominent.

■ *Paranoid Disorders*   Another type of functional psychotic disorder is **paranoid disorders.** People with paranoid disorders become seriously deluded but do not suffer the hallucinations and general personality disorganization usually associated with schizophrenic disorders. The delusions usually involve persecution. The person suffering from a paranoid disorder is highly suspicious of other people and often misinterprets their actions, remarks, or gestures as in-

---

## CASE IN POINT
## Disorganized Schizophrenia

Mehr (1983, pp. 300–301) describes some of the behavior of Pam, an institutionalized 24-year-old woman who suffers from the disorganized type of schizophrenic disorder:

1. At night, she often drinks many cups of coffee and then vomits it as she walks
2. Sometimes, she hugs and kisses staff and other patients; at other times, she becomes aggressive
3. She is usually bizarre and overactive

4. Her speech is disconnected and confused and speaks in fragments about her delusions and hallucinations
5. She ingests objects such as pens, pencils, and screws
6. She often sleeps on the floor

Pam has been treated with psychotherapy, several major tranquilizing medications, and an intensive behavior modification program, but none has been successful in helping her to change her strange behavior.

## CASE IN POINT
## Maladjustment and You

It is important for you to understand that it is normal to want to be alone from time to time, just as it is normal to suspect people's motives or to feel unusually happy or sad at times. These are not necessarily signs of maladjustment. The maladjusted person tends to do these things in such an exaggerated fashion that they begin to dominate his or her life. If, however, you have some serious concerns about your adjustment patterns, it may be worthwhile for you to discuss them with someone who has been professionally trained in human behavior, human relations, or some area of human services. Perhaps a visit to your campus counselor or psychologist would help.

tentional insults. Moreover, no evidence to the contrary can convince the person of the falsity of those delusions of persecution. Indeed, a vigorous attempt to convince the deluded person that his or her beliefs are false may result in new suspicion directed at the person attempting to help. In this manner, the delusional system of the individual may continue to expand until it dominates his or her world.

REVIEW
QUESTIONS

35. Psychotic disorders are those in which the individual loses contact with reality.
T F

36. _____ are inappropriate perceptions of sensory phenomena.

37. Delusions are false beliefs that the individual readily gives up when accurate information is presented to him or her. T F

38. _____ psychotic disorders are associated with brain damage.

39. Schizophrenic disorders are characterized by a split between _____ and

_____ .

40. A person with a paranoid disorder might likely suffer from delusions of persecution. T F

*The answers to these review questions are on page 437.*

## SUMMARY

■ Maladjustment is the relative failure to meet adequately the psychological demands of oneself, the group, or the situation. It has been attributed to supernatural, physical, and psychological causes.

■ There are many different types of maladjustment, each with its own set of symptoms and potential causes. The American Psychiatric Association has published a *Diagnostic and Statistical Manual* (DSM) of mental disorders that describes and catalogs maladjustments.

The most recent edition (DSM-III) was published in 1980.

■ Anxiety disorders are those in which anxiety is the predominant disturbance or the individual attempts to avoid anxiety by behaving in particular ways. Specific anxiety disorders include panic disorder, generalized anxiety disorder, phobic disorders, and obsessive compulsive disorder.

- Panic disorder includes recurrent, unpredictable, short-term panic attacks.

- Generalized anxiety disorder involves a general anxiety that persists for at least a month. The anxious individual is less terror stricken than in panic disorder.

- Phobic disorders involve intense and unrealistic fears. Agoraphobia is a fear of being alone or being in public places. Social phobia is a fear and avoidance of situations in which the person may be carefully observed by others. Simple phobia is a persistent, irrational fear and avoidance of various other objects and situations (snakes, insects, heights, enclosed places).

- Obsessive compulsive disorder involves recurrent obsessions and compulsions.

- Disorders of social concern are at least as much a problem for other people as for the person with the disorder. Three areas that include such disorders are sexual behavior, substance use, and personality.

- Psychosexual disorders include psychosexual dysfunctions, gender identity disorders, paraphilias, and other psychosexual disorders.

- Psychosexual dysfunctions involve inhibitions of sexual desire or psychophysiological functioning that prevent the individual from satisfactorily completing the cycle of sexual response. Erectile dysfunction, premature ejaculation, inorgasmic dysfunction, functional dyspareunia, and functional vaginismus are examples of psychosexual dysfunctions.

- In gender identity disorders, the individual has feelings of discomfort and inappropriateness about his or her anatomic sex and persistently behaves in ways generally associated with the other sex. In adults the maladjustment is called transsexualism; in children, gender identity disorder of childhood.

- Paraphilias are sexual disorders in which the individual requires unusual or bizarre imagery or acts for sexual excitement (for example, exhibitionism, fetishism, voyeurism).

- Ego-dystonic homosexuality occurs when a homosexual wants to change sexual preference to heterosexuality but has difficulty making the adjustment.

- Homosexuality and bisexuality are not classified by DSM-III as mental disorders, although they are considered deviations by many people within our society.

- Substance abuse is a maladjustment characterized by impairment in social or occupational functioning caused by a pattern of pathological drug use that lasts for at least one month.

- Physical substance dependence requires evidence of either tolerance or withdrawal. Psychological substance dependence occurs when the person needs a drug to cope or to function optimally from a psychological perspective.

- Alcohol, sedatives, opioids, stimulants, hallucinogens, and cannabis are examples of drugs that can be abused and that may cause dependence.

- Personality disorders are characterized by personality traits that deviate substantially from social norms and that prevent the person's achieving the satisfaction that comes with social acceptance.

- DSM-III specifies three main clusters of personality disorders: (1) odd or eccentric; (2) dramatic, emotional, or erratic; and (3) anxious or fearful.

- The most extensively researched personality disorder is antisocial personality disorder, which is characterized by continuous and chronic antisocial behavior that violates the rights of others.

- Psychotic disorders are maladjustments characterized by disturbances in thinking, feeling, and behaving that are so severe the person loses contact with reality. Organic psychotic disorders are those associated with brain damage. Functional (nonorganic) psychotic disorders are not associated with brain pathology, although chemical abnormalities have been found in the brains of some people with these disorders. Two classes of functional psychotic disorders are schizophrenic disorders and paranoid disorders.

## SELECTED READINGS

Coon, D. *Introduction to Psychology: Exploration and Application,* 2nd ed. St. Paul, Minn.: West, 1980. Chapter 20, "Deviance and Disorder: The Unhealthy Personality," and Chapter 21, "Psychosis." Two chapters from an introductory psychology text as interesting as it is informative.

*Diagnostic and Statistical Manual of Mental Disorders,* 3rd ed. Washington, D.C.: American Psychiatric Association, 1980. A manual that is complete, authoritative, and surprisingly easy to understand.

Loftus, E. F. "Alcohol, Marijuana, and Memory." *Psychology Today* (March 1980): 42–56, 92. A review of studies dealing with the effects of alcohol and marijuana on short- and long-term memory.

Mehr, J. *Abnormal Psychology.* New York: Holt, Rinehart and Winston, 1983. A complete and well-balanced text on abnormal psychology that provides an excellent general overview of maladjustment.

## GLOSSARY

**addiction:** a condition in which the individual is either psychologically or physically dependent on drugs, or both.

**agoraphobia:** fear of either being alone or being in public places.

**alcohol:** a central nervous system depressant that has both immediate and long-term effects on the person.

**alcoholism:** excessive use of alcohol to the extent that it seriously impairs personal, social, or occupational functioning, or physical dependence on alcohol.

**antisocial personality disorder:** a maladjustment characterized by continuous and chronic antisocial behavior that violates the rights of others.

**anxiety:** feelings of fear and apprehension usually accompanied by signs of autonomic nervous system arousal.

**anxiety disorder:** maladjustment in which anxiety is the predominant disturbance or the individual attempts to avoid anxiety by behaving in particular ways.

**avoidant personality disorder:** a maladjustment characterized by hypersensitivity to rejection, humiliation, or shame and by social withdrawal.

**bisexuality:** sexual attraction to members of both sexes.

**borderline personality disorder:** a maladjustment characterized by instability in various areas, including mood, self-concept, and interpersonal behavior, with no single feature invariably present.

**cannabis:** a drug, commonly called marihuana, that is a preparation of resin taken from the *Cannabis sativa,* or Indian hemp plant. Taken in large quantities, it has a mildly hallucinogenic effect.

**compulsion:** repetitive and seemingly purposeful behavior performed according to certain rules or in a stereotyped fashion.

**compulsive personality disorder:** a maladjustment characterized by conventionality and formality in everyday relationships, stinginess, demands for perfection regarding trivial details, and excessive devotion to work and productivity.

**delusion:** false belief that the individual refuses to let go of despite a wealth of information showing it to be false.

**dependent personality disorder:** a maladjustment characterized by an inability to function independently.

**disorders of social concern:** maladjustments as much a problem for other people as for the person who displays them. Examples: psychosexual disorders, substance use disorders, personality disorders.

**ego-dystonic homosexuality:** a maladjustment in which a homosexual wants to change sexual preference to heterosexuality but has difficulty making this adjustment.

**functional psychotic disorder:** psychotic disorder that is not associated with brain pathology (although chemical abnormalities have been found in the brains of some people with functional psychotic disorders).

**gender identity disorder:** maladjustment in which the individual has feelings of discomfort and inappropriateness about his or her anatomic sex and persistently behaves in ways generally associated with the other sex. In adults the maladjustment is called **transsexualism;** in children it is called **gender identity disorder of childhood.**

**generalized anxiety disorder:** a maladjustment characterized by a general anxiety that persists for at least a month.

**hallucination:** inappropriate perception of sensory phenomena.

**hallucinogen:** drug, such as mescaline and LSD, that produces sensory distortion.

**histrionic personality disorder:** a maladjustment characterized by dramatic, overemotional, and exaggerated behavior.

**homosexuality:** sexual preference for members of the same sex.

**insanity:** a legal term, often used in reference to psychotic disorders, but meaning specifically the state of being unable to be held accountable for one's actions, manage one's own affairs, or carry out one's social responsibilities.

**maladjustment:** the relative failure to meet adequately the psychological demands of oneself, the group, or the situation.

**narcissistic personality disorder:** a maladjustment characterized by an exaggerated sense of self-importance a preoccupation with fantasies of unlimited success, and an exhibitionistic need for constant attention and admiration.

**obsession:** recurrent, persistent idea, thought, image, or impulse experienced as involuntary and as senseless or repugnant.

**obsessive compulsive disorder:** a maladjustment characterized by recurrent obsessions and compulsions.

**opioid:** drug such as opium, morphine, or heroin that produces a floating feeling and can reduce the perception of pain.

**organic psychotic disorder:** psychotic disorder associated with brain damage.

**other psychosexual disorders:** a residual class of sexually related maladjustments. The primary disorder in this category is ego-dystonic homosexuality.

**panic disorder:** a maladjustment characterized by recurrent, intense, short-term anxiety attacks.

**paranoid disorder:** psychotic disorder in which the individual becomes seriously deluded but does not suffer the hallucinations and general personality disorganization usually associated with schizophrenic disorders.

**paranoid personality disorder:** a maladjustment characterized by pervasive and unwarranted suspiciousness and mistrust of others, hypersensitivity, and unemotionality.

**paraphilia:** maladjustment in which the individual requires unusual or bizarre imagery or acts for sexual excitement.

**passive-aggressive personality disorder:** a maladjustment characterized by resistance of demands for adequate performance in occupational and social functioning.

**personality disorder:** maladjustment characterized by personality traits that deviate substantially from the social norms and that prevent the person's achieving the satisfaction that comes with social acceptance.

**phobic disorder:** disorder characterized by intense and unrealistic fears, such as fear of being alone, of heights, or of harmless animals.

**physical substance dependence:** a substance use disorder that requires evidence of either tolerance or withdrawal.

**psychological substance dependence:** a condition in which the individual needs a drug to cope or to function optimally from a psychological perspective.

**psychosexual disorder:** one of a category of sexually related maladjustments that includes psychosexual dysfunctions, gender identity disorders, paraphilias, and other psychosexual disorders.

**psychosexual dysfunction:** maladjustment that involves inhibitions of sexual desire or psychophysiological functioning that prevent the individual from satisfactorily completing the cycle of sexual response.

**psychotic disorder:** maladjustment characterized by disturbances in thinking, feeling, and behaving so severe that the person loses contact with reality.

**schizoid personality disorder:** a maladjustment characterized by voluntary social isolation and an incapacity to form social relationships.

**schizophrenic disorder:** functional psychotic disorder characterized by a split between cognition and emotion and by the disorientation and confusion one would expect to accompany such a split.

**schizotypal personality disorder:** a maladjustment characterized by personality traits similar to those found in schizoid personality disorder, plus various oddities of thought, perception, speech, and behavior.

**sedative:** drug such as a barbiturate, tranquilizer, or hypnotic that can induce a relaxed state and sleep.

**simple phobia:** a persistent, irrational fear of and avoidance of objects and situations other than those included in agoraphobia and social phobia. Example: fear of insects.

**social phobia:** fear and avoidance of situations in which the person may be carefully observed by others.

**stimulant:** substance such as cocaine or amphetamine that stimulates rather than depresses the central nervous system.

**substance abuse:** drug use characterized by impairment in social or occupational functioning caused by a pattern of pathological use that lasts for at least one month.

**tolerance:** a condition in which there is a diminished effect with regular use of the same dose of a drug or in which increased amounts of the drug are necessary to achieve the same effect.

**withdrawal:** a substance-specific syndrome that follows cessation or reduction in intake of a substance.

# REFERENCES

Barber, J. X. *LSD, Marihuana, Yoga, and Hypnosis.* Chicago: Aldine, 1970.

Briddell, D. W., and Wilson, G. T. "The Effects of Alcohol and Expectancy Set on Male Sexual Arousal." *Journal of Abnormal Psychology* 85, no. 2 (1976): 225–234.

Cohen, S. "The Hallucinogens." In *Principles of Psychopharmacology.* Edited by W. G. Clark and J. del Giudice. New York: Academic Press, 1970.

Cohen, S. "Cocaine." *Journal of the American Medical Association* 236, no. 1 (1975): 74–75.

Doughty, P. L.; Carter, W. E.; Coggins, W. J.; and Page, J. B. "Marijuana—Here to Stay?" *APA Monitor* 7, no. 1 (1976): 5, 10.

[DSM-III.] *Diagnostic and Statistical Manual of Mental Disorders,* 3rd ed. Washington, D.C.: American Psychiatric Association, 1980.

Engs, R. "Drinking Patterns and Drinking Problems of College Students." *Journal of Studies on Alcohol* 38, no. 11 (1977): 2144–2156.

Goodwin, D. W. "Alcoholism and Heredity: A Review and Hypothesis." *Archives of General Psychiatry* 36, no. 1 (1979): 57–61.

Hare, R. *Psychopathy: Theory and Research.* New York: Wiley, 1970.

Hunt, M. *Sexual Behavior in the 1970s.* Chicago: Playboy Press, 1974.

Judd, L. L., and Grant, I. "Brain Dysfunctions in Chronic Sedative Users." *Journal of Psychedelic Drugs* 7, no. 2 (1975): 143–149.

Kinsey, A. C.; Pomeroy, W. B.; and Martin, C. E. *Sexual Behavior in the Human Male.* Philadelphia: Saunders, 1948.

Kunnes, R. "Double-Dealing in Dope." *Human Behavior* 2, no. 10 (1973): 22–27.

Lazarus, R. S. *Patterns of Adjustment.* 3rd ed. New York: McGraw-Hill, 1976.

Mann, D. "Marijuana Alert II: More of the Grim Story." *Reader's Digest* (November 1980): 65–71.

Margulies, R. Z.; Viessler, R. C.; and Kanded, D. B. "A Longitudinal Study of Onset of Drinking among High School Students." *Journal of Studies on Alcohol* 38, no. 5 (1977): 897–912.

Maugh, T. H., II. "Marihuana: The Grass May No Longer Be Greener." *Science* 185 (1974a): 683–685.

———. "Marihuana (II): Does It Damage the Brain?" *Science* 185 (1974b): 775–776.

Mehr, J. *Abnormal Psychology.* New York: Holt, Rinehart and Winston, 1983.

Millon, T. *Disorders of Personality DSM-III: Axis II.* New York: Wiley, 1981.

Nahas, G. G. "Marihuana." *Journal of the American Medical Association* 233, no. 1 (1975): 79–80.

NIDA. *Marihuana and Health.* Rockville, Md.: National Institute on Drug Abuse, 1977.

Pittel, S. M., and Hofer, R. "The Transition to Amphetamine Abuse." In *Uppers and Downers.* Edited by D. E. Smith and D. R. Wesson. Englewood Cliffs, N.J.: Prentice-Hall, 1973.

Pleck, J. H. "The Male Sex Role: Definitions, Problems, and Sources of Change." *Journal of Social Issues* 32 (1976): 155–164.

Post, R. M. "Cocaine Psychosis: A Continuum Model." *American Journal of Psychiatry* 132, no. 3 (1975): 225–231.

Redl, F., and Wineman, D. *Children Who Hate.* New York: Collier, 1962.

Reytula, R. E.; Wellford, C. D.; and DeNombreux, B. G. "Body Self Image and Homosexuality." *Journal of Clinical Psychology* 35 (July 1979): 567–572.

Rubin, V., and Comitas, L. *Ganja in Jamaica: A Medical Anthropological Study of Chronic Marijuana Use.* The Hague, Netherlands: Mouton, 1975.

Snyder, S. H. "Amphetamine Psychoses: A Model Schizophrenia Mediated by Catecholamines." *American Journal of Psychiatry* 130, no. 1 (1973): 61–66.

Tashkin, D. P.; Shapiro, B. J.; and Frank, I. M. "Acute Effects of Smoked Marihuana and Oral Delta-9—Tetrahydrocannabinal on Specific Airway Conductance in Asthmatic Subjects." *American Review of Respiratory Diseases* 109 (1974): 420–428.

Tashkin, D. P.; Shapiro, B. J.; Lee, Y. E.; and Harper, C. E. "Subacute Effects of Heavy Marihuana

Smoking on Pulmonary Functions." *New England Journal of Medicine* 294, no. 1 (1976): 125–129.

Wilson, G. T.; and Lawson, D. M. "Expectancies, Alcohol, and Sexual Arousal in Women." *Jour-*

*nal of Abnormal Psychology* 87, no. 3 (1978): 368–372.

Wolfe, L. "The Sexual Profile of That Cosmopolitan Girl." *Cosmopolitan* (September 1980): 254–257, 263–265.

## ANSWERS TO REVIEW QUESTIONS

**Page 412.**  *1.* oneself, group, situation  *2.* medical, psychological  *3.* T  *4.* F  *5.* F  *6.* agoraphobia, social phobia, simple phobia  *7.* obsessions  *8.* Compulsions

**Page 417.**  *9.* Psychosexual dysfunctions, cycle, sexual response  *10.* erectile  *11.* inorgasmic  *12.* T  *13.* T  *14.* F  *15.* Homosexuality  *16.* bisexuality  *17.* T  *18.* F

**Page 424.**  *19.* T  *20.* tolerance, withdrawal  *21.* psychological substance dependence  *22.* T  *23.* F  *24.* heroin  *25.* T  *26.* T  *27.* Hallucinogens  *28.* F

**Page 428.**  *29.* T  *30.* paranoid  *31.* Narcissistic  *32.* T  *33.* F  *34.* T

**Page 432.**  *35.* T  *36.* Hallucinations  *37.* F  *38.* Organic  *39.* cognition, emotion  *40.* T

# 14

# PSYCHOTHERAPY

On November 16, 1980, the *Miami Herald* reported that a man who had lived at the Salvation Army shelter in Miami, George David Quesenberry, had apparently committed suicide by kneeling in front of an oncoming train.

"The engineer sounded the train's horn several times, witnesses told Metro Homicide Detective John Parmenter. The witness said Quesenberry sat down on the tracks and was aware that the train was approaching for at least two minutes before the mishap occurred at 2:17 PM.

" 'The victim, from a sitting position, looked up at the train, then covered his ears and looked back at the ground,' Parmenter said. 'He had plenty of time to get off [the tracks] and he just didn't—he didn't even try. The train couldn't stop in time to avoid striking him.' "

Salvation Army officials reported that they had never heard Quesenberry discuss suicide. But he had said he had found it hard to "cope out in society," according to Salvation Army workers. "He needed the controlled, regimented environment of the Salvation Army," Detective John LeClaire said.

George David Quesenberry had needed help.

**14**

PSYCHOTHERAPY

## DISCUSSION: PSYCHOTHERAPY

**Psychotherapy** is a process involving the use of psychological techniques to help a person achieve better adjustment. There are many types of psychotherapy and several types of **psychotherapists**. This chapter will consider both therapies and therapists and will deal with a variety of considerations related to therapy. For example, when should a person consider entering therapy? How does a person choose a therapist? How does a person know whether a therapy is working? What does therapy cost? What is the effect of therapy on family life? When should therapy end? In short, you will be provided with a brief but fairly comprehensive overview of therapy.

### ■ Entering Therapy

People begin to sense that they may need some kind of help when they realize that things are not going well, but they do not know what to do to improve the situation. Examples might include: (1) *extreme moods*, such as depression, anxiety, hopelessness, continuing guilt, inability to concentrate, or forgetfulness; (2) *problems relating to others*, such as inability to get along with others, compulsive drinking, gambling, or drug use, sexual difficulties, repeated trouble with the law, or frequent arguing; (3) *problems with sleep*, such as insomnia, frequent awakening at night, frequent nightmares, or too much sleep; and (4) *stress-related disorders*, such as headaches, ulcers, stomach troubles, or asthma. (See Mishara and Patterson, 1979, pp. 13–15, for a more complete list.)

It is important to emphasize that a person who has one or more of the above-listed symptoms is not necessarily a candidate for therapy. The critical factor in the determination of whether therapy is warranted is the person's perceived need for relief. That is, does the person believe he or she really needs relief? If so, therapy is warranted. It is time to select a therapist.

> Janet is an alcoholic. Her drinking has led to strained relationships with her husband, her children, and her friends. It threatens her physical health and has led to a pattern of absenteeism at work that is placing her job in jeopardy. It would appear that Janet is a prime candidate for therapy.
>
> The problem is that Janet denies that she has a drinking problem. Members of her family, some of her friends, her doctor, the pastor of her church, and even her boss have suggested that she seek help, but to no avail. And as long as Janet denies that she needs help, she will not seek it. Janet is *not* a prime candidate for therapy.

### ■ Types of Therapists

There are several types of therapists. They can be differentiated by kind and amount of formal training, licensing requirements, accreditation, services performed, and approaches to therapy. Among others, they include **psychiatrists, psychologists, psychiatric social workers,** and **psychoanalysts.**

■ *Psychiatrists*   Psychiatrists are licensed physicians. They have either an M.D. (Doctor of Medicine) or a D.O. (Doctor of Osteopathy) degree. Their usual educational and training requirements include four years of undergraduate college study, three or four years of medical school, a one-year hospital internship, and three years of psychiatric residency in which they study the theory and practice of psychiatry. Thus, well-trained psychiatrists should be professionally competent to treat patients through the use of psychological methods as well as through drugs and other physical methods.

Psychiatrists in the United States are certified by the American Board of Psychiatry and Neurology through an approved residency, related work experience, and written and oral examinations. Many psychiatrists do not bother to take the examinations; and only about two-thirds of those who do, pass. Consequently, only approximately one-third of psychiatrists are *Board certified*. Those who have completed training in approved programs but who have not passed the examination usually refer to themselves as *Board eligible*. Psychiatrists may provide many types of therapy, depending on their particular training and interests. They are the only therapists who can legally prescribe drugs or provide electroconvulsive (electroshock) therapy.

■ *Psychologists*   The usual education and training of psychologists include four years of undergraduate college and four to five years of graduate school in which a Master's degree (M.S. or M.A.) and/or a Doctor's degree (Ph.D., Psy.D., or Ed.D.) are earned. Many psychologists are not trained as therapists. They specialize in research and teaching. Others spend a significant part of their graduate school training learning and practicing therapy skills, including a one-year internship of full-time supervised clinical work. They are referred to as *clinical* or *counseling* psychologists.

Psychologists are licensed by the states, and the regulations vary, sometimes considerably, from state to state. Often these regulations require not only an appropriate degree from an accredited university and supervised clinical work, but recommendations from superiors and a written examination as well. A small number of psychologists are certified by the American Board of Examiners in Professional Psychology. The *National Registry of Health Services in Psychology* lists all applicants who meet minimum requirements for clinical practice. Generally, psychologists provide all types of psychotherapy as well as several types of psychological testing.

■ *Psychiatric Social Workers*   Psychiatric social workers complete a four-year undergraduate degree, followed by two years of graduate school to complete either the Master of Social Work (M.S.W.) or the Master of Science in Social Work (M.S.S.W.) degree. Supervised clinical work usually takes up at least half their training in these programs. A few social workers earn a doctorate in social work (Ph.D. or D.S.W.) by completing a program of approximately three more years of graduate work.

Social workers are licensed by some states, although several states do not issue licenses. The usual licensing requirement includes the Master's degree plus approved training and two years of supervised clinical work. In addition, a written examination may be required.

Social workers are certified by the Academy of Social Workers through written examinations to applicants who have a Master's degree in social work and two years of clinical experience. In addition, the National Association of Social Workers and the National Federation of Societies of Clinical Social Work publish directories listing approved applicants. Generally, psychiatric social workers provide all types of psychotherapy, some through full-time private practices and others through hospitals, clinics, and family service organizations.

■ *Psychoanalysts*   Psychoanalysts are therapists who have received advanced training in the treatment technique developed by Sigmund Freud. The training takes place in psychoanalytic institutes such as the New York Psychoanalytic Institute. Most candidates are psychiatrists, although psychologists, social workers, or lay persons may also be trained. The training usually takes at least four years (sometimes as long as ten years), during which candidates take evening and weekend classes while continuing their regular professional work. All candidates must undergo a personal psychoanalysis as part of the training. In addition, they use psychoanalysis to treat, under supervision, two to four patients.

There is no licensing for psychoanalysis; however, psychoanalytic associations may accept as members graduates of approved institutes. A few psychoanalysts treat patients only through psychoanalysis. Many, however, use additional approaches according to their patients' needs.

■ *Others*   In addition to psychiatrists, psychologists, social workers, and psychoanalysts, there are many other types of therapists. **Sex therapists** help people to overcome sexual dysfunctions. All nurses receive some training and experience in **psychiatric nursing** and may therefore provide psychotherapy to their patients. Psychiatric nurses, of course, do this routinely and may become highly skilled therapists. **Pastoral counselors** are rabbis, ministers, or priests who have been trained in counseling techniques. Most universities have counselors available in student development centers or university services centers. These psychological and school counselors often play important roles in developmental, preventative, and career counseling, in addition to crisis counseling. Other types of therapists include occupational therapists, dance therapists, and vocational therapists. These and even other types of therapists may be well-trained people who can provide legitimate therapy. Some people who call themselves psychotherapists, however, may be charlatans, skilled only at taking money from unsuspecting clients.

## ■ Qualities of a Good Therapist

Personally, therapists should have a strong commitment to help. Their work should be more than just another job to them. They should be sensitive, empathic, and accepting. They should really care about people.

Professionally, therapists should have the technical skills necessary to help. They should be able to gather information quickly and efficiently. They should be good listeners willing to discuss any issue that might advance the therapy. They should be fluent in the language the client speaks, and they should have a reasonably good understanding of his or her lifestyle. They should be able to help the client formulate problems and goals and to outline a comprehensive plan for helping. Of course, therapists should be well trained in their particular approach to therapy and familiar with the kinds of problems the people they help are likely to have.

## ■ Choosing a Therapist

The best source of information concerning a therapist is a person who has consulted that therapist. Such a person is likely to provide candid information that may be difficult to obtain from other sources. One should realize, however, that many people are reluctant to discuss such highly private matters as their own therapy with others. Therefore, family members and close friends are perhaps the best people to approach and, even with them, prudence dictates a soft touch.

Another good source of information is people who are members of a helping profession. Physicians, nurses, members of the clergy, counselors, and teachers can often provide excellent referrals. The important thing is to talk with someone you know or someone referred to you by someone you know. This direct, informal contact usually provides candid information—the kind that is most useful.

Other informational sources include local clinics or hospitals, local professional societies, area mental health associations, telephone hotlines, and various community-service or interagency-council information and referral services. These sources provide information, but it usually is less than candid and, thus, restricted in its utility.

One last source of information needs to be mentioned: a listing in the yellow pages of the telephone directory. This is the least desirable source in that it provides almost no useful information other than the phone number of the therapist. Certainly one can tell very little about the skills and experience of a therapist from a listing in the telephone book.

> Eric's problems had been mounting for some time. Over the past year, he had suffered from periodic headaches and insomnia, anxiety and depression, and most recently, an increasing inability to get along with others. He needed help and he knew it.
>
> Unfortunately, Eric was reluctant to seek help in choosing a therapist because he thought people would think there was something wrong with him if they knew he was thinking about therapy. So Eric selected his therapist on the basis of an ad in the yellow pages of the telephone directory.
>
> Eight months into his therapy and $1,500 later, Eric is still suffering from headaches and insomnia, anxiety and depression, and an increasing inability to get along with others. He is coming to the conclusion that "therapy doesn't work," a thought that depresses him further. Ironically, be believes the only bright spot in all of this is the fact that no one else knows he has been seeing a therapist.

**WHAT DO YOU THINK?**

■ If you thought you needed therapy, how would you go about choosing a therapist?

■ If you started treatment with a therapist and you did not feel comfortable with him or her, what would you do?

**REVIEW QUESTIONS**

*1.* Psychotherapy is a process involving the use of psychological techniques to help a person achieve better adjustment. T F

*2.* People begin to sense that they may need help when they realize that things are not going well, but they do not know what to do to improve the situation. T F

*3.* The best source of information concerning a therapist is a local clinic. T F

*4.* Psychologists are the only therapists who can legally prescribe drugs. T F

*5.* Psychiatric social workers are required to have a Ph.D. T F

*6.* Psychoanalysis is a treatment technique rather than a type of therapist. T F

7. There is no licensing for psychoanalysis. T F
8. Psychiatrists are physicians. T F

*The answers to these review questions are on page 471.*

---

## DISCUSSION:  ANALYTIC THERAPIES

There are many therapies and several ways of classifying them. For example, some therapies are said to be *insight-oriented*. These therapies are designed to help clients understand what forces are impinging on them and why their adjustive responses are what they are. It is assumed that the understanding or insight, in and of itself, helps the person to cope better. Other therapies are *action-oriented*. These therapies are designed to help clients to act in new, more adjustive ways. It is assumed that understanding alone is not enough (indeed, it may not even be necessary) to change behavior; action is necessary.

Another classification scheme divides therapies into *directive* and *nondirective* approaches. Directive therapies are those in which the therapist takes an active role in interacting with, interpreting for, and otherwise generally counseling the client. In essence, the therapist either pushes or pulls the client in one direction or another. Nondirective therapies are those in which the client takes much greater responsibility for solving his or her problems. The therapist may provide information and discuss alternatives with the client, but the client decides which courses of action to pursue.

A third classification scheme identifies three approaches—*individual, family,* and *group*. Family therapy sessions include two or more family members and the therapist, although family therapists may conduct individual sessions with one family member or another from time to time. Group sessions include several clients and the therapist. Sometimes, because of the nature of a particular therapy, it is useful to have two therapists working together with a group at the same time.

While each of these three classification schemes is useful in differentiating one type of therapy from another, none is recognized as *the* way to classify therapies. In fact, there is no universally accepted classification.

Our discussion of therapies is based on a classification scheme developed by Joel Kovel (1976). It progresses along both historical and thematic lines and should serve as a means of both extending and integrating many of the ideas presented earlier in this book. Since the number of therapies in current use is extremely large, our discussion is necessarily selective. Still, we attempt to touch on all major approaches to therapy. The first section deals with the **analytic therapies**—those therapies that rely on verbal means to place the person in greater contact with fragmented parts of his or her mental life. The discussion begins with a consideration of psychoanalysis.

### ■ Psychoanalysis

The first psychotherapy to have wide-ranging impact was Sigmund Freud's **psychoanalysis**. As we saw in Chapter 2, Freud viewed personality dynamics in terms of the interplay of our desires (the id), our rationality (the ego), and our conception of morality (the superego). Invariably, at times the demands of the id conflict with those of the superego. Generally, we may resolve these conflicts adequately through defensive behavior (unconsciously deceiving ourselves about our true desires). However, fixations (unresolved early childhood conflicts) may be carried unconsciously into our adult lives. Ultimately, the fixated person begins to have adjustment problems because the ego, weakened through its continuous unconscious expenditure of psychic energy in dealing with the id and the superego, becomes too weak to cope with the demands of reality. This weakness manifests itself most often in anxiety and depression.

*See Chapter 2 for a discussion of the unconscious, defensive behavior, and fixations.*

■ *Free Association*   Having conceptualized personality dynamics in these terms, Freud (1969) devised an insight-oriented, directive therapy in which the present is linked inextricably to the past. The analysand (in psychoanalysis today, the patient or client is called the *analysand*; the therapist is called the *analyst*) is taught the method of **free association**, or what Freud called the *fundamental rule* of analysis—to say everything that comes to mind, even if it is disagreeable, nonsensical, or seemingly unimportant. The purpose of free association is to bring repressed thoughts and feelings into consciousness. Of course, the repressed material is rooted in fixations; therefore, the analysand is encouraged to focus on early childhood experiences. Information obtained through free association is interpreted by the analyst, who then explains the interpretation, thus providing the analysand's ego with knowledge of his or her own unconscious. This knowledge, in turn, presumably strengthens the ego and enables it to cope more effecitvely with the demands of reality.

■ *Resistances*   While free association may be successful in bringing some repressed thoughts and feelings into consciousness, the analysand may be blocked by other, more threatening thoughts and feelings. These blocks are referred to as **resistances**. The analyst helps the analysand to overcome resistances through interpretation, progressing in a slow and deliberate manner. Here Freud was concerned that the analysand's ego might be completely overwhelmed by learning too much too soon about his or her socially forbidden desires. For example, an analysand who became fixated in the phallic stage (see Chapter 2) because his mother denied him the physical contact and general love and affection he so desired might maintain an unconscious hatred toward his mother in his adult life. Of course, the hatred would be repressed, because one is supposed to love one's mother, not hate her. This repressed hatred toward the mother might manifest itself in a general suspiciousness directed at all women. In this situation the analyst would proceed cautiously, at first indicating that the analysand is repressing something and only later, when the analyst senses that the analysand has enough ego strength to withstand the truth, revealing that he has hated his mother since early childhood.

■ *Transference*   A curious phenomenon that occurs during therapy is called **transference**. The analysand begins to see the analyst as some important figure from childhood (often the mother or father) and transfers onto the analyst feelings and reactions that applied to that other person. In essence, the analysand begins to act toward the analyst in ways that are totally unrealistic and outside the range of the therapeutic relationship. For instance, the analysand, in an attempt to win a parent's love, may attempt to win the love and approval of the analyst by acting in more adjustive ways. Freud viewed this affectionate attitude as an advantage, because it tends to strengthen the analysand's ego. That is, under the influence of this affection, the analysand achieves things that would ordinarily be beyond his or her power. In addition, by putting the analyst in the place of one of the parents (who were the origin of his superego), the analysand gives the analyst the power the superego has over the ego. The new superego (the analyst) can reeducate the analysand by correcting the mistakes for which the parents were originally responsible.

Freud recognized that the influence of the analyst in this matter is awesome. He cautioned stringently against its misuse.

> However much the analyst may be tempted to become a teacher, model and ideal for other people and to create men in his own image, he should not forget that this is not his task in the analytic relationship, and indeed that he will be disloyal to his task if he allows himself to be led on by his inclinations. If he does, he will only be repeating a mistake of the parents who crushed their child's independence by their influence, and he will only be replacing the patient's earlier dependence by a new one. In all his attempts at improving and educating the patient the analyst should respect his individuality (1969, p. 32).

The affectionate attitude is only one part of the transference. Almost inevitably the affection eventually changes to hostility that is also rooted in past experience. As a child, the analysand sought his or her parent as a sex object. At some time during the transference, the same demand will press forward and seek satisfaction. Freud insisted, however, that real sexual relations between analyst and analysand are "out of the question, and even the subtler methods of satisfaction, such as the giving of preference, intimacy and so on are only sparingly granted by the analyst" (1969, p. 33). The analysand feels rejected and responds with hostility.

Ultimately, transference is useful in that it provides the therapist with an understanding of the analysand's conflicting attitudes toward his or her parents. However, it is also dangerous in that the analysand mistakes reflections of the past for current reality. For example, an analysand who senses the strong erotic desire that underlies the affectionate attitude may believe that he or she has fallen madly in love. If the affection changes to the hostile attitude, the analysand feels rejected, hates the analyst, and wants to quit the therapy. Either way, the analysand's behavior is totally unrealistic. The analyst's task is to show the analysand over and over that his or her thoughts, feelings, and behavior are reflections of the past and have nothing to do with current reality. If the analyst succeeds, the analysand will have taken a great step toward strengthening the ego and breaking down resistances.

■ *Dream Analysis*   One more aspect of psychoanalysis needs to be mentioned: **dream analysis**. In psychoanalysis the analysand is encouraged to tell his or her dreams to the analyst, who interprets them to the analysand. According to Freud, dreams may arise either from the id, as an unconscious wish that makes itself felt by the ego, or from the ego, as a conflict left over from waking life that is supported during sleep by an unconscious element. In either event, a demand is placed on the ego for the satisfaction of an instinct or for the solution of a conflict. The sleeping ego, however, wants to remain sleeping. It accomplishes this by symbolically fulfilling the wish and thus temporarily meeting the demands placed on it, while at the same time allowing itself to remain asleep.

In some dreams the symbols are fairly explicit representations of what they stand for. A hungry sleeping person may dream of eating a delicious meal. In this case, if the wish fulfillment is sufficient to meet the person's hunger (temporarily, of course), then he or she will continue sleeping. If the hunger persists, the person will wake up.

In other dreams, the symbols are not so explicit. Suppose, for instance, the sleeper desires a forbidden sexual object, the husband of one of her friends. This desire provokes so much anxiety in her that the ego defends itself by distorting the symbolic content of the wish fulfillment. She dreams of having sex with some other man, one to whom she is sexually indifferent, but who has the same name as her friend's husband. In this case, if the anxiety becomes too great for the wish fulfillment to deal with successfully, the person will wake up.

**WHAT DO YOU THINK?**
- Do you remember your dreams?
- Do these dreams delight, upset, or confuse you?
- Have you ever spoken with someone about your dreams?
- Did talking about your dreams help you sort them out?

■ *Summary of Psychoanalysis*   To summarize, psychoanalysis involves two steps: strengthening the weakened ego by extending its self-knowledge and breaking down resistances. The analyst gathers material from several sources: direct information supplied by the analysand and information conveyed through free associations, transferences, and the telling of dreams. The analyst then constructs interpretations of this material and gives them to the analysand. Great care is taken to avoid telling the analysand too much too soon. As a rule, the analyst refrains from providing an interpretation until the analysand is only a single step away from discovering it for himself or herself. Otherwise the information would produce either no effect or a violent outbreak of resistance. When resistances do occur, the analyst must proceed sensitively, patiently, and caringly, always showing the analysand how the present is linked with the past. In this manner, ego strength is restored and the analysand is able to cope more effectively with the demands of reality.

In traditional psychoanalysis, the analyst sits out of view of the analysand, who is lying on a couch, and, as described above, encourages the unfolding of the analysand's unconscious. A complete analysis usually requires four to five fifty-minute sessions per week for three to five years (Kovel, 1976). At $40 to $125 per session, depending on the analyst and the city in which he or she practices, the costs can be staggering.

## ■ Psychoanalytic Psychotherapy

**Psychoanalytic psychotherapy** is a modification of psychoanalysis that attempts to provide the patient with a shorter and less expensive treatment. Here, the therapist and patient confront one another, physically sitting up and engaging in a dialogue that focuses more on current problems in living than on fixations. The therapy is classified as psychoanalytic because Freudian principles underlie the general understanding of what is going on and because the goals include strengthening of the ego through the extension of its self-knowledge. There are usually only one to two sessions per week, and the therapy may be completed in half the time required for traditional psychoanalysis.

### ■ Neo-Freudian Analysis

Several of Freud's major disciples broke away from Freud and created therapies of their own. A few of these therapies, although different from one another in specific details, have enough in common that they may be considered variations of an identifiable type of therapy—**neo-Freudian analysis**.[1]

Neo-Freudian analysis places little emphasis on instinctual drives. Instead, it emphasizes the drive toward self-realization, assuring that each person has a unique, central inner force composed of specific potentialities. This self is influenced by culture in general and interpersonal relations in particular. Ultimately, the needs for security, love, and self-esteem (as opposed to sex) motivate behavior, and repression and unconscious thought are not considered nearly as important as in psychoanalysis. Generally, the neo-Freudians view people's problems as stemming from negative life experiences rather than from unresolved early childhood conflicts related to infantile sexuality.

Neo-Freudian analysis does not insist on strict adherence to the fundamental rule—to say whatever comes to mind. It is much less concerned with exploring the unconscious mind and past relationships. Rather, great emphasis is placed on conscious thoughts, feelings, and behavior in the here and now. Sometimes, future orientation in the form of goals is explored.

Generally, neo-Freudian analysis requires less total time, fewer sessions per week, and less expenditure of money than traditional psychoanalysis. There is less emphasis on free association, less use of the couch, and more intervention by the analyst. There is more concern with unrealistic attitudes and self-regard. The therapy tends to produce more immediately discernible change in what neo-Freudians hold to be the most important elements: strategies of living and feelings of self-worth.

### ■ Analytical Psychology

While the neo-Freudians deemphasized the unconscious, C. G. Jung, another major disciple of Freud, attempted to expand the unconscious far beyond what Freud had envisioned. Jung's school of psychological thought, including his method of therapy, is called **analytical psychology**.

Jung (1968) asserted that in addition to the Freudian personal unconscious, there is a vast transpersonal unconscious in which each and every person shares. This *collective unconscious* reflects the cosmic order, including all of human history. It contains mythic themes, such as the Great Mother and the Hero, which recur in one culture after another throughout history. These themes, called *archetypes*, are known through symbols that appear in dreams, in flights of creative imagination, in disturbed states of mind, and in the products of art and science.

Analytical psychology holds that neurosis is caused by a splitting off of parts of the self. The person has lost touch with the archetypes and with other psychological formations such as the *anima* (split-off female quality in the male), the *animus* (split-off male quality in the female), and the *shadow* (a negated or

---

1. Among the major contributors to neo-Freudian analysis are Alfred Adler, Otto Rank, Karen Horney, Harry Stack Sullivan, and Erich Fromm.

inferior self-image). The overriding goal of therapy, therefore, is the integration of the self with its transpersonal parts.

The therapy is divided into two overlapping phases that usually take one to two sessions per week for a year or more to complete. The first phase is down-to-earth and extremely supportive. The patient and analyst confront one another in a face-to-face dialogue in which the neurosis is dealt with on a conscious level. The analyst often provides practical advice and attempts to build a friendly, warm, positive relationship with the patient.

The second phase involves the exploration of the archetypes. This is done primarily through *dream analysis*. Jung, however, did not accept Freud's conception of the dream as a distorted representation of an unconscious wish. Rather, the dream is the vehicle through which archetypes can make themselves known. Thus, Jung devised a technique called *amplification* in which the dream content is first expanded dramatically within the patient's life, then placed within the human tradition of myth and symbol. For example, the patient might be asked to extend the dream by imagining a few additions to it. The analyst could then show how each form of the expanded dream reflected the collective unconscious. In this manner, the analyst puts the patient in contact with the deep unconscious, a process believed by Jung to be intrinsically healing.

## ■ The Existential Approach

Psychoanalysis, psychoanalytic psychotherapy, neo-Freudian analysis, and analytical psychology have in common a reliance on verbal means to put the person in direct contact with fragmented parts of his or her mental life. The therapist analyzes and the patient synthesizes. This also happens in the **existential approach**, the most radical type of analytic strategy. However, because it is so often woven into the fabric of various other therapies, the existential approach may be more accurately defined as an approach, a technique, or a strategy rather than as a complete therapy.

The existential approach has its roots in twentieth-century European philosophy and psychiatry, both of which include elements that emphasize the themes of personal alienation in mass society, the breakdown of traditional values, and the consequent loss of meaning in our lives. These themes illuminate the chaotic nature of the world in which we live, a world that produces in us a despair and, ultimately, a gnawing anxiety as we encounter the incompleteness, meaninglessness, and nothingness in the here and now.

It is, however, precisely from this encounter that a healthier self can be forged, for an analysis of the human condition reveals that the only certainty is that we can control our own lives. We have the capacity to choose, and it is through our choices that we may construct an orderly and meaningful life for ourselves. In fact, the failure to choose is a choice in itself. The responsibility to choose, then, is inescapable and heavy; but the exercise of that responsibility is the pathway to freedom and wholeness.

The existential approach involves a face-to-face, active dialogue between therapist and patient. The therapist focuses on the conscious, here-and-now relationship between himself or herself and the patient. There is no reference to the unconscious, or to anything else other than the dialogue currrently taking place. Often the focus of that dialogue is the patient's construction of a personal value system and the consistency of current life choices with that value system.

**WHAT DO YOU THINK?**

■ Do you believe you have choices in your life?

■ Do you think yourself solely responsible for what happens to you?

*9.* _____ therapy is designed to help clients understand what forces are impinging on them and why their adjustive responses are what they are.

*10.* The first psychotherapy to have wide-ranging impact was _____ .

*11.* The condition in which the analysand sees the analyst as some important figure from childhood and transfers onto the analyst feelings and reactions that applied to that other person is called _____ .

*12.* According to Freud, dreams may arise from either the _____ or the _____ . In either case, the function of the dream is to help the sleeping ego _____ .

*13.* Psychoanalysis involves two steps: strengthening the ego by extending its _____ and breaking down _____ .

*14.* Neo-Freudian analysis emphasizes the person's drive toward _____ .

*15.* Analytical psychology holds that in addition to the Freudian personal unconscious, there is a _____ unconscious that reflects the cosmic order, including all of human history.

*16.* According to the _____ _____ , it is through our own choices that we construct an orderly and meaningful life for ourselves.

*The answers to these review questions are on page 471.*

## DISCUSSION: EXISTENTIAL HUMANISM

A recent and distinctly American trend in therapy is **existential humanism**. This trend, often referred to as *humanist psychology* or the *human potential movement*, is composed of a vast array of therapies—from bioenergetics to encounter groups—that share the following characteristics:

> *1.* A blending of the direct experience component of the existential approach with a deep philosophical commitment to the notion of the perfectibility of human beings.
> *2.* A shift of concern to ordinary unhappiness and alienation.
> *3.* A concern with educating the public (that is, the movement tends to promote or sell itself to the public).

Specific techniques vary from one therapy to the next, but a spirit of spontaneous and honest self-expression and the goal of attaining personal happiness can be found at the base of them all.

### ■ Rogerian Therapy

Sometimes referred to as *client-centered therapy*, **Rogerian therapy** is perhaps the most influential brand of existential humanism. This nondirective therapy was devised by Carl Rogers (1961) and is consistent with his view of personality.

As we saw in Chapter 2, Rogers believes personality contains two basic components: the *potentialities* (our inherent capacities) and the *self* (a conscious

■ In Rogerian therapy, the therapist provides the unconditional positive regard that the client so desperately needs.

idea of who and what we are). The potentialities are genetically determined and are therefore not subject to modification by social or psychological forces. The self, however, is formed by social and psychological forces and is subject to further modification by those forces.

The basic life force is the drive to actualize potentialities. We also have a drive to actualize the self. When the self is consistent with our potentialities, we are in a state of congruence. As we actualize the self, we also actualize our potentialities. Conversely, when the self is inconsistent with our potentialities, we are in a state of incongruence. As we actualize the self, we do not actualize our potentialities. We are maladjusted.

Rogers views maladjustment as the last link in a developmental chain that begins when significant others give us *conditional positive regard*. They accept, support, and respect us only when we behave the way they want us to behave. To keep the approval of these significant others, we behave according to their ideas of who and what we should be, and our self develops consistently with those ideas. Next, we translate their "shoulds" into *conditions of worth*—standards by which we judge the value of our thoughts, feelings, and actions. When we fail to live up to these conditions of worth—and inevitably we will fail, because our self is based on someone else's idea of what we should be rather than on our own potentialities—we experience guilt and anxiety. These, in turn, lead to defensive behavior, which is an expression of a state of incongruence and therefore a maladjustment.

The basic technique of Rogerian therapy is for the therapist to encounter the client in an open, honest, and empathic manner, providing the *unconditional positive regard* the client so desperately needs. In such an atmosphere, the client is able to experience his or her potentialities and to develop an accurate self while remaining free from the guilt, anxiety, and defensive behavior associated with the old conditions of worth.

*See the discussion of love in Chapter 6 for further information on the role of empathy.*

---

## CASE IN POINT
## Demonstrating Unconditional Positive Regard

The therapist demonstrates unconditional positive regard by listening carefully and reflecting feelings back to the client accurately, always without the slightest hint of negative judgment. For instance, to the client who complains about being unfairly passed over for a job promotion, the therapist might say, "You feel frustrated and angry because you believe it was unfair."

To the client who is depressed because she does not have any close friends, the therapist might say, "You feel unhappy because you are lonely." In each case, the client is being given an opportunity to discuss feelings honestly with an accepting, caring, and understanding person. Note that Rogerian therapy emphasizes the present rather than the past.

---

As the therapeutic relationship progresses, the therapist encourages a more and more complete description of feelings; and as the client's true self emerges, the old neurosis breaks up. In many instances, the complete therapy may take only one session per week for a year or less.

### ■ Gestalt Therapy

Like Rogerian therapy, **Gestalt therapy** emphasizes human perfectibility; however, the Gestaltists place a much greater emphasis on nonverbal experience than do the Rogerians. In fact, as articulated by its principal founder, Frederick (Fritz) Perls (1969), Gestalt therapy places the body on the same level as the mind.

The basic idea of Gestalt therapy is that any organism seeks to maintain its internal organization through exchanges with its environment. It does this through the process of *awareness*: first, an awareness of an imbalance in its internal organization; second, an awareness of something in the environment that can restore balance. The organism's recognition of the relationship between itself and its environment as an integrated unit, an organized, meaningful whole, is called a *gestalt*. Perls explains as follows:

> *Let's assume that I walk through the desert, and it's very hot. I lose, let's say, eight ounces of fluid. Now how do I know . . . this? First, through self-awareness . . . called "thirst." Second, suddenly . . . something emerges as a gestalt, as a foreground, . . . say, . . . a pump—or anything that would have plus eight ounces. This minus eight ounces of our organism and the plus eight ounces in the world can balance each other. The very moment this eight ounces goes into the system, we get a plus/minus water which brings balance. We come to rest as the situation is finished, the gestalt is closed. (1969, pp. 14–15)*

**WHAT DO YOU THINK?**

■ Are you usually aware of your needs?
■ What do you do when you become aware of them?
■ Are you often thinking of the past or the future?
■ Do you often stop to make yourself aware of your needs as they occur?

The situation may be finished and the gestalt closed, but only to be replaced by another unfinished situation, another incomplete gestalt. Thus, life is an unending series of incomplete gestalts. When we are living well, we are aware of our needs. As these needs express themselves through our thoughts, feelings, and actions, we become aware of what in the environment will satisfy them and we move to close the gestalt.

When we are not living well, we are unaware of our needs. Consequently, we are unaware of what will satisfy our needs, and we do not move to close the gestalt. Failure to close the gestalt leads to a psychological fragmentation, which, in turn, leads to the anxiety, frustration, and conflict we experience as we blindly grope to put the pieces together again.

Gestalt therapy seeks to help by expanding conscious awareness so that the person can recognize needs and, through the process of gestalt formation, be restored to psychological wholeness. The therapist's job is to get the patient to focus awareness on the present so that the natural process of gestalt formation will take place. Attempts by the patient to interpret what is happening or to refer to the past or future are strictly prohibited. Gestalt therapy may be practiced on an individual basis; however, treatment is usually in groups. The function of the group is usually limited to providing approval for emotional expression by the patient. Also, treatment often takes place in workshops in which many hours of contact are concentrated into a small time frame (for example, a weekend). This workshop approach often allows therapy to be completed in a relatively short time.

The therapist usually works with only one patient at a time within the group setting, watching and listening to the patient carefully, keeping awareness focused on the here and now, and prodding the patient to express thoughts and feelings. When a conflict is uncovered, the patient is asked to act it out by alternately playing its different parts. Similarly, images from fantasies and dreams may be acted out. The parts of a conflict and images from fantasies and dreams are considered fragmented parts of the patient, and the dramatizations serve to heighten awareness that, despite the fragmentation, there is only one organism.

## ■ Biofunctional Therapy

While Gestalt therapy places the body on the same level as the mind, **biofunctional therapy** goes a step further by placing body above mind. There are a variety of biofunctional therapies, but all of them assume that both psychological health and neurosis are expressed directly through the body. Hence, the therapist works directly with the body of the patient.

The originator of biofunctional therapy is Wilhelm Reich, a disciple of Freud who rejects the later Freudian view that anxiety is a signal of impending disaster to the ego. Instead, he retains the earlier Freudian view that anxiety is an expression of blocked sexual energy (Kovel, 1976, pp. 128–129). Reich maintains that our attempts to defend ourselves against stress are expressed in the development of muscular armor, body postures such as the stiff neck, the ramrod back, or the fixed smile, which become more rigid with time. This muscular armor blocks the free flow of sexual energy, thus producing anxiety, frustration, psychological conflict, and neurosis.

The goal of Reichian biofunctional therapy is to release the flow of sexual energy, and the criterion of the therapy's success is sexual orgasm. The therapist carefully observes the patient's body and then begins to knead, squeeze, press, stick, and prod muscles. Sometimes there is an exchange of words; often there is not. Therapy progresses in a sequence, moving from blockages in the forehead down through the eyes, mouth, throat, neck, shoulders, thorax, diaphragm, belly, perineum, and genitals. Treatment sessions usually take place once a week and the therapy continues for an undetermined time (until a completely satisfactory orgasm can be achieved by the patient). It is important to note that

Reich, like Freud, is expressly opposed to sex between the therapist and the patient. Therefore, orgasm is to be sought outside the therapeutic relationship.

As mentioned, Reich's is not the only biofunctional therapy. A pupil of Reich, Alexander Lowen (1976), originated his own approach, called *bioenergetics*. Lowen devised a series of exercises to facilitate the flow of energy, and he does some analytic as well as biofunctional work with his patients. Another bio-functional therapy is *Rolfing*, or *Structural Integration*, developed by Ida P. Rolf, which is closer to the original Reichian approach in that no analytic work is done.

### ■ Primal Therapy

A recently conceived but notable existential humanist therapy is Arthur Janov's **primal therapy**. According to Janov (1970), neurosis is rooted in early child-hood experience, specifically the rejection of the child by the parents. What a child needs more than anything else is to be loved by his or her parents. Children who are accepted and loved grow into well-adjusted adults. However, children who are not accepted and loved experience a Pain (Janov often capitalizes terms to emphasize their significance) that sets the neurosis into motion. Janov con-ceptualizes the neurosis as consisting of symbolic attempts to avoid the Pain (for example, defensive behavior) and the chronic tension that inevitably engulfs the person.

The goal of primal therapy is to transform the patient's state of feeling. The therapy is divided into two phases, and the treatment is highly structured. The first phase takes three weeks to complete. During this phase, the patient isolates himself or herself from usual relationships and regular activities, abstains from drugs and tension-reducing diversions, and concentrates only on the treatment. There is an open-ended session with the therapist each day. The session ends when the therapist decides the patient has had enough (usually after two to three hours). Each session has as its specific goal to get the patient to express deep feelings toward his or her parents. Sessions tend to be highly emotional, including crying, moaning, and screaming, as the patient confronts Primal Pain (the pain of having been rejected by parents). The therapist does not let anything interfere with the patient's expression of feelings toward the parents—no thoughts, feelings, or actions related to anything else.

The second phase lasts approximately six months. The patient resumes normal life activities but continues therapy in a Primal Group. There is little interaction in the group; each patient works in isolation. Ultimately, the patient experiences his or her real self and is able to live autonomously.

### ■ The Transcendent Approach

One more aspect of the human-potential movement is the **transcendent ap-proach**. Like existentialism, the transcendent approach is used in conjunction with a variety of therapies, although it has at times taken the form of a complete therapy in itself (Watts, 1961). Whether in the form of Yoga, Zen, Sufism, Tibetan Buddhism, variants of Judeo-Christian mysticism, or mind-expanding drugs, the transcendent approach is concerned with the attainment of altered states of consciousness in which the usual boundary between subject and object becomes blurred.

Having transcended the usual state of consciousness, the person allows the emergence of a potential spectrum of experiential states.

> *At the one end is the attainment of the blissful state of reunion and unity; while the other faces the terror of repressed demonic fantasies. The situation is very much the same as having a good or bad drug trip. The agent of change, be it the drug or meditative ritual, succeeds in disengaging the person from everyday expectations and perceptions. (Kovel, 1976, p. 152)*

Thus, the transcendent approach provides a new perspective from which to view everyday life. This new perspective, when supported by an effort to change life circumstances, may produce therapeutic effects.

REVIEW
QUESTIONS

*17.* Existential humanism is concerned more with ordinary unhappiness and alienation than with the classical neurosis of psychoanalysis. T F

*18.* The basic technique of Rogerian therapy is for the therapist to provide the client with conditional positive regard. T F

*19.* Usually Rogerian therapy takes longer to complete than psychoanalysis. T F

*20.* In Gestalt therapy the therapist's job is to get the patient to focus awareness on the present so that the natural process of gestalt formation will take place. T F

*21.* Gestalt therapy is always provided in traditional fifty-minute sessions between therapist and patient. T F

*22.* The goal of Reichian biofunctional therapy is to release the flow of sexual energy, and the criterion of the therapy's success is sexual orgasm. T F

*23.* Primal therapy holds that neurosis is caused by dysfunctional relationships between either spouses or friends. T F

*24.* Like existentialism, the transcendent approach is used in conjunction with a variety of therapies. T F

*The answers to these review questions are on page 471.*

## DISCUSSION: GROUP THERAPY

The therapies discussed thus far focus either on the mind or on the body as a means to help the person change. Each of these therapies also has a social dimension, but it receives little or no attention as an agent of change.

Conversely, **group therapy** uses the social dimension as the predominant change agent. Within a group the individual becomes part of an ongoing system of relationships. Over time this web of relationships develops a set of objective realities (customs, social norms, belief and value systems, and so on) that may be powerful influences that can be brought to bear on the individual's thoughts, feelings, and actions.

### ■ Traditional Group Therapy

**Traditional group therapy** is most often associated with the psychoanalytic schools of therapy. Although the therapist must deal with both the individual patients within the group and with the group itself, there is a tendency to focus primarily on one factor or the other. Thus, some therapists are said to do psychoanalysis in groups, while others are said to do group psychoanalysis (see the Case in Point).

## CASE IN POINT
# Two Approaches to Traditional Group Therapy

A therapist focusing on the individual might note that patient A is behaving in a hostile manner and interpret this as the result of a slight received from patient B, who has been lavishing attention on patient C. The therapist might then refer this interpretation back to some specific facts known about patient A's childhood.

A therapist focusing on the group might note that the group was extremely passive as the dynamics of the A-B-C triangle unfolded before it. The therapist might interpret this passivity as members' need to behave as helpless infants because they fear their own jealousy and hostility. Here, the therapist would be relating the group members' behavior to a phase in their development as a group.

In traditional group therapy, transference feelings toward the therapist provide the opportunity for group members to act out their neuroses both as individuals and as a group. Extreme idealization of the therapist, truculence, provocation, jealousy, and flattery are grist for the mill of therapy.

Additional advantages are afforded by traditional group therapy. As the group progresses, the therapist can begin to withdraw from the position of dominance. This allows group members the opportunity for personal maturation. They can become less dependent on the therapist's authority and also can facilitate their identification with the therapist by helping other group members.

### ■ Encounter Groups

The human potential movement is represented in group therapy by **encounter groups**. These groups tend to be more concerned with adding something positive (such as joy, warmth, spontaneity) to their members' lives than with removing something negative (such as neurosis). Indeed, encounter group leaders often indicate that the group activities are designed for normal people who want to get more out of life and not for emotionally disturbed people seeking a cure for their adjustment problems.

There have been so many encounter groups representing such a great variety of goals and activities that it is virtually impossible to define them in any precise manner. However, whether small (six to ten members) or large (twenty to forty members), whether led by one therapist or by two or more, and whether focusing on body, mind, emotion, or spirit, encounter groups provide experiences in which the individual may approach life on new levels. The group itself becomes an instrument of support to encourage the individual to try out new thoughts, feelings, and actions.

While encounter groups have no doubt been of great benefit to many people by helping them discover hidden potentialities, they have also produced negative results for others (Lieberman, Yalom, and Miles, 1973). We therefore recommend that you get appropriate information and referrals before joining an encounter group.

■ Encounter groups provide experiences in which the individual may "try on" new thoughts, feelings, and actions.

■ est

Perhaps the most highly organized of all therapies is *est*, the recent creation of Werner Erhard. *Est* is Latin for *it is* and is also an acronym for Erhard Seminars Training. It must be pointed out that *est* is not therapy. Its stated purpose is not to change behavior, to make people "better," or to solve their problems, but rather to transform their experience of themselves, others, the world, and so on. The basic philosophy of *est* falls within the existential humanist tradition. Life is a series of conscious choices for which we are responsible. When we function according to this principle, we are psychologically healthy; when we do not (when we avoid responsibility, lie to ourselves, live in the past, and so on), we are psychologically ill.

The *est* group is a large (200–250 people) and extremely powerful device. The group meets in a hotel ballroom for two consecutive weekends and three evening seminars, led by a trainer. All together, the experience constitutes about sixty hours. The training has three major components: (1) *data* (lectures by the trainer); (2) *processes* (experiential exercises such as guided imagery and relaxation, led by the trainer, ordinarily done individually with the eyes closed); and (3) *sharing* (voluntary self-disclosure with the trainer and the group about experiences during the training). There are various forms of forced physical discomfort (uncomfortable chairs, hardly any breaks for eating, drinking water, going to the bathroom, and so on); but no one is required to speak out or, indeed, to do anything else except follow the rules and take responsibility for personal behavior.

The combination of the physical discomfort on the one hand and the sense of group sharing and psychological support on the other tends to break down defenses. The individual becomes open and receptive and begins to embrace the *est* philosophy.

## ■ Transactional Analysis

Although often used in individual therapy, **transactional analysis** (TA), a creation of Eric Berne (1961), may be used just as effectively with groups. In fact, TA is one of the more popular group therapies.

TA focuses on the way people interact with one another and the way they behave toward themselves. According to Berne, a person's behavior at any given time is dominated by one of three *ego states*: the *Parent*, which expresses prejudicial, critical, and nurturing behavior; the *Adult*, which tests reality, estimates probabilities, and computes dispassionately; or the *Child*, which acts impulsively, creatively, and selfishly. Although all three ego states are considered essential in a healthy personality, the Adult should be in charge. Thus, TA places a premium on rational, conscious behavior. Of course, it is acceptable to be critical or impulsive at times, but only when appropriate (that is, when the Adult has flashed a green light). Therefore, adjustment problems are to be approached through the individual's Adult.

In TA therapy, clients learn to identify their ego states and to determine which one seems to be taking control at any given time. This allows them to exercise greater choice in their behavior.

> Tina has always suffered from a terrible case of the "shoulds." She seems to have rules to govern all occasions and judgments concerning how well the rules are being followed. She is highly critical and overly responsible, and she rarely lets herself have fun, even when there is nothing wrong with what she keeps herself from doing.
>
> Recently, Tina joined a TA group. Now, when her "critical Parent" begins to take charge, her Adult makes a rational decision about the propriety of her desired behavior. If she believes there is nothing wrong with what she wants to do, then she does it—without guilty feelings.

Three additional major concepts of TA are *life scripts, life positions,* and *games.* Life scripts are much like theatrical scripts. Both include a cast of characters, dialogue, scenes, acts, plots, themes, and so on. The difference is that life scripts are for real. We go through life as though we were actors in a play, acting out our hopes, fears, desires, likes, and dislikes according to a drama that was written when we were young children.

Life scripts are jointly produced by parental teachings and early decisions we make about ourselves. Among these early decisions are the life positions we adopt; they concern how we relate to ourselves and others. There are four life positions: (1) I'm OK—you're OK, (2) I'm OK—you're not OK, (3) I'm not OK—you're OK, and (4) I'm not OK—you're not OK. According to TA, most of us settle upon one of the life positions in early childhood and continue to act from that position unless something unusual happens.

Games are manipulative ploys used to induce "pay-offs," which always are reactions that support the negative component of our life position. For example, a person with an *I'm not OK—you're OK* life position might express this position's negative component by believing "I'm stupid." One way of verifying this belief is to manipulate someone else, particularly someone whose intellect is respected, such as a teacher, into saying "You're stupid." Of course, games are never played from the *I'm OK—you're OK* life position, because this position has no negative component.

TA clients are taught to recognize their life scripts and life positions and the games they play and are encouraged to make positive changes in their lives (that is, to avoid games, to adopt the *I'm OK—you're OK* life position, and to "rewrite" the life script).

TA groups usually meet once a week for a predetermined length of time (often ten weeks). The therapist teaches the group the basic concepts of TA and then facilitates group interaction (transactions). The emphasis is on analysis of conscious behavior as it is displayed in transactions. The group provides emotional support, feedback, and help in analyzing these transactions.

## ■ Family Therapy

Since the mid-1950s, **family therapy** has steadily expanded to become one of today's most important treatment modes. Unlike the other groups discussed thus far, the family is a natural group; it contains the set of relationships within which the individual lives and within which his or her neurosis probably has its roots. Thus, the family is an excellent setting within which to deal with maladjustment.

Family therapists use various techniques. A psychoanalytically oriented therapist, for instance, might approach the therapy from either or both of the perspectives described in the section dealing with traditional group therapy. Many family therapists, however, are thoroughly grounded in *systems theory*. These therapists view the family itself as the primary unit of analysis and treatment. In this view, neurosis in one family member is an indication that something has gone wrong within the family and that the family itself needs treatment.

**WHAT DO YOU THINK?**

■ Are there any aspects of your behavior that would be easier to change in a family therapy situation?
■ Would other members of your family also benefit?
■ Are some of these problems simply a matter of mismanagement?

---

## CASE IN POINT
## Circular Communication

Suppose Johnny asks Father if he can stay out late on Saturday night and Father says "no." When Johnny asks again, Mother tells him not to ask his father that question again. Then Father tells Mother not to tell Johnny not to ask that question again. Then Mother tells Johnny to go ahead and ask again. Then Johnny asks again and Father says "no." In this case, the therapist would intervene, point out the dysfunctionality of the circular communication, and suggest some alternative. Perhaps some new rules concerning how late Johnny can stay out on certain nights need to be negotiated. In taking the family through the negotiation of the new rules, the therapist would be teaching a process for resolving disputes as well as helping to produce a more functional set of rules to govern future behavior.

A usual approach by a systems family therapist is to observe the family as interaction takes place within it. This can be done either in the therapist's office or in the family's home. Once the therapist has inferred the rules governing the family's behavior, he or she can begin to intervene, focusing on interaction as it takes place. "The goal is to interrupt the circular feedback of pathological communications, then replace it with a new pattern that will sustain itself without the crippling limitations imposed by the rules of the original setup" (Kovel, 1976, p. 188).

### ■ Couples Therapy

A variant of family therapy that has grown recently is **couples therapy**. The couple might be any two people, married or not, who share a significant relationship. The basic methods of couples therapy are essentially the same as those employed in other family therapy approaches, including an emphasis on communications and techniques designed to manage or eliminate conflicts. Couples therapy is of particularly great potential benefit to couples who are thinking about getting married. Such therapy allows the opportunity to look objectively at an emerging relationship at a time when people are not usually objective. And that might save a lot of problems in the long run.

REVIEW
QUESTIONS

25. Group therapy differs from individual therapy in that group therapy uses the _____ dimension as the predominant agent of _____ .

26. Traditional group therapy is most often associated with the _____ schools of therapy.

27. _____ groups tend to be more concerned with adding something positive to people's lives than with removing something negative.

28. Perhaps the most highly organized of all therapies is _____ .

29. Transactional analysis holds that behavior at any given time is dominated by one of three ego states: the _____ , the _____ , or the _____ .

30. The _____ contains the set of relationships within which the individual lives and within which his or her neurosis probably has its roots.

31. Many family therapists treat the family as a social _____ .

32. _____ therapy might include any two people, married or not, who share a _____ _____ .

*The answers to these review questions are on page 471.*

## DISCUSSION: BEHAVIORAL-DIRECTIVE THERAPIES

**Behavioral-directive therapies** assume that emotional problems have an *observable* source. Once the source is located, therapeutic activity is directed toward it so that it may be eliminated, or at least controlled. Thus, therapists using a behavioral-directive therapy would not concern themselves with whether patients having problems getting to sleep at night have unresolved conflicts from early childhood, lack self-esteem, feel unloved by parents, or have any other unobservable source of the sleep problem. Rather, such a therapist would carefully observe the antecedents to the problem behavior (what came before it) and its consequences (what followed it). Then, after having identified what he or she believed to be the observable source of the problem, the therapist would prescribe an appropriate treatment, which, in this case, might include rearranging the antecedents, teaching the patient relaxation techniques, or even directing the patient to take sleeping pills. There are many behavioral-directive therapies, and the following discussion surveys only a few.

*See Chapter 1 for a discussion of one behavioral-directive approach—Watson and Tharp's "ABCs of behavior."*

## ■ Somatic Therapy

**Somatic therapy** defines the source of the emotional problem as biological and attempts to treat the problem through some biological means such as drugs, shock treatment, or psychosurgery. There seems to be little doubt that a distinct, inherited somatic predisposition exists for schizophrenia and that some forms of severe depressive illness are inheritable (Kovel, 1976). Thus, there is a definite link between biology and some forms of extreme emotional disturbance. In these instances, drugs may be much more useful than other techniques in managing the disorders (for example, phenothiazine is used for schizophrenia; lithium for mania; tricyclic antidepressants for psychotic depressions, and so on).

*Chapter 13 contains a more detailed consideration of schizophrenia.*

Sometimes, *electroconvulsive*, or *shock, therapy* (ECT) is used to treat serious depressions and extreme states of excitement when the patient fails to respond to drug or other treatment. ECT involves the application of an electric current for a fraction of a second through two electrodes placed on the sides of the patient's head. The patient is unconscious throughout the procedure and does

■ Drugs are effective only in postponing the ultimate confrontation with reality.

not feel any discomfort. The treatment usually requires two to eight sessions and is administered at the rate of three sessions per week. The usual effects after two or three sessions include a return to a more normal emotional mood and general mental state, improved appetite and sleep, and temporary difficulty in remembering. The memory lapses usually go away gradually over several weeks after treatment stops, although some patients claim to have persistent memory difficulty after the therapy.

*Psychosurgery* is a surgical procedure in which seemingly healthy brain tissue is destroyed or nerve pathways severed to change brain functioning and, consequently, behavior. This radical therapy has been used primarily to treat prolonged severe depression, abnormal excitement, severe anxiety, and violent outbursts of anger. Psychosurgery is relatively rare today and is usually regarded as an experimental procedure, although it was used more frequently in the 1950s. The infrequency of use today is the result of permanent negative side effects that have been observed, including loss of motivation for constructive activities and deterioration of ordinary social habits such as concern for others or concern for personal appearance.

While biologically based treatment may be the only therapy that works in some of the cases mentioned above, it is not the only workable treatment in many instances in which some doctors prescribe it. This is particularly true of drugs. It is likely that everyone suffers from tension, frustration, anxiety, and slight depression from time to time. In the case of a brief crisis, taking a sedative might be a reasonable treatment. However, for a crisis of longer duration, psychological or social therapy is the preferred treatment. In short, drugs do not help you cope with life; they simply postpone your ultimate confrontation with reality.

### ■ Sex Therapy

While somatic therapy attempts to influence mind, emotions, and behavior by treating the body, **sex therapy** attempts to influence the body by treating mind, emotions, and behavior. Sex therapy seems to work best for couples who, because of the effects of inhibition or ignorance, are sexually frustrated. They have fairly intact relationships and reasonably good capacities for communication. There is a clear, behavioral aspect to their difficulty.

*See Chapter 13 for a discussion of sexual dysfunctions.*

Many approaches have been taken to treating sexual dysfunctions, from simple reeducation programs for transient problems to lengthy and intensive psychotherapy. Knowledge of the physiology of sex, simple techniques of arousal, and contemporary sexual practices may alter the attitudes of the sexual partners and thus improve their sexual lives. For example, knowing that an extensive use of fantasy during coitus is effective and widely practiced may enable one or both partners to respond more effectively. If sexual dysfunctions are found to be based on interpersonal conflicts or poor communication, couples counseling can help change the bedroom from a battleground to a focal point for mutually supportive activities. Personal problems rooted in past experiences may contribute to the couple's problems, and insight-oriented therapies may help the affected partner to gain an understanding of the unconscious conflicts relating to present sexual problems. Insight can improve performance.

Perhaps the most widely practiced sex therapy is the behavioral-directive therapy based on the work of William Masters and Virginia Johnson (1966,

1970), who employ an intimate educational approach. A treatment team of a woman and a man therapist interact with an involved couple. (Single people are not allowed into therapy because of legal and moral considerations.) After a complete background study has been completed, a relaxed atmosphere is established and training begins. Treatment consists of education pertaining to the sex organs and their functioning, sets of suggestions for pleasurable explorations leading to, but short of, intercourse, and a new awareness of the nature of a sound sexual relationship.

Certain concepts are introduced and reinforced during treatment:

1. No one is uninvolved and no one is at fault; it takes two to make love.
2. Sex is a natural function that requires relaxation, not heroics.
3. Each partner must learn self-arousal and communication skills.
4. Each must give as well as receive stimulation.
5. Orgasm will come in time, and there is nothing to be gained by seeking it anxiously.

## ■ Behavior Therapy

**Behavior therapy** is a behavioral-directive approach that is strictly psychological. It is a natural outgrowth of behavioral psychology, the academic tradition that focuses on observable, testable, quantifiable, and reproducible behavior. Thus, behavior therapy begins with analyzing a pattern of behavior and identifying an observable component such as a phobia. Then a set of directives is aimed at altering the behavior pattern so that the observable component is eliminated or controlled. The key to this method is to narrow the problem by continually defining and redefining it so that it can eventually be brought under control. Once the problem is narrowed sufficiently, treatment can begin.

There are many behavior therapy techniques. Generally, they involve the application of control over one piece of behavior, then another, then another, and so on until the whole problem has been brought under control. For example, a technique created by Joseph Wolpe (1969) for the treatment of phobias is *systematic desensitization*. This technique is often used when the patient suffers from some overt anxiety. The general notion is to construct a hierarchy of fear-inducing situations, beginning with one the patient can handle and then proceeding, step by step, to the target situation. Suppose, for instance, the patient is fearful of flying in a plane. Over a period of several weeks the patient might look at pictures of people flying in a plane; go to the airport and watch planes take off and land; get on a plane and imagine that it is taking off, flying, and landing; and finally, actually fly in a plane.

An integral part of systematic desensitization is relaxation training. One widely used relaxation technique is *progressive relaxation*, in which the alternate tensing and relaxing of muscles, together with breathing exercises, relaxes first one part of the body and then another, until the person is in a highly relaxed state. A variation of this technique involves the use of relaxing images rather than the tensing and relaxing of muscles. These techniques can be taught to the patient so that he or she can attain states of calm whenever desired, or they can be used to relax the patient, making him or her more susceptible to suggestion. (Another technique that can accomplish either of these objectives is *hypnosis*, although hypnosis does not appear to be widely used by behavior therapists.)

*Chapter 7 contains more information on progressive relaxation.*

One of the main currents of behavior therapy mixes Skinnerian operant conditioning and respondent conditioning (see Chapter 2). For example, a behavior therapist working with a couple might observe their interaction carefully and then show how a behavior emitted by one is a reinforcement for a negative response by the other, which in turn reinforces the reinforcer and so on, until they are literally at each other's throats. Here again, the behavior pattern can be broken down into small parts, which can be changed through conditioning until a new functional behavior pattern has been constructed to replace the older, dysfunctional one.

## ■ Cognitive Therapy

*See Chapter 5 for more about cognition.*

One more type of behavioral-directive therapy is **cognitive therapy**. This therapy has several versions, including Albert Ellis's (1962) *rational-emotive therapy*, William Glasser's (1965) *reality therapy*, and Aaron Beck's (1976) *cognitive therapy*. All of them are concerned with concepts, assumptions and values.

The general notion is that the patient displays maladjustive behavior because of some error or confusion with regard to beliefs or values. For example, we can easily understand the depression of a person who believes he or she should be thoroughly competent and adequate and who has just made a terrible blunder. The real blunder, according to the cognitivists, is not in making a mistake but in believing one has to be perfect. The truth of the matter is that *everyone* makes errors from time to time; although we do not look forward to making errors, doing so does not justify depression.

Cognitive therapists, therefore, point out to their patients faulty thinking and confusion with regard to value judgments. Then, they attempt to correct these errors by teaching more realistic and effective ways of thinking and methods by which patients can work out their own value systems. This approach is demonstrated in the second action plan in the Action Plans section, which provides a self-help model based on cognitive therapy.

**WHAT DO YOU THINK?**

■ What particular situation makes you anxious or insecure?
■ Why?
■ Is your position realistic?

REVIEW
QUESTIONS

*33.* Behavioral-directive therapies assume that emotional problems have observable sources. T F

*34.* A somatic therapist would never treat a patient with drugs. T F

*35.* Psychosurgery is a popular new type of surgery. T F

*36.* Sex therapy attempts to influence the body by treating mind, emotions, and behavior. T F

*37.* Behavior therapy is a behavioral-directive approach that is strictly psychological. T F

*38.* A widely used behavior therapy technique that was originally created for the treatment of phobias is systematic desensitization. T F

*39.* Progressive relaxation tends to make the person more susceptible to suggestion. T F

*40.* Cognitive therapy is nondirective in nature. T F

*The answers to these review questions are on page 471.*

# DISCUSSION: A FEW REMAINING CONCERNS

Thus far in this chapter, we have explored concerns related to the appropriate time to enter into therapy, different types of therapists, qualities of a good therapist, methods of choosing a therapist, and a variety of specific therapies. Now, in the last section, we will tie together the loose ends by answering a few remaining questions.

## ■ Choice of Therapy

The choice of a particular therapy may not be as important as the choice of a particular therapist or the decision to enter therapy in the first place. Once a person has willingly chosen to seek help and has selected a therapist who meets the criteria discussed earlier in this chapter, the chances of success are good regardless of the therapy employed.

Still, some therapies may be better suited than others to deal with certain problems. A person who wants to quit smoking, for example, might be well advised to try a behavioral-directive approach to therapy, rather than one of the analytic or existential humanistic approaches. By the same token, the person who has deeply rooted internal conflicts and who suffers the pangs of great anxiety and guilt might be a more likely candidate for an analytic therapy, and the person who is mildly depressed because he or she believes that "Life is passing me by" might better seek an existential humanistic therapy.

It is also important to point out that many therapists today blend elements of two or even more approaches in an attempt to tailor a therapy to the unique needs of their clients. The pure models of therapy discussed earlier are often not precisely followed. Common sense dictates that the selection of a particular therapy should be based on information gathered about that therapy, including factors such as time and money spent.

## ■ Price of Therapy

Therapy costs what the market will bear. Because of the relatively large fluctuation in inflation rates in the United States in recent years, prices for therapy have been unstable, and it is difficult to quote accurate figures. However, even if prices remain stable, the variation in price from one therapy to another can be great, depending on whether the therapy treats individuals or groups and on whether it is provided through private practice or a practice supported by public funds. For example, in some places in the United States individuals are willing to pay private practitioners as much as $125 an hour for therapy. In other parts of the country people are not willing to pay that much, and the same type of therapy may be bought from private practitioners for $40 an hour, or perhaps even less. Some group therapies tend to be relatively inexpensive (for example, TA or encounter group therapy may cost as little as $15 to $20 per session), while others may cost more (for example, *est* currently costs $425). Therapy provided through a practice supported by public funds (by some community agency or a public university or college, for example) may cost little or nothing. The main point here is that, since prices vary greatly, one should investigate them thoroughly before making a commitment to a particular therapy.

### ■ Other Costs of Therapy

Therapy may have other costs. The general expectation is that a person who enters therapy will achieve better adjustment. Thus, a person in therapy can expect to change. This change may involve thoughts, feelings, or actions and may manifest itself in the way the person treats himself or herself, others, or life in general.

Successful therapy may cost the person a relationship. Suppose the wife in therapy should discover that she has grown apart from her husband and that this growth threatens and may ultimately destroy their relationship. Costs such as this are inherent in the process of therapy. Certainly, not all the changes are so dramatic, but changes will occur. The change may "cost" the person in therapy and/or those who are close to him or her. Thus, the risks of successful therapy extend to family members and friends as well as to the person in therapy.

### ■ Evaluating Therapy

By definition, successful therapy helps the person to achieve better adjustment. Thus, to judge whether a therapy is successful, we can evaluate how well the goals of the therapy are being achieved. For example, the person who suffers frequent, severe anxiety attacks would, no doubt, want to eliminate the anxiety attacks. This person might conclude that the therapy is working well if the anxiety attacks decrease in both intensity and frequency.

*See the Conclusion for a consideration of goal setting.*

Note that in our example there is an implicit division of the goals of therapy into long-range and short-range goals. The long-range goal is the elimination of anxiety attacks. The short-range goal is a decrease in the intensity and/or frequency of the attacks. This division of goals is useful because it is through the achievement of short-range goals that we ultimately achieve our long-range goals, and it is through the evaluation of short-range goals that we can make reasonable judgments about whether the therapy is helping us to achieve our long-range goals.

One method in evaluating goal achievement is self-assessment. Ask yourself, "What evidence do I have that I am achieving my goal?" Another method is discussion with the therapist. Ask the therapist, "What evidence do you see that I am achieving my goal?" A third method is discussion with a family member or friend. Ask this person, "What evidence do you see that I am achieving my goal?" Gather information from all three sources, inspect it carefully, and make a judgment.

Therapy should end either when the goals have been completely achieved or when there has been no progress toward the achievement of goals for an inordinately long time. In either case, you have achieved what is possible for the time being, and it is time to move on.

REVIEW
QUESTIONS

41. Some therapies may be better suited than others to deal with certain problems. T F

42. Many therapists today blend elements of two or even more approaches in an attempt to tailor a therapy to the unique needs of their clients. T F

43. The monetary costs of all types of therapy are the same. T F

44. Generally, a person in therapy can expect to change. T F

*45.* The risks of successful therapy extend to family members and friends as well as to the person in therapy. T F

*46.* Therapy should end only when the goals of therapy have been completely achieved. T F

*The answers to these review questions are found on page 471.*

## SUMMARY

■ Psychotherapy is a process involving the use of psychological techniques to help a person achieve better adjustment. There are many types of psychotherapy and several types of psychotherapists.

■ People should consider entering therapy when they realize things are not going well, but they do not know what to do to improve the situation.

■ Therapists can be differentiated by kind and amount of formal training, licensing requirements, accreditation, services performed, and approaches to therapy. They include psychiatrists, psychologists, psychiatric social workers, psychoanalysts, sex therapists, psychiatric nurses, and pastoral counselors. Good therapists are sensitive, empathic, and accepting, in addition to being well trained.

■ The best source of information concerning a therapist is a person who has been in therapy with that therapist. Other sources of information include members of helping professions, local clinics or hospitals, local professional societies, area mental associations, telephone hotlines, and community-service or inter-agency-council information and referral services. The least desirable source is the yellow pages of the telephone directory.

■ A therapy may be classified as insight-oriented or action-oriented; as directive or nondirective; or as oriented toward individual, family, or group treatment. This chapter classifies therapies as analytic, existential humanistic, group, or behavioral-directive. There is some overlapping among these categories.

■ Analytic therapies rely on verbal means to place the person in greater contact with fragmented parts of his or her mental life. These therapies include psychoanalysis, psychoanalytic psychotherapy, neo-Freudian analysis, analytical psychology, and the existential approach.

■ Psychoanalysis involves two steps: strengthening the weakened ego by extending its self-knowledge and breaking down resistances. Using direct information supplied by the analysand and information conveyed through free associations, transferences, and the telling of dreams, the analyst acts as interpreter for the analysand.

■ Psychoanalytic psychotherapy is a modification of psychoanalysis that focuses more on current problems in living than on fixations. The treatment is shorter and less expensive than traditional psychoanalysis.

■ Neo-Freudian analysis emphasizes the drive toward self-realization and views adjustment problems as stemming from negative life experiences rather than from unresolved early childhood conflicts related to infantile sexuality. Therefore, the treatment focuses on conscious thoughts, feelings, and behavior in the here and now.

■ Analytical psychology is based on the notion that there is a collective unconscious, shared by all people, that reflects the cosmic order and contains archetypes that recur in human cultures and that can be known through dream symbols, creative imagination, disturbed mental states, and the products of art and science. It is assumed that neurosis results when the person has lost touch with the archetypes and other psychological formations such as the anima, the animus, and the shadow. The goal of treatment is to integrate the self with its transpersonal parts.

■ The existential approach emphasizes the themes of personal alienation in mass society, the breakdown of traditional values, and the consequent loss of meaning in our lives. It assumes that we can control our own lives through the individual choices we make. The treatment involves an active dialogue between therapist and patient that focuses on the patient's current choices.

■ Existential humanistic therapies share the following characteristics: (1) a blending of the direct experience component of the existential approach with a deep philosophical commitment to the notion of the perfectibility of human beings, (2) a concern with ordinary unhappiness and alienation as opposed to the classical neurosis of psychoanalysis, and (3) a concern with educating people. Existential humanistic therapies include Rogerian therapy, Gestalt therapy, biofunctional therapy, primal therapy, and the transcendent approach.

■ Rogerian therapy aims at getting the client to experience his or her potentialities and to develop an accurate self-concept. The therapist works toward these ends by providing unconditional positive regard in an open, honest, and empathic encounter.

■ Gestalt therapy assumes that maladjustment is the result of a person's failing to recognize and satisfy his or her needs. The therapist attempts to get the patient to focus awareness on the present so that needs and the means to satisfy them will come into focus. There is a distinct emphasis on nonverbal as well as verbal behavior.

■ Biofunctional therapy assumes that both psychological health and neurosis are expressed directly through the body. Hence, the therapist works directly with the body of the patient.

■ Primal therapy asserts that neurosis is rooted in early rejection of the child by the parents. The goal of treatment is to transform the patient's state of feeling. The therapist accomplishes this by getting the patient to express deep feelings toward his or her parents.

■ The transcendent approach is concerned with the attainment of a new perspective on life through altered states of consciousness in which the usual boundary between subject and object becomes blurred.

■ Group therapy uses social dynamics as the predominant change agent. Group therapies include traditional group therapy, encounter groups, *est*, transactional analysis, and family therapy.

■ Traditional group therapy is most often associated with the psychoanalytic schools of therapy. The therapist tends to focus on either the individual patients within the group or on the group itself.

■ Encounter groups tend to be more concerned with adding something positive to members' lives than removing something negative. The group functions as an instrument of support to encourage the individual to try out new thoughts, feelings, and actions.

■ *Est* attempts to transform the individual's experience of himself or herself, others, and the world in general, through highly organized training that emphasizes conscious choices and personal responsibility.

■ Transactional Analysis (TA) focuses on the way people interact with one another and the way they behave toward themselves. The therapist draws attention to people's interactions (transactions) and emphasizes the value of reality testing, probability estimating, and dispassionate computing in the establishment of adjustive behavior patterns.

■ Family therapy focuses on group dynamics within the family itself, which comprises the living set of relationships that probably gave rise to the patient's neurosis in the first place. A growing variant of family therapy is couples therapy.

■ Behavioral-directive therapies assume that emotional problems have observable sources. Once the source is located, therapeutic activity is directed toward eliminating, at least, controlling it. Behavioral-directive therapies include somatic therapy, sex therapy, behavior therapy, and cognitive therapy.

■ Somatic therapy defines the source of emotional problems as biological and attempts to treat the problem through such means as drugs, shock treatment, or psychosurgery.

■ Sex therapy attempts to treat sexual dysfunctions, such as premature ejaculation, by dealing with attitudes, expectations, emotions, and behavior. Treatment is usually given to a couple, with both partners being taught various techniques for enhancing erotic arousal.

■ Behavior therapy is a strictly psychological behavioral-directive approach that begins with analysis of a pattern of behavior and identification of an observable component, such as a phobia. Therapy is aimed at altering the behavior pattern so that the observable component is eliminated or controlled.

■ Proponents of cognitive therapy believe maladjustive behavior is caused by some error or confusion with regard to beliefs or values. The therapist points out the faulty thinking to the patient and then attempts to correct it by teaching more realistic and effective ways of thinking and of establishing values.

■ The choice of a particular therapy may not be as important as the choice of a particular therapist and/ or the decision to enter therapy in the first place. Still, some therapies may be better suited than others to deal with certain problems. Common sense dictates that the selection of a particular therapy should be based on information gathered about that therapy, including factors such as time and money spent.

■ Therapy costs what the market will bear, from literally nothing, as in the case of some therapy provided through practices supported by public funds, to as much as the $125 an hour charged by some private practitioners.

■ A person in therapy can be expected to change in various ways. Thus, the risks of therapy, particularly successful therapy, extend to family members and friends as well as the person in therapy.

■ We can judge whether a therapy is successful by evaluating how well the goals of therapy are being achieved. This evaluation might include self-assessment, discussion with the therapist, and discussion with a family member or friend.

■ Therapy should end either when the goals have been completely achieved or when there has been no progress toward the achievement of goals for an inordinately long time.

## SELECTED READINGS

Bergin, A. E., and Garfield, S. L., eds. *Handbook of Psychotherapy and Behavior Changes: An Empirical Analysis.* New York: Liley, 1971. A comprehensive review and evaluation of approaches to therapy, including practical implications inferred from the data presented. This book is somewhat technical in nature and therefore perhaps better suited to advanced psychology students.

Goleman, D., and Speeth, K. R., eds. *The Essential Psychotherapies: Theory and Practice by the Masters.* New York: New American Library, 1982. A compilation of essays by twenty-four well-known therapists, with each essay preceded by bibliographical information supplied by the editors.

Kanfer, F. H., and Goldstein, A. P., eds. *Helping People Change.* New York: Pergamon Press, 1975. A book that provides clear examples of the methods used by different kinds of psychotherapists.

Kovel, J. *A Complete Guide to Therapy: From Psychoanalysis to Behavior Modification.* New York: Pantheon, 1976. An excellent book that, though broad in scope, is relatively short and easy for the introductory student to understand.

Mishara, B. L., and Patterson, R. D. *Consumer's Handbook of Mental Health: How to Find, Select and Use Help.* New York: Signet, 1979. A handbook that tries to answer practical questions people often have about fees, insurance, financial help, the relationship between therapist and patient, and the legal rights and responsibilities of patients.

## GLOSSARY

**analytic therapy**: a therapy that relies on verbal means to place the person in greater contact with fragmented parts of his or her mental life. In essence, the therapist analyzes what has happened or what is happening to the person, who then synthesizes or puts the fragmented parts back together.

**analytical psychology**: C. G. Jung's system of psychological thought, including his method of therapy.

**behavior therapy**: a behavioral-directive approach to therapy that is strictly psychological.

**behavioral-directive therapy**: a therapy that assumes emotional problems have observable sources.

**biofunctional therapy**: an existential humanistic therapy that places body above mind.

**cognitive therapy**: a behavioral-directive therapy concerned with correcting incorrect or unrealistic concepts, assumptions, and values.

**couples therapy**: a variant of family therapy that deals with the relationship between two people.

**dream analysis**:   the process in which the analysand tells his or her dreams to the analyst, who interprets them and, in turn, reveals the interpretations to the analysand.

**encounter-group**:   existential humanistic group that tends to concentrate on adding something positive to rather than removing something negative from the lives of participants.

**est**:   a highly organized existential humanistic group therapy that attempts to transform the person's experience of himself or herself, others, the world, and so on.

**existential approach**:   a radical type of analytic strategy based on the idea that the individual is responsible for personal choices.

**existential humanism**:   a recent and distinctly American trend in therapy that blends direct experience with the concept of human perfectibility and deals more with ordinary unhappiness and alienation than with the classical neurosis of psychoanalysis.

**family therapy**:   the only type of group therapy that involves the natural group—the family—that contains the set of relationships within which the individual lives and within which his or her neurosis probably has its roots.

**free association**:   the method whereby the person says everything that comes into his or her mind.

**Gestalt therapy**:   an existential humanistic therapy that places the body on the same level as the mind.

**group therapy**:   a type of therapy in which one or more therapists meet with several patients or clients who form a social group that becomes a powerful influence that may be used to help change the behavior of its members.

**neo-Freudian analysis**:   an approach to therapy created by several of Freud's disciples. It emphasizes the realization of self as opposed to instinctual drives, present as opposed to past relationships, and conscious as opposed to unconscius thoughts, feelings, and behavior.

**pastoral counselor**:   member of the clergy trained in counseling techniques.

**primal therapy**:   an existential humanistic therapy designed to rid the person of the hurt feelings carried over from early childhood when he or she was rejected by parents.

**psychiatric nursing**:   training in psychotherapy, given to all nurses.

**psychiatric social worker**:   social worker trained in and practicing psychotherapy.

**psychiatrist**:   licensed physician who practices psychotherapy.

**psychoanalysis**:   Sigmund Freud's system of psychological thought. It includes both a theory of personality and a therapeutic method.

**psychoanalytic psychotherapy**:   a modification of psychoanalysis that attempts to provide the patient with a shorter and less expensive treatment.

**psychoanalyst**:   individual who has received advanced training in the psychotherapeutic technique developed by Sigmund Freud.

**psychologist**:   individual who has earned master's and/or doctor's degrees in psychology.

**psychotherapist**:   practitioner of psychotherapy.

**psychotherapy**:   a process in which psychological techniques are used to help a person achieve better adjustment.

**resistance**:   thoughts and feelings severely threatening to the person, who blocks them from consciousness through repression.

**Rogerian therapy**:   an existential humanistic therapy devised by Carl Rogers.

**sex therapist**:   pyschotherapist trained in techniques designed to help people overcome sexual dysfunctions.

**sex therapy**:   a behavioral-directive therapy that attempts to influence the body (that is, sexual dysfunction) by treating mind, emotions, and behavior.

**somatic therapy**:   a behavioral-directive therapy that defines the source of emotional problems as biological and that attempts to treat the problem through some biological means, such as drugs, shock treatment, or psychosurgery.

**traditional group therapy**:   a group therapy version of psychoanalysis.

**transactional analysis**:   a popular group therapy that focuses on the way people interact with one another and the way they behave toward themselves.

**transcendent approach**:   an approach to therapy that uses altered states of consciousness as a new perspective from which to view everyday life.

**transference**:   the process in which the analysand begins to see the analyst as some important figure from childhood and transfers onto the analyst feelings and reactions that applied to that important figure.

# REFERENCES

Beck, A. *Cognitive Therapy and Emotional Disorders*. New York: International University Press, 1976.

Berne, E. *Transactional Analysis in Psychotherapy*. New York: Grove Press, 1961.

Ellis, A. *Reason and Emotion in Psychotherapy*. New York: Lyle Stuart, 1962.

Freud, S. *An Outline of Psycho-Analysis*. Revised, translated, and edited by James Strachey. New York: Norton, 1969. (First German edition, 1940.)

Glasser, W. *Reality Therapy*. New York: Harper & Row, 1965.

Janov. A. *The Primal Scream*. New York: Putnam, 1970.

Jung, C. G. *Analytical Psychology: Its Theory and Practice*. New York: Pantheon Books, 1968.

Kovel, J. *A Complete Guide to Therapy: From Psychoanalysis to Behavior Modification*. New York: Pantheon, 1976.

Lieberman, M. A.; Yalom, I. D.; and Miles, M. B. *Encounter Groups: First Facts*. New York: Basic Books, 1973.

Lowen, A. *Bioenergetics*. New York: Penguin, 1976.

Masters, W. H., and Johnson, V. E. *Human Sexual Response*. Boston: Little, Brown, 1966.

_____. *Human Sexual Inadequacy*. Boston: Little, Brown, 1970.

*Miami Herald* (November 16, 1980): 4b.

Mishara, B. L., and Patterson, R. D. *Consumer's Handbook of Mental Health: How to Find, Select and Use Help*. New York: Signet, 1979.

Perls, F. *Gestalt Therapy Verbatim*. Lafayette, Calif.: Real People Press, 1969.

Rogers, C. *On Becoming a Person*. Boston: Houghton Mifflin, 1961.

Watts, A. *Pschotherapy East and West*. New York: Pantheon Books, 1961.

Williams, R. L., and Long, J. D. *Toward a Self-Managed Life Style*, 2nd ed. Boston: Houghton Mifflin, 1979.

Wolpe, J. *The Practice of Behavior Therapy*. New York: Pergamon Press, 1969.

## ANSWERS TO REVIEW QUESTIONS

**Page 443.** *1.* T  *2.* T  *3.* F  *4.* F  *5.* F  *6.* T  *7.* T  *8.* T

**Page 450.** *9.* Insight-oriented  *10.* psychoanalysis  *11.* transference  *12.* id, ego, remain sleeping  *13.* self-knowledge, resistances  *14.* self-realization  *15.* collective  *16.* existential approach

**Page 455.** *17.* T  *18.* F  *19.* F  *20.* T  *21.* F  *22.* T  *23.* F  *24.* T

**Page 460.** *25.* social, change  *26.* psychoanalytic  *27.* Encounter  *28.* est  *29.* Parent, Adult, Child  *30.* family *31.* system *32.* Couples, significant relationship

**Page 464.** *33.* T  *34.* F  *35.* F  *36.* T  *37.* T  *38.* T  *39.* T  *40.* F

**Page 466.** *41.* T  *42.* T  *43.* F  *44.* T  *45.* T  *46.* F

By reading, understanding, and reflecting on the material in this book, you have, no doubt, increased your understanding of yourself. You have gained insights into your own adjustment and growth patterns, into factors that have influenced your personality development, and into other factors that build up and tear down your self-esteem. You have considered the physical, cognitive, and emotional aspects of yourself and the impact of stress on your life. You have contemplated your own socialization and your relationships with others, including communication, intimacy, and leadership. You have also identified some of your dysfunctional behavior patterns and some of the general approaches that may be used to change them. Now, in the Conclusion, you will focus on the processes that may be used to put this self-knowledge to some practical use: goal setting and decision making.

# CONCLUSION: GOAL SETTING AND DECISION MAKING

## GOAL SETTING

To have a fulfilling and satisfying life, we need to make decisions that relate to our life goals. Goals give our lives direction and purpose. They let us know where we have been, where we are now, and where we hope to be in the future. Furthermore, life goals help us make personal adjustments. We should have goals in several areas: personal goals (say, to develop a healthier body), educational goals (to earn a master's degree), professional goals (to become a manager), and social goals (to develop skills in interpersonal interaction). By setting a variety of goals, we can avoid becoming too occupied with any one aspect of our lives.

Although goal setting is essential to healthy adjustment, we should not become so obsessed with our goals that we fail to enjoy the present. Some people are so preoccupied with the future that they fail to adjust to the present. College students who believe they cannot spend time in extracurricular activities because they must constantly prepare for a profession are not demonstrating healthy adjustment. Future goals are important, but they should facilitate rather than hinder our adjustment and enjoyment of the present.

### Goal-Setting Criteria

Before we can effectively formulate life goals, we need as much information about ourselves as possible. We must seek information about our strengths and values. An assessment of our strengths helps us determine our capabilities; an assessment of our values helps us determine what is most important to us. This information will enable us to set goal priorities. We must bear in mind, however, that our goals must be realistic. Therefore, we must choose them carefully. Goals that are beyond our capabilities may cause us frustration and disillusionment. On the other hand, if our goals are set too low, we will suffer boredom. The first step in setting goals, then, is to learn as much about ourselves as we can. You have begun this process with your involvement in the previous chapters.

We can test a goal to see if it is realistic by determining if we are motivated enough or want to expend the energy necessary to achieve it. Another criterion to consider is whether we have the time to achieve a particular goal. Often our expectations of ourselves are unrealistic in terms of the amount of time available.

A goal must be measurable. Thus, it should be stated as concretely and specifically as possible. To say that you are going to study harder in biology is vague and not measurable. It becomes measurable when you state, "I will read Chapter 8 in my biology book and answer all the study questions at the end of the chapter." When our goals are vague and not measurable, it is unlikely that we will ever achieve them to our satisfaction.

Knowing that procrastination is a common trait, we might go a step further and state, "I will read Chapter 8 and answer the study questions at the end of the chapter by Tuesday, October 18." The goal stated this way provides a deadline for completion. Without deadlines, most of us would seldom achieve our goals.

### Long-Range and Short Term Goals

From a time perspective, there are two basic types of goals. *Long-range goals* represent accomplishments we hope to achieve some time in the distant future—

for example, I hope to be a forest ranger in the Rocky Mountains; I hope to live in a beautiful house overlooking the Pacific Ocean; I hope to win a gold medal in the Olympics; or I hope to live to be a hundred years old and do it in good health. Long-range goals such as these certainly are attainable. However, just hoping for them will not bring them to be. Our long-range goals are relatively few in number and may take years or a lifetime to achieve. We usually achieve them by setting and accomplishing many related *short-term goals*. Short-term goals help us to move steadily toward the achievement of our long-range goals. Our short-term goals are usually more immediate and may be achieved within hours, days, weeks, or months. The goal profile included here will help you identify some long-range and short-term goals.

## Goal Priorities

It is important to establish some goal priorities for both long-range and short-term goals so we can determine which goals we should begin working toward first. Some goals will need to be achieved earlier as a prerequisite for later goals. Some earlier goals will be those we have the capability of completing successfully

## Goal Profile

List five long-range goals you are presently working toward. For each long-range goal, list three short-term goals that will lead you toward its achievement.

Long-Range Goals

1. _____

2. _____

3. _____

4. _____

5. _____

Short-Term Goals

A. _____

B. _____

C. _____

A. _____

B. _____

C. _____

A. _____

B. _____

C. _____

A. _____

B. _____

C. _____

A. _____

B. _____

C. _____

very soon. Goal setting for success is a very important consideration in estab-lishing goal priorities. Success is our greatest motivator. For this reason it is important to plan to complete some of our goals relatively soon; we may lose our determination if many of our goals seem too far in the future.

## Goal Setting for Success

There are no guarantees that we are going to attain our goals or that they will meet our expectations. However, the following points may help us increase our goal satisfaction:

*1.* Be careful not to invest too much of your life focusing on long-range ambitions. Seek satisfaction in the achievement of numerous short-term, day-to-day goals.

*2.* Choose long-range goals you can enjoy working toward as much as reaching. Even if you fail to reach a goal, you have the satisfaction and enjoyment of trying. Many of us have discovered that the journey is often more enjoyable than the destination. Having reached our goals, we may look back and realize that we have lived through the happiest moments of our lives without fully appreciating them.

*3.* If you have a goal that involves helping others, make sure your satis-faction comes from the act of helping, doing, or giving rather than from the appreciation, recognition, or respect you expect to receive from the recipients. When the accomplishment of a goal is to be measured by rec-ognition and appreciation from others, we often set ourselves up for disappointment.

*4.* Your goals should be chosen on the basis of your enjoymnent or your feeling of accomplishment rather than on the basis of impressing or pleasing others. People often go to college or enter a profession because they give in to parental pressure or because they want to impress others. The result is that they end up unhappy about their choices. It is important to remember that our first priority is to please ourselves and be happy. If then we impress or please others, we have an added reward.

*5.* Be flexible in choosing your long-term goals. We may discover that our primary goal is not realistically achievable. A goal to enter medical school should have some backup goal, such as pharmacy or biological or chemical research. We are less likely to be disappointed with the failure to reach a primary goal if we use the time and energy spent in a related way.

*6.* It is important to remember that failure in achieving a goal need not be devastating, for failure sometimes forces us to seek alternatives that may be more desirable for us. We may discover that by changing our goals we afford ourselves an opportunity to explore many paths we might otherwise have overlooked.

## Goal Setting as a Life-Long Process

In our rapidly changing, mobile world, the opportunities for everyone to con-tinue to grow and live a long, productive life are limitless. Once it would have seemed odd to encounter a middle-aged or older person as a student in college. Increasingly, we discover older people, both men and women, enrolled in part-time and full-time college programs. These people are taking advantage of their right to change their minds about their previously chosen goals (work, interests, and so on) or set new goals to improve the quality of their lives.

Every day we live affords us the opportunity to discover more about ourselves, our lives, our environment, our relationships to others, and our opportunities. This new information allows us to revise our goals and establish new ones. In short, life should be a never-ending process of goal setting.

## DECISION MAKING

A thorough understanding of the process of formulating and achieving goals is the basis for effective decision making. A decision is a choice that usually affects a future course of action. In other words, the choice we make from among available alternatives most often results in our making additional related choices in the future. These choices move us toward the achievement of our goals.

We make decisions every day that range from "What shall I wear?" to "Should I get married?" Decisions of lesser importance usually are made without much thought. Decisions of greater importance demand more time and thought, for we want to be sure we make the right choice; we want to guarantee success. Because we fear that we will make a mistake, we often procrastinate, fret, worry, and even avoid making these decisions. Decisions that greatly affect our lives do require much thought and planning. They become easier, however, when we follow a step-by-step process.

---

## Steps You Have Used to Make Major Decisions

Identify *two* major decisions you have made in your life. List the steps you used to arrive at each decision.

Major decision: _____

_____

Steps I used in the decision-making process:

1. _____

2. _____

3. _____

4. _____

5. _____

Major decision: _____

_____

Steps I used in the decision-making process:

1. _____

2. _____

3. _____

4. _____

5. _____

The following seven-step process is helpful:

*1.* You must identify the circumstance you are attempting to manage and state it clearly and specifically.

*2.* You should gather all the information available that relates to the circumstance. The most important information is information about you—your value priorities, interests, aptitudes, and goals; obstacles that may stand in your way; and so on.

*3.* You need information about significant others, people you care about who will be affected by your decision.

*4.* You need information about the available alternatives from which you will eventually choose. For example, if you are deciding what graduate school to attend, you will need information about the location, reputation, programs, and desirability of various graduate schools.

*5.* You need to weigh the evidence gathered in the previous steps. In other words, you must weigh the pros and cons of your alternatives.

*6.* You are now ready to choose among the alternatives (make the decision). If your information gathering has been thorough and honest, you should have confidence in your decision.

*7.* Finally, you are ready to take action—to follow through on your decision.

As an example of this process, let us look at how one person used it to make an important decision in her life.

The college Joanne attended required only freshman students to live on campus. Near the end of her freshman year, she felt the need to make a decision about where she would live during her sophomore year. Several of her friends had already decided to live off campus in college-approved housing; however, a few of her friends, including her roommate, had decided to stay in the college dormitories at least another year. Influenced by both sets of friends, Joanne vacillated between the two alternatives. She realized that the only way to approach this dilemma was to use a logical decision-making process.

Joanne began by identifying pertinent personal information such as value priorities, goals, interests, and obstacles. To help review the information carefully, she decided to write out the personal information on a sheet of paper, as shown.

Personal Information

| VALUE PRIORITIES | GOALS | INTERESTS | OBSTACLES |
|---|---|---|---|
| Personal growth | Education | Tennis | Lack of money |
| Honesty | Career | Backgammon | Parents' wants |
| Independence | Marriage | Acting | Loyalty to friends |
| Love relationship | Travel | | |
| Family | | | |
| Friendship | | | |

Joanne's next step was to identify the alternatives available to her. There appeared to be at least three alternatives: live on campus in the dormitory with a roommate, live off campus in an apartment with four friends, or live off campus in a private room by herself. She recorded the pertinent information for each alternative on a sheet of paper, as shown.

Alternatives

|  | ON CAMPUS | OFF CAMPUS APARTMENT | OFF CAMPUS ROOM |
|---|---|---|---|
| *Studying* | Some quiet time | More distractions | Ample quiet time |
| *Privacy* | Some | Minimal | Ample |
| *Interaction* | Ample | Ample | Minimal |
| *Freedom* | Moderate | Ample | Ample |
| *Parents' Wants* | Yes | No | Maybe |
| *Proximity* | Close to everything | 6 miles from campus | Walking distance |
| *Cost* | $100 per month | $185 per month | $135 per month |

Next, Joanne weighed the pros and cons of each of the alternatives. As shown, she listed each alternative and its pros and cons on a separate sheet of paper.

## Pros and Cons of Living on Campus

| PROS | CONS |
|---|---|
| 1. I have become good friends with my roommate, and we respect each other's privacy and needs (friendship). | 1. I feel restricted by some of the dormitory rules (freedom). |
| 2. There are designated times for studying and most people seem to respect this use of time (growth). | 2. During social time, people in the dormitory seem to impose and often borrow things (privacy, independence). |
| 3. The dormitory is close to the building where I have most of my classes, near the cafeteria, and near the tennis courts (proximity). | 3. The dormitory environment seems monotonous at times (freedom, personal growth). |
| 4. My parents prefer that I live on campus (parents' wants). | 4. I may be keeping myself from developing more responsibility and independence (independence, personal growth). |
| 5. I have adjusted to living on campus (comfort, security). | |
| 6. It is cheaper to live on campus (costs). | |

## Pros and Cons of Living off Campus in an Apartment

| PROS | CONS |
|---|---|
| 1. It will be a new experience and seems challenging and exciting (personal growth, freedom). | 1. The adjustment may get in the way of my homework (studying). |
| 2. It seems like the adult and mature thing to do (personal growth). | 2. It may require more self-discipline than I want (freedom). |
| 3. I will be able to spend more time with my boyfriend (love relationship). | 3. The additional time spent with my boyfriend may get in the way of my homework (studying). |
| 4. I will get to know my new roommates (friendship, interaction). | 4. Adjusting to three new roommates may take a lot of time and energy (studying, privacy). |
| | 5. It may be far from the campus, and I do not have my own transportation (proximity). |
| | 6. My parents do not believe it is the best choice (parents' wants). |
| | 7. My share of the rent, utilities, and other expenses may be more than I can afford, and I will have to get a part-time job (cost, studying). |

Pros and Cons of Living off Campus in a Rooming House

| PROS | CONS |
|---|---|
| 1. Complete privacy and freedom to come and go as I please (freedom, privacy). | 1. I may feel lonely and alienated at times (interaction). |
| 2. Complete freedom to spend intimate time with my boyfriend (love relationship). | 2. My boyfriend and I may have more freedom together than either of us is prepared to handle (studying, parents' wants). |
| 3. Optimal opportunity to study in peace and quiet (studying). | 3. The rooming house is within walking distance of campus but is far enough to require my getting up earlier in the morning. It would also require trips back and forth to campus for tennis and meals at the cafeteria (proximity, cost). |
| 4. Less expensive than the apartment (cost). | 4. More expensive than the dormitory (cost). |
|  | 5. Parents are reluctant (parents' wants). |

After weighing the pros and cons for each alternative and reviewing her value priorities and goals, Joanne was ready to choose what she believed to be the best alternative. Joanne chose to spend her sophomore year on campus in the dormitory.

This step-by-step decision-making process is designed to help you organize the essential information necessary to make good decisions. As you improve your decision-making skills, you gain greater control of your own life and your own destiny. It is to the realization of that end that this book has been written.

# PERSONAL ACTION PLAN
## Time Management

Perhaps the most practical first step in meeting the demands of college is to construct a time schedule, a budget of your time. In college you spend less time in class, and class time counts little toward your final grade. What does count is performance on tests, papers, and examinations. Therefore, study time really counts. You should consider constructing a formal plan for allocating your time because such a plan frees you from worry and makes time for pleasurable pursuits. It also improves your performance. The very act of planning encourages you to:

- Give attention to your future.
- Reflect on your present values.
- Select short-, intermediate-, and long-term goals.
- Establish priorities among your competing goals.

- Give consideration to obligations arising from noncollege demands.
- Set realistic standards for work, play, and study.

Carrying out a planned schedule provides many benefits, too:

- It gets you started.
- It keeps you busy on task-centered behavior rather than occupied with worry or daydreams.
- It allows you to do one thing at a time.
- It keeps you progressing toward your selected goals.
- It systematically varies your activities.
- It prepares you for special events, from exams to weekends.

**Step 1. Time Log**   If you wish to construct a time schedule for use during this term, it is best to begin with a realistic notion of how you are now spending your time. For one week record your actions in the time frame in which they occur. Be complete and accurate.

▶

Name _____ Class _____ Date _____

| Hours | Monday | Tuesday | Wednesday | Thursday | Friday | Saturday | Sunday |
|---|---|---|---|---|---|---|---|
| 7:00 AM | | | | | | | |
| 7:30 | | | | | | | |
| 8:00 | | | | | | | |
| 8:30 | | | | | | | |
| 9:00 | | | | | | | |
| 9:30 | | | | | | | |
| 10:00 | | | | | | | |
| 10:30 | | | | | | | |
| 11:00 | | | | | | | |
| 11:30 | | | | | | | |
| 12:00 Noon | | | | | | | |
| 12:30 | | | | | | | |
| 1:00 | | | | | | | |
| 1:30 | | | | | | | |
| 2:00 | | | | | | | |
| 2:30 | | | | | | | |
| 3:00 | | | | | | | |
| 3:30 | | | | | | | |
| 4:00 | | | | | | | |
| 4:30 | | | | | | | |
| 5:00 | | | | | | | |
| 5:30 | | | | | | | |
| 6:00 | | | | | | | |
| 6:30 | | | | | | | |
| 7:00 | | | | | | | |
| 7:30 | | | | | | | |
| 8:00 | | | | | | | |
| 8:30 | | | | | | | |
| 9:00 | | | | | | | |
| 9:30 | | | | | | | |
| 10:00 PM | | | | | | | |
| 10:30 | | | | | | | |
| 11:00 | | | | | | | |
| 11:30 | | | | | | | |
| 12:00 | | | | | | | |
| 12:30 | | | | | | | |
| 1:00 | | | | | | | |
| 1:30 | | | | | | | |
| 2:00 | | | | | | | |

After finishing your time log, complete the classification of time log data and the analysis of time log classification below.

**Step II. Classification of Time Log Data.** Using the information contained in your time log, fill in the hours spent in the following pursuits.

A. Fixed obligations

 1. Class and lab        _____

 2. Job                  _____

 3. Transportation       _____

 4. Required meetings
    and so on            _____

B. Variable obligations

 1. Individual needs

    a. Meals             _____

    b. Sleep             _____

    c. Rest              _____

    d. Exercise          _____

    e. Grooming          _____

    f. Other             _____

 2. Scholastic needs

    a. Study             _____

    b. Review            _____

    c. Research          _____

    d. Writing           _____

    e. Discussion        _____

 3. Social needs

    a. Family            _____

    b. Friends           _____

    c. Others            _____

C. Obligation—free time

 1. Recreation           _____

 2. New interests        _____

 3. Travel               _____

 4. Other                _____

             Total       _____

The total hours should equal 168, the number of hours in a week.

**Step III. Analysis of Time Log Classification.** Use your experience and the results of your time log classification to make reasonable evaluations of your present use of time.

Analyze the results by answering these questions.

■ What hours were spent in activities you value highly or consider essential? _____
_____
_____
_____

■ What hours were spent in activities that constitute a waste of your time? _____
_____
_____
_____

■ What hours were insufficient to complete what needed to be done? _____
_____
_____
_____

Record possible alternative allocations of time.

■ List activities that are low on your priority list and could be omitted or reduced. _____
_____
_____
_____

■ List activities that were omitted from the week's schedule but are important to you.

_____

_____

_____

■ List activities that could replace the wasteful or less essential activities. _____

_____

_____

_____

Now prepare your own time schedule.

**Step IV. Construction of a Time Schedule.** Using your analysis of the time log, construct a tentative schedule for your time this term. Consider these suggestions.

A. Keep study hours close to class periods. Schedule study time before class if you are expected to perform (class recitation or examination) and after class if the professor is expected to perform (class lecture or demonstration).
B. Allocate specific hours for each subject, not simply study time.
C. Maximize the use of daylight hours and minimize the use of dead hours when you are least alert.
D. Give attention to what follows what. One subject can interfere with the learning or remembering of another.
E. Allow ample time for eating, resting, exercising, and sleeping. Know your physical needs and respect them.
F. Schedule a quiet review period just before sleep.
G. Build in spare time each day and week to allow for any opportunity or emergency that may arise.

H. List points you want to keep in mind while constructing your time schedule.

1. _____
2. _____
3. _____
4. _____
5. _____
6. _____
7. _____
8. _____
9. _____
10. _____
11. _____

A workable time schedule contains three parts. The first is a calendar covering the entire semester and listing important dates for exams, papers, holidays, and so on. The second is a weekly calendar blocking out time for specific daily activities. The third is a note (one for each day) recording daily tasks to be accomplished. All three should be placed where they cannot be overlooked. The daily note can be carried with you. Once you have constructed your schedule, commit yourself to living by it and enjoy the returns in increased security, peace, and accomplishment.

Good Grades!

**Time Schedule**

Name _____ Class _____ Date _____

| Hours | Monday | Tuesday | Wednesday | Thursday | Friday | Saturday | Sunday |
|-------|--------|---------|-----------|----------|--------|----------|--------|
| 7:00 AM | | | | | | | |
| 7:30 | | | | | | | |
| 8:00 | | | | | | | |
| 8:30 | | | | | | | |
| 9:00 | | | | | | | |
| 9:30 | | | | | | | |
| 10:00 | | | | | | | |
| 10:30 | | | | | | | |
| 11:00 | | | | | | | |
| 11:30 | | | | | | | |
| 12:00 Noon | | | | | | | |
| 12:30 | | | | | | | |
| 1:00 | | | | | | | |
| 1:30 | | | | | | | |
| 2:00 | | | | | | | |
| 2:30 | | | | | | | |
| 3:00 | | | | | | | |
| 3:30 | | | | | | | |
| 4:00 | | | | | | | |
| 4:30 | | | | | | | |
| 5:00 | | | | | | | |
| 5:30 | | | | | | | |
| 6:00 | | | | | | | |
| 6:30 | | | | | | | |
| 7:00 | | | | | | | |
| 7:30 | | | | | | | |
| 8:00 | | | | | | | |
| 8:30 | | | | | | | |
| 9:00 | | | | | | | |
| 9:30 | | | | | | | |
| 10:00 PM | | | | | | | |
| 10:30 | | | | | | | |
| 11:00 | | | | | | | |
| 11:30 | | | | | | | |
| 12:00 | | | | | | | |
| 12:30 | | | | | | | |
| 1:00 | | | | | | | |
| 1:30 | | | | | | | |
| 2:00 | | | | | | | |

# PERSONAL ACTION PLAN
## Self-Help

The first section in this Personal Action Plan provides a model for self-help. This model is a modification of William Glasser's reality therapy combined with Watson and Tharp's ABCs of behavior. The second section applies the model to an area in which many people openly acknowledge they need help: cigarette smoking. Many of the remarks in this section are based on the discussion contained in Chapter 5 of R. L. Williams and J. D. Long, *Toward a Self-Managed Life Style*, 2nd ed. (Boston: Houghton Mifflin, 1979).

### A Model for Self-Help

**Step I.** *Make friends with yourself.* People who realize that things are not going well, but who do not know what to do to improve the situation, often treat themselves poorly. This tendency must be overcome if effective self-help is to be provided. Making friends with yourself might include the use of relaxation techniques, fantasy, or positive self-talk. The important thing is to see yourself as an OK person. You may need some help, but you are OK nonetheless.

**Step II.** *Ask yourself, "What am I doing now?"* This is simply a way of focusing awareness on the target behavior.

**Step III.** *Ask yourself, "Is it helping?"* This is a critical step because a thorough consideration of the answer to this question should provide the motivation to change your behavior. Think about it. If you have a clear picture of what you are doing (Step II) and what you are doing is not helping, then why not change your behavior?

**Step IV.** *Make a plan to do better.* This step involves: (A) gathering information about the kind of behavior you want to change; (B) studying carefully not only the behavior itself, but the antecedents and consequences of the behavior; and (C) applying the information from (A) to the conditions of (B) in the construction of a plan designed to change the target behavior.

**Step V.** *Make a commitment.* A plan to change behavior is worthless unless you carry it out. Thus, it is important to make a commitment to do what you have planned to do. Here, it is probably best to make the commitment to at least two people—to yourself and to some other person who cares about you. Choose a person whom you respect, who has known you for some time, and who is willing to spend time talking with you about what you are attempting to do.

**Step VI.** *Do not accept excuses.* If you fail to carry out the desired behavior change, accept the fact that you have not done what you wanted to do and try again.

**Step VII.** *Do not punish yourself, but do not interfere with reasonable consequences of your behavior.* If you continue to try but also continue to fail in changing your behavior, go back to Step IV and make a new plan to do better.

**Step VIII.** *Never give up.*

### A Self-Help Plan to Quit Smoking Cigarettes

**Step I.** Using one or more of the techniques suggested in the model for self-help, make friends with yourself. You are really an OK person, but one who has a habit that is not good for you or for anyone else.

**Step II.** Ask yourself, "What am I doing now?"

_____

_____

_____

_____

_____

**Step III.** Ask yourself, "Is it helping?"

_____

_____

**Step IV.** Make a plan to do better.

A. *Getting information.* Some things you ought to know about smoking and smokers:

1. There are *no* physiological benefits from smoking. Smoking is positively correlated with higher rates of heart attack, stroke, and lung cancer—three of the great causes of disability and death within our society. In fact, smoking does not even calm you down. It constricts blood vessels, raises blood pressure, and places the body in a condition of stress.

2. Research indicates that the attitudes of smokers toward their own smoking range from smoking without regret to smoking with considerable conflict. In all cases, however, smokers tend to resort to defensive coping to maintain their habit. Those who smoke without regret, for example, tend either to deny or to minimize the hazards of smoking. You may often hear them making statements such as the following: "I just had a complete physical exam and my doctor says I am as healthy as a horse. Smoking does not bother me." "I cannot understand why they make such a big deal about smoking. A person can get killed crossing the street." "If smoking is so bad for you, how come some doctors and nurses smoke?" Those who smoke with conflict often attempt to resolve the conflict by reducing their smoking, by telling themselves and others that they intend to quit in the future, by contending that if they quit smoking they will suffer some negative effect such as gaining weight, and by emphasizing that they simply lack control over the problem.

3. There is an alternative to all of the above rationalizations: one can *quit smoking.* In fact, millions of people have quit smoking and so can you. Some succeed with a gradual approach, reducing the amount of smoking little by little over a period of time. Others succeed by quitting "cold turkey." Thus, there is more than one way to quit smoking.

B. *Focusing on the ABCs.* Construct a log in which you record answers to each of the following questions for each cigarette you smoke during the day:

1. Amount smoked
(whole cigarette, 3/4, 1/2, 1/4)?
2. Time of day?
3. Place?
4. Who was present?
5. What were you doing?
6. What were the consequences of your smoking?

Continue to log information for one week. At the end of the week, study your log carefully. Look for patterns. When are you most or least likely to smoke? Where? With whom? Doing what? When was smoking most or least satisfying for you?

C. *Applying information.* Our suggested strategy combines aspects of the gradual and "cold turkey" approaches. When you begin, apply the following guidelines. For the next two weeks you will use the gradual approach to reduce your smoking. You will:

1. Set a long-range goal for the number of cigarettes you want to be smoking two weeks from now. We suggest that the number be about half the number you are currently smoking. If you now smoke two packs a day (forty cigarettes), your goal will be to smoke only one pack a day (twenty cigarettes) two weeks from now.
2. Construct a schedule that reflects short-range goals for the number of cigarettes you want to be smoking at three- to four-day intervals during the two-week period. If you currently smoke forty cigarettes a day, you will want to cut down by at least five cigarettes every three to four days to achieve

your long-range goal. Your schedule will look like this:

| | |
|---|---|
| Sunday (today) | 40 cigarettes |
| Wednesday | 35 cigarettes |
| Sunday | 30 cigarettes |
| Wednesday | 25 cigarettes |
| Sunday | 20 cigarettes |

3. Use information obtained from your smoking log to devise tactics that alter the antecedents and the consequences of your smoking. The following list of suggestions and examples might be useful to you.

a. *Antecedents.* (*1*) Alter the antecedents so that you become more aware of your behavior and thus eliminate impulsive smoking. For example, do not carry matches or a lighter (so you will have to ask someone for a light whenever you smoke), or change the place you usually carry your cigarettes (so you will have to think about what you are doing to find a cigarette). (*2*) Reduce the range of stimuli associated with smoking. For example, you might find that there are six or seven situations in which you are more likely to smoke (after eating, while studying, when driving, and so on). Try to break these associations. Deliberately *do not* smoke immediately after eating or while driving your car. Another excellent tactic is to confine your smoking to a limited number of places (perhaps one place at home, one at school, one at work). (*3*) Replace the antecedents with other antecedents over which you have no control. For example, you could set a time interval between cigarettes and gradually increase the interval. You might begin with an interval of at least half an hour between cigarettes and, three days later, increase the interval to forty-five minutes, and so on. In this manner, you would be controlling when you smoked.

b. *Consequences.* (*1*) Apply aversive consequences so that smoking is an unpleasant experience for you. For example, each time you light a cigarette, force yourself to think about the most disgusting and dehumanizing experience you have ever had. (*2*) Positively reinforce nonsmoking behavior. For example, each day you smoke less than the day before, reward yourself with something you really like. (*3*) Combine aversive and positive reinforcement tactics. Combining (*1*) and (*2*) is often a more effective tactic than applying either (*1*) only or (*2*) only.

4. While you are gradually reducing your smoking during the next two weeks, you will also be devising tactics to use when you quit completely. You will:

a. Devise tactics for dealing with the antecedents. You could: (*1*) Remove or reduce environmental cues that trigger impulsive smoking. For example, remove all ashtrays and table lighters from your home and office. (*2*) Avoid people, places, and activities that are most frequently associated with smoking. For example, if smoking is always a part of your behavior when you and a couple of your classmates stop at the campus cafeteria for a cup of coffee following your psychology class, then go to the library or some other place when your psychology class ends. (*3*) Concentrate on alternatives to the usual smoking antecedents. For example, become more involved in activities that you have never associated with smoking.

b. Devise tactics for altering the consequences. Here, you will focus on tactics that positively reinforce nonsmoking behavior. For example, construct a list of reinforcers, any of which can be used to reward yourself at predetermined intervals (say, once a day or once a week) for not smoking. It is important to continue to reinforce your nonsmoking behavior for some time after you have quit completely. We recommend indefinite periodic reinforcement. So, even if you have not smoked for ten years, give yourself a reward. You deserve it. Also, you should be aware that it takes about one week from the time you quit completely for your withdrawal symptoms to disappear. Thus, each time you crave a cigarette during that week, you will have moved one step closer to never craving a cigarette again.

5. Two weeks from now, you will quit smoking completely and put into action the tactics you have devised to use when you quit.

**Step V.**   Make a commitment. Make a solemn commitment to yourself to carry out the plan specified in Step IV. Also, locate another person to whom you can make the same commitment. Tell the person what you are attempting to do and explain carefully the plan you have constructed. Ask the person to be available to you for support and encouragement when needed and to help you evaluate your progress at predetermined intervals.

**Step VI.**   Do not accept excuses. If you have not lived up to your commitment, do not despair. Put your nose to the grindstone and try again.

**Step VII.**   Do not punish yourself, but do not interfere with reasonable consequences of your behavior. If you repeatedly do not live up to your commitment, go back to Step IV and make a new plan.

**Step VIII.**   Never give up. Smoking is usually a difficult habit to break. But millions of people have broken the habit and so can you. Like those who have succeeded in breaking the habit, you, too, will quit if you keep trying. We repeat, **never give up.**

# PERSONAL ACTION PLAN
# Stress Reduction

The purpose of this plan is to give you an opportunity to select an emotion, such as anger, that you believe constitutes a problem in living for you at this time. Your plan will enable you to make that emotion work for you.

■ Fill in the blank. My _____ is the emotion that is of most concern to me right now.
■ Fill in that same emotion whenever a blank line appears in the steps that follow.

You have written that _____ is a problem to you. If you wish to change the way you view and express this emotion, follow the steps outlined below. You may thereby gain a greater awareness of your emotional patterns, greater understanding of the functions this feeling plays in your life, and a greater possibility of successfully modifying your response when in situations that provoke this emotion.

**Step I. Accepting My _____ as a Legitimate Part of Me.** Relax and take a few deep breaths. Assume a very comfortable position. Now repeat at least five times the following statement: "I accept the fact that at the present time many situations provoke me to _____ . This emotion is a legitimate part of me and I accept myself."

Saying this sincerely to yourself in a calm voice helps in bringing your concern into the open and making it manageable. Note how the statement is worded. First, "at the present time" implies that it need not be for all time. It opens the possibility for change. Second, "many situations" implies that not all situations provoke this emotion. Your response is situational. These two basic beliefs—that situations control behavior and that change is possible—are essential to your success in bringing this emotion under control.

Have you been led to believe that this feeling style is part of your genetic makeup? "You're just like your father (or mother)" and so on. Accepting that your emotion is not a genetic flaw but a part of the self that is learned will help you to complete Step II.

**Step II. My _____ Assessment Log.** Keep a written log of your daily _____ responses for a period of not less than five days. Include the following information for each entry:

A. The date and time your problem feeling was provoked.
B. The place and the people present.
C. The events that were going on.
D. An indication of the intensity of your response (1 = little intensity; 10 = uncontrolled intensity).
E. The physiological sensations accompanying your feeling state (pulse rate, muscle tension, heart rate, and so on).
F. Your behavior (facial expressions, verbalizations, and so on).
G. The immediate consequences of the emotional exchange on yourself and on those around you.

This log must be complete and accurate. Do not rely on memory, but record the information as soon as possible. It is a great deal of work, but it is worth its weight in gold. After completion, use your daily log to complete Step III.

**Step III. My _____ Profile.** Study your log entries and search for specific patterns. Using concrete examples drawn from your log, complete the following form. Do not attempt to do this from memory before beginning your log. Misinformation is much worse than no information at all. (Note that your feeling was not associated with everyone, all the time, under all circumstances.)

A. Based on my written observations, I frequently display _____ when:

  1. I am with _____

  _____

  _____

  _____

  (Name the specific *persons* involved.)

  2. I am at _____

  _____

  _____

  _____

  (Name the specific *places* involved.)

  3. I am engaged in _____

  _____

  _____

  _____

  (Name the specific *activities* involved.)

B. When I am provoked:

  1. My sensations include _____

  _____

  _____

  _____

  (Describe your pulse rate,
  muscle tension, and so on.)

  2. My actions include _____

  _____

  _____

  _____

  (Describe what you do or say
  after being provoked.)

C. As a result of my display of _____ :

  1. I feel _____

  _____

_____

_____

(Describe your feelings, such as shame,
enjoyment, power, and so on.)

  2. Other patterned responses include ____

  _____

  _____

  _____

(Record any other insights that came from
a study of your log.)

**Step IV. An Explanation of My _____
_____ .** Study and reflect on your feeling
profile as outlined above, then answer the following questions:

A. I most frequently respond with _____
when I feel (check one or more) afraid
_____ , embarrassed _____ ,
disappointed _____ , anxious _____ ,
helpless _____ , threatened _____ ,
uncertain _____ , other _____

_____

B. By responding this way, I feel (check one
or more) in control _____ ,
powerful _____ , active _____ ,
justified _____ , other _____

_____

C. My emotion is accompanied by such self-
talk as _____

_____

_____

_____

(Recall and record what you said to yourself
during each episode.)

D. Other possible causes for my emotional display include _____

_____

_____

_____

(Describe other internal events that trigger your emotion.)

Remember, no one and no circumstance can *make you* feel _____ ; you have to choose to respond that way. This perception of personal choice is essential to control.

**Step V. The Costs of My _____ .** Now that you know the situations that provoke you to emit your problem emotion and some of the benefits you derive from expressing it, such as getting what you want, feeling better, looking stronger or more appealing, and so on, you are ready to focus realistically on the price you pay for these benefits. Review the immediate consequences of your response on yourself and others and answer the following questions:

A. Did my emotion disrupt completion of the task at hand? _____.

B. Did my display disrupt my thinking and reasoning? _____.

C. Did my emotion lead to impulsive behavior? _____.

D. Did I use unfortunate, hurtful words or actions? _____.

E. Did I use direct, personal attacks that hurt my self-esteem or that of others? _____

_____ .

F. Did my display invite others to be antagonistic toward me? _____.

G. Did my display invite others to take advantage of me? _____.

H. Did my display lead me or others to act defensively? _____.

I. Did my display lead others to seek to avoid me? _____.

J. Did my display leave me or others weak, exhausted, or in physical discomfort or pain?

_____.

K. Did my emotional display produce any other problems? _____

_____

_____

_____

_____

_____

**Step VI. Alternatives to My Problem Emotional Response Pattern.** Now that you are aware of the situations that provoke you, your typical patterns of response, and the costs and benefits associated with them, you are ready to consider some direct coping techniques—practical alternative responses to use when you again find yourself in these circumstances. Get comfortable, relax, and when you feel deeply relaxed, repeat the following slowly and calmly five times. "No one can make me _____ ;

I can only choose to become _____ ." Just as no one can make you fat, because you have to choose to take in more energy than you expend, no one can make you _____ . You have to choose to mobilize and expend your energy in that fashion.

*Review your emotional log* and list situations in which a more productive and rewarding emotional response on your part might have been:

A. Humor: _____

_____

_____

_____

B. Empathy: _____

_____

_____

_____

C. Compassion: _____

_____

_____

_____

D. Patience: _____

_____

_____

_____

List situations in which a more rewarding and productive attitude on your part might have altered the situation constructively. "I could have viewed the situation as":

A. One calling for reason and constructive

thought: _____

_____

_____

_____

B. A problem to be solved rather than a personal threat: _____

_____

_____

_____

C. A sign that additional support on my part was needed: _____

_____

_____

_____

_____

D. Other: _____

_____

_____

_____

**Step VII. Practicing an Alternate Response.** As you know, your problem emotion is, at least internally, a state of high arousal. A state of low arousal, or deep calm, is incompatible with that emotion. You cannot be deeply relaxed and _____ at the same time. The skill of deep relaxation can be learned and called on in _____ -provoking situations. To practice this response:

A. Set aside a five- to fifteen-minute period when you are not likely to be disturbed.
B. Sit or lie in a comfortable position.
C. Breathe slowly and regularly. Let your body "breathe itself."
D. Let your mind be still.
E. Beginning with your toes, concentrate on contracting muscles in an area, be aware of the tension, breathe out, and quickly let the tension go.
F. Concentrate only on the tension and the release of tension. Notice what it feels like to have your muscles completely relaxed.
G. Continue concentrating on and relaxing each set of muscles from your toes to the top of your head. Do not omit your genitals.
H. When you have finished, focus your attention on any areas that retain some tension or pain and repeat the process there.
I. Let your mind be still. If thoughts arise, let them go and refocus on your tension. Do not become annoyed at yourself.

Try to practice this procedure twice a day, every day, for five to fifteen minutes. You will gain skill as the days go by. While you are practicing, arrange for another person to help you modulate your emotional response. Perhaps you can work together to help each other.

**Step VIII. Rehearsing Behavior.** Using your daily log as a guide, construct brief, typical scenes that usually produce your unwanted emotion. Be specific as to time, place, events, and other details. With these scenes, prepare for future encounters by rehearsing alternate ways of looking at the situation or the people involved, alternate ways of feeling, and alternate ways of acting. Take care not to look for support or justification for your old behavior; rather, look for suggestions for new responses. Evaluate these in terms of staying relaxed, rational, and on task. Be sure to ask your partner to model appropriate, useful responses and then discuss them with you. Do not just talk. Act. It is also important for you to rehearse what you say to yourself during these practice episodes so that you can begin to monitor your self-talk and improve it.

**Step IX. Using Positive Self-Statements.** Thoughts lead to feelings, which lead to behavior. Review your log to be sure of what you typically say to yourself during emotional entanglements. "This is a catastrophe!" is an example of negative self-talk that leads to uncomfortable feelings and unfortunate behavior. As a direct coping technique, write out and rehearse one or more positive statements that are appropriate to your typical problem situation and that will help you modulate your response to it. Examples of such statements include, "I can handle this; I can stay on task."

**Step X. Responding on Cue.** You now have an understanding of your typical response patterns, their costs, and their benefits. You also have insight into direct coping techniques available to you in problem situations. You have, or soon will have, skill in producing the relaxation response at will. Review your log one last time to refresh your memory concerning the specifics of the incidents that provoke your unwanted emotion. Study them so that you are sensitized to any subtle cues that seem to occur just before you respond inappropriately. It is imperative that you be able to identify such cues, because you are now ready to make productive use of them.

There is a certain beauty in this step because, instead of attempting to ignore or escape people or situations that were troublesome in your past, you are going to actively look for them so that you may use them as cues or signs that tell you it is time to respond with one or more of your new skills.

**Step XI. Positive Reinforcement Log.** Iden tifying a problem situation early, maintaining

composure, and acting to reduce stress while staying on task are all reinforcing in themselves. It is important to realize that you will not always be able to do all of these things all of the time. Do not wait for perfection to feel good about yourself, but rather set up a system of small rewards for each of the components of emotional modulation that you successfully produce under real-life conditions.

Set up a daily log as you did in Step II. Add the following entries:

A. I was able to recognize the provoking signs early. _____

B. I was able to initiate the relaxation response. _____

C. I was able to maintain patience or composure. _____

D. I was able to maintain a problem-solving, nondefensive attitude. _____

E. I was able to be aware of and modulate my self-talk. _____

F. I was able to decide whether humor, anger, empathy, support, or another response was called for. _____

G. I was able to produce the reponse deemed appropriate. _____

H. I was able to stay on task. _____

I. I was able to prevent the escalation of the situation into unfortunate dialogue or actions.

_____

J. I was able to control the situation so that a need for my unwanted emotion never developed. _____

As you can see, there is plenty of room for partial success and little likelihood of complete success during any one encounter. Reward your partial successes, rehearse alternatives to your partial failures, and build on your increasing skills. The result can be a sense of self-mastery and a feeling of positive personal control.

# PERSONAL ACTION PLAN
# Career Choice

The selection of a career is one of the choices that seems to have a great impact on personal satisfaction, self-esteem, and feelings of happiness and contentment for many people in our society. The exercises in this Personal Action Plan should help you to generate information and insights that may be useful in either your initial choice of a career or your evaluation of your present career.

**Step I.** Think about a few career areas that seem interesting and/or exciting to you. It is important here to enter freely into your own world of fantasy. Let your mind wander, and when you come on an area, try to see yourself playing a specific career role. Repeat this procedure several times, each time focusing on a different career area. List the career areas in the spaces below.

_____

_____

_____

_____

**Step II.** Having identified several career areas that seem attractive, you are ready to gather pertinent information concerning those areas. A good place to start is with your reference librarian, or perhaps the career counseling department, if your campus has one. The important point is for someone to direct you to useful written information. The answers to three questions are particularly important:

A. What are the future prospects for the career itself? (Is the career area growing or shrinking? Will there be jobs available in that area five years from now? Ten years? Twenty years?)
B. What does a person holding a specific job in the career area actually do? (What is a typical workday like? A work week? A work year?)

C. What are the rewards and sacrifices? (What are the salary ranges and fringe benefits? Are there any noneconomic rewards? What are the less attractive aspects of the job?)

After you have gathered answers to these questions from the written sources you have located, you are ready to check them out against verbal reports from people actually working in the career areas. Arrange interviews with at least two people in each area. If possible, interview one relative newcomer to the field and one old pro. Be sure to ask them the same three general questions listed above. Take accurate and complete notes.

**Step III.** Study carefully the information you have gathered for each career area. Then analyze each area in terms of the following considerations:

A. What are some of the personality characteristics that seem necessary for a person to succeed in this career.

_____

_____

_____

_____

_____

_____

B. What are the underlying values on which this career seems to be built?

_____

_____

_____

_____

_____

_____

C. What is the capacity of this career to fulfill an individual's needs? (Refer to Chapter 2 for a discussion of Maslow's hierarchy of needs.) Describe the capacity of this career to fulfill each of the following needs:

1. Physiological:

    _____
    _____
    _____
    _____
    _____
    _____

2. Safety:

    _____
    _____
    _____
    _____
    _____

3. Belongingness and love:

    _____
    _____
    _____
    _____
    _____
    _____

4. Esteem:

    _____
    _____
    _____
    _____
    _____
    _____

5. Growth:

    _____
    _____

_____
_____
_____
_____

**Step IV.**

A. List your outstanding personality characteristics:

    _____
    _____
    _____
    _____
    _____
    _____

B. List the values that are most important to you:

    _____
    _____
    _____
    _____
    _____

C. Refer again to Chapter 2 for information concerning your needs. Write brief descriptions of the ways you are fulfilling your needs and an estimate of how well you are fulfilling each.

1. Physiological:

    _____
    _____
    _____
    _____
    _____

2. Safety:

    _____
    _____

3. Belongingness and love:

_____

_____

_____

_____

_____

_____

_____

_____

4. Esteem:

_____

_____

_____

_____

_____

5. Growth:

_____

_____

_____

_____

_____

_____

**Step V.** You are now in a position to make reasonable judgments concerning the suitability of several careers for you and your suitability for several careers. Compare and contrast your responses to Steps III and IV for each of the career areas you are investigating. Write answers to the following questions:

A. Do you have the personality characteristics that seem necessary for a person to succeed in this career? _____ Yes _____ No. If you checked *No*, are you willing to make the sacrifices necessary to acquire those characteristics?

_____

B. Are your personal values essentially the same as or substantially in agreement with the values you see as underlying this career? _____ Yes _____ No. If you checked *No*, are you willing to reorient yourself so that your values are consistent with those of this career?

_____

C. Does this career seem to have the capacity to fulfill your needs? _____ Yes _____ No. If you checked *No*, are you willing to accept the idea that your career will not fulfill some of your needs? _____

This Personal Action Plan should help you make some important judgments regarding the relative suitability of several careers. Once you have chosen the career you want to pursue, you will be ready to set appropriate goals and begin the process of achieving them. For help with this process, turn to the Conclusion.

# ■INDEX

(continued)

**Chapter Seven**
219 Photo Researchers, Inc.; 221 Cartoon by Kim Pickering; 234 Gregg Mancuso, Stock Boston; 239 John Maher, EKM-Nepethe; 293 Jean Boughton, Stock Boston.

**Chapter Eight**
265 Eric Kroll, Taurus Photos; 267 Robert V. Eckert, Jr., EKM-Nepenthe; 270 Will McIntyre, Photo Researchers, Inc.; 282 Arthur Grace, Stock Boston; 285 Frank Siteman, EKM-Nepenthe.

**Chapter Nine**
295 Rebecca Collette, Archive Pictures, Inc.; 297 Micheal Hayman, Stock Boston; 301 Frank Siteman, Tauras; 303 Ellen Pines Sheffield, Woodfin Camp & Associates; 306 Bruce Roberts, Photo Researchers, Inc.; 309 3M, Frost; 315 Paul Sequeria, Photo Researchers, Inc.; 320 Ellis Herwig, Stock Boston.

**Chapter Ten**
329 Robert George Gaylord; 332 Barbara Alper, Stock Boston; 333 Chester Higgins, Jr., Photo Researchers, Inc.; 336 Wendy Watriss, Woodfin Camp & Associates; 339 Abigial Heyman, Archive Pictures, Inc.; 343 Julie O'Neil, Stock Boston; 346 Chester Higgins, Jr., Photo Researchers, Inc.; 351 (left) Phyllis Graber Jensen, Stock Boston; 351 (middle) Owen Franklin, Stock Boston; 351 (right) Fredrick D. Bodin, Stock Boston.

**Chapter Eleven**
357 John Maher, EKM-Nepenthe; 359 Micheal O'Brien, Archive Pictures, Inc.; 363 Owen Franken, Stock Boston; 365 Micheal O'Brien, Archive Pictures, Inc.; 370 Les Mahon, Monkmeyer; 372 Martin Weaver, Woodfin Camp & Associates; 373 Hazel Hankin, Stock Boston; 378 Eric Kroll, Tauras.

**Chapter Twelve**
383 Arthur Tress, Photo Researchers, Inc.; 386 Jean-Claude Lejeune, Stock Boston; 387 Billy E. Barnes, Freelance Photographers Guild; 390 G. Gibbons, Freelance Photographers Guild; 393 Richard Laird, Freelance Photographers Guild; 395 Rick Smolan, Stock Boston.

**Chapter Thirteen**
405 Cathy Cheney, EKM-Nepenthe; 411 Cartoon by Kim Pickering; 415 Jean-Claude Lejeune, EKM-Nepenthe; 422 Peter Cunningham; 426 Bob Combs, Photo Researchers, Inc.; 430 Peter Southwick, Stock Boston.

**Chapter Fourteen**
439 Robert George Gaylord; 451 Ken Robert Buck, Stock Boston; 457 Robert George Gaylord; 461 Robert George Gaylord.